T0180954

Lecture Notes in Computer Science   12517

More information about this subseries at http://www.springer.com/series/7409

Iza Marfisi-Schottman · Francesco Bellotti ·
Ludovic Hamon · Roland Klemke (Eds.)

Games and
Learning Alliance

9th International Conference, GALA 2020
Laval, France, December 9–10, 2020
Proceedings

 Springer

Editors
Iza Marfisi-Schottman 🆔
Le Mans University
Laval, France

Ludovic Hamon 🆔
Le Mans University
Laval, France

Francesco Bellotti 🆔
University of Genoa
Genoa, Italy

Roland Klemke 🆔
Open University of the Netherlands
Heerlen, The Netherlands

ISSN 0302-9743   ISSN 1611-3349   (electronic)
Lecture Notes in Computer Science
ISBN 978-3-030-63463-6   ISBN 978-3-030-63464-3   (eBook)
https://doi.org/10.1007/978-3-030-63464-3

LNCS Sublibrary: SL3 – Information Systems and Applications, incl. Internet/Web, and HCI

This Springer imprint is published by the registered company Springer Nature Switzerland AG
The registered company address is: Gewerbestrasse 11, 6330 Cham, Switzerland

Preface

The 9th Conference on Games and Learning Alliance (GALA 2020) was organized by the Serious Games Society (SGS) and Le Mans University, France, and more specifically the researchers in the extension of this university in the city of Laval, France. Due to the COVID-19 crisis, the conference was exceptionally held online, in the Laval Virtual World.

The GALA series of conferences provide an excellent opportunity to foster the discussion of relevant topics in the growing field of serious games. The conference is a venue for academic researchers, industrial developers, teachers, and corporate decision-makers to meet and exchange experiences and knowledge in this multidisciplinary and challenging area.

In 2020, the GALA conference received 77 submissions. A total of 273 authors from 24 countries contributed their work to GALA 2020. The majority of authors are based in Europe (70%), including 17% of French authors, but North America and Canada (18%) were also quite well represented in the submissions for this online edition. On average, papers received 2.7 reviews from Program Committee members: 35 of these papers were selected for presentation at the conference (hence a 45% acceptance rate) and 10 papers for presentation at a poster session of the conference. These poster articles are included in these proceedings as short papers.

It was an honor to have Pr. Anna Cox from the UCL Interaction Centre (UCLIC) at the University College London, UK, and Anne-Gwenn Bosser from the Centre Européen de Réalité Virtuelle (CERV) at ENIB in France, as keynote speakers.

The conference featured seven sessions of paper presentations, and topics ranged from serious game design practices, gamification theories and applications, studies on engagement, learning, and usability of serious games, as well as virtual and mixed reality, storytelling, creativity, and awareness.

Instead of the traditional social event, the conference featured a treasure hunt game in the virtual world. The enigmas were related to women in computer science and to the history of the GALA conference itself.

Importantly for this year, the conference was accompanied by a serious game competition with a special focus on innovative human-computer interactions for learning. We received 30 submissions. With the help of a panel of experts, one serious game was awarded in each of the following categories: business, academic, and student.

As is the case every year, one of the highlights of the conference was the exhibition session. This year, it was hosted in the virtual exhibition hall of the Laval Virtual World. The exhibition featured 25 games developed by institutions and students as well as a selection of virtual and mixed reality tools developed by local industries.

As in previous years, selected best papers of the GALA conference will be published in a dedicated special issue of the *International Journal of Serious Games*, the scientific journal managed by the SGS, which is a great reference point for academics and practitioners to publish original research work on serious games, and be informed about the latest developments in the field. We thank the authors for submitting many interesting, field-advancing papers, the Program Committee for reviewing these papers, and the SGS and Le Mans University for organizing the conference.

October 2020

Iza Marfisi-Schottman
Francesco Bellotti
Ludovic Hamon
Roland Klemke

Organization

General Chair

Iza Marfisi-Schottman   Le Mans University, France

Program Chairs

Francesco Bellotti   University of Genoa, Italy
Ludovic Hamon   Le Mans University, France
Roland Klemke   Open Universiteit Nederland, The Netherlands

Exhibition Chair

Pierre Laforcade   Le Mans University, France

Tutorials and Keynotes Chair

Jannicke Baalsrud Hauge   BIBA, Germany, and KTH, Sweden

Competition Chair

Aous Karoui   University of Grenoble, France

Publication Chair

Riccardo Berta   University of Genoa, Italy

Communication and Promotion Chair

Mathieu Vermeulen   IMT, University of Lille, France

Administrative and Financial Chair

Francesco Bellotti   University of Genoa, Italy

Local Arrangements Chair and Support

Sébastien George   Le Mans University, France
Lachen Oubahssi   Le Mans University, France
Aicha Bakki   Le Mans University, France
Cathy Pons Lelardeux   National University Institute Champollion, France

Program Committee

Adam Mayes	Uppsala University, Sweden
Aida Azadegan	University of Reading, UK
Alessandra Antonaci	Welten Institute, Open University of the Netherlands, The Netherlands
Alessandro De Gloria	University of Genoa, Italy
Amel Yessad	Sorbonne University, France
André Czauderna	Cologne Game Lab, TH Köln, Germany
Angeliki Antoniou	University of Peloponnese, Greece
Avo Schönbohm	Berlin School of Economics and Law, Germany
Bibeg Limbu	Open University of the Netherlands and TU Delft, The Netherlands
Carolina A. Islas Sedano	Ubium Oy, Finland
Cathy Pons Lelardeux	National University Institute Champollion, France
Christos Sintoris	HCI Group, University of Patras, Greece
Davide Parmigiani	University of Genova, Italy
Dimitris Grammenos	FORTH-ICS, Greece
Dirk Ifenthaler	University of Mannheim, Germany
Emmanuel Guardiola	Cologne Game Lab, TH Köln, Germany
Erik Van Der Spek	Eindhoven University of Technology, The Netherlands
Frank Dignum	Utrecht University, The Netherlands
George Lepouras	University of Peloponnese, Greece
Georgios Fesakis	University of the Aegean, Greece
Georgios Kritikos	University of the Aegean, Greece
Giuseppe Città	CNR, ITD, Italy
Heide Lukosch	Delft University of Technology, The Netherlands
Heinrich Söbke	Bauhaus-Universität Weimar, Germany
Herre Van Oostendorp	Utrecht University, The Netherlands
Hugo Barbosa	Lusófona University of Porto, Portugal
Ioana Andreea Stefan	Advanced Technology Systems, Romania
Ioanna Lykourentzou	Utrecht University, The Netherlands
Ion Roceanu	National Defence University, Romania
Jan Dirk Fijnheer	Utrecht University, The Netherlands
Jean-Marc Labat	Sorbonne University, France
Jeffrey Earp	CNR, ITD, Italy
Joao Dias	INESC-ID, Portugal
Josef Wolfartsberger	University of Applied Sciences Upper Austria, Austria
Julian Alvarez	LudoScience, France
Katerina Mania	Technical University of Crete, Greece
Khaleel Asyraaf	Open University of the Netherlands, The Netherlands
Kostas Karpouzis	National Technical University of Athens, Greece
Krassen Stefanov	Sofia University, Bulgaria
Kurt Debattista	University of Warwick, UK
Lahcen Oubahssi	Le Mans University, France
Laura Freina	CNR, Italy

Lucia Pannese	Imaginary, Italy
Luis Miguel Encarnacao	Innovation by Design Intl. Consulting, USA
Maira B. Carvalho	Hrvatski Telekom d.d. Croatia
Margarida Romero	Université Nice Sophia Antipolis, France
Maria Popescu	Carol I National Defence University, Romania
Maria Tsourma	Centre for Research and Technology Hellas, Greece
Mario Allegra	CNR, ITD, Italy
Marius Preda	Institut Télécom, France
Mathieu Muratet	Sorbonne University, France
Matthias Teine	Paderborn University, Germany
Michael Derntl	University of Tübingen, Germany
Michael Kickmeier-Rust	Graz University of Technology, Austria
Michela Mortara	CNR, IMATI Genova, Italy
Nour El Mawas	University of Lille, France
Olivier Rampnoux	University of Poitiers, France
Panote Siriaraya	Delft University of Technology, The Netherlands
Pauliina Tuomi	Tampere University of Technology, Finland
Pedro A. Santos	Universidade de Lisboa, Portugal
Per Backlund	University of Skövde, Sweden
Petros Petridis	University of Thessaly, Greece
Pierre Laforcade	Le Mans University, France
Rafael Bidarra	Delft University of Technology, The Netherlands
Ralf Klamma	RWTH Aachen University, Germany
Riccardo Berta	University of Genoa, Italy
Rob Nadolski	Welten Institute, Open University of the Netherlands, The Netherlands
Rui Prada	Universidade de Lisboa, Portugal
Samir Garbaya	Arts et Métiers ParisTech, France
Samuel Mascarenhas	Universidade de Lisboa, Portugal
Sandy Louchart	The Glasgow School of Art, UK
Sobah Abbas Petersen	Norwegian University of Science and Technology, Norway
Spyros Vosinakis	University of the Aegean, Greece
Stelios Xinogalos	University of Macedonia, Greece
Teresa de La Hera Conde-Pumpido	Erasmus University Rotterdam, The Netherlands
Tharrenos Bratitsis	University of Western Macedonia, Greece
Theo Lim	Heriot-Watt University, UK
Thierry Nabeth	P-Val Conseil, France
Valentina Dal Grande	CNR, Italy
Vlasios Kasapakis	University of the Aegean, Greece
Wim Westera	CELSTEC, Open University of the Netherlands, The Netherlands
Yannis Skarpelos	Panteion University, Greece

Yoones A. Sekhavat   Tabriz Islamic Art University, Iran
Yurgos Politis   Technological University Dublin, Ireland
Zerrin Yumak   Utrecht University, The Netherlands

Contents

Serious Games for Instruction

Serious Game Applications and Studies

Posters

Serious Game Design

Accessibility and Serious Games: What About Entity-Component-System Software Architecture?

Mathieu Muratet[1,2]($\boxtimes$) and Délia Garbarini[3]

[1] CNRS, LIP6, Sorbonne Université, 75005 Paris, France
`mathieu.muratet@lip6.fr`
[2] INSHEA, Université Paris Lumière, 92100 Suresnes, France
[3] Université Paris Lumière, Paris 8, 93526 Saint-Denis, France

Abstract. Video games are an integral part of popular culture. The video game industry faces challenges with the increase in players' numbers and application areas including serious games. The increase in the number of players includes disabled players. Therefore, serious games have to consider these audiences who may be affected by one or more temporary or ongoing disabilities. Universally accessible games (UA-Games) aim to create interfaces that can be accessed and manipulated by the largest number of players. Currently few serious games include accessibility features, while accessibility should be considered at the beginning of the serious game design. Then how can we help designers and developers to include accessible features in an existing serious game? To this end, game engines must be efficient but also scalable and modular. This paper studies the interest of the Entity-Component-System (ECS) software architecture to integrate accessibility features in an existing serious game. As a case study, we will take a serious game developed with ECS yet not accessible: E-LearningScape. We will present the accessible features that we have integrated into the serious game and discuss the pros and cons of this approach. This feedback shows us that ECS provides very useful design flexibility to integrate unanticipated interaction features into serious games.

Keywords: Accessibility feature · Data oriented programming · Entity-Component-System · Serious games · Software architecture · Universal design

1 Introduction

Nowadays, video games have become a leisure activity for a large number of people. The Entertainment Software Association announces that 65% of American adults play video games [1]. 54% of them are male and 47% are female. On a global scale, video games represent an object of sharing, socialization, and learning that allows players to interact with the world, to be part of the community and meet people.

However, a large number of people face difficulties in playing video games due to one or more disabilities. Video games stimulate eyesight, hearing and touch, and require

© Springer Nature Switzerland AG 2020
I. Marfisi-Schottman et al. (Eds.): GALA 2020, LNCS 12517, pp. 3–12, 2020.
https://doi.org/10.1007/978-3-030-63464-3_1

players to analyze this multimodal information and perform motor actions in return (i.e.: ability to hold a joystick or perform large movements) [2–4].

The increase in the number of players includes disabled players whose temporary or chronic impairments reveal inaccessible gaming situations or interaction modalities. To offset this problem, video games have to be adapted to their entire audience. Various approaches attempt to tackle this problem and one is to design universally accessible video games (UA-Games) [2, 5–7]. This method aims to create many interfaces for everyone, so as to be accessible to as many players as possible with their abilities and disabilities. However, in their survey, Yuan *et al.* [4] found that small number of games incorporated the "design for all" paradigm and that few games implemented a multi-modal approach where multiple interfaces are designed for different impairments. One challenge is thus to help designers and developers to update existing games in order to incorporate accessibility features when they have not been anticipated.

To reach this objective, the game engine architecture must be flexible enough, during the game development process, to allow to add new features, to test different interaction modalities and to propose several representations of information. In this paper, we focus on Entity-Component-System (ECS) software architecture. This growing software architecture seems to embed mechanisms favoring modularity and scalability. It is a data-oriented approach based on the notion of composition. Several studies show that ECS can address objected-oriented programming limitations in the field of video games development [5, 8, 9].

Thus, our research question in this paper is: Does ECS architecture help to add unanticipated accessibility functionalities inside a serious game?

In the next section, we will discuss the challenges of adaptation in serious games. Then, in section three, we will present, the ECS software architecture used to develop the serious game studied in this article. In section four we will introduce the methodology we follow in this research and in section five, we will present results about the pros and cons of ECS architecture for integrating new accessibility features, before concluding.

2   Serious Games Adaptation Issues

Serious games are multimodal applications. They require players to have sensory, mental and motor skills. These skills are required to interpret stimuli produced by the game and to control the game through input device control (handle a controller, keyboard, mouse, touchscreen interface, etc.) [2–4, 10]. Yuan *et al.* [4] identified two categories of stimuli. The first one is essential to achieve a good understanding of the game, as a player who does not perceive these stimuli will not be able to play it. The second one complete the first and is not essential to understanding the game. In the majority of games, primary stimuli are essentially visual while secondary stimuli exploit hearing and haptic (controller vibration) features.

Thus, Bierre *et al.* [6] identified that the inaccessibility of video games is mainly due to the lack of perception of primary and secondary stimuli (because of visual or hearing impairments for instance) but also to the player's ability to analyze these stimuli and provide new actions in return. An overload of visual and hearing stimuli can place players with cognitive impairment in serious difficulty processing information and deciding which answer to provide. A motor impairment will limit the player's abilities to carry out the response if it results in in-game control manipulations, especially in a limited time context.

Much research contributes to producing knowledge on video game accessibility. Some studies analyze the difficulties met by players [4] and others focus on new functionalities to make video games more accessible [2]. The improvement of video game accessibility is also inspired by the standards initially developed for websites (WCAG[1] et W3C[2]). There are indeed similarities, in particular for interfaces and menu management (button spacing, alternative texts, subtitles, animations, contrast modification, text-to-speech). More specifically, in the field of video games, the Game Accessibility Guideline [11] initiative offers a full list of recommendations to improve the accessibility of video games according to the type of impairment.

The UA-Games approach and the works mentioned above are in line with research conducted in TEL (Technology Enhanced Learning) and especially on the three dimensions of adaptation [12] (adapted, adaptable and adaptive). Applied to the field of serious games, this theory allows us to define adapted, adaptable and adaptive serious games.

Adapted serious games target a particular profile of players. Interactions are set up during the design phase. As the environment creates disabilities, a serious game adapted to a particular impairment may consequently generate inaccessibility for other players. The serious game "A blind Legend" [13] is a singular example of this. This serious game puts the player in the shoes of a blind character for whom the only channel of communication used is sound. This serious game is therefore by nature inaccessible to players with a hearing impairment.

Adaptable serious games are the most widespread. Recent serious games integrate more and more menus allowing players to customize the interaction modalities as they wish (moving speed of the pointing device, colors/contrasts, keys/control buttons, difficulty level, etc.). These settings allow all players (including disabled players) to adapt the serious game to their skills in order to improve their playing experience.

Adaptive serious games have been less common because they have to include models (player's model and/or model of challenge resolution process) in order to automatically adapt interfaces and content to the difficulties encountered by the players.

Ergonomics research on activity theories provide knowledge that can help to understand how players master serious games. Activity theories aim to understand a subject's activity when trying to achieve a goal [14]. So, activity is different from a prescribed task. A task specifies what needs to be done (i.e. the goal) and the procedure to achieve this goal. An activity is singular, located, finalized and mediatized by an instrument [15]. Here, an instrument refers to an artifact associated with schemes. According to activity theories, we consider that a video game engine is an artifact on which the players will build schemes to interact with it. These schemes can only be built if the player is able to access the primary (or even secondary) stimuli and provide actions in return. A serious game uses an engine (the artifact) and offers objectives to the players in the form of a set of missions or quests to complete or a record to beat. The rules of the serious game constrain the player's actions and make it possible to calibrate the complexity of a game

---

[1] WCAG = Web Content Accessibility Guidelines.
[2] W3C = World Wide Web Consortium.

situation. Thus, a serious game can be abstracted as a task according to the activity theories. The player's activity is therefore what is accomplished by the player according to his/her skills and it depends on the accessibility of the engine and the complexity of the situations offered (including goals). This incremental process named instrumental genesis allows players to appropriate the artifact (transforming artifact into instrument) and involves two types of transformation: instrumentalization, where the player will adapt the artifact to his/her needs (dimension of adaptable serious games) and instrumentation, in which the artifact influences the player's actions (dimension of adapted and adaptive serious games).

Thus, improving serious game accessibility consists in supporting the instrumental genesis defined in activity theories and working on the three dimensions of adaptation (adapted, adaptable and adaptive).

3   Entity-Component-System: A Software Architecture Coming from Video Games

Video game and serious game developments are mainly based on the object-oriented programming paradigm (OOP), whose C#, C ++ and Java are the most used programming languages. However, OOP principles such as encapsulation, message sending and inheritance can make game engine maintenance and scalability difficult. With an object-oriented approach, developers model game elements in the form of classes that may be specialized into subclasses, etc. The video game development process is highly iterative, adding new game mechanisms or interaction modalities may request changes in the modeling initially designed. Then, these modifications may have significant consequences on developments and require code refactoring, which is expensive in development time and a possible source of bugs. The rigidity of the inheritance tree is a hindrance in this context.

The Entity-Component-System (ECS) is a software architecture mainly used for developing video games [16, 17]. This architecture uses a data-oriented approach and is built around three concepts. Entities (first concept) represent game objects but do not contain either data or methods. An entity is a simple reference to a collection of components (second concept) that contain data. Components describe an entity's aspects such as its color, size, speed, etc. A component may be added or removed dynamically to an entity. Systems (third concept) define the game logic. They access the components of the entities in order to process and update them. They modify the game data and then update the simulation.

ECS is a software architecture in which simulation is data-driven. ECS is based on composition whereas the object-oriented approach focuses on encapsulation and inheritance. ECS was developed to answer two issues: improving computer code modularity and improving game engine performance. As for modularity, the data-driven approach allows to add new game mechanisms or interaction modalities with a limited impact on the existing code. To integrate a new feature, the developer has to (1) define the components required to store the data, (2) add these components to the entities concerned and (3) implement systems that will process these components. Contrary to classes in OOP that contain data and logic, in ECS they are separated: data in components and logic in systems. From a performance point of view, ECS allows to control the organization of data in memory and optimizes access to components. In this paper, we are studying ECS for its modularity promises and we want to evaluate it to add accessibility features. We are not hereby studying questions of optimization.

Garcia *et al.* [5] also address this architecture based on component and data-driven approach for the development of accessible video games. They study the interest of ECS to create different game object representations that can be changed in real-time and without consequences on the game logic. Authors create components that contain the data of the different stimuli (graphic, audio, haptic) and specific systems to manage these components. When the game is running, the modal presentation sent to the player depends on the components attached to a game entity. It is therefore possible to switch from one representation to another in real-time, according to the needs and abilities of the player, offering a more accessible game experience. Moreover, this research highlights the advantage of this architecture for using an external data source (XML file) in order to define game-specific settings. Players could thus access this file and create a profile by customizing entities, modifying presets and creating default configurations adapted to their needs.

The runtime ECS advantages promoted by Garcia *et al.* [5] confirms our hypothesis that ECS architecture is adapted and useful to more easily modify an existing video game whose accessibility was not initially considered during the design step.

4 Methodology

As a preamble to this section let us introduce the artifact we have been working on. E-LearningScape (see Fig. 1) is a numerical adaptation of a physical escape game [19]. In this numerical adaptation, the participants (in teams of 2 to 5 players) play the role of a sandman immersed in the dream of Camille, a young lecturer on the eve of teaching her first lesson. Their challenge will be to help Camille structure her thought in her dream by solving puzzles using pedagogical concepts. The team members gather around a computer. One player controls the game and moves inside the virtual universe in a first-person navigation to discover fragments of dreams giving access to material in the real world. All members of the team solve puzzles inside and outside the game, these two facets feeding each other. E-LearningScape has several objectives, the main one being to test knowledge in the field of education and the other ones to promote team work and cohesion.

E-LearningScape was initially developed without accessibility constraints in mind. It is an open-source and totally designed with ECS architecture (it was developed with Unity and the FYFY plugin [18]).

This serious game is an interesting case study for our research question, which is: Does ECS architecture help to add unanticipated accessibility functionalities inside a serious game?

To tackle our research question, the serious game was analyzed with the Game Accessibility Guideline grid [11]. These guidelines are divided into six categories (motor, cognitive, vision, hearing, speech and general), each one broken down into three levels (basic, intermediate and advanced). This analysis, performed and discussed by two

Fig. 1. E-LearningScape screenshot

experts in accessibility, aimed to recommend accessibility functionalities suitable to the serious game. Based on these recommendations, a game developer incorporated the new functionalities inside the serious game. This developer was not part of the original team that developed the serious game and was not familiar with ECS architecture. The developer got support from an expert developer who was a member of the initial project. Each new functionality was studied to evaluate the advantages and drawbacks of ECS architecture. For each of them, the developer reflected on the following questions: Is it possible to integrate the functionality only using Unity editor (without a line of code)? How many Unity editor manipulations are required with a classical Unity script to integrate the functionality? Does a system in which the functionality can be integrated exist? Which components and systems have to be created to integrate the functionality? Which choices make future updates easier?

5 Results

5.1 E-LearningScape Analysis

Among the 121 recommendations included into the Game Accessibility Guideline grid [11], experts in accessibility have retained 67 criteria that make sense for E-LearningScape. For instance, they excluded recommendations on voice subtitles, multiplayer and chat features, and virtual reality and mobile devices because they were judged not consistent for the serious game. Among the 67 criteria identified by experts in accessibility, 10 were already integrated into the game (for instance: including tutorials, allowing reminders of current objectives during gameplay, ensuring no essential information is covered by sounds alone, etc.). The developer updated the game and added 34 supplementary recommendations to fulfill the basic level of motor, cognitive and vision categories (hearing and speech categories are not requested by E-LearningScape). Let us give some examples of new features that were incorporated: supporting more than one input devices, including options to adjust the sensitivity of controls, using simple clear text formatting, ensuring no essential information is covered by color alone, etc. The current version of the game includes 17 basic recommendations over the 18 suitable ones, 22 intermediate recommendations over the 35 suitable ones, and 5 advanced recommendations over the 14 suitable ones. Figure 2 shows details about accessibility completion of the game before and after the updates.

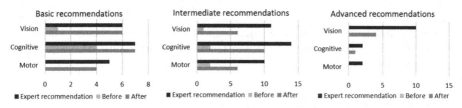

Fig. 2. Accessibility recommendations integrated into the game

5.2 Adapted Serious Game

Modifications have been made to change serious game interfaces and interactions. To complete the default mouse/keyboard inputs, the developer increased the diversity of control devices: the serious game is now playable with the Xbox one controller, the Microsoft Xbox adaptive (XAC), the Nintendo Nunchuck and specific controllers. The Unity environment provides native tools to abstract controllers. In this case, ECS did not bring any advantages. As for controllers' abstraction, the developer reviewed menu navigation and added visual effects to help players to easily identify the UI element focused on. Similarly, Unity's native tools are very efficient to define interface navigation order and highlight interactive UI elements. Other functionalities have been integrated without the ECS layer because they were relating to static graphical parameters: color review (limitation of red and green colors), black outline on textual elements, etc. All these accessibility features were editable inside Unity's editor and did not require programming.

In the first version of the serious game, in-game interactive objects were highlighted with visual effects. Experts' recommendations suggested dubbing this information with audio notifications. With a classic use of Unity, the developer would create a new script, add it manually to all interactive game objects and configure them in Unity inspector with the risk of forgetting one of them (the game contains more than 60 interactive game objects). In this case, ECS enables to easily add this functionality. Indeed, a system already existed to highlight interactive game objects. The developer just added one line of code in this system to dynamically add a new component on the highlighted game objects. This new component contains sound data to play. Then he created a new system to process sound components and play audio notifications. The developer could play sound directly inside the existing highlighter system, yet chose to separate it inside a new system. This makes the audio notification system independent from the highlighter system. Thus, the audio system can be turned off by the player without any consequence on visual notifications. Moreover, the audio system may be used in other cases that require audio notifications (changing room, enigma success/fail, etc.). The consequences of adding this new functionality to the existing code were very limited.

ECS was also useful to easily identify the different functionalities of the game that a developer could change. Indeed, each functionality is implemented inside a system, and updating a functionality consists in identifying the concerned system and focusing attention on it. Thus, the developer, who did not master ECS at the beginning of this work found it easier to study the list of systems to understand the game logic than parsing game objects hierarchy and components interdependences. He updated the system that manages interactive game objects to enable the player to hold down or successively press a button; or to drag and drop a game object without holding down a button. Finally, he modified the system that manages the camera to add a zoom function and to switch point of view (first/third person).

5.3 Adaptable Serious Game

Several recommendations concern menus, to enable players to personalize serious game interfaces according to their needs. The developer added functions to change controls, graphics, and sounds. For instance, the player can disable/enable animations, change moving speed and camera rotation speed, adjust music and effect volumes, grow cursor, and update scene luminosity. For all of these new features, the default tools of Unity were sufficient.

On the other hand, ECS was useful to apply massive changes to game objects. One recommendation is that players have to be able to change text font, to switch from the default non-accessible font to an accessible one. With a classical usage of Unity, the developer would have added a new script to each textual game object or created a text manager and bound each textual game object in (more than 570 game objects are concerned). In these two solutions, designers risk making errors when a new text is added to the game, and forgetting to add the accessible script to the game object or to bind the game object to the text manager. With the ECS approach, the developer added a new system and created a family to filter game objects that contain default text components. When the player switches text font, the system updates all textual game objects in the scene. Adding new accessible text into the game requests designers to simply add a default textual game object to the scene without taking into account any accessibility constraints (no script to add, no specific manager to bind). The same principle has been applied to manage windows' transparency.

5.4 Adaptive Serious Game

The adaptive dimension is present in this serious game with a monitoring module. This functionality generates in-game hints to help players depending on their difficulties. The monitoring module integrated into the game is compatible with ECS architecture [20] and enables to monitor players' activities either at the level of entities (local monitoring) or at the level of families (set of entities – global monitoring).

Integrating this monitoring module requires a set of modifications in the existing code, especially to produce tracks. The first challenge was to identify inside existing programs in which the player's actions were validated. ECS architecture helps to understand game design because each logic functionality is implemented inside a specific system. Then the developer easily identified systems that manage player inventory, moving, interactive objects, etc. Finally, producing tracks consisted in updating systems and adding one line of code to build the monitoring component (provided by the monitoring module) with action data. This monitoring component is processed by the monitoring module that labels the player's actions (correct, too late, useless, etc.).

The second step was to create a new system to process results from the monitoring module. This system chooses the next hint to be displayed to the player depending on labeled actions aggregated over time, player progression, and time left. Generated hints may suggest searching for a specific area, indicate a clue position, explain a bad answer, and validate the fact that players have all the elements to resolve an enigma.

6 Conclusion

We began this paper by pointing out the importance of taking into consideration the question of accessibility to serious games. We were interested in the cases in which accessibility had not been taken into account in the early phases of development and had to be integrated retrospectively. So, we studied the potential benefits of ECS architecture in this context. Our theoretical foundation is based on activity theories and the three dimensions of adaptation (adapted, adaptable and adaptive).

We analyzed the serious game E-LearningScape and we added 34 supplementary recommendations from the Game Accessibility Guideline grid [11].

The contribution of this paper concerns the analysis of updates made into the serious game E-LearningScape. We found that Entity-Component-System architecture does not bring added value to process singular and/or static game objects. In this case, the classical features of Unity seem to be more effective. However, this work showed that ECS is advantageous to carry out transformations impacting a large number of game objects and to avoid repetitive manipulations that are a source of errors. We also found that the principle of modularity and decomposition of the game's features into systems, allowed the developer to quickly identify the parts of the program to be modified.

Thus, the Entity-Component-System architecture seems to be interesting to help integrating accessibility features into serious games, especially when these have not been anticipated. In this research we worked on a serious game initially designed with ECS. However, we think that this approach is also practical for non ECS serious games made with Unity because FYFY and Unity perfectly fit together and complement each other. We plan to check this hypothesis in future research.

Acknowledgements. We thank Séverine Maillet for comments on the paper.

References

1. ESA Essential Facts About Computer And Video Game Industry. https://www.theesa. com/esa-research/2019-essential-facts-about-the-computer-and-video-game-industry/, last accessed 2020/03/19
2. Grammenos, D., Savidis, A., Stephanidis, C.: Designing universally accessible games. ACM Comput. Entertain. **7**(1), 29 (2009)
3. McCrindle, R.J., Symons, D.: Audio space invaders. In: Third International Conference on Disability, Virtual Reality and Associated Technologies (2000)
4. Yuan, B., Folmer, E., Harris, F.: Game accessibility: a survey. Univ. Access. Inf. Soc. **10**, 81–100 (2011)
5. Garcia, F.E., de Almeida Neris, V.P.: A data-driven entity-component approach to develop universally accessible games. In: Stephanidis, C., Antona, M. (eds.) UAHCI 2014. LNCS, vol. 8514, pp. 537–548. Springer, Cham (2014). https://doi.org/10.1007/978-3-319-07440-5_49

6. Bierre, K., Chetwynd, J., Ellis, B., Hinn, D.M., Ludi, S., Westin, T.: Game not over: accessibility issues in video games. In: Human-Computer Interaction (2005)
7. Grammenos, D., Savidis, A., Stephanidis, C.: Unified design of universally accessible games. In: Stephanidis, C. (ed.) UAHCI 2007. LNCS, vol. 4556, pp. 607–616. Springer, Heidelberg (2007). https://doi.org/10.1007/978-3-540-73283-9_67
8. Rafaillac, T., Huot, S.: Polyphony: programming interfaces and interactions with the entity-component-system model. In: 11th ACM SIGCHI Symposium on Engineering Interactive Computing Systems, Valencia, Spain (2019)
9. Gestwicki, P.: The entity system architecture and its application in an undergraduate game development studio. In: International Conference in the Foundations of Digital Games (2012)
10. Bierre, K., et al.: Accessibility in games: motivations and approaches. In: The International Game Developers Association (2004)
11. Game Accessible Guidelines. http://gameaccessibilityguidelines.com/full-list/, last accessed 2020/03/11
12. Hussaan, A.M.: Generation of adaptive pedagogical scenarios in serious games. Université Lyon 2, Lyon, France (2012)
13. A Blind Legend, http://www.ablindlegend.com/. Accessed 11 Mar 2020
14. Daniellou, F., Rabardel, P.: Activity-oriented approaches to ergonomics: some traditions and communities. Theor. Issues Ergon. Sci. **6**(5), 353–357 (2005)
15. Forcisi, L.A., Decortis, F.: Children's creativity at school: learning to produce multimedia stories. In: Bagnara, S., Tartaglia, R., Albolino, S., Alexander, T., Fujita, Y. (eds.) IEA 2018. AISC, vol. 826, pp. 683–692. Springer, Cham (2019). https://doi.org/10.1007/978-3-319-96065-4_72
16. Bilas, S.: A data-driven gameobject system. In: Game Developers Conference (2002)
17. Capdevila, B.: Serious game architecture and design: modular component-based data-driven entity system framework to support systemic modeling and design in agile serious game developments. Université Pierre et Marie Curie, Paris, France (2013)
18. FYFY, https://github.com/Mocahteam/FYFY. Accessed 11 Mar 2020
19. LearningScape. https://sapiens-uspc.com/projets-innovants/learningscape-2/. Accessed 11 Mar 2020
20. Muratet, M., Yessad, A., Carron, T.: Understanding learners' behaviors in serious games. In: Advances in Web-Based Learning – ICWL 2016, Rome, Italy (2016)

Generation of Adapted Learning Scenarios in a Serious Game: Lessons Learnt

Pierre Laforcade$^{(\boxtimes)}$ 🆔

LIUM (Computer Science Laboratory), University of Le Mans, Le Mans, France
pierre.laforcade@univ-lemans.fr

Abstract. This article presents the lessons we learnt during the development of a generation component in the *Escape it!* learning game. They are presented according to the different development stages of the generator. They may be considered useful by designers or researchers sharing similar contexts and objectives.

Keywords: Serious game · Adaptation · Design · Generation

1 Introduction

Adaptivity is an important success factor to enhance the learning facet æof serious games [11]. In this article we are interested in adaptive serious games and more specifically adaptive *learning games*. Adaptations may refer to some learning side targets (learning resources, activities, etc.), game side targets (difficulty, gameplay components, etc.) or both at the same time. Our concern is about personalizing the levels presented to the learner/player by only considering the learning dimensions (progress in the skill tree). Such adaptations at runtime are generally called generations. The perimeter of our research is then about learning games proposing the generation of adapted scenarios (ordered activities) according to the available game elements and learners' progress.

Even if some researches have dealt with the generation of serious game components [1,6,9,12], only a few research works [5] propose guides, generic frameworks or approaches to support the design and development of such generators. This led us to propose a dedicated $3 \times 3 \times 2$ approach [7,8] while developing a serious game in the *Escape it!* project. Our proposition is design-centered because it guides and supports the formalization of models and metamodels that capture three dimensions of the adaptation (context, game components, scenario) into three iterative perspectives (objectives, structures, features). Nevertheless, it impacts all stages of the development of the generator (analysis, design, implementation, and re-engineering). Because we met with different issues during the development of the generator, we intend to share the lessons we have learnt. Researchers and designers sharing similar objectives and context could benefit from this feedback information.

© Springer Nature Switzerland AG 2020
I. Marfisi-Schottman et al. (Eds.): GALA 2020, LNCS 12517, pp. 13–23, 2020.
https://doi.org/10.1007/978-3-030-63464-3_2

We propose the following organization. Section 2 presents the context of the *Escape it!* project and serious game. Section 3 gathers all lessons according to the development stages they refer to. Finally, Sect. 4 concludes this paper.

2 Context

2.1 The Escape It! Project

The project aims to develop a mobile learning game dedicated to children with ASD (Autistic Syndrome Disorder). The purpose of the game is to support the learning of visual skills derived from a curriculum guide [10]: matching an object to another identical object, sorting objects into different categories, making seriation of objects, etc. It will be used to reinforce and generalize the learning skills [2].

The project involves autism experts and parents. The main challenge is about the proposition of a large variety of playable scenes to learners in order to support the visual skills generalization. Because the engineering costs of hard-coded scenes could not be considered, it has been decided to study the development of a dedicated generator that will dynamically build playable game scenes in relation to learners' profile. A Design-Based Research method has been conducted on account of its usefulness as an exploratory research adapted to study research issues while producing designed artifacts.

2.2 The Escape It! Serious Game

Overview. The main gameplay consists, for players, in finding some relevant objects in the displayed scene, and dragging and dropping them to appropriate places in order to respect the association/match/sort/... objective. When all required actions are performed, the door is unlocked, giving access to the next level. The game design relies on the best practices from the literature [3,16] and the recommendations/requirements expressed by the ASD experts involved in the design sessions. Our game fits the ASD requirements by its targeted skills from the ABBLS curriculum [10] and the use of ABA pedagogical key features (fading guidance by the pairing adult, positive rewards, no task failure, etc.) [2]. The main concerns are listed below:

- Targeted skills: a subset of the visual performance skills derived from [10] (those that can be adapted for a mobile gameplay).
- Variable game sessions: the game proposes from 3 to 5 levels at the convenience of the pairing adults or the children themselves.
- Scenes as meaningful living places: for example, the *bedroom*, the *kitchen* and the *living room*.
- Adapted difficulty: the difficulty level is set according to the current child's progress related to the targeted skills. Basically, three successful activities for a same skill (along one or several game sessions) raise the difficulty level for this skill.

– Generalizing the acquired skills: scenes have to be changed in accordance with previous difficulty levels. Hence, the game proposes non-identical challenges for the same skill. We quote variation examples: changing the background elements of a scene, adding background elements to disrupt visual reading; changing the objects to find and handle; adding other objects that are not useful for the resolution; hiding objects behind or into others.

The Current Prototype. Various screenshots of the current prototype are illustrated in Fig. 1. To present them briefly, the children with ASD, supervised by adults, ask for a new game session (1) and choose the number of levels composing the session (3), for example a 4-level length. The generator is then called to provide an adapted scenario (4). Children can visualize the current

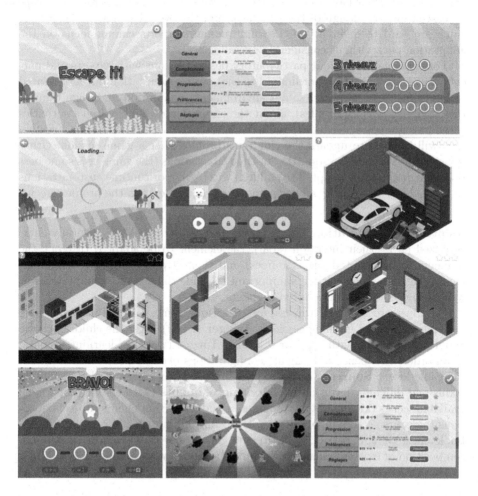

Fig. 1. Overview of the different screens during a learning game session

progress within the session (5). They successively solve the 4 levels (6–7–8–9). The progress screen (5) is updated and shown after each completed level. When the session is over, an end-game screen is shown (10), and a reinforcer element is won (11). The pairing adults can access the secured children' profile in order to see their progress (2 and 12), their history reports, etc.

3   Lessons Learnt While Developping the Generator

3.1   Preliminary Stage

Focus on the Design of the Generator. When the serious game is already developed, the integration of an adaptation component can benefit from a lot of information already delimited about the game. Nevertheless, when both learning game and generator have to be considered from scratch, as it was for the *Escape it!* case-study, the design of the generator and the overall design of the serious game are hard to differentiate. Learning domain experts cannot focus on the adaptation part without considering overall aspects.

For example, during our participatory design sessions with experts and parents, the discussions were not limited to the runtime adaptation but also related to the game aesthetics and sound environment (adaptation at design-time to the children's sensory profiles), about the regulation of the children's activities (prompts, guidance, feedback, reinforcements), or about the tracking system that will be used to update the children's profiles after a game session. Other information also concern some design-time adaptations (the game uses some best practices design to be adapted to children with ASD), or runtime customizations to be made by the pairing adult (parameters adjustments in the profile screen).

Identify the Generation Characteristics. Adaptations are generally characterized [4] by their intention (goal), the element to be adapted (target), the elements to be adapted with (sources) and their strategy [15]. We think that identifying these information is important to guide the design of adaptations as well as the generation of adapted elements.

We illustrate them for the *Escape it!* serious game. **Intention** (what for): individualization of learning sessions; **Trigger** (when): after the children choice about the session length (3, 4 or 5 levels); **Target** (what): a learning scenario as an ordered sequence of elements configurations declaring the initial setup of the game levels; **Sources** (according to what): current progress of the children (skills and difficulty levels); **Participating elements** (with the help of what): available scenes (kitchen, living room, etc.) and their components (objects, locations, hideouts...); **Level of automation**: full, no human intervention; **Feedback time of the result**: just after its generation; **Generation approach**: composition of existent elements within every scene, with random selections.

The Generator as a Black-Box Component. The learning game should be considered as a complex object composed of inter-related components. The generation part can then be analyzed as a black-box software component with inputs and outputs, or as a service consuming and producing data. It is useful to identify the generator role, avoiding considering related but external tasks as under the responsibility of the generator. As inputs we can distinguish the sources and the participating elements (cf. previous characteristics). Sources inputs may vary for each generation whereas participating elements are more likely to stay invariant.

The *Escape it!* generation component produces as output a scenario composing of 3 to 5 levels configurations including the initial location of objects to find, objects solution, hideouts, etc. The source input is the child's profile (current progression for each skill) including the context-sensitive choice of the session length. The additional input is the description of the game in terms of skills, scenes and game objects. The generator is not in charge of updating the children profiles according to their results during the learning sessions (tracking system concern). It is also not responsible of setting up the levels presented to learners according to the scenarios descriptions (game engine concern). By analogy with some existent procedural context generation taxonomy [14] the Escape it! generation could be considered *online* (during the runtime), *necessary* (the content has to be correct), *parameterized* (the generator takes as an input the game description model), *stochastic* (randomness is used when several combinations are possible), *constructive* (the algorithm never produces broken content).

3.2 Specification Stage

The main objective of the specification is to capture and model the elements (with their properties and relations) and the generation rules involved in the generation process. This specification will drive the implementation stage. It is important to identify these information, even more to avoid considering information not necessary to the generation.

An Iterative and Incremental Specification Centered on the Target. The generation design can be eased by decomposing the specification into successive but complementary perspectives. They are all centered on the specification of the target as a first class element.

The $3 \times 3 \times 2$ approach [7] suggests to consider at first the *Objective* perspective. It refers to the selection of targeted learning objectives according to the user's profile. In the *Escape it!* project, the scenario to generate is then an ordered sequence of the visual performance skills that will be considered; these skills are selected in accordance with the number of levels to generate, the considered skills available in the game and the child's progression.

The second additional perspective is about the *Structural* part of the scenario. It consists in the selection of learning game exercises or large grain game components that are compliant with the previous selected skills. In our context, we focus on the various scenes that are compliant with the previously chosen skills. This scenario specifies correspondences between the selected pedagogical large-grained resources (i.e. scenes) and their targeted skills.

Finally the third *Feature* perspective completes the scenario by specifying additional inner-resources/fine-grained elements along those which are compliant with the previous chosen skills and large-grain components. In the *Escape it!* project, this concerns the initial configuration of each scene in terms of additional background elements, objects to find, hideouts, etc.

Specification into 3 Inter-related Dimensions. Each of the three previous perspectives can be specified through 3 inter-related dimensions. The first one to consider is the scenario to generate. It will drive the other dimensions. The specification consists in modeling the generic domain concepts, properties and relations, required for the generation of scenarios. In our work we use metamodels representations to this aim but other formalisms, ontologies for example, could be considered.

In order to avoid repetitions we propose that the *Scenario description meta-model* elements that are known before the generation are captured into the *Game description metamodel* and referenced by the *Scenario metamodel*. That is a debatable choice because it complexifies metamodels and implies cross-references into the models. Nevertheless we consider it plays a valuable part in supporting the complex and subjective modeling work, improving the overall quality of the design.

The *Game description metamodel* is then the abstract syntax declaration of the additional elements required by the generation. These elements are considered as a model conformed to this metamodel. As a model they explicitly declare the game elements according to the 3 perspectives (objectives, structure and features): skills, resources or exercisers, in-game objects, etc.

The third metamodel to consider captures the description of the source context: the learner model and other context elements. Similarly to the game dimension, the metamodel specifies the abstract syntax describing all children's profiles, but only the elements that will be useful for the generation (the ones involved in the generation rules). Children's concrete profiles will be part of models in conformance with this metamodel. The 3 × 3 × 2 approach does not suggest to specify 9 different metamodels (3 perspectives and 3 dimensions) but to consider the iterative and incremental completion of only 3 metamodels (scenario, game and context).

As an illustration, we propose in Fig. 2 a visual representation of metamodels and models for the *objective* perspective in the *Escape it!* case-study. To explain briefly, the Scenario metamodel expresses that the Objective part is composed of various *TargetedSkill*. Each one of them has a *difficulty level* and references a concrete *Bxskill* among those defined in the description of the game. These *BxSkill* are part of the *Domain* section of the *GameDescription*. Each *Bxskill* has a textual description and can refer to another *Bxskill* as a *prerequisite* or refer to

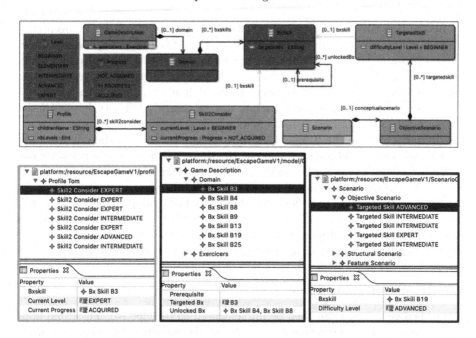

Fig. 2. Visual representations of the 3 inter-related metamodels (top), source input model (bottom left), game input model (bottom center), and output scenario model (bottom right), for the *Objective* perspective.

several ones as available *Bxskill* when the former will be achieved. On the *Profile* part, the desired number of levels is specified. Several *Skill2Consider* indicate the current *difficulty level* and *progress* for the referenced *Bskill*. The game description model concretely describes 7 *Bxskills* with their *prerequisite/unlockedBx* relations. The learner profile is for a fictive "Tom" who would like a 5-level length new game session according to his current difficulty levels and progress for the 7 considered skills. Finally, the scenario model is an example of generated model in conformance with its metamodel. It is composed of 5 targeted skills. We can notice that the first one concerns the B19 skill at an "advanced" difficulty level.

Consider Generation Rules at a *Meta* Level. Generation rules describe how to generate the scenario elements, properties and relations according to the information from a given child profile and the game description model. These rules can be specified based on the model information or the metamodel ones. They can be directed by the selection of input information to generate output ones or, on the contrary, be centered on the generation of target elements with respect to input conditions. In our case study, the generation rules are target-centered, at the meta level and expressed in a textual format with references to the named elements from the metamodels. These informal specifications are a reformulation of the information given by experts using the natural language.

In addition to the *Objective* perspective, the following rules have been considered: there are as many *TargetedSkill* as the *nbLevels* value; each of these *TargetedSkill* refers to an "eligible" Bxskill, i.e. 1/ that is referenced by a Skill2Consider, in the learner profile, which has an "in progress" *currentProgress*, and 2/ the potential *BxSkill* as *prerequisite*, if it exists, being also referenced by a *Skill2Consider* having at least an "intermediate" difficulty level. All the referenced *BkSkill* from a *TargetedSkill* must be different if possible. Finally, the difficulty level of the *TargetedSkill* has the same value as the one from the *Skill2Consider currentLevel* pointing at the shared *BxSkill*. These rules are not understandable by experts because of their expression close to the metamodels syntax. Nevertheless they are useful to drive their implementation. Experts do not refer to the metamodel elements obviously. For example, they stated that *the scenario to generate can only refer to skills that are currently in progress and for which their skill prerequisite has at least reached the 'intermediate' level.* That is simpler to express than the equivalent translation we specified.

3.3   Implementation Stage

A specified generation can then be implemented to be effective. The usual approach consists in implementing it as a part of the serious game, using the same frameworks, languages or architectures. But another solution is possible.

Machine-Readable Specification Models. Considering that the previous specifications have been modeled thanks to a practical *Model Driven Engineering* tooling, they can be used to generate code to load, save, and handle the previous metamodels and models. Only the generation rules still require to be coded. Other formal or semi-formal modeling frameworks, like ontologies tooling, can ease or support the use of the specified models as machine-readable models to be used at runtime by the generator.

In the *Escape it!* case study we used the *Eclipse Modeling Framework* [13]. The metamodels are *ecore* file, and the models are XMI-formatted files. The generation of scenarios is implemented as a model transformation written in Java/EMF mainly based on a Java code generated from the *ecore* (meta)models by the EMF tooling. The generation rules are then hard-coded into the generator code.

Integration of an Independent Generator. Having an independent generator from the serious game is helpful to develop and maintain it without any consideration for the game engine, mechanics, aesthetics, as well as the tracks collecting, the updating of the profile, etc. Nevertheless it is an integration challenge because of the potential gap between the required (scenario) and provided (learner profile, context...) formatting from the serious game perspective, and the ones required (profile...) and provided (scenario) from the generator perspective.

In our case study, the generator is deployed on a Web server and accessible through a Web service. The learner profile from the Unity-based serious game is an XML file that required some transformations, on the server side, to be in conformance with our metamodels. Similarly, the generated scenario is transformed before being sent to the serious game, in order to be compliant with the expected format.

3.4 Re-engineering

Similarly to the other parts of the serious game development, the generator cannot be designed and implemented without considering the evolving stakeholders' needs, the changes in the generation choices, the evolution of the game, etc.

Experts of the Learning Game Domain Are Not Experts in Adaptation. Serious game stakeholders are not adaptation or generation experts. They do not have a precise perception of the generation rules to consider. They need some feedback about their expressed rules and strategies to make some adjustments, or to remove/add some new rules.

In our project, some initial rules have been finally rejected ("80% of the considered skills in the scenario must concern mastered skills whereas 20% focus on new skills"). The rule was not relevant with a 3-to-5-level length for the scenario. Experts finally propose 5 difficulty levels to always generate appropriate difficulties. Some other rules have been adjusted like the one stating the minimum and maximum range for the different categories of objects (backgrounds, hideouts, objects to find, useless objects, etc.) to add in the scene, according to the current level difficulty.

Evolution of the Serious Game. There are many reasons leading to reconsider the current metamodels and models involved in the generation. The serious game can evolve on both learning and gaming facets. It can imply to update the game description model, if it only concerns content changes, or also the game description metamodel for deeper changes. The learner profile can also be impacted by these changes. Differently, new learner information or other context elements can be available to be used into the generation rules; the context model and metamodel can then be updated. Generation rules can also have to be updated in case of input metamodels changes. Finally, the scenario model and metamodels can also be updated according to deep changes in the serious game.

We only encountered the situation of adding new scenes into the *Escape it!* learning game. It implied to declare them appropriately in the game description model to be directly taken into account by the current generator.

4   Conclusion

This paper gives us the opportunity to present the lessons we learnt during the development of a generation component of the *Escape it!* learning game. We present them according to the different stages of the development. This may be considered useful by other designers or researchers sharing similar contexts and objectives: proposing the generation of adapted scenarios that take into account context information, including learners' profiles, and the different components provided by the learning game. This adaptation is necessary in order to propose a large variety of situations to learners. The generation can contribute to reducing the cost of hard-coded situations.

Nevertheless, our results also point out the difficulty to express, specify and validate the generation rules. It is an important obstacle to overcome in the future. Our current research works are focusing on this point.

References

1. Belahbib, A., Lotfi, E., Bouhorma, M., Yedri, O.B., Slimani, A., Fatiha, E.: Serious games adaptation according to the learner's performances. Int. J. Electric. Comput. Eng. **7**, 451–459 (2017)
2. Burton, L.R., McEachin, J.: A Work in Progress: Behavior Management Strategies and a Curriculum for Intensive Behavioral Treatment of Autism. DRL Books, New York (1999)
3. Ern, A.: The use of gamification and serious games within interventions for children with autism spectrum disorder (2014)
4. Grubišić, A., Stankov, S., Žitko, B.: Adaptive courseware: a literature review. J. Univ. Comput. Sci. **21**, 1168–1209 (2015)
5. Hussaan, A., Sehaba, K.: Consistency verification of learner profiles in adaptive serious games. In: Verbert, K., Sharples, M., Klobučar, T. (eds.) Adaptive and Adaptable Learning. EC-TEL 2016. Lecture Notes in Computer Science, vol. 9891, pp. 384–389. Springer, Cham (2016). https://doi.org/10.1007/978-3-319-45153-4_31
6. Janssens, O., Samyn, K., Van de Walle, R., Van Hoecke, S.: Educational virtual game scenario generation for serious games. In: Proceedings of the IEEE 3rd International Conference on Serious Games and Applications for Health (SeGAH'14) (2014)
7. Laforcade, P., Laghouaouta, Y.: Supporting the adaptive generation of learning game scenarios with a model-driven engineering framework. In: European Conference on Technology Enhanced Learning (ECTEL'18), pp. 151–165. Leeds, United Kingdom (2018)
8. Laforcade, P., Loiseau, E., Kacem, R.: A model-driven engineering process to support the adaptive generation of learning game scenarios. In: CSEDU, vol. 1. INSTICC, Funchal, Madeira, Portugal (2018)
9. Melero, J., El-Kechaï, N., Yessad, A., Labat, J.M.: Adapting learning paths in serious games: an approach based on teachers' requirements. In: Zvacek, S., Restivo, M., Uhomoibhi, J., Helfert, M. (eds.) Computer Supported Education. CSEDU 2015. Communications in Computer and Information Science, vol. 583, pp. 376–394. Springer, Cham (2016). https://doi.org/10.1007/978-3-319-29585-5_22
10. Partington, J., Analysts, P.B.: The Assessment of Basic Language and Learning Skills-Revised (the ABLLS-R) (2010)
11. Ravyse, W., Blignaut, S., Leendertz, V., Woolner, A.: Success factors for serious games to enhance learning: a systematic review. Virt. Real. **21**, 31–58 (2016)

12. Sina, S., Rosenfeld, A., Kraus, S.: Generating content for scenario-based serious-games using crowdsourcing. In: Proceedings of the Twenty-Eighth AAAI Conference on Artificial Intelligence, pp. 522–529. AAAI Press (2014)
13. Steinberg, D., Budinsky, F., Paternostro, M., Merks, E.: EMF: Eclipse Modeling Framework 2.0, 2nd edn. Addison-Wesley Professional (2009)
14. Togelius, J., Yannakakis, G.N., Stanley, K.O., Browne, C.: Search-based procedural content generation: a taxonomy and survey. IEEE Trans. Comput. Intell. AI Game. **3**(3), 172–186 (2011)
15. Vandewaetere, M., Desmet, P., Clarebout, G.: The contribution of learner characteristics in the development of computer-based adaptive learning environments. Comput. Hum. Behav. **27**, 118–130 (2011)
16. Zakari, H.M., Ma, M., Simmons, D.: A review of serious games for children with autism spectrum disorders (ASD). In: Ma, M., Oliveira, M.F., Baalsrud Hauge, J. (eds.) Serious Games Development and Applications. SGDA 2014. Lecture Notes in Computer Science, vol. 8778, pp. 93–106. Springer, Cham (2014). https://doi.org/10.1007/978-3-319-11623-5_9

Lessons Learned from Implementing a Serious Game in Higher Education – A Student and Trainer Perspective

Knut Erik Bonnier[1](✉) [ID], Rune Andersen[2], and Hege Mari Johnsen[3]

[1] Department of Working Life and Innovation, University of Agder, Jon Lilletunsvei 3, Kristiansand, Norway
knut.e.bonnier@uia.no
[2] Department of ICT, University of Agder, Jon Lilletunsvei 9, Kristiansand, Norway
[3] Department of Health and Nursing Science, University of Agder, Jon Lilletunsvei 9, Kristiansand, Norway

Abstract. Serious games (SGs) have shown great potential as student-active learning tools in education, as they enable experimentation with practice-related work environments and systems that may otherwise be challenging and/or impractical to facilitate in an educational institution. However, existing instructional design models are limited in use when it comes to how to implement and integrate SGs within the existing curricula. Furthermore, the trainer perspective is often neglected in literature about serious games. The aim of this study was to explore the experiences of both students and trainers after the implementation and use of a SG in a master level course in project management (PM). Data was collected using six focus group interviews (FGIs) comprising 38 students. In addition, trainers' experiences were gathered as written comments to the results from the FGIs. Data was analysed using inductive content analysis. Results identified several issues related to the implementation and use of the SG that can be summarized through the following main- and subthemes; 1) Integration (introduction, facilitation, feedback and debriefing) and 2) Usability and gameplay (user interface design, learnability and use, immersion and satisfaction). Results showed that when adopting an existing SG to a course it enhances the need for a good implementation process, especially when it comes to provision of information, instructions, and feedback from trainers. Thus, the purpose of this paper is to share some of the experiences, issues and important lessons learned from the implementation to inform trainers on what to focus on when considering implementing SGs in their program.

Keywords: Serious games · Simulation · Implementation · Integration

1 Introduction and Background

Serious games have been an integral part of education over the last couple of decades. Through a rapid developing technology, this approach to education has provided us with the opportunity to create a more "real life" adaptation of training. Although referred to as

© Springer Nature Switzerland AG 2020
I. Marfisi-Schottman et al. (Eds.): GALA 2020, LNCS 12517, pp. 24–33, 2020.
https://doi.org/10.1007/978-3-030-63464-3_3

"games" they are often closer to real life simulations. Abt [1] states that serious games have an explicit and carefully thought-out educational purpose and are not intended to be played primarily for amusement. Loh et al. [2, p. 13] define serious games as "...digital games and simulation tools that are created for non-entertainment use, but with the primary purpose to improve skills and performance of play-learners through training and instruction". This paper will mainly use the definition provided by Loh et al. Serious games can produce several positive effects among students, such as increased motivation and development of knowledge [3, 4]. Lee [5] points out that simulations provide opportunity to experiment with practice-related work environments and systems that would otherwise be too expensive or in other ways impractical to facilitate, and as such supports the process of experiential learning. Furthermore, he states that the uncertainties and dynamics related with project management make it an ideal topic for using games and simulation to teach, which is in line with other authors [6, 7]. The closer to reality a game/simulation seems, the more transferable the skills will be [8]. "Contextualization, personalization and choice positively influence a learner's intrinsic motivation, depth of engagement in learning and learning performance" [9, p. 13]. Thus, usability is considered as a key component in relation to the game development process and is closely tied to the user's overall experience [10]. According to Nielsen [11], usability is a quality attribute that can be defined by the following five components: Learnability, efficiency, memorability, errors, and satisfaction. In order to maximize the benefit of good interaction design, usability testing is vital [10].

Arnab et al. [12] state that gameplay in serious games should support intrinsic experiential learning and that learning should be obtained through game mechanics. In general, serious games are associated with experiential learning since they often provide contextualization [9] and arenas to experiment [4], and enable decision making without facing serious consequences [13]. Kolb's Experiential Learning Cycle [14] suggest that effective learning is achieved when a person advances through a cycle of four stages, for which a learner can enter from any stage (Fig. 1). This process includes the following stages: concrete experience, reflective observation, abstract conceptualization, and active experimentation. In the first stage novel or modified experiences or contexts (i.e., serious games) are encountered and experienced. In the subsequent stages the experience is processed, and emerging theories and knowledge constructed through reflection. Kolb [14] sees learning as an integrated process and as such the learner needs to execute all four stages for efficient learning to take place. It is in relation to these stages that debriefing is particularly useful for ensuring deep learning. Crookall [15] states that; "debriefing is the processing of the game experience to turn it into learning". In the final stage of Kolb's cycle [14], the learner applies the newly acquired knowledge. According to Kolb [14] it is the learners own experience and reflection that creates knowledge, understanding and skills.

Serious Games Instructional Design (SGID) models are intended for the design and development of serious games [16] and are of limited use to anyone simply wanting to adopt a game rather than develop one. Hence, there is a lack of knowledge on how to integrate games with the rest of the course [17, 18]. Furthermore, the trainer perspective is often neglected in literature about serious games [19]. Younis and Loh [17] express the need for effective instructional design models which consider the adoption

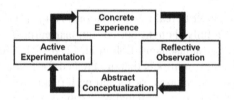

Fig. 1. Kolb's Experiential Learning Cycle

of serious games. However, instructional design can be seen as a wicked problem that cannot be easily understood and where minor changes can produce disproportionately major consequences. The way to approach such a problem is according to Snowden and Boone [20], "…to allow the path forward to reveal itself". Thus, one need to probe first, then sense, and then respond. Taking heed, the instructional design in this study is defined as iterative and experimental, since the trainers were on their own learning journey with regards to using games in an educational context. The introduction of a serious game for teaching project management was a new experience to us. Through the process we encountered several obstacles and learned valuable lessons, which ties to our research question: "What are the most important issues to address in the introduction and implementation of a serious games as viewed from student and trainer perspectives?".

2   Materials and Methods

The serious game used in this study is titled "The Project Management Game" (PM Game) and is developed by Media Engineering Institute (MEI) at HES-SO, Switzerland. In the PM game students take the role of a project manager (group-play) and manage an entire virtual project. The educational concept includes computer-based simulation, teamwork (solution searching, production of documentation) and real-world role-playing (selling the project to clients, reporting to the steering committee). The objective of the game is to transform an innovative idea into a concrete realization. The gameplay is based on Kolb's [14] experiential learning theory and facilitates both formative (in-game) and summative (after-game) assessment of students' knowledge and skills. Summative assessment is conducted through written reflective reports. After receiving feedback on all assignments, students resubmit their work for grading. The game was introduced and implemented during the Fall semester of 2019 as a module in a master level Project Management course with 58 students at UiA.

An explorative qualitative design was used. Data collection entailed 1) Focus group interviews (FGIs) with students, and 2) Trainer´s comments on the results from the FGIs. FGIs aim to capture the range of ideas, perspectives or feelings that people have about something [21]. Students were recruited based on their enrolment in the course. Participation was voluntary. Six FGIs were conducted comprising in total 38 students of the 58 which were enrolled. The FGI groups ranged in size from five to nine students. First the participants were asked if they had previous experience with serious games. The main interview question was open-ended; How did you experience the implementation and use of the PM Game? They were told that this included information, log-in, playing the game, facilitation and help from lecturers, including related task outside of the game, feedback and other issues. The analysis was informed by Braun and Clarke's [22] thematic content analysis. The analytic process was inductive, and data driven. All authors took part in the analysis and the results were discussed until agreement was reached. Based on the results from the FGIs, the trainer's experiences and point of view were provided through written notes.

This study was approved by the Norwegian Centre for Research Data (Number: 852540). All participants received oral and written information about the project and signed informed consent forms.

3   Results

None of the participants claimed to have previous experience from using serious games. Further, the analysis of the FGIs identified two main themes that influenced student experiences of implementation and use of the PM game. The main themes and subthemes are displayed in Table 1.

Table 1. Main Themes and Subthemes from Focus Group Interviews

Main themes	Subthemes
Integration	Introduction
	Facilitation
	Feedback and debriefing
Usability and gameplay	Learnability and use
	User interface design
	Immersion and satisfaction

In the next sections, results will be presented according to the main- and subthemes and include both students and trainers' experiences of implementation and use of the serious game.

3.1   Integration

Integration is defined as "the action or process of combining two or more things in an effective way" [23]. In our case this can be translated to the action or process of combining the game with other didactics, with an emphasis on issues that were not directly tied to the game itself.

Introduction and Facilitation
Several students expressed that they missed information and instruction about the game and how to play. One expressed: "Wish we knew more what we were in for before we started. I felt that when we had played maybe 50% of the game, we understood the concept" (FGI 3). Further, students felt confused with regards to the chosen instructional

strategy based on learning by doing (flipped classroom). One student said: "We were thrown into deep water and received a lifejacket after struggling for some time first" (FGI 4). However, students expressed that the provision of relevant information, instruction and materials improved during the course. Despite the above comments.

The trainers pointed out that game manuals were made available to the students and this was communicated both in writing and orally. There were also manuals available in the game, but they were written in English and not intuitively accessible.

Students perceived a mismatch in allocated time and expected effort. It was also perceived that trainers had varied knowledge about the game. This caused some confusion. Like the students, the trainers experienced different issues during the introduction of the module. For example, a change in the curricula caused a mismatch between time allocated to the game and its impact on the grading. Consequently, students´ workload increased. Furthermore, the trainers had different roles in the module; one was responsible for issues directly related to the game. The two other trainers were responsible for providing the additional components such as subject material, student supervision. The trainer responsible for game related issues could not attend the first session. Consequently, the introduction suffered greatly from this. The trainers expressed that their learning curve had been quite steep. However, they felt they had learned a lot from the iterative integration process and had managed to correct and improve the instruction design during the course.

Feedback and Debriefing

Some students expressed that the trainer's feedback on students´ assignments could have been more specific and tailored to each group. The trainers agreed to some extent with this but insisted that oral feedback and debriefing had been provided during the sessions but not in a structured fashion. Some students also criticized the limited word count permitted in reports, as this decreased the opportunity for more thorough reflection on their mistakes. Students also proposed that they should have got an opportunity to hear how other students had solved the same tasks in the game.

3.2 Usability and Gameplay

The other main theme "Usability and gameplay" is comprised of issues that are directly tied to the game.

Learnability and Use

Several students expressed that they had to learn using the game by playing it, and that this was a time-consuming process. One student said that; "we used three to five hours playing and doing things the wrong way, before we realized how the game should be played" (FGI 4). Several of the students suggested that the game should have included in-game information, instructions, and alerts. Similar, many students wished for more in-game feedback on their performance, particularly regarding what was incorrect and correct. The trainers agreed that the game should have provided more feedback, at least as an option.

Some students also expressed that they wished the gameplay were more flexible. For example, they wished for the ability to go back and change their decisions. As one student said, "If you move to the next phase you are not able to go back and change your mind in the prior phase" (FGI 1). In addition, many students called for an opportunity to replay the game. The trainers explained that the developers had not conducted any usability testing of the game, and that this could explain the perceived usability issues.

User Interface Design

Some students expressed that information could easily be overlooked, as some important messages disappeared in too much text or was hidden in e-mails within the game. It was also perceived as difficult to play the game using only one screen or playing alone. Consequently, it was challenging to get a holistic overview of the game and their group performance.

Immersion and Satisfaction

Several students expressed that they liked the concept of learning through experience and got quite immersed during gameplay. For instance, one student said; "the group got a bit too much immersed at sometimes, and it created quite hot discussions" (FGI 1). Similar, another student, asserted that this concept of learning created a higher degree of engagement among students. However, one student claimed that; "the game was not boring but not so exciting either" (FGI 5).

The experience of relevance and authenticity varied among the students. One student declared that: "This is actually a scenario that you easily can meet in a real job-situation" (FGI 3). Others found it hard to relate to. However, several students believed the serious game enabled them to get a different perspective on project management compared to a more traditional teaching approach. One group said: "We learned a lot by seeing all the elements we hadn't thought of come together. You don't really think about the problems that might appear. If we had been able to play again, we would have done other things than we did this time" (FGI 3). The trainers stated that they believed that the game as a virtual environment provided the students with a somewhat realistic experience of managing a project. However, the fact that the game was developed for a Swiss context made it sometimes difficult to relate all elements to a Norwegian context.

Even if many students perceived it as quite exhausting to play in the beginning, most of the students expressed that playing went smoother and became more fun towards the end. Some said that it was fun watching the scoring indicators moving up and down as consequences of their performance and got intrigued by it. Despite the experienced issues during implementation and use, learning by gameplay was proposed by several students as better than reading a book or attending lectures.

4 Discussion

In this section, results will be discussed according to the main themes from the results; integration and usability and gameplay.

4.1 Integration

Like in the study by Rumeser and Emsley [7], both students and trainers experienced several issues related to the integration of the PM game. Integration is explicitly highlighted as the key to a successful implementation of serious games [8] and flipped classroom settings [24]. Issues experienced during integration were partly related to trainers' inexperience on how to integrate the game within the course [17, 18], and their provision of information to students on how to play the game. In addition, usability issues experienced by students influenced the integration. A lot of time was spent figuring out how to play the game instead of focusing on the learning objectives in the course.

Evidence [25, 26] show that applying games via trial and error often leads to ineffective practice. However, in our case a cyclical approach in integration seemed appropriate to facilitate the learning process of both students and trainers. After learning to play the game, many students preferred gameplay before lectures. As trainers' knowledge about the game and its usability issues increased, they gained awareness on what was needed of supplemented information and manuals in future courses using the game. We agree with Crookall [15], who argues that having competent trainers is important in relation to the learning potential of games. Fortunately, the experiences related to the introduction of the game gave valuable lessons. For example, an instructional video would simplify the process immensely. One should also in a much larger extent make use of "superusers" of the game in future courses. Superusers should also include students. We also suggest introducing the game before playing it, to allow the students to explore and become familiar with the user interface [8, 27]. Issues in relation to the game can then be resolved early.

Many teachers/trainers are reluctant to use games as part of their pedagogical "toolbox". A major reason is a lack of knowledge on how to integrate games within courses. Younis and Loh [17] and Giessen [18] express the need for effective instructional design models which consider the use of serious games and fulfil the trainer's needs. However, instead of just reading manuals about the content of the game and how to play it, we recognize that all the trainers involved in a PM course should have explored the game substantially before introducing it to students.

Feedback and debriefing enable students to reflect on their experiences and integrate and retain new knowledge [14, 15]. Reflection on action refers to reflecting on experiences from clinical practice situations, or reflection on reflection [28]. Reflection on experiences from the PM game was facilitated through group discussions and written reports based on problem-based learning through PM gameplay. However, some students expressed that the trainers' feedback could have been more specific and tailored to each group. As suggested by Crookall [15], the learning potential of games can only be activated in full by having competent game managers and debriefers. The need of more feedback was recognized by the trainers. As the trainers became more familiar with the PM game, more comprehensive and specific feedback were provided. The trainers asserted that feedback and debriefing were deemed important in the course.

Socialization in terms of interacting with other students may also facilitate reflection and experiential learning. As results showed, students had quite hot discussions based on their gameplay. If the students had played the game all by themselves, they would have missed this. Thus, an additional way to facilitate debriefing after game play is using peer assessment. Student mentioned that they were interested to hear how other students would solve the same tasks. This peer assessment will be employed in upcoming project management courses. Future courses will also provide more instant feedback by trainers and make better use of a forum functionality available in Canvas (Learning Management System). Crookall [15] suggest that such forums can be designed in a manner that facilitate formalized guidance for more structured discussion. Topical discussions tied to each project phase is an example of a feedback mechanism that relates to this suggestion.

4.2 Usability and Gameplay

According to Nielsen [11] usability is a "quality attribute that assesses how easy user interfaces are to use". Several usability issues were identified in the PM game, particularly regarding learnability and efficiency of use. For instance, it was cumbersome to learn and time-consuming to play. Consequently, students spent a lot of time and effort on learning how to play the game, which may have impacted the cognitive capacity to focus on the content and fulfill the learning objectives of the game [29]. Arnab et al. [12] state that gameplay in serious games should support intrinsic experiential learning and that learning should be obtained through game mechanics. This relates to Kolb´s experiential learning theory, which proposes that important components are situated learning and reflection [14]. Thus, experiential learning is dependent on both the quality of the experience (gameplay) and quality of the (in-game) reflection. In relation to reflection during gameplay, students missed in-game instructions and feedback particularly if wrong decisions were made. Reflection in action represents thinking that modifies what is being done in the moment of execution [28]. Lack of ability to reflect in action (during gameplay) may influence the process whereby knowledge is created through transformation of experience [14]. Crookall [15] states that in general it is easy to collect data during gameplay, and that this data can provide feedback during in-game debriefing. He points out that in-game feedback could enable a richer debriefing process since participants have to confront the hard facts instead of denying them, which can happen during debriefing after gameplay.

Experiential learning (i.e., through serious games) may help students recognize cues in new situations and aid their information-processing [14]. Thus, in relation to experiential learning Lamb et al. [8] suggest that students should be able to replay a game if they wish to improve their performance. Students clearly expressed that lacking the ability to undo choices and play the game several times, affected their learning process. The trainers agreed that such functionality would be beneficial.

This PM game was developed for a different social system in Switzerland, which sometimes influenced the experience of realism and authenticity, which adds to the evidence [8] that a contextualized game is important. Consequently, this project is developing a game that will fit the Norwegian context and better supports our instructional design (experiential learning theory) when it comes to feedback and debriefing.

5 Conclusion

From the implementation process we experienced the introduction of the game as particularly challenging. We advise using time to explain the instructional strategy and how the game will be used in the beginning of the course. An instructional video or a similar option should be implemented. We also recommend that all trainers explore and learn the game properly to ensure instructional assets suffice.

Feedback and debriefing are crucial and should be available in several formats, both within the game and elsewhere. We recommend using multiplayer games since they facilitate unstructured and informal debriefing and reflection. Further, it is recommended to use games that has built in feedback, and supplement with activities outside of the game which enable further debriefing. By exploring and developing competence on the game, it will be easier for the trainer to design a holistic integrated system for debriefing and reflection.

Usability was a major issue. Students struggled to grasp the game in the beginning, this was partly caused by the introduction issues, but could have been avoided or mitigated by conducting comprehensive usability testing.

References

1. Abt, C.C.: Serious Games. University Press of America, London (1987)
2. Loh, C.S., Sheng, Y., Ifenthaler, D.: Serious games analytics: theoretical framework. In: Loh, C.S., Sheng, Y., Ifenthaler, D. (eds.) Serious Games Analytics. AGL, pp. 3–29. Springer, Cham (2015). https://doi.org/10.1007/978-3-319-05834-4_1
3. Whitton, N.: Digital Games and Learning: Research and Theory. Routledge, New York (2014). https://doi.org/10.4324/9780203095935
4. Boyle, E.A., et al.: An update to the systematic literature review of empirical evidence of the impacts and outcomes of computer games and serious games. Comput. Educ. **94**, 178–192 (2016). https://doi.org/10.1016/j.compedu.2015.11.003
5. Lee, W.L.: Spreadsheet based experiential learning environment for project management. In: Proceedings of the 2011 Winter Simulation Conference (WSC), pp. 3877–3887. IEEE (2011). https://doi.org/10.1109/wsc.2011.6148079
6. Saenz, M.J., Cano, J.L.: Experiential learning through simulation games: an empirical study. Int. J. Eng. Educ. **25**(2), 296 (2009)
7. Rumeser, D., Emsley, M.: Lessons learned from implementing project management games. Int. J. Ser. Game. **6**(1), 71–92 (2019). https://doi.org/10.17083/ijsg.v6i1.130
8. Lamb, R.L., Annetta, L., Firestone, J., Etopio, E.: A meta-analysis with examination of moderators of student cognition, affect, and learning outcomes while using serious educational games, serious games, and simulations. Comput. Hum. Behav. **80**, 158–167 (2018). https://doi.org/10.1016/j.chb.2017.10.040
9. Breuer, J., Bente, G.: Why so serious? on the relation of serious games and learning. J. Comput. Game Cult. **4**(1), 7–24 (2010)
10. Olsen, T., Procci, K., Bowers, C.: Serious games usability testing: how to ensure proper usability, playability, and effectiveness. In: Marcus, A. (ed.) DUXU 2011. LNCS, vol. 6770, pp. 625–634. Springer, Heidelberg (2011). https://doi.org/10.1007/978-3-642-21708-1_70
11. Nielsen Norman Group. https://www.nngroup.com/articles/usability-101-introduction-to-usability/. Accessed 01 Jul 2020
12. Arnab, S., et al.: Mapping learning and game mechanics for serious games analysis. Br. J. Educ. Technol. **46**(2), 391–411 (2015). https://doi.org/10.1111/bjet.12113
13. Marsh, T.: Serious games continuum: between games for purpose and experiential environments for purpose. Entertain. Comput. **2**(2), 61–68 (2011). https://doi.org/10.1016/j.entcom.2010.12.004

14. Kolb, D.A.: Experiential Learning: Experience as the Source of Learning and Development. Prentice-Hall, Englewood Cliffs, NJ (1984)
15. Crookall, D.: Serious games, debriefing, and simulation/gaming as a discipline. Simul. Gaming **41**(6), 898–920 (2010). https://doi.org/10.1177/1046878110390784
16. Becker, K., Parker, J.R.: The Guide to Computer Simulations and Games. Wiley, New York (2011)
17. Younis, B., Loh, C.S.: Integrating serious games in higher education programs. In: Paper presented at Academic Colloquium 2010: Building Partnership in Teaching Excellence. Ramallah, Palestine (2010)
18. Giessen, H.W.: Serious games effects: an overview. Proc. Soc. Behav. Sci. **174**, 2240–2244 (2015). https://doi.org/10.1016/j.sbspro.2015.01.881
19. Becker, K.: Choosing and Using Digital Games in the Classroom - A Practical Guide. Springer, Cham (2017). https://doi.org/10.1007/978-3-319-12223-6
20. Snowden, D.J., Boone, M.E.: A leader's framework for decision making. Harv. Bus. Rev. **85**(11), 68 (2007)
21. Krueger, R.A., Casey, M.A.: Focus Groups: A Practical Guide for Applied Research, 5th edn. Sage, Los Angeles (2015)
22. Braun, V., Clarke, V.: Using thematic analysis in psychology. Qual. Res. Psychol. **3**(2), 77–101 (2006). https://doi.org/10.1191/1478088706qp063oa
23. Cambridge Dictionary. https://dictionary.cambridge.org/dictionary/english/integration, last accessed 2020/07/08
24. Tucker, B.: The flipped classroom. Educ. Next **12**(1), 82–83 (2012)
25. Takeuchi, B.L.M., Vaala, S.: Level Up Learning: A National Survey on Teaching with Digital Games (2014)
26. Kenny, R., Gunter, G.: Factors affecting adoption of video games in the classroom. Education **66**, 11–24. J. Interact. Learn. Res. **22**(2), 259–276 (2011)
27. Bollin, A., Hochmüller, E., Mittermeir, R.T.: Teaching software project management using simulations. In: 2011 24th IEEE-CS Conference on Software Engineering Education and Training (CSEE&T), pp. 81–90. IEEE (2011). https://doi.org/10.1109/cseet.2011.5876160
28. Schön, D.A.: The Reflective Practitioner: How Professionals Think in Action. Basic Books, New York (2007). https://doi.org/10.4324/9781315237473
29. Kiili, K.: Digital game-based learning: towards an experiential gaming model. Internet High. Educ. **8**(1), 13–24 (2005). https://doi.org/10.1016/j.iheduc.2004.12.001

User-Centred Design Method for Digital Catalogue Interfaces

Maho Wielfrid Morie[1]([⊠]) [iD], Iza Marfisi-Schottman[2], and Bi Tra Goore[1]

[1] Institut National Polytechnique Felix Houphouët-Boigny, Yamoussoukro 1093, Côte d'Ivoire
{maho.morie,bitra.goore}@inphb.ci
[2] Le Mans Université, EA 4023, LIUM, 72085 Le Mans, France
iza.marfisi@univ-lemans.fr

Abstract. Digital catalogues must be intuitive and easy to use. However, designing their interfaces is a complex task because there is so much available information and such little space. The choice of search filters, their format, their position, including the way to represent the results, are not trivial decisions. This paper presents the *User-Driven Interface Design* (*UDID*) method that offers five steps with specific material to help end users produce mock-up interfaces for digital catalogues. This method recommends letting participants compose their interfaces according to their needs. In this article, we present how the UDID method offered several befts for designing the interface of a Learning Game catalogue. 17 participants followed this method to produce five mock-up interfaces that we then analysed and compared to create the final interface.

Keywords: Interface design · User-centered design · Digital catalogue · UX design method · Learning games

1 Introduction

Digital catalogues are useful to filter a large number of resources in order to find those that meet ones needs. Such catalogues are used in many domains such as education (e.g. *Le Catalogue Collectif de France*[1]) or commerce (e.g. *Amazon*). Users should be able to find resources without assistance or significant intellectual effort [1]. Therefore, digital catalogues must provide simple and intuitive interfaces [2]. Yet, digital catalogue interface design is a complex task. Available resources in these catalogues are described with metadata that usually contain a lot of information. For example the Learning Object Metadata (LOM) has 69 fields of information such as title, type of resource, age of the public, cost, etc. [3]. However, it would not be relevant to offer a filter for each of these fields, as this would overload the interface. The problem therefore concerns the choice of the few relevant filters and the format that will facilitate the search. The way the resources, resulting from the search, are displayed is also important to help users make a quick choice.

---

[1] https://bbf.enssib.fr/consulter/bbf-2011-02-0071-001.

I. Marfisi-Schottman et al. (Eds.): GALA 2020, LNCS 12517, pp. 34–44, 2020.
https://doi.org/10.1007/978-3-030-63464-3_4

These difficulties appear more marked in domains where there are no satisfying catalogues to draw inspiration from. This is the case for Learning Games (LGs): the existing LG catalogues do not offer filtering systems that facilitate the selection of LGs adapted to teachers' specific needs [4]. To illustrate, the *SeriousGamesClassification*[2] catalogue, offers a filter system based on three criteria: the purpose of the LG (e.g. education, information or marketing), the market (*e.g.* health, communication or politics) and the public (*e.g.* children, general public or professionals) [5]. The *Mobygames*[3] catalogue offers filters based on the platform (*e.g.* PC, Nintendo), the year of the LG, the game theme (visual, board game or shooter) and the game rating (*e.g.* ESBR, PEGI). First of all, these catalogues do not comply with the basic UX design models [6]. The filters on *SeriousGamesClassification* for example, are all in checkbox format, whether the possible values are numerical, textual or require choosing a range of values. The filters of *Mobygames* are available as links that open up another page, which complicates the search process, because the users are most likely to go back to the first page to try other filters. In addition, the thumbnails that represent the result LGs only contain an image, the title of the game and the year of publication, which is not sufficient to help teachers. Most importantly, the existing catalogues that inventory LGs (e.g. *SeriousGamesClassification, Mobygames, Serious Games FR*[4], *MIT Step*[5], *LearningGamesForKids*[6]) do not allow to search for LGs depending on their educational goal. This is probably because these catalogues are not primarily intended for teachers. They are designed by video game experts and offer more non-education games than LGs. The existing catalogues therefore do not answer the teacher's need for an intuitive tool to find LGs for their classes.

In a previous study, we show that it is possible to browse LG web sites and automatically collect 23 items of information, compliant with the Learning Games Metadata Definition (LGMD) [7]. These items include the educational topic for which the LG may be relevant, its game type and the platform requirement to play it. Each of these 23 items can be transformed into a filter but there is only room for a few on the catalogue's homepage. Moreover, each filter can be implemented in various formats such as checkbox, drop-down list, radio button etc. Search results (*i.e.* LGs that meet the search criteria) can also be represented in different ways. In addition, the layout of these filters and results is important to create a good user experience. Given the many choices that need to be made, it seems paramount to consult the end users at the very beginning of the interface design process. Thus, we propose a digital catalogue interface design method, inspired by the user-centred approach [8].

Section 2 presents a state of the art of interface design methods. In Sects. 3 and 4 we present the UDID method and how it was used for designing a LG catalogue interface. Finally, in Sect. 5, we discuss the difficulties observed by teachers when using UDID and the relevance of the proposed interface mock-ups, followed by the conclusion and perspectives.

---

[2] http://serious.gameclassification.com/.

[3] https://www.mobygames.com/.

[4] https://www.serious-game.fr/.

[5] https://education.mit.edu/.

[6] https://www.learninggamesforkids.com/.

2 Interface Design Methods

There are several methods for interface design [9]. The **UX (User eXperience) design** methods, for example, give guidelines on the colours to adopt, the type of widgets and their layout on the interface, etc. [2]. This method is interesting because it allows structuring the web pages content to be more pleasant for the users by highlighting the important content with appropriate style choices. However, these methods do not involve the end users for the beginning [10] and may lead to redesigning the interfaces when the final product is confronted to them, which is very expensive.

The **Agile method** is an approach that consists in developing applications incrementally by asking the user's appreciation at each design step [11]. This validation is important for further application design because it allows to improve the interface and functionalities but it provides limited information on the interface that users actually want [12]. Indeed, end users will tend to make minimal changes on the already designed interfaces, without thinking of the interface they would really like. When it comes to creating a catalogue interface, one of the most complex tasks lies in the interface organization. Out of the dozens possible ways of organizing the interface, the designers will make one choice that will not necessarily be the end users' choice.

The **User-Centred Design (UCD) approach** therefore seems to be most suitable because it delegate the interface design and all non-technical parts of application to the end users [13]. It is an interactive approach that allows knowing users' needs and preferences. However, in the case of LG catalogue design, UCD should be implemented with caution because there are no existing satisfactory examples to build on [14]. To solve this problem, we propose a design method adapted from UCD with clearly defined steps and material to help the end users design their ideal interface.

3 UDID Catalogue Interface Design Method

The User-Driven Interface Design (UDID) method is inspired by Learning Analytics Dashboard (LAD) method [8], which generates dashboards for learning in which the end users are involved. The UDID method also requires the involvement of volunteer participants who are representative of the catalogues' end users. These participants are mobilized to design the mock-up interfaces themselves and not to evaluate proposed mock-ups. Participants must be organized in teams of three or four to boost creativity but also to encourage them to explain their choices in order to clearly understand their approach. They also need to be guided through this process with a step by step method and specific material.

3.1 Material for the UDID Method

The material for the UDID methods consists of:

- A white A3 cardboard that represents a computer screen. One could also choose a phone or tablet depending on the context of use.

- Filter cards, representing all available product information. For each filter, six formats are available: *drop-down list*, *checkbox*, *radio button*, *textbox*, *word cloud* and *range sliders* (Fig. 3).
- Post-it notes, which are used to represent thumbnails of the products matching the search. Participants can list the information they want to have for products' summary descriptions.

The size ratio of these items should represent the screen without having to scroll down. The filter cards should show both filter name and format design with possible examples of available information. Each filter should have a card in each available format, unless this format is not suitable for the type of information carried by this filter (Fig. 3). Finally, participants should have empty post-it notes, pens and markers to modify the given material or create new ones.

3.2 Five Steps of the UDID Method

The participants follow five steps in which they use the above material (Fig. 1):

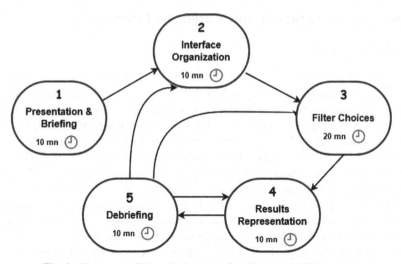

Fig. 1. Five steps of *User-Driven Interface Design* (UDID) method

- **Step 1** – The person organizing the design session **presents the goals** (i.e. create a catalogue interface mock-up) to the participants and explains how to use the material while insisting on the possibility to create new material. It is also important to indicate the time required for each step of the process.
- **Step 2** – The participants **organize the interface** by deciding where to place the search and result areas.

- **Step 3** - The participants **choose the filter cards** they want to place in the search area and determine their **layout.** To help them, all filters should be visible on the table, grouped by filters types. This step can be quite time-consuming because of the large number of filters.
- **Step 4** – The participants have to determine how they would like to see the **research results displayed** on the interface. They can use Post-it notes to represent the result thumbnails, on which they can draw the information they would like to see (i.e. description information, image, key words, etc.).
- **Step 5** – A **debriefing** should be carried out at the end of session to help the participants review their choices and make changes to the proposed interface based on new ideas that emerge from the discussions.

It is important to film the design session to help identify the components and displays on which there was immediate consensus and those for which the decision was much more difficult. This information is precious for designing the final mock-up interface. In the next section, we will present how UDID was applied, through several design sessions with teachers, to design a LG catalogue.

4   Design of a Learning Game Catalogue Interface

4.1   Participant Profiles

The purpose of this catalogue is to allow education stakeholders find LGs adapted to specific teaching needs. Hence, we solicited 17 volunteers with the right profile: 12 teachers, 3 librarians and 2 educational designers. Educational designers are experts in computer technologies for education. Their ability to design and manage training devices is an asset to evaluate a learning resource platform. In addition, they have a good appreciation of how to describe the needs of teachers, since they train them. The librarians chosen were familiar with classic learning resource catalogues, such as those found in libraries and online learning resource platforms. They also recently created the *Nantilus*[7] online catalogue for medical learning resources. Although these participants are not representative of the end users, we assumed they would provide us with interesting ideas. The teachers were chosen to represent a diversity of domains and levels: 4 teachers for pre-school and primary school, 4 for middle school and 4 for higher school. None of them was familiar with searching online learning resources. Table 1 summarizes the number of participants for each of the five teams.

---

[7] https://nantilus.univ-nantes.fr/vufind/.

Table 1. Distribution of participants by co-design team

	Team 1	Team 2	Team 3	Team 4	Team 5
Date	24/01/2020	31/01/2020	07/02/2020	07/02/2020	07/02/2020
Place	Université du Mans	Université de Nantes	CBCG Daloa	CBCG Daloa	CBCG Daloa
Nb participants	2	4	3	4	4
Participant profiles	1 teacher (high school) 1 educational designer	3 librarians 1 educational designer	3 teachers (high school)	4 teachers (college)	4 teachers (preschool)

We planned three co-design sessions: two in France with team 1 and team 2 and another session in Côte d'Ivoire, with the three remaining teams (Fig. 2). Even though two different researchers carried out the experiments in France and Cote d'Ivoire, we provided the same material and followed the same strict experimental protocol.

Fig. 2. Co-design sessions in Le Mans (A), Nantes (B), and Daloa (C)

4.2 Experimentation Material and Protocol

The filter card we create with the 23 information items of the LGMD metadata model [8]. For each filter, we created up to six card that represented the available formats depending on the type of values (Fig. 3).

The co-design sessions followed the one-hour UDID process. However, all the sessions exceeded this time limit, with some teams working up to two hours. The debriefing was particularly rich and provided valuable insight on the co-design method. We filmed

Fig. 3. Different formats for the educational domain filter

all the sessions in order to analyse each step and points of conflict. This was crucial to design the final catalogue interface, based on the five mock-up interfaces designed by the teams (Fig. 4). In the next section, we analyse these mock-up interfaces and explain how they helped us answer the four questions for designing digital catalogues: which filters should be chosen, in what format should they be, how should the interface be organized and how should the results be presented?

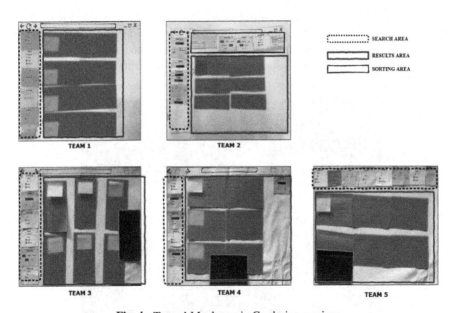

Fig. 4. Teams' Mock-ups in Co-design sessions

4.3   Results of Interface Design Sessions

In this section, we analyse the mock-up interfaces designed by the five teams and decide which design choices should be kept for the final LG catalogue interface.

Interface Organization

We observed almost the same result for all teams regarding the web page organization: four teams placed the search area on the left, in which they placed filters vertically. For the result area, four out of five teams create thumbnails in a row (Fig. 4). We therefore decided to choose the interface organization that most of the teams used. In addition, we add a sorting area, above the result area, as proposed by Team 2, composed of librarians, who already had experience in designing such catalogues.

Choice of Search Filters

The analysis of the five mock-up interfaces shows that each team chose an average of six filters for the search area. Team 2 also proposes four additional filters, in a new area labelled "sorting area". For the final mock-up, we decided to keep the filters *Language, Platform requirements, Public and Domain* that were chosen by at least three teams (in yellow in Table 2). We also added the filters *Keywords* and *Age,* considered as sub-criteria of the filters *Domain* and *Public* by the participants. In addition, we added the filters *Game Mode* and *Cost,* chosen by two teams, but with default options already activated. We also chose to place the filter *Date* in sorting area. Finally, we added the *Motivation* filter, which carries essential information, especially in primary and pre-school level, as expressed by team 5, composed of this profile.

Table 2. Filters chosen per team

Filters	Team 1	Team 2	Team 3	Team 4	Team 5	Total
Title						0
Language	X	X	X	X	X	5
Description						0
Keywords	X	X				2
Version						0
Contribution						0
Date		X		X		2
Format		X				1
Size						0
Location						0
Platform requirements		X		X	X	3
Public	X	X	X	X	X	5
Age	X			X		2
Motivation		X			X	2
Knowledge Validation				X		1
Game Type				X	X	2
Game Mode		X	X			2
Domain	X		X	X	X	4
Progress Indicators			X			1
Cost	X	X				2
Rights		X				1
Gameplay			X	X		2
Rating						0

Search Filter Formats

The analysis of the mock-up interfaces shows that the teams chose different formats for a given filter. We therefore followed the following tendencies. In all, the *drop-down list* format was used the most (7 times for the filters chosen above). It was particularly appreciated for filters containing over three values and requiring a single choice such as *Domain* and *Public,* because it takes up little space on the interface. The *checkbox* format was also use 7 times. This format was uses for the filter *Platform,* which allows several choices of values. The *range sliders* format was preferred for filters with numerical information such as *Age.* The *text box* format was chosen for filters with free information such as *Keywords.* Finally, filters containing two values such as *Language, Game Mode* and Cost were placed in the sorting area in *radio button* format with default options.

Presentation of LG Research Results
Concerning the design of the LG thumbnails on Post-it notes, all teams reserved space for an illustrative image of the LG with several information fields. The information presented was quite diverse with 17 fields chosen out of 23. However, all teams chose *Title* and three teams chose *Gameplay* and *Cost.* The other fields were selected by maximum two teams and the films show that their choice was not particularly motivated. For the final interface, we therefore decided to use *Title, Gameplay* and *Cost* and add the fields used in the search area (i.e. *Domain, Keywords, Public, Age* and *Platform*) since this information can help them selected LGs that meets their search criteria. Finally, we added information on the *Motivation* and *Progress Indicator* as participants mostly showed interest about the LG's pedagogical characteristics. We arranged the fields according to space that information could occupy since participants did not give importance to information's order or appearance (Fig. 5).

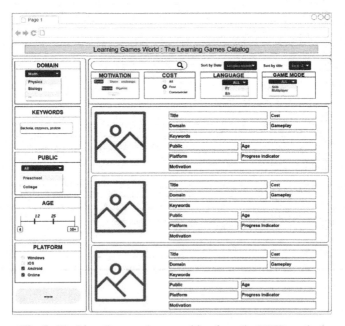

Fig. 5. Final interface mock-up resulting from the UDID method

4.4 Discussion

As we noted throughout the discussions with the participants, all the teams managed to apply the UDID method without difficulty and found it was a helpful for designing interfaces. They particularly appreciated the use of paper materials that encouraged them to take part in the design sessions. Being able to customize and move the cards seemed to help them express their needs and organize the interface the way they wanted. The team of librarians also expressed a preference for this approach rather than the Agile method they have recently used to design their educational resource catalogue. However, we identified several limitations. First, the time allocated to each design session was clearly insufficient. Choosing the filters and placing them on the interface was the most time-consuming. The format of the filter were also subject to a lot of discussion, which was not unanimous in all teams. A solution may be to pre-select filter formats based on the type of content. Another delicate choice we made was to involve five teams. It might be better to involve fewer teams to simplify the final design choices, based on their mock-ups that were sometimes quite different. This might also be because the participants were grouped by profile. This fact underlines why it is important to film all sessions in order to understand the dynamics behind the participants' choices and their priorities regarding the search filters.

5 Conclusion and Perspectives

The User-Driven Interface Design (UDID) method allows us to meet the challenge of designing a Learning Games (LG) catalogue interface. Thanks to its clear step-by-step method and the material it provided, five teams of teachers and other educational stakeholders were able to design mockup models of the interface. By comparing the similarities of these mockups and analyzing the discussions that the participants had during the design phase, we were able to design a final interface for the LG catalogue.

Nevertheless, we need to verify that the final interface truly allows teachers to find the relevant LGs quickly. To do this, we will carry out another experimentation with the final LG catalogue. UDID could also be adapted to the design of mobile application interfaces. Indeed, it raises similar challenges such as choosing and organizing a lot of potential information in on a very small screen.

References

1. dos Santos, F.A., Tiradentes Souto, V.: Graphic design and user-centred design: designing learning tools for primary school. Int. J. Technol. Des. Educ. **29**(5), 999–1009 (2018). https://doi.org/10.1007/s10798-018-9480-1
2. Kurniawan, S., Zaphiris, P.: Research-derived web design guidelines for older people. In: Proceedings of the SIGACCESS Conference, pp. 129–135. ACM (2005)
3. Neven, F., Duval, E.: Reusable learning objects: a survey of LOM-based repositories. In: Proceedings of the Conference on Multimedia, pp. 291–294. ACM (2002)
4. Morie, M.W., et al.: Information extraction model to improve learning game metadata indexing. ISI **25**, 11–19 (2020)

5. Djaouti, D., Alvarez, J., Jessel, J.-P.: Classifying serious games: the G/P/S model. In: Handbook of Research on Improving Learning and Motivation through Educational Games: Multidisciplinary Approaches (2011)
6. Leavitt, M.O., Shneiderman, B.: Based web design & usability guidelines. Background and Methodology (2006)
7. Morie, M.W., Marfisi-Schottman, I., Goore, B.T.: LGMD: optimal lightweight metadata model for indexing learning games. In: Hamlich, M., Bellatreche, L., Mondal, A., Ordonez, C. (eds.) SADASC 2020. CCIS, vol. 1207, pp. 3–16. Springer, Cham (2020). https://doi.org/10.1007/978-3-030-45183-7_1
8. Ines, D., et al.: User centered approach for learning analytics dashboard generation. In: Proceedings of Conference on Computer Supported Education, Heraklion, Greece, pp. 260–267 (2019)
9. De Troyer, O.M.F., Leune, C.J.: WSDM: a user centered design method for Web sites. Comput. Netw. ISDN Syst. **30**, 85–94 (1998)
10. Sutcliffe, A.: Assessing the reliability of heuristic evaluation for Web site attractiveness and usability. In: Proceedings of the Hawaii International Conference, pp. 1838–1847 (2002)
11. Maleki, N.G., Ramsin, R.: Agile Web development methodologies: a survey and evaluation. In: Lee, R. (ed.) SERA 2017. SCI, vol. 722, pp. 1–25. Springer, Cham (2018). https://doi.org/10.1007/978-3-319-61388-8_1
12. Torrecilla-Salinas, C.J., et al.: Estimating, planning and managing Agile Web development projects under a value-based perspective. Inf. Softw. Tech. **61**, 124–144 (2015)
13. Schnall, R., et al.: A user-centered model for designing consumer mobile health (mHealth) applications (apps). J. Biomed. Inform. **60**, 243–251 (2016)
14. Vredenburg, K. et al.: A survey of user-centered design practice. In: Proceedings of SIGCHI, pp. 471–478. ACM, Minneapolis (2002)

Approaching Quantum Entanglement Developing a Serious Game in Quantum Computing for IT Professionals

Isabell Heider[1,2(✉)], Harald Bendl[1], Jan-Rainer Lahmann[2], and Frauke Mörike[3] ⓘ

[1] DHBW Mannheim, Coblitzallee 1-9, 68163 Mannheim, Germany
Isabell.heider@ibm.com
[2] IBM Deutschland GmbH, Am Weiher 24, 65451 Kelsterbach, Germany
[3] Technische Universität Berlin, Straße Des 17. Juni 135, 10623 Berlin, Germany

Abstract. Quantum Computing (QC) has gained a constantly rising level of attention and interest in the last years from academic institutions and research teams in the industry alike. Although several serious games (SG) for QC are available to date, the specific learning needs of IT professionals are not sufficiently covered to equip them with a knowledge base on the fundamental concepts of QC. Based on an analysis of 12 current SGs in QC, we have identified the concept of Entanglement as an underrepresented learning objective and have developed a SG around Quantum Entanglement using the Greenberg-Horne-Zeilinger (GHZ) experiment as a joint project in cooperation with the IBM Quantum Ambassadors team.

This paper advances the knowledge base within the field of SGs and learning across three dimensions: (1) it identifies Quantum Entanglement as underrepresented learning topic in the array of QC concepts covered by SGs, (2) provides a case study on the development of a SG in the application domain QC for a business context, and therefore (3) fundamentally adds to the understanding how and with whom such a SG is used in the advanced professional computing industry.

Keywords: Quantum computing · Entanglement · GHZ experiment · Serious games · Application of serious games · IT professionals

1 Introduction

Quantum Computing (QC) is a topic of increasing popularity both in academia and even more in applied research contexts in the Industry [1, 2], which build on its promising potential to approach increasingly complex computing tasks [3, 4]. At the same time, however, the topic yields several fundamental concepts utterly incompatible with the accepted properties of classical physics and computing theory [5]. This is illustrated by Einstein's famous quotes "God does not throw dice" and "spooky action at a distance" (own translation) referring to Quantum Superposition and Quantum Entanglement [6].

Conveying knowledge about QC depicts a major challenge with the consequence that skillsets such as the ability to program Quantum Computers are a rare token and the

© Springer Nature Switzerland AG 2020
I. Marfisi-Schottman et al. (Eds.): GALA 2020, LNCS 12517, pp. 45–54, 2020.
https://doi.org/10.1007/978-3-030-63464-3_5

awareness for the increasing importance of QC is dragging behind the rising interest of QC application in both academia and industry.

Serious games (SG) feature an impressive list of successful achievements on learning in various challenging fields including the physical/mathematical sciences, game theory or problem solving [7–10] and have also been successfully used to convey the theory of quantum mechanics [11]. With their potential to unleash an immersive learning experience, SGs provide a promising approach to address the complex topic of QC while being geared towards the needs of specific and specialized audiences [11–13]. IBM research has one of its foci in the field of QC and contributes to spreading the subject among a broader audience, targeting at (future) IT professionals such as university students or developers on the one hand and decision makers in different companies on the other. Accordingly, the ways to address those different target groups vary, but one way to attract interest in quantum mechanics and QC is by using SGs highlighting the specific effects that distinguish Quantum Computers from classical computers.

Although several SGs for QC are available to date, the specific learning needs of IT professionals are not sufficiently covered to equip them with a knowledge base on the fundamental concepts of QC. Based on an analysis of the current SGs for QC, we have identified the concept of Entanglement as an underrepresented learning objective. In accordance with this finding, we have developed a concept for a SG around Quantum Entanglement in cooperation with the IBM Quantum Ambassadors team by using the Greenberg-Horne-Zeilinger (GHZ) experiment [2, 5]. Our prototype[1] has already been included in the workshop concept for applied QC at both practitioner-oriented Meetup™ Sessions [14] and IEEE QC conferences [15].

This paper aims to advance the knowledge base within the field of SGs and learning in three dimensions: (1) it identifies Quantum Entanglement as underrepresented learning topic in the array of QC concepts covered by SGs, (2) provides a case study on the development of a SG in the application domain QC for a business context, and therefore (3) adds to the understanding how and with whom such a SG is used in the advanced professional computing industry.

2 Related Work and SG Evaluation

2.1 Quantum Computing as a Field of Interest

A classical computer used today is based on classical physics. Information is stored in bits that can be either 0 or 1. In contrast to that, a Quantum Computer is based on quantum mechanics and the basic unit to store information is a quantum bit, also called qubit [5]. A qubit as a normal bit can only return $|0\rangle$ or $|1\rangle$ as result of a measurement. However, its true state can take on infinitely many linear combinations of these two basis states [16]. Using operations from quantum mechanics, a Quantum Computer can perform calculations on several input values at the same time and therefore QC is projected to support many different areas including finance (stock market forecasts), the medical field (drug development), chemistry (identification of new molecules and materials), or machine learning (provision of more accurate models) [17].

---

[1] Available under CC-license on github (https://github.com/JanLahmann/Fun-with-Quantum).

Although the first Quantum Computers with 2 qubits were introduced in 1998, two decades later the nowadays existing Quantum Computers with around 50 qubits [18], still are not capable to run the previously developed algorithms in a way that exceeds the capabilities of classical computers [19]. While QC has long existed as a primarily theoretical subject, its practical application was largely unfeasible due to the lack of a real Quantum Computer. But as hardware innovation in this field is catching up, QC is increasingly becoming a subject of practical relevance.

The idea of QC is to use Quantum Gates and quantum effects such as Superposition, Interference and Quantum Entanglement. Quantum Gates perform basic operations on qubits similar to the classical operations "and", "or," "not" and so on [5]. Superposition basically states that any two (or more) quantum states can be added together ("super-posed") and the result will again be a valid quantum state [ibid]. Quantum Interference allows the Superposition to happen constructively or destructively, i.e. the states may amplify or cancel each other out. In QC, Interference is used to increase the probability of getting a right answer and decrease the chance of getting a wrong one [20].

The last key effect, the Quantum Entanglement, creates a strong dependency between several qubits and enables a Quantum Computer to solve problems that were previously impossible to solve [5]. Experiments such as the GHZ experiment [21] illustrate problems which cannot be solved with classical logic but can be solved by exploiting Quantum Entanglement. The GHZ experiment therefore can be used to show the additional potential of Entanglement.

2.2   Serious Games for Quantum Computing: Selection Criteria

Games are following a long tradition and play an important role in the learning process of humans [22]. The element of gamification takes advantage of the natural play instinct to set a focus on the task and increase the motivation to solve the presented problem in the best way possible. This can motivate people to spend more time with higher concentration [23]. These positive effects can also be used for learning. Therefore, SGs are a good way to learn about a new technology such as QC.

With the rising interest in QC, many different forms of learning material come to the fore, including different types of game applications. They can be distinguished into two types of games: (1) Games explaining aspects of QC but are themselves not running on Quantum Computers. This type includes analogue board and card games, as well as video games that explain or exploit the basic principles of QC. (2) Games running on a quantum device or a quantum simulator. This second type is an absolutely recent phenomenon, as it is closely connected to IBM's launch of the IBM Quantum Experience on May 4th, 2016 [24], which enables the public to access IBM's Quantum Computers via cloud. Using Qiskit [25], IBM's open source QC software framework, these Quantum Computers can be programmed either using Python or a graphical interface.

The games in this second type are designed for various purposes. Some of the first games were developed to proof that games can run on Quantum hardware. Other games have the purpose to teach the player principles of QC and some are developed mostly for the developer himself to learn how to program a Quantum Computer. Across type (1) and (2), there are roughly 50 games in different forms concerning QC which are developed from different individuals and companies. For this paper, only those games which are (a) digital, (b) target on aspects of QC and/or quantum mechanics and are (c) publicly available free of charge in a playable version, have been analyzed. According to these criteria, we have included 11 SGs of type 2 into our analysis. Additionally, the board game "Entanglion" (Type 1) has been included as it is covering a broad variety of concepts in the field of QC and appeared to meet most criteria of a SG in providing an introduction to the subject. Even though it is not digital, it is available as a printing version free of charge on GitHub [26].

2.3 Evaluation of Learning Topics

A systematic review of the included SGs for QC in relation to the addressed learning topics reveals major differences in relation to covered QC concepts and intended audiences. Table 1 provides an overview on the main learning objective of each of the SGs in conjunction with the Quantum concepts it explicitly addresses. As the level of depth at which these concepts are covered varies significantly, a four-tiered classification concept was introduced: (T) - teaches, (L) - links additional information, E - exposes and (U) - uses. (T)eaching means, that background information for the general application of the concept is provided, while (L) does not provide information about the application of the concept in general but only for the use case in the SG. However, the name of the concept or references to further information about the concept are provided so that it is easy to obtain further inform about it. (E) only highlights the difference in the use of a Quantum Computer but does neither link any references nor mention the exact term of the concept used. (U) only uses the concept as a consequence of the game mechanics and does not mention it in any further way.

The outcomes of the evaluation (Table 1) illustrate that most of the evaluated SGs make use of the four fundamental concepts of QC but typically do not address the subjects in a depth required to create awareness beyond the fact that there are some differences between QC and classical computing. Surprisingly, none of the SGs follows the intention to provide a complete introduction to all of the concepts of QC. Furthermore, the only fundamental concept not covered by SGs on a teaching level (T) is the concept of Quantum Entanglement, although it is (U)sed in many SGs. This is a clear gap in the field of SGs for QC and hence this paper is aiming to close it.

3   Development and Implementation of a New Serious Game on Quantum Entanglement

3.1   The GHZ-Experiment as Conceptual Background to Approach Quantum Entanglement

Quantum Entanglement is one of the four fundamental concepts in QC and only few of the SGs have attempted to explain the concept behind it or show how it can be incorporated in a program running on a Quantum Computer. The reason might be that Entanglement is quite difficult to grasp as it conflicts with our intuition. Entanglement strongly connects two or more qubits – regardless of their physical distance - so that their quantum states are no longer independent [38].

Table 1. Overview of learning objectives

Name	Main objective	Quantum Concepts				
		Superposition	Interference	Entanglement	Quantum Gates	Other
"Hello Quantum" [27]	Enable public to explore quantum gates	U	U	U	L	
"QPong" [28]	Program game on Quantum Computer to experience the functionalities of different quantum gates	U	U	U	L	
"Quantum Coin Game" [29]	Teach how to use Superposition and Interference on a Quantum Computer and how to program it	T	T		U	L (Qiskit)
"Battleship with partial NOT gates" [30]	Show that it is possible to program a multiplayer game on a real Quantum Computer	U			U	
"Hunt the Quantpus" [31]	Show the effects of Superposition and Entanglement in scope of a game	L	U	L		
"Quantum Solitaire" [32]	Provide taste of quantum world possibilities			E		
"Quantum TicTacToe" [33]	Expose player to basic quantum concepts & Introduce new possibilities to the game	L	U	L		
"Quantum Poker" [34]	Provide engaging tool to expose player to basic quantum concepts	L	U	L	L	
"Qiskit Blocks" [35]	Introduction to QC and programming with Qiskit	U	U	U	T	
"Quantum Awesomeness" [36]	Test the capabilities and quality of Quantum Computers			U		L (error rate, QC hardware)
"Quantum Chess" [37]	Expose player to basic quantum concepts & Introduce new possibilities to the game	L	U	U		
"Entanglion" [26]	Expose player to basic quantum concepts	L	L	L	L	L (error and components)

The effects of Entanglement have been shown in several experiments, e.g. the GHZ experiment [21]. The GHZ Game involves a simple puzzle. A team of three players collaborates to agree on a winning strategy. At a certain time, they are then either asked for an X value or a Y value (One may think of X and Y being the shape and color of an object, respectively). Each player can answer either with 1 or -1 but needs to answer immediately without any consultation with the fellow players.

The variables - which represent the pre-agreed answers of each player to each of the possible questions - can only be chosen in a way to win for some, but not all four of the question sets [39]. When introducing moves (i.e. strategies to answer the questions) based on quantum mechanics, however, it becomes possible to constantly win the game for each of the four sets of possible questions. If the three players share three qubits in a GHZ state and each player measures the X or Y value of their qubits according to the question they were asked, the answer is always correct. This means the players can succeed in a game impossible to win under conditions based on classical physics.

3.2 Development and Implementation of a SG on Quantum Entanglement

Harnessing the setup of this experiment the learning objective of the GHZ SG is to introduce the concept of Entanglement, show how it can be programmed using Qiskit and make the players become acquainted with the additional possibilities QC can provide. The targeted audience are IT professionals who can be classified as beginners in the field of QC who want to understand the principle of Quantum Entanglement and are interested in learning how to program a Quantum Computer. In the current prototype version, interactions are limited to a dropdown choice in the classical version and interactive code cells in the quantum part of the game. The game is designed for a single player. For the implementation of the concept presented above, Jupyter Notebooks[2] and Qiskit [25] are being used.

Fig. 1. Starting screen

The game starts with an introduction of the user interface and the explanation of the rules for the GHZ-game. Then the experiment is represented interactively, so that the player can choose the actions his team is taking in the classical version of the experiment Fig. 1. He can test his choices by running a game simulation. When thinking about it in more detail or testing several options the player finds out, that he is unable to constantly win the game. With the classical version, the maximum winning probability is 75%.

However, after introducing Quantum Computing, it becomes possible to develop a 100% winning strategy. Therefore, the player is taught how to write a simple quantum circuit to derive the necessary information out of a GHZ state to win the game Fig. 2. At the end of the notebook further explanation of the GHZ state and the GHZ experiment as well as references to further learning material are provided.

---

[2] Documents that can contain interactive code cells (programmed in Python), equations, visualizations and explanations.

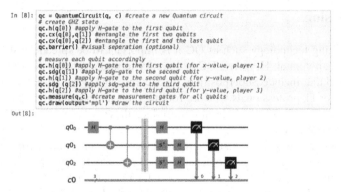

Fig. 2. Learning to write a quantum circuit

The SG is now an integral part of IBM's QC introduction and hands-on sessions, such as Meetups and various client presentations on QC. Before development of the GHZ SG, a SG (a "Quantum Coin Game" [29]) was used, that could solely explain Superposition and Interference, but not Entanglement. These games demonstrate the potential power of quantum algorithms over classical algorithms in an engaging and plausible way.

4 Discussion

On purpose, the covering story and the gamification elements incorporated into the SG are limited, and a simple riddle which is played in two teams is chosen. With the SGs main focus being on teaching the concept of Entanglement and showing its capabilities as well as how to program it using the quantum framework Qiskit, the visualization is deliberately basic with an emphasis on accurate provision of the content. However, an increased user experience with more visualizations might attract more players beyond the immediate workshop attendees.

As the objective of the game is to provide an on-the-spot introduction to Quantum Entanglement it is not designed to be played repeatedly. Nonetheless, the SG can help to develop a basic understanding of Entanglement and the additional possibilities it may provide. It is the first SG, to the best of our knowledge, that provides an extensive introduction to Quantum Entanglement. Therefore, despite its limited user experience it is well suitable to be used as an introductory tool.

An initial version of the SG has already been used with a small number of IT Professionals. The first release will be piloted in a tutorial at an IEEE Quantum conference ("IEEE QCE20") [15] in October 2020 and then will be used in Meetups conducted by the IBM Quantum Ambassador and Qiskit Advocate teams. Based on these inputs, a follow-up study is planned to provide a relevant empirical data base.

A potential extension could be to add additional levels to the game that broaden the gameplay and the concepts being illustrated. We could imagine using the application of Quantum Entanglement to other problems that are not solvable in a classical way but have a solution when using Quantum Entanglement.

5 Conclusion

For an emerging technology such as QC it is important to be spread for the public to understand its potential. However, QC is not easy to understand, and the fundamental concepts used that include Superposition, Interference and Quantum Entanglement are challenging for IT professionals who are rooting their understanding in classical computing. Therefore, SGs can be helpful to introduce these concepts to a wider audience in an entertaining way.

The 12 SGs that have been evaluated in our review study have shown a heterogeneous field of objectives, purposes and target audiences. In spite of this finding we were able to clearly identify the transfer of knowledge about the Quantum Concept of Entanglement as a gap in the field. Accordingly, we have conceptualized and developed a SG based on the GHZ-experiment targeted at IT Professionals. Our paper, therefore, not only provides a systematic analysis of the current landscape of SGs in QC, but also delineates a case study on how to design and implement a SG in that field.

Acknowledgements. We would like to thank Dr. James Wootton (IBM Research) for discussing our ideas of the game and design of a Serious Game for Quantum Computing and for his help in streamlining our setup for the target group of IT professionals.

References

1. Chow, J.; Gambetta, J.: Quantum Takes Flight: Moving from Laboratory Demonstrations to Building Systems. IBM Research Blog (2020). https://www.ibm.com/blogs/research/2020/01/quantum-volume-32/. Accessed 22 June 2020
2. Mermin, N.D.: Quantum Computer Science: An Introduction. Cambridge University Press, Cambridge (2007)
3. Woerner, S., Egger, D.J.: Quantum risk analysis. npj Quantum Inf. 5 (2019). Paper 15. https://doi.org/10.1038/s41534-019-0130-6
4. Airbus Innovation: Airbus Quantum Computing Challenge. https://www.airbus.com/innovation/tech-challenges-and-competitions/airbus-quantum-computing-challenge.html. Accessed 08 July 2020
5. Nielsen, M.A., Chuang, I.L.: Quantum Computation and Quantum Information. Cambridge University Press, Cambridge (2010)
6. Einstein, A., Born, M.: Briefwechsel 1916-955. Müller Verlag, Langen (2005)
7. C. Conati, Zhao, X.: Building and evaluating an intelligent pedagogical agent to improve the effectiveness of an educational game. In Proceedings of the 9th International Conference on Intelligent User Interfaces (IUI 2004). Association for Computing Machinery, New York, pp. 6–13 (2004). https://doi.org/10.1145/964442.964446
8. Johnson, W.L.: Serious use of a serious game for language learning. In Proceedings of the 2007 Conference on Artificial Intelligence in Education: Building Technology Rich Learning Contexts That Work, pp. 67–74. IOS Press, NLD (2007)
9. Millis, K., Forsyth, C., Butler, H., Wallace, P., Graesser, A., Halpern, D.: Operation ARIES!: a serious game for teaching scientific inquiry. In: Ma, M., Oikonomou, A., Jain, L.C. (eds.) Serious Games and Edutainment Applications, pp. 169–195. Springer, London (2011). https://doi.org/10.1007/978-1-4471-2161-9_10

10. Rowe, J.P., Shores, L.R., Mott, B.W., Lester, J.C.: Integrating learning, problem solving, and engagement in narrative-centered learning environments. Int. J. Artif. Intell. Educ. **21**(1–2), 115–133 (2011)
11. Dorland, B., et al.: Quantum physics vs. classical physics: introducing the basics with a virtual reality game. In: Liapis, A., Yannakakis, Georgios N., Gentile, M., Ninaus, M. (eds.) GALA 2019. LNCS, vol. 11899, pp. 383–393. Springer, Cham (2019). https://doi.org/10.1007/978-3-030-34350-7_37
12. Bommanapally, V., Subramaniam, M., Chundi, P., Parakh, A.: Navigation hints in serious games. In: Beck, D., et al. (eds.) Online Proceedings from First Immersive Online Learning Network Conference, Technische Universität Graz (2018)
13. Abeyrathna, D., Vadla, S., Bommanapally, V., Subramaniam, M., Chundi, P., Parakh, A.: Analyzing and predicting player performance in a quantum cryptography serious game. In: Gentile, M., Allegra, M., Söbke, H. (eds.) GALA 2018. LNCS, vol. 11385, pp. 267–276. Springer, Cham (2019). https://doi.org/10.1007/978-3-030-11548-7_25
14. Meetup. https://www.meetup.com/de-DE/meet-and-think-at-ibm/events/268534178/. Accessed 05 July 2020
15. IEEE QCE20. International Conference on Quantum Computing & Engineering. https://qce.quantum.ieee.org/tutorials/. Accessed 05 July 2020
16. Homeister, M.: Quantum Computing verstehen: Grundlagen – Anwendungen –Perspektiven. Springer Vieweg, Wiesbaden (2018). https://doi.org/10.1007/978-3-658-22884-2
17. Baumhof, A.: Quantum leap: why the next wave of computers will change the world. World Economic Forum (2019). https://www.weforum.org/agenda/2019/10/quantum-computers-next-frontier-classicalgoogle-ibm-nasa-supremacy/. Accessed 05 July 2020
18. Statista (2020). https://www.statista.com/statistics/993634/quantum-computers-by-number-of-qubits/. Accessed 05 July 2020
19. Wilhelm, F.K., et al.: Status of Quantum Computer development. BSI, Federal Office for Information Security (2019). https://www.bsi.bund.de/EN/Topics/Crypto/Cryptography/QuantumComputing/quantum_computing_node.html. Accessed 05 July 2020
20. Guidotti, R.: The Power of Destructive Interference in Quantum Computing (2015). https://doi.org/10.13140/rg.2.1.2067.4008. Accessed 05 July 2020
21. Vaidman, L.: Variations on the theme of the Greenbeger-Horne-Zeilinger proof. Found. Phys. **29**, 615–630 (1999)
22. Huizinga, J.: Homo ludens: Versuch einer Bestimmung des Spielelementes der Kultur. Pantheon, Amsterdam (1939)
23. Dörner, R., Göbel, S., Effelsberg, W., Wiemeyer, J. (eds.): Serious Games. Springer, Cham (2016). https://doi.org/10.1007/978-3-319-40612-1
24. Gambetta, J.; Chow, J.: Quantum computing: it's time to build a quantum community (2016). https://www.ibm.com/blogs/research/2016/05/quantum-computing-time-build-quantum-community/. Accessed 05 July 2020
25. Qiskit: Welcome to Quantum (2020). https://qiskit.org. Accessed 05 July 2020
26. IBM Research: Entanglion (2019). https://entanglion.github.io. Accessed 05 July 2020
27. IBM: Hello Quantum (2018). http://helloquantum.mybluemix.net. Accessed 05 July 2020
28. Huang, J.: QPong: a quantum version of the classic Pong using Qiskit and pygame. https://github.com/HuangJunye/QPong. Accessed 20 Apr 2020
29. Lahmann, J.R.: How Quantum Power Helps to Win a Coin Game (2020). http://ibm.biz/QiskitCoinGame. Accessed 05 July 2020
30. GitHub: Quantum Battleships with partial NOT gates. Github (2019). https://github.com/Qiskit/qiskit-community-tutorials/blob/master/games/battleships_with_partial_NOT_gates.ipynb. Accessed 05 July 2020
31. Decodoku: Hunt the Quantpus. https://decodoku.itch.io/hunt-the-quantpus. Accessed 05 July 2020

32. Decodoku: Quantum Solitaire. https://decodoku.itch.io/quantum-solitaire. Accessed 05 July 2020
33. Quantum TicTacToe: Play the game (2019). https://quantumtictactoe.com/play. Accessed 05 July 2020
34. GitHub: Quantum Poker. Github (2020). https://github.com/sintefmath/QuantumPoker. Accessed 05 July 2020
35. GitHub: Qiskit Blocks. Github (2019). https://github.com/JavaFXpert/QiskitBlocks. Accessed 05 July 2020
36. GitHub: Quantum Awesomeness (2018). https://github.com/decodoku/A_Game_to_Benchmark_Quantum_Computers/blob/master/README.md. Accessed 05 July 2020
37. Truly Quantum Chess: Truly Quantum Chess Alpha (2017). https://truly-quantum-chess.sloppy.zone. Accessed 05 July 2020
38. Thomas, A.T.: Hidden in Plain Sight 10: How to Program a Quantum Computer. Createspace Independent Publishing Platform (2018)
39. Mohrhoff, U.: A Quantum Game. This Quantum World (2018). https://thisquantumworld.com/the-mystique-of-quantum-mechanics/a-quantum-game/. Accessed 05 July 2020

Serious Game Analytics

Interactive Gamification Analytics Tool (IGAT)

Nadja Zaric[1](✉) [iD], Rene Roepke[1](✉) [iD], Manuel Gottschlich[2](✉),
and Ulrik Schroeder[1](✉) [iD]

[1] Learning Technologies, RWTH Aachen University, Ahornstr. 55, 52704 Aachen, Germany
{zaric,roepke,schroeder}@cs.rwth-aachen.de
[2] RWTH Aachen University, Templergraben 55, 52062 Aachen, Germany
manuel.gottschlich@rwth-aachen.de

Abstract. This paper presents the current state-of-the-art in applying Gamification Analytics (GA) techniques in the e-learning context and presents the design, implementation, and early evaluation of the Interactive Gamification Analytics Tool (IGAT) for the learning management system Moodle. By exploring existing work on GA, we provide insights into current problems and challenges of gamification monitoring. Next, we reflect on a GA requirements model and analyze existing GA tools. From this, we incorporate key aspects in the design and development of IGAT.

Keywords: Gamification analytics · Gamification · Learning analytics · E-learning

1 Introduction

Gamification signifies the application of game elements for developing game-like experiences in non-game tasks and concepts [1]. A game-like experience describes users' emotions and satisfaction of using a gamified application, which should, if positive and consistent, ensure gamification achieves its goals (e.g. encourage users' engagement, motivation, or goal achievement [2]). Gamification as a process can be divided into two phases—*monitoring* and *adapting*. In the *monitoring* phase, designers gain knowledge on user-gamification interaction which should, in the later phase, be used to adapt design flaws that do not work as intended [3]. Gamification Analytics (GA) describes methods and tools that support gamification designers to monitor the success of gamification projects, to understand a user's behavior and to adapt gamification design accordingly [4]. The main task of GA is to identify and implement metrics that provide comprehensive insights into the user interaction with a gamified system, from which designers should be able to draw conclusions regarding their gamification design. Besides, GA should support the identification of different user types as the heterogeneity of users' traits is recognized as one of the main challenges in obtaining positive gameful experience [4]. For this, GA applies methods from data science and machine learning to gamification data to analyze and visualize the results to the different stakeholders.

Despite the highlighted importance of monitoring and adapting gamification, GA has not yet received significant attention from the community. Namely, the literature

© Springer Nature Switzerland AG 2020
I. Marfisi-Schottman et al. (Eds.): GALA 2020, LNCS 12517, pp. 57–68, 2020.
https://doi.org/10.1007/978-3-030-63464-3_6

review reports only four existing GA tools and emphasizes that the progress in research on gamification is highly dependent on GA tools [5]. To reduce this gap, we developed an Interactive Gamification Analytics Tool (IGAT) for gamification in online education. IGAT is a plugin for the Learning Management System Moodle that provides various metrics for students and teachers to help the reflection on the gamification design and success. Further, to ensure IGAT's contributes the current research needs a literature review on most recent publications regarding GA tools was conducted.

2 Theoretical Background and State of the Art

Since gamification emerged, numerous studies have applied game elements in education and especially in online learning contexts. However, various open questions and challenges need to be addressed. One such issue is the inconsistency of gamification evaluation approaches, which directly question the validity of the results reported in the studies [6]. Therefore, reviewers seek to find new methods that will reduce the existing restrictions and increase the credibility of results. For example, more data on user-gamification interaction are needed as these can provide comprehensive insights into the relationship between a gamified system and users' behavior. Methods and approaches to realize such requirements are merged in the GA research domain. To support the development of GA tools, Heilbrunn et al. developed a design framework for the gamification monitoring process (see Table 1) [7].

Table 1. List of requirements and the evaluation of IGAT design regarding them.

Requirements groups	Requirement	Result
Application KPI monitoring—provide insight into undesirable behavior to help designers understand causal relations between gamification design and resulting application KPI values	R1: Definition of custom KPIs	LA
	R2: Definition of pattern-based KPIs	LA
	R3: Definition of KPI goal values	LA
	R4: Dashboard	LA
	R5: Change markers	LA
	R6: Goal markers	LA
Game Element Analytics—provide an understanding of user interactions with the gamified system. Observing how the system components work, which parts are (not) often used or are used only by a specific group of users give important insights into user behavior and lead to major gamification improvements	R7: Feedback rate	↑
	R8: Point distributions	↑
	R9: Achievable game elements statistics	↑

(*continued*)

Table 1. (*continued*)

Requirements groups	Requirement	Result
	R10: User distributions on game element state	↑
	R11: Temporal statistics	↑
	R12: User characteristics	↑
	R21: Tracking Intercations with the GUI	↓
	R22: Alerting	↓
Game Design Adaptation—enable the integration of A/B testing to conduct experiments and real-time changes to the system	R13: Experiment creation	↘
	R14: Experiment result analysis	↘
	R15: Direct design adaptation	↘
User Groups of Interest—enable the reflection of different user types that show varying behavior when interacting with the gamification	R16: Definition based on criteria	↑
	R17: Definition based on cluster analysis	↓
	R18: Definition based on manual selection	↓
	R19: Filtering of overviews by user groups	↑
Simulation—provide designers a possibility to simulate a gamified system to support early design decisions	R20: Simulation and result analysis	↓

Note*: ↑ = fulfilled, ↗ = mostly fulfilled, ↘ = partly fulfilled, ↓ = not fulfilled, LA = fulfilled by suitable LA tools

The framework describes the data-driven process of monitoring and adapting gamification design, and the analytics-related activities for gamification interventions. The framework defines 22 requirements a GA tool should fulfill to provide valuable support for gamification phases. In this paper, we use their requirements model to assess the state of the art on the currently available tools for integrating GA in a gamification project, and, to design the IGAT tool.

Literature Review. Trinidad et al. [5] examined relevant scientific papers on GA to locate studies that deal with the monitoring phase of the gamification process, and identify challenges and problems in the field. In this regard, we applied their methodology to also cover the most recent publications (until Dec. 2019). Our literature review should answer two research questions (RQ): (1) what are the available GA tools and (2) what are the main problems and needs that require to be addressed regarding the gamification monitoring phase? The selected scientific databases are IEEE Xplore, Web of Science, Springer Link, ACM Digital Library and Scopus. The used search string is "gamification AND monitor*". Searches were carried out applying the following inclusion criteria (C):

- C1: The retrieved study is written in English.

- C2: The retrieved study deals with the field of the gamification monitoring process.
- C3: The study introduces a tool for supporting the gamification monitoring process.

The search led to 337 retrieved papers that were assessed concerning the inclusion criteria. The inclusion criteria were applied by reading the title and abstract from the articles which left us with only one (that from Dichev et al. [9]) corresponding publication to be considered as a primary study. These literature reviews revealed that possibly only three studies [7–9] exist that deal with the gamification monitoring process. From them, we identify four GA tools which are discussed in Table 2.

Table 2. The description and analysis in regard to GA requieremnt model

Reference numer	Description of the tools	Fullfiled requirements
[7]	*Bunchball*[a] is a commercial, cloud-based platform that offers gamification solutions to improve user loyalty and online engagement as a Software-as-a-Service model. Bunchball incorporates several basic monitoring features like predfined gamification-related reports and a user segmentation feature. *Gigya*[b] is part of the "SAP Customer Data Cloud" and mainly targets the gamification of online communities. It embeds analytics that provides a set of predefined reports which accordingly focus on social metrics. However, its documentation states that it will be deprecated on 31.01.2021	1/22
[8]	A framework that can be used directly by domain experts without dealing with implementation details. Experts can use a visual editor to create a gamification strategy model, which then, automatically gets compiled into a runtime environment. Further, GA metrics can be modeled using the editor. The gamification analysis is then sent to the strategy experts via email	10/22
[9]	Analytics dashboard for teachers and students in the OneUp gamified learning platform. These dashboards used timelines as a key aspect of the feedback process. Aside from various learning analytics (LA) metrics, the dashboards also included some game elements statistics like number and category of awards acquired and virtual currency obtained and high/low/mean points	3/22

[a]https://www.bunchball.com/, last accessed on 12.04.2020
[b]https://developers.gigya.com, last accessed on 12.04.2020

This review of currently available GA solutions shows that there is currently a severe lack of tools that support the gamification monitoring process. The discussed GA tools can be adopted to fulfill gamification monitoring purposes to some degree but are not designed for this purpose. Thus, we conclude that none of the currently existing solutions support the majority of the requirements and therefore do not offer sufficient support for assessing the gamification design in the monitoring and adaptation phase.

Concerning the RQ2, we did not found any new studies discussing the current challenges and problems in the field, thus we summarize the conclusion from the work of Trinitad et al. as follows: The main problems and needs in gamification monitoring phase are categorized in three groups: General (the complexity of the field, existing GA tools do not satisfy a large portion of the GA requirements), Metrics (lack of GA solutions on defining and monitoring KPIs and solutions that allow experts to discover different user types), and Testing (lack of solution providing the support for early gamification design phases and simulation) [5].

3 Interactive Gamification Analytics Tool

IGAT supports teachers and gamification designers to understand students' interactions with gamification in the e-learning environment. Further, IGAT helps students to accept and understand the gamified system, by providing notifications, and in-depth feedback on their current state and progress in gamification-related activities, and the possibility to control and justify certain gamification features. IGAT is developed as a Moodle block-plugin and therefore is built upon available gamification features—experience points (XPs) and levels provided by the *Level up!* plugin[1], and the Moodle badge system[2]. Analytics on these game elements are presented and available in two main Views - Student and Teacher Dashboards. IGAT is accessable within the right-side block in the course.

The Student dashboard consists of four tabs: Progress, Badges, Leaderboard, and Settings (see Fig. 1). The Progress tab merges all information regarding the students' current state concerning available game elements. This includes the overall progress depicted in a progress bar displaying the ratio of completed levels and acquired badges, current XPs and the points required for reaching the next level. Next, the level overview shows the current level and its description as well as a list of all available levels and the points required to achieve them. A badge overview shows already achieved and yet to be achieved badges. Besides, a statistics box informs the students about the percentage of students in the course, that are at a higher level, lower or the same level as the current student.

To inform the student on how to progress further, another module displays ten random activities that he/she can take to earn more points and thus level up. The Badges tab provides an overview of achieved and available badges. For achieved badges, the issue date is stated and for badges that are still available the criteria for earning are listed.

Finally, the Leaderboard tab consists of a table of students which are ranked by their current points. By default, the leaderboard displays only 5 students below and above

---

[1] https://moodle.org/plugins/block_xp, last accessed on 12.04.2020.

[2] https://docs.moodle.org/38/en/Badges, last accessed on 12.04.2020.

Fig. 1. Screenshot of progress tab

the rank of the current student, however, the student can change this in the Settings tab to view the full leaderboard or completely hide it. Students can also choose if the leaderboard shows their full or anonymous name.

The Teacher Dashboard is designed based on the gamification requirements model. It is composed of two views: *Gamification Elements Analytics* and *Gamification Dashboard Analytics*. Gamification Elements Analytics provides insights on students' interaction with each game elements separately, while Gamification Dashboard Analytics provides insights on their interaction with the Students' Gamification Dashboard. The following metrics concerning the GA requirements are available:

- The gamification feedback rate (R7) measures the number of state changes in the gamification per day. These include gathering points, achieving badges and reaching levels. The metrics should indicate to the teacher how much feedback is provided by the current gamification configuration.
- The point's distribution (R8) is displayed in a bar chart showing the number of students in the predefined XPs range (e.g. [0–200], [201–400]). Also, a level distribution (R10) is provided which visualizes how many students have reached each available level. Finally, badges distribution (R9) plots the number of students who have achieved the available badges on a bar chart. This supports evaluating the design of badges in the course and their reception by students.
- Complementary to level and badges distribution, the average days it took for students to reach each level and average days needed to earn a badge (R11), are presented as a bar chart. This statistics should enable further insights into game elements design.
- The 'gamification tab view metric' (R10) measures how often the students visit each of the four tabs (see Fig. 2). This line chart plots all dates from the course begging on the x-axis and the no. of page views for each tab on the y-axis. This should allow us to reflect on user-gamification interaction and detect changes in user behavior.
- To provide more insights on how the student browse through the dashboard, a 'gamification dashboard subsequent pages' (R10) graph has been added (see Fig. 3). This graph shows which pages students move to when they left a tab on the students' view.
- The 'average tab viewing duration' calculates the time student spent on each dashboard tab. This metric is visualized as a bar chart for easy comparison between the tabs.

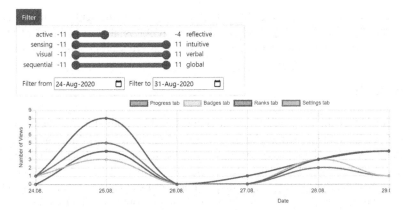

Fig. 2. Gamification tab-view metric with filters

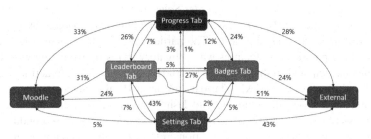

Fig. 3. Gamification dashboard subsequent chart preview

- The 'leaderboard visibility' (R10) chart shows student's configuration concerning the leaderboard visibility (full, limited -five places above and below their position or hidden leaderboard). Analyzing which settings have been chosen by the students can provide insights into the students' perception of the leaderboard.
- The 'leaderboard anonymity' (R10) chart shows the proportion of students that chose to hide their full name i.e. show as anonymous in the leaderboard.
- IGAT includes the possibility to filter each GA metric based on students' learner type (see Fig. 3). The information on students' learner type is derived from a third-party Moodle plugin that integrates a questionnaire based on the Felder and Silverman learning style model [10]. With this R12, R16 and R19 are fulfilled.

The design of IGAT was able to completely fulfill 10 of the 22 requirements, (see Table 1). Three requirements regarding Game Design Adaptation are considered to be *partly fulfilled* as A/B testing experiments are easily realizable by dividing students between two Moodle courses with identical learning materials and comparing the GA provided by IGAT. Simulation requirements (R20) could not be realized, because the Level up! plugin and the badge system differ considerably regarding their software architecture and have not been designed in a way that allows simulating gamification use. Finally, as the KPI in the e-learning context is used to measure learning success through LA data, these requirements (R1-R6) are already supported. Namely, this area is very well supported by several Moodle plugins and thus the KPI requirements are not considered as an IGAT feature. To conclude, IGAT is able to meet 17 of the 22 requirements at least partially when adequate LA tools are used in combination.

4 Evaluation

The evaluation of the proposed GA tool is addressed by both students' and teachers' perspectives. First, the student dashboard design was evaluated regarding students' experience and opinions. Next, professors evaluated the teacher's dashboard to examine its design and usefulness. The design evaluation aims to identify aspects that succeed in achieving their desired effects and highlight shortcomings to point to directions on how these could be improved. The evaluation of usefulness should assess if used GA metrics are valuable and useful in identifying gamification design flaws.

The IGAT was applied in a one-month online JavaScript course offered to Bachelor students at the Department of Computer Science at the RWTH Aachen University. Students could collect XPs, progress through levels, and earn badges by completing different learning activities and tasks. The participation in the course was voluntary, and none of the gamification features was obligatory or restrictive in any way. In total, 38 students participated in the course. The student-gamification interaction data were collected and displayed in IGAT. The data are used for the quantitative measures to capture first insights on game elements and dashboard usage. After the course, interview invitations were sent to course participants and five interviews were conducted. The semi-structured interviews included questions referring to their perception and experience with the student dashboard and each dashboard tab individually. The interviews were analyzed to gain the first insights into the design process, which will be used for further improvements in IGAT design.

The evaluation of the teachers' dashboard and GA features was conducted through semi-structured interviews with six professors at the RWTH Aachen University. The interviews began with a short introduction to the JavaScript course and the IGAT on a computer that was accessible during the whole interview. After the introduction, participants were free to interact and get familiar with IGAT. The main objective of the interview was to address the metrics available in the teacher's view. For each metric, the participants were asked to describe what it measures and how they interpret it. The teachers were asked if the visualization of each metric is appropriate and what conclusions can be drawn. The teachers then were asked to evaluate the usefulness of this metric for assessing and improving gamification. The interviews concluded with closing questions to summarize their opinion and address additional aspects that have not been covered. Teachers' answers are used to gain insights on current metrics provided within IGAT and to evaluate metrics readability and interpretations.

4.1 Results and Discussion

Students' dashboard. IGAT interaction data collected from the JavaScript course showed 44% students actively[3] interacted with game elements. On average students leveled up every 5th day, and earned 1.5 badges per week. Regarding their interaction with the gamification dashboard, IGAT data showed that the most visited tab was the leaderboard tab with an average retention of 2.31 s per visit. Opposite, the least visited is the progress tab with retention of 0.6 s per visit. Concerning the settings configuration, 42% students switched the visibility setting of the leaderboard to 'show full', while none of the students choose to hide the leaderboard. Further, none of the students had completely hidden their full name on the ranking list.

The semi-structured interviews with students revealed most students had an overall positive perception of the gamification and its integration in the course. They all think the inclusion of game elements is interesting and harmless and would like to see it in other courses as well. Besides, they perceived the layout clear and well-structured. The importance of the leaderboard noted from the data collected in course was underlined by the interviewed students as they explicitly stated that the leaderboard was most important to them. One of the students stated "While looking at the leaderboard I was focused on my point count and the points of the first student above me. Each time I completed an exercise I went back to leaderboard to check if I managed to overtake his/her place". Another student stated "If there was no leaderboard I think I would not do as many assignments as I did. I really wanted to reach a high rank". Regarding badges and progress bars interviews indicated two main reasons for their low visits. First, 2/5 students said they were unnecessary as the leaderboard tab already showed all information there were interested in. Other students, however, said they didn't even see the tabs as they used only the direct link to the leaderboard tab and did not pay attention to others. This indicates that the block's placement on the right side next to the course' learning materials does not sufficiently capture a student's attention.

To conclude, the students' view was evaluated positively by students, however, some improvement is needed especially concerning the progress and badges tabs that have not been used very frequently. Further, the links leading to the gamification dashboard need to be placed more prominently and notification feedback should be provided at the moment the student reaches a new level or earns a badge.

Teachers' Dashboard. Evaluation with teachers revealed that IGAT is interesting, the overall layout structure was intuitive to use, and the existing metrics covered some important aspects of gamification. However, the metrics should be extended to provide a clearer picture of student-gamification interaction. Further, two participants said the Gamification Dashboard Analytics are more useful for the gamification developers, while the Gamification Elements Analytics are also interesting for teachers. The results and derived improvements are summarized in Table 3.

---

[3] Every student who earned at least one badge or reached minimum level 2 is considered as active.

Table 3. Results of semi-structured interviews with teachers including derived improvements

Evaluated metrics	Participants' comments and observations	Derived improvements
Gamification page views	Useful for comparing which game elements are interesting and which are irrelevant to students	Correlate data to the overall student activity to provide deeper conclusions
Dashboard subsequent pages graph	The graph was perceived as an advanced metric	Improve the readability of visualization by coloring the edges of the graph and the data values, the thickness of the edges should be changed based on the data and it would be helpful to be able to filter nodes
Leaderboard settings metrics	The metrics are clear, understandable, and useful for gaining insights into students' attitudes towards leaderboards	The system should prompt the user to specify the desired leaderboard settings before accessing it. Also, information on how the settings have changed over time should be included
XPs, levels, and badges distribution	Helpful to get an overview of the current state of gamification and assess how challenging levels and badges are	The metrics should be extended to provide a clearer picture of student-gamification interaction The form of visualization should change more frequently to keep the viewers' interest
AVG tab view duration	Good indicators for gamification achievement in students' engagement	Enrich the data with the median, and upper and lower quartile

5   Conclusion

In this study, we have conducted a literature review on the current state of GA, which included an investigation of available GA tools focusing on the gamification monitoring process, as well as the general discussion on problems and gaps in the field. Further, we designed IGAT – a GA tool for the LMS Moodle to provide insights into the interaction of students with game elements in the e-learning environment. The results from evaluation showed students had an overall positive perception of the developed gamification dashboard and would enjoy having it in other courses as well. Similarly, teachers stated that provided metrics are easily accessible and are valuable to draw meaningful conclusions regarding gamification design and success. However, this work was subject to some limitations. Namely, not all requirements identified in literature could be realized. As Moodle's system architecture and the used plugins came with some limitations it was not feasible to implement features like e.g. simulation during this project. Also, the design was restricted to the game elements introduced by the Moodle. In the evaluation, no gamification experts were available for the interviews, thus, raising these numbers would have provided more reliability. Regarding the evaluation, we are aware that, due to the small number of participants and the early stage of our work, those results can not be quantifiable or generalized. Instead, they are taken as a first step guide towards improvements that are necessary for IGAT to become a suitable GA tool.

To overcome the technical limitations, learning analytics could be integrated into a future version of IGAT to enable a compact picture of how gamification can assist learning. Another interesting aspect that can be explored is making GA accessible to students. Expending statistics into the students' view could help students reflect on gamification as a tool for enhancing learning. Further, A/B testing with two gamified courses from which one uses IGAT and the other does not, would be beneficial for understanding if and to what extend available GA improves students' perception and attitudes toward gamification. Finally, since Moodle is a widely used platform, IGAT could be easily integrated into courses from various domains. This could gain valuable info on what metrics should be provided in GA tools concerning the diverse nature of different educational subjects, and thus deepen the current evaluation issues.

References

1. Landers, R.N., Auer, E.M., Helms, A.B., Marin, S., Armstrong, M.B.: Gamification of adult learning: Gamifying employee training and development. In: The Cambridge Handbook of Technology and Employee Behavior, pp. 271–295. Cambridge University Press, New York (2019)
2. Dicheva, D., Dichev, C., Agre, G., Angelova, G.: Gamification in education: A systematic mapping study. J. Educ. Technol. Soc. **18**, 75–88 (2015)
3. Herzig, P., Ameling, M., Wolf, B., Schill, A.: Implementing Gamification: Requirements and Gamification Platforms. In: Reiners, T., Wood, Lincoln C. (eds.) Gamification in Education and Business, pp. 431–450. Springer, Cham (2015). https://doi.org/10.1007/978-3-319-10208-5_22
4. Heilbrunn, B., Herzig, P., Schill, A.: Gamification analytics—Methods and tools for monitoring and adapting gamification designs. In: Stieglitz, S., Lattemann, C., Robra-Bissantz, S., Zarnekow, R., Brockmann, T. (eds.) Gamification. PI, pp. 31–47. Springer, Cham (2017). https://doi.org/10.1007/978-3-319-45557-0_3
5. Trinidad, M., Calderón, A., Ruiz, M.: A systematic literature review on the gamification monitoring phase: How SPI standards can contribute to gamification maturity. In: Stamelos, I., O'Connor, R.V., Rout, T., Dorling, A. (eds.) SPICE 2018. CCIS, vol. 918, pp. 31–44. Springer, Cham (2018). https://doi.org/10.1007/978-3-030-00623-5_3
6. Rincón-Flores, E.G., Montoya, M.S.R., Mena, J.: Engaging MOOC through gamification: Systematic mapping review. In: Proceedings of the 7th International Conference on Technological Ecosystems for Enhancing Multiculturality, pp. 600–606. ACM, León (2019)
7. Heilbrunn, B., Herzig, P., Schill, A.: Tools for gamification analytics: A survey. In: 2014 IEEE/ACM 7th International Conference on Utility and Cloud Computing, pp. 603–608. IEEE, London (2014)
8. Calderón, A., Ruiz, M., O'Connor, R.V.: A multivocal literature review on serious games for software process standards education. Comput. Stand. Interfaces **57**, 36–48 (2018). https://doi.org/10.1016/j.csi.2017.11.003

9. Dichev, C., Dicheva, D., Irwin, K.: Gamification driven learning analytics. In: Proceedings of the 13th International Conference on e-Learning, pp. 70–76. Academic Conferences International Limited, Kidmore End (2018)
10. Zaric, N., Judel, S., Roepke, R., Schroeder, U: ILSA—An integrated learning styles analytics system. In: Proceedings of the International Conference on Education and New learning Technologies, Palma de Mallorca (Spain), 1–3 July 2019

A Scalable Architecture for One-Stop Evaluation of Serious Games

Iván J. Pérez-Colado$^{(\boxtimes)}$ (iD), Víctor M. Pérez-Colado (iD), Iván Martínez-Ortiz (iD), Manuel Freire (iD), and Baltasar Fernández-Manjón (iD)

Department of Software Engineering and Artificial Intelligence, Complutense University of Madrid, C/Profesor José García Santesmases, 9, 28040 Madrid, Spain
ivanjper@ucm.es

Abstract. Evaluating a serious game is a time-consuming task. However, good evaluations are necessary to improve the effectiveness of serious games, and to prove this effectiveness to stakeholders. Computer support of evaluations requires addressing several problems, including security, privacy protection, data collection from both questionnaires and in-game activities, data analysis, and management of the experimental workflow. We describe improvements to the Simva architecture to add scalability and a bridge to exploratory data science to our one-stop serious games evaluation platform. Simva supports evaluations ranging from small-scale pilots to full-fledged validations with complex experimental designs. The improvements described in this paper greatly increase ease of deployment, interoperation with existing authentication infrastructure, and scalability of Simva, and can be readily applied to tools with similar goals.

Keywords: Serious games · Evaluation · Learning analytics

1 Introduction

Serious games are currently expensive to evaluate. Additionally, traditional questionnaire-based evaluations are limited in scope, and require substantial effort to yield additional insights. Our evaluation platform, Simva, streamlines evaluations by bringing all required steps under a single roof. We present a new architecture for Simva that makes it easier to install and use; and which allows extracting more insights from collected data by interoperating with common data science tools, such as Jupyter Notebooks.

The next section of the paper describes how serious games are generally evaluated and includes examples of common experimental setups for evaluating serious games. Then, we present improvements to Simva to simplify validation by automating all steps, and simultaneously simplifying the roles of the system administrators which install and integrate Simva and the researchers that use it to run their experiments and look at the resulting data. Finally, we describe our conclusions and planned future work.

© Springer Nature Switzerland AG 2020
I. Marfisi-Schottman et al. (Eds.): GALA 2020, LNCS 12517, pp. 69–78, 2020.
https://doi.org/10.1007/978-3-030-63464-3_7

2   Evaluating Serious Games

Serious games are often evaluated with pre-post experiments, in which participants fill in questionnaires both before (pre) and after (post) playing the game [1]. Improvements in questionnaire scores are attributed to in-game learning, and when statistically significant, result in games that are formally evaluated as effective.

To perform a pre-post test, experimenters need to prepare, distribute among participants, and score both the pre and post versions of the questionnaire. They also need to ensure that each post-test is paired with its corresponding pre-test. This can be automated through online forms, such as LimeSurvey; but online forms are generally not designed to support this workflow, and even when programmable, require significant effort to do so.

Experimental designs often include the use of control groups. For example, members of a control group could be asked to play a second game, of equal duration but unrelated to the serious game under study. Improvements in pre-post scores from control group participants allow learning effects from the tests themselves to be measured and quantified. In a more complex approach, a counter-balanced experimental approach would include two sequences of experiments for each of two groups: participants in the first group would be requested to fill in a pre-questionnaire, play the intervention game, fill in a post-questionnaire, perform the control activity, and then fill in a final questionnaire. Those in the second group would reverse the order of the control activity and the intervention game. The advantage of this approach is that all participants end up performing all activities, avoiding unfairness. As a final example, a recall experiment measures test-score variations several days or weeks apart from the interventions. Logistically, they are harder to carry out, since additional experimental sessions must be scheduled in addition to the main experiment where the game is played.

In a recent literature review on serious games to address bullying and cyber-bullying [2], 45% of the 42 publications describing experiments used paired pre and post-tests, 90% of the experiments used a single session of gameplay (as opposed to several), and 42% of the 26 games used control groups for their experiments. While not a representative sample of all serious games, these numbers hint at the difficulty of carrying out more complex experiments

2.1   Collecting Interaction Data to Improve Evaluations

Interactions between the players and serious games can also be collected and analyzed, either in real-time or after the session is through. Several standards for reporting these interactions are currently in use. General interactions between the learning system and learners can be formatted and sent to a server for analysis using standard formats, such as ADL's xAPI statements [3] or IMS' Caliper events [4]. Using game-specific vocabularies to describe these interactions decreases ambiguity by using standard definitions of most game-relevant concepts; this is the purpose of the xAPI Serious Game profile, proposed in [5].

Game Learning Analytics is the combination of Game Analytics and Learning Analytics and is dedicated to gaining insights from such interactions [6]. To use GLA in an evaluation, playthrough data for each participant must be linkable with their pre and post-test responses.

3   The Simva Approach

In [7], we described the main functionality of the initial version of Simva, which integrated LimeSurvey, an open-source survey management system, with RAGE Analytics, a serious game analytics platform developed for the RAGE H2020 project [8]. By managing identifiers and handling pre-post questionnaires, in addition to collecting user interaction data, this version of Simva addressed many of the requirements for experiments such as those described in [2]. Indeed, based on our experience managing large experiments [9], we have identified multiple tasks that usually are problematic and cumbersome in evaluations, and sought to address them with Simva.

Improvements to Simva further streamlined the process, adding support for more complex experiments [10]. In addition, we identified the opportunity to integrate evaluation into game authoring, so that game authors using tools that support Simva (uAdventure) could enjoy built-in validation support [7]. However, those authors would still need to install the Simva platform to be able to enjoy these advantages.

3.1   Integrating Simva

Our goal is to simplify game evaluation. The rest of this work motivates and describes the architectural changes needed to make Simva (and evaluation tools in general) easier to install, scale and integrate, both for small (local installation) and large (cloud/institutional) deployments.

Figure 1 illustrates the new architecture of Simva, with the main modules as rounded boxes. Modules are currently distributed as docker containers and configured to interoperate together through docker-compose (docs.docker.com/compose). Docker containers generally encapsulate or all dependencies of a service and can be seen as lightweight virtual machines. Use of these containers strikes a balance between ease of testing in single-workstation scenarios and scalability in larger installations: many public clouds, such as those offered by Amazon, Microsoft and Google, support kubernetes containers. However, they are harder to work with locally; and the greatest leap, architecture-wise, is from a monolithic to a distributed system—once a system has been split up into collaborating containers, changing the type of containers is relatively straightforward.

In addition to cloud support, containers such as docker have several advantages for development. First, it is possible to use trusted and tested containers for common functionality with minimal or no modification, thus avoiding costly implementations and gaining access to free maintenance in the form of bugfixes and newer versions. In this sense, Kafka and Kafka-Connect, Minio, KeyCloak, Traefik and LimeSurvey (depicted in Fig. 1) are existing open-source projects that we did not need to reimplement, potentially saving several years of development efforts. Additionally, as these actively maintained projects are updated, we will have the chance to upgrade to newer versions with minimal additional effort on our part. We are the authors of RAGE Analytics, but it is also an open-source project distributed as a collection of docker containers.

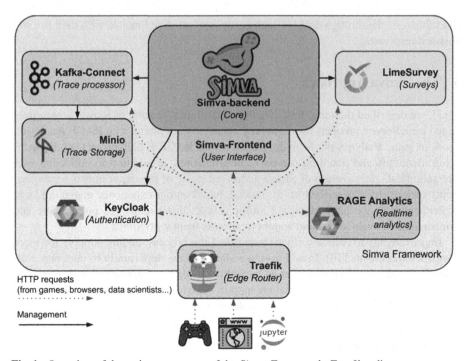

Fig. 1. Overview of the main components of the *Simva* Framework. *Traefik* redirects requests to each service, while *Simva-Backend* is the core that manages all other components.

An additional advantage is that changes to one container are, by the very nature of containers, isolated from each other; so that use of incompatible library versions from within different containers can never be an issue.

However, bringing together multiple systems does have a cost. In particular, users rightfully expect to be spared from the internal complexity of the system. To this end, Simva's modules are hidden behind an application gateway (Traefik). Single-Sign-On (SSO), provided by KeyCloak, allows the whole platform to appear as a single coherent web application to the outside world, with 3 main entry-points, depicted at the bottom of Fig. 1:

- Web access to the front-end, after suitable authentication, allowing studies to be configured, managing groups of participants and their activities, and accessing collected data once through a browser once it is available
- Ingress of xAPI-Serious Game statements describing how players interact with games, to be stored for later analysis; and, in the case of activities where real-time analysis is enabled, to be made available as dashboards that display real-time analytics based on player activity.
- Authenticated access to stored experimental results for access from external data-science tools, such as Jupyter Notebooks.

To achieve interoperation between all modules required some effort, mostly related to enabling and configuring SSO and streamlining communication between them. For example, LimeSurvey was modified to use a SAML plugin to interoperate with KeyCloak for SSO purposes; and we made additional changes to its RemoteControl API to better manage surveys from the Simva backend. Minio, KeyCloak and Kafka-connect were similarly customized to interoperate better.

The move to a containerized architecture has brought the following advantages to Simva:

- Easy deployment. Containers are extensively used in cloud deployments, covering scalability; and docker containers are lightweight enough to be deployed locally for testing or smaller deployments, with minimal dependencies.
- KeyCloak supports major SSO technologies such as OpenID or SAML, allowing integration of Simva into existing institutional authentication systems, so that users need not memorize additional passwords.
- Traefik hides the inner complexity of the system, and as a fully featured application gateway, can protect against API abuse via throttling and other configurable policies.
- Simva can quickly incorporate upstream improvements to its component modules; for example, should newer versions of LimeSurvey be released, minimal effort would be required to incorporate them into Simva, as changes would be limited to that particular container.

3.2 Workflow of a Simple Evaluation

To illustrate the comparative ease of evaluating a serious game with Simva, we now briefly explore the steps involved, assuming we are interested in evaluating a game with participants from a local high school and have an unrelated serious game available for use as a control group.

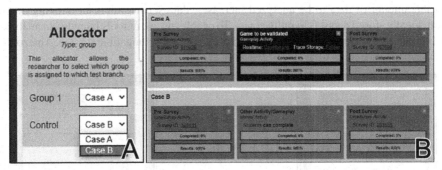

Fig. 2. Researchers can create multiple test branches and assign them to participants (A). Each branch can be assigned different sequences of activities (B)—in this case, the bottom-right row is the control group, while the top-right group plays the game under study.

First, the experimenters would need to download and launch the installation script (github.com/e-ucm/simva-infra), following the instructions included in the repository.

Given an environment where docker and docker-compose can be installed, this script downloads, configures and connects all relevant containers, launching a fully functional Simva platform locally. Experimenters would next need to enter into Simva and configure the participant groups for the study; this can be as easy as requesting Simva to generate two sets of random tokens, one set for the intervention group and another for the control group. Experimenter would then download the token sets as printable PDF files, where tokens can be torn off to give them physically to each participant according to group; for a more in-depth discussion of token use to provide anonymization, see [11]. Studies are configured by determining participant groupings and assigning a sequence of activities to each group, as illustrated in Fig. 2. Examples of activities include playing a serious game or filling in a questionnaire. Figure 3 illustrates how Simva users interact with the questionnaire module, provided by LimeSurvey but accessible through SSO as if it were built in. For this evaluation, experimenters could author two surveys, one for use as a pre-test and another for use as a post-test.

As participants log into the system through links (using their experimenter-provided token), they would be requested to fill in the questionnaire, to play the game that corresponds to their grouping only once the pre-test is complete, and, only after finishing the game, to fill in the post-test. Interaction between games and Simva is optional, and performed through an HTTP API; but if enabled, games can query whether participants with particular tokens have finished required activities before allowing the player to play; and can report player progress to Simva.

Finally, once an experiment is finished, data for each participant is available for download. In this case, experimenters would determine a scoring procedure for tests, and measure score increase from pre-test to post-test in both the experimental and control groups. Survey data can be downloaded as CSV or JSON files, while game interactions are available as JSON using xAPI-SG structure.

3.3 Cloud Storage and Access to GLA

As the amount of data to be analyzed increases, data-science tools are moving away from locally stored datasets to online ones. To enable the use of tools intended to analyze online datasets, the updated Simva architecture uses an S3-compatible storage. Amazon's

Fig. 3. Screenshots illustrating the process of creating a new survey in *Simva*, using the *LimeSurvey* module: (A) launching the survey module to create a new survey; (B) survey authoring environment; and (C) choosing an existing survey to use.

Simple Storage Service (S3) is a de-facto standard for cloud storage; we use the open-source, S3-compatible Minio cloud-storage server for trace storage in Simva. This allows us to support the many data-science packages and libraries that are already compatible with AWS S3, due to the frequent choice of S3 to host data lakes

Figure 4 illustrates how Simva handles storage. Incoming traces from game inter-actions are queued into Kafka and stored by Minio for later retrieval. Use of Kafka, a scalable fault-tolerant queue, ensures that traces will not be lost, even in the presence of potential processing delays on the part of different modules of Simva, most notably complex analyses in RAGE Analytics. Simva includes a trace reallocator process that periodically builds downloadable versions of per-user traces. This allows traces to be stored per-activity but retrieved per-user with suitable access controls.

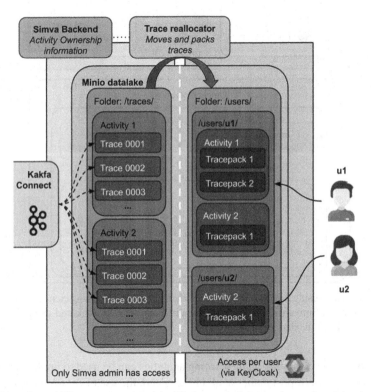

Fig. 4. Incoming xAPI traces are stored in Minio per-activity; and transformed using a trace reallocator to enable per-user access.

Access to interaction traces is targeted at external data science tools such as Jupyter Notebook, which have plugins that support S3 storages (see Fig. 5). Jupyter allows quick generation and testing of hypotheses, for example segmenting users according to their in-game actions to determine the impact of player behaviors on learning. During preliminary tests of games, such rapid iterations are key to forming insights of what works and what does not, and to build better learning analytics models (LAMs; see

[12]) for the final dashboards to be used in future versions of that game. For example, teachers often desire simple and understandable dashboards to see what is going on during gameplay sessions, particularly if the games are used as a class activity. To create these dashboards requires significant time and effort to build a data analysis pipeline; if real-time updates are required, this would require stream-analysis technologies such as Apache Spark, Apache Storm, or Kafka Connect, which are hard to prototype with. A usual approach is therefore to start by applying a data science approach to perform coarse-grained analysis, establishing and testing hypothesis in quick succession. Once finished, it is much simpler to go to a data-engineering approach that applies streaming technologies to build real-time dashboards.

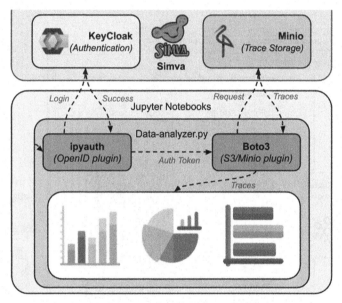

Fig. 5. Researchers using Jupyter Notebooks or other S3-compatible data-science tools can access the traces stored in Simva (Minio) by authenticating against KeyCloak and using the returned access token to fetch the data from Minio.

Once the game is mature, game learning analytics can be used to predict knowledge gain without using pre-post games at all [13]. Indeed, the use of data-science tools with serious games is most often related to prediction tasks, according to a recent literature review [14].

4   Conclusions and Future Work

Streamlining the evaluation of serious games can greatly reduce the efforts required to perform such evaluations, lowering the cost and risk associated with serious game deployment. We have described improvements to the Simva serious game validation platform that further lower the associated costs, by moving Simva to a containerized architecture based on solid open-source modules, and by adopting cloud storage for GLA data, which is readily accessible from existing cloud-based data science tools.

We described how a typical evaluation experiment for a serious game with the updated Simva architecture would work, highlighting the main advantages it provides to experimenters interested in evaluating or improving such a game. As a working tool, the new version of Simva will be used to illustrate the evaluation workflow during the following semesters in several graduate and post-graduate courses on Serious Games and E-Learning Technologies in the Complutense University in Madrid, Spain.

However, development of Simva is still ongoing. In particular, we are working on adding support for IMS' Learning Tools Interoperability (LTI) [15], to enable integration of Simva-managed activities into LTI-supporting LMSs such as Moodle, and to facilitate the development of Simva-compatible plugins and games. Simva would therefore act as both an LTI Tool Consumer, to host/interoperate with games and plugins; and as a Tool Provider, to be accessible from LMSs as an additional activity. This would remove two large hurdles for running experiments with serious games in LMS-equipped classrooms: it would remove the need to pre-configure games with Simva activity-ids (as the games would receive this information via LTI); and it would allow launching of Simva-managed experimental activities from within the LMS as one more task, allowing one-click launching of activities by relying on LMS-supplied information for authentication and group configuration.

Although the present work has been focused on applying Simva to evaluate games, it can also be used to evaluate any other educational tool that can be integrated as an activity, for example with IMS LTI; and more so if it can generate xAPI statements, such as H5P or Articulate content.

Acknowledgements. This work has been partially funded by Regional Government of Madrid (eMadrid P2018/TCS4307), by the Ministry of Education (TIN2017-89238-R), by the European Commission (Erasmus+IMPRESS 2017-1-NL01-KA203-035259) and by the Telefonica-Complutense Chair on Digital Education and Serious Games.

References

1. Boyle, E.A., Hainey, T., Connolly, T.M., Gray, G., Earp, J., Ott, M., et al.: An update to the systematic literature review of empirical evidence of the impacts and outcomes of computer games and serious games. Comput. Educ. **94**, 178–192 (2016). https://doi.org/10.1016/j.com pedu.2015.11.003
2. Calvo-Morata, A., Alonso-Fernández, C., Freire, M., Martínez-Ortiz, I., Fernández-Manjón, B.: Serious games to prevent and detect bullying and cyberbullying: A systematic serious games and literature review. Comput. Educ. (accepted), (2020)
3. Advanced Distributed Learning Initiative: Experience API. https://github.com/adlnet/xAPI-Spec/releases/tag/xAPI-1.0.3. Accessed 10 July 2020
4. IMS Global Learning Consortium Inc.: Caliper Analytics Specification, version 1.1. https://www.imsglobal.org/sites/default/files/caliper/v1p1/caliper-spec-v1p1/caliper-spec-v1p1.html. Accessed 10 July 2020
5. Serrano-Laguna, Á., Martínez-Ortiz, I., Haag, J., Regan, D., Johnson, A., Fernández-Manjón, B.: Applying standards to systematize learning analytics in serious games. Comput. Stand. Interfaces **50**, 116–123 (2017). https://doi.org/10.1016/j.csi.2016.09.014

6. Freire, M., Serrano-Laguna, Á., Iglesias, B.M., Martínez-Ortiz, I., Moreno-Ger, P., Fernández-Manjón, B.: Game learning analytics: Learning analytics for serious games. In: Spector, M., Lockee, B., Childress, M. (eds.) Learning, Design, and Technology, pp. 1–29. Springer, Cham (2016). https://doi.org/10.1007/978-3-319-17727-4_21-1

7. José, P.I., Manuel, P.V., Iván, M., Manuel, F.: Simplifiying serious games authoring and validation with uAdventure and SIMVA, pp. 106–108 (2020). https://doi.org/10.1109/ICALT49669.2020.00039

8. RAGE Consortium: RAGE realizing an applied gaming eco-system. http://rageproject.eu/. Accessed 10 July 2020

9. Calvo-Morata, A., Rotaru, D.C., Alonso-Fernandez, C., Freire-Moran, M., Martinez-Ortiz, I., Fernandez-Manjon, B.: Validation of a cyberbullying serious game using game analytics. IEEE Trans. Learn. Technol. **13**, 186–197 (2020). https://doi.org/10.1109/TLT.2018.2879354

10. Alonso-Fernandez, C., Perez-Colado, I., Calvo-Morata, A., Freire, M., Martinez-Ortiz, I., Fernandez-Manjon, B.: Applications of Simva to simplify serious games validation and deployment. IEEE Rev. Iberoam. Tecnol. del Aprendiz, p. 1 (2020). https://doi.org/10.1109/RITA.2020.3008117

11. Alonso-Fernández, C., Perez-Colado, I.J., Calvo-Morata, A., Freire, M., Martinez-Ortiz, I., Fernández-Manjón, B.: Using Simva to evaluate serious games and collect game learning analytics data. In: LASI Spain 2019: Learning Analytics in Higher Education (2019)

12. Perez-Colado, I., Alonso-Fernandez, C., Freire, M., Martinez-Ortiz, I., Fernandez-Manjon, B.: Game learning analytics is not informagic! In: 2018 IEEE Global Engineering Education Conference (EDUCON), pp. 1729–1737. IEEE (2018). https://doi.org/10.1109/EDUCON.2018.8363443

13. Alonso-Fernández, C., Caballero Roldán, R., Freire, M., Martinez-Ortiz, I., Fernández-Manjón, B.: Predicting students' knowledge after playing a serious game based on learning analytics data: A case study (in press). J. Comput. Assist. Learn. (2019). https://doi.org/10.1111/jcal.12405

14. Alonso-Fernández, C., Calvo-Morata, A., Freire, M., Martínez-Ortiz, I., Fernández-Manjón, B.: Applications of data science to game learning analytics data: A systematic literature review. Comput. Educ. **141**, 103612 (2019). https://doi.org/10.1016/j.compedu.2019.103612

15. IMS Global Learning Consortium, I.: Learning tools interoperability core specification, version 1.3. https://www.imsglobal.org/spec/lti/v1p3/. Accessed 10 July 2020

Employing an IoT Framework as a Generic Serious Games Analytics Engine

Luca Lazzaroni, Andrea Mazzara, Francesco Bellotti$^{(\boxtimes)}$, Alessandro De Gloria, and Riccardo Berta

DITEN, University of Genoa, Via Opera Pia 11A, 16145 Genoa, Italy
{francesco.bellotti,alessandro.degloria,riccardo.berta}@unige.it

Abstract. This paper proposes the use of a new data toolchain for serious games analytics. The toolchain relies on the open source Measurify Internet of Things (IoT) framework, and particularly takes advantage of its edge computing extension (namely, Edgine), which can be seamlessly deployed cross-platform on embedded devices and PCs as well. The Edgine is programmed to download from Measurify a set of scripts, that are periodically executed so to get data from sensors, pre-process them and send the extracted information to the Measurify APIs. Virtual sensors can be built in game engine scripts. This paper describes the implementation of the plug-in which deploys Edgine in Unity 3D, allowing an easy delivery of virtual sensor information to Measurify. Just as a proof of concept, we present the utilization of the whole chain within a trivial game scene, showing the application development efficiency provided by a tool which is made available open source to researchers and developers.

Keywords: Internet of Things · System architecture · Game development · Game engine plug-in · Virtual sensors · Reality-enhanced games

1 Introduction

Serious game analytics is an emerging research field, which aims at turning gameplay data into "valuable analytics or actionable intelligence for performance measurement, assessment, and improvement" [1]. Not only does this high-level goal require the need for developing serious games able to provide didactically relevant quantitative information, but also efficient integration of modules for analytics collection and management [2].

Dealing with big data is a general and common problem, particularly in the context of the Internet of Things (IoT), for which several solutions have been developed, especially using cloud-based frameworks. In this paper, we are interested in investigating the application to the serious game context of Measurify (previously known as Atmosphere), an open source IoT framework built around the concept of measurement, which looks quite relevant to the goal of assessing and supporting a learner [3].

Actually, that article already briefly reports the experience of a University spin-off company applying Measurify to design a data management model for the use case of a 3D virtual reality simulator for emergency room personnel instruction. The goal of the

© Springer Nature Switzerland AG 2020
I. Marfisi-Schottman et al. (Eds.): GALA 2020, LNCS 12517, pp. 79–88, 2020.
https://doi.org/10.1007/978-3-030-63464-3_8

instructional tool was to assess the performance of a doctor by evaluating the effects of his interventions on the various patients. To this end, the Measurify data model was designed to record (i) the state of a patient, that is characterized by a set of time-evolving parameters; (ii) the actions performed by the doctor (e.g., how he interacted with the available simulation tools); and (iii) the events in the simulation (e.g., changes in medical equipment availability).

In this paper, we intend to go more in depth about the utilization of Measurify as an analytics engine, particularly investigating its extension towards edge computing [4], namely the recently released Edgine module [5], aimed at supporting a configurable provision of measurements from the field.

The remainder of the paper is organized as follows. Section 2 provides the related work, while Sect. 3 and 4 describe the Measurify and Edgine systems, respectively. Section 5 is devoted to the application of the IoT framework to a gaming environment. Section 6 draws the conclusions on the presented work and outlines possible directions for future research.

2   Related Work

Serious games analytics is a research field involving empirical research methodologies, including existing, experimental, and emerging conceptual frameworks, from various areas, such as: computer science, software engineering, educational data mining and statistics information visualization [1].

The literature provides several examples of serious game analytics (or game learning analytics) applications. [6] explored players' gameplay patterns to understand player dropout in the Quantum Spectre science game. Based on their results, the authors argue that modeling player behavior can be useful for both assessing learning and for designing complex problem solving content for learning environments. [7] present a novel method that suggests curricular sequencing based on the prediction relationship between math objectives. The authors argue that their method can potentially be applied to data from a wide range of games and digital learning platforms, enabling developers to better understand how to sequence educational content. [8] explore existing log files of the VIBOA environmental policy game. Our aim is to identify relevant player behaviours and performance patterns. The correlation analysis suggests to the authors a behavioural trade that reflects the rate of "switching" between different game objects or activities. The authors also established a model that uses switching indicators as predictors for the efficiency of learning. [9] developed a mobile game to support the transfer of theoretical knowledge on resuscitation training in case of cardiac arrest. To analyse a large and heterogeneous (in terms of sources and quality) data-set collected from 171 players, the authors applied different types of data modeling and analyses. This approach showed its usefulness and revealed some interesting findings.

[10] discuss a conceptual model (ecosystem and architecture) aimed to highlight the key considerations that may advance the current state of learning analytics, adaptive learning and SGs, by leveraging SGs as an suitable medium for gathering data and performing adaptations. [11] describe two key steps towards the systematization of game learning analytics: 1), the use of a newly-proposed standard tracking model to exchange

information between the serious game and the analytics platform, allowing reusable tracker components to be developed for each game engine or development platform; and 2), the use of standardized analysis and visualization assets to provide general but useful information for any SG that sends its data in the aforementioned format.

3 Measurify APIs

Measurify is a cloud-based Application Programming Interface (API) designed to support an efficient workflow for preparing different measurement-based data-rich applications, especially but not exclusively from IoT devices [Atmos]. The framework integrates APIs implementing Representational State Transfer (REST) services [12], that provide a platform-independent HTTP interface (e.g., [13]). Measurify exploits the open source MongoDB non relational database technology for data management, and on the NodeJS programming language, supporting by design seamless cross-platform portability, without being locked to a specific cloud vendor technology (e.g., Amazon Web Services for the Internet of Things (AWS IoT) [14] or Microsoft Azure cloud platform [15]), which is an important limit of current approaches. According to the RESTful programming paradigm, the API exposes a set of resources, A resource is an object with a type, associated data, relationships to other resources, and a set of methods that operate on it. Measurify defines a limited but powerful set of resource types (Table 1), that have been suited to create applications in international research projects in the automotive and health domains [16–18].

Table 1. Outlook of the measurify resources

Resource	Description
Measurement	Is the actual data taken from the field (e.g., a temperature value)
Feature	Is the type of a measurement. A type could be complex, with several dimensions, of various numeric/text types (e.g., sets of position records). Measurements could be of different types
Device	Is the instrument (e.g., a thermometer) through which the measurement is obtained
Thing	Is the subject of a measurement (e.g., a weather station located on a mountain)
Tag	Labels that can be attached as attributes to other resources – typically measurements, features, things and tag themselves
Constraint	A generic relationship between two resources (e.g., to support automatic generation of graphical user interfaces)
Computation	Is the actual data taken from the field (e.g., a temperature value)

The first step of the workflow supported by Measurify consists of the domain modeling, where the field objects (i.e., the objects involved in the measurements) are mapped to the API's resources. In this phase, the IoT application designer has to define features devices, tags, and constraints. In the configuration (or deployment) step, the above designed model resources are straightforwardly encoded in a.json file, which is POSTed to the framework APIs, so to create the Application Database (ADB) structure. In the regime phase, the framework manages the ADB, allowing (i) dynamic insertion/update of users, things, field measurements and computation requests; and (ii) retrieval of results in terms of things, measurements and computation outcomes. The ADB structure can be updated during the operation as well, by POSTing/PUTting/DELETEing features, devices, and tags. All these actions happen only through the exposed resource routes (i.e., standard functions through which objects can be accessed), with the well known advantages of the RESTful approach in terms of scalability, encapsulation, security, portability, platform independence, and clarity of terminology and operations.

In the next section, we present the extension of Measurify in the direction of the edge computing, namely the Edgine (Edge Engine) module.

4   Edgine

Measurify is a cloud-based system designed to host applications receiving measurements data through a REST API. According to the edge computing paradigm, computation is being moved towards the edge, in order to optimize exploitation of resources. Availability of computing capabilities on the edge, close to the field sensors implies the possibility to implement sensor hubs, typically represented by microcontrollers, that can be configured from remote in order to deliver the dynamically needed information.

This is the founding idea of Edgine, an edge system designed to support efficient development of integrated IoT applications. Edgine features an HTTP communication interface with the cloud (particularly with the Measurify APIs) in order to download configuration settings and scripts that are executed locally.

The system code consists of two main parts: an initial one and a loop one. In the start phase, which is implemented inside the setup() function, the Edgine software authenticates itself and connects to the APIs to download its configuration parameters and the list of scripts to be executed. Then, during the infinite cycle loop, the software continuously executes each assigned script in sequence, processing the data and sending them to the Measurify APIs.

Each device associated with Measurify is described by a JSON (JavaScript Object Notation) file which includes, among others, the feature field, describing the expected type of the measurements to be delivered, and the scripts field, including all the scripts to be downloaded and executed by the particular device. A script consists of a sequence of instructions that typically conclude with the delivery of the processed data to Measurify. The raw data processing instruction types currently include simple arithmetic functions, computation of simple statistic operations (e.g., min, max, mean, median, stdev), and accumulation of values in a (sliding) window.

A key design requirement for Edgine is platform independence, in order to make this paradigm widely available across edge devices. Thus, we strived to keep the system as independent as possible from the hardware. To that end, classes have been created to allow developers to switch from Windows/Linux/Mac PC platforms to Arduino through the use of C preprocessor macros.

The differences between the two main platform types concern the Internet connection. In the Arduino case, an automatic connection to a WiFi network (predefined in the code) is performed, and the system is also designed to perform a reconnection in case of signal loss. In the Edgine version for PC-type machines, on the other hand, the system waits until a network connection becomes available, before trying to perform the initial authentication operations. At runtime, data that cannot be sent due to lack of connectivity are accumulated in a buffer, waiting for a connection.

Up to now, Edgine has been used in some IoT applications, concerning the monitoring of environmental parameters such as temperature, humidity, light conditions [19].

5 Serious Game Application

While Edgine has a clear application to edge devices, such as microcontrollers, mobile phones and automotive electronic central units (ECUs), its concept is abstract and can be applied to any device processing raw data. Thus, the Edgine can also be employed in a serious game with a goal to get measurements from it and pre-process them according to some basic scripts. Everything is dynamically programmed from remote. Conceptually, this corresponds to applying the IoT sensor measurement concept not only to reality but also to a game's virtual reality.

To achieve this goal, it is necessary to insert the Edgine system inside the target serious game. This can be achieved by integrating Edgine inside a game engine. This is a general solution, that could be seamlessly applied to any game implemented with a given game engine.

For the case of Unity 3D, a widely used game engine, the idea is to develop a plug-in that would wrap Edgine, making it available to any game. For instance, it would be possible to configure the Edgine so to send to the measurement API (i.e., the generic analytics engine) information such as: the average distance covered by a virtual character in the last minute, the number of collected objects, the number of correctly answered quizzes, etc. The key advantage – especially in a software engineering perspective of efficient development - is the abstract and generic architectural approach, which makes the solution generally applicable.

In the following, we describe the implementation of Edgine in Unity 3D. In this game engine, C# scripts are usually employed to create components and specify their behaviour. Scripts can exploit libraries of additional functionalities, made available in Unity as plug-ins. Plug-ins are platform-specific native code libraries that can access operating system functions and other third-party libraries, that would not otherwise be available to Unity developers.

A Unity plug-in is equivalent Dynamic-Link Library (DLL), and can be efficiently developed with Visual Studio, which is quite similar to the Unity Integrated Development Environment (IDE). In the DLL, we implemented a single class, which wraps the methods intended to be exposed to Unity C# scripts. Inside the header, it is necessary to define such functions with the declspec(dllexport) attribute. Moreover, through the extern "C" label, it is indicated to the compiler that the C linking conventions should be employed for such function. This is necessary for a correct export, because, otherwise, C++ compilers would perform the mangling process, making them unreachable from Unity. The mangling is a technique used to distinguish functions that have the same name (overloading). The technique manipulates the name during compilation, so that it becomes unique. But this would make the final name unknown to the Unity developer. The C language, on the other hand, does not support function overloading, thus does not perform the mangling. Thus, the binary file generated by the compilation process contains the original method names. However, since the C linking convention is adopted, it is necessary that the input and output data types are those of the C, even if the body of the function is written in C++.

According to the Edgine programming model presented in the previous section, the class exposes two methods: Setup() and Action(). The first one will be used at start-up, the second one will be employed inside the game engine's update loop. For the Unity implementation, we let that the service descriptive features (device, thing, feature, username e password) can be specified by the Unity user as parameters of the two exposed functions and are not hard-wired in the source code, which is the approach employed in the edge/embedded environment. Intuitively, the user can specify the names of the resources related to a correct delivery of measurements to Measurify. The Action() function, takes in input the name of the feature and the measurement value, which will need to be delivered to the cloud.

The compiled Edgine project produces five dll files: NativeCppLibrary.dll, pcred.dll, PocoFoundationd.dll, PocoNetd.dll, zlibd1.dll, of which the first one is the dynamic library containing the two functions mentioned above. In order to use the plug-in inside Unity, it is necessary to copy all these .dll files in the project directory.

As a proof of concept, we implemented a very simple application example of collection of data from a game scene and their delivery to the cloud. Particularly, we tracked the collisions of a ball with the borders of a squared region (Fig. 1). Every time a collision is detected with the wall, a variable is incremented. When the number of collisions becomes a multiple of 5, the value, added with the time stamp, is sent to the Measurify APIs, from where it can be manipulated, also in real-time, by other applications and/or user interfaces.

Fig. 1. Simple game scene in Unity3D

This goal is achieved by following the standard steps of the workflow of an Edgine-extended Measurify application. The first step consists in POSTing to Measurify (e.g., through a common collaboration platform for API development, such as Postman) the names and, particularly for the Script resource, the contents of the resources needed to configure the environment so that it will be able to receive measurements from our application. In our case, the names are reported in the second column of Table 2. The Measurify APIs will create the corresponding resources, that will be available at the URLs in the third column, where the base url is http://students.atmosphere.tools/

Table 2. Measurify resources for the example application

Resource type	Resource	Resource URL
Thing	Ball	url/v1/things/ball
Feature	Collision	url/v1/features/collision
Device	Unity	url/v1/devices/Unity
Script	Collisions-count-send	url/v1/scripts/collisions-count-send

The next step concerns the development of the C# script that detects the collision and exploits the Edgine plug-in to transmit the corresponding value to Measurify. As anticipated, for the sake of flexibility, in the Unity implementation the Setup() and Action() functions are parametric, thus we allow the Unity user to specify through the Inspector module (Fig. 2) the values that will be passed to such functions.

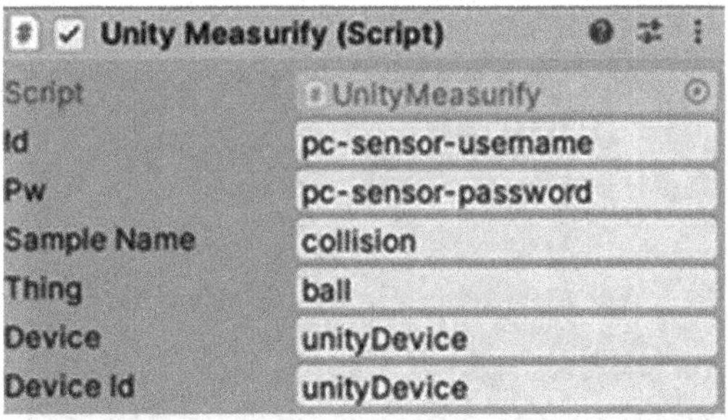

Fig. 2. Variables set by the user inside the Unity Inspector

The Unity scripts are organized in a structure that strictly corresponds to the Edgine programming model, with an initial Start() method, executed only once at the beginning of the programme, and an Update() method, which is continuously called, at each frame's update. The mapping for an Edgine application in Unity is thus straightforward: the Setup() method is called inside the Start(), while Action() inside Update(), (Fig. 3).

Start() accomplishes the task of initializing all the StringBuilder public variables involved in the script. Once such user-defined parameters are collected, the plug-in's Setup() is executed, which performs the authentication in Measurify, getting the Json

```
// Start is called before the first frame update
void Start()
{
    idSB = new StringBuilder(id);
    pwSB = new StringBuilder(pw);
    sampleSB = new StringBuilder(sampleName);
    thingSB = new StringBuilder(thing);
    deviceSB = new StringBuilder(device);
    deviceIdSB = new StringBuilder(deviceId);

    Setup(idSB, pwSB, thingSB, deviceSB, deviceIdSB);
    threads = new Queue<Thread>();
}
```

```
// Update is called once per frame
void Update()
{
    if (MoveBall.collisionCount % 5 == 0 &&
        MoveBall.collisionCount != 0 &&
        oldCollisionCount != MoveBall.collisionCount)
    {
        Thread t = new Thread(Play);
        threads.Enqueue(t);
        if(!threads.Peek().IsAlive)
            threads.Peek().Start();
    }
    oldCollisionCount = MoveBall.collisionCount;
}
```

Fig. 3. Start and update methods in the Unity script

Web Token (JWT) that will be used in all the subsequent accesses to the cloud APIs. A Queue<Thread> object is also initialized, that will be useful during the game loop. The creation of a Thread object, in fact, is necessary when sending data to the cloud, in order not to block the continuous game update cycle. The threads are inserted in a queue to simplify their management, as they are created, executed once at a time and destroyed in order, making use of the Enqueue(), Peek() and Dequeue() methods.

The Update() method first makes a check on the number of accumulated collisions (a measurement is sent to the cloud only when a multiple of 5 is hit). Then, if the sending condition is met, a thread is created, consisting of the Play() function calling the plugin's Action(), and added to the queue. Once created, a thread is ready to be executed as soon as no other thread is still alive. In this way, the application is not overloaded with threads. If some threads are still in the queue when the game is completed and quitted by the player, the OnApplicationQuit() method launches the missing threads before the actual end of the program execution. Finally, Fig. 4 shows an example of measurement received by Measurify in JSON format.


```
{
    "visibility": "private",
    "tags": [],
    "_id": "5f05e7608b005e6b0dedcdce",
    "thing": "ball",
    "feature": "collision",
    "device": "unityDevice",
    "script": "collisions-count-send",
    "samples": [
        {
            "values": [
                25
            ]
        }
    ],
    "startDate": "2020-07-08T15:33:50.492Z",
    "endDate": "2020-07-08T15:33:50.492Z"
}
```


Fig. 4. The measurement received from the Unity game at the Measurify's end

6 Conclusions and Future Work

This paper has proposed the use of a new data toolchain for serious games analytics. The toolchain relies on the open source Measurify IoT framework for measurement management, and particularly takes advantage of its edge computing extension (Edgine), which can be seamlessly deployed cross-platform on embedded devices and PCs as well. The Edgine is programmed to download from Measurify a set of scripts, that are periodically executed so to get data from sensors, pre-process them and send the extracted information to the Measurify APIs.

Thanks to its powerful abstractions, this model can be seamlessly employed also in the virtual reality and gaming domain. Virtual sensors can be built in game engine scripts. This paper has presented the implementation of the plug-in which deploys Edgine in Unity 3D, allowing an easy delivery of virtual sensor information to Measurify. Just as a proof of concept, we have presented the utilization of the whole chain within a trivial game scene. We plan to employ and test the system with more complex serious game analytics, and this opportunity is possible for every researcher and practitioner thanks to the open source release of the whole Measurify framework [20].

There is another aspect beside the general applicability of the toolchain to any virtual sensors. In fact, the same software engineering approach (and actual Edgine tool) could be used also for measuring real world parameters, connected to the game. This opportunity is particularly relevant to augmented reality games and reality enhanced serious games (e.g., [21–23]). Moreover, the same system can be used also the physiological parameters of the player. To the best of our knowledge, no tool exists that is able to process information from such heterogeneous sources as physical and virtual sensors. For instance, the Edgine toolchain could be used to simultaneously get data about a game session and a player's physiological status.

References

1. Loh, C.S., Sheng, Y., Ifenthaler, D. (eds.): Serious Games Analytics. AGL. Springer, Cham (2015). https://doi.org/10.1007/978-3-319-05834-4
2. Alonso-Fernández, C., Pérez-Colado, I., Freire, M., Martínez-Ortiz, I., Fernández-Manjón, B.: Improving serious games analyzing learning analytics data: lessons learned. In: Gentile, M., Allegra, M., Söbke, H. (eds.) GALA 2018. LNCS, vol. 11385, pp. 287–296. Springer, Cham (2019). https://doi.org/10.1007/978-3-030-11548-7_27
3. Berta, R., Kobeissi, A., Bellotti, F., De Gloria, A.: Atmosphere, an open source measurement-oriented data framework for IoT. IEEE Trans. Ind. Inf. https://doi.org/10.1109/tii.2020.2994414
4. Lin, L., Liao, X., Jin, H., Li, P.: Computation offloading toward edge computing. Proc. IEEE 107, 1584–1607 (2019)
5. https://github.com/measurify/edge
6. Hicks, D., Eagle, M., Rowe, E., Asbell-Clarke, J., Edwards, T., Barnes, T.: Using game analytics to evaluate puzzle design and level progression in a serious game. In: Proceedings of the Sixth International Conference on Learning Analytics & Knowledge (LAK 2016), pp. 440–448. ACM, New York (2016). https://doi.org/10.1145/2883851.2883953

7. Peddycord-Liu, Z., Cody, C., Kessler, S., Barnes, T., Lynch, C.F., Rutherford, T.: Using serious game analytics to inform digital curricular sequencing: what math objective should students play next? In: Proceedings of the Annual Symposium on Computer-Human Interaction in Play (CHI PLAY 2017), pp. 195–204. ACM, New York (2017). https://doi.org/10.1145/311 6595.3116620

8. Westera, W., Nadolski, R., Hummel, H.: Serious gaming analytics: what students' log files tell us about gaming and learning. Int. J. Serious Games **1**(2) (2014). https://doi.org/10.17083/ ijsg.v1i2.9

9. Lukosch, H., Cunningham, S.: Data analytics of mobile serious games: applying bayesian data analysis methods. Int. J. Serious Games **5**(1) (2018). https://doi.org/10.17083/ijsg.v5i 1.222

10. Baalsrud Hauge, J.M., et al.: Learning analytics architecture to scaffold learning experience through technology-based methods. Int. J. Serious Games **2**(1) (2015). https://doi.org/10. 17083/ijsg.v2i1.38

11. Alonso-Fernandez, C., Calvo, A., Freire, M., Martinez-Ortiz, I., Fernandez-Manjon, B.: Systematizing game learning analytics for serious games. In: 2017 IEEE Global Engineering Education Conference (EDUCON), Athens, pp. 1111–1118 (2017). https://doi.org/10.1109/ EDUCON.2017.7942988

12. Solapure, S.S., Kenchannavar, H.: Internet of Things: a survey related to various recent architectures and platforms available. In: International Conference on Advances in Computing, Communications and Informatics (ICACCI), Jaipur, pp. 2296–2301 (2016). https://doi.org/ 10.1109/ICACCI.2016.7732395

13. Jiong, S., Liping, J., Jun, L.: The integration of azure sphere and azure cloud services for Internet of Things. MDPI J. Appl. Sci. **9**(13), 2746 (2019). https://doi.org/10.3390/app913 2746

14. Amazon Web Services AWS IoT. https://aws.amazon.com/iot/solutions/industrial-iot

15. Azure IoT, Microsoft (2019). https://azure.microsoft.com/en-us/overview/iot/

16. Cirimele, V., et al.: The fabric ICT platform for managing wireless dynamic charging road lanes. IEEE Trans. Veh. Technol. **69**(3), 2501–2512 (2020)

17. Hiller, J., et al.: The L3Pilot data management toolchain for a level 3 vehicle automation pilot. Electronics **9**, 809 (2020)

18. Monteriù, A., et al.: A smart sensing architecture for domestic moniotring: methodological approach and experimental validation. Sensors **18**(7) (2018). https://doi.org/10.3390/s18 072310

19. http://students.atmosphere.tools/

20. https://github.com/measurify

21. Massoud, R., Bellotti, F., Poslad, S., Berta, R., De Gloria, A.: Towards a reality-enhanced serious game to promote eco-driving in the wild. In: Liapis, A., Yannakakis, G.N., Gentile, M., Ninaus, M. (eds.) GALA 2019. LNCS, vol. 11899, pp. 245–255. Springer, Cham (2019). https://doi.org/10.1007/978-3-030-34350-7_24

22. Massoud, R., Poslad, S., Bellotti, F., Berta, R., Mehran, K., De Gloria, A.: A fuzzy logic module to estimate a driver's fuel consumption for reality-enhanced serious games. Int. J. Serious Games **5**, 45–62 (2018). https://doi.org/10.17083/ijsg.v5i4.266

23. Fijnheer, J.D., van Oostendorp, H.: Steps to design a household energy game. Int. J. Serious Games **3**(3) (2016). https://doi.org/10.17083/ijsg.v3i3.131

Virtual and Mixed Reality Applications

Use of Virtual Reality Technology for CANDU 6 Reactor Fuel Channel Operation Training

Ziqi Fan[1], Kaitlyn Brown[1], Stephanie Nistor[1], Karishma Seepaul[1], Kody Wood[1], Alvaro Uribe-Quevedo[1(✉)], Sharman Perera[1], Edward Waller[1], and Shawn Lowe[2]

[1] Ontario Tech University, Oshawa, ON, Canada
{ziqi.fan,kaitlyn.brown,stephane.nistor,karishma.seepaul, kody.wood}@ontariotechu.net
{alvaro.quevedo,sharman.perera,edward.waller}@ontariotechu.ca
[2] Ontario Power Generation, Burlington, ON, Canada
shawn.lowe@opg.com

Abstract. The CANDU (CANada Deuterium Uranium) 6 nuclear reactor core consists of 380 horizontal fuel channels that hold the fuel in the reactor core and allow for the expansion of the fuel channel components. Fuel channel assembly enables the heat transfer from the nuclear fuel to heavy water coolant. Heavy water coolant under elevated pressure ($\sim 10\,\mathrm{MPa}$), carries the heat generated from nuclear fission reaction to heat exchangers located outside the reactor core to generate steam that will turn the turbine to generate electricity. The fuel channel assembly also allows the fueling machine to perform online refueling of nuclear fuel and provide shielding protection to safeguard the nuclear workers while providing structural integrity during the regular operation of the nuclear reactor. The physical configuration and coolant flow path of the CANDU fuel channel assembly is very complex, and teaching and training associated with the fuel channel assembly employ pictures and computer simulations. However, these traditional approaches lack the immersion and interactivity that virtual reality can provide to realistically expose learners in a safe and controlled manner otherwise difficult to achieve in real life due to the dangers of radiation exposure. In this paper, we present the development of virtual reality (VR) fuel assembly prototype generated for teaching CANDU concepts. Our preliminary study focused on understanding face validity and usability perceptions regarding the virtual interactions. Preliminary feedback from content exports provided us with valuable insights on improvements regarding usability, fidelity, and gamification.

Keywords: CANDU · Calandria · Fuel channel · Reactor core · Educational · Nuclear Science · Virtual reality

I. Marfisi-Schottman et al. (Eds.): GALA 2020, LNCS 12517, pp. 91–101, 2020.
https://doi.org/10.1007/978-3-030-63464-3_9

1 Introduction

The CANDU (CANada Deuterium Uranium) 6 reactor core consists of hundreds of horizontal fuel channels that hold the fuel in the core and allow for the expansion of the fuel channel components. Each fuel channel assembly includes a pressure tube containing a string of twelve fuel bundles, within a calandria tube, with pressurized heavy water coolant flowing through it [1,2].

Throughout the reactor's operational life, the components of the fuel assembly, especially the pressure tubes experience high stress, high temperature, and high neutron flux, resulting in changes to the tubes' geometric and material properties, a phenomenon called sag deformation. The downward sag of the pressure tube may lead to contact between the hot pressure tube and the relatively cold calandria tube (Pressure Tube - Calandria Tube (PT-CT) contact), leading to the pressure tube's failure. The calandria tubes provide the structural rigidity to the calandria vessel and insulate the coolant flowing through the pressure tube from the lower temperature (less than 100 °C) of the moderator [3]. PT-CT contact can force a reactor shutdown and result in losses of millions of dollars of revenue [4,5].

Companies invest time and money into routine inspections to ensure PT-CT contact does not occur [6,7]. The enormous cost associated with replacing a failed fuel channel following PT-CT contact and the time and resources allocated to inspections requires that nuclear engineers become knowledgeable about the CANDU fuel channel for optimizing its operation.

Virtual reality (VR) has been gaining momentum as a disruptive technology in several fields, including health care [8], education [9], and training amongst others. More specifically, the nuclear industry has seen a growth in VR developments for improving safety and training workers at various levels. VR allows recreating scenarios otherwise impossible in real life. That itself presents with opportunities to explore decision making under extreme duress circumstances to assess training outcomes, such as simulating cyber security attacks and visualizing the possible outcomes in a more immersive and meaningful manner [10].

In this paper, we present a CANDU VR assembly environment prototype for teaching purposes. Our goal is to understand our system's face validity and usability perceptions when employing VR. We chose VR technology as it can help to overcome the limitations of safety and physical constraints found if students were to work with the real tubes, or workers were to work with used fuel channel components since they are highly radioactive.

2 Background

Virtual Reality technologies are currently being used as a medium that provide safe immersion for training and education in several industries including medical, automation, automotive, aviation, and nuclear amongst others. For example, VR can help training and preparedness of safety culture [11], and due to its affordability as a consumer-level technology [12], is being adopted for radiation

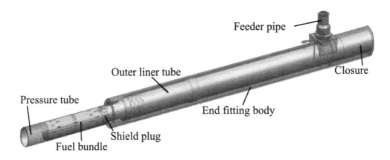

Fig. 1. 3D CAD model of a CANDU 6 fuel channel end fitting area created using the NX 12 CAD software [9].

training practices involving an accident, a leak, or when an emergency exposure occurs [13]. Radiation visualization combined with VR allow increasing awareness protection to avoid health-risks [14].

Furthermore, VR is helping to address training challenges by providing unlimited access to complex virtual nuclear reactor systems and components, including control rooms [15], estimated radiation dose for minimizing exposure during maintenance [16], and safe construction [16]. In the classroom, VR can be used to teach nuclear reactor operation, fission and fusion principles and criticality accidents by presenting simulated power plants with immersive visuals about the process [17], basic theoretical study, and professional skills training [18].

Additionally, VR technologies are being coupled with serious games (i.e., games for learning purposes) and gamification (i.e., use of gameful design in non-game context to create experiences similar to that of games to boost engagement and motivation) are being used to enhance simulation and training by providing engaging environments providing novelty and motivating experiences [19]. The addition of game design includes the employment of dynamic elements (e.g., constraints, narrative, and progression), mechanics (e.g., rules, challenge, feedback, resource management, rewards) and game components (e.g., achievements, badges, and points) [20].

3   CANDU Fuel Channel VR Development

The CANDU fuel channel VR environment development required the analysis and characterization of the steps involved in understanding its operation to transfer suitable interactions done in simulation software. A 3D CAD model of one of the end-fittings of a CANDU 6 fuel channel assembly built using NX 12 computer assisted design (CAD) software is shown in Fig. 1.

The simulated velocity vectors plots of the heavy water flowing through this section are shown in Fig. 2. The vectors are coloured accordingly to the static pressure of the same section. NX 12 allows users to rotate, zoom, and

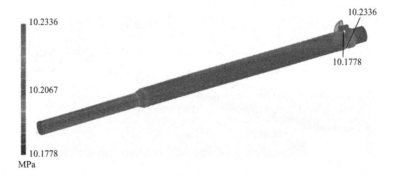

Fig. 2. Simulated velocity vector plots colored by Static Pressure (MPa) of CANDU 6 fuel channel end-fitting area generated using NX 12 simulation software [21]. (Color figure online)

pan the camera position to navigate the virtual tube and the numerical simulation results. However, the simulation is observed through regular 2D screens and it does not convey an immersive experience where students can visualize and explore the tube as if they had access to the real system with overlaid simulated data in Lagrangian and Eulerian frames of reference.

Building on top of the curriculum for Nuclear Engineering undergraduate students at Ontario Tech University, our design process focused on mapping the instructions provided by video and lectures into a narrative where users interact with the CANDU fuel channel and, in the end, take a quiz. For the VR development, we chose the Oculus Quest head-mounted display (HMD) as it provided a stand-alone experience that could help reduce VR's entry barrier associated with costs. Additionally, the Oculus Quest tracks the environment and the user through inside-out sensors supporting seated, standing, and room-scale interactions. The Oculus Quest Headset offers six degrees of freedom (DOF) tracking on the HMD and controllers through four wide-angle cameras located on each corner of the headset. Furthermore, the device can track hand and finger movement within the cameras field of view.

3.1   Graphical User Interfaces (GUI)

Our proposed simulation presents all interactions occurring in a large room where students are greeted with a big screen on the front wall, showing all the menu items and instructions. User interactions occur through the GUI by accessing menu buttons that branch into different VR experiences. For example, students can decide whether they prefer to start with the fuel channel interactions, visit a collection of information, know about the development team, or exit the application. The students can access the GUI buttons by employing the Oculus Quest controller or their hands projecting a ray cast that can be used to aim at the desired interactive trigger. After the student selects the *Start*, they will go to a *Ready* screen asking for confirmation to continue with the experience. Alternatively, the students can return to the *Main Menu* by selecting the *Back* button.

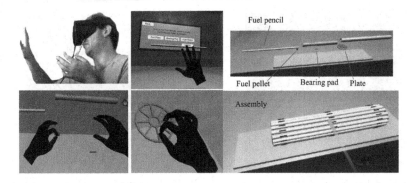

Fig. 3. *Fuel Bundle* assembly employing hand tracking in VR. (Color figure online)

3.2   Virtual Environment

In addition to the screens presenting the fuel channel assembly related information (as shown in Fig. 3), the environment also includes a bench for performing the assembly tasks and a real life-size CANDU 6 reactor face 3D model from which the fuel channel parts were obtained. Figure 4 displays the 3D model of the reactor. The assembly process presents the users with the choice of performing the task with the VR controller or hand tracking. These two methods were chosen as they both present intuitive forms of interaction that allow reaching, grasping, and positioning elements within the workspace. The assembly process requires the users to identify the components and assembly them in the following order: i) the fuel pellet, ii) the end plate, and iii) the fuel pencil. When the simulation starts, the reactor face and the end fitting of the fuel assembly of a CANDU 6 reactor appear on the top of the bench. The students can select the part displayed on the screen, and a virtual representation appears in front of them. Once the part is enabled for visualization, the students can grab it and manipulate it employing the Oculus Quest's grip button, or by grabbing the object performing a cylindrical grasp captured through hand tracking Fig. 3. Tube interactions trigger pop-up information used for evaluation purposes of measuring attention after the interaction.

Labels were added to all parts of the fuel channel assembly to help the students identify individual parts and components. The labels are only shown when in the proximity of the controller, or when secured and facing the HMD, then fade away when the item is released. Figure 4b shows labels on the visualized parts when grabbed and in the proximity of the user input device.

3.3   Assessment

Once the calandria tube has been examined, users can take the test, or go back to review previous information. If the test is selected, the first task requires the students to build the *Fuel Bundle* by assembling it correctly. After completing the assembly, the second part presents ten multiple-choice questions with four

(a) Model of Nuclear Reactor face.   (b) Fuel bundle part selection in VR.

Fig. 4. Elements in virtual scene.

answers to choose from. It is important to highlight that we have chosen to present the quiz within VR to avoid breaking immersion and presence [22].

After reading the question, the answer is chosen by selecting the corresponding colored button associated with the answer displayed on the virtual screen. A thirty-seconds timer starts and it is displayed on screen to answer a question; after the timer ends, the system shows the right answer and a button leading to the next question (Fig. 5). Time constraints were added to the questionnaire as a resource to improve student engagement and promote rapid thinking that may be necessary for emergencies. The choice to display the correct answer after the timer runs out aims to provide immediate feedback for the students to consider without requiring them to go through the entire assembly process. The score of each question will be based on the correctness and response speed. Wrong answers will result in a zero; if correct, the score is modified so that instructors can identify areas of difficulty. After completing all the ten questions, a panel displays the final score factoring the time taken to answer and its correctness. Finally, we decided to leave the questionnaire within the VR environment to avoid breaking immersion and facilitate reviewing materials after the quiz is completed.

4   Preliminary Assessment

A preliminary assessment was conducted to understand the usefulness and usability perception of the prototype as a potential complementary teaching tool. The assessment was conducted in two parts. First, we focused on gathered opinions for face validity from A content expert, a laboratory technician, and a fourth-year undergraduate student from a Nuclear Engineering program volunteered to watch a live remote demonstration of the VR tool providing them with a first-person view of the process. This approach was necessary due to the physical distancing restrictions in place to prevent the spread of COVID-19.

(a) User interacting with a menu.

(b) Answer selection through colored push buttons.

Fig. 5. User interactions with the menu and questions employing the Oculus Quest controllers.

The content expert and the student expressed not having prior immersive VR experience, while the laboratory technician did.

The live demonstration was conducted on Mozilla Hubs, a browser-based virtual collaborative platform, where the participants experience a live demonstration of the prototype. The demonstration included assembling the calandria tube and then they were asked open questions about perceived challenges and suggestions for in-class use.

Four participants comprised of two graduate students, a fourth-year nuclear engineering student, and a Game Development Professor volunteered to try on the project inside the Oculus Quest. The reason for this diverse pool of participants was to gather usability opinions from different points of view. After using the VR environment, the participants were asked to provide their usability perceptions through the System Usability Scale [23].

The System Usability Scale (SUS) consists of ten questions that are answered on a scale of one to five. The usability score is calculated by subtracting one mark from every odd question while subtracting five from every even question. Once completed, the addition of all the results is multiplied by 2.5, which provides the system's usability score. Typically, a score above 68/100 means the system is usable, and little to no changes are required to make the system more usable. However, if their score is below 68/100, the system requires significant changes [24]. Table 1 presents the SUS questions, where usable results will see odd questions obtaining responses oriented to 'Agree' and 'Strongly Agree,' whereas even questions should see a trend towards 'Disagree' and 'Strongly Disagree.'

The preliminary overall SUS score was 69/100, indicating that there are improvements to be made.

Table 1. System usability scale questions [23].

Question	System usability scale questionnaire
Q1	I think that I would like to use this system frequently
Q2	I found the system unnecessarily complex
Q3	I thought the system was easy to use
Q4	I think that I would need the support of a technical person to be able to use this system
Q5	I found the various functions in this system were well integrated
Q6	I thought there was too much inconsistency in this system
Q7	I imagine that most people would learn how to use this system quickly
Q8	I found the system very cumbersome to use
Q9	I felt very confident using the system
Q10	I needed to learn a lot of things before I could get going with the system

5 Discussion

The participants who attended the video recording demonstrations liked the tool and expressed their interest in using it as a complement to their traditional teaching materials. However, two participants, the student and the content expert did not feel confident using the tool since this was the first-time using Mozilla hubs for a remote VR experience. The combination of controller and hand-tracking input caused interest, but live testing is needed to understand the efficacy of both system when performing the tasks.

Regarding the preliminary usability perceptions, the system requires improvements associated with the technical assistance. While the system was found easy to use, there were problems with hand tracking and physical interactions with the fuel pellet. On one occasion, the participant dropped the pellet and the simulation had to be restarted as it disappeared from the scene. We believe that while hand tracking is appealing, VR controllers are more effective because of the higher tracking accuracy and decisive actions performed by using the buttons. In contrast, hand tracking required several tries, proper lighting conditions and moving back and forth to get the hands and interactions properly detected.

Overall, the feedback associated with challenges and suggestions about the experience, provided us with the following considerations: i) Level of fidelity of the fuel channel assembly: The content expert highlighted that there were some important pieces of the fuel bundle missing that students often have difficulty understanding, ii) Accessibility features: Make the prototype available to all students, iii) Ease of use: The student found the concept simple to follow and understand the fuel channel parts, while expressing concerns with the controllers and the need for more practice to perform virtual tasks better, iv) Gamification: The content expert highlighted the importance of considering other forms of input to award scores that require students to provide argumentative responses in addition to multiple choice questions, and v) Natural user interactions: Including speech to text can facilitate interactions with some GUI elements as an alternative to controller/hand tracking inputs.

6 Conclusions

Here we have presented the development of a CANDU 6 fuel channel VR prototype for potential teaching purposes. Employing VR offers the opportunity to bring nuclear reactor systems closer to the students as they can explore, interact, and navigate the environment in a safe and controlled manner with meaningful interactions. Our preliminary assessment indicates there is interest in such tool for complementing traditional teaching of CANDU-related materials. The fidelity, content, user interactions, and gamification require further work to understand their impacts on learning. The current VR prototype allowed us to gather preliminary information to assess both face validity and usability, along with identified and perceived challenges to meet the expectations in future development.

Future work will focus on increasing fidelity, narrative, gamification improvements, testing with more content experts, and students to compare how the fuel channel assembly VR approach helps learning when compared to traditional methods. Moreover, we will add emergency conditions to study the effects of stress on decision making when working with radioactive reactor components by adding non-invasive physiological measures as interactive metrics. Furthermore, we will study the effects on retention and in VR and outside VR assessment with a larger pool of participants.

Acknowledgment. The financial support of the *Natural Sciences and Engineering Research Council of Canada* (NSERC) in the form of a Discovery Grant RGPIN-2018-05917 awarded to Alvaro Uribe Quevedo, supporting Kody Wood and Ziqi Fan's research. The support of the Sigma Lab from the Faculty of Energy Systems and Nuclear Sciences and Callan Brown, Rob Ulrich is acknowledged.

References

1. Safa, M.: CANDU fundamentals, December 2010. https://canteach.candu.org/ContentLibrary/20040700.pdf
2. Wijayaratne, U., Bereznai, G., Perera, S.: A review of flow accelerated corrosion in CANDU feeder pipes
3. Tapping, R.: Corrosion issues in pressurized heavy water reactor (PHWR/CANDU®) systems. In: Nuclear Corrosion Science and Engineering, pp. 581–633. Elsevier (2012)
4. Cziraky, A.: Pressure tube-calandria tube thermal contact conductance. Ph.D. thesis, McMaster University (2009)

5. Shokralla, S., Krause, T.W.: Methods for evaluation of accuracy with multiple essential parameters for eddy current measurement of pressure tube to calandria tube gap in candu® reactors. CINDE J. **35**(1), 5–8 (2014)
6. Krause, T., Klein, G., Luloff, M., Morelli, J.: Finite element model of eddy current measurement of pressure tube to Calandria Tube gap. NDT.net, December 2016. https://www.ndt.net/search/docs.php3?id=20390
7. Candlish, J., Dalton, K., Marshall, B.: Computer simulation of fuel channel replacement (1988)
8. Chanchaichujit, J., Tan, A., Meng, F., Eaimkhong, S.: Healthcare 4.0. Springer, Singapore (2019). https://doi.org/10.1007/978-981-13-8114-0
9. Horn, M.B.: Virtual reality disruption: will 3-d technology break through to the educational mainstream? Educ. Next **16**(4), 82–84 (2016)
10. Cho, H.S., Woo, T.H.: Cyber security in nuclear industry-analytic study from the terror incident in nuclear power plants (NPPs). Ann. Nuclear Energy **99**, 47–53 (2017)
11. Xiyun, L., Xi, W., Chenchen, L., Shaohua, W.: Application of virtual reality technology in nuclear power plant control room simulator. In: 2018 26th International Conference on Nuclear Engineering. American Society of Mechanical Engineers Digital Collection, London, England (2018)
12. Velev, D., Zlateva, P.: Virtual reality challenges in education and training. Int. J. Learn. Teach. **3**(1), 33–37 (2017)
13. Carroll, M., Shaw, S., Schrader, P.: Virtual reality for career and technical education. In: E-Learn: World Conference on E-Learning in Corporate, Government, Healthcare, and Higher Education, pp. 1355–1363. Association for the Advancement of Computing in Education (AACE), San Diego, CA, USA (2019)
14. Cryer, A., Kapellmann-Zafra, G., Abrego-Hernández, S., Marin-Reyes, H., French, R.: Advantages of virtual reality in the teaching and training of radiation protection during interventions in harsh environments. In: 2019 24th IEEE International Conference on Emerging Technologies and Factory Automation (ETFA), pp. 784–789. IEEE (2019)
15. Lee, H., Cha, W.C.: Virtual reality-based ergonomic modeling and evaluation framework for nuclear power plant operation and control. Sustainability **11**(9), 2630 (2019)
16. Wang, L., Du, W., Chu, S., Shi, M., Li, J., et al.: Intelligent science and technology assists safety culture construction. In: Abu Dhabi International Petroleum Exhibition & Conference. Society of Petroleum Engineers (2019)
17. Fradika, H., Surjono, H.: Me science as mobile learning based on virtual reality. J. Phys. Conf. Ser. **1006**, 012027 (2018)
18. Wu, P., Shan, J., Zhang, B.: Application of virtual simulation experiment in teaching of major of nuclear engineering and technology. Res. Explor. Lab. **4**, 27 (2018)
19. Majuri, J., Koivisto, J., Hamari, J.: Gamification of education and learning: a review of empirical literature. In: Proceedings of the 2nd International GamiFIN Conference, GamiFIN 2018. CEUR-WS (2018)
20. Werbach, K., Hunter, D.: The Gamification Toolkit: Dynamics, Mechanics, and Components for the Win. Wharton School Press, Philadelphia(2015)
21. Grigor, R.M., Vaitheeswaran, M., Zhang, F., Karam, J.: Computational fluid dynamics: gray-lock hub to first fuel bundle, November 2019

22. Putze, S., Alexandrovsky, D., Putze, F., Höffner, S., Smeddinck, J.D., Malaka, R.: Breaking the experience: effects of questionnaires in vr user studies. In: Proceedings of the 2020 CHI Conference on Human Factors in Computing Systems, pp. 1–15 (2020)
23. Brooke, J., et al.: SUS - a quick and dirty usability scale. Usability Eval. Ind. **189**(194), 4–7 (1996)
24. Sauro, J.: Practical Guide to the System Usability Scale: Background, Benchmarks & Best Practices. CreateSpace Independent Publishing Platform, Scotts Valley (2011)

Dynamic Difficulty Adjustment Through Real-Time Physiological Feedback for a More Adapted Virtual Reality Exposure Therapy

Sorelle Audrey Kamkuimo K.[1](✉) ⓘ, Benoît Girard[2], and Bob-Antoine J. Menelas[1] ⓘ

[1] Department of Computer Sciences and Mathematics, University of Quebec at Chicoutimi, Quebec, Canada
{sorelle-audrey.kamkuimo-kengne1,bamenela}@uqac.ca
[2] La Futaie Therapy Center, Boulevard Tadoussac, Saint-Fulgence, QC, Canada
beni.girard@gmail.com

Abstract. Like many researchers, we think that the use of dynamic difficulty adjustment (DDA) to offer an appropriate balance between the skills of the player and the difficulty of the gameplay is an appropriate avenue to maintain the flow of a user. We analyze this approach in a virtual reality serious game dedicated to people suffering from post-traumatic stress disorder (PTSD). Knowing that heart rate is a good indicator of the emotional state of people with PTSD, we collect this variable in real-time to propose a virtual reality dynamic adjusted system based on the emotional state of the subject. The proposed adaptation system can be approached in three modes: the offline mode which consists on therapist selections before launching the game, the manual online mode during which the therapist can adapt the virtual environment while the subject is exposed, and the computational online mode that runs a DDA algorithm to automatically adjust the game.

Keywords: Serious game · Adaptivity · Virtual reality · PTSD · Heart rate · Physiological feedback

1 Introduction

One of the main advantages of serious games (SG) is that they offer a suitable environment for learning [1]. Like many other researchers, we see SG as a medium of active learning based on problem-solving with multiple interactions. In this view, we are particularly interested in the fact that SG players have in-game objectives whose achievement involves solving one or more challenges in some specific contexts. Hence, it appears that the more adapted the situation is to the player's profile, the more efficient they may be in the game. This approach can be found in the dynamic difficulty adjustment (DDA). To maintain an appropriate balance between the skills of the player and the difficulty level of the gameplay, some SGs offer static difficulty levels that the player can select before entering the gameplay. However, this may not be meaningful enough for the players because they may not know exactly what level of challenge to expect when selecting a difficulty level. To address that issue, many studies have looked at the possibility of

I. Marfisi-Schottman et al. (Eds.): GALA 2020, LNCS 12517, pp. 102–111, 2020.
https://doi.org/10.1007/978-3-030-63464-3_10

adapting the challenges of the game according to the personal characteristics of each player [2–4]. While several techniques have focused on the players' performances in the game, others have studied the players' emotional analysis, for example by tracking their face in real time to adjust the game's scenario according to their attention [5]. This approach could be particularly interesting when it comes to SG with therapeutic vocation because the profiles of end users are very varied on the cognitive and psycho-affective levels alike. In this paper, we propose the contribution of the DDA for a virtual reality SG that uses prolonged exposure therapy [6] to treat people suffering from post-traumatic stress disorder (PTSD).

The adjustment modes that are commonly seen in virtual reality exposure therapy (VRET) systems for the treatment of PTSD are essentially manual, meaning that the therapist adjusts the virtual environment (VE) through a menu that lists the different possible scenarios and situations of the virtual world [7]. In this work, in addition to manual adjustment modes, the proposed DDA system includes a computational online mode through an algorithm that provides a treatment tool capable of adapting itself automatically and in real-time according to the patient's emotional state. This algorithm collects the patients' heart rate (HR) online in order to offer them a therapy situation corresponding to their current level of stress. We integrated our algorithm into a truck driving simulator developed for VRET for truckers suffering from PTSD following an accident. Such a way of understanding therapy can give the opportunity to analyse the level of immersion and presence of the patients in the VE and allow them to self-regulate their physiological reactions by perceiving their self-efficacy while interacting with the VE. We start the paper by analysing some works that come close to our subject. This allows us to understand how DDA can be applied in a therapeutic context. Thereafter we present the DDA system with the algorithm for the online computational adjustment that we propose for a self-adaptive therapy system.

2 Related Works

In this review, we analyse how subjects' physiological feedback are exploited in DDA systems and we discuss how heart rate (HR) is exploited in PTSD treatment.

Liu et al. proposed a DDA approach based on the users' emotional feedback to offer a level of difficulty adapted to the level of anxiety while playing the game [8]. They exploited a regression tree technique to determine the emotional state of the player based on a set of physiological characteristics. Their DDA algorithm used three difficulty levels and three anxiety levels. During the game, they inversely matched the difficulty level to the anxiety level of the player. Hence, the difficulty level of a game was easy when the player was anxious, and vice versa. To compare this affect-based DDA system with a performance-based DDA system, the authors integrated this algorithm into the game *Pong*. They observed a high precision in real time of the affect-based DDA system. They also underlined an improvement in the performances of participants, a better in-game challenge, an increased player satisfaction, and a reduced level of perceived anxiety among many of the participants during game sessions using the affect-based DDA model, compared to those with a performance-based DDA model. Their study highlighted the benefits of using emotional feedback to adjust the difficulty of a game.

Van Rooij et al. proposed a VR biofeedback breathing game named DEEP [9]. It is a self-adaptive relaxation SG that immerses players in a fantastic underwater world that they can explore while moving freely. In their game, the respiratory rates of players are measured to adapt several aspects of the game accordingly. One aspect of adaptation is at the level of the monitoring of players' breathing using a circle whose diameter varies according to their breathing. In addition, the movement of the player in the game is easier or more difficult depending on whether their breathing rate is slow or fast. Following a seven-minute experience of immersion by 86 children aged between eight and twelve, the authors point out a significant decrease in the general anxiety state of the subjects, whose levels of relaxation, satisfaction, boredom, or pressure were evaluated. This finding of reduced anxiety suggests that the DEEP system may be valid for limiting the anxiety levels of children.

In a digital game-based emergency personnel training, Ninaus et al. evaluated the feasibility of a heart rate-based DDA system in which players had to learn to manage three critical emergency scenarios (Traffic Accident, Buildings Fire and Train crash) [10]. Each scenario had three difficulty levels (easy, medium, and hard). Authors assessed participants' preferences for the non-adaptive and adaptive versions of the game. In the non-adaptive version, participants had to play the game scenarios normally in the time allotted. In the adaptive version, the game scenarios were adjusted so that the game became more difficult if the player's heart rate dropped below a certain predefined threshold—and easier if the heart rate exceeded this threshold. Their study revealed that gamers found the adaptive version of the game to be more exciting, fascinating, challenging and engaging. These results, therefore, show that heart rate can be a good physiological parameter that can be used to optimise DDA systems in a game-based learning.

As in the studies reviewed above, it is possible to consider parameters other than the user's performance in the game. One could be interested in the subject's affects through more objective measures such as HR or respiratory rate. When it comes to PTSD, HR has been shown to be an objective indicator of the patient's stress level in the presence of trauma cues. First, it is a good indicator for the risk of developing PTSD following a traumatic situation [11]. Second, the values of the patients' HR retrieved at regular time intervals during treatment can be used to assess the evolution of their emotional state [12]. In this case, a positive outcome of the treatment may be in the attenuation of the subject's HR when facing anxiety-provoking stimuli. This attenuation would correspond to a decrease in the response to these stimuli as expected when using prolonged exposure therapy [6, 12]. Therefore, in the current proposition, we are interested in the emotional state of the patient, measured by means of the HR, to offer an adaptative VRET system for treating PTSD.

3   Truck Driving Simulator Integrating a DDA System

In a previous work, we proposed a new approach named Action-Centered Exposure Therapy (ACET) in the use of virtual reality for the treatment of people suffering from PTSD [13]. This approach promotes active learning of safer and healthier coping strategies combined with systematic exposure to reduce the psychological distress associated with PTSD. In the ACET approach, the gamification relies on three main phases. The first is dedicated to the trivialization of the stimuli associated to the trauma, the goal being to denature the environment to allow the patient to appropriate it. By doing so, this stage allows the patient to experiment with the actions on which the therapy is centred. The second stage brings the patient into a realistic universe. In this potentially anxiety-provoking environment, it is expected that the patient will cling to the action as his centre of interest and thus eventually be able to make other non-problematic associations with these stimuli. In the last stage, there is an indirect exposure to the anxiety-provoking stimuli. The overall goal is to define a framework that will be able to detect which situations appear to be appropriate to the player's mental state.

As a continuation of that work, here we present a truck driving simulator integrating a DDA system. Our dynamic adjustments are made on scenarios and environments. Indeed, scenarios and environments could be adjusted according to the user's learning curve [14]. The environments allow for the definition of a global context for the development of the gameplay and the scenarios define the flow of events in the environment.

3.1 Devices

The truck driving simulator was developed using the Unity 3D game engine (www.unity. com) and was installed on a Windows operating system. The simulator can be visually operated using the Oculus Rift headset [15]. As control device, we have the Logitech G27 (https://www.logitechg.com) which is a system consisting of an electronic steering wheel with pedals and a gear lever. The set consists of different buttons to which we could attach computational functionality for interacting with the VE. To retrieve the subject's HR in real time, we use the Hexoskin (www.hexoskin.com), which is a sleeveless garment fitted to the body that measures different physiological data (including HR, HR variability, respiration rate) more precisely than commercial heart rate monitors that synchronise an abdominal belt with a wristwatch (Fig. 1).

Fig. 1. Devices used

3.2 Main Mechanics

In this simulator, apart from visual exploration using the headset, we have a total of three main mechanics linked to the Logitech G27: moving mechanics, selection mechanics and driving mechanics.

3.3 Virtual Environment and Scenarios

In addition to the fairy environment (in which the subject drive a flying carpet) described in our previous studies [13, 16], this simulator consists of two virtual open driving environments: 'city and countryside' and 'road by the lake' (see Fig. 2). Several scenarios can arise from these environments by changing the weather, the time of the day, and contents (traffic and accident).

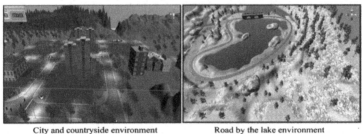

City and countryside environment   Road by the lake environment

Fig. 2. Virtual open driving environments

The 'city and countryside' environment offers several possible scenarios related to the season (summer or winter), including snowfall in winter (no snow, light wind, heavy snowstorm, etc.), the weather in summer (rain or no rain), the time of day (dawn, dusk, night, day, etc.) and the type of day (sunny or overcast). In addition, traffic lights and road traffic in this world are managed by artificial intelligence. This environment could also include accidents at different points (see Fig. 3 for scenario and accident examples). The 'road by the lake' environment offers just one scenario. This scenario consists of driving on a road by the lake, in summer, during daytime and without rain. The process in each of these environments takes place in two phases: a parking phase in which the user chooses a truck to drive using moving and selection mechanics, and a truck-driving phase in which the user effectively drives the chosen truck using driving mechanics.

Winter at day time   Accident

Fig. 3. Examples of a scenario and an accident

3.4 Dynamic Difficulty Adjustment Module

In our system, we have developed a module that is responsible for linking the simulator and the Hexoskin to collect the user's HR in real time. The simulator can be adapted in three ways: offline adaptation, manual online adaptation, and computational online adaptation. For both offline and manual online adaptation, the system offers the therapists an easy-to-use menu (see Fig. 4) from which they can select environments, and scenarios with eventually some accidents, according to the patient's characteristics. For offline adaptation, selections are made immediately after the simulator is launched. Thus, in this adjustment mode, in addition to the patients' HR, therapists may use the data they have about their patients' background and their evolution in the previous sessions to choose which environment and scenario will be most appropriate for the current session. In the manual online mode, therapists have the possibility to manually change the environment or scenario according to their observations of the patient's state while the latter is being exposed. For the computational online mode, the system uses a DDA algorithm that automatically change the environment or scenarios according to the emotional state of the patients, as evaluated by their HR. Thus, patients' HR is collected in real-time and transmitted to the simulator using a dedicated plugin. The algorithm therefore uses HR and the current situation of the VE to adjust scenarios and/or the VE.

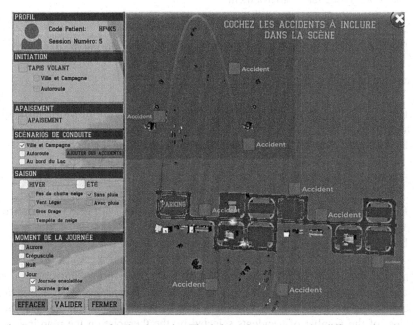

Fig. 4. Easy-to-use menu for the therapist. The left section presents the different situations that the therapist can select by checking the corresponding checkbox. The right section is a window that is only activated when the therapist clicks on the 'add accident' button (orange button) in the left section. It shows the map in the top view of the 'city and countryside' environment, with the checkboxes (in orange) for the various accident positions. By default, accidents are deactivated in this environment. If the therapist checks an accident position on this map, the corresponding accident will be activated in the 3D environment after validation. (Color figure online)

In the following section, we detail how the computational online mode is implemented.

Categorisation of Anxiety Levels

The goal of prolonged exposure therapy is for the patient to be able to reach a relatively normal HR in situations which could elicit high anxiety [12, 17, 18].

Thus, we begin by defining the different possible scenarios to be integrated into the simulator and classifying them by 'anxiety level'. We did this based on the study [19], presenting statistics on traffic accidents. Indeed, apart from accidents caused by internal conditions specific to the driver, as much as 21% of road accidents in the United States have causes associated with bad weather conditions. Almost 71% in this category are related to rain and 26% to snow, depending on the ampleness. Poor weather conditions can affect driver visibility, traffic speed, travel time, lane obstruction, and vehicle stability. This statistical information allowed us to define three main anxiety levels from 1 (can evoke low anxiety in the subject) to 3 (can evoke high anxiety in the subject). Each anxiety level is associated to a VE and/or a scenario.

- Scenarios of anxiety level 1:

  - The 'road by the lake' environment
  - The 'city and countryside environment, in winter or summer, without snowfall and without rain, during dawn, dusk, day or night
  - The 'city and countryside environment, with light snow, during the day

- Scenarios of anxiety level 2:

  - The 'city and countryside' environment, with light snow, during dawn, dusk, or at night
  - The 'city and countryside' environment, with rain, during the day

- Scenarios of anxiety level 3:

  - The 'city and countryside' environment, during winter, with heavy thunderstorm or snowstorm, during dawn, dusk, day, or night
  - The 'city and countryside' environment with rain during dawn, dusk, or night

The system is made to allow the addition of new anxiety-provoking stimuli in the 'city and countryside' environment, such as accidents. The presence of one or more accidents in the scenario will increase the anxiety level of the current scenario by 1, regardless of the number of accidents selected by the therapist on the map in Fig. 4. Indeed, having several accident positions makes it possible to increase the chances that the patient will encounter at least one of them on their way.

DDA Algorithm

The DDA algorithm operates in two main stages: the first consists in evaluating the emotional state of the patient according to their HR and the second consists in using this information to adapt the VE to the current state of the patient. To do so, the algorithm takes as parameters the patient's current HR and an integer representing their anxiety level. The algorithm runs until the patient reaches a situation where they maintain a relatively normal HR while a scenario of maximum 'anxiety level' is presented. In each session, their resting HR is collected before the exposure.

The variables used by this algorithm are as follows:

- A: Unsigned integer used to store the anxiety level of the current situation in the VE. The initial value of A is set according to the parameters selected by the therapist at the beginning of the session. For example, if at the beginning the therapist selects the 'road by the lake environment', A is set to 1.
- maxA: Unsigned integer used to store the anxiety level of the most anxiety-provoking situation for the patient among the main scenarios defined.
- m: Unsigned integer equivalent to the number of additional anxiety-provoking events added to the predefined situations. For example, this parameter can have a value of 1 if the therapist adds an accident to the selected initial scenario.
- time: Unsigned integer used to store the time the subject must spend in a situation trying to regulate their physiological response. In accordance with previous studies that evaluate patient HR during exposure therapy [12], we have fixed the value of time to 5 min here.
- HR: Unsigned integer used to store the patient's current HR transmitted to the simulator by the Hexoskin.
- normalHR: Unsigned integer used to store the HR of the patient collected at the baseline. This variable constitutes the patient's normal HR for the current session and may vary from one session to another.
- r: Unsigned integer allowing flexibility in the value of the patient's normal HR. r can either take a value of 40 bpm, because the normal HR of an adult at rest varies between 60 and 100 bpm [20]; or it can be defined by the therapist at the start of exposure depending on the evolution of the patient's HR in previous sessions.

The body of our DDA algorithm is as follows:

```
do
{
  if (HR>normalHR+r)
  {
    A = A-1;
  }
  else
  {
      A = A+1;
  }
  Load (a situation with anxiety level A);
  wait (time);
}
while (A>=maxA+m and HR<=normalHR+r);
```

By running this algorithm, a recovery after treatment would mathematically correspond to A = maxA and HR <= normalHR + r. Although this algorithm offers a self-adaptive simulator for VRET, the therapist's presence remains crucial during treatment. Thus, in parallel with the computational system, the simulator offers the therapist the possibility of ensuring that adequate changes are made in response to the patient's HR, according to the communication with the latter and vis-à-vis the observations made. We have also given the therapist the possibility of activating or deactivating the computational online DDA system. Therefore, an example of a practical case would be that where A = 3 and HR> normalHR + r; while the DDA algorithm is running, the therapist may decide to interrupt it and switch from a situation of A = 3 to a situation of A = 1 in order to quickly stabilise the patient's HR — just as the therapist can also decide to keep the patients at A = 3 for longer than time to help them learn strategies for self-regulation of their physiological responses. The role of the therapist will also be to decide when or whether to stop exposure depending on the patient's condition.

4   Conclusion

The use of VRET for the PTSD treatment is an area of vigorous ongoing research; the aim is to find approaches that would facilitate the exploitation of VR and produce even more appreciable results. The evaluation of treatment efficacy in this area is generally made either by subjective measurements or by observing the patient's HR at regular intervals. In this work, we proposed the integration into a VR truck driving simulator of a DDA system that can be executed according to three modes: (1) the offline mode, which consists in configuring the system according to the characteristics of the patient before the launch of the simulator; (2) the manual online mode, which consists of the therapist modifying the scenarios during the exposure; and (3) the computational online mode, which uses an algorithm to dynamically adjust the scenario according to the current state of the patient. In the latter mode, the patient's HR is collected in real time using Hexoskin and included directly into the system using a module developed for this purpose. The HR variable is then used to dynamically adjust the system during the exposure sessions so that at each stage of therapy, subjects can have a better experience through scenarios adapted to their current emotional state. In the future, we will evaluate the effectiveness of our proposed system with subjects suffering from PTSD. We have already received ethics approval from our university to conduct this research with truckers whose PTSD is linked to road accidents. This will be done with patients in residence at "La Futaie therapy center", with which we collaborate. Thereafter, several other experiments will have to be conducted to validate such a system for VRET.

References

1. Menelas, B.-A.J., Benaoudia, R.S.: Use of haptics to promote learning outcomes in serious games. Multimod. Technol. Interact. 1(4), 31 (2017)
2. Delmas, G., Champagnat, R., Augeraud, M.: Plot monitoring for interactive narrative games. In: Proceedings of the International Conference on Advances in Computer Entertainment Technology (2007)

3. Hunicke, R., Chapman, V.: AI for dynamic difficulty adjustment in games. In: Challenges in Game Artificial Intelligence AAAI Workshop, San Jose, pp. 91–96 (2004)
4. Spronck, P., et al.: Adaptive game AI with dynamic scripting. Mach. Learn. **63**(3), 217–248 (2006)
5. Perreira Da Silva, M., Courboulay, V., Prigent, A., Estraillier, P.: Real-time face tracking for attention aware adaptive games. In: Gasteratos, A., Vincze, M., Tsotsos, J.K. (eds.) ICVS 2008. LNCS, vol. 5008, pp. 99–108. Springer, Heidelberg (2008). https://doi.org/10.1007/978-3-540-79547-6_10
6. Foa, E., Hembree, E., Rothbaum, B.O.: Prolonged Exposure Therapy for PTSD: Emotional Processing of Traumatic Experiences Therapist Guide. Oxford University Press, Oxford (2007)
7. Rizzo, A., et al.: Virtual reality applications for the assessment and treatment of PTSD. In: Bowles, S.V., Bartone, P.T. (eds.) Handbook of Military Psychology, pp. 453–471. Springer, Cham (2017). https://doi.org/10.1007/978-3-319-66192-6_27
8. Liu, C., et al.: Dynamic difficulty adjustment in computer games through real-time anxiety-based affective feedback. Int. J. Hum. Comput. Interact. **25**(6), 506–529 (2009)
9. Van Rooij, M., et al.: DEEP: a biofeedback virtual reality game for children at-risk for anxiety. In: Proceedings of the 2016 CHI Conference Extended Abstracts on Human Factors in Computing Systems (2016)
10. Ninaus, M., Tsarava, K., Moeller, K.: A pilot study on the feasibility of dynamic difficulty adjustment in game-based learning using heart-rate. In: Liapis, A., Yannakakis, G.N., Gentile, M., Ninaus, M. (eds.) GALA 2019. LNCS, vol. 11899, pp. 117–128. Springer, Cham (2019). https://doi.org/10.1007/978-3-030-34350-7_12
11. Bryant, R.A.: Acute Stress Disorder: What it is and How to Treat it. Guilford Publications, New York (2016)
12. Wood, D.P., et al.: Combat-related post-traumatic stress disorder: A case report using virtual reality graded exposure therapy with physiological monitoring with a female Seabee. Milit. Med. **174**(11), 1215–1222 (2009)
13. Kengne, K., et al.: Action-centered exposure therapy (ACET): a new approach to the use of virtual reality to the care of people with post-traumatic stress disorder. Behav. Sci. **8**(8), 76 (2018)
14. Lopes, R., Bidarra, R.: Adaptivity challenges in games and simulations: a survey. IEEE Trans. Comput. Intell. AI Games **3**(2), 85–99 (2011)
15. Desai, P.R., et al.: A review paper on oculus rift-a virtual reality headset. arXiv preprint arXiv: 1408.1173 (2014)
16. Menelas, B.-A.J., et al.: Use of virtual reality technologies as an Action-Cue Exposure Therapy for truck drivers suffering from Post-Traumatic Stress Disorder. Entertainment Comput. **24**, 1–9 (2018)
17. Rothbaum, B.O., et al.: Virtual reality exposure therapy of combat-related PTSD: a case study using psychophysiological indicators of outcome. J. Cogn. Psychother. **17**(2), 163–178 (2003)
18. Walshe, D.G., et al.: Exploring the use of computer games and virtual reality in exposure therapy for fear of driving following a motor vehicle accident. CyberPsychol. Behav. **6**(3), 329–334 (2003)
19. Transportation UDO, How Do Weather Events Impact Roads? Federal Highway Administration Washington, DC (2015)
20. website, American Heart Association. All About Heart Rate (Pulse)

Analysis of Mixed Reality Tools for Learning Math in Primary and Secondary School

Sofiane Touel[1]([✉]), Iza Marfisi-Schottman[2]([✉]), and Sébastien George[2]([✉])

[1] Plaisir Maths Lab, 75011 Paris, France
Sofiiianos@outlook.com
[2] Le Mans Université, EA 4023, LIUM, 72085 Le Mans, France
{iza.marfisi,sebastien.george}@univ-lemans.fr

Abstract. In our study, we provide a state of the art on Mixed Reality (MR) learning tools for teaching math in primary and secondary school. Through a detailed analysis of eight representative applications, we provide an overview of the MR applications currently used, their educational objectives, the augmentations and interactions they offer, the technologies they use, their advantages and their limitations. We conclude by identifying several remaining challenges that need to be addressed in order to benefit from the full educational potential of MR for teaching math in schools.

Keywords: Learning · Augmented reality · Mixed reality · Math · Serious game

1 Mixed Reality to Help Children Learn

Teaching methods have evolved a lot in the recent decades. The use of digital tools has become widespread because they are essential in modern professional and non-professional life, but also because they have many educational benefits. Among these digital innovations, we will focus on Mixed Reality (MR).

As defined by Drascic and Milgram [1], "MR refers to the incorporation of virtual computer graphics objects into a real three-dimensional scene, or alternatively the inclusion of real world elements into a virtual environment. The former case is generally referred to as Augmented Reality (AR), and the latter as Augmented Virtuality." The augmentations are displayed on a screen, in glasses or directly on real objects using a video projector. It is possible to interact with these augmentations.

The educational potential of MR comes from several factors. First, **the manipulation of real objects** has an impact on **embodied cognition** and would allow to significantly reduce mental load [2]. Object manipulation also motivates learners and encourages them to carry out their activities [3]. In addition, Chandler and Tricot's study [4] demonstrates the positive impact of **physical activity** that accompanies this object manipulation, especially for young children. Physical movement seems to be especially relevant for mathematical cognition. It is through the explanation of mathematical concepts that one can notice different types of gestures (pointing, representation and metaphorical gestures) which make it possible to externalize information and improve memory

© Springer Nature Switzerland AG 2020
I. Marfisi-Schottman et al. (Eds.): GALA 2020, LNCS 12517, pp. 112–121, 2020.
https://doi.org/10.1007/978-3-030-63464-3_11

management [5]. Finally, MR makes it possible to **create multimodal (visuo-haptic) activities**, which have a superior pedagogical potential over unimodal (visual) activities for children [6]. MR allows, for example, displaying different types of contextualized information directly on physical objects (*e.g.* 3D animated model of the solar system, organ names). MR can also give students more autonomy by displaying information to guide them (e.g. contextual information or step-by-step guide on the actions to be performed) or even validate the activities once they have been completed (*e.g.* validation of the objects position).

Some studies also show that students using AR have better understanding of the course and memorization, compared to those using only books [7]. In addition, MR improves the involvement and engagement of learners in learning tasks [8] and is confirmed by Kun-Hung Cheng's study of 267 middle school students [9]. However, these previous studies also revealed some negative points. Some students think MR is responsible for reducing imagination and obstructing their reading skills. In addition, the equipment used can be expensive but also complicate the activities [10]. This equipment can also be tedious to set up for teachers but also to use for students (*e.g.* wearing glasses for a long time).

Despite the undeniable potential of MR, its integration into schools therefore raises a certain number of questions related to the type of activities and equipment that should be used to maximize its educational potential without constraining teachers and students. In the rest of this article, we focus on MR for math. As we will present, this is an area which has a strong impact on other scientific fields and which could particularly benefit from the advantages of MR.

1.1 Learning Math with Mixed Reality

At school, all subjects are important, but math represents the knowledge from which most other sciences derive. According to the study of Watts *et al.* [11], the skills of children aged four to five would predict their scientific skills in adolescence. Another study [12] shows that succeeding in math generally implies future success in other fields such as reading. In addition, many primary school students find science to be a masculine, elitist and consider math as a difficult subject. Using a motivating medium like MR, for learning mathematics, has a positive effect on the motivation of learners [13] and could be a good solution to avoid blockage [14]. MR interactions are also very well suited to convey notions of geometry and algebra by displaying virtual 3D shapes or showing 2D information directly on 3D figures. MR applications for math are numerous and varied by the interactions they offer (display of information, help, validation), the targeted educational objectives (*e.g.* additions, fractions, 3D geometry), but also by the equipment they require (*e.g.* tablets, projectors, markers, glasses). In this article, we offer an analysis of existing MR applications, in order to understand their different characteristics and their impact on learning.

2 Analysis of Mixed Reality Applications for Math

To our knowledge, even though there are a considerable number of MR applications for learning math, there is still no state of the art on this subject. We therefore propose to analyze a representative selection of these applications. We searched on *Google Scholar*, which indexes the articles from the main publishers (*Springer, IEEE, HAL archives ouvertes*, etc.) by combining the following keywords: *(teaching or learning and (augmented reality or mixed reality)) or (math or fraction or geometry), (learning or teaching) and (object manipulation or physical movement) or (digital) or (preschool or primary)*. This research allowed us to select about 30 scientific studies.

In this paper, we will only present eight out of these 30 studies. Given the rapid technological evolution of the RM, we only chose recent studies, published after 2015, and that offer a functional prototype. The eight applications presented bellow were also selected because they come from different countries (Asian, European, American), teach various fields of math, provide a variety of interactions and require different types of equipment. The objective of this selection is to provide a good overview of existing applications (Fig. 1).

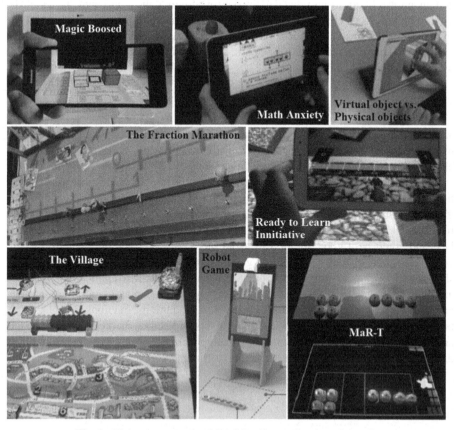

Fig. 1. Eight representative Mixed Reality applications for math

In the next section, we analyze these eight applications according to four points. First we identify the context in which they were created and their educational objectives. Then, we identify the nature of the MR interactions they offer. Thistly, we list the necessary equipment and the software used to develop the application. Finally, if the application was tested, we present the advantages and limitations identified by the authors.

2.1 Magic Boosed

The *Magic Boosed* [15] app comes from Indonesia. Its objective is to improve the spatial perception of geometric shapes for children aged 7 to 12.

The students need to answer basic geometry questions (*e.g.* what is the surface of this 3D figure?). The application helps then by provides AR information (*e.g.* 3D objects, height, formulas). These augmentations offer no interaction.

Students are equipped with a paper exercise textbook and a smartphone with the application. The article does not provide information on the MR technology.

According to the authors, the experimentations lead with two teachers and eight students showed that the application increases the motivation and interest of the students and facilitates exchanges between them and the teacher.

2.2 Math Anxiety

Math anxiety is a Taiwanese study [16] to reduce anxiety related to learning maths.

Eight quizzes are scattered around the classroom to review topics such as fractions and geometry. In addition to displaying 3D objects in AR, the application also triggers videos when it recognizes real objects to help students answer the quizzes. These virtual items are not interactive.

The quizzed are printed out on sheets of paper. The students use tablets this the app. The application was developed with HP Reveal and Augment.

The experiment, carried out with 137 students, showed that AR app decreases anxiety in math, increases attention, motivation, confidence and student satisfaction compared to the mobile application without AR. The authors would like to add interactions and virtual 3D objects and use more efficient tools than HP Reveal and Augment as they could not customize the content and interactions according to their needs.

2.3 Virtual Object vs. Physical Object

This Turkish study compares the use of AR virtual objects and physical objects for learning geometry [17]. The objective is to teach 5 to 6 year-old children how to recognize geometric shapes, including 2D (eg triangle, square) and 3D (eg: sphere, cube).

Students have to classify cards with images of geometric shapes. They can use the AR app to view the 3D version if the geometric shapes, change their size, position, orientation and manipulate them. This app was developed with Augment.

The experimentation, lead with 72 children, showed that the application seemed to have effectively supported the learning process, and created excitement. The authors argue that it would be beneficial to add educational feedback to help children understand the type of each object based on the choices they make.

2.4 The Fraction Marathon

The Fraction marathon uses number lines to teach fractions (addition and subtractions) to 11-year-olds Greek children [18].

The game scenario features several runners interrupted in their 2 km race due to rain. The students must place the runners back where they stopped. Their position is given as a fraction relative to the finish point (*e.g.* 2/3 of the finish), the position of other runners or elements of the scene. If the students make a mistake, they lose points and are prompted to click on the help button. This triggers a video with voice instructions that guides them on how to handle the lines and solve the problem. Students can measure the size between two objects by resize and moving the MR number line. They can also update the fractional unit with a physical button. The MR also automatically validates the position of the runners.

The game involves a miniature wooden stadium, a projector, a camera, a laptop, two Makey Makey boards (is an electronic invention kit that allows you to connect "everyday objects" to the computer program without any technical knowledge). The technology used to develop the game is not given in the article.

After a study lead with 28 students, the authors argue that the game immerses and amuses the students. The feedback and help mechanisms were particularly effective for empowering them. The authors also believe that it would be more effective to present the game without mentioning fractions to reduce stress at the beginning of the game. The authors also wish to enlarge the play space so that more children can play at the same time and find a less expensive solution.

2.5 Ready to Learn Initiative

Ready to Learn initiative [19] aims to study the potential of AR for learning certain mathematical themes (Geometry, Fraction, Counting, etc.) in the US. Among other applications, they offer an AR application for introduce fractions to children aged 6 to 9.

Childrens place real objects on a number line and the application automatically measures the position of the object and displays it as a fraction. Students can change the denominator of the fraction, and the app automatically updates the numerator.

The app requires to print out a sheet of paper with markers and a tablet with the app. It was developed with a web version of scratch 2.

Even if it was not tested by the students, three teachers were able to evaluate the prototype and noted that the presence of interactions with 3D objects would be likely to capture the attention of their students as well as a good potential pedagogic.

2.6 The Village

The village is a Greek project designed to teach fractions to elementary school children aged 6 to 12 years old [20].

The game scenario features a child visiting his grandparents in their partially destroyed village. Using two virtual characters, the player's goal is to repair the infrastructure of the village (eg: the pipe, the bridge represented by legos), by measuring the damaged part (in red) with the number line. Players can adjust the size, numerator and denominator of the MR digital line by manipulating screwdrivers and knobs. The game automatically detects if the damaged part of the infrastructure is correctly measured.

The game consists of a Makey Makey board, a projector, a table and accessories. The game was developed with MIT Scratch (block-based visual programming).

This game was not tested in an educational context. The authors' perspectives are to use mobile devices in order to simplify the game.

2.7   Robot Game

The Uruguayan robot game, aims to teach additions [21] to children aged 5 to 6.

The players must choose enough blocks (lengths from 1 to 5) to extend a robot's arm by placing physical blocks in front of the tablet so that it can reach a screw. The system provides continuous real time feedback by extending the robot's arm.

To be able to use the game, children need a tablet, a tablet holder, as well as a mirror and a wooden block set. The game was developed with the open source platform CETA, OpenCV, libgdx and TopCode libraries.

After testing the game with 19 students, the authors argue that it provides cognitive offload, increases commitment and joy and empowers students through the feedback system. Their perspectives are to use a markerless technology, improve the feedback by making it fluid and add animations and advice from the robot.

2.8   MaR-T

This Turkish study aims to help children aged 3 to 5 understand non-symbolic numbers and compare values [22].

The children must help Momo, a fictional character, to get home by placing objects in the designated locations to allow Momo to cross obstacles (e.g. river, ditch). Momo then asks them to point to the side where there are the most objects or to put their hand in the middle if there are as many on both sides. If the children give the correct answer they are congratulated, otherwise Momo asks questions such as "Why do you think this side has more than the other?".

This game requires a camera and a projector and was been developed with OpenCV, Royale SDK, IR image, Lottie and Bodymovin libraries.

After testing the game with ten children, the authors argue that the interactions with Momo helps children keep focused. The feedback and reward systems also seemed to help the children complete the activities.

3   Global Analysis

3.1   Variety of Educational Objectives

The examples analyzed above show that MR can be used for learning math at all levels. For example, MR can be used for learning the **basics of math** such as the *Robot Game* and *MaR-T*. There are many other MR applications that teach additions and subtractions. For example, the *Counting With Paula* AR app [7] or the *AR Flashcards Addition* application [23]. The effectiveness of MR for teaching the basics of math appears to be due to its capacity to immerse students in a fun environment and arouse their curiosity [3] which leads to a better understanding and motivation [24].

AR is also well adapted to teach **geometry**, such as *Magic Boosed, Math anxiety and Virtual object vs Physical object.* There are many MR applications for this topic, certainly due to the fact MR technology improves spatial intuition of students, which is an effective way to learn geometry [25].

Finally, AR seems particularly effective for teaching **fractions**, which often discourage students and push them to dislike math. The use of MR, such as *The Fraction Marathon, Ready To Learn Initiative* or *The Village*, can transform this complex and unpopular matter into a fun and captivating experience.

3.2 Analysis of Mixed Reality Interactions

The applications analyzed above present two types of MR interactions. The first group offers **very light or non-existent AR interactions**, such as *Ready To Learn Initiative, Virtual Object vs Physical Object and Magic Boosed*. These applications only use AR to display virtual information on real objects. At best, the students can manipulate, turn and change the size of the virtual augmentations. These applications have the advantage of being easy to set up since they only require a tablet or smartphone and printed out markers on paper or cardboard.

The second group of applications offer **rich MR interactions**, in which we find *MaR-T, The Village, The Fraction Marathon, Robot Game* and *Math anxiety*. In addition to the AR augmentations, the manipulation and the position of the real objects have an impact on the applications. In *MaR-T* for example, it is the position of the cubes that triggers the next level in the game. Some of these applications also offer personalized feedback and help. Such rich interactions have undeniable advantages for different areas of learning. For example, studies in the medical field show that the presence of feedback contributes to the development of psycho-motor and cognitive skills [26]. Another study [27] shows that students appreciate this type of rich interaction, and in particular the feedback, which promotes self-regulated learning, at their own pace. However, the applications mentioned above all require specific equipment such as projectors, 3D objects, as well as space, thus making their use in a school complicated.

3.3 Analysis of Mixed Reality Hardware and Software

The most common hardware to support MR applications are **Smartphone and tablets. This is for example the case** of Ready *To Learn Initiative, Virtual Object vs Physical Object and Magic Boosed*. According to a study in Switzerland, on more than 1,000 students, 78% from age 6 to 13 use mobile phones regularly and 3/4 of students aged 12 to 13 already owned one [28]. The figures for tablets are similar. The fact that the majority of children are already familiar with this equipment is an important advantage to using them in class. On the other hand, tablets or smartphones do not allow having both hands free to handle objects. In addition, some devices do not support advanced technologies such as *Vuforia*'s Ground Plane technology, which allows placing digital content on a table [29].

The other hardware used for the MR is **projectors and cameras.** This is for example the case of *The Village, The Fraction Marathon* and *Math anxiety*. They have the advantage of being moderately expensive and users have their hands free to manipulate objects. In addition, projectors have a wide field of vision, and allow group work [30]. However, they take up allot a room and are complex to set up. Indeed, the projector and the tracking camera need to be calibrated and placed directly above the working area. The *Robot Game* is a simplified version of this setup because it uses a holder and a mirror to use the tablet's camera. It is simple to set up but offers a narrow field of vision.

Finally, even though none of the applications above use this technology, it is important to cite **AR glasses and headsets** mostly used for professional training, due to their very high cost. These have the advantage of offering good perception of depth [31]. Their mobility is also a major asset since the devices can be transported everywhere and leave the user's hands free. However, they can cause visual fatigue and nausea.

There are several types of software to design MR applications. Teachers can use **AR application editors** that allow them to create AR applications without any development skills such as *Augment* [32] and *Aurasma* [33]. Thanks to simple interfaces, they can record their markers (object, image or QR Code) and associate them with different 3D models or documents. Applications, created with these editors, only support very light AR interactions, which consist in simply displaying digital content on the detected marker. Such application do not support feedback and automatic activity validation.

There are several **open source technologies** such as *Artoolkit* [34] or *OpenCv* for example, used to develop *MaR-T* and *Robot Game*. However, these open source and free technologies require advanced expertise in image processing.

Finally, there are several **paying technologies**, generally offering a free version, which allow developers to create MR applications, without being an expert in image recognition. The most popular is *Vuforia* [29] which offers good quality, stable and efficient services. *Wikitude* [35] and *Kudan* [36] are other alternatives.

4   Conclusion and Discussion

Through the analysis of eight Mixed Reality (MR) applications for teaching math in primary and secondary schools, we show that this technology offers several educational benefits such as cognitive offloading, captivating students' attention and making them learn while having fun. The experimentations, led by the authors of these applications, show that, even more than the AR augmentations (virtual information and object projected on real objects), it is the **rich interactions**, the **custom feedback** and **help provided** by the MR applications that have the highest impact on engagement and learning.

As we stand, the only technology capable of creating such rich MR interactions are paying technologies such as *Vuforia*, that requires solid programming skills. If we want MR to be accessible in schools, is it important to provide similar open-source technologies or MR editors that could allow teachers to create their own complex MR applications. In addition, the only way to develop the use of MR in schools is to provide applications that function with tablets since most schools are usually equipped with them and they are simple to set up. However, their use deprives children for using their hands at the same time. This constraint therefore needs to be taken into account when designing activities by clearly identifying when the children should be manipulating real objects and when they should pick up the tablet to get feedback or validate the exercises. Another method would be to design collaborative activities in which the children take turns in holding the tablet, while the other manipulates the objects. The experimentation also show that the MR applications should also function with markers teachers can easily print out on paper or cardboard. Another interesting perspective would be to help them create augmentations on material they already have in their class (*e.g.* cubes, globe) by using custom marker stickers.

References

1. Drascic, D., Milgram, P.: Perceptual issues in augmented reality. In: Stereoscopic Displays and Virtual Reality Systems III, vol. 2653, pp. 123–134 (1996)
2. Wilson, M.: Six views of embodied cognition. Psychon. Bull. Rev. **9**(4), 625–636 (2002)
3. Liou, H.-H., et al.: The influences of the 2D image-based augmented reality and virtual reality on student learning. j-ets **20**(3), 110–121 (2017)
4. Chandler, P., Tricot, A.: Mind your body. Edu. Psycho. Rev. **27**(3), 365–370 (2015)
5. Alibali, M.W., Nathan, M.J.: Embodiment in mathematics teaching and learning: evidence from learners' and teachers' gestures. J. Learn. Sci. **21**(2), 247–286 (2012)
6. Kalenine, S., et al.: The visual and visuo-haptic exploration of geometrical shapes increases their recognition in preschoolers. IJBD **35**(1), 18–26 (2011)
7. Weng, C., et al.: Mixed reality in science education as a learning support: a revitalized science book. JECR **57**(3), 777–807 (2019)
8. Hughes, C.E., et al.: Mixed reality in education, entertainment, and training. IEEE Comput. Graph. Appl. **25**(6), 24–30 (2005)
9. Cheng, K.-H.: Surveying students' conceptions of learning science by augmented reality and their scientific epistemic beliefs. Eurasia J. Math. Sci. Tech. Edu. **4**(4), 1147–1159 (2018)
10. Lin, H.-C.K., et al.: Establishment and usability evaluation of an interactive AR learning system on conservation of fish. TOJET **10**(4), 181–187 (2011)
11. Watts, T.W., et al.: What's past is prologue: relations between early mathematics knowledge and high school achievement. Edu. Res. **43**(7), 352–360 (2014)
12. Sarama, J., Clements, D.H.: Early Childhood Mathematics Education Research: Learning Trajectories for Young Children. Routledge (2009). 242 p
13. Backlund, P., Hendrix, M.: Educational games-are they worth the effort? A literature survey of the effectiveness of serious games, VS-GAMES, pp. 1–8 (2013)
14. van der Stappen, A., et al.: MathBuilder: a collaborative ar math game for elementary school students. In: Proceedings of CHI PLAY, Spain, pp. 731–738 (2019)
15. Andrea, R., et al.: Magic Boosed' an elementary school geometry textbook with marker-based augmented reality. Telkomnika **17**(3), 1242–1249 (2019)
16. Chen, Y.: Effect of mobile augmented reality on learning performance, motivation, and math anxiety in a math course. J. Educ. Comput. Res. **57**(7), 1695–1722 (2019)
17. Gecu-Parmaksiz, Z., Delialioglu, O.: Augmented reality-based virtual manipulatives versus physical manipulatives for teaching geometric shapes to preschool children. BJET **50**(6), 3376–3390 (2019)
18. Palaigeorgiou, G., Tsolopani, X., Liakou, S., Lemonidis, C.: Movable, resizable and dynamic number lines for fraction learning in a mixed reality environment. In: Auer, Michael E., Tsiatsos, T. (eds.) ICL 2018. AISC, vol. 917, pp. 118–129. Springer, Cham (2019). https://doi.org/10.1007/978-3-030-11935-5_12

19. Radu, I., et al.: Discovering educational augmented reality math applications by prototyping with elementary-school teachers. In: IEEE VR, pp. 271–272 (2016)
20. Kazanidis, I., et al.: Dynamic interactive number lines for fraction learning in a mixed reality environment. In: Proceedings of the SEEDA, Greece, pp. 1–5 (2018)
21. Marichal, S., et al.: CETA. In: Proceedings of the MobileHCI, pp. 1–13 (2017)
22. Beşevli, C., et al.: MaR-T. In: Proceedings of the IDC, Austria, pp. 280–292 (2019)
23. Bujak, R., et al.: A psychological perspective on augmented reality in the mathematics classroom. Comput. Educ. **68**, 536–544 (2013)
24. Radu, I.: Augmented reality in education: a meta-review and cross-media analysis. Pers. Ubiquit. Comput. **18**(6), 1533–1543 (2014). https://doi.org/10.1007/s00779-013-0747-y
25. Kaufmann, H.: Geometry education with augmented reality. na (2004)
26. Kotranza, I., et al.: Real-time in-situ visual feedback of task performance in mixed environments for learning joint psychomotor-cognitive tasks. In: Proceedings of ISMAR, U.S.A, pp. 125–134 (2009)
27. Birt, J.R., et al.: Mobile mixed reality for experiential learning and simulation in medical and health sciences education. Information **9**(2), 31 (2018)
28. Süss, D.D., et al.: Ergebnisbericht zur MIKE-Studie 2019. In: MIKE, p. 100 (2019)
29. Vuforia library (2020). https://library.vuforia.com/. Accessed 15 July 2020
30. Anastassova, M., et al.: Ergonomics of augmented reality for learning: a review. Travail Humain **70**(2), 97–125 (2007)
31. Van Krevelen, D.W.F., Poelman, R.: A survey of augmented reality technologies, applications and limitations. IJVR **9**(2), 1–20 (2010)
32. Augment (2020). https://www.augment.com/. Accessed 25 June 2020
33. Aurasma (2020). https://www.aace.org/. Accessed 15 July 2020
34. ARToolKit (2020). http://www.hitl.washington.edu/. Accessed 25 June 2020
35. Wikitude (2020). https://www.wikitude.com/. Accessed 04 July 2020
36. Kudan Inc. (2020). https://www.kudan.io/. Accessed 04 July 2020

Gamification Theory

Gamification and Beyond: The Case of Ludification

Bo Kampmann Walther$^{(\boxtimes)}$ and Lasse Juel Larsen

University of Southern Denmark, Odense, Denmark
{walther,ljl}@sdu.dk

Abstract. This paper discusses the relatively new concept of ludification with the attempt of laying the theoretical groundwork for further studies. Although ludification ties in with both gamification and the concept and practice of transmedia it possesses unique characteristics and qualities of its own, primarily evolving around playful ways of creating and interacting with stories. The focus point is especially how traditional media such as tv-series and movies incorporate game-like structures into their narrative structure. This concerns both the narrative structures that users can and cannot interact with. Among other things, we consider a deep understanding of ludification vital for the more practically oriented approach to learning through (serious) games and game mechanics. Thus, this paper serves as a prolegomenon to the interpretation of works of ludification, as well as to the diverse field of deploying ludified material in didactical and pedagogical context.

Keywords: Ludification · Gamification · Play theory · Game design · Learning

1 Introduction

In an American perspective ludification has come to mean the use of game systems for business and government use. However, there is no clear-cut consensus about terminology in the literature. For instance, the term ludification is now a stable in cultural studies where it very broadly signifies the introduction of elements of playfulness into our lives and culture (Dippel and Fizek 2017). Therefore, we need a concept that makes it possible to differentiate between gamification, on the one hand, and ludification on the other hand. Initially, we understand ludification as a concept that uncovers how storytelling across media, tv series and movies, integrate computer game structures in their narrative composition. We propose the term ludification, rather than transmedia, because the question is not just how stories migrate between different media, but rather, and more specifically, how *games* influence a host of different media. However, we comprehend 'ludification' as a robust enough concept to not become merely a subset included in the terminology of gamification and/or transmedia. Ludification is connected to both, gamification and transmedia, and yet it possesses unique characteristics and qualities of its own. The goal of this paper is thus to show how computer games influencen 'traditional' and especially cinematic storytelling; further to pinpoint how play elements and game structures can be explored using what we call ludo-interpretation, i.e. reading traditional

© Springer Nature Switzerland AG 2020
I. Marfisi-Schottman et al. (Eds.): GALA 2020, LNCS 12517, pp. 125–134, 2020.
https://doi.org/10.1007/978-3-030-63464-3_12

media through the lens of games. Although this can of course only be hinted at here, such scrutiny should make way for a better understanding and a more fitting classification of ludification, and in addition provide a theoretically informed working model for the serious use of ludified material in assorted contexts.

First, we outline the conceptual framework of gamification, followed by the second section in which we look more closely at the underlying design principles of using game elements and game mechanics in non-game settings, which would typically be traditional storytelling. Third, we discuss how gamification rests on rewards as triggers for situational motivation. Fourth, play and playfulness are discussed vis-à-vis games and ludification, while the fifth section examines the sociological claims about the 'rationalization' of play bringing about specific forms of social order. Finally, in the concluding section, we tentatively offer some thoughts on the connection between ludification and learning.

2 Gamification

Gamification is often interchangeably understood as ludification (Kirkpatrick 2015). The conflation of the two terms is unfortunate, especially since there are a number of differences between the two. The fate of gamification has been the subject of hot debates (Bogost 2014). In those debates, gamification associates with terms like 'gameful' (McGonigal 2014), 'gamified', and 'gamefulness'. But what do these terms mean? 'Gameful' and 'gamefulness' seem to point toward the experience of the player engaged in game-like activities. 'Gamified', on the other hand, signals design, that is, how one may apply game-like traits to a wide range of topics and areas typically located outside the realm of video games. This has led to a tentative, porous, broad, and accepted definition of gamification: '[The] use of game design elements in non-game contexts' (Deterding et al. 2011, para. 1). To clearly separate gamification from ludification we propose the following definition of ludification as *the use of game design elements in non-game contexts with a special emphasis on 'ludifying' story structures and story objects residing in (linear) stories.*

Despite its far-reaching scope gamification hints at a specific design practice by which game elements are applied to a wide sample of topics and activities in a host of different contexts. This practice has been labelled 'gameful design', 'gamified design', 'applied game', as well as 'applied game design' (Schmidt et al. 2015).

Another difference between ludification and gamification has to do with learning and motivation. Central to this is the notion of how interaction with game-like features in non-game contexts promote engagement and accelerate learning, usually through some kind of reward system (Walz and Deterding 2014; Huotari and Hamari 2011). Overall, the rationale for gamification rests on the somewhat dubious reasoning that video games are heavily dependent upon rewards, and that players like and respond well to being rewarded. Furthermore, this implicit behavioristic rationale is merged with the observation that video games engage players. Ergo, the thinking seems to suggest that players get engaged in video games because they get rewarded. Following this line of thinking points toward mesmerizing possibilities of harvesting the sway video games hold on players and apply it outside the realm of games. The sheer thought of the endless possibilities is enough to cloud even the fiercest critic – games are, commercially and conceptually, a goldmine.

3   The Design Practice of Gamification

Let us focus a bit more on the design approach of gamification with its declared ambition to use video game elements to engage and motivate users to accelerate learning (Bogost 2011, 2014). One difficulty that quickly emerges involves understanding how video games actually work. This question can lead to several different answers as the growing catalogue of research into video games demonstrates. However, an important and unclear border exists between the machinery of games, in general, and designing for gamification. This border has to do with how players recognize the interactive gamified system and its properties. Do players see the system as gamified content, or do they see it as a video game? Another important and unclear border loops around the question of learning, namely what kind of learning and knowledge the gamified system is designed to promote. Yet another vital and unclear issue concerns motivation, specifically whether the gamified system relies on intrinsic or extrinsic motivation to engage players (Ryan and Deci 2000; Csikszentmihalyi 2000).

A deeper and transcendental question concerns what it takes to make a system engaging to interact with (Hunicke et al. 2004), be that the need for clear goals, manageable challenges, or transparent and quantifiable outcomes. All this questioning, from the nature of gaming to the valorization of goals, leads to fundamental design reflections on how to understand formal game elements and combine them in relation to an intended learning outcome. As such, the conceptual scrutiny of games (what they are) and the functional applicability (what they are good for) weave into one another. For instance, posing the question, does it make sense to reward the user with a star when she is trying to learn a new language, implies a causal connection between practical upshot (language skills) and the conceptual premise that games are splendid tools with which to reward users when they achieve a goal.

All of these borders are blurred. Nevertheless, they rise from the same rift in the rationale of gamification; the gap between aspects of games on the one side and fully-fledged games on the other. This rift has not been bridged. One thing is sure: it generates these blurred borders. One only has to ask oneself the question how many game aspects – and specifically which ones – are needed before a 'gamified' system tilts and becomes a fully-fledged video game. Until now the focus, in research, has been on game aspects such as clear goals, feedback in the form of quantified rewards and measurable progress normally in the shape of badges, levels, and leader boards (Walz and Deterding 2014).

4   Reward

Common knowledge dictates that reward systems are connected with motivation. However, the question of how to design a reward system that can drive behavioral changes is another matter. Despite this challenge almost all research on gamification dodge the explanation of how to design a reward system beyond the meagre notion of handing out a badge for a job well done.

This illustrates a curious lapse of attention. Since motivation and reward go hand-in-hand in the *raison d'être* of gamification, it would seem obvious that research would center on principles for designing reward systems in order to monitor their behavioral effect (on playful humans). However, let us be more specific: How does a reward system trigger the activity levels of the user? Noteworthy in this regard is John Hopson's (2001) investigation of behavioral game design. Hopson is inspired by neo-behaviorism and contemporary behavioral psychology. He argues that it is possible to a certain degree to 'filter' structural parameters and their effects. What we have, then, is a design structure of rewards.

Hopson further explains how reward systems can be designed through contingencies and schedules (Hopson 2001, p. 1). A contingency is a rule, which governs when a reward is given out (hence the scheduling). Essentially, there exits two different kinds of contingencies, ratios and intervals, which can be both fixed and variable. Each produce different patterns in player activity.

Ratio schedules are dependent on the user's activity. They provide the user with a reward after a specific number of actions have been taken. When this is translated into a task, it would sound something like this: the game presents the player with a task of killing X orcs or to solve Y math assignments (Larsen 2012). In both of these cases, the player will be rewarded following a specific number of actions. This is called a fixed ratio schedule since it requires a finite number of actions before the reward is provided. Note that the specific number of actions required have been announced beforehand and that the number of actions never change. If the player begins the game anew the same task will require the exact same number of actions before the reward is given. Nothing changes. Most noteworthy, however, in the fixed ratio where player activity begins very slowly with a short sudden burst of energy toward the end. The opposite happens with the variable ratio. Here, the player activity levels are constant and fairly high. In other words, the player performs the same action over and over again in anticipation of a reward even though the reward fails to materialize itself.

This design structure is contrasted by the interval schedules, which also can be both fixed and variable. When they are fixed, they depend on the internal clock of the game system, i.e. interval schedules provide rewards after a certain amount of time has passed. There is no need for player activity. The reward will be provided regardless of player actions or not. The opposite holds for the variable interval schedule, which constitutes a reward after a variable time period. Sometimes, the reward is provided after 30 s, while at other times the reward is revealed after five minutes. Here, the players' activity levels follow the fixed (slow in the beginning accelerating toward a burst in the end) and variable (steady and fairly high) pattern of behavior. The correlation between the structural design of rewards and the users' response and behavior seems to escape the studies of motivation within the field of gamification, i.e. how the structural design of rewards drives behavioral changes both in the short, intermediate, and long term.

5 Play and Playfulness

Studies of ludification have mostly been related to media production and how playfulness and a certain gaming sensibility create new cultural practices (Raessens 2006).

They involve the consumption of new media and how it reconfigures, reshapes, and transforms both the media itself and the wider ecology around it (Frissen et al. 2015). Such approaches express a change 'from a predominantly narrative to a predominantly ludic ontology' (Raessens 2006, p. 54). This change is particular true of the role of play in modern culture (Raessens 2014).

Media convergence, as defined and discussed by Henry Jenkins (Jenkins 2006), can be seen as the combined product of ludification and play. Convergence represents the flow of content across media platforms added with an emergent and increasingly powerful participatory culture where users playfully distribute, produce, and engage with content to make meaningful connections (Jenkins et al., 2013; Kerr et al. 2006). Identities do not emerge as mere reflections or effects of media consumption. Instead, the dynamic of ludic identity creation is reciprocal and tied to new media practices and (re)configurations.

In light of this ludification can be viewed as a cultural and social practice situated at the intersection between play and game (Lindtner and Dourish 2011). Play and games find themselves 'at the heart of a dispersed ecology of practice, diffused from local identity creation to global cultural production and usage' (Larsen 2019, p. 458).

This view, one that springs from the disruption of the sharp border between production and reception, is influenced by Johan Huizinga's ([1938] 2014) seminal definition of play. According to Huizinga play acts as an inspirational force, which propels the development of culture. Play is different from work, Huizinga writes, in that it does not have a utilitarian purpose. Play seems to 'float' awaiting materialization either in the shape of an arena or board of sorts or by the contextualization of playful activities. Huizinga's distinction between work and play is echoed by Caillois ([1958], 2001) when he describes play as 'pure waste' (p. 5). Huizinga and Caillois' shared epistemology of play, it could be argued, originates from Protestant ideology as it is portrayed by Max Weber (Weber 1958). The overall perspective is that play is unproductive as opposed to work, which is a productive and meaningful activity. Thus, play exists outside ordinary life, adheres to its own rules and carries no material interest. Accordingly, play is an unserious activity even though it has the capacity to fully absorb its participants and pose as a vital drive in cultural production.

Contrary to this view, Stevens (1978) regards Huizinga and Caillois' split between play and work as 'a false dichotomy' (p. 17). He criticizes Huizinga and Caillois for mixing and confusing the formal characteristics of play with the experience of being in play. This polarity blurs the boundaries, since 'we are taking the behavior for the experiencing of that behavior' (Stevens 1978, p. 21). Stevens' solution is to separate form from experience or poetics from aesthetics, which further means separating the formal markers of play from the experience of being-in-play. This approach in drawing clear boundaries reflects several research traditions within the humanities, which can be illustrated with an example from Russian formalism.

The Russian formalists were not interested in play *per se*. Instead, they wanted to distance themselves from 'aesthetics' or 'experience' especially in an effort to formally divorce literature from non-literature.

Shklovsky, in his essay *Art as Technique* (1917), draws a defining line between what can be considered art and what cannot. This line, Shklovsky says, belongs to the concept of 'defamiliarization'; a device or perceptional trigger that forces the reader to see the already acquainted in a new light. Guided by Shklovsky's device of defamiliarization, Tomashevsky, in his essay *Thematics* (1925), meticulously outlines the specific units and the order of narrative elements that are present in literature. Two distinct layers exist within the narrative design of literature: on the one hand, story (*fabula*) emerging as the chronological order of events; on the other hand, that which appears as the presented story (*sjuzet*). A story is thus the unedited sequence of events as opposed to the plot, which is the edited and defamiliarized composition of the chronological order of the story.

What is relevant here is that Stevens seems to echo the overall mode of thinking of the Russian formalists, especially in the cut between 'play form' and 'play experience'. This does not mean, however, that Stevens is a straight-faced formalist; on the contrary, Stevens illuminates the flipside of the formalist coin, the experience. Such focus on the experience of play resemblances Hans George Gadamer's ([1960] 2013) phenomeno-logical analysis of play. He too separates the experience of being in play from the formal structure of play (Larsen 2015).

Stevens' turn away from the formal analysis in return of an investigation of the inner workings of the experience of being in play opens up a novel approach to play. This approach allows for play to be seen as a particular and pleasurable attitude to an on-going, prosaic activity.

Thus, play is 'a mode of human experience [...] a way of engaging the world whatever one is doing' (Malaby 2007, p. 100). This rather totalizing view upon play implies for Malaby that we can think of 1) play as a mode of experiencing; 2) play as a particular way of engaging with the world; and 3) play as a possibility, which can happen in all kinds of places and in any number of activities.

In a more recent study Malaby redefines his position. Now play is regarded as a disposition 'characterized by a readiness to improvise in the face of an ever-changing world that admits of no transcendently ordered account' (Malaby 2009, p. 206). Malaby's approach to play means: 1) To prioritize play over any given activity or practice; and 2) a specific and situational stance which resonates in Sicart's (2014) take on play. According to Sicart play is an appropriative power that has the ability to 'take over' or colonize any unfolding activity. Play is furthermore an activity, which always happens in a context. 3) Finally, play seems to be always-already tied to a specific situation, the specific role of play, which lend itself to navigating the indeterminateness of an ever-changing world. We have now, with the help of Malaby, Stevens, and Sicart abandoned the traditional and 'false' dichotomy of work versus play. When the work/play distinction is left behind, we see instead in ludic practice a more useful contrast between a cultural form (a game-like activity, regardless of the level of playful engagement) and a mode of cultural experience (a playful disposition towards activities no matter how game-like) (Malaby 2009, p. 209).

However, what Malaby is hinting at here is the important dichotomy between 'play' and 'game'. Or, a separation between 'play' and 'game' activities (gaming). When play is estranged from actual game activities, it is possible to treat play as an autonomous, conditional unit fundamental to the human condition. Play becomes, almost in a Hedeg-gerian fashion, a disposition or a mode of experiencing the world – i.e. play being the a priori framework for aposteriori and actualized gameplay (Larsen and Walther 2019).

6   Rationalization

But there is a darker side hidden in the entanglement of the dichotomy between 'play' and 'game'. Grimes and Feenberg 2009) writes about play being mixed up with a form of social rationalization, which takes place at the junction of play experience and game systems. According to them 'play', in itself, reproduces 'the larger processes of rationalization at work within modern capitalist societies' (p. 105). Silverman and Simon (2009) use the term 'power play', which they see as an act of 'machination', a submission of the player shaped by the game system. In pragmatic terms one can think of (the experience of) play transforming itself from being fun and engaging to a tiresome, boring and work-like activity. Players no longer enjoy the game. Instead they mechanically respond to the demands of the video game system as their playful attitudes sublimate into rationalization. Rather than players playing the game, it is the game that plays and drives the players toward future rewards.

The silver lining in this dystopian perspective is Grimes and Feenberg's observation that players increasingly become part of the production of game content, which means that we should couple the view on the dark side of play with the 'social, cultural, and political conditions within which a game is appropriated and contested by its players' (Grimes and Feenberg 2009, p. 107). The premise of this claim is, similar to Stevens and Malaby, the transgression of the work and play dichotomy. Rationalization may be a process that basically simulates 'work'; but it must be measured against the appropriating act of cultural counter production that play offers. Not only does play entail the dialectic of tyrannizing players from within the game system as well as to harvest a potentially liberating annexation. Play also creates 'a form of social order' (p. 108): "[It] is not that social order recapitulates certain features of games, but rather that games have themselves become forms of social order" (p. 109). This implies a dual set of premises: First, the distinction between the poetics of the system and the aesthetics of the play experience; and second, a peculiar flip-side version of Huizinga's claim: Namely, the idea that play not only propels forward the fruition of culture, but also that play is laden with interest, rather than being mere fun and dis-interested stuff. Since play, then, really can exist as a kind of realization of its own promise, because it can foster a disruption of the hegemonic one-way-street of brute game systems; the vital (and perhaps sad) point here is that rationalization may come back to haunt players in the shape of not just the social ordering of games, as Grimes and Feenberg writes, but also as the instrumentalization of play.

Nevertheless, play itself holds transformational capabilities; not statically, but dynamically, while percolating from play mode to game mode. Play passes from an undifferentiated state of playfulness to a rationalized configuration adjusted to fit the video game system. This transformative process takes place through a series of differentiations (Walther 2003, 2011), which end up subjugating play in such a way that play bends to the will of the game system. This is not the instrumentalization of play, but, rather, the inherent and almost evolutionistic dynamic of the activity: play lends itself to and is drawn towards the game. The continuum of play mode and game mode alludes to Caillois' conceptualization of play, which equally takes place in a band between *paidia* and *ludus*. *Paidia* (mostly translated as 'free play') embraces the precipitateness and spontaneity of play, play mode, and is contrasted by the much more disciplined *ludus*, or game mode. Caillois himself explains the two poles respectively as 'diversion, turbulence, free improvisation, and carefree gaiety [and] ever greater amount of effort, patience, skill, or ingenuity' (Caillois 2001, p. 13).

To play a game is to be swept away by and drawn into a series of transformations, a rationalization process which ends up quelling play, according to Grimes and Feenberg. Callios sees it differently. What could be called game mode is merely the maturation of 'diversion' and 'turbulence' as well as the effect of *paidia* gradually 'becoming' *ludus* with all its 'effort, patience and skill'. One could say, partly conclusive, that there lies an inherent ideological stance in play's subjugation to game, *pace* Grimes and Feenberg. Callios, on the other hand, is much more akin to the idea of the evolutionary and dynamic processualism of play and games. In addition, play mode and game mode resemble Malaby's 'cultural form' and 'mode of cultural experience'. Both evolve in an overlapping continuum while keeping both aspects open for on-going configurations.

The procedurality of play also represents the process of ludification. Play activities transform from undifferentiated to differentiated states though optimization, discipline, and self-referential awareness. It is this process that ascribe to the social order while simultaneously creating opportunities for user resistance and creativity. One could say that the procedural wave of play turning into game means both to 'fit in' to the power structure of games but also to make play 'stand out'. Ultimately, there is an element of instrumentalization in the dominance of the game mode and the way it takes control over and disciplines play. And yet there is equally, and simultaneously, an imaginative resonance in the very same playfulness that sparks the process as such. Ludification, thus, is a process which injects playfulness and gamefulness (game structures) into tv series and movies. In contrast to this process, gamification insert game-like progress patterns and reward structures outside the realm of games, especially within the domain of learning.

Together, ludification and gamification reside in a circular and recursive formation accelerating and expanding the ludic presence of game-like traits outside the realm of (proper) games.

7   Conclusion: Learning from Ludification

Gamification means introducing and enhancing game elements and game mechanics in non-game objects, installations, and situations; in fact, gamification can be regarded as a subset of applied behavioral psychology because of the profound emphasis, as we saw above, on motivation, feedback, progress, and reward. Ludification relies on the same kind of infusion of game elements – but in another domain. Ludification concerns the enhancement specifically of game elements in stories and their combination (e.g. interactive fiction).

Thus, one could say that a *gamified* structure and object are non-game structures and objects endowed with components and traits from the gaming regime; while *ludified* structures and objects are non-game story-structures and story-objects endowed with similar game components and traits whose focus, however, is not so much motivation, feedback, and reward but, rather, ways of 'designing' and 'telling' stories in new and exciting, i.e. 'ludified' fashions. The terminology that we propose here, and which we outlined above, constitutes a shift from ludification being merely a subset of gamification intended for specific non-game purposes to contemporary media productions and consumption practices where the co-existence of elements of play, game structures, and game mechanics together with modes of storytelling – preferably across media – become more and more dominant.

Ludology, the academic study of computer games, evidently pawed the way for the understanding of games on a formal level (their ontology) as well as for insights into the experiences, community making, and playfulness associated with games, i.e. the epistemology of games. Tentatively, one could envision the same kind of progression undertaken by the study of ludification – ludified story-structures and story-objects – as that of the science of ludology: From the formalistic enquiry into the nature or ontology of games (or story-structures and story-objects behaving like games); to studies of playful practices and reception communities arising from these structures and objects and the way they are ludified; to, finally, modes of 'extracting' situational knowledge and learning from these structures and objects. In other words, a journey from the underlying, theoretical strata of understanding and categorizing structures and objects to new and fruitful ways of *using* these structures and objects – and the deep understanding of them – in instrumentalized contexts. Will ludification be the next wave of serious, mediated learning? This paper has tried to sketch the base theory of such structures and objects; and, of course, only time will tell.

References

Bogost, I.: Why gamification is bullshit. In: Walz, P.S., Deterding, S. (eds.) The Gameful World. MIT Press, Cambridge (2014)

Caillois, R.: Man, Play and Games. University of Illinois Press, Urbana (2001)

Csikszentmihalyi, M.: Beyond Boredom and Anxiety – Experiencing Flow in work and Play. Jossey-Bass Publishers, San Francisco (2000)

Deterding, S., Sicart, M., Nacke, L., O'Hara, K., Dixon, D.: Gamification: using game design elements in non-gaming contexts. In: CHI 2011, Vancouver, BC, Canada (2011)

Dippel, A., Fizek, S.: Ludification of Culture, The Significance of play and games in everyday practices of the digital era. In: Koch, G. (ed.) Digitalization: Theories and Concepts for Empirical Cultural Research. Routledge, London (2017)

Frissen, V., Lammes, S., De Lange, M., De Mul, J., Raessens, J. (eds.): Playful Identities: The Ludification of Digital Media Cultures. Amsterdam University Press, Amsterdam (2015)

Gadamer, H.G.: Truth and Method. Bloomsbury Academic, London (2013)

Grimes, S.M., Feenberg, A.: Rationalizing play: a critical theory of digital gaming. In: The Information Society, vol. 25, pp. 105–118. Routledge Taylor and Francis Group (2009)

Hopson, J.: Behavioral Game Design in *Gamasutra* (2001). http://www.gamasu-tra.com/view/feature/131494/behavioral_game_design.php. Accessed 15 Dec 2015

Huizinga, J.: Homo Ludens: A Study of the Play-Element in Culture. Martino Publishing (2014)

Hunicke, R., Leblanc, M., Zubek, R.: MDA: a formal approach to game design and game research (2004). http://www.cs.northwestern.edu/~hunicke/pubs/MDA.pdf. Accessed 15 Dec 2015

Huotari, K., Hamari, J.: "Gamification" from the perspective of service marketing. In: CHI 2011, Vancouver, BC, Canada (2011)

Jenkins, H., Ford, S., Green, J.: Spreadable Media. New York University Press, New York (2013)

Jenkins, H.: Convergence Culture – Where Old and New Media Collide. New York University Press, New York (2006)

Kerr, A., Kücklich, J., Brereton, P.: New media – new pleasures? Int. J. Cult. Stud. **9**(1), 63–82 (2006)

Kirkpatrick, G.: Ludefaction: fracking of the radical imaginary. Games Cult. **10**(6), 507–524 (2015)

Larsen, J.L.: Objects of desire: a reading of the reward system in world of warcraft. Eludamos J. Comput. Game Cult. **6**(1), 15–24 (2012)

Larsen, J.L.: Play and space - towards a formal definition of play. Int. J. Play. Taylor & Francis (2015). http://www.tandfonline.com/doi/full/10.1080/21594937.2015.1060567

Larsen, J.L.: Play and gameful movies: the ludification of modern cinema. Games Cult. **14**(5) (2019). https://doi.org/10.1177/1555412017700601

Larsen, L.J., Walther, B.K.: The ontology of gameplay: toward a new theory. Games Cult. (2019). https://doi.org/10.1177/1555412019825929

Lindtner, S., Dourish, P.: The promise of play: a new approach to productive play. Games Cult. **6**(5) (2011)

Malaby, T.M.: Anthropology and play: the contours of playful experience. New Literary History **40**(1), 205–218 (2009)

Malaby, T.M.: Beyond play: a new approach to games. Games Cult. **2**(2), 95–113 (2007)

McGonigal, J.: I'm not playful, i'm gameful. In: Walz, P.S., Deterding, S. (eds.) The Gameful World. MIT Press, Cambridge (2014)

Raessens, J.: Playful Identities or the Ludification of Culture in Games Cult. **1**(1), 52–57 (2006)

Raessens, J.: The ludification of culture. In: Fuchs, M., Fizek, S., Ruffino, P., Schrape, N. (eds.) Rethinking Gamification. Meson Press, Lüneburg (2014)

Ryan, R.M., Deci, E.L.: Intrinsic and extrinsic motivations: classic definitions and new directions. Contemp. Educ. Psychol. **25**, 54–67 (2000)

Schmidt, R., Emmerich, K., Schmidt, B.: Applied games – in search of a new definition. In: Chorianopoulos, K., Divitini, M., Hauge, J.B., Jaccheri, L., Malaka, R. (eds.) ICEC 2015. LNCS, vol. 9353, pp. 100–111. Springer, Cham (2015). https://doi.org/10.1007/978-3-319-24589-8_8

Sicart, M.: Play Matters. Playful Thinking Series. The MIT Press, Cambridge (2014)

Silverman, M., Simon, B.: Discipline and dragon kill points in the online power game. Games Cult. **4**(4), 353–378 (2009)

Stevens, P.: Play and work: a false dichotomy. Assoc. Anthropol. Study Play **5**(2), 17–22 (1978)

Walter, B.K.: Playing and gaming: reflections and classifications. Game Stud. Int. J. Comput. Game Res. **3**(1) (2003)

Walter, B.K.: Reflections on the philosophy of pervasive gaming with special emphasis on rules, gameplay, and virtuality. Fibreculture J. **19**

Walz, P.S., Deterding, S. (eds.): The Gameful World. MIT Press

Weber, M. (1958). *The Protestant Ethics and the Spirit of Capitalism*, trans. Parsons, T. New York, Scribners

The Empirical Investigation of the Gamified Learning Theory

Nadja Zaric$^{(\boxtimes)}$ (ID), Vlatko Lukarov$^{(\boxtimes)}$, and Ulrik Schroeder$^{(\boxtimes)}$ (ID)

Learning Technologies, RWTH Aachen University, Ahornstr. 55, 52704 Aachen, Germany
{zaric,lukarov,schroeder}@informatik.rwth-aachen.de
https://learntech.rwth-aachen.de

Abstract. The use of gamification in education is increasing, but it is still not clear exactly how or which game elements are conducive to learning. The research on gamification in learning is hindered by the users' heterogeneity, whose personal and professional traits can moderate the impact of gamification on learning success. This study aims to experimentally investigate the moderator role of learners' learning tendencies on gamification success concerning students' academic participation, engagement, and experience. In our study, 85 students were randomly assigned to one control and two treatment groups. Our results showed gamification design positively contributes to the academic participation, affects learners' engagement in gamified environments, and that students' engagement was moderated by students' learning tendencies.

Keywords: Gamification · Gamified learning theory · Engagement · Gamified experience · Personalization · Learning tendencies

1 Introduction

Landers defines gamification as "the use of game elements (GEs) outside the context of a game to affect learning-related behaviors or attitudes" [1]. Learner-related behavior, just as any behavior, can influence learning. Gamified learning theory (GLT) implies that gamification does not affect learning directly, but is rather used to stimulate learning-related behavior in a moderating process, which means gamification affects learning when an instructional designer intends to encourage a behavior or attitude which increases depends on the third variable – the moderator [1]. The moderators are "psychological constructs that affect how gamification interventions work across different people" [2]. In education, learners' learning tendencies (LTs) are regarded as one of the moderators of the relationship between instructional design and learning outcomes. LTs refer to "cognitive, affective and psychological behaviors that serve as relatively stable indicators of how learners interact with and respond to the learning environment" [3].

This work empirically evaluates the GLT by exploring the moderating effect of LT on students' academic participation (ACP), engagement, and gameful experience in a given course. Students' engagement is composed of behavioral, cognitive, and emotional

I. Marfisi-Schottman et al. (Eds.): GALA 2020, LNCS 12517, pp. 135–145, 2020.
https://doi.org/10.1007/978-3-030-63464-3_13

engagement and defines time, energy, effort, and feelings students invest in their learning. ACP refers to students' interactions and involvement in online learning activities and is a part of students' behavioral online engagement [3]. Gameful experience is a psychological state in which one perceives presented goals as non-trivial and achievable, is motivated to pursue those goals, and believe that one's actions are volitional [1].

2   Background

According to [3] LTs assert individuals have preferences along four bipolar dimensions of learning. These dimensions are described as a 'double-pan scale', where 'pans' present the two opposite poles (active/reflective pan of processing dimension, sensing/intuitive pan of perceiving, sequential/global pan of understanding and visual/verbal pan of presenting new information). Which pan will weigh depends on the strength of the tendency the student has toward a particular dimension' side. The stronger the tendency toward one side of the scale, the greater the chance that the student will resort to the 'more likely' behavior for that side of the dimension [3]. The underlying idea of LT is that instructional design should be in line with learners' LTs to provide learners a possibility to fulfill their potential. However, in the light of the ongoing critical discussions about LTs and their miss-interpretation [4], we further define what this work does (not) entail under the term 'LTs', how LTs are (not) used in this study and how they fit the propositions of the moderating process in GLT.

First, the goal of identifying LTs is not to label students but to use what we know about LTs to create an effective and balanced learning environment. The balanced environment is one in which students are sometimes taught in a manner that matches their LTs, and sometimes oppositely, so they are forced to stretch and grow in the direction they might be inclined to avoid [3]. In other words, the quality of the instructional design is responsible for learners learning, not their LTs. This is in line with GLT proposition that effective instructional content is crucial to the success of gamification, that is, gamification cannot be used to replace, but instead to improve the instruction [1]. Next, LTs describe learner's behavioral tendencies, not their learning outcomes. If a student is confronted with different learning situations she will tend to behave in a manner characteristic to their LTs. However, not every learning behavior is relevant for a certain learning outcome, e.g., active participation in the course discussion will probably not affect one's performance. Thus, gamification should be used to directly target the behavior that is shown to influence instructional success [1]. If the impact of gamification interventions differs among different groups of people, then the characteristics that make people different are called personal moderators. This interrelationship among gamification, behavior, personal characteristics, and outcomes is called moderation. Translated to the context of our study, the effect of gamification on intended outcomes is moderated by learners' behavior (which is defined by learners' LTs).

3   Related Work

Literature showed that attitudes towards learning, age, and gender moderate the effect of gamification on its intended outcomes. For example, positive attitudes contribute to higher learning outcomes and positive reactions to training while negative attitudes are correlated with lower outcomes [5]. Next, age can influence gamification success, as elder people found gamified environments harder to use [6]. Gender also affects the design of gamification, as males are motivated by achievement, and females are motivated by collaborative GEs [7]. Regarding the scope of this work, we found only one study exploring the relationship between LTs and gamification. Namely, authors questioned if LTs affect how gamification influences users' perception, participation, and overall performance in an online course. As reported, students with active processing tendencies had a more positive perception comparing to reflective. Students with global understanding expressed a more positive attitude and had higher scores then sequential [8]. However, due to the lack of a control group, it is not possible to determine whether gamification affected performance enhancement or the differences occurred exactly because of the presence of GEs.

In the absence of satisfactory evidence on the links between LT and game elements, we conducted an exploratory study to investigate gamification contribution to students' engagement by taking into account their LTs [9, 10]. For that, the PBL system (Badges, Points, and Leaderboards) was implemented in the different course activities and tasks, after which the exploratory experiment was conducted. This study revealed that our gamification design increased students' engagement, students' engagement differed depending on one's LT, and gamification did not affect all students in the same way. Further, the qualitative analysis showed students' had positive attitudes towards gamification, which encourage further investigation in this direction. However, due to the nature of the exploratory study, it was not possible to draw a conclusion on the relationship between game elements and LTs, hence, this study aims to exceed presented limitations by creating one control and two treatment groups in which each treatment is designed with one game element. With this, we investigate: (i) whether LTs moderate gamification influence upon students' ACP, engagement and experience, and (ii) which gamification design is more appropriate for which LT.

4 Research Questions

This study investigates three research areas (RA). In RA1 we question "Whether gamification improves the targeted outcomes in comparison to traditional learning?". For this, we compare the ACP and engagement of students who have the same LT but are attending different courses (gamified and non-gamified). In RA2 and RA3 we focus only on the treatment groups. First, we question "Are there differences among students with opposite LTs inside each gamified group?" to see if and how LTs moderated the effect of gamification design. Finally, RA3 question "How the two gamification approaches influence the engagement and experience of students with a particular LT, and whether influential differences exist?". The conceptual model of our RAs and the hypothesis (H) is given in Fig. 1.

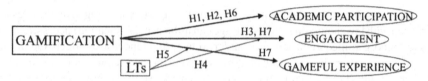

Fig. 1. The conceptual model of research areas and hypothesis

5 Method

The online JavaScript (JS) course was created for Bachelor Computer Science (CS) students, who registered for the "Web Technologies" course taught every winter semester at the RWTH Aachen University. Participation in the JS course was voluntary and the students had the opportunity to earn five bonus points as entry points for the course. The JS course was organized as a one-month course (October to November 2019), realized within the Moodle LMS. The course covered six topics consisted of various learning materials, lecture videos with practical examples, code examples, and supplementary materials. The instructor involved in the course only when an announcement had to be made, or a student (virtually) asked for an assignment feedback or had a questions.

Targeting the Behavior for Gamification Intervention. CS education combines both theoretical and practical concepts which indicate that CS students should be inclined towards practicing or solving exercises by using principles and theories to discover new relationships and find innovative solutions. In which of these two 'directions' (practical or theoretical skills) students are *likely* to develop strengths, that is, weaknesses are defined by their tendencies towards a perception dimension of learning [3]. The sensing side of the perception dimension describes students who perceive things by observing, listening, and feeling. They tend to solve problems by standard methods, using facts and experimentation, they dislike complications and theories (practical skills). The intuitive side, describes perceiving information through the imagination and instincts. Intuitive like innovations and challenges, they avoid repetition and seek to discover new relationships (theoretical shill). Studies on LTs showed that every learner can use both perception ways, but most of the time they use only one of them – which, in the case of CS students is the sensing way [2]. Thus, it is important to establish a balance between what learners must learn or work on to master a subject - and what and how they prefer to learn. Due to the majority of CS students having sensing LTs, this work aims to encourage *sensing* students to engage in tasks that they might, because of their sensing nature, avoid.

Selecting Game Elements. The first treatment group (T1) was gamified with the Trading GE. Trading is "an incentive exchange of some kind of items between the player and the game" [11]. The second treatment group (T2) was gamified using the PBL system. Table 1 describes how GEs were designed regarding the 'intuitive behavior' they indent to encourage.

Data and Feedback Collection. LTs were measured with the Index of Learning Style (ILS) questionnaire [12] that was given to students before the beginning of the course. For

Table 1. Overview of included GEs and experimental manipulations

Aim: Encourage students to try new solutions on their own	
T1	**Collecting puzzle pieces:** Puzzle pieces were hidden inside the coding challenges. A student could pick up a piece (by clicking on the item image) when a submission is made and unlock the instructor's solution. When all six pieces are collected, students trade them with the 'getaway card' to freely skip one of the tests for bonus points.
T2	**Badges**: Badges were automatically awarded to students when they submit a coding challenge. If all six badges are earned students get the 'getaway card'
Control	Submitting coding challenges was optional, and the solutions were open. Skipping the test was not possible
Aim: Encourage students to watch videos with theoretical explanations and concept	
T1	**Collecting coins:** Students collected coins by watching a theoretical video. Coins could be traded with 10 extra minutes for two Bonus tests of their choice
T2	**XPs and levels**: Students collected 45 XP points by watching theoretical videos. When they collect 450xp, respectively, 900xp they unlock the 30-min tests
Control	No awards for watching the videos. No possibility to extend the Bonus Tests time
Aim: Encourage students to explore the course, doing additional exercises and quizzes	
T1	**Collecting food ingredients**: the ingredient items were hidden inside additional activities like self-assessment quizzes. Once all ingredients are collected student unlocks a new learning section with supplementary materials on advanced JS concepts
T2	**Levels and leaderboard:** By doing self-assessment exercises and quizzes students were given additional XPs. When a certain amount of XP is being collected students leveled up. When the ultimate level 7 is reached, additional learning materials are unlocked. Students' current XPs and levels are shown in the leaderboard
Control	The additional material section was available from the beginning

the students' engagement, we created a self-reporting instrument and included: *behavioral scales* (Online Active (OA) scale that measures how actively students use e-learning systems to enhance their learning and Online Engagement (OE) scale that measures the degree to which students have applied the e-learning system into their academic studies) adapted from the Student Engagement Questionnaire[1], *emotional* (Interest and enjoyment (EE)) and *cognitive scales* (the invested effort in the course (IE)) from the Intrinsic Motivation Inventory[2] and *cognitive scale* ('effort/regulation' (ER)) from the Motivated Strategies for Learning Questionnaire[3]. Behavioral engagement scales used a 4-point Likert scale (1 = never to 4 = very often), while emotional and cognitive scales use a 7-point Likert Scale (1 = strongly disagree to 7 = strongly agree). Students' experience was measured with a Gamefulquest [13], an instrument used to assess users' gameful

---

[1] https://www.acer.org/au/ausse/survey-instruments.

[2] http://selfdeterminationtheory.org/intrinsic-motivation-inventory.

[3] http://stelar.edc.org/instruments/motivated-strategies-learning-questionnaire-mslq.

experience when using a gamified system. From the Gamefulquest playfulness (PL), accomplishment (AC) and challenge (CH) scales were used. The surveys were optional and given to students after the course ended. Table 2 summarizes the data used in this study.

Table 2. Measures and data used in the study

	RA	Data set
LTs	RA1-2	ILS test results
Engagement	RA1-2	Students engagement survey
Experience	RA2-3	Gamification engagement survey - Gamefulquest
ACP	RA1-3	*Time spent in course, Activities (No. of* events, course visits), *Self-assessment (No.* of completed self-assessment quizzes and exercises), *Coding challenges* (No. of submitted coding challenges), *Learning materials (*visits to lecture notes, additional material), *Gamified videos (No. of watched gamified videos)*

6   Analysis and Results

This study gathered 85 Bachelor CS students from RWTH Aachen University randomly assigned to one of the three groups. However, as this investigation is focused on students' behavior concerning their LTs, for the data analysis, only 69 students who completed the ILS questionnaire were taken into account (see Table 3). All extracted data were analyzed by using the IBM SPSS tool. Based on the assessment of the data normality, for measuring differences among groups parametric (Independent t-test) or non-parametric (Man Whitney U and Kruskal-Wallis) were used. Further, a simple regression was used to investigate the moderating effect of LTs [14]. The significance is measured at a level of 5% (p-value $< .05$).

Table 3. Students' distribution in the experiment

	Control Group 20 students		T1 Group 26 students		T2 Group 23 students	
	Intuitive	Sensing	Intuitive	Sensing	Intuitive	Sensing
	5	15	11	15	9	14
Engagement survey	9 students		21 students		14 students	
Gamefulquest	NA		24 students		14 students	

H1: Our gamification design contributes to ACP of sensing students: ACP will be higher for sensing students in the treatment (gamified) vs. control (non-gamified) conditions;

Table 4 presents the results of a Kruskal-Wallis test. The test revealed differences in ACP of sensing students between the three groups. Namely, in the T1 sensing students (n = 15) had significantly more actions, watched more gamified videos, and accessed more learning materials than their peers from the control group (n = 15). Similarly, in the T2 group sensing students (n = 14) were significantly more active than the peers from the control group. From this we conclude that gamified interventions had a direct impact on students' ACP in the course, thus *H1 is confirmed.*

Table 4. Comparison of ACP between control and treatment groups

	df	H	p	Control	T1	T2	Control - T1	Control - T2	T1 - T2
Time	2	3.69	.15	17.33	24.93	25.43			
Actions	2	10.67	.005**	14.30	29.47	23.82	.001**	.04*	.23
CC[a]	2	9.25	.01**	5.87	23.17	28.89	.08	.002**	.18
SA[b]	2	6.90	.11	17.73	25.70	24.18			
LM[c]	2	10.10	.006**	14.20	28.57	24.89	.002**	.03*	.44
GV[d]	2	13.76	.001**	13.37	30.67	23.54	.033	.02*	.13

Note: * = p < .05, ** = p < .01, [a] Coding Challenge, [b] Self-assessments, [c] Learning materials, [d] Gamified videos

H2: Our gamification design does not contribute to ACP of intuitive students: there are no significant differences in ACP of intuitive students among control and treatment groups; Kruskal-Wallis test (Table 4) results did not reveal significant differences between intuitive students' (n = 25) across the three groups thus *H2 failed to be rejected.*

H3: Our gamification design contributes to students' engagement: Engagement of intuitive and sensing students will be higher in gamified treatment. A Kruskal-Wallis results (see Table 5) showed no significant differences in the effect of our gamification design on students' engagement, *thus H3 is not confirmed.*

H4: LTs moderate gamification effect on engagement: there will be differences between intuitive and sensing students in the treatment groups. The T-test revealed in the T1 group EI of sensing students (n = 14) was statistically higher than EI of intuitive students (n = 7) (see Table 6). Further analysis with simple regression established tendency towards sensing perception could significantly predict EI, $F (1, 21) = 4.72$, $p < .05$ and that tendency accounted for 18.4% of the explained variability in EI. T-test also showed sensing students in the T2 group (n = 7) had higher OAE and EE in comparison to intuitive (n = 7). The analysis showed the sensing tendency could significantly predict OA, $F (1, 12) = 11.21$, $p < .005$, and accounted for 48.3% of the explained variability. Further, the tendency could significantly predict EE, $F (1, 12) = 6.55$, $p < .005$ as it

Table 5. Engagement comparisons among groups, Kruskal-Wallis

	Intuitive students						Sensing students				
	df	H	p	Control[a]	T1[b]	T2[c]	df	H	p	Control[d]	T1[e]	T2[f]
OA[i]	2	1.69	.43	12.0	7.94	10.58	2	3.67	.16	12.83	13.27	19.88
OE[j]	2	1.73	.42	9.67	8.0	11.67	2	.563	.76	13.5	14.67	16.75
EE[k]	2	.96	.63	11.50	9.83	8	2	3.0	.22	14	13.07	19.38
ER[l]	2	1.66	.43	12.67	8.17	9.92	2	2.84	.24	10.08	15.6	17.56
EI[m]	2	1.33	.51	11.67	8.11	10.5	2	3.1	.21	9.92	17.3	14.81

Note, [a.] n = 3, [b.] n = 7, [c.] n = 6, [d.] n = 6, [e] n = 14, [f] n = 8, [i] Online Active, [j] Online Engagement, [k] Emotional Engagement, [l] Effort Regulation, [m] Effort Invested.

accounted for 35.3% of the explained variability. From this, *we conclude H4 is partially confirmed.*

Table 6. Comparison engagement and gameful experience between intuitive and sensing students

	T1 group				T2 group			
	t(21)	p	Intuitive	Sensing	t(12)	p	Intuitive	Sensing
OA[a]	−1.79	.08	2.13 ± .68	2.70 ± .65	−2.52	.02*	2.46 ± .54	3.25 ± .59
OE[b]	−1.99	.05	2.41 ± 1.07	3.1 ± .61	−.06	.94	3.12 ± .70	3.15 ± .99
EE[c]	−.74	.43	4.0 ± 1.74	4.4 ± .88	−2.54	.02*	3.64 ± 1.23	5.14 ± .97
EI[d]	−2.17	.04*	3.86 ± 1.2	4.74 ± .75	−.61	.55	4.5 ± 1.65	4.9 ± .80
ER[e]	−1.28	.21	3.86 ± 118	4.5 ± .94	−.54	.59	4.13 ± .90	4.55 ± 1.68
AC[f]	.108	.91	4.11 ± .71	4.02 ± 1.97	−1.63	.12	4.72 ± 1.9	6.0 ± .99
CH[g]	.257	.79	3.22 ± 1.58	3.05 ± 1.59	−1.85	.08	3.64 ± 1.62	5.18 ± 1.40
PL[h]	.591	.56	3.87 ± 1.32	3.45 ± 1.88	−1.37	.19	4.14 ± 1.64	5.27 ± 1.41

Note, [a]Online Active, [b]Online Engagement, [c]Emotional Engagement, [d]Effort Invested, [e]Effort Regulation, [f]Accomplishment, [g]Challenge, [h]Playfulness.

*H5: LTs **moderate gamification effect on students' gameful experience** in the course: there will be differences between intuitive and sensing students in the treatment groups.* A T-test revealed no differences between sensing and intuitive students regarding their gamified experience (Table 6), thus H5 is not confirmed.

*H6: Our gamification designs **differently contribute to ACP**: ACP will be different between sensing and intuitive students across the two treatment groups.* The results of the Kruskal-Wallis (Table 4) test showed no differences in ACP, thus the H6 is not confirmed.

H7: Our gamification designs differently contribute to students' engagement and gamification experience: engagement and gamified experience will differ between students

across the treatment groups. Table 7 showed OA of sensing students in T2 was statistically higher in comparison to sensing students of the T1 group. Further, sensing students in the T2 group had a higher gameful experience. However, there were no differences between intuitive students among T1 and T2 thus *H7 is partially confirmed.*

Table 7. Comparison of engagement and gameful experience of students with same LT

	Intuitive				Sensing			
	t(14)	p	T1[a]	T2[b]	t(19)	p	T1[c]	T2[d]
OA[a]	1.04	.31	2.13 ± .68	2.45 ± .49	−2.39	.03*	2.7 ± .64	3.37 ± .52
OE[b]	1.57	.13	2.41 ± .07	3.14 ± .64	−.09	.92	3.1 ± .63	3.14 ± 1.07
EE[c]	.31	.75	4.0 ± 1.74	3.75 ± 16	−1.86	.07	4.43 ± .90	5.24 ± 1
EI[d]	−.62	.54	4.19 ± 1.1	4.06 ± 53	−.63	.53	4.62 ± .75	4.85 ± 85
ER[e]	−.35	.72	3.87 ± 1.18	4.06 ± .85	.11	.91	4.74 ± .75	4.68 ± 1.78
AC[f]	−.65	.52	4.26 ± 1.71	4.72 ± 1.88	−2.63	.004**	4.02 ± 1.97	6.0 ± .99
CH[g]	−.50	.62	3.22 ± 1.58	3.64 ± 1.62	−3.18	.004**	3.05 ± 1.59	5.18 ± 1.4
PL[h]	−.35	.72	3.92 ± 1.32	4.14 ± 1.64	−2.38	.02*	3.45 ± 1.88	5.27 ± 1.41

Note: * = p<.05, ** = p < .01, [a] n = 9, [b] n = 7, [c] n = 7, [d] n = 14, [a] Online Active, [b] Online Engagement, [c] Emotional Engagement, [d] Effort Invested, [e] Effort Regulation, [f] Accomplishment, [g] Challenge, [h] Playfulness.

7   Discussion and Conclusion

This study makes four primary contributions to the growing research on the GLT and gamification. First, we introduced a theoretical rationale to the usage of LTs for the identification of a learning-related behavior. Specifically, tendencies for the *perception* learning dimension were discussed concerning how they shape student' strengthens i.e. weaknesses in solving practical or theoretical tasks. From this, a learners' likely behavior in the course is identified and used as a framework for gamification design. Second, this study provides possible indications for the causal gamification effect explained in GLT i.e. that gamification can produce change only if the targeted behavior can itself be changed. Namely, GEs were incorporated in activities, that sensing students tend to avoid, that is, in activities intuitive students by their nature tend to do. Hence, this study assumed that the change will happen only in the behavior of sensing students. This assumption was indicated (H1 and H2). Third, this study supports the moderating GLT theory: 1) a sensing tendency had a significant positive effect on students' effort and interest in the T1 group. This indicates that implementing Trading GE in learning activities that (sensing) students tend to avoid, can increase their cognitive engagement; 2) sensing tendency increased the usage frequency of learning materials (Online Active engagement) and had a positive effect on students' emotional engagement in the T2 group. Specifically, sensing students expressed higher interest and enjoyment while interacting with PBL, in comparison to intuitive. To summarize, having a sensing tendency statistically improved students' behavioral and emotional engagement in T2 and cognitive engagement in the T1 group. Finally, by showing a significant difference in the effect of two gamified interventions on students' engagement and experience, this study highlights the importance of exploring and comparing multiple GEs to find the most effective gamification design for a particular user group [8]. Further, despite the ongoing criticism of using the PBL in gamification intervention [11], this study showed that if designed properly, the PBL can positively influence users' engagement and experience.

Aside the contributions, we also identified limitations of this study. First, the subjective nature of the engagement survey may have shown an inaccurate engagement picture and thus affected the H3 results. Next, because this study is a pioneer in investigating LTs as personal moderators of gamification, it is not possible to state that the outcomes of this study are generalizable, however, they do provide indications for further research. Further, the extrinsic motivator (the bonus points) may affect students' intrinsic motivation. Also, since students were able to meet face-to-face during the course, there is a possibility that they have discussed the gamified vs. non-gamified course version, producing a possible bias. Finally, the empirical work is based on a comparative study which concerns a limited number of students and for which the variables are not controlled (random distribution in the different groups, influence of the conditions of the tests, etc.). Therefore, the results obtained may be debatable and could be attributed to factors other than those discussed (LTs).

To overcome these limitations and reduce the possibility of validity errors new interventions will be created. First, the PBL and the Trading system will again be applied, but in a way to encourage intuitive students to behave 'more like' sensing students. If such an environment succeeds in enhancing ACP and the engagement of intuitive students, it will once again confirm that gamification can succeed only if it targets behavior that can truly change. On the other hand, if no changes occur this will mean that PBL and Trading GE do not affect intuitive students. Results like these would then require further investigation for other GEs that can lead to improvement. Besides, results on the moderating effect of LTs in a gamified environment that is adjusted to fit sensing students' needs will provide broader knowledge on how LTs influence gamification outcomes concerning different gamification design and to both 'panes' of perception dimension.

References

1. Landers, R.: Developing a theory of gamified learning: linking serious games and gamification of learning. Simul. Gaming **45**(6), 752–768 (2014)
2. Cassidy, S.: Learning Styles: An overview of theories, models, and measures. Educ. Psychol. **24**(4), 419–444 (2004)
3. Felder, M., Brent, R.: Teaching and Learning STEM, 2nd edn. Josses Bass (2016)
4. Kirschner, P.A.: Stop propagating the learning styles myth. Comput. Educ. **106**, 166–171 (2017)
5. Armstrong, M., Landers, R.: An evaluation of gamified training: using narrative to improve reactions and learning. Simul. Gaming (2018)
6. Greenberg, B.S., Sherry, J., Lachlan, K., Lucas, K., Holmstrom, A.: Orientations to video games among gender and age groups. Simul. Gaming **41**(2), 238–259 (2010)

7. Koivisto, J., Hamari, J.: Demographic differences in perceived benefits from gamification. Comput. Hum. Behav. **35**, 179–188 (2014)
8. Buckley, P., Doyle, E.: Individualizing gamification: an investigation of the impact of learning styles and personality traits on the efficacy of gamification using a prediction market. Comput. Educ. **106**, 43–55 (2017)
9. Zaric,N., Lukarov, V., Schroder, U.: The Exploratory study of Personalized Gamification Application, submitted to the International Journal of Serious Games, 10th edn. (2020)
10. Zaric, N., Scepanovic, S.: Gamification of e-learning based on learning styles–design model and implementation. In: Proceedings of the World Conference on E-learning in Corporate, Government, Healthcare, and Higher Education (2018)
11. Toda, A.M.: A taxonomy of game elements for gamification in educational contexts: proposal and evaluation. In: 19th International Conference on Advanced Learning Technologies (ICALT), Brazil, pp. 84–88 (2019)
12. Felder, R., Spurlin, J.: Applications, reliability and validity of the Index of Learning Styles. Int. J. Eng. Educ. **21**(1), 103–112 (2005)
13. Högberg, J., Hamari, J., Wästlund, E.: Gameful experience questionnaire: an instrument for measuring the perceived gamefulness of system use. User Model. User-Adap. Inter. **29**, 619–660 (2019)
14. Field, A.: Discovering Statistics Using SPSS, 4th edn. SAGE Publications Ltd., London (2013)

7 P's of Gamification: A Strategic Design Tool for Ideation of Gamified Solutions

Helder Ferreira[1,2](✉), Catarina Roseira[1](✉), and Rui Patrício[2](✉)

[1] FEP - School of Economics and Management, University of Porto, Rua Dr. Roberto Frias, 4200-464 Porto, Portugal
`hld.ferreira@gmail.com`, `catarina.roseira@fep.up.pt`
[2] UNIDCOM/IADE - Unidade de Investigação em Design e Comunicação, Av. D. Carlos I, 4, 1200-649 Lisboa, Portugal
`rui.patricio@universidadeeuropeia.pt`

Abstract. The creation of a strategic design tool to develop multidisciplinary teams' gamification capability can contribute to a better understanding of this concept, stimulate collaborative work, and contribute to the ideation of creative gamified solutions. In this context, the paper proposes a structured method - '7 P's of gamification - which offers a broad and comprehensive perspective of gamification based on a step-by-step process. It allows team members with limited knowledge of gamification to understand it and start to use it in a real case scenario. This method was tested in a fully online workshop that challenged four teams (nineteen students in total) to ideate gamified solutions for a Lisbon municipality, which established the conditions and desired goals. The collaborative effort between team members and facilitators during the entire process was supported by digital collaborative tools (digital workspace and communication platform). Before the workshop, a training session was conducted with all participants, followed by a survey and semi-structured interviews, conducted immediately after the workshop. Based on the findings, it was possible to conclude that participants positively assessed the '7 P's of gamification' method. This type of approach engages participants in the ideation process and facilitates the ideation of gamified solutions. The presence of facilitators was also positively highlighted, which reinforces the importance of having this type of 'actors' when conducting gamification practices. Further research is needed to assess this method in other work contexts as well as the influence on adoption, implementation, and outcomes of gamification.

Keywords: Gamification · Ideation · Management

1 Introduction

Gamification has been increasingly used in many areas of business attracting scholars and practitioners [1–3]. However, many doubts remain about the actual influence of gamification tools in work contexts. As referred by Morschheuser et al. [4] most gamification efforts fail due to poor understanding of how gamification should be designed

© Springer Nature Switzerland AG 2020
I. Marfisi-Schottman et al. (Eds.): GALA 2020, LNCS 12517, pp. 146–156, 2020.
https://doi.org/10.1007/978-3-030-63464-3_14

and implemented. Lack of managerial knowledge may also be a barrier to introducing gamification in organizations [5]. Thus, adequate training on design processes [6] and practical guidance on designing gamification solutions [4] seem needed.

Building on existing literature on gamification frameworks, a strategic design method (the 7 P's of gamification) was developed to help users ideate gamified solutions. Moreover, this method helps users understand the gamification concept, e.g., its principles, benefits, applicability, and usability.

The method was tested in a two-week online event with the participation of four groups of university students from several backgrounds (e.g., design, computer management, marketing, and publicity). The event's main goal was the ideation of a gamified solution to a challenge set by the Lisbon municipality (hereinafter, LM). LM presented the challenge and defined its conditions, rules (e.g., time, physical resources) and specific goals. One week after, the '7 P's of gamification method' was presented to participants, who had a week to explore ideas and the concept of gamification. The following week, each team had four hours to work cooperatively in virtual rooms to ideate a gamified solution and later present to LM. After the completion of the event, all participants were invited to fill a survey to evaluate the gamification design method. Adding to this we interviewed six of them and the representative of the LM.

This study provides critical contributions to the existing literature. The results suggest that the use of this gamification strategic design process may contribute to enhance and accelerate knowledge on gamification in organizational contexts and ideation. By linking these two separate streams of literature, this study proposes that a structured gamification process is essential to motivate and ensure that participants understand the gamification concept when doing and facilitating ideation. Besides these theoretical implications, it also provides some practical insights. This method facilitates the design of gamified solutions in a short time, event with participants with limited knowledge of gamification, by engaging participants in the ideation process. It also allows aligning different participants' perspectives in a gamification solution's ideation.

This article is structured as follows. Section 2 reviews relevant literature on gamification and ideation. Section 3 presents the gamification strategic design method. Section 4 presents the research methodology and Sect. 5, the results. Section 6 closes paper with the discussion of findings, conclusions, and suggestions to further research.

2 Literature Review

2.1 Gamification on Management Field

Gamification aims to motivate and influence people to change behaviours, develop skills, drive innovation [7] and, essentially, to solve problems [2]. However, there are a lot of barriers to introduce gamification in work contexts, as the lack of managerial knowledge [5]. Hassan and Hamari [8] refer several gaps in understanding what gamification is, if it effectively works, or how it can be applied. For instance, poor design gamified experiences [3] and the use of inappropriate game design elements [9] can generate conflicts, tensions [10] and social pressure over employees [11]. This reinforces the importance of how to design inspirational gamified experiences [12] and to define the desired goals and metrics to assess the gamified process [3].

In the same line, Landers [6] claims for adequate training or knowledge of design processes to legitimate gamification implementation. Also, Morschheuser et al. [4] call for methodological insights on designing gamification. So, despite the existence of various design approaches [13], there is still a lack of knowledge of the gamification concept in the academic and business field and a lack of methodological guidelines to ideate, design, and adopt gamification in work contexts. Particularly, the ideation stage has received less attention in the building of gamified experiences which seems critical to design gamified solutions [4]. Responding to Morschheuser et al. [4] call, this study proposes a strategic design method that can be used by people with different backgrounds and distinct levels of knowledge about gamification. This method follows a step-by-step process to promote and increase participants' understanding and experience about gamification, stimulate collaborative behaviours [9] and encourage teamwork [14] to facilitate the ideation of customized gamified solutions.

2.2 Ideation

Idea generation (ideation) has been studied in both fields of creativity and innovation management [15] and is a key step to solve complex problems [16], and a key factor to the success of organizations [17]. The increased generation of new ideas includes other types of solutions (i.e., not only products and services) and has been expanding the traditional sources of ideation [15, 18]. Moreover, some of the challenges for organizations in the ideation stage lie in understanding the individual motivation of participants, the best incentives for people to participate, and the quality of their inputs [18], which reinforces the importance of how to measure the ideation quality [16, 19]. Björk and Magnusson [15] state that to support and facilitate the ideation process, knowledge about what influences the quality of the ideas created is critical what led them to suggest the creation of 'arenas' to support and facilitate innovation to take place. The idea is to enable the interaction between people increasing connectivity with other people inside or outside the company, stimulate cooperation and creativity, and promote knowledge-sharing. Diversity of members (e.g. with different backgrounds) contribute to the process of creating innovative proposals (ideation) [20]. However, despite unclear answers about what it is the best option (i.e., formal or informal), this study follows a formalization of activities providing a clear direction in the ideation stage [15], although taking some risks such as missing of more peripheral opportunities.

Following, the next chapter describes the proposed gamification design method.

3   Ideation of Gamified Solutions with the 7 P's of Gamification

Werbach and Hunter [21] suggest a design framework to develop gamified systems constituted by six steps: define business objectives, delineate target behaviours, describe players, devise activity cycles, don't forget the fun, and deploy the appropriate tools. Based on these guidelines and considering the importance of ideation stage to the process of creating gamified experiences [4], a full online and strategic design method - 7 P's of gamification - was developed to train multidisciplinary people about gamification and

Fig. 1. Elements of 7 P's of gamification ideation method

to help them to ideate gamification solutions. The method is structured in seven stages that are illustrated in Fig. 1.

Each step has a set of activities: (1) identify the Problem and the need for a gamified solution instead of other solution; (2) identify the Players, i.e. the target audience, (3) identify the 'driving Purpose' to engage the target audience and preserve their interest; (4) select the Place (physical, online or both) where the game will be played; (5) define the Procedures, i.e. rules, components, mechanics and dynamics; (6) design the Player Experience i.e., the player journey; and (7) strategically build the Program Evaluation, defining the main goals, key performance indicators, desired behaviours as well the metrics and analytical tools to assess and monitor the gamified experience.

The method is delivered in a full online and collaborative design tool (Fig. 2). Participants must go through every step but not necessarily in a pre-determined sequence.

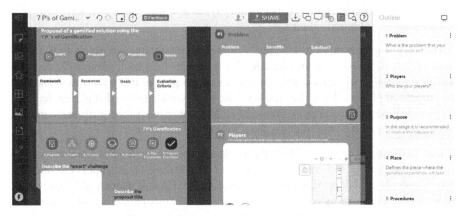

Fig. 2. Collaborative and online environment

As illustrated in Fig. 2, the participants should check the explanations about each 'P' on the sidebar that was designed to be an encouraging and learning tool for participants. It also allows the search of examples of game design elements, components, mechanics, and dynamics [22]. As a result, it is expected an increase in the quality of suggestions of potential gamified solutions to use in work contexts.

Current times increasingly call for online design processes. This method facilitates cooperative work online allowing participants from different locations to brainstorm ideas to achieve the best gamified solution. The collaborative screen (Fig. 2) has two blocks. On the right side, each 'P' has an available white space for teams to express their opinions and ideas in a free and creative way. On the left side, the block is divided into two parts. The block on top describes the challenge, i.e. the context, resources allocated to the project, goals, and criteria to evaluate the gamified proposal. The part below of left block is reserved for the presentation of the proposed solution in a structured way covering and detailing each 'P'. Videos, photos, slide presentations and other types of files are welcome to strengthen the gamified solution proposal.

The 7 P's of Gamification uses digital collaborative tools, e.g. a workspace for visual collaboration and a video communication platform, to provide an immersive online experience. It also includes facilitators specifically trained by the researchers to help the teams with the digital tools and the 7 P's gamification method and guide them along the online process. Next, each 'P' is described in more detail.

Problem: In this first step, participants must identify the problem that needs to be solved and why a gamified solution should be used. The right identification of the problem requires an understanding of its nature and causes, which calls for participants to research, collect and analyse data, namely about the organization that owns the problem, the relationships between people and their needs, and the resources available (e.g., time, budget, technology) for the gamified solution.

Players: An in-depth knowledge of the target audience, e.g. customers, employees, or communities, is necessary to understand what drives them. Players are different and what motivates one person may have the opposite effect on someone else [7]. Thus, it is crucial to be aware of players' personality types and individual characteristics [23] when ideating a gamified solution.

Purpose: For gamification to effectively influence behaviours and psychological outcomes [7], it is necessary to inspire affective responses [12] from players. To do so, it is critical to design a gamified solution that fits the purpose of the organization and also the purpose of players. Thus, the ideation must be player-centric so that players feel that the gamification solution aims at producing results that answers their goals and concerns and makes them part of the solution, thus 'touching their hearts'.

Place: In this stage, the space where the gamified experience occurs is defined: it can be virtual, physical (e.g., web and mobile applications, software, boardgame) or a combination of both [24, 25]. It provides the context where players will interact and engage with each other, corresponding to the social dimension. Participants must analyse available resources as they condition feasible alternatives.

Procedures: The engagement of the target audience cannot depend solely on extrinsic motivators [7]. Gamification's success calls for more intrinsic than extrinsic features. Thus, it is necessary to define the type of gamification, e.g., content or structural [26]; the rules, components, mechanics and dynamics; and if it will be a multiplayer or solitary player [24].

Play (er) Experience: At this stage, the experience should be presented as a play journey [7] showing the architecture of the gamified solution, i.e., how it looks like and which effects are expected. Gamification requires a strategic view [3] that considers the specific circumstances where the gamified solution is needed and justified.

Program Evaluation: The sweet spot for gamification [24] is achieved when organizations' and the players' goals are aligned: when players achieve their goals, organizations also achieve theirs [7]. Thus, this alignment is a main aspect of gamification [3] and deserves full attention during the ideation stage. To evaluate a gamified solution, it is necessary to previously determine (i) the objectives (e.g., behaviours that need change); (ii) what desired individual and business outcomes are we trying to achieve; (iii) appropriate metrics (as the progress of players) to measure its success; (iv) a revision cycle to make adjustments to maintain players engaged with the experience, something that is not always done after the implementation of gamification [27].

After ideation, if the organization's decision-maker approves gamified solution, the following steps are to prototype, implement e.g., test a pilot, and monitor the results [4]. Those steps are beyond the scope of this study.

4 Research Methodology

This study adopts an exploratory case study approach [28] to better understand the 7 P's of gamification as an online strategic ideation method. Specifically, this study seeks (1) to understand the 7 P's of gamification as a tool to the ideation of gamified solutions, (ii) identify limitations, opportunities and suggestions to improve the 7 P's of gamification method to apply in work contexts, (iii) the importance of facilitators in the process, and (iv) what are the motivations and expectations for using gamification hereafter in organizational settings and individual level.

Case Study: The case selected was the 'OnBoard' event, where nineteen students from distinct areas gathered in four multidisciplinary groups to answer a call to develop a gamified solution for a problem proposed by LM. The teams used the '7 P's of gamification', a method that was developed for and first used in this event to support participants on the ideation of gamified solutions. Figure 3 presents an overview of the event.

Fig. 3. 'OnBoard' Event

Data Collection and Analysis: The study used a mixed methods approach, combining data from an online survey, direct observations and semi-structured interviews [29]. Regarding direct observation, researchers were 'silent' observers along the event to analyse how participants interacted with each other, with facilitators and with the 7 P's of gamification; their notes were a relevant complement to interpret data from the survey and the interviews. After the closing of the event, three participants and three facilitators covering the four groups and a representative from LM accepted to be semi-interviewed to get their perceptions about the process; participant interviews average 30 min and LM interview lasted one hour. Also, 16 participants were surveyed about the outcomes of participating in the 'OnBoard' event.

The data from the interviews was content analysed, a method that analyses written, oral or transcribed texts [30]. NVivo 12 software was used, which is recommended for this type of study [31]. Also, descriptive statistics was used to analyse data from the survey. In the Results section, interviewed participants are identified as P2, P4 and P6, facilitators as F1, F3 and F5, and the representative of LM as E1.

5   Results

Findings reveal the incipient diffusion of gamification concept, at least in the university context of this event, as 38% of respondents did not know the term gamification. As lack of knowledge can hinder the development and adoption of gamification, it is suggested that organizations evaluate participants' knowledge before launching a gamification process.

Regarding the two stages i.e., the presentation of the event and the gamification workshop, a 5-point Likert scale (1-not at all; 5-very much) was used for participants to evaluate how motivating the challenge was and how useful was the work session about gamification. Participants considered the challenge very motivating (mean: 4.69; SD: 0.48) and evaluated rather positively the workshop session (mean 4.44; SD 0,73).

The interviews reveal participant perceptions about the event, which is viewed as a means to (i) encourage new ideas and creativity, (ii) contribute to the understanding of the concept of gamification, and (iii) guide the participants on the ideation of a gamified solution. As P4 says, *"it was only after the presentation that I found a proposal that turned out to be the final; it helped me a lot to organise my mind and to idealize how I could come up with a viable solution, as it also ended up organising* [my ideas about] *what gamification was.* F3 considers that *"with the workshop, the teams, in addition to being more motivated, started working to find solutions, as well as understanding a little bit about what gamification is and what are the steps, I think that helped a lot"*. In a similar vein, P6 believes that *"the second moment was very important because it explained what gamification is and what you expected from this project"*. Thus, findings suggest that events as the intermediate workshop are crucial to train participants about gamification, making them more at ease and motivated to use it.

Participants were asked to evaluate their experience using a 1-10 scale (1-very negative; 10-very positive). 88% of respondents answered between 8-10, revealing a very positive perception of the overall experience. When asked to rate the possibility of recommending the 7 P's of gamification using a 1-10 scale (1- not at all likely; 10-extremely likely), 62,6% of respondents answered between 8 – 10, 18.1% answered 7, 6.3% answered 6 and the others 12,5% answered 4. These are encouraging results about the use and recommendation of the '7 P's of gamification'.

The interviewees confirmed its usefulness on the ideation of a gamified solution and revealed the factors for this positive evaluation: design (e.g., useful and easy to work; referred by all) and guidance of participants (mentioned by P2, F3, P4, F5, P6); motivation (mentioned by F3, F5), and objectivity, innovation, teamwork, integration with digital tools and a holistic view (each mentioned by one interviewee).

From the perspective of the 'customer' of the gamified solution (the LM representative), the proposed method is well structured and facilitates the creative and cooperative work of teams as well the presentation of all gamified solutions. In his own words, "*I recognize two advantages immediately: one is that it is a set of structured steps that stick in the memory and the other is that they [the steps]focus on specific gamification issues. I had never even seen a methodology that addresses this various concepts and that made a lot of sense for the practical case; if I were to present solutions, the subjects that I would like to address are all defined in this methodology*" (E1). Interviews with participants and researchers' observation revealed interesting factors about the role of facilitators. Their role is based on more experience and knowledge about the topic and leadership skills. Essentially facilitators' role comprises helping, supporting, and motivating the participants as well as offering other perspectives to solve problems and find solutions. This reveals the importance of adding this role of facilitators with the '7 P's of gamification' in the ideation stage of designing gamified solutions.

To get a full evaluation from participants, the interviewees were asked to identify possible caveats in the use of the method. Findings reveal aspects that can limit its use even if they are not dimensions of the 7 P's of gamification alone; here, the most prominent difficulty was the learning curve of digital tools (F1, P2, F3, P4) that is distinct for each participant, followed by the short duration of the experience (P2, F3), and the lack of early availability of the digital workspace (F3) or even restrictions of digital workspace e.g., zoom amplitude (P4, F5). Other limitations are related with doubts about specific steps that delayed the overall understanding of the method (P2, P4). F3 also identified a lack of competences of some participants in this level of complexity.

As both the method and this study have an exploratory nature, suggestions from participants on how to improve the 7 P's of gamification were collected. As expected, some suggestions are linked with the identified caveats. Interviewees provided the following ideas of improvement: add one more workshop about gamification to gain more experience, provide the digital workspace earlier to facilitate their use and to make participation and to brainstorm easier (referred by F1, P2, F3, F5); review some aspects of the design (e.g., space extra to write, revision of texts about the P's, namely the extension; referred by F5); include more participants with different backgrounds to leverage multidisciplinary skills and perspectives to benefit the final solution (F1); increase the duration of the event (F1, P6); test the 7 P's in an analogical and physical environment (F5); and test integration with other digital tools (P4). The survey provided some additional suggestions, as follows: "*Placing extra space for extra work*" (R1); "*the only change I would make would be the way of presentation…otherwise, I loved the methodology used.*" (R7); "*I really loved having participated in the project! I just believe that like many, I was unaware of the digital tool, we could have had a little more time in the workshop*" (R11). It confirms the need for revision and the opportunity to improve the '7 P's of gamification' method and the overall participant experience.

Moving from the ideation to the future use of gamification in work contexts, interviewees expect to have the opportunity to create or customize gamified solutions to produce innovative solutions. F5 states that "*I think it makes perfect sense and it makes the work of organizations much easier and it can thus create very interesting ideas for the company and also for the consumer*". Survey results confirm the interest of gamification to solve organizations' problems (mean: 4.13; SD:0.81, in a 5-point Likert Scale). This reveals the importance of extending the training of gamification in educational and business contexts to help people get better results with gamification tools.

As to the use of gamification in organizations, the representative of LM believes that to adopt and implement gamified solutions successfully, organizations should have (i) a 'champion' who owns the gamification project; (ii) a proper organizational context (e.g., culture, leadership, adequate work environment), (iii) a voluntary participation strategy and (iv) a strategic and long-term vision to gather positive results. In his own words, "*the implementation phase implies that organization has someone, a 'champion' who takes this forward, believes and has resources and power for that*" (E1).

6 Discussion and Conclusions

This exploratory case study unveils the perceptions of participants in the first '7 P's of gamification' event, an online and strategic method to ideate gamified solutions. This method integrated with digital tools (e.g., digital workspace and communication platform) follows a design process to help people, either internal or external of organization, with distinct backgrounds and levels of expertise on gamification to collaborate in the ideation stage of a gamification process. In line with existing concerns about the quality of ideas [19], the '7 P's of gamification' looks for quality rather than quantity of gamified solutions, which can be achieved with the use of a structured process, as the method proposed in this study.

The main goal of the paper was to evaluate the '7 P's of gamification' as a tool to ideate gamified solutions, namely, to identify its strengths and areas of improvement, and its potential of application in organizational and work contexts. Findings show a very positive evaluation from participants. The study supports the idea that the quality of gamified solutions benefits from the use of this type of approach, as it helps, guides and engages participants in the gamification' ideation process. Results also confirm that increasing the knowledge about the gamification concept facilitates the creation of gamified solutions in a short time. This contributes to answer to Landers [6] concerns about the need of adequate training to legitimate gamification implementation.

Another interesting finding regards the importance of facilitators, which emerged in this study as a consensually recognized means to facilitate collaboration and encourage innovation [7], help with technology, explain the gamification concept, explore the 7 P's of gamification's usability and flexibility, motivate teams to cooperate and guide them to achieve a gamified solution. Despite the global positive evaluation, some caveats (above all technical) and suggestions were identified, which encourage practitioners and researchers to improve, use and test this design method, e.g. in work contexts.

At the end of the event, participants were rather receptive to adopt gamification to solve problems in organizational contexts. It is important to recall that this was their participation in the ideation of a gamified solution. This suggests that more training and knowledge on gamification is an effective way to promote good practices, avoid misalignments and misunderstandings as argued by some authors [3, 6], and foster its use.

Finally, the results of this first test in an educational context reveal the importance of the ideation stage on the development of gamified solutions, in line with Morschheuser et al. [4] encourage additional research, namely the validation of these findings in organizational and work contexts. For instance, researchers may focus on the role of middle managers as facilitators of the ideation process and, more broadly, of the adoption and implementation of gamification solutions. Future work may take the ideation output (i.e. the gamified solutions) of the '7 P's of gamification' method to the following phases of a gamification process: prototyping, implementing and monitoring, as a way to test its effectiveness and potential to leverage the use of gamification. Finally, this study envisions the '7 P's of gamification' to be used in a multidisciplinary and bottom-up approach, e.g. in a collaborative process between MM of different departments. Future research may compare this bottom-up approach with top-down approaches (e.g. gamified solutions imposed by top managers), in terms of process and of organizational and individual outcomes of the gamification experiences.

References

1. Werbach, K.: (Re)Defining gamification: a process approach. In: Spagnolli, A., Chittaro, L., Gamberini, L. (eds.) PERSUASIVE 2014. LNCS, vol. 8462, pp. 266–272. Springer, Cham (2014). https://doi.org/10.1007/978-3-319-07127-5_23
2. Huotari, K., Hamari, J.: A definition for gamification: anchoring gamification in the service marketing literature. Electronic Markets 27(1), 21–31 (2016). https://doi.org/10.1007/s12 525-015-0212-z
3. Wanick, V., Bui, H.: Gamification in Management: a systematic review and research directions. Int. J. Serious Games 6(2), 57–74 (2019)
4. Morschheuser, B., et al.: How to gamify? A method for designing gamification. In: Proceedings of the 50th Hawaii International Conference on System Sciences. University of Hawai'i at Manoa (2017)
5. Woźniak, J.: Some factors hindering acceptance of three gamification solutions in motivation systems, in small and medium enterprises. Manag. Dyn. Knowl. Econ. 5(4), 663–680 (2017)
6. Landers, R.N.: Gamification misunderstood: how badly executed and rhetorical gamification obscures its transformative potential. J. Manag. Inquiry 28(2), 137–140 (2019)
7. Dale, S.: Gamification: making work fun, or making fun of work? Bus. Inf. Rev. 31(2), 82–90 (2014)
8. Hassan, L., Hamari, J.: Gameful civic engagement: a review of the literature on gamification of e-participation. Government Inf. Q. 101461 (2020)
9. Koivisto, J., Hamari, J.: The rise of motivational information systems: a review of gamification research. Int. J. Inf. Manage. 45, 191–210 (2019)
10. Perryer, C., et al.: Enhancing workplace motivation through gamification: transferrable lessons from pedagogy. Int. J. Manag. Educ. 14(3), 327–335 (2016)
11. Mitchell, R., Schuster, L., Jin, H.S.: Gamification and the impact of extrinsic motivation on needs satisfaction: making work fun? J. Bus. Res. 106, 323–330 (2020)
12. Robson, K., et al.: Is it all a game? Understanding the principles of gamification. Bus. Horiz. 58(4), 411–420 (2015)

13. Mora, A., Riera, D., González, C., Arnedo-Moreno, J.: Gamification: a systematic review of design frameworks. J. Comput. Higher Educ. **29**(3), 516–548 (2017). https://doi.org/10.1007/s12528-017-9150-4
14. Morschheuser, B., et al.: How games induce cooperation? A study on the relationship between game features and we-intentions in an augmented reality game. Comput. Hum. Behav. **77**, 169–183 (2017)
15. Björk, J., Magnusson, M.: Where do good innovation ideas come from? exploring the influence of network connectivity on innovation idea quality. J. Prod. Innov. Manag. **26**(6), 662–670 (2009)
16. Briggs, R.O., Reinig, B.A.: Bounded ideation theory. J. Manag. Inf. Syst. **27**(1), 123–144 (2010)
17. Heising, W.: The integration of ideation and project portfolio management—a key factor for sustainable success. Int. J. Project Manage. **30**(5), 582–595 (2012)
18. Zimmerling, E., et al.: Exploring the influence of common game elements on ideation output and motivation. J. Bus. Res. **94**, 302–312 (2019)
19. Reinig, B.A., Briggs, R.O., Nunamaker, J.F.: On the measurement of ideation quality. J. Manag. Inf. Syst. **23**(4), 143–161 (2007)
20. Hartson, R., Pyla, P.S.: The UX Book: Agile UX Design for a Quality User Experience. Morgan Kaufmann (2018)
21. Werbach, K., Hunter, D.: For the Win: How Game Thinking Can Revolutionize Your Business. Wharton Digital Press (2012)
22. Friedrich, J., et al.: Incentive design and gamification for knowledge management. J. Bus. Res. **106**, 341–352 (2020)
23. Hamari, J., Koivisto, J., Sarsa, H.: Does gamification work? A literature review of empirical studies on gamification. In: 2014 47th Hawaii International Conference on System Sciences, pp. 3025–3034 (2014)
24. Burke, B.: Gamify: How Gamification Motivates People to Do Extraordinary Things. Bibliomotion. Inc., (2014)
25. Patrício, R., Moreira, A.C., Zurlo, F.: Gamification approaches to the early stage of innovation. Creativity Innov. Manag. **27**(4), 499–511 (2018)
26. Darejeh, A., Salim, S.S.: Gamification solutions to enhance software user engagement - a systematic review. Int. J. Hum.-Comput. Interact. **32**(8), 613–642 (2016)
27. Rosmansyah, Y.: Gamification framework for designing online training and collaborative working system in statistics Indonesia. In: 2016 International Conference on Information Technology Systems and Innovation (ICITSI). IEEE (2016)
28. Yin, R.K.: Case Study Research: Design and Methods, vol. 5, 3rd edn. Sage, Thousand Oaks (2003)
29. Creswell, W.J.: Research Design Qualitative, Quantitative, and Mixed Methods Approaches (2009)
30. Insch, G.S., Moore, J.E., Murphy, L.D.: Content analysis in leadership research: examples, procedures, and suggestions for future use. Leadersh. Q. **8**(1), 1–25 (1997)
31. Feng, X., Behar-Horenstein, L.: Maximizing NVivo utilities to analyze open-ended responses. Qual. Rep. **24**(3), 563–571 (2019)

Motivation in Gamification: Constructing a Correlation Between Gamification Achievements and Self-determination Theory

Brunella Botte[1](✉), Sander Bakkes[2](✉), and Remco Veltkamp[2](✉)

[1] DASIC, Digital Administration and Social Innovation Center, Link Campus University, Rome, Italy
b.botte@unilink.it
[2] Utrecht Center for Game Research, Utrecht University, Utrecht, The Netherlands
{s.c.j.bakkes,r.c.veltkamp}@uu.nl

Abstract. This paper presents an analysis of the general concept of motivation and how it is fostered in gamified solutions for learning, particularly in the context of self-determination theory. The analysis leverages academic literature on the topics of motivation, player engagement, basic psychological needs, and the ability of video games to potentially satisfy these needs. Specifically, the paper contributes to the field of game-based learning by (1) proposing a correlation between gamification achievements and basic psychological needs, as derived from self-determination theory, (2) analysing an already effective game-based learning platform (SOLOLEARN) for mechanics that do – and that do not – contribute to the basic psychological needs of individual users.

Keywords: Gamification · Self-determination theory · Adaptive gamification · Gamification design

1 Introduction

In recent years, one may observe a rapid increase in adopting gamified solutions for non-gaming contexts (i.e., the use of gamification and game mechanics for purposes other than entertainment) [1]. Repurposing of such gamification techniques is typically aimed at supporting and enhancing a user's motivation, creating engagement for specific activities of everyday life, and fostering the training of specific skills. More specifically, the diversity of domains in which gamification is adopted is noteworthy; from personal improvement to learning, from business training to marketing. As a result, the target audience of gamified solutions is highly diverse too. As gamification deals with motivation, it has to be taken into account – when designing gamified solutions – that distinct people are usually motivated by different things in different ways, and therefore, by distinct game interactions (i.e., as resulting from distinct game mechanics like rewards, achievements, etc.).

© Springer Nature Switzerland AG 2020
I. Marfisi-Schottman et al. (Eds.): GALA 2020, LNCS 12517, pp. 157–166, 2020.
https://doi.org/10.1007/978-3-030-63464-3_15

Indeed, many scholars have investigated the nature and origin of human motivation, highlighting a difference between the motivation that arises from the individual, compared to that which is fueled by the desire to achieve an external goal [2–4]. Behaviourists considered behaviour as the result of the stimulus-response relation [2] and the studies carried out by Skinner introduced the concept of reinforcement [3], as a fundamental element that fosters the acquisition and performance of a specific behaviour. As studies about the psychology of motivation developed, it was indicated that reinforcement was typical of extrinsic motivation. White [4] in 1959 stated that behaviour is driven by *innate psychological tendencies*, in particular, *competence*. Activities and behaviour performed to satisfy these psychological tendencies are considered by White as intrinsically rewarding and satisfying [2].

Leveraging White's work, Ryan & Deci analysed intrinsic motivation [5] and identified the psychological needs that, according to self-determination theory (SDT), are the basis of a users' intrinsic motivation[1]. At its core, SDT proposes that three main intrinsic needs are involved in self-determination of an individual; needs which motivate the self to initiate behavior and specify nutrients that are essential for psychological health and well-being. These needs are considered to be universal and innate, and concern the need for competence, autonomy, and social relations (relatedness). Ryan *et al.*, building upon the foundation provided by SDT, extensively investigated how motivation is fostered in video games, and concludes that players may indeed experience gameplay as an intrinsically rewarding experience [6]. Follow-up studies by Przybylski *et al.* [7] and Ryan *et al.* [8] strongly argued that the video game medium, because of the experiences that it often creates for its users, may perfectly fit and satisfy the three basic psychological needs of SDT: autonomy, competence and relatedness [7, 8].

As we will show in the remainder of this article, one may safely assume that the basic psychological needs that are essential for creating intrinsically motivating video game experiences, are indeed similarly important for creating intrinsically motivating gamified learning experiences. In the upcoming sections, we will specifically contribute to the field of game-based learning by (1) proposing a correlation between gamification achievements and basic psychological needs, as derived from self-determination theory, (2) analysing an already effective game-based learning platform (SOLOLEARN) for mechanics that do – and that do not – contribute to the basic psychological needs of individual users. This study represents the first step of a broader research that intends to investigate if adaptivity in gamification, based upon the satisfaction of the basic psychological needs can improve the effectiveness of gamified solutions.

2   SDT and Motivation in Video Games

According to self-determination theory (SDT), personal growth and well-being of people are dependent on the satisfaction of three basic psychological needs [5], namely autonomy, competence and relatedness. Focusing specifically on video game experiences, studies have examined the ways by which video game engagement shapes psychological processes and influences well-being [7], and have indicated that both the appeal and

---

[1] The topic of intrinsic motivation itself is explored in more detail by cognitive evaluation theory (CET); one of the six sub-theories of which self-determination theory (SDT) is composed [5].

well-being effects of video games are based in their potential to satisfy basic psychological needs for competence, autonomy, and relatedness [8]. The question that Ryan *et al.* attempts to answer is "Why do so many people spend so much time engaged in video games?" The first answer is that videogames are typically fun – unsurprisingly – but, more specifically, the engaging power of videogames lies in the experiences they provide [7]. The research carried out in order to apply SDT – and in particular SDT's sub-theory called cognitive evaluation theory (CET) [5] – to the domain of video games, illustrates that when autonomy and competence are supported through gameplay, video games were significantly more enjoyable and satisfying for players [9]. Subsequently, the study reveals that games with substantial social components such as Massive Multiplayer Online Role Playing Games (MMORPGs) were also able to satisfy the basic psychological need for relatedness.

It is important to note that, of course, other perspectives on video game motivation exist. A highly influential model that is applied to games in the communications domain, is the uses and gratifications theory [11], upon which Sherry and Lucas [12] have built a statistically validated taxonomy of reasons that individuals hold for engaging in video games (i.e., competition, challenge, diversion, fantasy, social interaction, arousal). However, an essential point to make about taxonomies that are focused on a player's individual goals for engaging in video games, is that SDT has a long tradition of showing that people's goals, even when fulfilled, do not always yield need satisfaction, and therefore do not always predict persistence or well-being outcomes [13].

Autonomy. The first of the three needs identified by the SDT and analyzed in relation to games is Autonomy [5], namely the sense of willingness in accomplishing tasks: the more the interest in the activity derives from personal interests, the higher is autonomy [5, 8]. This basic psychological need is fostered in video games, for instance, by providing choices, by using rewards as informational feedback or by giving non-controlling instructions. On the other side, all mechanics that implies lack of choice, control or freedom are perceived negatively and can undermine intrinsic motivation [8]. In regard to video games, the choice of playing a specific game, or to play a game at all, is already a manifestation of autonomy. But, at a deeper level, autonomy must be fostered through gameplay design choices: game designed to allow flexibility (and therefore the chance for the player to strategize), to offer the possibility to make significant choices over tasks and goals, and to assign rewards structured to provide feedback, are more effective in fostering autonomy than games that don't include those design elements.

Competence. The second basic psychological need analyzed in SDT is Competence, that is fostered by the chance to acquire new knowledge, skills or abilities, by the possibility to receive positive feedback and to participate in optimally structured challenges [5]. In games, the need for competence is largely satisfied: most gameplays are based on player's competence to accomplish game missions.

Relatedness. The third basic psychological need discussed in SDT is Relatedness, namely the feeling of being connected with others and to be relevant in the community [5]. This need is often satisfied in games where the multiplayer option is present or, even mostly, in MMORPGs, founded on the simultaneous interaction among players.

3   SDT and Motivation in Gamification

Focusing more specifically on gamification and game-based training, it is important to note a major distinction to video games. To reiterate, Ryan *et al.* [8] observes that the SDT basic psychological needs may be satisfied by video-game playing, and therefore can be considered predictors of enjoyability and engagement during the gaming experience. However, the choice to start playing a video is typically autonomous, and as such, intrinsically motivated – yielding an experience that is distinct to one that is initiated by force, coercion, or other external stimuli [7, 9]. This suggests a substantial difference between typical gamification & game-based training, and video games for two reasons. First, participation in gamified activities is not always voluntary, since performing these activities is often mandatory (*e.g.*, in learning contexts). Second, users that engage in gamified activities may not experience the activities as play (but, *e.g.*, as training); thereby imposing substantial constraints on the subjective experience – and by implication, need satisfaction – of the player.

Considering that activities targeted by a gamification strategy often cannot be changed, as they generally are part of, *e.g.,* a predefined training programme, a natural avenue for enhancing the effectiveness of gamified training programmes is to more directly target need satisfaction of the individual user [5]. Analogously to how user retention and general satisfaction in video games is often facilitated by considering individual differences between players – *e.g.*, via dynamic difficulty adjustment (DDA) [15] and experience-driven procedural content generation (EDPCG) [16] – one may investigate to what extent individual preferences for the satisfactions of distinct psychological needs can be modeled automatically from training interactions, and to what extent such a model can be used to automatically adapt gamification strategies to the individual user.

As a first step towards this overarching goal, we will now explore how distinct types of gamified achievements may be related to SDT psychological needs, and how these relationships can be exploited to the designer's advantage.

3.1   Gamification Achievements and Need Satisfaction

Here, we explore the relationship between gamification achievements and basic psychological needs – as derived from self-determination theory – and propose a (general) correlation table based on academic literature (Table 1). Taking input from SDT basic psychological needs, Kapp defined a taxonomy of achievement in games and gamification [17]. We build upon this taxonomy as a starting point to construct an analysis which includes the most commonly used achievements in gamification and show their expected impact on the three basic psychological needs of SDT.

For each achievement area of impact, we will now discuss the expected impact on the three basic psychological needs of SDT. The discussion is summarized in Table 1; different achievements impact distinctly on the three basic psychological needs: in some cases, they are satisfied (+), in others they have negative impact (−) and in still others no specific impact may be expected (NA).

- *Evaluation* achievements, and more specifically measurement ones, are strongly related to users' performance in accomplishing a target activity. On one side, this

Table 1. General correlation table of gamification achievements in relation to SDT basic psychological needs. Different achievements impact distinctly on the three basic psychological needs: in some cases, they are satisfied (+), in others they have negative impact (−) and in still others no specific impact may be expected (NA).

Area of impact	Achievement type	SDT Basic psychological needs		
		Autonomy	Competence	Relatedness
Evaluation	Measurement	−/+	+	NA
	Completion	*Cf.* completion contingent achievements		
Completion	Performance contingent	−	+	NA
	Non-Performance contingent	NA	NA	+
Goal orientation	Performance oriented	NA	+	NA
	Mastery oriented	+	+	NA
Predictability	Expected	+	+	NA
	Unexpected	NA	NA	NA
Functionality	Cosmetic	+	NA	+
	Functional	+	+	NA
Flexibility	Achievement as gift	−	NA	+
	Achievement as currency	+	+	NA
Clustering criteria	Incremental	NA	+	NA
	Meta-achievements	−	+	NA
Competitiveness	Competitive	+	+	+/−
	Non-competitive	NA	+	+

type of reward is perceived as strongly controlling, but the evaluative nature of the achievement, necessitating competence to be awarded, softens its controlling side [8, 13, 17, 18]. Evaluation achievements are very close in their function to positive feedback [18], considered effective in fostering intrinsic motivation. Completion achievements, namely achievements awarded just for participating in an activity, are examined in the *Performance* area of impact.

- *Completion* includes the two types of achievements that aim at giving to the player feedback just for participating in an activity, without evaluation. As measurement achievements, performance ones are awarded for completing activities that require competence, hence the perception of control is balanced by the need for competence [8, 13, 17, 18]. On the other hand, non-performance achievements are perceived as strongly controlling and therefore not fostering intrinsic motivation [8, 13, 17, 18].
- *Goal Orientation* area of impact is referred to the reasons why users are involved in target activities included in a gamified solution. *Performance contingent achievements*

are similar to evaluation achievements and are awarded in relation to how well a player performs in a single task [17]. On one side, this is perceived as controlling, but the evaluative nature of the achievement softens the controlling side [8, 13, 17, 18]. *Mastery oriented achievements* are awarded in relation to the effort the player puts in a task with the main objective to get better at it, in the long period [17]. The will to improve one's skill is mostly autonomous, and the final objective is competence, for this reason mastery-oriented achievements are mainly perceived as supporting motivation [8, 13, 17, 18].

- *Predictability* is the area of impact that makes explicit the relation between task performance and achievements. *Expected achievements* are directly related to the target activity, and therefore can be perceived as controlling [18], while *unexpected achievements* are totally unrelated to the target activity, and hence considered having no impact on intrinsic motivation [18].
- *Functionality* area of impact does not consider the nature of the reward, but rather the use of the reward that can be done within the gamified system. Established that both *cosmetic* and *functional* achievements are material achievements [18], they can have different roles within the gamified system. *Cosmetic* achievements can be exhibited, and as a consequence have meaning in the social context of the activity, enhancing relatedness [8, 13, 17]. *Functional achievements*, on the other hand, given their potentially strategic role in the gamified system, offer to users the chance to strategize, and therefore take advantage of competence.
- *Flexibility* area of impact is similar to the *Functionality* one. *Achievements as gifts* are awarded as a consequence of a target behavior, which may reasonably be expected to be perceived as controlling [18]. On the other hand, achievements as currency give to users the chance to use that currency according to their own will, fostering autonomy [8].
- *Clustering criteria* area of impact includes achievements that, although perceived as controlling [18], require competence to be awarded [8, 13, 17, 18].
- *Competitiveness* area of impact achievements can be *competitive* or *non-competitive*. Both of them have impact on competence, required to carry out the target activity, but have a slightly different impact on relatedness [8, 13, 17].

4   The SOLO LEARN Case Study

To provide an illustrative example of how the general correlations that are summarized in Table 1 can be utilized, we here present a case study of the popular and effective SOLOLEARN training platform for learning how to code[2]. We will show that – while SOLOLEARN is rated by gamification scholars among the best gamified applications for learning [19] – it still falls short in catering for specific psychological needs. In the case study, we will highlight potential venues for improvement, which indeed can reasonably be assumed to be applicable for other gamified applications for learning.

SOLOLEARN is a mobile application for learning coding skills, with elements of gamification as support for users' motivation. Specifically, here we examine SOLOLEARN Pro Version's training structure and achievement system, analyzing it

---

[2] Application website: https://www.sololearn.com/.

in light of the investigated correlation between achievements and SDT basic psychological needs (cf. Table 1). We decided to analyse The Pro Version of the application because it includes all the gamified features available for learners.

- *Evaluation achievements:* In SOLOLEARN there are no *measurement achievements*. The user performance is not evaluated in any way. *Completion achievements*, on the other hand, are extensively used (*cf. Completion*).
- *Completion* achievements: In SOLOLEARN all achievements are *performance-contingent*, meaning that there is no evaluation of the performance, but competence is required in order to solve exercises correctly. Users have to complete small exercises in order to gain experience points, that can then be used to level up and to buy hints. Solving exercises requires competence, but there is no difference in the amount of experience gained, based on the evaluation of the performance. Exercises have just two status: correct and incorrect. *Non-performance contingent achievements* are used in some cases in order to encourage the user to perform basic tasks: for instance, it is possible to obtain a badge just for verifying the email address or to complete a course.
- *Goal Orientation:* In SOLOLEARN it is possible to set daily learning goals. Different types of goals are available, depending on the amount of time users chose to spend studying, (from 5 min to 60 min per day). Even though the application's final objective is supposed to be the mastery of the subject, there is no sense of progression in the learning path toward it, since all achievements are performance-contingent and there is no evaluation of performance nor increasing exercises difficulty.
- *Predictability:* All achievements in SOLOLEARN are *expected*.
- *Flexibility:* The main achievements in SOLOLEARN are badges and experience points. Considering their characteristics, badges can be considered as *achievements as gifts*, while experience points can be considered as *currency*, since they can be spent to buy hints during exercises, even if the only choice available is whether to spend them or not.
- *Functionality:* In SOLOLEARN, badges can be considered as *cosmetic achievements*, since their role is just to show others (and oneself) the goals achieved in the application, set by the application itself. Experience points, as previously stated in Flexibility, can be considered as *functional achievements*, since they can be spent to buy hints. In spite of that, it has to be considered that there is just one way to spend experience points, therefore the level of strategy applied can be considered to be low.
- *Clustering criteria:* In SOLOLEARN experience points seem to be not incremental, since it is not possible to infer the amount of experience points gained for each exercise correctly done. On the other hand, badges, occasionally, require the user to perform the same task incrementally (*e.g.* at first 5 times, then 10 and so on). There are no *meta-achievements* in the application.
- *Competitiveness:* Experience points and badges can be achieved both performing individual exercises/tasks, at the end of every learning fragment, and competing with other players answering questions about the course topics.

4.1 Autonomy in SOLOLEARN

In SOLOLEARN, as in many different gamified applications or activities, the majority of achievements may reasonably be expected to be perceived as controlling, and therefore,

164 B. Botte et al.

not fostering autonomy [18]. Furthermore, the only choice given to the user is the topic to be studied. Badges are predefined and are obtained through the same sequence of activities by all users; it is not possible, for instance, to decide how to achieve a specific goal: it can be achieved only in one way, and it is the same for everyone. Furthermore, it has to be considered that not everyone has interest in reaching the same objectives or goals. As investigated by Ryan *et al.*, in fact, there are not only different reasons behind the choice to pursue a specific goal [13], but also a different preference for them, according to the individual value assigned to the goal itself [13]. While previous motivation theories considered motivation and amotivation as the only two states possible, SDT states that the quality of motivation depends on the degree of autonomy or control that impact on the behavior[3] [13].

Usually, gamification reward structure, as it is also in SOLOLEARN, leverages above all on external and introjected extrinsic motivation, since the rewards are totally separated from the activity itself. These are the extrinsic motivations with the lower level of autonomy, and therefore the less effective in fostering autonomy.

4.2 Competence in SOLOLEARN

Competence is usually the basic need mostly taken into account in learning gamified apps, and this is also true for SOLOLEARN, it having as primary objective to support users in acquiring new knowledge. However, we argue that for the adopted gamification mechanics in SOLOLEARN this is not the case.

That is badges are used as feedback to acknowledge competence, in some way, but most of the time they are used just as milestones in a highly controlling manner. To have gained a badge for completing a learning unit, for instance, doesn't mean necessarily to have acquired knowledge (or competence): as discussed, no measurement achievement is adopted. Furthermore, the effort undertaken by users is not taken into account: do I deserve/would I like the same badge of a person that had less difficulty than me to learn something (or to accomplish a given task)? And vice versa. Considering the different perception of a task being boring or interesting (*cf.* [13, 17, 18]), the level of satisfaction perceived for receiving that same feedback, or reward, probably will be different and, consequently, the level of motivation in proceeding through the learning path can be expected to decrease.

---

[3] Autonomous behaviors are shown to have a highly positive impact on motivation [13], compared to controlled behaviors. What is indicated is that the amount of motivation derived from a person's being autonomous or controlled can be exactly the same, but what really changes is the quality of the motivation [13] and this difference has a significant impact at a functioning level [13]. Two persons can indeed perform the same task with the same engagement, but for different reasons: one motivated by interest, engagement and enjoyment, the other one because of the fear of punishment or to satisfy other people [18]. The result will maybe be the same but there is a substantial difference. Motivation can thus be intrinsic or extrinsic, according to the locus of causality [13]: while with intrinsic motivation, both in achieving the fixed goal or in performing a specific behavior, the reward is the enjoyment of performing the activity itself, extrinsic motivation foresees an external reward, that is separated and has no necessary correlation with the activity itself [5].

The other gamified element in SOLOLEARN that has an impact on competence need-satisfaction, is the chance to start a challenge, and to confront another player using a specific knowledge as "weapon" for the confrontation. This is a good way to test the acquired competence but can have a side effect in discouraging the losing user. Also, the consequences of the challenge should be interesting for the player, otherwise it risks becoming just a meaningless confrontation to obtain a badge.

What has been said about objectives and goals in regard to the autonomy basic psychological need, is true also for competence but with a lower impact on the effectiveness of external and introjected motivations [17].

4.3 Relatedness in SOLOLEARN

Only limited functionality is included in SOLOLEARN that may cater for the need of relatedness. In SOLOLEARN it's possible to interact with other people, in an asynchronous way, for instance by posting code projects and receiving comments from other users, by discussing with peers about micro-unit topics and by starting one-on-one challenges about a chosen topic. By accomplishing tasks referred to interaction with others, users can also obtain experience points and specific badges. While this for sure helps people to feel related with each other, on the other hand compel to interact also with people who do not typically display a strong need for relatedness, or that would like to relate to others in different ways, like cooperate for a common purpose for instance, rather than competing. This choice is not available.

5   Conclusions and Future Work

This paper presents an analysis of the general concept of motivation and how it is fostered in gamified solutions for learning, particularly in the context of self-determination theory. The analysis leveraged academic literature on the topics of motivation, player engagement, basic psychological needs, and the ability of video games to potentially satisfy these needs. Specifically, the paper contributes to the field of game-based learning by (1) proposing a correlation between gamification achievements and basic psychological needs, as derived from self-determination theory, (2) analyzing an already effective game-based learning platform (SOLOLEARN) for mechanics that do – and that do not – contribute to the basic psychological needs of individual users. While the findings are drawn from a case-study with the SOLOLEARN environment, they may reasonably be expected to apply to other game-based learning environment too.

Furthermore, it could be beneficial to highlight that, in order to design an effective reward system, it is recommended to distinguish boring tasks from interesting ones [13, 17, 18]. As stated by Deci, Koestner & Ryan [18], indeed, tangible achievements, in contrast with positive feedback, are effective when the task performed is considered boring by users [13, 18]. This can be considered a limitation, since gamified activities target an heterogeneous audience, especially in the case of learning activities, a task is not interesting or uninteresting to everyone in the same way.

For future work, we will investigate to what extent individual preferences for the satisfactions of distinct psychological needs can be modeled automatically from training interactions, and to what extent such a model can be used to automatically adapt gamification strategies to the individual user.

References

1. Deterding, S., Dixon, D., Khaled, R., Nacke, L.: From game design elements to gamefulness: defining "gamification". In: Proceedings of the 15th International Academic MindTrek Conference: Envisioning Future Media Environments, pp. 9–15, September 2011
2. Thorndike, E.L.: Educational psychology, The original nature of man, vol. 1 (1913)
3. Skinner, B.F.: Operant conditioning. Encycl. Educ. **7**, 29–33 (1971)
4. White, R.W.: Motivation reconsidered: the concept of competence. Psychol. Rev. **66**(5), 297 (1971)
5. Ryan, R.M., Deci, E.L.: Self-Determination Theory: Basic Psychological Needs in Motivation, Development, and Wellness. Guilford Publications (2017)
6. Csikszentmihalyi, M., Csikzentmihaly, M.: Flow: The Psychology of Optimal Experience, vol. 1990. Harper & Row, New York (1990)
7. Przybylski, A.K., Rigby, C.S., Ryan, R.M.: A motivational model of video game engagement. Rev. Gen. Psychol. **14**(2), 154–166 (2010)
8. Ryan, R.M., Rigby, C.S., Przybylski, A.: The motivational pull of video games: a self-determination theory approach. Motivat. Emot. **30**(4), 344–360 (2006)
9. Ryan, R.M.: Basic psychological needs across cultures: a self-determination theory perspective. In: International Workshop in Developing Countries, Bremen, Germany (2004)
10. Vallerand, R.J.: On passion for life activities: the dualistic model of passion. In: Advances in Experimental Social Psychology, vol. 42, pp. 97–193. Academic Press (2010)
11. Blumler, J., Katz, E.: The Uses of Mass Communications. Sage, Beverly Hills (1974)
12. Sherry, J., Lucas, K.: Video game uses and gratifications as predictors of use and game preference. In: Presented at the Mass Communication Division, International Communication Association Annual Convention, San Diego, CA (2003)
13. Ryan, R.M., Sheldon, K.M., Kasser, T., Deci, E.L.: All goals are not created equal: an organismic perspective on the nature of goals and their regulation (1996)
14. Lombard, M., Ditton, T.: At the heart of it all: the concept of presence. J. Computer-Mediated Commun. **3**(2), JCMC321 (1997)
15. Zohaib, M.: Dynamic difficulty adjustment (DDA) in computer games: a review. In: Advances in Human-Computer Interaction (2018)
16. Yannakakis, G.N., Togelius, J.: Experience-driven procedural content generation. In: 2015 International Conference on Affective Computing and Intelligent Interaction (ACII), pp. 519–525. IEEE, September 2015
17. Kapp, K.M.: The Gamification of Learning And Instruction: Game-Based Methods and Strategies for Training and Education. Wiley, Hoboken (2012)
18. Deci, E.L., Koestner, R., Ryan, R.M.: A meta-analytic review of experiments examining the effects of extrinsic rewards on intrinsic motivation. Psychol. Bull. **125**(6), 627 (1999)
19. Yu-kay chu blog. https://yukaichou.com/education-gamification/top-10-education-gamification-examples-for-lifelong-learners/. Accessed 01 July 2020

Gamification Applications

Bloxxgame – A Simulation Game for Teaching Blockchain

Walter Dettling$^{(\boxtimes)}$ ⓘ and Bettina Schneider ⓘ

Institute for Information Systems, School of Business, University of Applied Sciences and Arts
Northwestern Switzerland FHNW, Basel, Switzerland
{walter.dettling,bettina.schneider}@fhnw.ch

Abstract. Bloxxgame is a software tool evolving from a whiteboard-based blockchain game to a web-based simulation game with a variety of teaching scenarios. It is a simulation of a public blockchain, mostly similar to Bitcoin. Each player acts as a node with all possibilities of creating coin-transactions and blocks as well as the capability to experience the consensus algorithm by checking transactions and blocks. Bloxxgame supports experience-based instruction of blockchain concepts and can be used in class or for online teaching. Moreover, the simulation offers students the opportunity to experiment with all relevant operations of a blockchain such as signing, creating transactions, block building, etc. In this paper, we aim to share our practical experiences from teaching the emerging technology of blockchain to business or business information technology students on Bachelor and Master level applying a newly developed gamified teaching approach. The research was guided by the methodology of design-based research. We elaborate the process starting from problem identification, to designing the bloxxgame tool and demonstrating its applicability in the 2020 Corona lockdown.

Keywords: Teaching blockchain · Gamification · Design-based research

1 Introduction

In this paper, we present a structured analysis of five years of experimenting with various blockchain simulation scenarios in classroom. The result is a teaching solution we name bloxxgame. Bloxxgame is a software tool, which was developed from a whiteboard-based blockchain game in classroom to a web-based simulation game with a variety of teaching scenarios. It is a simulation of a public blockchain, mostly similar to Bitcoin, in which each player acts as a node with all possibilities of creating coin-transactions as well as blocks. Bloxxgame enables students to learn the consensus algorithm by checking transactions and blocks. It supports experience-based instruction of blockchain concepts and can be used in class or for online teaching. Moreover, the game offers students the opportunity to experiment with all relevant operations of a blockchain such as hashing, signing, block building, etc. The game experience supports the understanding of the abstract and complex blockchain mechanism. This is especially the case for the consensus algorithm, which bloxxgame simulates very closely.

© Springer Nature Switzerland AG 2020
I. Marfisi-Schottman et al. (Eds.): GALA 2020, LNCS 12517, pp. 169–178, 2020.
https://doi.org/10.1007/978-3-030-63464-3_16

This paper summarizes the first teaching experiences, especially in the 2020 Corona lockdown, where it was used for instruction and as examination tool in a blockchain elective course. In addition, an outlook to further research on the impact of this tool, and to next steps in the development are provided.

2 Methodology

The methodology used to develop this teaching tool comes closest to design-based research [1]. This method is appropriate to the complexity of teaching blockchain and building artifacts. It is a common approach in information system research, which is another argument for this method, as we look at blockchain in regard of its role in this field. According to Pfeffers et al. [2], the research design consists of the following steps:

1. Problem identification and motivation; 2. Objectives of a solution; 3. Design and development; 4. Demonstration; 5. Evaluation; 6. Communication

Although the research design is nominally ordered and structured, the research process often does not follow these steps in a linear order [2]. In this ex post report of our research, the chapter sequence follows the six-step structure. Nevertheless, throughout the real research process, we made different loops and side steps. This paper is neither a general introduction to blockchain, nor a user manual for bloxxgame. The description of the software and its functions are restricted to the minimum, which is necessary for the explanation of the design process. Details about bloxxgame are available at: https://bloxx-wiki.herokuapp.com/.

3 Problem Identification and Objectives of the Solution

Although blockchain has been used and taught for a couple of years, it remains a very abstract concept, mostly described by its properties such as distributed ledger or storing transactions in blocks. To understand these blockchain elements, cryptographic functions such as hashing or signing must be introduced. When the term 'mining' comes up, explanations become harder. Building a block of transactions, solving a hash puzzle, attaching it to the longest valid chain and creating new cryptocurrencies, etc. are complex subjects. Finally, when the 'consensus algorithm' must be explained the gap between reality and abstraction grows even more. This is due to the dynamics emerging from the interaction of many independent actors following the rules of the consensus protocol. However, the mechanism or protocol of a blockchain is a complex, dynamic process, which involves many elements in various ways. Only when the interaction of the elements is recognized, the mechanism of blockchain can be fully understood.

Following Dettling [3] in "How to Teach Blockchain in a Business School", blockchain courses can address three dimensions: First, the building blocks of blockchain, which are necessary to understand the basic mechanism of blockchain. Topics such as hashing, signatures, consensus algorithm, etc. belong to this category. Second, the relevance or the impact of blockchain in business, which is for the time being represented by topics such as cryptocurrencies, smart contracts, legal issues, etc. Third, the applications of blockchain where nowadays most blockchain startups are active and which is a very dynamic field. Here, almost each industry has its own ecosystem requiring specific solutions for various use cases.

We focus on the first dimension, the mechanism of blockchain. This by the conviction, that a basic understanding of blockchain is a necessary precondition to fully understand the impact and application of blockchain. This assumption could change in the future, when blockchain has been universally adopted and seamlessly integrated into software systems. Today, software developers and business strategists are still searching for another 'killer' application besides Bitcoin. Consequently, qualified knowledge is still necessary to make strategic business decisions aiming at the use of blockchain. As our developed teaching approach incorporates gamification, the next section will focus on reviewing the relevant literature in this field.

3.1 Literature Review

Background of Gamification as Teaching Approach

To understand the term gamification, it is necessary to turn to the origin of this concept, namely the play. Piaget [4], a pioneer and enduring influencer in educational research, laid the foundations for integrating the idea of 'play' into didactic scenarios. He was the first to introduce the theory of constructivism, a learning situation in which the learners' knowledge and meanings are 'constructed' through the interaction of their ideas and experiences. Constructivist learning presupposes the necessity of experiential learning through social interaction with the environment and peers [5]. A statement of Piaget [4] confirms this: "You cannot teach concepts verbally; you must use a method founded on activity". One such activity may be 'playing', and the play is regarded as one central pattern for active and spontaneous children's learning.

Transferring the idea of 'play' to adult education and the corporate learning setting has led to the term gamification. As additional concept, the term serious games has gained relevance and it denotes games designed to convey learning material [6].

State of Gamification as Approach to Teach Blockchain

A systematic literature review of studies published in the scientific databases Web of Science, IEEE Xplore, ACM Digital Library, google scholar and SpringerLink was performed. The term 'blockchain' was combined with the keyword 'gamification' and subsequently with keywords like 'teaching', 'learning' and 'education'. From the result set we excluded studies that investigate the use of blockchain technology as a means of supporting processes in the education sector or that use blockchain technology as a technological basis for virtual games. We focused on studies in English language that deal with the question of how blockchain can be taught or learned as a subject. Furthermore, only studies that are available online as full text were considered for this review.

Most of the identified publications examine ways in which blockchain can be integrated into existing curricula of higher education institutions. Toleva-Stoimenova et al. [7] share their experience concerning the incorporation of blockchain content into existing data science curricula for master's programs. Purden et al. [8] generally advocate using a blockchain application in the cloud for classes thus avoiding the need for hardware; Dettling [3] proposes specific subject structures for teaching business students. In line with the latter, teaching blockchain to non-technical students is the focus of Negash and Thomas [9]. They developed seven use cases from industry (e.g. aviation, healthcare car, supply chain) to achieve the learning objectives. Kursh et al. [10] evaluate blockchain as a topic in Fintec curricula and offer categorization according to several dimensions such as level of detail, format, and emphasis.

Few more detailed approaches towards blockchain teaching can be found in recent publications. The first example is a role play combined with 3D animations [11]. The game simulates a classroom and offers a puzzle to the learners, where questions related to blockchains have to be answered to get to the next levels. A second research result is a Java application called 'ChainTutor', enabling users to experiment with important blockchain concepts through a graphical user interface [12]. The application is capable of simulating low-level details of a blockchain such as the generation of keys, hashes, transactions, blocks and wallets. As a third approach, Rao and Dave [13] explain how they developed a hands-on lab using a Raspberry Pi to instruct students on embedded systems with elements of cloud and blockchain technology.

3.2   Application of Gamification Theory in Bloxxgame

As evidenced by the literature research, the application of gamification to the topic of blockchain is still in its infancy. Adding game elements to a learning situation does not per se add value; rather an appropriate didactic concept is an important prerequisite for successful implementation [14]. For this reason, we proposed different teaching scenarios, which have been developed based on practical experience.

In all scenarios, bloxxgame offers a simulation of a blockchain. A simulation can be defined as a method of implementing a representation of a system, an entity, a phenomenon, or a process over time [15]. Simulations attempt to capture relevant aspects of a topic or phenomenon to allow learners to interact in order to observe the effects of their interactions [16]. These simulations are not only effective in situations where real-world contact is dangerous or expensive (e.g., flight simulators), but also in situations where the topic in focus is very abstract or complex (e.g., [17]). Blockchain is a highly challenging subject that requires the learner to understand concepts in the field of economics, finance, and information technology, in particular cryptography. In addition, the mechanisms of blockchain are inherently very abstract, given that they occur in cyberspace. Therefore, it is very promising to simulate the essential operations of blockchain to help individuals 'experience' the technology and see the impact of own actions.

3.3   Objectives of the Solution

The solution we were looking for was a teaching method and/or a tool, which enables learners to gain a profound understanding of the basic blockchain mechanism. We expected that after the instruction, students should be able to describe the main elements and give a coherent explanation of the mechanism of a blockchain. At best, the tool should also provide means to evaluate this understanding. Once the tool was developed, we recognized that it was more than just a demonstrator or teaching lab in the classroom, but that it could also be used as a blockchain simulation game. Therefore, another objective of this solution could be added: It should provide an authentic experience of the consensus algorithm.

4   Design and Development of the Solution

When designing bloxxgame, it was important to reduce complexity, without neglecting relevant aspects of the topic. We decided to focus on a public blockchain, which issues coins and only allows transactions of integer coins from one address to another. This comes very closely to Bitcoin although there are some important differences to the Bitcoin protocol.

4.1   Design of the Software

In the beginning, we used paper and whiteboards to simulate coin transactions and build blocks with them. It helped the students to visualize the different steps of the blockchain algorithm, but the necessary reduction of reality was disadvantageous since many important things such as hashing, or signing were left out. Thus, the idea of a software-based simulation became imminent. The main elements of the software were derived from the classroom experience.

Fig. 1. Bloxxgame Play-Board. Nine boxes represent all relevant functions for blockchain transactions and display the status of the active blockchain seen as a node in real-time.

Normally, simplicity in software design is achieved by automating processes to help the user easily accomplish complex tasks. In bloxxgame we aimed at the opposite. No automated operations are implemented; only basic functions such as hashing, asymmetric encryption and decryption, as well as broadcasting data to the blockchain network are provided as encapsulated functions.

All design decisions were based on two main criteria — simplicity, and transparency.

The result of this was a one-screen-board containing a complete set of functions, which are used in blockchains (Fig. 1). These functions are organized in logical units, which are called boxes. In total, nine boxes comprise the game front-end: Nodes, Wallet, Signature, Unspent Transactions, Mempool, Blockchain, Hasher, Merkle, Block. Each box consists of a set of data and functions, which can be treated as a single learning topic.

There is a second screen (called 'admin') only for teachers (Fig. 2). The admin can reset or initiate a new blockchain by sending coins to the wallets of each player when creating the genesis block. The difficulty and reward for mining can also be adjusted. When the admin marks a new block as 'confirmed', all related transactions get the same status for all players. There is also a 'view'-mode where the admin can see all nodes and the transactions initiated or received by them. In bloxxgame, the students stay anonymous, only the node address of active players is shown to the teacher.

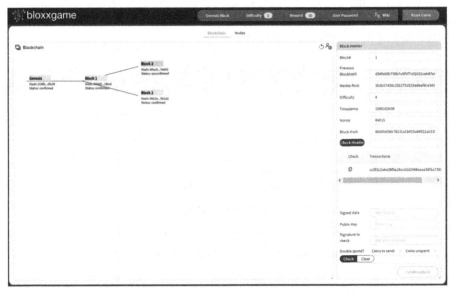

Fig. 2. Bloxxgame Admin-Board. Teacher can start, overview and influence the outcome of a bloxxgame session within the limits of the bloxxgame consensus algorithm.

4.2 Teaching Scenarios with Bloxxgame

We propose three elementary teaching scenarios when applying bloxxgame. For students with little or no knowledge in blockchain, it is recommended to start with scenario 1, before trying scenario 2 or 3. However, it would also be possible to start immediately with a blockchain-building session without instructions. In any case, all scenarios are suitable for class instruction or for online teaching.

Scenario 1: Understanding the Basic Elements of Blockchain
In this initial scenario, the boxes can be used for explanation or experimenting with the various core concepts of blockchain, e.g. hashing, signing data, building a Merkle tree, etc. One important aspect is the 'check function', which shows up in several boxes. The check function supports the comparison of hash values or is executed to confirm the validity of signed data. Students using the bloxxgame tool for the first time can be supported by teachers in different ways. For example, teachers can start with bloxxgame as a demonstrator tool for instruction and then let the students have their own experiences. In class, this can be done either in groups or each student can work on a separate node.

Scenario 2: Interacting with the Blockchain
After a first inspection of the basic boxes (Fig. 1), the next step would be to use functions, which have an impact on the blockchain status. Before students can start with this activity, the teacher must create the genesis block. The main operations at this level are the creation of transactions or blocks. Both operations are complex activities with several steps and involve multiple boxes simultaneously. At this point, each player will get in contact with the activities of other players. For example, transactions, which are broadcast, will show up in the mempool box of each player, and blocks, which are published, will be attached to the existing blockchain in the blockchain box. At this level latest, the learning process takes on a dynamic of its own for each player.

After experimenting, different topics can be reflected in class: In addition, the creation of transactions and blocks, the most important topics are the checking of transactions in the mempool, the checking of blocks as well as the process of block confirmation. The role of teachers in this scenario can vary from individual coaching to additional class instructions on topics such as forking or double spending. In addition, the teacher must decide on the block status. Only when a block gets the status 'confirmed', the transactions in the block are considered in the mempool, in the wallets and in the unspent transactions. In this scenario, individual or group work is possible.

Scenario 3: Immerging into the Blockchain
When students are familiar with the functions and operations of bloxxgame, the next level is a scenario where the whole blockchain is reset and all players acting as nodes have to login again. After the creation of the genesis block, the students can start to create transactions and blocks. Teachers can guide the students by announcing tasks they should perform, e.g. sending coins to a specific address, creating a block with a specific number of transactions, identifying inconsistent transactions in the mempool, etc. There is no fixed 'finish line' in the game, so it would make sense to either limit the number of blocks, which should be built or the time until the game is closed. In this scenario, the teacher only must observe the block creation and decide, on which branch the blockchain will grow. Normally students behave competitively without further instruction. The fact that they can earn coins by coinbase transactions with each block they create, and which is confirmed, results in a high intensity for all participants.

In a later chapter, we will show that scenario 3 gives ground for further analysis and development of bloxxgame. Again, this approach enables individual as well as group work.

5 Demonstration of Bloxxgame

The demonstration phase in the research process should prove that the solution works and achieves the objectives set for this solution [2]. So far, we have used bloxxgame in different classes with students of varying technical skills (bachelor in business economics, in business information technology, and executive master). We always could properly work with the software and focus on the teaching experiences. Exemplarily, we describe the case of one class in the next paragraphs.

In spring 2020, bloxxgame was used for teaching an elective class for students of information systems. We used bloxxgame to instruct and train the understanding of underlying algorithms and the mechanism of using a blockchain for distributed transaction handling. After four sessions in class, the Corona lockdown forced distance teaching in this course. The combination of online-teaching software with the web-based playground of bloxxgame was a good setting for this new situation. Especially the one-screen design was helpful for online classes. Students could follow the instructions in the teacher's screen and experiment in a separate window on their own node of bloxxgame. Teachers and students agreed on using a game session (scenario 3) for the final grading of the practical part of the course. The students had to perform a couple of actions such as hashing, signing, creating, and checking transactions, as well as creating an own validated block in the blockchain. The grading based on the blockchain data, which could be linked to the students by their submission of the respective node address with hashes of transactions or of the performed actions. The outcome was positive and allowed a clear distinction between different levels of blockchain understanding.

6 Evaluation

Once the demonstration of the solution proved its feasibility, a formal evaluation of the outcome of bloxxgame becomes necessary. Gamification, which was not in focus of the solution at the beginning emerged as an important characteristic of bloxxgame. Especially in teaching scenario 3, students began to engage more emotionally. In discussions after the game, students showed more interest and awareness regarding networks or the social aspect of cooperation. This opened the field for advanced teaching topics about the role of blockchain in society. Additionally, feedback from students was used for the further development of the game. For example, the possibility to change the difficulty for mining was induced by students' wish for more competition. So far, formal feedback from students about bloxxgame was part of the overall evaluation of blockchain courses. Now, having a tool which can be used for a stand-alone activity, a systematic evaluation can be considered. For a formal evaluation, the following aspects are of interest: Topic mastery, entertainment, socialization. The next paragraph elaborates on more information about planned research.

7 Communication and Outlook

Communication in design science research has the purpose to expose the result of the study to other experts and researchers to prove or improve the result. So far, bloxxgame has only been communicated within a small group of teachers and blockchain experts. With this paper, we hope to increase attention and receive feedback from other teachers, which could help to improve our solution. The order of reaction and the grade of interest in this teaching approach will also be relevant for further development, such as making bloxxgame publicly available.

Bloxxgame will need further improvement if it should become a publicly available teaching tool. The following activities are ongoing or planned. A research project examines the impact of bloxxgame on the learning success of students. With pre- and post-game surveys we will compare the knowledge increase induced by different learning scenarios. In addition, students will be asked about their subjective learning experience and for ideas to improve the outcome. A second project will extend the technical infrastructure of bloxxgame. So far, bloxxgame is only usable in one instance. To become a multi-teacher, multiclass software and some additional programming will be necessary.

8 Conclusion

By exploring, experimenting, and playing bloxxgame, students will learn and understand how the most elementary components of an information system, the transaction, is handled in the blockchain. Although this looks like a very technical perspective, it will be understandable for everybody through the demonstrative form.

The second thing learners should experience and understand is the social and economic aspect of a public blockchain. For most people, the term 'consensus algorithm' is very abstract. When playing bloxxgame, they can experience the role of (social) interaction implied by the consensus algorithm. In bloxxgame each player will experience how the behavior of all participants decides on the outcome of the game.

For teachers, bloxxgame also offers many opportunities for discoveries and experiments. Bloxxgame is a playground with transparent functions and no automated checks or autofill functions, etc. Like in a board game, users are free to follow the suggestions of the game manual or to define own actions and procedures, as long as they are possible within the existing framework.

References

1. Hevner, A.R., March, S.T., Park, J., Ram, S.: Design science in information systems research. MIS Q. **24**(1), 75–105 (2004).
2. Peffers, K., Tuunanen, T., Rothenberger, M.A., Chatterjee, S.: A design science research methodology for information systems research. J. Manag. Inf. Syst. **24**(3), 45–77 (2007)
3. Dettling, W.: How to teach blockchain in a business school. In: Dornberger, R. (ed.) Business Information Systems and Technology 4.0. SSDC, vol. 141, pp. 213–225. Springer, Cham (2018). https://doi.org/10.1007/978-3-319-74322-6_14
4. Piaget, J.: La naissance de l'intelligence chez l'enfant. Delachaux et Niestle, Geneva (1936)

5. York, J., deHaan, J.W.: A constructivist approach to game-based language learning: student perceptions in a beginner-level EFL context. Int. J. Game-Based Learn. **8**(1), 19–40 (2018)
6. Deterding, S., Dixon, D., Khaled, R., Nacke, L.: From game design elements to gamefulness: defining "gamification". In: Proceedings of the 15th International Academic Mindtrek Conference: Envisioning Future Media Environments, Mindtrek 2011. ACM Press, New York, New York, USA (2011)
7. Toleva-Stoimenova, S., Christozov, D., Rasheva-Yordanova, K.: Introduction of emerging technology into higher education curriculum: the case of blockchain technology as part of data science master program. In: 9th International Conference the Future of Education, Florence Italy (2019)
8. Purdon, I., Erturk, E.: Perspectives of blockchain technology, its relation to the cloud and its potential role in computer science education. Eng. Technol. Appl. Sci. Res. **7**(6), 2340–2344 (2017)
9. Negash, S., Thomas, D.. Teaching blockchain for business. In: 2019 IEEE Canadian Conference of Electrical and Computer Engi-neering (CCECE), pp. 1–4. IEEE (2019)
10. Kursh, S.R., Gold, N.A.: Adding FinTech and blockchain to your curriculum. Bus. Educ. Innovation J. **8**(2), 6–12 (2016)
11. Weng, T., Li, C.-K., Wu, C.-H.: Integrating the combination of blockchain and RPG into undergraduate learning. In: Rønningsbakk, L., Wu, T.-T., Sandnes, F.E., Huang, Y.-M. (eds.) ICITL 2019. LNCS, vol. 11937, pp. 513–524. Springer, Cham (2019). https://doi.org/10.1007/978-3-030-35343-8_55
12. Liu, X.: A small java application for learning blockchain. In: 2018 IEEE 9th Annual Information Technology, Electronics and Mobile Communication Conference (IEMCON), pp. 1271–1275. IEEE (2018)
13. Rao, A.R., Dave, R.: Developing hands-on laboratory exercises for teaching STEM students the internet-of-things, cloud computing and blockchain applications. In: 2019 IEEE Integrated STEM Education Conference (ISEC), pp. 191–198. IEEE (2019)
14. ter Vrugte, J., de Jong, T.: How to adapt games for learning: the potential role of instructional support. In: De Wannemacker, S., Vandercruysse, S., Clarebout, G. (eds.) ITEC/CIP/T 2011. CCIS, vol. 280, pp. 1–5. Springer, Heidelberg (2012). https://doi.org/10.1007/978-3-642-338 14-4_1
15. Fujimoto, R., Bock, C., Chen, W., Page, E., Panchal, J.H.: Research Challenges in Modeling and Simulation for Engineering Complex Systems. Springer, Heidelberg (2017). 10.1007/978-3-319-58544-4
16. Hays, R.T.: The Effectiveness of Instructional Games: A Literature Review and Discussion. Technical report (2005). http://faculty.uoit.ca/kapralos/csci5530/Papers/hays_instructionalGames.pdf. Accessed 03 June 2020
17. Schwarzenbach, M., Schneider, B.: Teaching data standards using learning applications: a game-based example from supply chain management. In: Dermol, V. (ed.): Integrated Economy and Society: Diversity, Creativity, and Technology. Proceedings of the MakeLearn and TIIM International Conference, pp. 581–587. ToKnowPress, Bangkok, Celje, Lublin (2018)

Pointer Attack: Lessons Learned in Computer Concept Gamification

Andrew Droubay$^{(\boxtimes)}$ and Durell Bouchard

Roanoke College, Salem, VA 24153, USA
awdroubay@mail.roanoke.edu, bouchard@roanoke.edu

Abstract. Many early students of computer science struggle with a theoretical understanding of new concepts and their programmatic implementations. However, the difficulties associated with the necessary learning often frustrate newer students. Thus, any educational strategy must be able to both engage and motivate. Based on previous research, we developed a small game to teach undergraduate computer science students about pointers, which are variables that reference computer memory indirectly. We did not find that our attempt at gamification yielded significant improvement in student engagement, learning or motivation, but our experience indicates that future research into a sandbox type game has potential to encourage students to learn independently.

Keywords: Game-based learning · Pointers · Serious game

1 Introduction

A computer science education frequently requires students to struggle through learning new concepts without providing sufficient learning resources that can engage them. This is readily apparent when students learn pointers. Pointers differ from preceding computer science content because they store data indirectly, referencing the data location in computer memory instead of referencing the data itself. Their use requires a student to visualise this reference in computer memory and then use it in a program. In our experience, students find the pointer syntax intimidating and wrestle with implementing this abstract concept.

Pointers represent an early step that moves a student beyond simple programming and towards understanding how data works, helping transition the student into a computer scientist. Introductory programming is straightforward and explicit, but pointer programming necessitates an understanding of the abstract, causing many students to stumble. One paper studied pointers as a threshold concept, which generally elevate the student's understanding but are often counter-intuitive and challenging to learn [4]. This is especially true for pointers, and traditional teaching methods such as practice problems and visualisations are often insufficient to offset the struggles pointers present.

Programming is best learned by practice and repetition. This is effective, but it can be difficult to entice students to study and practice consistently through

© Springer Nature Switzerland AG 2020
I. Marfisi-Schottman et al. (Eds.): GALA 2020, LNCS 12517, pp. 179–188, 2020.
https://doi.org/10.1007/978-3-030-63464-3_17

traditional teaching methods. Teaching students in an enjoyable environment would facilitate the necessary engagement for learning [3]. This paper describes a computer game we created to provide a venue for students to practice their programming skills and build their knowledge driven by their enjoyment. We hoped that such a model would motivate learning. Although the data does not show that the game is more academically effective or motivating than traditional teaching methods, we observed students engaging with the material when they deviated from the strict confines of the level design and experimented within the game environment. Future research exploring this aspect of gamification may be beneficial.

2   Related Work

Because of the difficulties often presented by learning pointers, traditional teaching methods have directly targeted them in the past, specifically using visualisation [7] and practice problems [8]. Though these tools are statistically effective at increasing a student's knowledge of coding, it is currently unclear whether this knowledge directly translates to a student's ability to code, as knowledge of programming does not always engender programming ability [7]. In addition to coding difficulty and conceptual understanding, traditional teaching methods fail to account for student engagement. While practice problems may be academically effective, students often quickly lose motivation in a strictly pedagogical setting, inhibiting the necessary repetition for continued, sustained learning [11]. To address this, many researchers have incorporated educational games into their curriculum.

Educational games are not foreign to the field of computer science [2]. Computer games naturally force a player to learn the mechanics of the game, doing so in an enjoyable, rewarding, and ultimately engaging setting [13]. This engagement promotes repetition. A student is far more willing to apply the additional practice necessary to learn new content if they are having fun. In this way, educational games have been consistently shown to increase learning [6,16]. In addition, games can be very visual. A visualisation can lead to a better understanding of a topic that, when combined with entertainment value, results in repetition of practice and comprehension, inciting education. However, despite these well-documented benefits, a systematic review of educational computer science games from 2000 to 2016 showed no results for a game using the principles of pointers [2].

3   Design Decisions

We emulated the style of the tower defence genre to integrate pointers organically into our game, *Pointer Attack*. The game's primary goal is to defend a castle by creating catapults to defeat marauding enemies. Because a pointer references a location in computer memory, any created catapult in the game will point to a literal grid location (Fig. 1), giving the student a more explicit understanding of the computer processes through an interactive visualisation. The player interacts by physically typing C++ code to create the appropriate catapults. They then hit the compile button (Fig. 1) (as if they were compiling computer code), which will cause the enemies to move according to a predetermined pattern. If the player's code has created a catapult that points to where each enemy lands, they win. This forces the player to read the enemy's movement, represented above the game grid (Fig. 1), and intelligently plan how they implement the pointer catapults. The student earns different levels of stars based on the criteria for level completion. This style of gameplay reinforces a student's ability to write code and problem solve. Code tracing like this is an effective tool for increasing coding ability [9]. Thus, the game design emphasises fun, giving a sense of accomplishment while also educating the player through visualisation and repetition.

 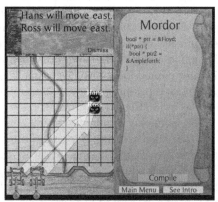

Fig. 1. Labelled game layout   **Fig. 2.** Win state

To increase engagement, we used stars as a system of positive reinforcement [5]. At the end of every level, students receive 1–3 stars based on their performance. For example, in Level 1, players are told to code with a conditional statement, a coding expression that will execute a block of code depending on the evaluation of an expression. The game awards three stars for doing so in one try, two stars for multiple tries, and only one star if the player completes the level without using the conditional statement. This encourages good behaviour without punishing bad behaviour.

We used a story-motivated approach to design the puzzles. Because there are many different ways to program an answer to any problem, we used the story to guide the player to perform a specific action. In Level 1, the player could create two pointers, but we wanted them to associate pulling the value of a pointer reference with a conditional statement, so we phrased the following prompt. "Well done! More enemies lie beyond. These two will always move side by side. We must attack them at the same time. Any mistakes could be deadly. For safety, we must attack the second enemy only if the first one has been targeted. Using the fact that the location grid-points are Boolean variables and an if statement, destroy our enemies." This use of story-driven design has been effectively used in other fields, such as second language acquisition, suggesting that an emphasis on story can better invest students in the material [10].

We spent much time discussing gameplay. We wanted to reinforce the connection between coding and the visualisation. So, we designed the controls of the game to rest solely in typing code. Anytime the player wants to interact with the game, they have to code. We also wanted the enemy movement to be predictable to integrate it into puzzles.

4   Methods and Level Design

Although the game was developed in Unity using the C# programming language, the student coding environment uses regular expressions to interpret C++ input code. *Pointer Attack* accepts most basic C++ commands including variable assignment, printing, looping, pointer creation and reassignment, and arrays. The game displays the computer memory as a grid, in which enemies move to different named locations every time the player presses the compile button. This movement is pre-programmed and predictable, and is constantly displayed above the play grid (Fig. 1).

For gameplay, students enter C++ code into an input box. They can finish a level by creating a pointer directed at the predicted locations of their enemies. Every grid location has a Boolean value of true or false, indicating whether that square is occupied by an enemy. For example, if a lone enemy was moving to the square `Amarillo` the next turn, winning code would be `bool * ptr = &Amarillo`, creating a catapult/pointer to the proper location (Fig. 2). This basic functionality expands as the levels progress. Each level is intended to reinforce a certain aspect of pointers, such as dereferencing and use with arrays. At the beginning of every level, the game presents the player with text introducing the relevant content.

Level 0, the tutorial, introduces the concept of the game to the player. It begins tying the story, gameplay and visual elements together. "Hello! Welcome to *Pointer Attack*. In this game, each grid square represents a Boolean variable that is true or false based on whether it is occupied by one of the evil cats. You can see the name of the square by dragging you mouse over it. Our scout in the top left will tell you where our enemies will move next. To attack them, create a pointer to the location they will move to. You can create a pointer in C++ using this format: `<type> pointerName= &pointingToVariable;` Now, destroy our enemies!" In this way, we hoped to motivate students to complete the game using the anthropomorphic cats within the context of defending a kingdom (Figs. 3, 4 and 5).

Level 1 asks the student to retrieve the value that a pointer is referencing and use it in a conditional statement. To make this a puzzle, we had two enemies running in parallel, and the student would fire on a grid square only if the

Fig. 3. Level 1: initial   **Fig. 4.** Level 1: with code   **Fig. 5.** Level 1: final state

adjacent grid cell is occupied. We contextualized this puzzle using storytelling, saying that the catapults had to be created correctly on the first try. "Well done! More enemies lie beyond. These two will always move side by side. We must attack them at the same time. Any mistakes could be deadly. For safety, we must attack the second enemy only if the first one has been targeted. Using the fact that the locations grid points are Boolean variables and a conditional statement, destroy our enemies." Because the conditional statement was unnecessary from a programming point of view, we hoped that connecting it to the story would help the students play the game.

We wanted the students to practice using arrays (lists of data) with pointers, as pointers are commonly used in early programming iterate over the elements of an array. We also used a story motivated design here to incorporate every element of the code into the story. "Very good! More enemies remain. For their records, the scribes ask that we use a list for our attacks. In C++, we can create a pointer to an array, which will point to the first element of that array automatically. We can then iterate that pointer to go to the next objects in the array." Unlike Level 1, where the conditional statement has no context, the array is described by how it relates to the story; it is a record for the "scribes".

Level 3 introduces the students to looping mechanics (repeating lines of code) with pointers. This builds on the previous level's puzzle and integrates the story and mechanics by removing the predictable enemy movement. The following level text explains: "Well done on the last wave, but we have terrible news! Our scout has been captured. We have replaced him with a cardboard cutout of his likeness. We cannot tell where the enemies will go any longer. However, there is still hope. Use a for loop, an array and a conditional statement to destroy our enemies!" This develops on Level 1 and Level 2 by using the mechanics to drive the story so that the story can motivate player behaviour.

5   The Experiment

We provided the game to two classes of computer science, an introductory programming course, and a software engineering class. Between the two groups, we had a total sample size of 32 students, consisting mostly of first- and second-year students. The introductory group had been introduced to pointers the previous week and the software engineering class had at least a year of experience with them. We included both groups to increase the sample size and to investigate whether the gaming experience was influenced by pointer experience.

Each class was divided into a control and an intervention group. Both groups were presented with a five-question practical short answer quiz asking for the output of certain programs involving pointers; some questions were derived from an assessment for a similar pointer game, *If Memory Serves* [12]. In addition to the quiz, we included a question asking a student about their conceptual knowledge of pointers. The experimental group played four levels of the game, and the control group completed a programming exercise that was similar to their coursework. After the experiment portion, the students repeated similar quizzes to give a comparison between their before and after grades. Using these quizzes, we hoped to measure increases in code tracing ability between the game and the traditional teaching methods. All students were assessed for their enjoyment of their activity using questions drawn from an Intrinsic Motivation Inventory (IMI) Scale from the Center for Self-Determination Theory [1, 14].

We asked the control group to execute two simple assignments using pointers and arrays, with an additional, optional, bonus assignment. The experimental group received the game and were given instructions to complete levels 0–3 (of five levels total) with three stars each. In this way, we could measure quantitative score improvement and enjoyment using both the IMI score and conceptual knowledge of pointers.

6   Data

The data did not necessarily bear out any difference between the two treatments. Quantitatively, the mean change in quiz score (graded 0–5) for the experimental group was 0.79, and the mean quiz score change for the control group was 0.11. Performing a two-sample t-test gets a t-value of -1.09 and p-value of 0.14. The mean enjoyment of control group was 56.722 on the IMI scale, and the mean enjoyment of experimental group was 57.482, giving a t-value of -0.183 and a p-value of 0.428. Neither of the results can be considered statistically significant. We had to reject our null hypothesis that playing the game increased academic ability or enjoyment of the activity.

7   Experience Report

The project faced several challenges and issues which skewed the data. First and foremost, the game was not engaging. It was evident during testing that the experimental group exhibited the typical frustrations of any computer science student stuck on a project, and the little cats hopping around the screen were insufficient to offset that frustration. As a result, many students did not try very hard to complete the quiz after finishing the game. In fact, multiple post-experiment quiz entries (three from the control group and one from the study group) were left blank, diminishing the student's score. Evidently, because these quizzes had no impact on their grade, the students were more interested in being done than in doing well. In addition to the interactions we had with the students while administering the experiment, students could comment on the game after they completed the last quiz. This allowed us to gather more qualitative information to supplement the quantitative data from the quizzes.

A lot of our focus went into trying to address the academic side of the problem. As discussed earlier, we used code-tracing, visualisations and story motivated puzzles, but none of them was sufficient to engage. Visualisations and code-tracing on their own are merely academic and do little to motivate the students, and although the story exists throughout the game, the overall lack of consequences and mechanics based puzzles meant students forgot about it after closing the introductory text bubble. The introduction of interesting concepts and the integration of visualisation and code does not necessarily make a fun game. Ultimately, even though the game educated as well as the programming exercises, the lack of enjoyment and motivation resulted in a game that felt purely academic.

The different degrees of story integration seem to affect student engagement. Level 1 poorly integrates the story, Level 2 uses the story to drive player decision and Level 3 utilises game mechanics and story in tandem. While observing and helping student's during the experiment, Levels 1 and 2 seemed much more frustrating for the students to complete. They did not understand why they had to complete the level in a certain way. However, students that reached Level 3 needed less intervention. While it is possible that the students were able to improve and learn the game by Level 3, it is more likely that the integration of story and mechanics made the level much stronger than story alone did. This merits future research.

From in-class student feedback, we could tell that the game failed to be engaging. The balance of time spent on development is likely partially responsible. About 90% of our time was spent on developing and implementing a compiler that would accept most code inputs. Even then, the compiler was not perfect, and the result was a game that had been insufficiently tested for enjoyment, had little to no design iterations, and exhibited a lack of time to develop a level design that made sense to the students.

The game's level design was a recurring issue. The levels present specific challenges to the user, and there is a specific set of codes that the game expected. Any solution that does not satisfy the strict requirements is either not accepted or receives only one star. This frustrated many students. Because they were instructed not to move on until they received three stars, they treated the one-star rating as a poor grade. Although the stars should have acted as a carrot, they ended up more like a stick.

On the other hand, one student gave up quickly, and instead of trying to complete the given task, attempted to break the game. He spent much more

Fig. 6. Student Experimentation

time with the code in hopes of causing an unexpected bug, generating a large number of pointers (Fig. 6). As a result, he spent much more time with the game than other students, which gave him more practice and his attempt to create a bug actually engaged him with the material. He was not the only student to experiment like this, and it points to the most engaging part of the game. When the students could see their code interact in a new environment, they experimented and enjoyed experiencing unregulated and unplanned discoveries. This concept could be well expanded in the future. The strict linear game limited enjoyment, but turning the focus to a more sandbox environment and free-play approach encouraged learning.

8   Conclusion and Future Steps

We developed *Pointer Attack* to engage students and to help them visualise the difficult concept of pointers. We hoped to directly integrate learning with enjoyment. Unfortunately, the data did not show that our game increased learning, engagement or motivation any more than traditional teaching methods. However, based on student experiences and surveys, some hypothesis can be drawn, which in turn could be used to great effect in the future.

First, this developmental experiment implies that technological focus does not necessarily lead to higher engagement. Instead, future creators should spend the time to assess how changes affect user engagement, employing an iterative design with lots of play-testing to produce a more enjoyable and engaging program [15]. Next, the story can be completely ineffective if it is not integrated with the game mechanics. In one level, students ignored the story because it had no bearing on the game. A different level used the story as a motivator for the mechanics and was received much better by students. Exploring a narrative structure that integrates story and gameplay in this way could prove fruitful on a larger scale. Finally, the linear nature of *Pointer Attack* proved to be a hindrance. We believe restricting options like this (as many programming games do) is an impediment, and an environment that rewards creativity and experimentation would produce the necessary engagement in students.

References

1. Intrinsic Motivation Inventory (IMI). https://selfdeterminationtheory.org/intrinsic-motivation-inventory
2. Battistella, P., von Wangenheim, C.G.: Games for teaching computing in higher education-a systematic review. IEEE Technol. Eng. Educ. **9**(1), 8–30 (2016)
3. Blasco-Arcas, L., Buil, I., Hernández-Ortega, B., Sese, F.J.: Using clickers in class. The role of interactivity, active collaborative learning and engagement in learning performance. Comput. Educ. **62**(C), 102–110 (2013)
4. Boustedt, J., et al.: Threshold concepts in computer science: do they exist and are they useful? In: Proceedings of the 38th SIGCSE Technical Symposium on Computer Science Education, SIGCSE 2007, pp. 504–508. Association for Computing Machinery, New York (2007). https://doi.org/10.1145/1227310.1227482
5. Gaston, J., Cooper, S.: To three or not to three: improving human computation game onboarding with a three-star system. In: Proceedings of the 2017 CHI Conference on Human Factors in Computing Systems, CHI 2017, pp. 5034–5039. Association for Computing Machinery, New York (2017). https://doi.org/10.1145/3025453.3025997
6. Hakulinen, L.: Using serious games in computer science education. In: Proceedings of the 11th Koli Calling International Conference on Computing Education Research, Koli Calling 2011, pp. 83–88. Association for Computing Machinery, New York (2011). https://doi.org/10.1145/2094131.2094147
7. Kumar, Amruth N.: Learning programming by solving problems. In: Cassel, Lillian, Reis, Ricardo A. (eds.) Informatics Curricula and Teaching Methods. ITIFIP, vol. 117, pp. 29–39. Springer, Boston, MA (2003). https://doi.org/10.1007/978-0-387-35619-8_4
8. Kumar, A.N.: Data space animation for learning the semantics of c++ pointers. In: Proceedings of the 40th ACM Technical Symposium on Computer Science Education, SIGCSE 2009, pp. 499–503. Association for Computing Machinery, New York (2009). https://doi.org/10.1145/1508865.1509039
9. Kumar, A.N.: A study of the influence of code-tracing problems on code-writing skills. In: Proceedings of the 18th ACM Conference on Innovation and Technology in Computer Science Education, ITiCSE 2013, pp. 183–188. Association for Computing Machinery, New York (2013). https://doi.org/10.1145/2462476.2462507
10. Lane, N., Prestopnik, N.R.: Diegetic connectivity: blending work and play with storytelling in serious games. In: Proceedings of the Annual Symposium on Computer-Human Interaction in Play, CHI PLAY 2017, pp. 229–240. Association for Computing Machinery, New York (2017). https://doi.org/10.1145/3116595.3116630
11. Mathrani, A., Christian, S., Ponder-Sutton, A.: PlayIT: game based learning approach for teaching programming concepts. J. Educ. Technol. Soc. **19**(2), 5–17 (2016). http://www.jstor.org/stable/jeductechsoci.19.2.5

12. McGill, M.M., et al.: If memory serves: towards designing and evaluating a game for teaching pointers to undergraduate students. In: Proceedings of the 2017 ITiCSE Conference on Working Group Reports, ITiCSE-WGR 2017, pp. 25–46. Association for Computing Machinery, New York (2018). https://doi.org/10.1145/3174781.3174783

13. Muratet, M., Torguet, P., Jessel, J.P., Viallet, F.: Towards a serious game to help students learn computer programming. Int. J. Comput. Games Technol. **2009**, 1–12 (2009). https://doi.org/10.1155/2009/470590

14. Ryan, R.M., Mims, V., Koestner, R.: Relation of reward contingency and interpersonal context to intrinsic motivation: a review and test using cognitive evaluation theory. J. Personal. Soc. Psychol. **45**(4), 736 (1983)

15. Schell, J.: The Game Improves Through Iteration, pp. 75–95. Morgan Kaufmann, Burlington (2010)

16. Virvou, M., Katsionis, G., Manos, K.: Combining software games with education: evaluation of its educational effectiveness. J. Educ. Technol. Soc. **8**(2), 54–65 (2005). http://www.jstor.org/stable/jeductechsoci.8.2.54

Antecedents of the Adoption of Gamification in Strategy Alignment: An Exploratory Study of Middle Managers' Perspective

Helder Ferreira[✉] and Catarina Roseira

FEP - School of Economics and Management, University of Porto, Rua Dr. Roberto Frias, 4200-464 Porto, Portugal
hld.ferreira@gmail.com

Abstract. The use of gamification in management, namely in strategic alignment is still under researched. Due to the pivotal role of Middle Managers (MM) in business strategy, this study investigates their perspective on the organizational, individual, and gamification-related factors that may influence the adoption of gamification as a strategic alignment tool. Four focus groups with MM revealed the most relevant antecedents for participants. The paper offers companies some suggestions on how to design and implement successful gamified experiences. Namely, it suggests that clear support of top managers and the involvement of MM in the adoption of gamification may avoid MM' resistance and enhance their motivation and engagement in the process. Also, to assure an effective contribution of MM, it is advisable to evaluate their gamification competences and provide them with adequate training when needed. Finally, due their pivotal position, MM can offer valuable insights to design and communicate the gamification modalities that are the most adequate to participants, thus reducing the identified risks and fostering success.

Keywords: Strategic alignment · Middle managers · Gamification

1 Introduction

Gamification has become present in business [1, 2], and in other various sectors [3, 4]. Despite the research attention it has been attracting, the field still lacks empirical research [5] in the context of management [6] e.g., in work gamification [7]. For instance, Ruhi [8] argues that little empirical research exists on which factors determine the success or failure of enterprise gamification initiatives. Wünderlich et al. [9] call for more research to understand how and when gamification in intra-organizational settings leads to favorable outcomes. This paper responds to the call for further research of gamification in management strategy [10] and explores the use of gamification as a tool of strategy implementation and alignment. Considering MM pivotal role in the implementation of strategy [11] this study reveals specially concerns with MM' perceptions about the potential of gamification application in work contexts and about the factors that may influence its adoption. Specifically, the goal of this study is to understand the Middle

© Springer Nature Switzerland AG 2020
I. Marfisi-Schottman et al. (Eds.): GALA 2020, LNCS 12517, pp. 189–199, 2020.
https://doi.org/10.1007/978-3-030-63464-3_18

Managers' perspective on the factors that may influence the adoption of gamification as a strategy implementation and alignment tool. Two research questions further this issue: (1) what is the role of MM on organizational strategic processes and how may it influence their perceptions on the adoption of gamification?; and (2) which factors can influence the adoption of gamification from the perspective of the MM?

Building on literature on strategy alignment, middle managers and gamification, a theoretical framework proposes that three types of factors – organizational-related factors, individual-related factors, and gamification related factors - may influence the adoption of gamification in this specific setting. Due to its exploratory nature and to the fact that it aims at capturing the perceptions of MM, this study adopts a qualitative methodology, specifically four focus groups, to collect the insights of thirty-four MM from different industries on the research questions. The findings confirm MM's key role in organizations, which can be crucial to the adoption of gamification. Organizational factors (e.g., organizational environment, MM role) and individual factors (e.g., MM resistance, individual characteristics) were identified as influencers of the adopting of gamification. Furthermore, gamification-related benefits (e.g., increase of strategy knowledge and alignment and of engagement with the organization and teams, enhancement of internal communication, and positive influence on employee experience) and risks (e.g., doubts on how to implement gamification and on its advantages, conflict and tensions between employees, time-constrains, lack of top management support, lack of competences to design and apply gamification tools) may influence the adoption of gamification. This paper is structured as follows. Next, it reviews the literature on strategic alignment, middle managers, and gamification. Section 3 presents the research framework and Sect. 4 the research design and methodology. Section 5 discusses the results and Sect. 6 presents the main findings and suggestions to further work.

2 Literature Review

Strategic alignment and Middle Managers: This study adopts Trevor and Varcoe [12] understanding that strategic alignment exists when all elements of a business (including functional strategies) are arranged to best support the fulfillment of its long-term purpose. Namely, a better performance is expected when the operations strategy adequately supports the business strategy [13]. Strategic alignment is widely accepted as a prerequisite for a firm's success [14] and is one of the top concerns of executives and managers [15]. In this sense, organizations that want to stay competitive need to engage employees [16] to achieve high organizational performance [17]. Moreover, employees must understand the strategy, and be committed [18] to execute it successfully [19].

As Baker and Singh [20] mention failure of strategic alignment can be due to inadequate methods of communication and employees disconnected from business strategy. MM can help to prevent this risk, as they hold knowledge and power of influence [21] that facilitates the communication along the organization. MM play the role of intermediaries between top managers and employees [22]. They can participate, influence upward and downward, and make divergent or integrative cognitive contributions to the management strategy [23]. Also, Darkow [24] considers that the top management is not able to develop and implement a strategy successfully without the commitment of MM.

So, it is the interest of the organizations that MM recognize and support the strategy and implement it [11]. Thus, to sustain, develop and promote the involvement of MM with the strategy, organizations should create positive conditions to motivate and engage consistently their employees [25] without disregarding the fact that if MM believe that their self-interest is being compromised, they can delay, reduce the quality or sabotage the strategy implementation [26].

Gamification has been used in various contexts with distinct aims [27] e.g., to solve problems, increase employee motivation [28], change behaviors [3], or to engage and mobilize people to achieve goals [29]. Various studies provide evidence of gamification's positive effects [3, 7, 30] but others show that perceived usefulness, enjoyment and playfulness tend to diminish with time and ease of use [31] and that it is difficult to sustain user engagement with a gamified information system [32]. Even when play is mandatory people have a tendency to give up quickly [30]. Engaging people in gamification experiences requires care and understanding of the player experience, the players themselves [33] and the alignment of intrinsic and extrinsic incentives with business goals [34]. So, it is important that organizations know how to motivate their employees [25] if the employees 'buy' the idea of gamification [35] or if they feel manipulated or intimidated [34]. Despite gamification potential applications in management [34], its influence in this context is still under researched [10, 30]. For instance, Wanick and Bui [34] call for a better understand of management and gamification in a holistic way as well the benefits for both management and employees. To sum-up, this study assumes that strategic alignment is an important process for firm's success, which makes supporting tools relevant for firms and managers. In this context, this study explores gamification as a potential tool to support strategic implementation and alignment. And, due to MM's role, focuses on their views on the adoption of gamification.

3 Research Framework

This study proposes a research framework (cf. Fig. 1) that integrates the antecedents of the adoption of gamification as a strategic implementation and alignment tool.

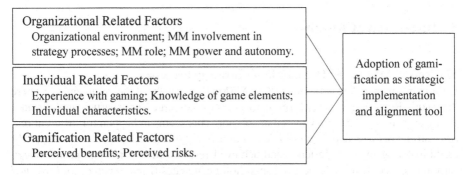

Fig. 1. Research framework

It suggests that MM' views on this issue are influenced by three types of factors: organization-related factors; individual-related factors and gamification perceived benefits and risks.

At the organizational level, Amar [25] claims that to succeed, 'knowledge organizations' have to develop a work environment [34] that consistently motivates and engage their employees e.g., making professional activities more like pleasant games [36]. Ouakouak et al. [37] also highlight the need to involve MM in the organization strategy processes to successfully implement the management strategy. Additionally, their level of power and autonomy may condition the adoption of management tools. At the individual level, this framework proposes that MM's knowledge about game design elements, experience with gaming and individual characteristics as players may influence the adoption of gamification [4]. At the gamification level, as in Guth and MacMillan [26] it seems that the degree to which MM believe that gamification may be aligned with their self-interest (e.g. personal risks and benefits) influence their willingness to adopt gamification tools.

4   Research Design and Methodology

This exploratory study adopts a qualitative approach and focus group technique, an effective way to gather information when little is known about an issue [38]. Focus groups are suitable to allow individuals (MM in this case) to express their experiences, opinions and feelings about a topic [39]. In line with other studies [40], four focus group sessions were organized with 8–9 participants. This allowed to reach data and theoretical saturation [41]. The moderators used a script of open questions to generate data across the sessions [42]. Data was recorded, transcribed, and then coded with the support of NVivo 12 to explore the insights of data [43]. Participants filled a short questionnaire about their knowledge of gamification and demographic and professional details. Thirty-four MM from several hierarchical positions and sectors participated in this study. The sample is balanced in terms of gender. 85% of the sample is aged between 31 and 50 and 91% holds at least a bachelor's degree. Most participants (65%) work in large companies (more than 250 employees); the others are equally distributed between medium (51–250 employees) and small companies (up to 50 employees).

5   Discussion of Results

The Role of MM on the Organization's Strategy Processes
Participants were asked about the role of MM in the strategy of the organizations where they work. Regarding strategy formulation, opinions diverge: some participants consider themselves as contributors while others do not. This seems to happen for different reasons: structure (size, departments, and resources), organizational processes or even MM credibility (e.g. work experience and achieved results). MM participation in strategy formulation seems to influence their psychological states (*I feel involved and satisfied that I can be heard, P24*; *People who saw their ideas implemented felt good, P19*). This study confirms the key role of MM in implementation [11, 21] (*MM distribute strategic*

information across the team and functions, P17; MM know the base of the pyramid to gather and evaluate the best resources, P15) and in strategic alignment (*I can do it in different ways as long as the organization's goal is achieved, P5*).

Antecedents' of Gamification: Organizational Factors

Participants identified organizational environment (e.g., culture, leadership, structures, and departments), the involvement of MM in strategy processes, the role of MM, and the autonomy and power of MM, as relevant factors to the adoption of gamification.

Organization Culture is believed to impact the decision to adopt gamification. Some participants feel that strategies are defined mainly by top managers and MM just implement them. This study confirms a variety of organizational structures and dynamics, which may influence the gamification process as anticipated by Koivisto and Hamari [4]. Conflicts between departments were mentioned as counterproductive to implementation and strategic alignment [44] and to the adoption of gamification tools.

Involvement of MM in Strategy Processes: Findings confirm the need to offer the right conditions to motivate their employees [25]. Reward systems and the work environment (e.g., stimulating of talent, team spirit, sense of belongingness, transparency and clarity of communication and employee participation) impact the involvement of participants with companies and strategy management, e.g., with the adoption of gamification.

Role of MM: Participants identified three roles that may impact gamification: adjust internal communication between different internal audiences, be agents of change, and motivate 'players' to participate and involve them in gamified experiences.

Autonomy and Power of MM to Adopt Gamification in Work Contexts: Participants mentioned some factors that impact their autonomy and power and consequently the implementation of gamification: MM leadership competences, experience and knowledge (*top management does not understand the operation; it's up to us, MM, to manage the operation, P30*), MM's negotiation skills (*my conquered power depends on my attitude when I present the pros and cons, P28*), credibility gained from results (*I have autonomy because I provide quantifiable results, P28*) and support of top managers (*it takes superior sponsorship from the organization, P9*). The global feeling is that without enough 'power', MM are not able to effectively involve their teams [45] or convince top managers to accept gamification.

MM Resistance: In line with Fenton-O'Creevy [45], this study identified several constraints to the implementation of management strategy that also apply to the adoption of gamification, namely: block information or/and implementation, aversion to change; disagree and misalignment with the management strategy and demotivation.

Antecedents' of Gamification: Individual Factors

Experience with gaming and knowledge of games were previously indicated as individual factors that may influence the adoption of gamification. In this case, while only a few participants reported gaming experience and knowledge of game elements, 85% said they were 'interested' or 'very interested' to adopt gamification tools. Although knowledge and experience do not seem determinant in the decision to adopt gamification tools, they may influence their implementation. Individual characteristics of MM, such as skills, motivation and personalities, were also identified as factors that affect gamification in works contexts, which is in line with Buckley and Doyle [46].

Gamification - Related Factors
This study identified a set of perceived risks and benefits that may negatively or positively condition the adoption of gamification tools, as detailed below.

Risks: Perceived risks may block or delay the adoption of gamification (see Table 1).

Table 1. Gamification perceived risks

Level	Risks	Interview excerpts
Organizational	Doubts about gamification	*To MM to adopt gamification, it is necessary to know how it works (…) and show the benefits (P2)*
	Conflict and tensions between employee's	*Considering the conflicts between departments, when you adopt gamification you may intensify those conflicts (P13)*
	Lack of top management support	*It needs sponsorship from the Board and then each MM with its own style can use it or not (P9)*
Individual	Lack of knowledge and skills in gamification	*You have to teach us how we to design the game (P25); For a specific context, someone more trained is needed to design the (gamification) tool (P3)*
	Individual characteristics and personality	*Gamification must be framed by the culture of the people who report to MM, otherwise it is a problem (P17); It is more interesting for some people than for others (P32)*
	Time constrains	*You need to see how much time is going to be wasted in the game, as we have projects to complete (P22)*

In line with Hassan and Hamari [47] participants showed concerns about the possibility of gamification generating conflicts and tensions between employees and teams. This can in fact occur as result of using poor design gamified experiences [4], among other factors. Ignorance of gamification advantages and unsatisfactory results are seen as good reasons for not adopting gamification until the concept prove its effectiveness. Lack of top management support may also hinder the adoption of gamification tools. At the individual level, the lack of knowledge of MM on how to design and apply gamification

(35% of participants were not familiar with the concept) highlights the importance to carefully design carefully gamification [48] that take into account participants' level of expertise in this area. Participants identified other issues that can jeopardize the adoption of gamification: the heterogeneity of players (MM and other employees) [49] namely their motivations [33] mindset and dispositions [8]. Finally, time consumed with gamification was identified as a risk mainly because it is perceived as non-core activity that requires extra time and effort. MM fear that the gamification experience may be an extra to their worktime instead of being part of it.

Benefits are mainly associated with the organizational level (see Table 2).

Table 2. Gamification perceived benefits

Level	Benefits	Interview excerpts
Organizational	Knowledge of management strategy	*To know better the reasons why teams are involved in tasks, perceive better the goals, results and strategy* (P10)
	Alignment with management strategy	*This tool may help to disseminate what is important and crucial for the organization* (P15); [gamification]*make it clear how to achieve medium and strategic goals* (P17)
	Engagement with the organization and with teams	*The need to retain MM is so great that leads to the creation of games to retain people* (P19); *It is an interesting way of interacting, learning and training* (P3); *Team members will get involved and gain additional motivation* (P2)
	Internal communication	*If gamification is adopted by the company it can improve company communication* (P13)
Individual	Employee experience	*We know that it has an emotional effect* (P11); *Stimulate the person's curiosity, take the stress out for a few moments and focus on something more fun* (P24);

Participants refer the gain of knowledge of management strategy, sense of alignment with the management strategy, engagement with the organization and with teams, and enhanced internal communications. They also hope that the employees' experience may improve with the adoption of gamification tools in work contexts (e.g., less stressful, and more stimulate). These findings are in line with Wünderlich et al. [9] that found out much potential in implementing gamification in intra-organizational settings.

6   Conclusion

This study responds to calls for empirical research of gamification [5, 9, 27] in management [6], and focuses on MM perspective on the factors that may influence the adoption of gamification as a strategic alignment tool.

The study involved four focus groups with the participation of thirty-four MM from companies of different industries, sizes, and structures. In line with existing literature, it confirms MM's key role in strategy management, particularly in the implementation process, which suggests that they may also play a crucial role on the implementation of gamification experiences.

This study identifies factors at the organizational, individual, and gamification levels that seem to influence the adoption of gamification. At the organizational level, the organizational environment (e.g., culture, leadership, structures, and departments), the role of MM and their involvement in strategy processes emerge as the most relevant influencing factors. At the individual level, previous experience with gaming and knowledge of games seems indifferent to the interest of adoption of gamification; however, lack of knowledge and skills in the area is seen as a deterrent to its implementation. Thus, to increase the possibility of success of gamification, and specially considering the pivotal role of MM, it is advisable to evaluate their gamification competences and provide them with adequate training if needed. Other issues like MM's power and autonomy, and potential resistance to gamification if they believe it may harm their individual interests, should also be considered as they impact their willingness to collaborate and to effectively support the adoption and implementation of gamification. Regarding the individual characteristics of employees and in line with previous research [33], this study suggest that the adoption of gamification in management requires solutions (e.g. specific configuration of game elements) that are customized to MM and other players characteristics to produce the intended results.

Lastly, the paper identifies several benefits associated with gamification by MM (e.g., increase of knowledge and alignment with management strategy, increase of engagement with the organization and with the teams, and enhancement of internal communication processes), which may positively impact MM attitude towards gamification. On the contrary, identified perceived risks (e.g. increase of conflict and tension between employees, teams and departments, resistance based on doubts, unknown advantages or absence of positive results, lack of top management support, lack of gamification competences) may contribute to negative attitudes towards the use of gamification tools. Thus, when adopting it, companies should be aware of the benefits and pitfalls that different modalities of gamification may accrue.

This paper focuses on the perspective of MM due to their pivotal role. However, there are other relevant stakeholders (e.g. gamification providers, gamification consultants, top managers, MM teams, customers) in the process. Thus, future studies may explore the factors that influence the adoption and outcomes of gamification from a multi-stakeholder perspective. Other fruitful research areas with useful contributions to academics and practitioners can be the role of MM as ignitors of gamification in work contexts and the influence this may have on the outcomes; the impact of distinct models of gamification adoption (bottom-up, top-down) on the implementation process and outcomes of gamification; and the impact that successful or failed gamified experiences can have on MM role in the organization and also on further adoption of gamification.

References

1. Robson, K., et al.: Is it all a game? Understanding the principles of gamification. Bus. Horiz. **58**(4), 411–420 (2015)
2. Hanus, M.D., Fox, J.: Assessing the effects of gamification in the classroom: a longitudinal study on intrinsic motivation, social comparison, satisfaction, effort, and academic performance. Comput. Educ. **80**, 152–161 (2015)
3. Hamari, J., Koivisto, J., Sarsa, H.: Does gamification work? – a literature review of empirical studies on gamification. In: 2014 47th Hawaii International Conference on System Sciences, pp. 3025–3034 (2014)
4. Koivisto, J., Hamari, J.: The rise of motivational information systems: a review of gamification research. Int. J. Inf. Manag. **45**, 191–210 (2019)
5. Hamari, J., Koivisto, J.: Why do people use gamification services? Int. J. Inf. Manag. **35**(4), 419–431 (2015)
6. Landers, R.N.: Gamification misunderstood: how badly executed and rhetorical gamification obscures its transformative potential. J. Manag. Inq. **28**(2), 137–140 (2019)
7. Cardador, M.T., Northcraft, G.B., Whicker, J.: A theory of work gamification: something old, something new, something borrowed, something cool? Hum. Resour. Manag. Rev. **27**(2), 353–365 (2017)
8. Ruhi, U.: Level up your strategy: towards a descriptive framework for meaningful enterprise gamification. Technol. Innov. Manag. Rev. **5**, 5–16 (2015)
9. Wünderlich, N.V., et al.: The great game of business: advancing knowledge on gamification in business contexts. J. Bus. Res. **106**, 273–276 (2020)
10. Hamari, J., et al.: Theoretical perspectives and applications of gamification in business contexts. J. Bus. Res. (2017)
11. Mair, J., Thurner, C.: Going global: how middle managers approach the process in medium-sized firms. Strateg. Chang. **17**(3–4), 83–99 (2008)
12. Trevor, J., Varcoe, B.: A simple way to test your company's strategic alignment. Harv. Bus. Rev. Digit. Artic. (2016)
13. Avison, D., et al.: Using and validating the strategic alignment model. J. Strateg. Inf. Syst. **13**(3), 223–246 (2004)
14. Acur, N., Kandemir, D., Boer, H.: Strategic alignment and new product development: drivers and performance effects. J. Prod. Innov. Manag. **29**(2), 304–318 (2012)
15. Cao, R., Baker, J., Hoffman, J.: The role of the competitive environment in studies of strategic alignment: a meta-analysis. Int. J. Prod. Res. **50**, 567–580 (2012)
16. Bakker, A.B.: Strategic and proactive approaches to work engagement. Organ. Dyn. **46**(2), 67–75 (2017)
17. Walter, J., et al.: Strategic alignment: a missing link in the relationship between strategic consensus and organizational performance. Strateg. Organ. **11**(3), 304–328 (2013)
18. Kaplan, R.S., Norton, D.P.: The Execution Premium: Linking Strategy to Operations for Competitive Advantage. Harvard Business Press, Brighton (2013)
19. Box, S., Platts, K.: Business process management: establishing and maintaining project alignment. Bus. Process Manag. J. **11**(4), 370–387 (2005)
20. Baker, J., Singh, H.: The roots of misalignment: insights on strategy implementation from a system dynamics perspective. J. Strateg. Inf. Syst. **28**(4), 101576 (2019)

21. Ahearne, M., Lam, S.K., Kraus, F.: Performance impact of middle managers' adaptive strategy implementation: the role of social capital. Strateg. Manag. J. **35**(1), 68–87 (2014)
22. Huy, Q.N.: In praise of middle managers. Harv. Bus. Rev. **79**(8), 72–79 (2001)
23. Floyd, S.W., Wooldridge, B.: Middle management involvement in strategy and its association with strategic type: a research note. Strateg. Manag. J. **13**(S1), 153–167 (1992)
24. Darkow, I.-L.: The involvement of middle management in strategy development—development and implementation of a foresight-based approach. Technol. Forecast. Soc. Chang. **101**, 10–24 (2015)
25. Amar, A.D.: Motivating knowledge workers to innovate: a model integrating motivation dynamics and antecedents. Eur. J. Innov. Manag. **7**(2), 89–101 (2004)
26. Guth, W.D., MacMillan, I.C.: Strategy implementation versus middle management self-interest. Strateg. Manag. J. **7**(4), 313–327 (1986)
27. Seaborn, K., Fels, D.I.: Gamification in theory and action: a survey. Int. J. Hum.-Comput. Stud. **74**, 14–31 (2015)
28. Friedrich, J., et al.: Incentive design and gamification for knowledge management. J. Bus. Res. **106**, 341–352 (2020)
29. Kim, B.: Understanding Gamification. ALA TechSource, Chicago (2015)
30. Deterding, S.: Gamification in management: between choice architecture and humanistic design. J. Manag. Inq. **28**(2), 131–136 (2019)
31. Koivisto, J., Hamari, J.: Demographic differences in perceived benefits from gamification. Comput. Hum. Behav. **35**, 179–188 (2014)
32. Suh, A., et al.: Gamification in the workplace: the central role of the aesthetic experience. J. Manag. Inf. Syst. **34**(1), 268–305 (2017)
33. Tondello, G.F., et al.: Empirical validation of the gamification user types hexad scale in English and Spanish. Int. J. Hum.-Comput. Stud. **127**, 95–111 (2019)
34. Wanick, V., Bui, H.: Gamification in management: a systematic review and research directions. Int. J. Serious Games **6**(2), 57–74 (2019)
35. Landers, R.N., Bauer, K.N., Callan, R.C.: Gamification of task performance with leaderboards: a goal setting experiment. Comput. Hum. Behav. **71**, 508–515 (2017)
36. Mancilha Da Silva, A.M., Pinho, A.F.: Definition of a framework for organisational management. Knowl. Manag. Res. Pract. **18**, 1–16 (2020)
37. Ouakouak, M.L., Ouedraogo, N., Mbengue, A.: The mediating role of organizational capabilities in the relationship between middle managers' involvement and firm performance: a European study. Eur. Manag. J. **32**(2), 305–318 (2014)
38. Masadeh, M.A.: Focus group: reviews and practices. Int. J. Appl. Sci. Technol. **2**(10), 63–68 (2012)
39. Herington, C., Scott, D., Johnson, W.L.: Focus group exploration of firm-employee relationship strength. Qual. Mark. Res.: Int. J. **8**(3), 256–276 (2005)
40. Morgan, D.L.: Planning and research design for focus groups. Focus Groups Qual. Res. **16** (1997)
41. Onwuegbuzie, A.J., Leech, N.L.: A call for qualitative power analyses. Qual. Quant. **41**(1), 105–121 (2007)
42. Creswell, W.J.: Research design qualitative, quantitative, and mixed methods approaches (2009)
43. Feng, X., Behar-Horenstein, L.: Maximizing NVivo utilities to analyze open-ended responses. Qual. Rep. **24**(3), 563–571 (2019)
44. Hatch, M., Schultz, M.: Are the strategic stars aligned for your corporate. Harv. Bus. Rev. **79**, 128–134 (2001)
45. Fenton-O'Creevy, M.: Employee involvement and the middle manager: evidence from a survey of organizations. J. Organ. Behav.: Int. J. Ind. Occup. Organ. Psychol. Behav. **19**(1), 67–84 (1998)

46. Buckley, P., Doyle, E.: Individualising gamification: an investigation of the impact of learning styles and personality traits on the efficacy of gamification using a prediction market. Comput. Educ. **106**, 43–55 (2017)
47. Hassan, L., Hamari, J.: Gameful civic engagement: a review of the literature on gamification of e-participation. Gov. Inf. Q. **37**, 101461 (2020)
48. Mitchell, R., Schuster, L., Jin, H.S.: Gamification and the impact of extrinsic motivation on needs satisfaction: making work fun? J. Bus. Res. **106**, 323–330 (2020)
49. Mulcahy, R., Russell-Bennett, R., Iacobucci, D.: Designing gamified apps for sustainable consumption: a field study. J. Bus. Res. **106**, 377–387 (2020)

Using Gamification to Improve Students' Typing Skills

Szabina Fodor$^{(\boxtimes)}$ (iD) and Márton Varga

Corvinus University of Budapest, Budapest, Hungary
szabina.fodor@uni-corvinus.hu,
marton.varga7@stud.uni-corvinus.hu

Abstract. Educational systems are under increasing pressure to use information and communication technologies (ICTs) and to teach students the knowledge and skills they need. While tablets have become important tools in education today, typing on the computer is still a crucial skill for students to learn. In this paper we describe the design, implementation, and evaluation of a gamified application which aims to improve 10-finger typing skills. Evaluation of our application revealed that the users showed a solid improvement in typing skills. Overall, our development got positive feedback and a broad demand for the application was received.

Keywords: Gamification · 10-finger typing · Joyful learning

1 Introduction

The coronavirus (COVID-19) pandemic has significant impact on the importance of digital learning as it has disrupted the usual didactic education and in parallel, it has reinforced the importance of some competencies [1, 2], like 10-finger typing. Unplanned school closures caused by COVID-19 could negatively affect the academic interest and performance of students [1].

The gamification, which is defined as *"using game-design elements in any non-game system context to increase users' intrinsic and extrinsic motivation, help them to process information, help them to better achieve goals, and/or help them to change their behaviour"* [3, 4] has become one of the most popular strategies to strengthen motivation and commitment to learning. The popularity of gamification used in education is understandable as there are overlaps between game and the classroom. Players work to achieve one (or more) certain goals and ultimately win, while students work to achieve specific learning goals and deliver adequate academic performance. Players progress from level to level based on their performance, and students must achieve different levels of courses and master specific topics for their academic development [5].

One of the essential features of gamification is that the gamified application is mostly based on online, digital technology. An important consideration is that the current student base is made up of members of Generation Z (born in the mid-to-late 1990s to the early 2010s) whose learning and information-gathering habits are vastly different from those

© Springer Nature Switzerland AG 2020
I. Marfisi-Schottman et al. (Eds.): GALA 2020, LNCS 12517, pp. 200–206, 2020.
https://doi.org/10.1007/978-3-030-63464-3_19

of previous generations. Generation Z uses the Internet and social media comfortably, naturally and often, as they have been an integral part of their lives and socialization processes from an early age [6, 7]. Another important feature of members of Generation Z is that a decrease in the ability to maintain attention can be observed. Gamification can be a solution to this as it helps to break down the learning process into smaller steps, and students' motivation can be increased with different styles and degrees of positive reinforcement [6].

The impact of gamification can be even greater if we can gather information about gamified platforms. The results of analyses based on such information allow learners to tailor educational gamification goals and principles to their specific needs and learning paces [8].

There are many examples of the applications which use the concept of gamification in education and educational activities. Markets and Markets reports that the value of the educational gamification market is expected to grow from $9.1 billion in 2020 to $30.7 billion by 2025. Key elements of growth include the increasing use of digital learning and the growing use of cloud-based services among organizations [9]. However, gamification should not be considered as an elixir that solves all teachers' problems immediately, but rather as one of the many efficiency-enhancing tools.

In this paper, we present a gamified application (*Dungeon Typer*) which aims to improve the 10-finger typing skill. Its target audience is the youth, particularly students of middle school and lower secondary school. In the following section related work is discussed. Section 3 presents the game design that was used. Section 4 presents the implementation of our game and the students' feedbacks. Finally, conclusions are drawn in Sect. 5.

2 Related Work

Many studies have been published on the use of gamification in elementary, secondary, and higher education to promote students' motivation. The evidence of the effectiveness of gamification is mainly empirical. Wrzesien and Raya published a study [10] that found no significant correlation between children who were taught via games and the control group. The students reported enjoying the class more, being engaged more than the control group.

So far, there have been a few proposals (RapidTyping[1], Felhos[2]) to apply gamification techniques to teach typing to children using the Hungarian keyboard. One of the challenges in teaching typing skills is that it is highly language specific, since most languages use unique characters in addition to the English alphabet.

Currently, Hungarian students use a program called ABC[3] in secondary education for learning the 10-finger typing technique. This program is not considered a gamified solution as it does not include any game elements or mechanisms; it only shows the proper finger usage and provides some typing tasks for practicing.

---

[1] https://rapidtyping.com/.

[2] egyszervolt.hu.

[3] gepokt.hu.

3 Game Design

There are several theories and frameworks of gamification like PBL[4], Wu's [11], Bartle's [12], Kim's [13] models, Octalysis [14], and MDA framework [15] which can help to create an effective gamified application. In our project we used the Gamification Model Canvas which based on the MDA framework. Ms. Bella who has been teaching typing for many years at BGSZC Secondary School of Buda[5], helped a lot in developing the game mechanisms. We have developed the principles of our gamification design based on numerous personal discussions with her and class visits.

According to the Gamification Model Canvas we set our main tasks:

- **setting challenges** (traditional assignment):

  - The curriculum needs to be articulated and multiple levels created from it. This way, everyone can learn at a speed that is not too difficult, but not too easy for them.
  - During the learning we need to keep track of which character is next in the text, and you also need to show which finger to use to hit that character.
  - We should not use meaningless 3-letter words to build proper finger-muscle memory.
  - When displaying a word, it is very important that it remains legible and does not overlap with another word. It should always be clear which word belongs to which game element.

- **motivation** (the dynamic and aesthetic layer of MDA): currently, we use only elements of the PBL and Wu's reward models.

  - The scoring system should be designed to look more like positive feedback.
  - The increase in difficulty level must be assigned to a specific point amount. This point amount increases with each level, so the more points are collected, the harder the game will be.
  - To awaken the spirit of competition, it is important to have a multiplayer mode or leaderboard.

- **making stress-free setting**: we try to eliminate the most important sources of stress in these situations.

  - It is important to assure our players that they can run into the task several times. The goal is to get the best out of them. This means making a "*mistake okay, trying again is good*" slogan as failure is not only an option, it is expected. Our game starts with multiple lives because it is assumed students are going to need them.
  - It is important to raise awareness of the acquired knowledge and skills, even though the incorporation of a follow-up training.
  - We use only local leaderboard which lists only nearby players.

---

[4] Points, badges and leaderboards.
[5] https://budaikozepiskola.hu/.

3.1 Framing the Vocabulary

It was essential to collect the right number of words to avoid the words being repeated too often. Our vocabulary based on a Web-based frequency dictionary was created in 2006 by the MOKK Centre for Media Research and Education[6] [16]. After filtering out the improper words (like dirty words, terms of reproach) we selected the approximately 2000 most common words while preserving the distribution of initial letters of the original dictionary. We divided this selected word list into three further sub-lists based on length of the word (containing five or fewer characters, from six to eight, or more than eight characters). According to this grouping, the words were included in the list of short, intermediate or long words and were used such in our game.

4   Our Gamified Solution: Dungeon Typer

Dungeon Typer is built around the concept that the player needs to escape from a prison guarded by skeletons. Skeletons try to make the escape attempt difficult with obstacles and soldiers. Deactivating these obstacles and eliminating enemies play the role of sub-tasks. By completing each subtask, the player brings the protagonist closer to reaching his goal. The following snapshot (Fig. 1) shows a subtask in which the player must defeat a soldier by typing correctly the appearing word within the time limit.

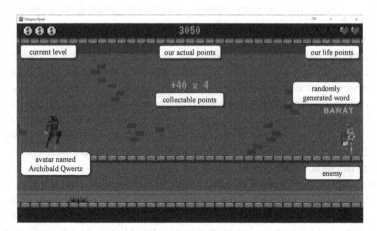

Fig. 1. Dungeon *Typer*: screen capture of a randomly generated track in early game level

During the typing, the program checks each keystroke to see if the current character is correct or not. If correct, no feedback will be given, if not, an audible signal will alert the player and will be deducted from the collectible points. If the player manages to type the active word correctly within the time frame, he gets a point and the avatar defeats, jumps out or rolls under the enemy. If the player fails and the animated opponent reaches

---

[6] http://mokk.bme.hu/en/.

the avatar, then a sword stroke animation will play, and a life point will be deducted from the player.

At the end of the game, the user can save his/her current points to a personal list and have the option to query the local leaderboard which lists only three nearby players.

4.1 Validating Our Gamified Solution

We implemented our game in C# using the Unity[7] development platform to design imagery which is captivating to our target audience.

Originally, we planned that we would validate our game with the help of students of BGSZC Secondary School of Buda. Our game was planned to be used by students with different ages and different levels of typing. However, an unscheduled closure of all schools was on March, 2020 due to coronavirus disease (COVID-19) outbreak in Hungary. Unfortunately, the originally planned intensive validation of the system could not be performed. Thanks to teachers' generous help we managed to perform the test of our program in a limited way. We sent the program and a questionnaire to 50 students and we asked them to try out the program as many times as they can and give their feedbacks using a questionnaire. During a two-week test period, 37 (8 male/29 female) students completed the questionnaire. We consider this as a great progress, particularly since the installation of the program was an extra task for the students.

At first, we were curious about how happy the users were to try the game. This question was intended to assess the attitude of the users before starting the game. This had to be marked on a scale of one to five, where a score of one means you are reluctant and a score of five means you are very enthusiastic. Roughly thirty percent of the students rated it neutrally, thirty-two percent chose the value of four, and the remaining thirty-eight percent were very happy to try it. Those who gave a neutral rating did not know what to expect about such a game or did not want to use a new program. Answer four was chosen by students who were interested in the software to be tested, but they found it difficult to put it into practice. Those are also in this group who were curious about the game itself but were unsure of their own abilities. Curiosity and interest were also expressed by those who were very happy to try the game, but there were also responses referring to the topic of the game or the control mechanism.

The next question was about how the testers liked the game. This question aimed to assess the experience of the users after obtaining experience with the game. The answer could be given on a scale of one to five. It is interesting how much their rates have changed after trying the game. Far more students rated the game positively than in the previous question. The number of five-point responses more than doubled (see in Fig. 2 Panel A).

In the third question, we asked whether players perceived an improving trend in the score of consecutive rounds played. This question was intended to show how successful the game has been in improving the 10-finger typing skills. In the present survey, this is only indicative and requires further comprehensive examination, but Fig. 2. Panel B clearly shows that eighty-one percent of the students who tried the game felt that their typing ability had improved.

---

[7] http://unity.com/.

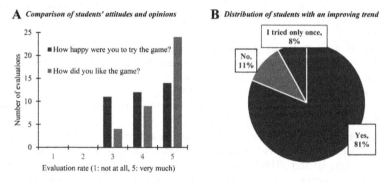

Fig. 2. Students' feedbacks

In the last question, we were curious about how willing students would be to use this game if it were made compulsory in school education. For example, if it is used by teachers at school as part of the curriculum or as an assessment method. We used a scale from one to five, where one meant that respondent would not like to see this game at all, and five meant that he/she would fully enjoy using it. The average of the responses received was 4.7, and 87% of response was 5 (data not shown). Overall, the users' feedback shows that students have improved their typing skills. In addition, students would be happy to use this program in their lessons.

We should mention that our study is limited by the fact that the feedback responses is self-reported, we could reach just small number of students due to coronavirus disease outbreak. Use of self-reported data is highly to affect the results as the users responding are most probably actively engaged with the service, and eager to participate in activities related to it. We are planning to perform a more comprehensive validation of our solution.

5 Conclusion

In this paper we presented a gamified application, *Dungeon Typer*, designed with the goal of improving 10-finger typing skills among secondary school students. We evaluated our game with secondary school students and the results showed its effectiveness in improving typing skills. Moreover, the students found the typing practice more enjoyable using gamified solution than the current one.

In the future, aside from refining the game we are planning to incorporate some new features based on additional feedback already received from the students. For example, in the current version of the game, only one avatar, Archibald can be selected and only his story was included in the game. We are planning to incorporate more persons. Future studies could also incorporate control groups to examine the effects of the gamification of the application. Such better-controlled experiments would be able to reveal subtle differences in a very precise manner on the effect of gamification in a secondary school education setting.

Acknowledgements. We highly appreciate Ms. Bella for her continuous and generous help and the students of BGSZC Secondary School of Buda who volunteered to test our game.

References

1. Onyema, E.M., et al.: Impact of coronavirus pandemic on education (2020)
2. Händel, M., et al.: Do students have the means to learn during the coronavirus pandemic? Student demands for distance learning in a suddenly digital landscape (2020)
3. Hamari, J., Koivisto, J., Sarsa, H.: Does gamification work?–a literature review of empirical studies on gamification. In: 2014 47th Hawaii International Conference on System Sciences. IEEE (2014)
4. Treiblmaier, H., Putz, L.-M., Lowry, P.B.: Setting a definition, context, and theory-based research agenda for the gamification of non-gaming applications. Assoc. Inf. Syst. Trans. Hum.-Comput. Interact. (THCI) **10**(3), 129–163 (2018)
5. Jackson, M.: Gamification in education: a literature review. Center for Faculty Excellence (2016)
6. Horovitz, B.: After Gen X, Millennials, what should next generation be. USA Today **4**, 2012-0503 (2012)
7. Koivisto, J., Hamari, J.: Demographic differences in perceived benefits from gamification. Comput. Hum. Behav. **35**, 179–188 (2014)
8. Barna, B., Fodor, S.: An empirical study on the use of gamification on IT courses at higher education. In: Auer, M.E., Guralnick, D., Simonics, I. (eds.) ICL 2017. AISC, vol. 715, pp. 684–692. Springer, Cham (2018). https://doi.org/10.1007/978-3-319-73210-7_80
9. Markets, M.A.: Gamification in education market by offering (software and services), deployment mode (cloud and on-premises), end user (academic (K12 and higher education) and corporate training (SMEs and large enterprises)), and region - global forecast to 2023 (2019)
10. Wrzesien, M., Raya, M.A.: Learning in serious virtual worlds: evaluation of learning effectiveness and appeal to students in the E-Junior project. Comput. Educ. **55**(1), 178–187 (2010)
11. Wu, M.: Level up your gamification to solve big business problems. In: Gamification World Congress (2015)
12. Bartle, R.A.: Designing Virtual Worlds. New Riders, USA (2004)
13. Kim, A.J.: Putting the fun in functional. Applying Game Mechanics to Functional Software (2008)
14. Chou, Y.-K.: Actionable Gamification: Beyond Points, Badges, and Leaderboards. Packt Publishing Ltd., Birmingham (2019)
15. Hunicke, R., LeBlanc, M., Zubek, R.: MDA: a formal approach to game design and game research. In: Proceedings of the AAAI Workshop on Challenges in Game AI (2004)
16. Kornai, A., et al.: Web-based frequency dictionaries for medium density languages (2006)

Designing an Online *Dungeons & Dragons* Experience for Primary School Children

Rosalba Spotorno[1], Marco Picone[2], and Manuel Gentile[3,4(✉)]

[1] Scuola Secondaria I grado G. A. Borgese-XXVII Maggio, Palermo, Italy
rosalba.spotorno@gmail.com
[2] Dipartimento di Architettura, Università degli Studi di Palermo, Palermo, Italy
marco.picone@unipa.it
[3] Institute for Educational Technology, National Research Council of Italy,
Rome, Italy
manuel.gentile@itd.cnr.it
[4] Dipartimento di Informatica, Università di Torino, Turin, Italy
manuel.gentile@unito.it,
http://www.itd.cnr.it/

Abstract. In this work, we present the results of a role-playing game experience carried out with a group of 9- to 12-year-old children during the COVID-19 emergence. The 'harmony in education' approach has been used to adapt the game design to the constraints imposed by the online context and the young age of the students involved. The results show the effectiveness of the approach in terms of 21st-century skills training with particular evidence on perspective-taking.

Keywords: D&D · RPG · Primary school · Serious games design

1 Introduction

The theme of life skills, what they are, their role in promoting the well-being and health of the citizens of the future, how they impact on the development of active citizenship and, of course, how to train them, is undoubtedly one of the most debated topics in scientific literature. In 1994, the World Health Organization (WHO) [14] identified the life skills and grouped them into five areas: 1) Decision-making and problem-solving, 2) Creative thinking and critical thinking, 3) Communication and interpersonal skills, 4) Self-awareness and empathy, 5) Coping with emotions and coping with stress. Moreover, WHO indicated in the school the ideal environment for training them and ensure the health and well-being of children and young adults.

In 2006, the European Parliament and the Council of the European Union adopted a Recommendation on Key Competences for Lifelong Learning [6]. A recent Recommendation of European Council [8] redefined these competences by integrating several themes like inclusion, sustainability, gender equality and

© Springer Nature Switzerland AG 2020
I. Marfisi-Schottman et al. (Eds.): GALA 2020, LNCS 12517, pp. 207–217, 2020.
https://doi.org/10.1007/978-3-030-63464-3_20

global citizenship. The Recommendation focused on the values of curiosity, creativity and the ability to relate to "the other" (intended as a person, context, culture, diversity), alongside the abilities of critical thinking and resilience. The document takes into account the importance of knowing how to evaluate the risks associated with transformations, the ability to read contexts, the need for a continuous state of self-reflection as well as the control of communication and relational phenomena.

All these steps led to the definition of what today is identified as 21st-century skills, that are the skills that human beings need to train to be good citizens, successful workers and to be able to cope with a context (the 21st century) [10] and that also UN 2030 agenda [5] reports as critical goals.

This perspective requires a careful approach to the design of learning spaces, and the necessity to reorganize the structure of the classroom in study groups to allow students to experience an environment based on peer education and cooperative learning. To do this, frontal teaching and fear or derision are not only useless, but can even dramatically prevent the learning process.

The need to rethink the teacher role and the very essence of teaching, moving from a mere transfer of information to the idea of building knowledge in action, is a matter of fact.

Piaget [15] argued that the methods used to obtain or create knowledge influence the validity of the resulting knowledge. Indeed, the pedagogy of the last century, which for brevity cannot be examined in detail, has widely debated the role of games within the child's learning process, because playing is the natural way of learning from birth, starting by social rules in a controlled situation, and if properly guided by an adult, it can serenely stretch towards the zone of proximal development (ZPD) to discover new horizons [23].

A huge number of authors have published examples of activities useful for the development of life skills in the classroom [12] also through the use of storytelling [4,18] or role-playing games [1,16,19].

The gamification of learning develops and enhances in an exemplary way most of the skills and competences, bringing out the hidden talents of children and teenagers and bringing out the potential mix of multiple intelligence of which each person is the expression [9], all to be developed according to the different cognitive styles.

In this paper, after presenting the core principles of that empirical approach that goes under the name of 'harmony in education', we try to understand how these principles, which seem to respond naturally to the demands imposed by 21st-century skills, can guide the design of role-playing experiences. In particular, we try to make explicit those design rules that have guided the creation of a *Dungeons & Dragons*-based educational activity.

2   Harmony in Education Through Role-Playing Games

In the last decades many projects, initiatives, realities and experiences have been born, realized above all by educators [11], but also by teachers [20] and psychotherapists [17], as well as by connected didactic or experiential laboratories at major fairs in the recreational sector, such as Lucca Comics and Games and Play Modena [2, 21], just to mention the best known.

Over the years of teaching, the authors of this paper have progressively developed an empirical and integrated teaching methodology called 'Harmony in Education.' One of the pillars of this method is the use of games and playing, employing a playful approach to traditional disciplines, the constant use of role-playing (especially to solve relationship problems) for the development of personal and social skills as well as peer collaboration.

The fundamental points for a true playful teaching cannot be separated from:

- Stimulation of the recognition of one's own and others' emotions to work with emotional intelligence and develop empathy and the ability to interact with others in a socially effective and constructive way (Goleman 2011);
- Continuous reflections on fair play and use of breathing techniques. This leads to an awareness and acceptance of negative emotions, which are encouraged to flow, including the fear of losing in competitive games, the sense of revenge on the partner who has won and who is considered an enemy instead of an opponent, the desire to collaborate to solve a problem, an enigma or develop a project by combining different intelligences and sensitivities to create something new and more creative;
- A humorous approach to things that happen at school (Sclavi and Giornelli 2014), to learn not to take themselves too seriously and not to dramatize the negative experiences that inevitably happen, trying to welcome them with all the wealth of useful comments they bring with themselves. This allows an acceptance of error not as an enemy but as a valuable ally and useful tool for knowledge and bad marks as an indicator of performance and not of the value of the person;
- The desire to have fun discovering, so the teacher does not drop all the knowledge from above but provides stimuli so that students can become curious, research and use creativity in learning also through the use of games or the playful approach to educational experiences;
- An interdisciplinary approach, linked to the reality of the topics addressed in school.

The techniques developed constitute real 'motivational hooks' that work well even in difficult cases, improving inclusion at school: even initially very unmotivated and oppositional pupils towards school change their attitude and become positive examples of transformation and agents of diffusion of the method. It should almost be taken for granted that in a society where hyper-specializations in all areas tend to lose sight of the general concepts and uniqueness of the person, the way of thinking and approaching knowledge is more important than knowledge itself; knowing how to think is more important than remembering every single detail, which is impossible. These reflections were employed in the design of the case study that will be addressed in Sect. 4 of this paper. In particular, our goal is to provide readers with tools that can help them adapt this case to other similar cases in primary and secondary schools.

3   Dungeons & Dragons: From Tabletop Game to Educational Tool

Dungeons & Dragons (D&D) is arguably the most famous tabletop role-playing game (RPG) and still actually the one which is most played all over the world [13]. Originally published in 1974, D&D has known many iterations, up to the 5th edition (D&D 5e) which was published in 2014 and met with a very high success: in 2017, Wizards of the Coast (the publishing company) estimated that the player base of D&D 5e includes 8.6 million American players [24], while more recently Wizards of the Coast estimated there to be more than 40 million D&D fans since the game was first released in 1974.[1] D&D 5e's primary goal was to make the game simpler and provide younger generations with the possibility to access the world of tabletop RPGs quickly and easily. In order to further increase this process and to exploit the commercial success of such popular TV shows as *Stranger Things* and *The Big Bang Theory*, both heavily influenced by D&D, Wizards of the Coast released a Starter Set aiming at attracting even younger players (Fig. 1).

Fig. 1. D&D Starter Set - Wizards of the Coast©.

Although the Starter Set[2] suggested a starting age of 12+, the case study we address in this paper proved that even 9-year-old children can be easily introduced to the world of D&D, as we will describe in the following Section. Implementing the use of the game with young children brings us to reflect on the role of D&D as an education tool. There are several studies showing how to use D&D to integrate curricula in elementary schools [3] or in higher grades [22]. Since the restrictions due to the COVID-19 lockdown made it impossible to physically meet at the table to play, the case study described in the following

---

[1] https://www.cnbc.com/2020/03/14/critical-role-helped-spark-a-dungeons-dragons-renaissance.html.

[2] https://dnd.wizards.com/products/tabletop-games/rpg-products/rpg_starterset.

Section required the use of an online platform to run a D&D 5e adventure for the educational experience we are discussing in this paper. Therefore, we decided to use Roll20,[3] probably the most used online virtual tabletop to play D&D. Roll20 was already used before the pandemic events of 2020, but its number of users peaked in the first half of 2020 [7], as a consequence of the lockdowns. Roll20 provides the users with a clean and easy-to-use UI (Fig. 2), and the children involved in our case study did not have any hard time learning how to move and manage their player characters (PCs) on the map. The results of using the D&D Starter Set, along with its introductory adventure called *The Lost Mine of Phandelver*, with the Roll20 platform are fully described in the next Section.

Fig. 2. *The Lost Mine of Phandelver* map on Roll20

4   The Case Study

The experience reported in this paper did not stem out of a pre-designed pedagogic experience, although its results suggest that it could be designed as such. Actually, this experience has been triggered by the concerns about the possible negative effects of the lockdown period highlighted by a friend of the authors who is also the parent of a nine-year-old student. The parent, worried about the time spent by his son playing competitive video games and compulsively watching videos on YouTube, shared his worries with a group of parents of the same class. Starting from these considerations and relying on a shared passion about role-playing games, the parent asked the first author of this paper to lead as a master a D&D game activity to utilise the playing time of their children for a more educational purpose. The main issue for the master was the need to

---

[3] https://roll20.net/.

adapt the game design to the constraints imposed by the online context and the young age of the students involved. Another issue for the master was her role as a schoolteacher who usually stimulates her students with the importance of life skills and the promotion of empathy, inclusion and solidarity: therefore, promoting a game based on combat and defeating imaginary foes would be unacceptable, as it would generate a distorted idea of what RPGs can be for young children, already overstimulated by the competitiveness of traditional video games. By playing tabletop face-to-face games, the master senses if the emotions generated by the situation he/she presents to his/her players are too intense and can mitigate them, but at a distance this becomes much more difficult because some communication channels, such as body language, are missing. In role-playing with adults it is not a problem to deal with a bloody fight or to extract useful information from an enemy by any means, but if players are children some issues must be treated with all the pedagogy and psychology necessary to avoid creating traumas. Therefore the group was created with four 9-year-old males and a 12-year-old female (one of the other players' sister) with the agreement that the parents would be physically beside them, in order to manage both the technical and linguistic aspects of the game software (Roll20) and any emotional problems that could appear. None of the players and none of the parents (except one) had ever played a RPG or knew what it was. The experience last about two months with one session per week (every Sunday afternoon) for 2.5–3.0 h per session. The Roll20 platform was used to simulate the game table with static maps to display, on which the player characters can move and interact, as stated in Sect. 3.

4.1   How to Adapt D&D to Primary School Children: Some Hints for the Dungeon Master

When designing the experience, one of the authors of this paper decided to run the adventure as a Dungeon Master (DM, the conductor of the game), exploiting her skills as an emotional teacher, and shared her decision with the parents of the five players.

The DM decided to use the RPG as a tool to stimulate the identification of the other as much as possible, even at the cost of losing dynamism in the game. The goal was to avoid bringing the typical criteria of first-person shooter (FPS) games or competitive video games into the RPG as it would have been natural for young Fortnite players.

However, such a new and different approach could have bored the children. Fortunately, the strength of the storytelling and the discovery of being together (even if virtually) and reasoning together by developing mutual listening, appropriately guided by the DM, would lead to unexpected success.

The DM adapted the spirit and rules to use D&D as a tool to stimulate empathy towards non-player characters (NPCs) even when they were not really friendly. All the NPCs were played by the DM, as usual for RPGs.

The Dungeon Master's role mixes the skills of a narrator and director of a show, in which, however, the actors work on a canvas without following any predetermined line. The DM frames the history and the environment in which the PCs move, but cannot predict what will really happen because this depends on the interactions between the PCs. Two different groups, while playing the same adventure with the same DM, could find themselves building two completely different stories.

Starting from the initial game, therefore, the DM studied the attitudes and behaviors of the children, to address them and their PCs towards fair play and prevent potential issues of prevarication and lack of inclusion. As a reminder, the players included 4 nine-year-old boys and 1 eleven-year-old girl and some of them did not previously know the others. In the case of children, thus, it was necessary to establish rules and objectives that were more important than the plot itself. The first rule was certainly linked to enhance active listening and respect for the opinions of others: the DM's initial task was therefore to find a spontaneous method to stimulate the group to listen to the opinions of others and effectively communicate their thoughts, which was not simple for the players.

To encourage this activity, the DM provided differentiated information to the individual PCs who would succeed in a certain skill check[4] and then invited those who had succeeded to move temporarily to a private audio channel to describe the details of the scene that was perceived or the insight that was gained. This forced the other players to wait for the PC who was in the private audio channel to come back to the group and then provide some elements of reflection on the data collected, provided that he/she wanted to share them.

Everyone has always been given the possibility of conscious choice to share their information or not. In the same way, some problematic situations were solved thanks to the fact that the characters had different abilities and backgrounds and that this diversity allowed to solve some game situations through different modes. For example, a potentially critical situation occurred when it became necessary and urgent to gather information from a group of goblins (monstrous and generally evil creatures) who had been arrested. Initially, the players had thought of torturing the unfortunate goblins (reenacting a very common scene in violent films and video games). However, the DM explained that an RPG is generally based on the interpretation of a role linked to the so-called alignment, i.e. the attitude of the PC towards the law (lawful, neutral or chaotic) and towards ethics (good, neutral or evil). If even a single PC had a Lawful Good alignment, then the torture action would become an ethically impossible choice, since that PC would never allow his/her companions to carry out any form of torture.

Therefore, the debate among children has focused on how to gather information in any case while remaining consistent with one's alignment. This ethical dilemma is generally not addressed by groups of adult players, who already master the notions related to moral choices; with children of this age, however, the moral issue has become a priority and is connected to the topic of 'harmony in education', as it was mentioned in the previous Sections. Even the idea of iden-

---

[4] In D&D, each PC has several skills (Athletics, Insight, Perception, etc.) and an individual's proficiency in a skill demonstrates a focus on that aspect.

tifying oneself as an imprisoned goblin, at the request of the Dungeon Master, helped the children to understand a different point of view.

The results were not long in coming. The parents, initially worried about technical difficulties and bearing some biases about role-playing, were continuously present alongside their children as assistants, but saw the attitudes and behaviors of their children change both in game and at home.

The children moved from an initial and generalized difficulty in expressing their thoughts clearly, from overlapping in verbal interventions and initiatives, from the tendency to perform reckless actions or aggressive dialogues with each other or with NPCs, to more mature reflections on the possible consequences that each word or action entails in the evolution of the characters and the story. During the narrative phases, the DM has often used increasingly complex synonyms to increase the language skills of the young players and discussed the systems of government and production of goods of the (fantasy) medieval period in which history took place and in which the PCs were interacting.

The DM implemented the investigative aspects of the plot to leave clues to be transcribed in a logbook that would help the players make notes and rework them critically. To this end, the DM introduced non-player characters that would help players reflect aloud on clues found during the game session. The results were a drastic reduction in fights (only 2 fights over 6 game sessions and without victims, but only prisoners) and increased attention to details.

The DM played a low-volume background music to help the PCs' immersion in the game. The players gradually sensed that the type of music could also be a clue to understand if there was to be on alert or if they could walk quietly. The most interesting initial episode that gave a twist to their superficial attitude occurred when a player who had to ingratiate himself with a potential NPC ally, in order to hurry up and move forward with the plot, decided instead to threaten the NPC with retaliation, in case the NPC did not want to collaborate. Critical success in the threat resulted in the potential ally being turned into an enemy. Faced with this change of perspective, all players felt challenged and began to think before acting, calculating the potential consequences of an uselessly aggressive attitude.

The story developed so that each player defined the psychology of their character by trying to think and identify with him/her, learning many new words and new meanings, describing at the moment what each of them would do if faced with a problem or a decision to be taken or a social interaction to be developed.

The DM thus led the players to develop the stories of their PCs and the interactions among them, by constantly asking to:

- Develop their abilities to translate their thoughts into words and sentences that the other players could easily understand and deal with. This revolves around the ideas of communication and interpersonal skills, the 3rd goal described in the life skills section above.
- Define the psychology of their PCs, by trying to think as the PCs would think and immerse themselves in their respective roles; describe their feelings and

understand that a PC's feelings could differ from a player's feelings; express their likes and dislikes about the other PCs and share all of these reflections with the group. All these topics revolve around the ideas of self-awareness and empathy, the 4th goal described in the life skills section above.

– Explore creative thinking by focusing on alternative ways to solve the situations that arise in the game and the social interactions to be developed. This revolves around the ideas of creative thinking and critical thinking, the 2nd goal described in the life skills section above.

– Learn how to get to a common decision and discuss the various hypotheses, analyzing their pros and cons in emotionally immersive modes. These topics revolve around the ideas of decision-making and problem-solving, as well as coping with emotions and stress, respectively the 1st and the 5th goal described in the life skills section above.

4.2   The Parents' Point of View

In this section, we report and comment on the feedback from three parents of the children involved in the experience.

One element that emerges in all the observations reported by parents is the ability of RPGs to create an environment that naturally stimulates social skills. A parent states: *"Right from the start, the game led them to socialize with other children they did not know."* This form of complicity crossed the boundaries of the game session; in fact, they were used to *"call a friend to comment on the game, or to draft the logbook."*

Closely related to social skills are the opportunities offered by the game to develop negotiation skills. A parent states: *"The game has undoubtedly developed complicity in reaching common goals, has improved relationships between children, has given a positive image of the comparison and made them understand that even a 'conflict' in decision-making was often the only way to reach the goal they had"* On a related note, another parent adds: *"His relational skills have improved, especially in negotiating and respecting the rules."* The rules were easily and naturally introjected by the children, as confirmed by the mother of the two brothers: *"In just a few game sessions, the children immediately understood the rules and strategies, tackling with the problem-solving abilities of a 9-year-old boy, of course, the small hindrances they gradually encountered."*

Another cognitive and emotional dimension developed by RPGs is that of imagination and creativity, a feature that clearly distinguishes this type of game from traditional games. A parent states: *"His attention has finally been diverted from video games and, contrary to the video game, in which the player's imagination is harnessed rigidly by the mechanics of the format, with RPGs he has finally started to make his fantasy work again. He is enthusiastic about the adventures, and the creative process continues beyond the hours of play."* An opinion shared by the mother of the two little brothers who says: *"Both give a positive opinion: they say it is fun and that while they play, they imagine the places and characters (and also the other players, with whom they have never met in person).*

They compared this process of imagination to what happens when reading a book, stressing that in the game, it is even more intense [...]."

Other comments recall the active role perceived by the children in the activity: *"They feel they have an active role in an activity in which they interact with others, making it indeed more pleasant and probably more effective."*

Finally, it is significant to quote a comment that shows how RPGs can profoundly affect the behaviour of participants. A parent says: *"albeit always wanting to win, my son is now mainly interested in adventure, fun and cooperation."*

5 Conclusions

In this paper, we presented a role-playing experience with a group of 9 to 12-year-old children during the COVID-19 lockdown period. An experience that has not been conceived following a scientific and structured approach, but whose results confirm the solidness of this way of engaging children and provide several valuable insights for further investigation. The analysis of the literature shows a lack of validated theoretical framework able to support the DM in the design of a D&D role-playing educational activity. The experience showed how the design of a role-playing game like D&D, given the complex context due to the young age of the players and the online gameplay, is all but a trivial task. The DM had to adapt the game design elements (e.g. rules, story and interactions with students) in the absence of validated guidelines but could take into account her own experience on the promotion of life skills in the classroom. The present study presents limitations both in terms of numbers of players involved and quantitative data. Nevertheless, the changes observed in the children involved both by the DM itself and by their parents demonstrate the effectiveness of the proposed approach. This work is only a first step in the broader definition of an evidence-based design methodology to support the DM in the design of a D&D role-playing educational activity. Such an activity can also promote and develop life skills, as discussed in the previous section and witnessed by the parents.

References

1. Angiolino, A., Giuliano, L., Sidoti, B.: Inventare destini: i giochi di ruolo per l'educazione; [metodi, esperienze e giochi per iniziare subito a scuola e nei gruppi]. Ed. la Meridiana (2003)
2. Bertolo, M., Mariani, I.: Game and play as means for learning experiences. In: INTED2013 Proceedings, pp. 698–707 (2013)
3. Carter, A.: Using *Dungeons and Dragons* to integrate curricula in an elementary classroom. In: Ma, M., Oikonomou, A., Jain, L.C. (eds.) Serious Games and Edutainment Applications, pp. 329–346. Springer, London (2011). https://doi.org/10.1007/978-1-4471-2161-9_17
4. Catala, A., Theune, M., Gijlers, H., Heylen, D.: Storytelling as a creative activity in the classroom. In: Proceedings of the 2017 ACM SIGCHI Conference on Creativity and Cognition, C&C 2017, pp. 237–242. Association for Computing Machinery, New York (2017). https://doi.org/10.1145/3059454.3078857

5. Colglazier, W.: Sustainable development agenda: 2030. Science **349**(6252), 1048–1050 (2015). https://doi.org/10.1126/science.aad2333. https://science.science mag.org/content/349/6252/1048
6. Council, E.: Recommendation of the European parliament and the council of 18 December 2006 on key competencies for lifelong learning. Bruss.: Off. J. Eur. Union **30**(12), 2006 (2006)
7. Coward-Gibbs, M.: Why don't we play *pandemic*? Analog gaming communities in lockdown. Leis. Sci. **42**, 1–7 (2020)
8. Europea, U.: Council recommendation of 22 May 2018 on promoting common values, inclusive education, and the European dimension of teaching (2018/c 195/01) (2018)
9. Gardner, H.: Frames of Mind: The Theory of Multiple Intelligences. Hachette Uk, London (2011)
10. Larson, L.C., Miller, T.N.: 21st century skills: prepare students for the future. Kappa Delta Pi Rec. **47**(3), 121–123 (2011). https://doi.org/10.1080/00228958.2011.10516575
11. Ligabue, A.: Didattica Ludica. Competenze in gioco. Erickson, IT (2020)
12. Marmocchi, P., Dall'Aglio, C., Zannini, M.: Educare le life skills: come promuovere le abilità psicosociali e affettive secondo l'Organizzazione Mondiale della Sanità. Edizioni Erickson (2004)
13. Mona, E.: From the basement to the basic set: the early years of *Dungeons & Dragons*. In: Harrigan, P., Wardrip-Fruin, N. (eds.) Second Person: Role-Playing and Story in Games and Playable Media, pp. 25–30. The MIT Press, Cambridge (2007)
14. World Health Organization, et al.: Life skills education for children and adolescents in schools. World Health Organization, Tech. rep. (1994)
15. Piaget, J.: L'epistemologia genetica. Edizioni Studium Srl (2016)
16. Qian, M., Clark, K.R.: Game-based learning and 21st century skills: a review of recent research. Comput. Hum. Behav. **63**, 50–58 (2016). https://doi.org/10.1016/j.chb.2016.05.023. http://www.sciencedirect.com/science/article/pii/S0747563216303491
17. Scicchitano, M.: Metodo LabGDR: Un manuale operativo per l'utilizzo del gioco di ruolo in clinica, educazione e formazione. Franco Angeli (2019)
18. Sidoti, B.: Giochi con le storie. Modi, esercizi e tecniche per leggere, scrivere e raccontare. edizioni la meridiana (2005)
19. Sourmelis, T., Ioannou, A., Zaphiris, P.: Massively multiplayer online role playing games (MMORPGs) and the 21st century skills: a comprehensive research review from 2010 to 2016. Comput. Hum. Behav. **67**, 41–48 (2017). https://doi.org/10.1016/j.chb.2016.10.020. http://www.sciencedirect.com/science/article/pii/S074756321630721X
20. Taurisano, R.: Progetto giocaruolando. https://giocaruolando.it/giocaruolando/
21. Uriarte, Y.T., DeFillippi, R., Riccaboni, M., Catoni, M.L.: Projects, institutional logics and institutional work practices: the case of the Lucca Comics & Games Festival. Int. J. Proj. Manag. **37**(2), 318–330 (2019)
22. Valença, M.M.: Disciplinary Dungeon master. In: Frueh, J. (ed.) Pedagogical Journeys through World Politics. PP, pp. 209–218. Springer, Cham (2020). https://doi.org/10.1007/978-3-030-20305-4_18
23. Vygotskij, L.: Il ruolo del gioco nello sviluppo mentale del bambino. JS Bruner, A. Jolly K. Sylva, Il gioco 4 (1981)
24. Witwer, M., Newman, K., Peterson, J., Witwer, S.: *Dungeons & Dragons* Art & Arcana; [A Visual History]. Ten Speed Press, Berkeley (2018)

Serious Games for Instruction

Flow Experience and Situational Interest in an Adaptive Math Game

Antero Lindstedt[1]([⊠]) [iD], Antti Koskinen[2] [iD], Jake McMullen[3] [iD],
Manuel Ninaus[4,5,6] [iD], and Kristian Kiili[2] [iD]

[1] Faculty of Information Technology and Communication, Tampere University, Pori, Finland
antero.lindstedt@tuni.fi
[2] Faculty of Education and Culture, Tampere University, Tampere, Finland
{antti.koskinen,kristian.kiili}@tuni.fi
[3] Department of Teacher Education, University of Turku, Turku, Finland
jamcmu@utu.fi
[4] Department of Psychology, University of Innsbruck, Innsbruck, Austria
manuel.ninaus@uibk.ac.at
[5] LEAD Graduate School and Research Network, University of Tübingen, Tübingen, Germany
[6] Leibniz-Institut für Wissensmedien, Tübingen, Germany

Abstract. The purpose of this study was to investigate flow experience and situational interest in a math learning game that included adaptive scaffolding. Fifty-two Finnish 5th graders played the game about fractions at home during COVID-19 enforced distance learning. The results showed that flow experience correlated positively with situational interest. Importantly, a deeper analysis of the Flow Short Scale (FSS) subscales revealed that only absorption by activity but not fluency of performance explained variance in situational interest. That is, at least in game-based adaptive learning, situational interest is mostly related to immersive aspects of flow. Results also revealed that students with better in-game performance had higher flow experiences, but their levels of prior knowledge were not related to flow levels. In contrast, students with lower prior fraction number knowledge showed higher situational interest, which might be partly attributed to the additional game elements provided to struggling students in the form of adaptive scaffolds. Moreover, the study demonstrated that the developed adaptive scaffolding approach and in-game self-reporting measures worked well. Finally, the implications of these findings for flow experience and situational interest research in game-based learning context are discussed.

Keywords: Flow experience · Situational interest · Game-based learning · Adaptive scaffolding · Mathematics

1 Introduction

Digital learning environments and game-based learning offer various tools to support learning in students, such as real-time feedback and adaptivity. Recent research indicates that adaptive learning can be more effective than non-adaptive forms of learning (for a

© Springer Nature Switzerland AG 2020
I. Marfisi-Schottman et al. (Eds.): GALA 2020, LNCS 12517, pp. 221–231, 2020.
https://doi.org/10.1007/978-3-030-63464-3_21

review, see [1]) and might be particularly useful for challenging topics. In the domain of mathematics education, fractions are considered to be one of the most difficult topics and many students struggle to understand fraction magnitudes (e.g. [2]). Appropriate adaptive feedback or scaffolds might be helpful to support students in learning fractions, including increasing their engagement. Scaffolding refers to support provided during the learning processes to assist a student in achieving something that would be hard or even impossible without assistance [3]. That is, scaffolding temporarily reduces the demands of the task to facilitate learning. With respect to game-based learning, the extended three-channel model of flow [4] suggests that scaffolding may also increase players' engagement as it helps to balance the challenge and skills of struggling players leading to higher possibilities for flow experiences.

1.1 Playing Experience

The evaluation of playing experience is important in educational game design. The enjoyment level that game-based learning produce is a key factor in determining whether a player will be engaged in the gameplay and achieve the desired learning objectives [4]. Flow experience is one of the most popular constructs to describe playing experience [4, 5] and it can be used to evaluate the quality of the playing experience as well as game-based learning solutions [4, 6]. Flow refers to optimal experience, where an activity is so pleasant that a person wants to perform it again and again without being concerned with what he will get out of it [7]. "The state of flow is characterized by a combination of several specific aspects, namely, (1) concentration, (2) a merging of action and awareness, (3) reduced self-consciousness, (4) a sense of control, (5) a transformation of time, and (6) an experience of the activity as intrinsically rewarding" [8]. Flow can be considered as a special form of enjoyment [9, 10] involving several requirements such as clear goals, immediate feedback, undivided attention to the task at hand, and skills matching the challenge or demands of the activity. Flow experience seems to be positively related to playing performance (e.g. [4, 11]) and can be divided into dimensions, such as fluency of performance and absorption by activity [12].

Situational interest is another construct that may explain students' engagement in game-based learning [13]. Situational interest refers to attentional and emotional reactions induced by the environment, for example, a learning environment (e.g. [14]). There is a growing body of literature suggesting that situational interest increases attention, cognitive processing, and persistence (e.g. [15]) that seem to be in line with several characteristics associated with flow experience. Although excitement and fascination are common characteristics of situational interest, it is distinct from enjoyment, as it also includes elements relating to the subjective value of the interest object or involvement in the activity [16].

1.2 Present Study

In this paper, we examine flow experience and situational interest in a math game that includes adaptive scaffolding. One aim of game-based learning is to elicit situational interest and flow experience, but to our knowledge, the relation of these constructs has not been examined in a game-based learning context yet. Further, it is of great interest to game designers and learning material producers to understand how the level of prior knowledge and in-game performance are related to situational interest and flow experience in learning solutions that include adaptive scaffolding features, as this knowledge might help to optimize the playing experience. Therefore, the aim of the present study was to investigate relations between prior knowledge, game performance, flow experience, and situational interest. Additionally, the implementation of the developed adaptive scaffolding system, and in-game self-report measures was evaluated.

To investigate the associations of flow with prior knowledge, game performance, and situational interest, we had three hypotheses. (H1) As flow and situational interest constructs share several common characteristics, we did expect that flow experience and situational interest have a positive relation. (H2) As subjective flow experience should be associated with high performance [12], we did expect that in-game performance and the level of flow are positively related. According to the knowledge-deprivation hypothesis, perceived lack of knowledge leads to situational interest [17]. (H3) Thus, we did expect that situational interest and prior knowledge are negatively related.

2 Method

2.1 Participants

This study included 52 fifth graders (age approx. 10–11 years) from eight schools in Helsinki, Finland. The study was approved by the city of Helsinki's ethical board and all students had parental permission. Originally, over 200 students had permission to participate, but as the study was held in spring 2020, the COVID-19 pandemic, unfortunately, forced the schools into a lockdown, which greatly affected our data gathering.

2.2 Description of the Game

We used our math game research environment, an extended version of the Semideus game engine [e.g. 11], to create a Number Trace fraction game for this study. The basic mechanic of the game is based on a number line estimation task, which requires users to indicate the position of a given number on a horizontal line with only its endpoints specified (e.g., where goes 4/5 on a number line ranging from 0–1). Ample research indicates that the number line estimation task can be used to assess, as well as train, students' understanding of number magnitude (for a review, see [18]).

The player controls a dog character and tries to locate bones hidden in the forest. The location of the bone is displayed as a symbolic fraction, visual representation, or mixed number. The player has to estimate the location and walk the dog to it. On some tasks, the walking is replaced with sequential jumping where the jump length is fixed to some mathematically meaningful sequence (usually unit fraction of the task). For example, if the estimated value is 3/7, the dog would need three jumps (3 * 1/7) to move from the left side of the number to the bone. Some tasks also included enemies that had to be avoided or destroyed. The number line ranged either from 0 to 1 or from 0 to 5.

Adaptive scaffolding was based on players' competences on three categories: fractions on a number line from 0 to 1, fractions on a number line from 0 to 5, and mixed numbers. The competence level of the category was the mean of student's five most recent answers to tasks relevant to the category. Adaptive scaffolding was triggered to assist the player based on their competence levels. That is, if the system identified that a player had minor difficulties with a certain competence, in subsequent tasks dealing with the same competence, scaffolding would trigger and assist the player if the initial answer was incorrect. If the player had more severe difficulties, the assistance was provided immediately at the beginning of the task.

The scaffolds included in the game:

- Shows the improper fraction as a mixed number. For example: 5/2 → 2 ½
- Shows the fraction number as a pie graph to provide visual representation.
- Subtracts the fraction to the smallest common factor. For example: 4/8 → 1/2
- Summons birds to divide the number line into equal sections based on the denominator of the fraction to be estimated. For example: 3/8 → divide into eight sections
- Summons worms to visualize improper fractions or mixed numbers (see Fig. 1).
- Jumping shoes activates the jump movement (as described above).

Fig. 1. *On the left*: A game task on a number line ranging from 0 to 5. The player has to estimate a mixed number 2 ¾. A scaffold "Worm" has been activated, which fills the number line with worms thus dividing it into five sections. *On the right*: A task from the flow questionnaire level. The answer is given on a continuous scale from 1 to 7 with the exact value shown.

The game also supports text-based questions that were used to implement in-game questionnaires (self-report measures). Instead of an estimation task, the student would see a question. The answering is still done using the number line by walking the dog character to a position that reflects the wanted value. The exact value is clearly visible above the dog, so the student knows exactly what he/she is about to answer. The number line range defines the used answer scale. For example, range from 1 to 5 means the question has a continuous scale from 1 to 5.

2.3 Measures

Prior knowledge was measured with a pretest that was conducted using a browser-based, non-gamified platform, developed by the authors. It contained eight number line items, where the student estimated the location of a fraction by dragging a marker on a number line. The answer was deemed correct if its accuracy was at least 92% for number lines ranging from 0–1. For number lines ranging from 0–5, an accuracy of 90% was enough for the answer to be considered correct. In addition, there were six ordering items, where the student had to drag boxes (3 or 4 per task), each containing a fraction or a mixed number, into an ascending order based on given values. Prior knowledge was calculated by taking the percent of correct answers.

Game performance in the Number Trace game was measured using the estimation accuracy percent of the initial answer on each task in levels 10–18 (see procedure). If the student answered incorrectly, the game offered another attempt, but the latter answer was not taken into account in our performance measurements. *Scaffold count* was calculated by tracking the number of tasks, where the student was scaffolded.

Situational interest was measured with a question "The tasks of this game level were interesting", which was asked at three different stages of the levels included in this study. *Flow experience* was measured with a slightly modified version of the Flow Short Scale [12] using a total of 10 items (6 items for fluency of performance; 4 items for absorption by activity). The statements were changed to past tense and made the activity to refer to game playing (see Appendix A).

2.4 Procedure

The teachers were supposed to hold five school classes (45 min each) within a four-week period, in which the students would complete the pretest, and play the Number Trace game. During this period, the teachers were instructed not to teach fractions in any other way. But, as mentioned, school lockdowns interrupted the intervention, which forced us to re-evaluate our participant inclusion criteria for this study. Some teachers decided not to continue playing, but with the classes that continued the playing at home, we faced another issue: as different classes had progressed at different schedules, there were some variations on how far the students had progressed on the game content before the lockdown that we had to take into account.

Fig. 2. The planned procedure of the study, which was interrupted by distance learning due to COVID-19. The parts marked with "Excluded" were not included in the data used in the study. We were unable to conduct the posttest. Situational interest item in levels: 10, 13 and 16.

Every student had completed the pretest at school. As Fig. 2 shows, we included levels 10–18 and the subsequent flow questionnaire level in the data. The levels 1–9 had too much variance in had those been played at school or at home and therefore had to be omitted. Levels 19–24 were excluded because too many students had not reached those during the intervention. Each level contained 10 fraction estimation tasks, meaning there were a total of 90 tasks included in this study. Of these tasks, 60 had potential scaffolding available. We were unable to conduct the planned posttest.

Situational interest was measured in levels 10, 13 and 16 using an in-game question (see Sect. 2.2). After level 18, the students completed a level that included the modified Flow Short Scale. The level started with one training item, which was not included in the data, to remind students how to answer the in-game questionnaire items, and to clarify that tasks in this level are not like the previous level's mathematical tasks.

3   Results

The descriptive statistics and reliabilities of the used scales for the measured variables are listed in Table 1. The modified Flow Short Scale (and its subscales), the situational interest items, and the pretest's prior knowledge questions all had at least good internal consistency (Cronbach's alpha). Additionally, we explored the data for anomalies, such as answering patterns and too short answer durations. As a result, we identified two students, who both had very short answering durations and all their answers were at default value. They were omitted from the flow experience measurements. It seems that our in-game self-reporting measures worked well, as we had to exclude only two students and the internal consistency of the measures were good.

Table 1. Descriptive statistics and reliabilities of the used scales for the measured variables.

	Mean	SD	Median	Scale
Flow experience	4.44	1.23	4.44	1-7 (α = .870)
Fluency of performance	4.72	1.23	4.85	1-7 (α = .852)
Absorption by activity	3.87	1.52	4.04	1-7 (α = .765)
Situational Interest	3.36	1.08	3.55	1-5 (α = .773)
Prior Knowledge	52.3	25.8	50.0	0-100% (α = .836)
Game Performance	93.9	2.04	93.9	0-100%
Scaffold Count	5.85	6.07	4.00	-

The combined average of all flow items was $M = 4.44$ ($SD = 1.23$). This was slightly below the overall Flow Short Scale mean (4.7) attained with various activities and across various previous studies [12]. Fluency of performance subscale ($M = 4.72$, $SD = 1.23$) scored above the overall mean, while absorption by activity subscale ($M = 3.87$, $SD = 1.52$) scored below. The correlation between the subscales was large ($r = .60, p < .001$) that is consistent with [12].

In this study, the correlation between several variables, such as flow experience, was studied (see Table 2). In line with *Hypothesis 1*, we found that flow experience was related to situational interest ($r = .41, p = .003$). In order to get a deeper understanding of this relation, we ran a multiple regression analysis with situational interest as a dependent variable and the two subscales of flow - i.e. fluency of performance and absorption by activity - as predictors. The results of the forced-entry multiple regression indicated that absorption by activity (*standardized Beta* $= 0.59, p < .001$) explained 27.2% of the variance [$F(2, 49) = 9.15, p < .001$; adjusted $R^2 = .24$]. Fluency of performance, however, did not account for a unique part of the variance in situational interest (*standardized Beta* $= -0.13, p = .41$). In line with *Hypothesis 2*, we found a correlation, albeit only a small one, between experienced flow and in-game performance ($r = .33, p = .016$). This suggests that the students with better in-game performance, had a higher experience of flow.

Table 2. Correlations (Pearson's r †) between the measured variables.

		1	2	3	4	5
1	Flow Experience	1				
2	Situational Interest	.414**	1			
3	Prior Knowledge	.092	-.380**	1		
4	Game Performance	.329*	.016	.368**	1	
5	Scaffold Count	-.176	.065	-.386**	-.659***	1

Note. * $p < .05$, ** $p < .01$, *** $p < .001$

† The same analysis with Spearman's correlation did not change the results substantially.

Addressing *Hypothesis 3*, we found a medium negative correlation ($r = -.38, p = .002$) between prior knowledge and experienced situational interest. Students with less prior knowledge were more likely to experience higher situational interest than students with higher prior knowledge. However, there was no correlation ($r = .02, p = .909$) between situational interest and in-game performance.

Out of the 90 total tasks included in the study's game level, 60 tasks included scaffolding features. The best players completed the game without seeing any scaffolds, while the most struggling student saw scaffolds on 23 tasks ($M = 5.85$, $SD = 6.07$). As designed for, the adaptive scaffolding system provided more scaffolds to students with weaker prior knowledge as indicated by the medium negative correlation ($r = -.39, p = .005$) between scaffold count and prior knowledge. The large negative correlation (r

$= -.66, p < .001$) between scaffold count and in-game performance was also expected as the scaffolds were targeted for low performing players.

Finally, a paired-samples t-test was conducted to compare estimation accuracy in the pretest and in the game levels (10–16) that included similar estimation tasks. Only the first answer for each task was included. The answers affected by scaffolds (0.5% of all answers) were excluded. The accuracy was significantly higher in the game ($M = 94.1$, $SD = 1.82$) than in the pre-test ($M = 84.3$, $SD = 7.18$), $t(51) = 10.6$, $p < .001$, $d = 1.47$.

4 Discussion and Conclusion

Player enjoyment is a crucial goal of games and game-based learning. If players do not enjoy the game, they will not play the game at all or they will play the game only super-ficially without investing cognitive resources to consider the challenges and the content of the game deeply enough. The purpose of the current study was to build a better under-standing of engagement in game-based learning. Particularly, we investigated students' playing experience in an adaptive math game through flow experience and situational interest and reflected these findings in relation to students' prior knowledge and in-game performance.

In line with *Hypothesis 1*, we found a positive relation between flow experience and situational interest, indicating that these constructs are partly parallel. Importantly, a more detailed analysis revealed that the flow subscale, absorption by activity, explained situational interest, while the fluency of performance subscale did not contribute to it. As expected in *Hypothesis 2*, we found that students who performed better in the game also experienced more flow, which is in line with previous research [12]. This would support the use of adaptive scaffolds as they may help the students with less competence to perform better and thus, presumably, experience higher flow as well. In contrast, in-game performance was not related to situational interest. In fact, this can partly explain why fluency of performance subscale did not predict situational interest. Although flow was not related to prior knowledge, it seems that flow is more competence-oriented construct than situational interest. With respect to *Hypothesis 3*, our finding that prior knowledge was inversely related with situational interest further supports our inference about the meaning of competence in flow and situational interest. The results are in accordance with Rotgans and Schmidt's [17] study indicating that knowledge accumulation tends to be inversely related to situational interest. Further, their study indicates that perceived lack of knowledge leads to situational interest, which in turn leads to learning. Thus, it is important that the game provides immediate feedback on players' competences, which helps to trigger and maintain situational interest.

In the current study, learning analytics of the game was successfully used to identify students that needed assistance. Consequently, weaker students were scaffolded, which balanced the game's challenge for them. As mentioned, students with lower prior knowl-edge experienced higher situational interest, which we, in addition to lack of knowledge, attribute to the additional game mechanics offered to them through adaptive scaffolding. Likely, the used scaffold mechanics have triggered situational interest in players as they may have perceived the scaffolds as novel and personally relevant events that have also helped them to identify the existing knowledge gaps. The downside of scaffolding is that it only supports students who need assistance. We believe that flow and situational interest could have been facilitated with adaptive features that consider also the needs of well-performing students. In the current implementation, better-performing students missed some of the game features as the scaffolds were not shown to them. This could be compensated by including features that increase the difficulty, like extra enemies to make playing harder, or ways to increase the mathematical difficulty. For example, one of the scaffolds subtracts the fraction number to the lowest common factor. This could be reversed by expanding the original fraction number into "larger" and more difficult factors. With respect to better-performing students, the increased difficulty would prob-ably facilitate flow as the challenge would be better balanced with skills, and the novel features and possibly aroused knowledge gaps would facilitate also situational interest.

We used in-game questions to measure flow and situational interest. The study demonstrated that we managed to successfully utilize the game's core mechanics to embed self-report items into the game. The answering was fluid and did not distract the students or disrupt the playing experience. Only the answers of two students had to be removed from the analyses, as they were clearly invalid. That is, the results suggest that such in-game self-report measures do not encourage careless responding. In fact, our approach was an effective way to collect the students' experiences during game-play as answering the questions was mandatory in order to progress in the game. The in-game approach works well to measure especially situational interest, as it allows an easy and non-distracting way to collect repeated measures providing more exhaustive insights in what happens during the gameplay compared to common before or after game measurement approaches.

The limitations of this study revolve much around the pandemic-enforced school lockdowns, which altered the research design quite a bit from the original. First of all, it greatly reduced the sample size (N = 52), reducing the statistical power of the study. It also forced us to exclude some early game levels from our analyses that complicates the interpretation of the results. We were also unable to conduct the planned posttest, so we had to evaluate learning outcomes by comparing the estimation accuracy of the pretest to an "ad-hoc posttest", i.e. estimation accuracy of the selected levels of the game. This comparison indicated that playing the Number Trace game significantly improved students' conceptual fraction knowledge. However, the large improvement needs to be interpreted cautiously as the tasks of the pretest and game were not entirely comparable. Further, the lack of a proper posttest also meant that we could not include a control group in the analyses. Even though we did manage the difference in playing surroundings by making sure that the measured game content was not played partly at school and partly at home, but only at home, we expect that there were variations at students' home surroundings. Things like distractions, technical issues, or parental help during the play might have affected the results.

To conclude, the current study advances the game-based learning field by shedding light on the unaddressed relationship between situational interest and flow experience. The results indicated that although these constructs are positively related, there are also differences. It seems that the immersive aspects of flow experience, rather than the competence related aspects, are associated with situational interest. Unlike flow, situational interest seems to be inversely related to knowledge accumulation and is triggered by perceived lack of knowledge. Thus, adaptation of feedback (ensuring that player perceives knowledge gaps) should facilitate situational interest, and challenge adaptation (balancing challenge to player's skills) should facilitate flow. On the practical side, as both the flow and situational interest constructs aim to explain why people engage in activities, they are useful measures for game design that can be used to evaluate playing experience as well as the quality of game-based learning solutions. Further, the results provide some validation for the proposed use of game's core mechanics to collect self-reported playing experience data.

Acknowledgments. Research was funded by the Academy of Finland (grant numbers: 326618 and 310338).

Appendix

Appendix A. Modified flow short scale questions

	Question	Fluency of performance	Absorption by activity
1	The game provided just the right amount of challenge.		x
2	My thoughts/activities ran fluidly and smoothly.	x	
3	I didn't notice time passing.		x
4	I could concentrate on playing.	x	
5	My mind was completely clear.	x	
6	I was totally absorbed in playing.		x
7	The right thoughts/movements occurred of their own accord.	x	
8	I knew what I had to do in the game.	x	
9	I felt that I had everything under control.	x	
10	I was completely lost in thought.		x

References

1. Aleven, V., McLaughlin, E.A., Glenn, R.A., Koedinger, K.R.: Instruction based on adaptive learning technologies. In: Handbook of Research on Learning and Instruction, pp. 522–560 (2016)
2. Siegler, R.S., Fazio, L.K., Bailey, D.H., Zhou, X.: Fractions: the new frontier for theories of numerical development. Trends Cogn. Sci. **17**(1), 13–19 (2013)
3. Wood, D., Bruner, J., Ross, G.: The role of tutoring in problem solving. J. Child Psychol. Psychiatry **17**, 89–100 (1976)
4. Kiili, K., Lainema, T., de Freitas, S., Arnab, S.: Flow framework for analyzing the quality of educational games. Entertain. Comput. **5**(4), 367–377 (2014)
5. Procci, K., Singer, A.R., Levy, K.R., Bowers, C.: Measuring the flow experience of gamers: an evaluation of the DFS-2. Comput. Hum. Behav. 2012 Conf. **28**(6), 2306–2312 (2012)
6. Perttula, A., Kiili, K., Lindstedt, A., Tuomi, P.: Flow experience in game based learning – a systematic literature review. Int. J. Serious Games **4**(1), 57–72 (2017)
7. Csikszentmihalyi, M.: Flow: The Psychology of Optimal Experience. Harper Perennial, New York (1991)
8. Keller, J., Landhäußer, A.: The flow model revisited. In: Engeser, S. (ed.) Advances in flow research, pp. 51–64. Springer, New York, NY (2012). https://doi.org/10.1007/978-1-4614-2359-1_3
9. Baumann, N., Lürig, C., Engeser, S.: Flow and enjoyment beyond skill-demand balance: the role of game pacing curves and personality. Motiv. Emot. **40**(4), 507–519 (2016)
10. Kiili, K., Lindstedt, A., Ninaus, M.: Exploring characteristics of students' emotions, flow and motivation in a math game competition. In: Koivisto, J., Hamari, J. (eds.) Proceedings of the 2nd International GAMIFIN Conference, pp. 20–29. CEUR Workshop Proceedings, Pori (2018)
11. Kiili, K., Ketamo, H.: Evaluating cognitive and affective outcomes of a digital game-based math test. IEEE Trans. Learn. Technol. **11**(2), 255–263 (2018)
12. Engeser, S., Rheinberg, F.: Flow, performance and moderators of challenge-skill balance. Motiv. Emot. **32**(3), 158–172 (2008)
13. Eccles, J.S., Wigfield, A.: Motivational beliefs, values, and goals. Ann. Rev. Psychol. **53**(1), 109–132 (2002)
14. Knogler, M.: Situational interest: a proposal to enhance conceptual clarity. In: O'Keefe, P.A., Harackiewicz, J.M. (eds.) The Science of Interest, pp. 109–124. Springer, Cham (2017). https://doi.org/10.1007/978-3-319-55509-6_6
15. Hidi, S.: Interest, reading, and learning: theoretical and practical considerations. Educ. Psychol. Rev. **13**(3), 191–209 (2001)
16. Plass, J.L., et al.: The impact of individual, competitive, and collaborative mathematics game play on learning, performance, and motivation. J. Educ. Psychol. **105**(4), 1050–1066 (2013)
17. Rotgans, J.I., Schmidt, H.G.: Situational interest and learning: thirst for knowledge. Learn. Instr. **32**, 37–50 (2014)
18. Schneider, M., Thompson, C.A., Rittle-Johnson, B.: Associations of magnitude comparison and number line estimation with mathematical competence: a comparative review. In: Lemaire, P. (ed.) Cognitive Development from a Strategy Perspective: A Festschrift for Robert S. Siegler. Psychology Press, London (2018)

Design and Evaluation of an Adventure Videogame Based in the History of Mathematics

Mariana Rocha[✉] and Pierpaolo Dondio

Technological University Dublin, Kevin Street, Dublin, Ireland
`mariana.rocha@tudublin.ie`

Abstract. The present paper describes the design and evaluation of an adventure videogame developed to cover the mathematics primary school curriculum. The narrative of the game is based in the history of mathematics and, to win, the player needs to travel through time, starting from the ancient Egypt and finishing at the modern world. To achieve that, the player interacts with real-life characters, such as Pythagoras of Samos, learning about their contributions to the field and using this knowledge to solve puzzles. The aim of the research presented in this paper is to understand the effects of the game on students' mathematics performance and levels of mathematics anxiety, a clinical condition where feelings of tension emerge during the manipulation of numbers. The game was tested by children from the first and second classes of Irish primary schools (n = 88). Students played the game for 3 weeks on weekly sessions of 45 min to 1 h. The experiment had a pre post-test design and students answered the Modified Abbreviated Math Anxiety Scale (mAMAS), and a mathematics test designed based on the content of the game. Statistical analysis suggested the game significantly improves students' mathematics performance. However, it increases the levels of mathematics anxiety on female students, opening discussion for considering what aspects of game design influences the levels of mathematics anxiety for this specific group.

Keywords: Mathematics anxiety · Primary school · History of mathematics

1 Introduction

International concerns about mathematics education involve factors related to children's poor level of understanding abstract concepts and their application to real life [1]. Traditional educational tends to focus on procedural and inflexible knowledge, leading students to look at mathematics as a cold-blooded subject that cannot be mastered by everybody. A research proposed 1,496 students from primary and secondary schools to write an essay with the theme "Me and Maths" [2]. The results suggest many of the essays are characterized by failures and unease, and students show a low perceived competence joint to the instrumental vision of mathematics. This is, according to the authors, reinforced by repeated experiences perceived as failures, when students feel they do not control their performance and conclude to be useless to work on it. Besides, students described they used to have a positive relationship with mathematics during

© Springer Nature Switzerland AG 2020
I. Marfisi-Schottman et al. (Eds.): GALA 2020, LNCS 12517, pp. 232–241, 2020.
https://doi.org/10.1007/978-3-030-63464-3_22

primary school, but it became negative in secondary school. This can be related with the development of a clinical condition known as maths anxiety, a collection of negative feelings associated with activities that involve the manipulation of numbers and calculations [3, 4]. This condition can lead to poor performance at school and at work [5]. Different interventions are proposed to overcome or prevent mathematics anxiety, such as the adoption of a game-based learning approach. Educational games can bring maths to a context of problem-solving, making it more recognizable and less frightening. This paper contributes to exploring the impact of a mathematics videogame on learning outcomes and levels of anxiety. The game's narrative is based in the history of mathematics and allows the player learns mathematics while using it to solve problems.

2 Background

2.1 Learning Mathematics Through a Historical Perspective

Using the history as a teaching tool allows pupils to experience mathematics as a field that is constantly in development [6], avoiding them to think about mathematics as a given science ready to be used. Learning through history is not a new approach. In 1899, the Italian historian Gino Loria advocated for the use of a historical perspective in maths education, indicating teachers should adopt it to revisit elementary concepts. This helps students to understand that mathematics results of a contribution from different cultures, connects with other disciplines, and stimulates scientific, technical, artist and social development [7]. Other researchers consider using history as a tool to teach mathematics may motivate students while sustaining their interests and excitement [8]. Moreover, a historical approach humanizes mathematics, making it less frightening, and students may find comfort in knowing that concepts they find hard to learn took thousands of years to shape into their final form [9]. Today, the use of history to teach mathematics is part of initiatives from established organizations and is subject of conferences, papers and international discussions [10], such the History and Pedagogy of mathematics, a study group affiliated to the International Commission on Mathematical Instruction (ICMI) created in the 1970s. Still, teachers face some challenges while implementing this approach in their classroom. The time is already limited to the curriculum coverage and the addition of the history of mathematics may be time-consuming; besides, teachers find it hard to locate material about this topic [11]. This paper describes a game designed considering these and other challenges involved in the integration of history to mathematics.

2.2 Mathematics Anxiety and the Challenges Behind It

Due to a lack of understanding of how mathematics can be useful in daily life, students can feel frustrated and develop low confidence during the learning process. This can lead to the development of mathematics anxiety, a condition that can cause adverse effects on career choice and professional success [12]. A longitudinal study with 413 middle-school students showed that there is a significant growth of mathematics anxiety at the end of sixth grade, highlighting the importance of early interventions [13]. A variety of strategies have been studied in an attempt to prevent mathematics anxiety, such as guided imagery sessions [14], cognitive tutoring [15], mindfulness sessions [16], and games [17, 18]. Still, more research is needed to better comprehend how these interventions act and when they should be implemented. Researchers have identified that student's gender plays an important role in the levels of this condition. Female students tend to have higher levels of anxiety than male students [19, 20]. Besides, a study with second-grade students showed that the levels of mathematics anxiety only moderated mathematics performance in girls [21]. Therefore, early school interventions to reduce mathematics anxiety should also consider gender-specific aspects.

2.3 Learning Mathematics During the Primary School

The primary school level is essential for children's cognitive development. What a student learns during this phase of school can be crucial for later mathematics. For example, if a child cannot understand fractions during primary school, there are few chances of understanding simple algebraic equations in the future. This is shown by a longitudinal study designed and implemented by [22]. The study had two samples. The first sample had 3,677 students from the United Kingdom that had their mathematics proficiency assessed when they were 10 years old, followed by another test when they were 16 years old. The second sample had 599 students from the United States that had their mathematics proficiency tested when they were 10–12 years old and again when they were 15–17 years old. Both samples tested revealed that primary school students' knowledge about fractions and division uniquely predicted their knowledge and achievements in high school. Thus, it is important to invest in looking for strategies and solutions that can improve a better education in mathematics during the primary school.

3   Research Design

3.1 Description of the Game Design

The game designed and tested during this research is entitled Once Upon a Maths, a free adaptation of the historical facts as an attempt to give a meaningful background to mathematics. The game is composed of different phases containing short minigames. This allows teachers to adopt the game in the classroom even if they do not have a lot of time available. The player assumes the role of a time traveler protagonist, who decides to go back in time. To achieve that, the player should interact with ancient characters by watching animations where those characters describe how mathematics was used to solve daily life problems during their times. The animation not only ignites the narrative but also works as a brief tutorial to make clear to the player what is the aim of the minigame that follows that animation. The character then challenges the player to solve a challenge using what s/he just learned. If the player succeeds, the character gives him/her a passport stamp, allowing the player to move to the next phase of the game. The game can be accessed by any device with an internet connection and the child can play by opening a browser and typing the address to the game website. When accessing the game, the player finds a landing page where s/he can insert his/her details to log into the system. After that, the user has access to the page that shows 9 islands, each

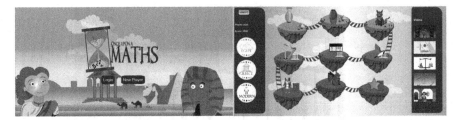

Fig. 1. Landing page and phases page of Once Upon a Maths.

representing one of the challenges according to the historical period (Fig. 1). If the player is accessing the game for the first time, all levels will be locked except for the first one.

The first phase of the game presents the mathematics from ancient Egypt (3100 B.C.E – 30 B.C.E). It is hosted by Nebamun, a sculptor who invites the player to visit his house and presents the large collection of vases designed by himself. This phase contains 3 minigames and each one covers one concept from the Ancient Egyptian mathematics: the use of parts of the body to measure objects (Fig. 2), the use of maps, and the implementation of pieces of metal to weigh animals and food.

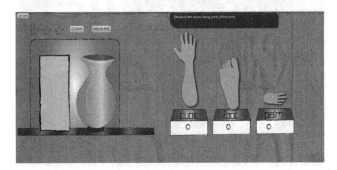

Fig. 2. In this minigame, student must measure the vase using parts of the body.

The second phase of the game comprises the mathematics from the ancient Greece period (1100 BC – 600 AD), presented by the philosopher Pythagoras of Samos, who describes the connection between mathematics and music. The animation was inspired by the registers that describe a moment where, while Pythagoras heard hammers in a blacksmith's forge and discovered that a balance between the hammers' weight resulted on a pleasant sound. This episode resulted on Pythagoras creating what is now known as music harmony. The 3 minigames of this phase challenges the player to play a song considering the relation between numbers and musical notes (Fig. 3).

The third phase of the game focuses on the mathematics concepts discovered in the Modern era (from the 19th century until nowadays), and the three minigames are open by an animation of the character Ada Lovelace, an English mathematician that is considered by many researchers the first computer programmer [23]. Lovelace explains what an algorithm is and tells a story from her childhood, when she was fascinated about the idea of flying [24]. The player is then challenged to use algorithms to teach an

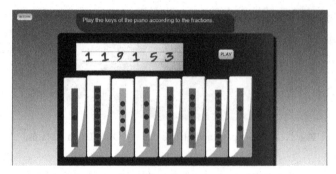

Fig. 3. The student has to play the piano according to the numerical music sheet.

animal how to fly. The minigames in this phase consist of dragging and dropping pieces of instruction to teach the animal how to fly among the clouds (Fig. 4).

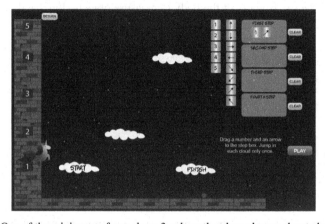

Fig. 4. One of the minigames from phase 3, where the player learns about algorithms.

3.2 Empirical Experiment

This research is motivated by the following research question (RQ):

RQ: What are the effects of a digital game based on the history of mathematics on the learning outcomes and anxiety in the primary school level?

Irish schools were recruited to be part of the experiment, which lasted 5 weeks. Each participant class was visited once per week and the visit had a duration between 45 min and one hour. The first visit consisted in a pre-test phase when students answered two questionnaires. The first is the modified Abbreviated Mathematics Anxiety Scale (mAMAS) [25], a reliable and validated questionnaire that measures the levels of mathematics anxiety in students from primary school. The second questionnaire consisted of a list of mathematics questions related to the content covered by the game, measuring students' performance on those topics. The mAMAS is based on the Abbreviated Math Anxiety Scale (AMAS) [26], and consists of a self-report questionnaire with nine items. Children use a 5-point Likert scale to indicate how anxious they feel when dealing with certain situations that involve maths, being 1 equal to low anxiety and 5 equals to hight anxiety. The higher is the result, the more anxious the child is. Both questionnaires were formatted so that it was more readable for young children, printed with large font size. The mAMAS included sad and happy emoticons at the endpoints of the Likert-scale to aid students in their responses. Each item of the mAMAS questionnaire was read out loud and the students answered the questions by themselves. The next three visits consisted of letting the students play each one of the three main phases of the game. In Ireland, the average class size is around 25 students [27]. Therefore, 30 tablets computers were brought to the classrooms for the game playing sessions. Students received printed passports with their username and password to access the game. The passport had three pages for students to get three different stickers as a reward for finishing each phase of the game, besides a page where they could get stickers for each colleague they helped. There was also a collection of pages for students to draw/register their adventure through the history of mathematics. Then, in the final fifth visit, students answered the mAMAS questionnaire again, and a modified version of the mathematics questionnaire. As participation was anonymous, researchers did not have access to students' names, only their game usernames. Teachers were responsible for filling a spreadsheet linking those details to students' usernames in the games, so researchers could link students' demographic data to their game performance and questionnaire results. The results were collected and inputted in a database and the analysis was carried out through statistics techniques using the software IBM SPSS Statistics 21. Statistics methods were applied to evaluate if Once Upon a Maths had any effect on the levels of maths anxiety of primary school students. First, Wilcoxon signed-rank test was conducted to evaluate if there was a significant difference between the pre and post-mAMAS test. Mann-Whitney U Test was used to evaluate if students' gender had an impact on the level of maths anxiety considering both pre and post-mAMAS tests. We also aimed to identify if Once Upon a Maths had any effect on students maths learning outcomes. The Wilcoxon signed-rank test was applied considering the pre and post-Maths test.

4   Results

Once Upon a Maths was tested by users in three different classrooms from two schools (Fig. 5). The first school is a catholic rural co-educational (mixed gender) school located in county Kildare, Ireland. It is a primary level school and has around 200 students registered currently. The game was played by 28 students from the second class of this school. The second school is also a catholic co-educational school. Located in Dublin, Ireland, this primary school has almost a thousand students enrolled currently. Two first class classrooms of this school played the game, in a total of 60 students. Therefore, a total of 88 students played Once Upon a Maths. From those students, 43 were females and 45 males.

Fig. 5. Students testing Once Upon a Maths.

4.1 Effects on the Game on Mathematics Performance

The Wilcoxon signed-rank test was also used to identify if Once Upon a Maths had any effect on students' performance in mathematics considering the pre and post-maths test. The test revealed a significant increase in maths performance after playing Once Upon a Maths ($z = -4.407$, $p < .001$, $r = .5$), with a medium effect. When evaluating if this increase of performance was significantly different considering gender (male and female) and maths performance group (low, medium and high), no significance was found (gender: $F (1, 67) = .953$ and $p > 0.05$; maths performance: $F (2, 67) = 2.699$ and $p > 0.05$).

4.2 Effects of the Game on Mathematics Anxiety

We evaluated students' levels of mathematics anxiety through mAMAS, a validated test designed for primary school students. The maximum score is 45, which results from the high level of mathematics anxiety, and the minimum is 1, resulting in a low level of mathematics anxiety. To identify if Once Upon a Maths has any effect on the levels of maths anxiety, statistical analysis was conducted to compare the pre and post-mAMAS test answered by the students. The test revealed no reduction in mathematics anxiety after playing Once Upon a Maths ($z = -1.242$, $p = .214$). However, considering the gender, there was a significant increase in the level of mathematics anxiety for the female group of students, with $F (1, 71) = 12.480$ and $p = 0.001$.

5 Conclusions

The novelty of this research consists of evaluating the use of a game based on the history of maths as a tool to improve learning outcomes and reduce anxiety. Games, in general, are a great way to approach the development of deep thinking and, if there is a good narrative behind them, to show how certain puzzles represent real-life challenges. Once Upon a Maths significantly increased the learning outcomes, which might be related to the fact narrative-based learning leads students to connect the concepts learned to the human experience [28], which can result in making abstract concepts more meaningful.

Once Upon a Maths did not affect the levels of maths anxiety considering the whole group of students but seems to increase those levels for female students. The gender differences about maths anxiety are already well described [29] and it is known that girls tend to be more anxious than boys, even when they have similar levels of performance [21]. Once Upon a Maths considered design principles that make the game more attractive to girls, like high use of visual learning approach [30], storytelling elements [31], and reduction of competitiveness [32]. Many reasons should be considered to explain why girls tend to have a higher level of mathematics anxiety than boys. Exposure to negative attitudes about maths by role models like parents and teachers, a higher possibility of feeling anxious when seeing another child with anxiety, and exposure to gender stereotypes are only a few reasons that might lead girls to have higher anxiety than boys [21, 33, 34]. The way students build their social relationships plays huge importance in their learning outcomes [35], further studies should evaluate the role social aspects play on the levels of maths anxiety.

References

1. Conway, P., Sloane, F.: International Trends in Post-Primary Mathematics Education: Perspectives on Learning, Teaching and Assessment, p. 295 (2006)
2. Di Martino, P., Zan, R.: "Me and maths": towards a definition of attitude grounded on students' narratives. J. Math. Teach. Educ. **13**, 27–48 (2010). https://doi.org/10.1007/s10857-009-9134-z
3. Caviola, S., Carey, E., Mammarella, I.C., Szucs, D.: Stress, time pressure, strategy selection and math anxiety in mathematics: a review of the literature. Front. Psychol. **8**, 1–13 (2017). https://doi.org/10.3389/fpsyg.2017.01488
4. Jansen, B.R.J., Louwerse, J., Straatemeier, M., Van der Ven, S.H.G., Klinkenberg, S., Van der Maas, H.L.J.: The influence of experiencing success in math on math anxiety, perceived math competence, and math performance. Learn. Individ. Differ. **24**, 190–197 (2013). https://doi.org/10.1016/j.lindif.2012.12.014
5. Mcmullan, M., Jones, R., Lea, S.: Math anxiety, self-efficacy, and ability in British undergraduate nursing students. Res. Nurs. Heal. **35**, 178–186 (2012). https://doi.org/10.1002/nur.21460
6. Kool, M.: An extra student in your classroom: how the history of mathematics can enrich interactive mathematical discussions at primary school. Math. Sch. **32**, 19–22 (2003)
7. Clark, K., Kjeldsen, T., Schorcht, S., Tzanakis, C.: History of mathematics in mathematics education. Recent developments. To cite this version (2016)
8. Farmaki, V., Paschos, T.: Employing genetic "moments" in the history of mathematics in classroom activities. Educ. Stud. Math. **66**, 83–106 (2007). https://doi.org/10.1007/s10649-006-9056-y
9. Bakker, A., Gravemeijer, K.P.E.: An historical phenomenology of mean and median. Educ. Stud. Math. **62**, 149–168 (2006). https://doi.org/10.1007/s10649-006-7099-8
10. Fried, M.N.: Can Mathematics Education and History of Mathematics Coexist? (2001)
11. Dejić, M., Mihajlović, A.: History of mathematics and teaching mathematics. Teach. Innov. **27**, 15–30 (2014)
12. Ma, X.: A meta-analysis of the relationship between anxiety toward mathematics and achievement in mathematics. J. Res. Math. Educ. **30**, 520–540 (1999). https://doi.org/10.2307/749772

13. Madjar, N., Zalsman, G., Weizman, A., Lev-Ran, S., Shoval, G.: Predictors of developing mathematics anxiety among middle-school students: a 2-year prospective study. Int. J. Psychol. **53**, 426–432 (2018). https://doi.org/10.1002/ijop.12403
14. Henslee, A., Klein, B.: Using brief guided imagery to reduce math anxiety and improve math performance: a pilot study. J. STEM Educ. **18**, 32 (2017)
15. Supekar, K., Iuculano, T., Chen, L., Menon, V.: Remediation of childhood math anxiety and associated neural circuits through cognitive tutoring. J. Neurosci. **35**, 12574–12583 (2015). https://doi.org/10.1523/JNEUROSCI.0786-15.2015
16. Samuel, T.S., Warner, J.: "I Can Math!": reducing math anxiety and increasing math self-efficacy using a mindfulness and growth mindset-based intervention in first-year students. Commun. Coll. J. Res. Pract. **00**, 1–18 (2019). https://doi.org/10.1080/10668926.2019.166 6063
17. Reyes, J.D.C.: Increasing self-efficacy and alleviating anxiety using touch math and instructional games: an intervention for low performing seventh graders. J. Humanit. Educ. Dev. **1**, 59–74 (2019). https://doi.org/10.22161/jhed.1.2.2
18. Verkijika, S.F., De Wet, L.: Using a brain-computer interface (BCI) in reducing math anxiety: evidence from South Africa. Comput. Educ. **81**, 113–122 (2015). https://doi.org/10.1016/j.compedu.2014.10.002
19. Hunsley, J., Flessati, S.L.: Gender and mathematics anxiety: the role of math-related experiences and opinions. Anxiety Res. **1**, 215–224 (1988). https://doi.org/10.1080/089177788082 48720
20. Rubinsten, O., Bialik, N., Solar, Y.: Exploring the relationship between math anxiety and gender through implicit measurement. Front. Hum. Neurosci. **6**, 1–11 (2012). https://doi.org/10.3389/fnhum.2012.00279
21. Van Mier, H.I., Schleepen, T.M.J., Van den Berg, F.C.G.: Gender differences regarding the impact of math anxiety on arithmetic performance in second and fourth graders. Front. Psychol. **9**, 1–13 (2019). https://doi.org/10.3389/fpsyg.2018.02690
22. Siegler, R.S., et al.: Early predictors of high school mathematics achievement. Psychol. Sci. **23**, 691–697 (2012). https://doi.org/10.1177/0956797612440101
23. Fuegi, J., Francis, J.: Lovelace & Babbage and the creation of the 1843 "Notes". Ada User J. **36**, 89–98 (2003)
24. Essinger, J.: Ada's Algorithm? How Lord Byron's Daughter Ada Lovelace Launched the Digital Age. Melville House, London (2014)
25. Carey, E., Hill, F., Devine, A., Szucs, D.: The modified abbreviated math anxiety scale: a valid and reliable instrument for use with children. Front. Psychol. **8**, 1–13 (2017). https://doi.org/10.3389/fpsyg.2017.00011
26. Hopko, D.R., Mahadevan, R., Bare, R.L., Hunt, M.K.: The abbreviated math anxiety scale (AMAS): construction, validity, and reliability. Assessment **10**, 178–182 (2003). https://doi.org/10.1177/1073191103252351
27. Kelleher, C., Weir, S.: Class size and student-teacher ratio at primary level in Ireland and other OECD countries. Irish J. Educ. **41**, 39–60 (2016)
28. Hobbs, L., Davis, R.: Narrative pedagogies in science, mathematics and technology. Res. Sci. Educ. **43**, 1289–1305 (2012). https://doi.org/10.1007/s11165-012-9302-5
29. Stoet, G., Bailey, D.H., Moore, A.M., Geary, D.C.: Countries with higher levels of gender equality show larger national sex differences in mathematics anxiety and relatively lower parental mathematics valuation for girls. PLoS One **11**, 1–24 (2016). https://doi.org/10.1371/journal.pone.0153857
30. Pruet, P., Ang, C.S., Farzin, D.: Understanding tablet computer usage among primary school students in underdeveloped areas: students' technology experience, learning styles and attitudes. Comput. Human Behav. **55**, 1131–1144 (2016). https://doi.org/10.1016/j.chb.2014.09.063

31. Giannakos, M.N., Chorianopoulos, K., Jaccheri, L., Chrisochoides, N.: "This Game Is Girly!" Perceived enjoyment and student acceptance of edutainment. In: Göbel, S., Müller, W., Urban, B., Wiemeyer, J. (eds.) Edutainment/GameDays -2012. LNCS, vol. 7516, pp. 89–98. Springer, Heidelberg (2012). https://doi.org/10.1007/978-3-642-33466-5_10
32. Hartmann, T., Klimmt, C.: Gender and computer games: exploring females' dislikes. J. Comput. Commun. **11**, 910–931 (2006). https://doi.org/10.1111/j.1083-6101.2006.00301.x
33. Beilock, S.L., Gunderson, E.A., Ramirez, G., Levine, S.C.: Female teachers' math anxiety affects girls' math achievement. Proc. Natl. Acad. Sci. U. S. A. **107**, 1860–1863 (2010). https://doi.org/10.1073/pnas.0910967107
34. Maloney, E.A., Sattizahn, J.R., Beilock, S.L.: Anxiety and cognition. Wiley Interdiscip. Rev. Cogn. Sci. **5**, 403–411 (2014). https://doi.org/10.1002/wcs.1299
35. Patrick, H., Anderman, L.H., Ryan, A.M.: Social motivation and the classroom social environment. In: Goals, Goal Structures, and Patterns of Adaptive Learning, pp. 85–108 (2002)

Motivational Potential of Leaderboards in a Team-Based Math Game Competition

Manuel Ninaus[1,2,3](✉) ⓘD, Sara De Freitas[4], and Kristian Kiili[5]

[1] Department of Psychology, University of Innsbruck, Innsbruck, Austria
manuel.ninaus@uibk.ac.at
[2] LEAD Graduate School and Research Network, University of Tübingen, Tübingen, Germany
[3] Leibniz-Institut für Wissensmedien, Tübingen, Germany
[4] Department of Computer Science and Information Systems, Birkbeck University of London, London, UK
sara@dcs.bbk.ac.uk
[5] Tampere University, Tampere, Finland
kristian.kiili@tuni.fi

Abstract. Leaderboards are a popular way to implement competition, trigger social comparison, increase participation, and provide goals and performance-based feedback to the players. Even though game-based learning has become more common in education, relatively little is known about the motivational power of leaderboards in team-based educational settings. This paper aims to contribute to this gap by exploring to what extent leaderboards motivate players in collaborative and competitive game-based learning context. The meaning of leaderboards was studied in a team-based math game competition relying on intra-classroom collaboration and inter-classroom competition. The findings suggest that the team rank, team commitment, and enjoyment of the game predicted leaderboard motivation. The results revealed that even though leaderboards were motivating in general, players whose team did not succeed well in the competition were less motivated. It seems that leaderboards may facilitated collaboration but the collaborative element of the competition did not totally reduce the negative effects of the used infinite leaderboard. These findings disclose some drawbacks of an infinite leaderboard design. To overcome this problem, we suggest some ways to redesign leaderboards for educational use. Finally, we discuss implications of the research for using leaderboards in game-based learning settings, factors affecting leaderboard motivation, and leaderboard design in general.

Keywords: Leaderboards · Game-based learning · Mathematics · Team competition · Collaboration

1 Introduction

Game-based learning and gamification of learning is utilized to motivate learners by using game elements to enhance learners' interest and engagement in learning content [1]. Several meta-analyses have provided evidence that digital game-based learning can

© Springer Nature Switzerland AG 2020
I. Marfisi-Schottman et al. (Eds.): GALA 2020, LNCS 12517, pp. 242–252, 2020.
https://doi.org/10.1007/978-3-030-63464-3_23

produce better learning outcomes than conventional learning approaches [2–4], but the subject domain as well as study design can remarkably influence the outcomes [3]. Accordingly, a meta-analysis of game-based mathematics learning reported statistically significant learning effects, however, the overall effect size was rather small [5]. Although several studies have indicated that game-based learning engages learners more than conventional instructional methods, the results of a meta-analyses by [3] did not support this common belief. The quality of digital game-based learning solutions tends to vary a lot that may partly explain these mixed results. Recent research has suggested that the effectiveness of different game features such as feedback, adaptivity, collaboration, competition, etc. should be more exhaustively studied with respect to learning and motivation [6]. This study contributes to this open question by exploring the motivational power of leaderboards included in a team-based math game competition.

1.1 Background

Competition is a common game element in which players compete with one another or with the game system. Previous results on the usefulness of competitive elements in game-based learning are mixed. Some studies have shown that competition can enhance engagement and playing performance (e.g., [7, 8]). For example, [7] found that leaderboards in a game enhanced students' motivation and performance. On the other hand, the competitive game element did not have such a positive effect in several other studies (e.g., [9, 10]). Competitive elements have been reported to result even in detrimental effects on learning outcomes (e.g. [11]). For instance, [11] found that competitive play in a math game resulted in the dominance of high achievers, which, in turn, decreased participation of low achievers. Furthermore, the study revealed that competition negatively affected collaborative learning for below-average students and positively for above-average students. A recent meta-analysis further revealed that competition in digital game-based learning was effective for math, science, and language, but not for social science and other subjects [12]. In general, the previous research has shown that competition is a multifaceted phenomenon, and the implementation, as well as contextual factors of the competition, can influence learning and motivational outcomes.

The use of a leaderboard is one popular way to implement competition, which seems to offer several advantages in game-based learning environments [13]. For instance, leaderboards may increase participation, provide specific goals for the learner, and provide means to evaluate learning progress. Accordingly, leaderboards provide feedback to the learner on their performance. Even though feedback has consistently been shown to positively affect students [14], it has also been demonstrated that the position in leaderboards affects its impact [15]. In particular, learners' reaction to receiving rather negative feedback (i.e. their performance is below a standard or below many other learners) can vary. Learners could increase their effort, reject the provided feedback or even abandon the activity (e.g., [15, 16]).

Leaderboards are also one of the simplest forms to facilitate social interaction (e.g., [15, 17]). In context of the self-determination theory, both collaboration and competition are factors addressing relatedness as well as the feeling of competence [18]. Enabling collaboration allows learners, for instance, to compete in teams to master challenges rather than overcoming them alone. Importantly, according to a recent meta-analysis on the effects of gamification competition combined with collaboration rather than competition alone seems to be particularly effective for improving behavioural learning outcomes as well as motivation [2]. Accordingly, the authors argued that competition alone might be suboptimal for at least some learners under certain circumstances. Utilizing a combination of collaboration and competition might help to reduce negative effects of leaderboards. Importantly though, collaboration can take many forms and to harness the potential of collaboration the task should require team members to share a common team goal and the success of reaching this goal should depend on all members of the group (e.g., [19, 20]).

Besides these reported specific effects of leaderboards, general learning related constructs such as learners' self-efficacy or the feeling of competence, respectively, and learning domain specific anxiety (e.g., math anxiety) have been considered as crucial factors in educational settings (e.g., [21]). In the domain of mathematics learning, it has been repeatedly demonstrated that low self-efficacy and high math anxiety negatively affects performance and motivation in traditional learning scenarios (e.g., [22–25]).

1.2 Present Study

In the present study, we applied the 'Teams-Game-Tournament' (TGT) model [11]. The TGT model is one of the most well-known competitive collaborative models in which students both collaborate in teams as well as play individually to compete as a team against other teams. In particular, we organized a math game competition in Finland to support rational number instruction. The game utilized the so-called number line estimation task [26], which is an established way to assess and train students number magnitude understanding (e.g., [27–29]). In this task, students have to estimate the position of a target number (e.g. 1/4) on a horizontal line with only its endpoints specified (e.g. where goes 1/4 on a number line ranging from 0 to 1). Students were organized in teams or classes, respectively, and competed across the country in a math game. Students' (team) scores and the respective rankings were shown on a dedicated competition webpage and in the game. Accordingly, the design of the math game competition aimed at facilitating inter-classroom competition as well as intra-classroom collaboration. The overall objective of the current study was to exploratively examine factors that contribute to the motivational potential of the provided leaderboards. In particular, we were interested to investigate whether the rank of the team affects the perceived motivation of the leaderboard, as it is the case for individual competition settings (e.g., [15]). Motivation experienced by the provided leaderboards might also depend on the commitment (e.g., [8, 19, 20]). Besides that, we examined whether motivation is also driven by the overall enjoyment with the game as well as other more general learning related constructs such as math anxiety and self-efficacy (e.g., [21–25]).

2 Methods

We organized a nation-wide game competition in which we utilized a mathematics game designed to foster rational number knowledge. The competition for elementary school students, allowed students from Finland to climb the ladders of online team-based and individual leaderboards to rehearse and improve their mathematics skills. The current study is part of a larger project investigating the use of math game competitions to support rational number instruction. Using the same sample but different research questions and partly different variables, a previous study explored the educational potential of the math game competition and demonstrated that students increased their performance over the course of the competition (see [30]). The current study, focused on the motivational potential of the competition and leaderboards, respectively.

2.1 Participants

The competition was open for all Finnish 3–6 graders. Approximately 1,500 students from 35 different municipalities around Finland participated in the game competition. Participation was voluntary but students needed approval from their parents. From these 1,500 students 271 students (mean age $= 11.62$ years; SD $= 1.03$ years) filled in a questionnaire about the game competition and thus were considered for analyses in the current study. Of these 271 participants 116 were females and 155 were males. The median of self-reported mathematics grade was 9. In the Finnish classification scheme, 10 reflects the best and 4 the lowest grade. Most of the participants were experienced players as 62% of the participants reported that they play digital games at least a couple of times per week and 78% of the participants reported that they usually do well or extremely well in digital games.

2.2 Description of the Game-Based Math Competition

The competition was based on the Semideus game [28] which utilizes number line estimation task mechanics and it was organised around one randomized game level that can be completed in a couple of minutes. In each task participants had to estimate the position of a target rational number (fraction or decimal) on a number line (see Fig. 1). The tasks could include visual hints, mathematical traps, enemies, and player-activatable in-game skills that reduced the task demands (see details in [30]). The educational goal of the game was to foster students' rational number knowledge. To support social interaction, each participating class formed a team that competed against other classes. Furthermore, municipalities competed with each other. The web page of the competition included leaderboards for both teams and municipalities. We used the classic infinite leaderboard design in which positions are presented as an ordered ranking. Additionally, students could check their individual and team high scores and rankings through the game. Thus, the design of the competition included inter-classroom competition as well as intra-classroom cooperation to facilitate social interaction, which might counteract potential negative side effects of competition within a classroom.

Participants received feedback on their personal performance in several ways. The success of each task of the game was immediately communicated through points. More accurate estimates yielded more points. Moreover, after every estimation the correct location was shown by a green marker on the number line and in case of successful estimation (accuracy $>= 92\%$) the respective accuracy percentage was shown. For inaccurate estimates (i.e., estimates more than $\pm 8\%$ away from the correct location) the avatar was struck by lightning and the player lost virtual energy. The points earned in

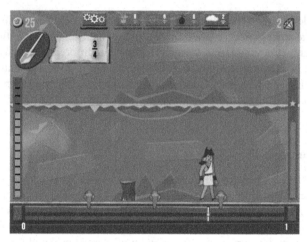

Fig. 1. The player had to estimate the position of the target number 3/4 on a number line from 0-1. In this particular instance, the player activated the in-game bird skill that divided the number line into four equal sized parts. (Color figure online)

the level formed an individual high score. Number line estimation accuracy formed 70% of the level score and 30% of the score was given by remaining energy (energy bonus) when player completed the level. The player could lose energy by inaccurate estimates, stepping on traps (locations shown with rational numbers) and being hit by enemies. That is, the game score reflected player's conceptual understanding of rational numbers quite well and thus provided clear feedback about player's skill-level (maximum score was 100 points). After completing a level, the player received additional feedback via a star rating system: one star for completing the level, one star for collecting enough points, and one star for completing the level within the set energy loss limit. On the other hand, leaderboards were used to provide feedback on a team level. The team rankings were based on the average value of each team member's highest game score. That is, every member of the team contributed to the team score/ranking.

2.3 Measures

Math self-efficacy was measured using three items on a Likert scale from 1 (Strongly disagree) – 5 (Strongly agree): (i) "I believe I will receive an excellent grade in math"; (ii) "I am certain I can understand difficult material presented in math"; (iii) "I am confident I can learn the basic concepts taught in math".

Maths anxiety was measured on a Likert with scale from 1 (Not at all anxious) – 5 (Very anxious) using three items: (i) "When I think about doing math, I feel …"; (ii) "When the teacher calls on me to answer a math problem, I feel …"; (iii) "When I make a mistake in math, I feel …".

As the competition heavily revolved around the integrated leaderboards we assessed whether players were motivated by them [*leaderboard motivation:* "Leaderboards were very motivating". Likert scale from 1(strongly disagree) – 5 (strongly agree)]. Related to this, players had to rate how much they enjoyed the game [*game enjoyment*: "I liked the game". Likert scale from 1(strongly disagree) – 5 (strongly agree)].

Moreover, to better understand whether teams worked together well, we developed a questionnaire to assess *team commitment,* which was measured using four items on a Likert scale from 1 (Strongly disagree) – 5 (Strongly agree): (i) "Our team had clear goals during the competition"; (ii) "We thought it was important to reach the team's goals."; (iii) "We had a good team spirit."; (iv) "We wanted to perform well in the math game competition as a team.".

2.4 Procedure and Data Collection

Participants had the opportunity to play the game as much as they wanted during a three-week period. Participants could play the game in school or in their free time. During the competition participants were allowed to share tips with their teammates and they were allowed to ask for help from their teacher. After the three-week period of the competition participants were asked to fill in a questionnaire.

3 Results

On average students played through 210 ($SD = 312$, *Median* $= 122$) number line estimation tasks. Table 1 shows descriptive statistics about student's performance and self-reported measures.

Table 1. Means and standard deviations of variables and construct reliabilities (n = 271)

Variable	M	SD	Scale
Math self-efficacy	3.74	1.10	1–5 ($\alpha = .86$)
Math anxiety	2.04	0.92	1–5 ($\alpha = .79$)
Team commitment	3.77	0.98	1–5 ($\alpha = .86$)
Individual rank	360.06	270.56	In this data set 1-891
Team rank	27.81	22.98	In this data set 1-74
Leaderboard motivation	3.25	1.28	1–5
Game enjoyment	3.41	1.14	1–5

By using multiple regression analyses, we aimed at investigating which self-reported measures and leaderboard metrics predicted students' perceived motivation caused by leaderboards. Accordingly, we used the leaderboard motivation score as dependent variable and following variables as potential predictors in a multiple regression analysis: i) math self-efficacy, ii) math anxiety, iii) team rank, iv) personal rank, v) team commitment, and vi) overall enjoyment of the game. The forced-entry multiple regression model explained 38.49% of variation in perceived leaderboard motivation [$F(6,264) = 27.99$, $p < .001$, *adj.* $R^2 = .37$]. When inspecting the beta weights math anxiety (standardized

$\beta = -0.04$, *n.s.*) and self-efficacy (standardized $\beta = 0.05$, *n.s.*) did not account unique parts of the variance in leaderboard motivation. However, a lower/better team rank (standardized $\beta = -0.18$, $p < .01$) and higher enjoyment of the game (standardized $\beta = 0.32$, $p < .001$) as well as higher team commitment (standardized $\beta = 0.29$, $p < .001$) were predictive for higher leaderboard motivation. Personal rank did not explain additional unique parts of the variance in leaderboard motivation (standardized $\beta = -0.05$, *n.s.*; see Fig. 2).

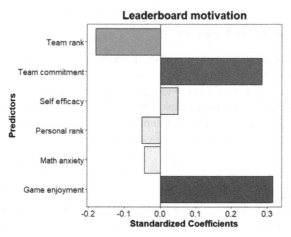

Fig. 2. Standardized beta weights of predictors of leaderboard motivation

4 Discussion

The current study utilized a nation-wide math game competition to realize inter-classroom competition as well as intra-classroom collaboration. Current results indicated that even though leaderboards in the competition were motivating, students with worse team-rank were less motivated. Students personal rank, however, did not contribute additionally to the perceived motivation by the leaderboards but team commitment and overall game enjoyment did. In the following, we will discuss these results in greater detail and provide practical implications.

The leaderboards used in the current math game competition were only partially successful in motivating students. In particular, we observed that students in teams with better team rank were motivated by the leaderboards used. This seemed to be not the case for students in poorly performing teams. Students personal rank did not additionally contribute to leaderboard motivation. Even though this is somewhat in line with previous research on the effects of individual competition [9, 11]. Contrary to our expectations, the integrated collaborative element did not reduce negative effects of leaderboards enough as initially assumed and suggested by previous results on the combination of collaboration and competition [2]. Importantly, team commitment did significantly contribute to perceived leaderboard motivation – even more so than team rank. This is in line with previous research indicating that collaboration is only successful when individuals in team members work in concert and share common goals (e.g., [8, 19, 20]). Additionally, we found overall enjoyment with the game itself to be another contributing factor to the perceived motivation gained from the leaderboards. In contrast, math anxiety and math self-efficacy did not explain additional variance of leaderboard motivation. This might indicate, that leaderboards can motivate players despite of individual differences on these learning related math anxiety and self-efficacy constructs. However, it is not clear whether this can be attributed to the leaderboards itself. For instance, this effect might be related to the general use of games as instructional tools. Because previous studies demonstrated that math anxiety can be lower in game-based than in conventional instructional tools (i.e. paper-based assessment: e.g. [31]).

Implications: Although personal rank or performance, respectively, was not a crucial predictor of leaderboard motivation, results of the current study emphasized some of the downsides of an infinite leaderboard design. Results clearly indicated that a worse team-rank negatively affected motivational power of the leaderboard. In its current implementation, leaderboard feedback mechanisms are a double-edged sword offering advantages for well performing teams, but not for teams who are struggling. Leaderboards provide a summative way to provide feedback about players' and teams performance and may facilitate collaboration. However, it is clear that the traditional infinite leaderboard approach – team based or personal – does not motivate all users in the same way.

To overcome this problem, the infinite leaderboards should be redesigned in the way that the position in the leaderboard does not demotivate even the weakest players or teams. That is, that all players or teams could be engaged by showing manipulated (sliced) leaderboards where they are performing relatively well and reaching the top 10 or top 20 does not seem totally impossible. The similar design is sometimes utilized in entertainment games. Further, in social gaming platforms this design is boosted by positioning player's friends just above and below the player. Generally, these kinds of manipulated leaderboards might support the feeling of competence and social interaction more than static infinite leaderboards. Moreover, leaderboards might utilize more and different metrics and thereby provide different goals for the players, such as persistence (e.g. most tasks completed) or gained experience points in a game (see Fig. 3).

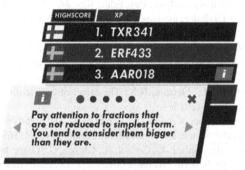

Fig. 3. Redesign of the leaderboard with personalized feedback and different metrics, i.e. highscore and experience points.

Additionally, the limited information that traditional leaderboards provide do not facilitate optimal learning or provide support for struggling learners/teams. Therefore, leaderboards or games in general should also provide feedback on players' actions that facilitate reflective thinking on players' conceptions and strategies towards increasing self-efficacy in the learning process [32]. Leaderboards can come with personalized feedback, which has the potential to influence players' performance. For example, a leaderboard could provide details about what a player could improve on and how they could do this (see Fig. 3). Next-generation leaderboards should provide feedback that goes beyond evaluative feedback (e.g. interpretive and supportive). Moreover, future studies need also to consider personality traits of learners as it has been shown, for instance, that introverts and extroverts might experience leaderboards and other game elements differently [33, 34].

Conclusion: Taken together, leaderboards motivated participating students, however, only when the teams of the students were performing well. Importantly, overall game enjoyment as well as team commitment were additional crucial factors contributing to the perceived motivation by the leaderboards. This suggests that in such team-based competitions team commitment needs to be fostered to benefit motivation but even with the collaborative aspect of having teams' negative side-effects of infinite leaderboards cannot be mitigated in its current form.

References

1. Ryan, R.M., Rigby, C.S.: Motivational foundations of game-based learning. In: Plass, J.L., Mayer, R.E., Homer, B.D. (eds.) Handbook of Game-Based Learning. pp. 153–176. MIT Press, Cambridge (2020)
2. Sailer, M., Homner, L.: The gamification of learning: a meta-analysis. Educ. Psychol. Rev. 32(1), 77–112 (2019). https://doi.org/10.1007/s10648-019-09498-w
3. Wouters, P., van Nimwegen, C., van Oostendorp, H., van Der Spek, E.D.: A meta-analysis of the cognitive and motivational effects of serious games. J. Educ. Psychol. 105, 249–265 (2013)
4. Clark, D.B., Tanner-Smith, E.E., Killingsworth, S.S.: Digital games, design, and learning: a systematic review and meta-analysis. Rev. Educ. Res. 86, 79–122 (2016)
5. Byun, J., Joung, E.: Digital game-based learning for K-12 mathematics education: a meta-analysis. Sch. Sci. Math. 118, 113–126 (2018)
6. Graesser, A.C.: Reflections on serious games. In: Wouters, P., van Oostendorp, H. (eds.) Instructional Techniques to Facilitate Learning and Motivation of Serious Games. AGL, pp. 199–212. Springer, Cham (2017). https://doi.org/10.1007/978-3-319-39298-1_11
7. Cagiltay, N.E., Ozcelik, E., Ozcelik, N.S.: The effect of competition on learning in games. Comput. Educ. 87, 35–41 (2015)
8. Plass, J.L., et al.: The impact of individual, competitive, and collaborative mathematics game play on learning, performance, and motivation. J. Educ. Psychol. 105, 1050–1066 (2013)
9. Lin, C.-H., Huang, S.-H., Shih, J.-L., Covaci, A., Ghinea, G.: Game-based learning effectiveness and motivation study between competitive and cooperative modes. In: 2017 IEEE 17th International Conference on Advanced Learning Technologies (ICALT), pp. 123–127. IEEE (2017)

10. Vandercruysse, S., Vandewaetere, M., Cornillie, F., Clarebout, G.: Competition and students' perceptions in a game-based language learning environment. Educ. Tech. Res. Dev. **61**(6), 927–950 (2013). https://doi.org/10.1007/s11423-013-9314-5

11. ter Vrugte, J., de Jong, T., Vandercruysse, S., Wouters, P., van Oostendorp, H., Elen, J.: How competition and heterogeneous collaboration interact in prevocational game-based mathematics education. Comput. Educ. **89**, 42–52 (2015)

12. Chen, C.-H., Shih, C.-C., Law, V.: The effects of competition in digital game-based learning (DGBL): a meta-analysis. Educ. Technol. Res. Dev. **68**, 1855–1873 (2020). https://doi.org/10.1007/s11423-020-09794-1

13. Nebel, S., Schneider, S., Beege, M., Rey, G.D.: Leaderboards within educational videogames: the impact of difficulty, effort and gameplay. Comput. Educ. **113**, 28–41 (2017)

14. Hattie, J., Timperley, H.: The power of feedback. Rev. Educ. Res. **77**, 81–112 (2007)

15. Nebel, S., Beege, M., Schneider, S., Rey, G.D.: The higher the score, the higher the learning outcome? Heterogeneous impacts of leaderboards and choice within educational videogames. Comput. Hum. Behav. **65**, 391–401 (2016)

16. Kluger, A., DeNisi, A.: The effects of feedback interventions on performance: a historical review, a meta-analysis, and a preliminary feedback intervention theory. Psychol. Bull. II **119**, 254–284 (1996)

17. Wang, H., Sun, C.T.: Game reward systems: gaming experiences and social meanings. In: Proceedings of the 2011 DiGRA International Conference Think Design Play (2011)

18. Rigby, C.S., Ryan, R.M.: Glued to Games: How Video Games Draw Us In and Hold Us Spellbound. Praeger, Santa Barbara, CA (2011)

19. Lou, Y., Abrami, P.C., Spence, J.C., Poulsen, C., Chambers, B., D'Apollonia, S.: Within-class grouping: a meta-analysis. Rev. Educ. Res. **66**, 423 (1996)

20. Slavin, R.E.: Cooperative learning and student achievement. Educ. Leadersh. **46**, 31–33 (1988)

21. Hung, C.-M., Huang, I., Hwang, G.-J.: Effects of digital game-based learning on students' self-efficacy, motivation, anxiety, and achievements in learning mathematics. J. Comput. Educ. **1**, 151–166 (2014). https://doi.org/10.1007/s40692-014-0008-8

22. Skaalvik, E.M., Federici, R.A., Klassen, R.M.: Mathematics achievement and self-efficacy: relations with motivation for mathematics. Int. J. Educ. Res. **72**, 129–136 (2015)

23. Peters, M.L.: Examining the relationships among classroom climate, self-efficacy, and achievement in undergraduate mathematics: a multi-level analysis. Int. J. Sci. Math. Educ. **11**, 459–480 (2013). https://doi.org/10.1007/s10763-012-9347-y

24. Pajares, F., Miller, M.D.: Role of self-efficacy and self-concept beliefs in mathematical problem solving: a path analysis. J. Educ. Psychol. **86**, 193–203 (1994)

25. Clute, P.S.: Mathematics anxiety, instructional method, and achievement in a survey course in college mathematics. J. Res. Math. Educ. **15**, 50 (1984)

26. Siegler, R.S., Opfer, J.E.: The development of numerical estimation: evidence for multiple representations of numerical quantity. Psychol. Sci. **14**, 237–243 (2003)

27. Ninaus, M., Kiili, K., McMullen, J., Moeller, K.: Assessing fraction knowledge by a digital game. Comput. Human Behav. **70**, 197–206 (2017)

28. Kiili, K., Moeller, K., Ninaus, M.: Evaluating the effectiveness of a game-based rational number training - In-game metrics as learning indicators. Comput. Educ. **120**, 13–28 (2018)

29. Fazio, L.K., Kennedy, C.A., Siegler, R.S.: Improving children's knowledge of fraction magnitudes. PLoS One **11**, e0165243 (2016)

30. Kiili, K., Ojansuu, K., Lindstedt, A., Ninaus, M.: Exploring the educational potential of a game-based math competition. Int. J. Game-Based Learn. **8**, 14–28 (2018)

31. Kiili, K., Ketamo, H.: Evaluating cognitive and affective outcomes of a digital game-based math test. IEEE Trans. Learn. Technol. **11**, 255–263 (2018)

32. Shute, V.J.: Focus on formative feedback. Rev. Educ. Res. **78**, 153–189 (2008)

33. Codish, D., Ravid, G.: Personality based gamification – educational gamification for extroverts and introverts. In: CHAIS 2014 - Conference for the Study of Innovation and Learning Technologies: Learning in the Technological Era, pp. 36–44 (2012)
34. Tondello, G.F., Wehbe, R.R., Diamond, L., Busch, M., Marczewski, A., Nacke, L.E.: The gamification user types hexad scale. In: Proceedings of the 2016 Annual Symposium on Computer-Human Interaction in Play - CHI Play 2016, pp. 229–243 (2016)

A Serious Game for Studying Decision Making by Triage Nurses Under Stress

Jarle Hulaas[1], Dominique Jaccard[1(✉)], Assunta Fiorentino[2], Philippe Delmas[2], Matteo Antonini[2], Séverine Vuilleumier[2], Guy Stotzer[2], Aurélien Kollbrunner[2], Olivier Rutschmann[3], Josette Simon[3], Olivier Hugli[4], Charlotte Gilart de Keranflec'h[5], and Jérôme Pasquier[6]

[1] School of Management and Engineering (HEIG-VD), HES-SO, 1401 Yverdon, Switzerland
{jarle.hulaas,dominique.jaccard}@heig-vd.ch
[2] La Source School of Nursing, HES-SO, 1004 Lausanne, Switzerland
[3] Emergency Department, Geneva University Hospital (HUG), 1205 Geneva, Switzerland
[4] Emergency Department, Lausanne University Hospital (CHUV), 1011 Lausanne, Switzerland
[5] School of Health Sciences (HESAV), HES-SO, 1011 Lausanne, Switzerland
[6] Institute of Social and Preventive Medicine, CHUV, Lausanne, Switzerland

Abstract. At patient intake in emergency departments, triage is a key step in ensuring optimal patient care and good use of hospital resources. Triage nurses must be able to make correct clinical judgements and triage decisions despite extremely stressful working conditions including noise and task interruptions. This article presents a new serious game designed to closely reproduce the conditions of a typical emergency department. Its purpose is to provide a generic testbed both for teaching and for research, notably in order to enable studying the impact of stressors on the quality of decisions made. A study involving 49 professional triage nurses shows that, despite its relatively modest technological requirements, this serious game is considered by the participants as highly attractive and very close to their professional experience.

Keywords: Decision making · Triage · Emergency · Nursing · Serious game · Simulation

1 Introduction

Clinical decision making is an essential competency within nursing practice, especially in emergency departments (ED) [1]. The ability of nurses to make optimal decisions is the end result of a complex cognitive process and is one of the main factors affecting quality of patient care [2]. When a nurse makes a decision, the outcomes may be positive (improved quality of life or reduced symptoms) or negative (medication errors, inadequate prioritization of patients in the waiting room) [3]. Nevertheless, ED professionals are seeing an intensification of their activity and an increase in the complexity of the clinical situations they encounter [4]. Besides these heavy responsibilities, triage

---

HES-SO stands for "University of Applied Sciences and Arts Western Switzerland" in English.

© Springer Nature Switzerland AG 2020
I. Marfisi-Schottman et al. (Eds.): GALA 2020, LNCS 12517, pp. 253–262, 2020.
https://doi.org/10.1007/978-3-030-63464-3_24

nurses must be able to make correct triage decisions in the middle of difficult working conditions, which include pervasive background noise and task interruptions.

Currently, the training of triage nurses and the evaluation of their competences are mainly based on printed clinical vignettes[1], personal coaching and observational methods [5–7]. The triage process can also be reproduced using classical simulation with standardized patients or high-fidelity manikins. But these solutions are very costly and difficult to integrate in a resource-strained ED environment. Therefore, considering the limited realism of the first approaches, the cost of the latter and the stakes involved in decision making at EDs, we decided to explore the use of a simulation-based serious game as a training and research tool.

Serious games are already widely used for training and evaluating healthcare professionals in specific technical procedures such as surgery or the development of the cognitive process involved in the evaluation of a patient [8, 9]. However, few serious games are suitable for post-graduate nursing education, particularly in the field of ED [9]. Also, surveys of serious games in health professions [9, 10] show that triage games seem to mostly focus on specific disaster responses, not on day to day ED operations.

This article presents a new serious game designed to closely reproduce the conditions of a typical emergency department by means of an affordable and easy-to-deploy 2D HTML technology. Its purpose is to provide a flexible infrastructure both for teaching/training and for research. Thus, we needed not only to validate this approach, by having its realism and acceptability assessed by a panel of triage nurses, but also to use it as a research tool, by conducting a pre-study on the impact of stressors such as noise and task interruptions on the quality of decisions made by triage nurses.

This work was carried out in Switzerland, following a multidisciplinary co-development process including emergency specialists from four hospitals, nursing sciences and stress specialists, statisticians and serious games developers.

The next section presents project objectives and methods, then we describe the resulting game. In the following section we present a field test with experienced triage nurses and the analysis of their answers to various questionnaires. Finally we discuss the success factors before concluding.

2   Objectives and Methods

Some authors point out that the nurse's decision making at the intake of an ED is different from other care contexts because: 1) it requires a high level of continuous concentration in an environment with many environmental distractors (noise, task interruptions or random workload), which may affect the quality of the decision-making; 2) it must be carried out in an extremely short time (often less than 5 min) and 3) it is often carried out autonomously and with a limited amount of information available [2, 11]. Task interruptions, for example, lead to delays in the execution of an activity, loss of information and reduced concentration leading to impaired decision making [12].

The objective of this project was to design and develop a serious game that would constitute a valid basis for teaching/training as well as for research. To validate this

---

[1] Clinical vignettes are patient-related cases and scenarios with educational value.

approach, we had to define a research methodology and organize a small-scale user test before presenting the game to a full group of participating nurses. The methodological framework chosen for this study is a 2×2 factorial trial to verify the impact of stressors on the nurses' decision making. Four equally-sized groups (a control group, a group exposed to noise, a group subject to task interruptions, and a group with an equal combination of noise and task interruptions) were formed randomly at each participating ED. The nurses needed to be active as intake and triage professionals in a hospital using the Swiss Emergency Triage Scale (SETS®) [13] and to consent to participate in the study. The following variables were collected by the game:

1. At the beginning of the game, sociodemographic data related to the nurses' professional background and experience.
2. During the game, the correctness of the emergency levels attributed by the nurses to the vignettes (data not disclosed to the participants). The durations of different phases and medical acts were also collected for future analysis.
3. After each vignette, the nurses' level of confidence in their own evaluation, by means of a visual analog scale from 0 to 10 (this data has not yet been analyzed at this writing).
4. At the end of the game, the AttrakDiff^{TM} usability questionnaire, in order to determine its acceptability, and the perceived realism, by means of a visual analog scale from 0 to 10.

In the following section, we describe the resulting simulation-based serious game.

3   The Triage Serious Game

Triage is a dynamic activity based on patient-nurse interactions. To reproduce this activity, our starting point was an existing interactive simulator enabling simple question-answer interactions based on clinical vignettes [13]. Then, to create a more realistic simulator, we added a dynamic 2D virtual environment replicating an ED waiting room (see Fig. 1). We created 20 clinical vignettes, the accuracy and consistency of which were tested by nurse experts. The vignettes were brought to life with a number of 2D figures reproducing patient arrival on foot, stretcher or wheelchair, with or without accompanying persons.

We integrated 10 task interruptions and 10 sound effects representing stressors frequently found in an ED. They were programmed to interfere in a reproducible way with specific player actions such as anamnesis or vital sign measurement. Game players have to wear a well-defined model of headphones to ensure consistent sound playback levels.

A permanent background noise with air conditioning and sounds of doors, footsteps and voices is played back at a level varying between 40 dB and 50 dB, depending on the occupancy of the waiting room. The above-mentioned intermittent sound effects, played at levels up to 80 dB, consist of phone calls, drilling, helicopter landing, baby cries, medical equipment alarm and thunderclaps. Finally, task interruptions are implemented using modal pop-ups with an image of the disturbing person or phone, whose request is displayed textually. The player then has to think of an answer to be typed into a text

Fig. 1. Waiting room in the serious game (© 2020 Archives Fondation La Source)

input field (the relevance of this answer is not analyzed by the game). It is allowed to dismiss a phone call, but it will then occur again a minute later.

The serious game was developed on Wegas[2] and is hosted on the same platform. Wegas is a web-based game authoring and execution platform, which supports the generation of trace data, in order to systematically log all choices made by the player. This feature opens the door to highly refined learning analytics [14], e.g. for eliciting and comparing problem-solving strategies developed by the players [15].

The Triage Serious Game records the nurse's anamnesis, vital sign measurements and their entry into the SETS input form, the attributed level of emergency and presenting complaint (i.e. the actual reason why the patient came to the ED) according to the SETS® scale. This data is collected in a way that preserves player anonymity and is stored in a database according to the Experience API (xAPI) specification [16].

Since the game is web-based, some technological constraints apply. It requires a relatively recent web browser and a steady network connection for saving trace data and periodically persisting game variables. Specific measures had to be implemented for detecting accidental page reloads inside the browser, which might invalidate some measurements. Moreover, sound management is complicated by the browser, whose security rules prevent the playback of sound at random moments, independently of user activity. The volume was calibrated and its consistency monitored using a sound level meter.

Figure 2 shows the patient examination screen, which is divided into two parts. On the left, the interaction with the virtual patient (keyword-driven anamnesis questions, measurement of vital parameters) and a glimpse of the waiting room (in case another patient should fail). On the right, in the blue area, the input form of the SETS® scale, where

---

[2] Project homepage: www.albasim.ch.

the nurse is to enter measured vital parameters, answers to recommended anamnesis questions, and finally the chosen presenting complaints and emergency degree.

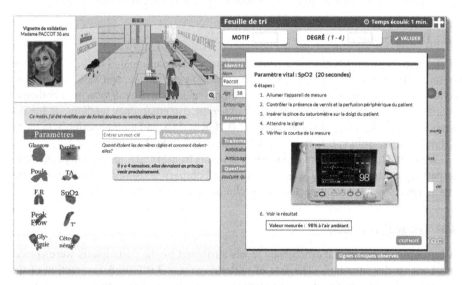

Fig. 2. Patient examination screen with sample vital parameter measurement (texts are in French). (© 2020 Archives Fondation La Source)

On top of the blue zone in Fig. 2, there is a pop-up window showing a vital parameter measurement in progress. The measurement of vital parameters is unfortunately a repetitive and tedious task in this setting where all phases are supposed to have realistic durations, since the nurse then has an entirely passive role, as opposed to the same situation in real life. In order to mitigate this, we added some simple animations (progress bar, slideshow of a real measurement) and shortened somewhat the durations.

4   Project Outcomes and Discussion

The Triage Serious Game was tested by a group of experienced nurses. The main goal of this study was to evaluate the feasibility and acceptability of the serious game, as follows:

- acceptability was measured using the AttrakDiff[TM] scale;
- realism was rated using a visual analogic scale, where nurses evaluated their perception of this simulation of triage activities;
- the research team used a research diary to note all technical difficulties during the sessions while nurses were playing the serious game on their on-loan laptops.

4.1 Preparations

Four equally-sized participant groups were created randomly at each ED: the control group, the "Interruption" group, the "Noise" group, and the "Interruption+Noise" (I+N) group. A set of identical laptops and headphones was prepared before each session. Each participant had two test vignettes to get acquainted with the game, while a member of the research team was available for additional explanations and technical support.

4.2 Demographics

Forty-nine triage nurses recruited from four Swiss EDs participated in the study. Their mean $\pm$ SD age was 37.7 ± 8.9 years; 73% (n = 36) were female, and 78% (n = 38) had followed a specific training in triage. Their employment activity rate was greater than or equal to 80% for 69.3% (34 nurses), their experience in emergency medicine 8.3 ± 6.1 years (min = 0.3, max = 30.0, median = 7.0, IQR = 7.0), and their experience in triage 7.9 ± 5.1 years (min = 0.3, max = 20.0, median = 7.0, IQR = 8.0).

We would like to emphasize that 80 participants from six EDs are actually scheduled to participate, but our study was suspended in February 2020 due to the coronavirus crisis. This may have an impact on the preliminary conclusions of Sect. 4.4.

4.3 Triage Performance

All groups combined, the emergency levels attributed by the participants were correct in 91.4% of the situations. The rate of undertriage was 3.9% (underestimation of the emergency level) and the rate of overtriage was 4.7% (overestimation of the emergency level). The frequency of correct level attributions is quite high and shows that the SETS® scale is strongly prescriptive: the probability of making errors remains low unless one ignores certain vital parameters recommended by the scale.

4.4 Comparing Error Rates Between Groups

When applied to the respective error rates, the Wilcoxon signed-rank test indicates that there are no significant differences between the control group and the three groups exposed to noise and/or interruptions, nor between any of the latter groups. To this end, we computed the odds ratio of correctly estimating the emergency level for a participant of each group relatively to a participant of any other group. Considering that participants came from different sites, that each participant evaluated several vignettes, and that each vignette was evaluated by several participants, we adjusted odds ratios for these variables. The outcome is that no difference in attributed emergency levels can be demonstrated between any groups at this stage. We found a similar result concerning attributed presenting complaints.

This preliminary result suggests that the stressors implemented in the serious game did not have any significant impact. If confirmed after participation of all enlisted nurses, it could be attributed to at least two factors. First, that the SETS® scale is very prescriptive and leaves little room for errors of judgement, even in presence of environmental stressors. Second, that we slightly underestimated the frequency and intensity of real-life stressors, a fact that was already pointed out by participants during debriefing sessions. It should be noted that we were very concerned about not exceeding legal sound levels inside the game. The difficulty of the vignettes, although reviewed by professional triage nurses, might also be revised upwards.

This result could lead to another interesting research question: at what threshold will hardened triage nurses start making more frequent errors?

4.5 Realism

At the end of each session, participants were asked to evaluate the realism of the simulation as compared to their own experience of a real-world ED. On a scale from 0 to 10, we obtained a global mean value of 8.08 (SD: 1.79). We give in Table 1 and Table 2 the respective results for the four participating ED sites and the four groups.

Table 1. Comparing perceived realism among ED sites

	Site 1	Site 2	Site 3	Site 4
Mean value	8.27	7.86	8.00	8.16
SD	0.89	2.51	1.54	1.80

Table 2. Comparing perceived realism among participant groups

	Control	Interruption	Noise	I+N
Mean value	8.08	7.76	8.26	8.17
SD	2.58	2.06	1.40	1.03

These tables show that there are no significant differences among sites and among groups. This positive result confirms previous work on the notion of fidelity in simulation-based serious games [17, 18], i.e. that depending on the application domain, players will feel immersed even without advanced technologies such as virtual reality devices. The present serious game seems to be doing its job with simple stereo headphones and 2D graphics without animations. This choice was also led by the need to limit development costs and to simplify the organization of field tests and, later, of classrooms.

4.6 Acceptability

Participants were asked to fill out the AttrakDiff[TM] questionnaire [19] regarding their user experience inside the game. This questionnaire is a reference tool for UX researchers and is used to assess the hedonic and pragmatic qualities of interactive systems. AttrakDiff has 4 subscales of 7 questions each, for a total of 28 questions presented as Likert scales. Answers receive values from −3 to +3.

According to Table 3, the serious game is perceived in a clearly positive way by its users. With a global attractiveness of 1.75 we conclude that the game is highly acceptable to its target audience. This is good news, as it means that it constitutes a good testbed for further research questions and does not need any fundamental redesign.

Table 3. Results of the AttrakDiff questionnaire

Subscale	Mean	SD
Pragmatic	1.04	0.72
Hedonic-stimulation	1.90	0.80
Hedonic-identity	0.99	0.67
Global attractiveness	1.75	0.83

4.7 Success Factors

We believe that the perceived quality of the serious game is largely due to the collaborative work of the development team. This work was indeed carried out following a multidisciplinary co-development approach including emergency specialists from four hospitals, nursing sciences and stress specialists, statisticians and serious games developers. This serious game therefore results from the combination of several fields of expertise:

- Clinical expertise: the SETS® scale, clinical vignettes, competences in triage and stress factors.
- Research expertise: methodological approach, human factors theory, creation of a realistic ED environment with stressors.
- Technological expertise: serious games development, a tried and tested execution platform, collection of execution traces.

Each step of the triage process was specified and implemented to be as similar as possible to real life: this was ensured by the participation of several ED and triage professionals (nurses and doctors). All participant actions were logged for later analysis: the research methodology was designed in collaboration with two statisticians. The agreement on the right emergency level for each vignette was based on a "gold standard" previously defined by four emergency medicine and nursing experts.

In the end, as reported by one field test participant, even if the game still needs to increase the level of stressors, it is very respectful of the nurse's professional mindset. Moreover, its attractiveness is high even though few specific accommodations have been made to increase the playing pleasure.

5 Conclusion

This article presented an innovative serious game designed as a flexible tool for training triage nurses and for studying the performance of triage nurses in realistic conditions. As a research tool, it should help improving the quality of the triage process, i.e. the accuracy of the attributed emergency levels and presenting complaints. Further research is planned, which consists of quantifying perceived emotions and adding clinical reasoning analysis. A study with 49 professional triage nurses shows that the game already is considered as realistic and acceptable in its current version. It has thus become a promising generic testbed for exploring and analyzing complex triage activities, and should become a valuable teaching and training tool without substantial redesign.

Acknowledgements. This work was supported by the Health Sciences Faculty Fund of the University of Applied Sciences and Arts Western Switzerland (HES-SO).

References

1. Stanfield, L.M.: Clinical decision making in triage: an integrative review. J. Emerg. Nurs. **41**(5), 396–403 (2015). https://doi.org/10.1016/j.jen.2015.02.003
2. Simmons, B., Lanuza, D., Fonteyn, M., Hicks, F., Holm, K.: Clinical reasoning in experienced nurses. West. J. Nurs. Res. **25**(6), 701–719 (2003). https://doi.org/10.1177/0193945903253092
3. Johansen, M.L., O'Brien, J.L.: Decision making in nursing practice: a concept analysis. Nurs. Forum **51**(1), 40–48 (2016). https://doi.org/10.1111/nuf.12119
4. McLeod, S.L., et al.: Interrater reliability, accuracy, and triage time pre- and post-implementation of a real-time electronic triage decision-support tool. Ann. Emerg. Med. **75**(4), 524–531 (2020). https://doi.org/10.1016/j.annemergmed.2019.07.048
5. Dallaire, C., Poitras, J., Aubin, K., Lavoie, A., Moore, L., Audet, G.: Interrater agreement of Canadian Emergency Department Triage and Acuity Scale scores assigned by base hospital and emergency department nurses. CJEM **12**(1), 45–49 (2010). https://doi.org/10.1017/s148180350001201x
6. Göransson, K.E., von Rosen, A.: Interrater agreement: a comparison between two emergency department triage scales. Eur. J. Emerg. Med. **18**(2), 68–72 (2011). https://doi.org/10.1097/MEJ.0b013e32833ce4eb
7. Göransson, K.E., Ehnfors, M., Fonteyn, M.E., Ehrenberg, A.: Thinking strategies used by Registered Nurses during emergency department triage. J. Adv. Nurs. **61**(2), 163–172 (2008). https://doi.org/10.1111/j.1365-2648.2007.04473.x
8. de Ribaupierre, S., Kapralos, B., Haji, F., Stroulia, E., Dubrowski, A., Eagleson, R.: Healthcare training enhancement through virtual reality and serious games. In: Ma, M., Jain, L.C., Anderson, P. (eds.) Virtual, Augmented Reality and Serious Games for Healthcare 1. ISRL, vol. 68, pp. 9–27. Springer, Heidelberg (2014). https://doi.org/10.1007/978-3-642-54816-1_2
9. Haoran, G., Bazakidi, E., Zary, N.: Serious games in health professions education: review of trends and learning efficacy. Yearb. Med. Inform. **28**(1), 240–248 (2019). https://doi.org/10.1055/s-0039-1677904
10. Ricciardi, F., De Paolis, L.T.: A comprehensive review of serious games in health professions. Int. J. Comput. Games Technol. (2014). https://www.hindawi.com/journals/ijcgt/2014/787968/. Accessed 23 Sept 2020
11. Reay, G., Rankin, J.A., Then, K.L.: Momentary fitting in a fluid environment: a grounded theory of triage nurse decision making. Int. Emerg. Nurs. **26**, 8–13 (2016). https://doi.org/10.1016/j.ienj.2015.09.006
12. Rivera-Rodriguez, A.J., Karsh, B.-T.: Interruptions and distractions in healthcare: review and reappraisal. Qual. Saf. Health Care **19**(4), 304–312 (2010). https://doi.org/10.1136/qshc.2009.033282
13. Rutschmann, O.T., et al.: Reliability of the revised Swiss Emergency Triage Scale: a computer simulation study. Eur. J. Emerg. Med. **25**(4), 264–269 (2018). https://doi.org/10.1097/MEJ.0000000000000449

14. Ferguson, R.: Learning analytics: drivers, developments and challenges. Int. J. Technol. Enhanc. Learn. **4**(5/6), 304–317 (2012)
15. Jaccard, D., Hulaas, J., Dumont, A.: Using comparative behavior analysis to improve the impact of serious games on students' learning experience. In: Bottino, R., Jeuring, J., Veltkamp, R.C. (eds.) GALA 2016. LNCS, vol. 10056, pp. 199–210. Springer, Cham (2016). https://doi.org/10.1007/978-3-319-50182-6_18
16. Fernández-Manjón, B., et al.: xAPI Application Profile for Serious Games, 18 March 2019. https://doi.org/10.13140/rg.2.2.31241.29284
17. Rooney, P.: A theoretical framework for serious game design: exploring pedagogy, play and fidelity and their implications for the design process. Int. J. Game-Based Learn. **2**(4), 41–60 (2012). https://doi.org/10.4018/ijgbl.2012100103
18. Ye, X., Backlund, P., Ding, J., Ning, H.: Fidelity in simulation-based serious games. IEEE Trans. Learn. Technol. **13**(2), 340–353 (2020). https://doi.org/10.1109/TLT.2019.2913408
19. Hassenzahl, M., Burmester, M., Koller, F.: AttrakDiff: Ein Fragebogen zur Messung wahrgenommener hedonischer und pragmatischer Qualität. In: Szwillus, G., Ziegler, J. (eds.) Mensch & Computer 2003. BGCACM, vol. 57, pp. 187–196. Vieweg+Teubner Verlag, Wiesbaden (2003). https://doi.org/10.1007/978-3-322-80058-9_19

Factors Affecting Success in a Digital Simulation Game for Nurse Training

Daria Novoseltseva[1]([✉]) [iD], Catherine Pons Lelardeux[2], and Nadine Jessel[3]

[1] IRIT, Université Paul Sabatier, Toulouse, France
`Daria.Novoseltseva@irit.fr`
[2] IRIT, Université de Toulouse,
INU Champollion, Serious Game Research Lab, Albi, France
`Catherine.Pons-lelardeux@irit.fr`
[3] IRIT, Université Toulouse Jean Jaurès,
Toulouse, France
`Nadine.Baptiste@irit.fr`

Abstract. Serious games have been developed in recent years as an essential tool for the improvement of students' decision-making skills and performance. They evolved in various domains, especially in the healthcare field. Healthcare professional experts and trainers indicate the importance of designing educational environments and educational programs in order to reproduce with high fidelity the professional context. Therefore, data gained through gaming is explored and exploited to extract information about the learning strategies. In this work, we explore data that was collected during courses in which students used a simulation game called CLONE (Clinical Organizer Nurse Education). This serious game has been designed to train nursing students in work organizations. With the implementation of statistical approaches, we intended to study factors that impact on the success of the game. Considering game sessions from 3 different angles, we try to answer the following questions: 1) Does the duration of the game session has an impact on gaming outcomes? 2) Which errors do students commit during the game? 3) Do students achieve learning progress by repeating the game? Eventually, we discussed obtained results and future work.

Keywords: Serious game · Simulations · Nurse training · Performance

1 Introduction

Serious games help to teach people about a certain subject, expand concepts, reinforce development, or assist students in skills acquisition or change their behavior. They are expected to contribute to deeper and more active education, through which students learn from their own experiences [1,19]. Thus, serious games are essential tools for delivering a message, teaching a lesson, or gaining knowledge supported by interactivity, motivation, and engagement.

© Springer Nature Switzerland AG 2020
I. Marfisi-Schottman et al. (Eds.): GALA 2020, LNCS 12517, pp. 263–272, 2020.
https://doi.org/10.1007/978-3-030-63464-3_25

In recent years, many reports and experts point the importance to design educational environments and educational programs to reproduce with high fidelity the professional environment [6,12,23]. Thus, Flin et al. [9] emphasize the significance of non-technical skills that are not directly linked to anesthetist's technical expertise. Non-technical skills are divided into interpersonal and cognitive. Interpersonal skills as communication, leadership, coordination are skills that make teamwork effective to reach a common goal [18]. Cognitive skills include task management, situation awareness, and decision making.

Hence, elaborating inter-professional simulations in the healthcare field is a perfect way to train medical specialists. Simulation is a technique that enables to replace or amplify real experiences with guided experiences that evoke or replicate substantial aspects of the real world in a fully interactive manner [11]. A simulation, in terms of healthcare training, is used to provide a safe environment for education without any real risk of accident or disease for the patient. Practically, modern simulation in healthcare education corresponds to using equipment, sometimes a computer software, a mixed reality system "which is a combination of both real and virtual" or a standardized patient for replicating a medical environment and/or a clinic situation and/or a specific pathology.

In this work, we consider dataset which was collected from game-based simulation for students from Nursing Schools, which is called Clinical Organizer Nurse Education (CLONE). The game aims at training students to organize their daily schedule, to delegate specific tasks to the nurse assistant, in order to educate professional nurses on scheduling skills, situation awareness, and decision-making [20]. The study demonstrates the analysis of data with implementation of statistical tools. We intended to find out factors that might help to predict game success or to display in-game feedback through analysis of game sessions duration, errors which students committed, and characteristics of repeated sessions.

2   Research Frameworks

2.1   Related Work

As many benefits of using games as an educational environment exist, a vast variety of applications were developed in past decades [5]. Serious games have various shapes, such as simulations or queries, and domains, such as well-being, cultural heritage, and even healthcare [17]. The importance of designing educational environments and educational program is marked by healthcare professional experts and trainers. Therefore, they intend to create an experiential learning environment, which helps students to develop inter-professional skills [6]. The majority of digital training in healthcare is designed for medical specialists and focused on technical skills and surgery [13]. Some of them are designed to train caregiving teams to improve coordination and efficiency at their operative unit [7,16]. Others simulate an operating room to train the inter-professional team activity [14,21].

The interaction students with virtual training environments gathers data, that might reflect important information about the learning process. Therefore, the methods of Game Learning Analytics (GLA) has been evolved in recent years. The game system usually represents data in a form of log files that determine records of events in the system. Extraction and prepossessing of meaningful data for further analysis is a challenging task related to the purpose of the research. Depending on the application purpose GLA methods study performance [2,15], in-game players behaviors [4], student profiles [8], and motivation [10,24]. Another challenging task is to find appropriate techniques for data analysis. In this context, GLA can be considered as an area which exploits a set of various methods such as machine learning, information retrieval, statistics, sequential mining, and visualization, in order to enhance learning experiences [3].

This work represents an analysis of data gathered from the virtual training environment CLONE, which is designed to support teachers in the Nursing Schools. We implement the methods of GLA to examine features of game sessions, which were played by students.

2.2 CLONE

The project CLONE (Clinical Organizer Nurse Education) is a Real-time Digital Virtual Environment for Training of nursing students in real-life-like professional situations. It proposes a large library of educational cases where a nurse-student plays the role of a regular nurse. This digital environment includes game mechanisms and interactive features such as a scheduling system, a task shifting, and a decision-making system.

The player chooses a game scenario from the library of educational cases, which proposes a brief description of the actual and expected situation. A scenario provides interactions that allow the players to complete the mission, it is composed of locks (educational locks or playful locks) to prevent the player to succeed. Hence, outcomes are compared to expected objectives, and results of the game are immediately displayed at the dashboard. Each proposed scenario contains a certain set of patients, unpredictable events, medical dynamic events, and the actors involved in the medical process. The player has to deal with patients' diseases (to provide care) and to deal with the nurse assistant (to share the work). To complete the mission, the medical staff (nurse and nurse assistant) has to provide the required care for each patient according to their medical profiles. The designing process of CLONE contained three steps: (i) the domain analysis, (ii) the human activity modeling, and (iii) the scenario. A more detailed description of the designing process is exposed in [22]. The graphical user interface is presented in Fig. 1.

The game process contains the following steps: the briefing, the communication with the night shift, the scheduling, the activity, and the communication with the afternoon shift with debriefing. Firstly, a student reads information about the mission of the game; then at the communication step a student receives information from the night shift about the current situation when they shift at 6:30 am; afterward, a student inspects patients' records and organizes the daily

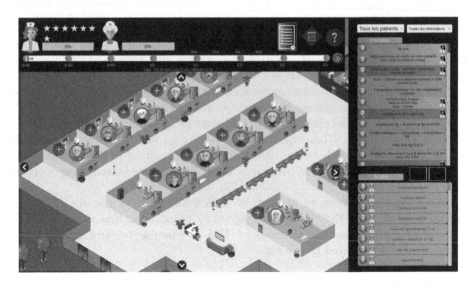

Fig. 1. The graphical user interface

activity; at the activity step a student provides care, organizes medical examination, professional phone calls, patient discharge or arrival; and finally - informs the next staff about the current situation when they shift at 1:30 pm.

2.3   Research Questions

To investigate the factors affecting the game success, this study addresses the following research questions:

RQ1: Does the duration of the game session impact on gaming outcomes?
RQ2: Which errors do students commit during the game?
RQ3: Do students achieve learning progress by repeating the game?

In responding to these research questions we aim at helping domain experts to understand learners and improve the learning process by provision data-based decision-making.

3   Methodology

To explore stated above research questions empirically, we gathered data for 353 game sessions which were played by 222 students from 11 Nursing Schools during the 2018–2020 time period. Students played according to the same scenario, which includes 5 patients, who require a low-level of care. The game proposes short storytelling of what is the actual situation and what is the expected situation at the end. The current situation starts at 6:30 am and stops at 2:00 pm. The main goal aims at elaborating a care plan for all the patients, delivering care and managing potentially hazardous situations. Students should carefully inspect patients' profiles, doctor prescriptions, and develop personalized care plan for all patients (except one, who is expected to arrive later in the morning). Then, CLONE provides interactions that allow the players to complete the mission avoiding locks (educational locks or playful locks), which prevent the player to succeed. Eventually, outcomes are compared to expected objectives, and performance indicators are immediately displayed at the end of a game session.

A list of established constraints (e.g. delivering drug, and taking blood sample) is attached to each patient. To complete a mission students have to respect to them. In case of discrepancy, the student accumulates errors: risk errors – break of soft constraints which do not have an important impact on the patient's health, and critical errors - break of hard constraints that strongly affect the patient's health. If the student exceeds the maximal number of allowed critical errors at least for one patient - the game is over.

4   Results

4.1   RQ1: Does the Duration of the Game Session Impact on Gaming Outcomes?

Answering RQ1, we investigated both the time of game sessions and the number of actions committed per session. The average duration of the game session according to the scenario with 5 patients is 46 min, while the average number of actions per game session is 175. Hereby, we compared these game session features depending on their results. Among 353 game sessions, 261 are lost and 92 are successful. In order to find out the difference between them we examined 2 hypotheses:

H1. The success of the session depends on the duration of the session.
H2. The success of the session depends on the number of actions, which were made by the player during the session.

To check these hypotheses, we applied non-parametric test due to a significant difference between analyzed indicators and normal distribution. According to Mann-Whitney U test for independent variables, the duration of the successful sessions is significantly higher ($p < 0,0005$) than the duration of lost games (Left panel in Fig. 2). Meanwhile, the number of actions for successful sessions is significantly higher ($p < 0,0005$) than the number of actions for lost games (Right panel in Fig. 2). Therefore, the assumed hypothesis can be accepted.

4.2   RQ2: Which Errors Do Students Commit During the Game?

Each patient has a list of constraints that have to be respected during the game session. In the considered scenario, 7 hard constraints are attached to Patient 1 and Patient 2, 3 hard constraints are attached to Patient 3 and Patient 4, and 4

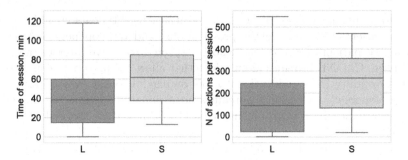

Fig. 2. Left panel: Boxplots of time distribution for lost/successful game sessions. **Right panel:** Boxplots of N of actions distribution for lost/successful game sessions. A box corresponds to the distribution of values according to 25%–75% confidence interval. The line at the center is the median. Here, L denotes lost sessions and S denotes successful sessions.

hard constraints are attached to Patient 5. In case of breaking hard constraints, student accumulates critical errors that lead to the fail of the game.

The distribution of critical errors according to their type shows that the majority of critical errors is related to omitting the delivery of medicines (e.g. a patient did not get paracetamol) as well as missing cares (e.g. a patient did not get a meal) (Left panel in Fig. 3). Meanwhile, less frequent errors were committed due to not following prescription (e.g. a patient overdosed with inappropriate medicine), missing procedures (e.g. missing an injection), and lack of monitoring parameters.

The distribution of the critical errors according to patients shows strong dependence on the number of constraints (Right panel in Fig. 3). Herein the majority of the errors corresponds to Patient 1 and Patient 2, while the minority corresponds to Patient 3, which requires less attention.

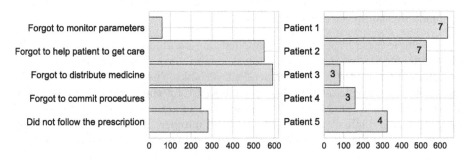

Fig. 3. Left panel: Distribution of critical errors by the type. **Right panel:** Distribution of errors by the patient. Here numbers on the bars denote number of constraints for each patient.

4.3   RQ3: Do Students Achieve Learning Progress by Repeating the Game?

Finally, in order to investigate the playing progress, the repeated sessions were examined. Among 222 students, who played a game, 81 students played more than one session (Table 1). During the first session 94% of students failed, while the percentage of failed games during the second session is 75% and during the third session is 76%. Furthermore, with increasing session order the average number of actions made per session is decreasing as well as the average time. This can be caused by the following reasons:

1. When a student launches a new session and restarts a scenario, the game saves modifications of schedule from previous sessions and a student continues playing. This simplifies the game process and cuts time during the second and further sessions due to the absence of necessity to plan.
2. Knowledge, gained during first sessions, helps some students to achieve a better result in the next session.

Table 1. Characteristics of repeated sessions.

Feature	1st session	2nd session	3rd session
N of sessions	81	81	29
Average time for session, min	50	23	14
Average N of actions per session	232	59	35
Lost sessions	94%	75%	76%
Successful sessions	6%	25%	24%

5   Discussion

In our study, we analyzed data gathered from game-based simulation for students from Nursing Schools CLONE. The game aims at training nurses to organize their daily schedule, to delegate specific tasks to the nurse assistant, in order to educate professional nurses on scheduling skills, situation awareness, and decision-making. With the implementation of statistical approaches such as non-parametric criteria and distribution analysis, we examined factors that have impact on the success of the game.

Comparing duration of lost and successful games, we found out that time and number of committed actions for successful sessions are significantly higher than for lost sessions (RQ1). Along with scheduling and delegating, students may inspect additional information, such as medical reports or patients' profiles. Likewise, they may set and modify schedule panel without any restriction. This activity requires time and numerous interactions. Consequently, students, who devoted more attention to these details, achieved better results.

Responding to the RQ2, we considered the distribution of critical errors that lead to the fail of the game. The most frequent committed errors are related to missing the delivery of medicines or cares. At the same time the less frequent errors were made by the reason of not following prescription, missing procedures, and lack of monitoring parameters. The distribution of critical errors by patients is strongly depends on the number of hard constraints, where Patient 1 and Patient 2 require more attention and Patient 3 less.

Finally, repeated sessions were examined in order to analyze learning progress during the game (RQ3). The percentage of won games is growing with the increase of session order, while the duration and number of committed actions are decreasing. This can be caused either by simplifying the game process during the second and further sessions due to the absence of necessity to work with schedule either by gaining knowledge and experience from the first sessions that help some students to improve the performance.

The obtained results point that students' learnability and acquisition can be improved in part through involvement and repetitions in game process. Indeed, the student's success progresses until it reaches a critical threshold of stability. It means that the students did not acquire totally the expected skills thanks to the repetitions and involvement. It highlights the need to add complementary theoretical courses to the serious game.

6   Conclusion and Future Work

A game-based simulation CLONE enables to train of professional skills of students from Nursing Schools. The analysis of collected data from the gaming sessions might help domain experts to understand learners' strategies and behavior. It should help to improve the educational process by providing data-based decision-making. For instance, it may be useful for an indication of struggling students and maybe even offer specific remediation actions for them.

The use of GLA techniques can be applied in order to evaluate student performance, determine their in-game behavior as well as to enhance the design of other serious games. Therefore, in future work, we will focus on student profiling through analysis of action sequences that students commit during the game.

Acknowledgements. This work is a part of a global innovative IT program whose partners are University Champollion and the French Regional Healthcare Agency (Occitanie).

References

1. Alonso-Fernández, C., Calvo-Morata, A., Freire, M., Martínez-Ortiz, I., Fernández-Manjón, B.: Applications of data science to game learning analytics data: a systematic literature review. Comput. Educ. **141**, 103612 (2019). https://doi.org/10.1016/j.compedu.2019.103612. http://www.sciencedirect.com/science/article/pii/S0360131519301654

2. Baker, R., Clarke-Midura, J., Ocumpaugh, J.: Towards general models of effective science inquiry in virtual performance assessments. J. Comput. Assist. Learn. **32**(3), 267–280 (2016). https://doi.org/10.1111/jcal.12128. https://onlinelibrary.wiley.com/doi/abs/10.1111/jcal.12128

3. Chatti, M.A., Dyckhoff, A.L., Schroeder, U., Thüs, H.: A reference model for learning analytics. Int. J. Technol. Enhanc. Learn. **4**(5/6), 318–331 (2012). https://doi.org/10.1504/IJTEL.2012.051815

4. Cheng, M.T., Lin, Y.W., She, H.C.: Learning through playing virtual age: exploring the interactions among student concept learning, gaming performance, in-game behaviors, and the use of in-game characters. Comput. Educ. **86**, 18–29 (2015). https://doi.org/10.1016/j.compedu.2015.03.007. http://www.sciencedirect.com/science/article/pii/S0360131515000767

5. Connolly, T., Boyle, E., Macarthur, E., Hainey, T., Boyle, J.: A systemic literature review of empirical evidence on computer games and serious games. Comput. Educ. **59**, 661–686 (2012). https://doi.org/10.1016/j.compedu.2012.03.004

6. Cornes, M.: Review of interprofessional education in the United Kingdom (1997–2013). J. Interprof. Care **29**(1) (2014). https://doi.org/10.3109/13561820.2014.981479. Hugh Barr, Marion Helme, and Lynda D'Avray, Fareham: Caipe (2014). 131 p. ISBN 978-0-9571382-2-3. http://caipe.org.uk/silo/files/iperg-review-15-4-14-with-links-pdf.pdf

7. Petit-dit Dariel, O., Raby, T., Ravaut, F., Rothan-Tondeur, M.: Developing the serious games potential in nursing education. Nurse Educ. Today (2013). https://doi.org/10.1016/j.nedt.2012.12.014

8. Denden, M., Tlili, A., Essalmi, F., Jemni, M.: Implicit modeling of learners' personalities in a game-based learning environment using their gaming behaviors. Smart Learn. Environ. **5**, 29 (2018). https://doi.org/10.1186/s40561-018-0078-6

9. Flin, R., Patey, R., Glavin, R., Maran, N.: Anaesthetists' non-technical skills. Br. J. Anaesth. **105**(1), 38–44 (2010)

10. Forsyth, C., et al.: Operation ARIES!: methods, mystery, and mixed models: discourse features predict affect and motivation in a serious game. J. Educ. Data Mining **5**, 147–189 (2013)

11. Gaba, D.M.: The future vision of simulation in health care. BMJ Qual. Saf. **13**(suppl 1), i2–i10 (2004)

12. Gough, S., Hellaby, M., Jones, N., MacKinnon, R.: A review of undergraduate interprofessional simulation-based education (IPSE). Collegian **19**(3), 153–170 (2012)

13. Graafland, M., Schraagen, J.M., Schijven, M.: Systematic review of serious games for medical education and surgical skills training. Br. J. Surg. **99**, 1322–1330 (2012). https://doi.org/10.1002/bjs.8819

14. Hu, J., Feijs, L.: A distributed multi-agent architecture in simulation based medical training. In: Pan, Z., Cheok, A.D., Müller, W., Chang, M. (eds.) Transactions on Edutainment III. LNCS, vol. 5940, pp. 105–115. Springer, Heidelberg (2009). https://doi.org/10.1007/978-3-642-11245-4_10

15. Kerr, D., Chung, G.K.W.K.: Identifying key features of student performance in educational video games and simulations through cluster analysis. In: EDM 2012 (2012)

16. Kilmon, C., Brown, L., Ghosh, S., Mikitiuk, A.: Immersive virtual reality simulations in nursing education. Nurs. Educ. Perspect. **31**, 314–7 (2009)

17. Laamarti, F., Eid, M., El Saddik, A.: An overview of serious games. Int. J. Comput. Games Technol. **2014**, 15 (2014). https://doi.org/10.1155/2014/358152

18. Lelardeux, C.P., Panzoli, D., Lubrano, V., Minville, V., Lagarrigue, P., Jessel, J.P.: Training the operating room staff in a virtual multiplayer and real-time environment to prevent adverse events: study of team situation awareness and decision making using the learning game 3D virtual operating room (2016)

19. Petri, G., Gresse von Wangenheim, C.: How games for computing education are evaluated? A systematic literature review. Comput. Educ. **107**, 68–90 (2017). https://doi.org/10.1016/j.compedu.2017.01.004. http://www.sciencedirect.com/science/article/pii/S0360131517300040

20. Pons Lelardeux, C., Galaup, M., Pingaud, H., Mercadier, C., Lagarrigue, P.: A method to balance educational game content and lesson duration: the case of a digital simulation game for nurse training. In: Auer, M.E., Hortsch, H., Sethakul, P. (eds.) ICL 2019. AISC, vol. 1134, pp. 125–136. Springer, Cham (2020). https://doi.org/10.1007/978-3-030-40274-7_13

21. Lelardeux, C.P., et al.: 3D real-time collaborative environment to learn teamwork and non-technical skills in the operating room. In: Auer, M.E., Guralnick, D., Uhomoibhi, J. (eds.) ICL 2016. AISC, vol. 544, pp. 143–157. Springer, Cham (2017). https://doi.org/10.1007/978-3-319-50337-0_12

22. Lelardeux, C.P., Pingaud, H., Galaup, M., Ramolet, A., Lagarrigue, P.: The challenge of designing interactive scenarios to train nurses on rostering problems in a virtual clinical unit. In: Auer, M.E., Tsiatsos, T. (eds.) ICL 2018. AISC, vol. 916, pp. 589–601. Springer, Cham (2020). https://doi.org/10.1007/978-3-030-11932-4_56

23. Riem, N., Boet, S., Bould, M., Tavares, W., Naik, V.: Do technical skills correlate with non-technical skills in crisis resource management: a simulation study. Surv. Anesthesiol. **58**, 15 (2014). https://doi.org/10.1097/SA.0000000000000020

24. Tlili, A., Essalmi, F., Jemni, M., Kinshuk, D.: An educational game for teaching computer architecture: evaluation using learning analytics, pp. 1–6, December 2015. https://doi.org/10.1109/ICTA.2015.7426881

Towards a Methodology to Co-design a Learning Game by Nursing Students

Sebastian Gajewski$^{(\boxtimes)}$, Nour El Mawas$^{(\boxtimes)}$, and Jean Heutte$^{(\boxtimes)}$

Université de Lille, Laboratoire CIREL, équipe Trigone EA 4354 Cité Scientifique, 59655 Villeneuve d'Ascq, France

{sebastian.gajewski.etu,nour.el-mawas,jean.heutte}@univ-lille.fr

Abstract. Nowadays medical errors are one of incidents and death causes involving nurses with poor clinical reasoning skills. Teachers in nursing schools need to improve these skills. Existing research works show the role of game-based learning to increase the students' learning. Furthermore, many game design software exist, they are available and easy-to-use even by students without any technical knowledge. Game-based learning includes gameplay-based learning and game design-based learning. This paper studies existing game design-based learning approaches and identifies a methodology to co-design a learning game in the clinical reasoning field by nursing students themselves. This methodology is composed of 11 steps starting from the specification of pedagogical objectives until the game evaluation. This research work is dedicated to Technology Enhanced Learning community and more specifically to pedagogical engineers, game designers, researchers, and teachers in nursing schools who encounter difficulties in improving the clinical reasoning learning.

Keywords: Learning · Clinical reasoning · Motivation · Co-design · Learning game · Nursing student

1 Introduction

Patient safety is a major concern of healthcare facilities. Between 44 000 and 98 000 Americans die each year as a result of medical errors [1]. Deaths due to medical errors are the 8th leading cause of death [1]. More people die as a result of medical errors than from motor vehicle accidents, breast cancer or AIDS [1]. These preventable adverse events sustained by patients are an international major public healthcare problem [2]. Medical errors can be classified into 4 types of errors [1]: diagnostic, treatment, preventive and other errors (like failure of communication). Furthermore, clinical reasoning is a complex process including, among others, data collection, problem identification (diagnostic), implementation of actions (treatment and preventive) and assessment of these actions' effectiveness. [3]. These adverse events, cited above, are clearly related to a very low level of clinical reasoning skills [2]. Medical errors do not involve only doctors but nurses too. Indeed, critical patient incidents often involve nurses with poor clinical reasoning skills [2]. 70% of nurses in the USA have an unsafe level of clinical reasoning skills [2].

I. Marfisi-Schottman et al. (Eds.): GALA 2020, LNCS 12517, pp. 273–282, 2020.
https://doi.org/10.1007/978-3-030-63464-3_26

Therefore, patient safety depends on nurses' clinical reasoning skills. So, there is a need to improve clinical reasoning skills in nursing education.

Moreover, motivation is a problem that teachers try to solve in all educational settings. Teachers often associate motivation to academic success with the idea that the more learners are motivated, better their outcomes would be [4]. Therefore, teachers seek to develop attractive learning tools, arousing learners' curiosity.

According to Kafai [5], there are 2 different game-based learning methods: instructionism (gameplay-based learning) and constructionism (game design-based learning). In the instructionist approach, learners play a serious game to learn. Whereas, in the constructionist approach, students learn by designing their own game. That is why this research work is in the game-based learning field.

In this paper, we are focusing on the game co-design-based learning in nursing education. Particularly, we are interested in important steps in game co-design-based learning and the evaluation of students' motivation and learning through this co-design.

This paper is structured as follow. Section 2 presents existing methodologies of game design and details research works in the game design-based learning. Section 3 presents learning games in nursing and more specifically in the clinical reasoning field and their evaluation. Section 4 concludes this research work and presents its perspectives.

2 Game Design-Based Learning

This paper seeks to identify a methodology to design a learning game in the clinical reasoning field by nursing students themselves. First, we review existing methodologies of game design. Second, we study existing game design works in order to identify the co-design steps used in these research works.

2.1 Methodologies of Game Design

The content-centric development process model is a methodology which places the experts in the content domain in the center of the process [15]. Indeed, the storyboard, which is the experts in the content domain's main activity, drives the game development. This methodology requires collaboration between experts in the content domain and the programmers. Indeed, without any developer's supervision, the game risks of being unsuccessful. However, if the developers spotlight first the technical limitations, the creativity of the experts in the content domain risks of being restricted. Developers equip experts in the content domain with a suitable language. This methodology is based on an iterative cycle. At each step, a supervisor approves or rejects each game design step. Each time the supervisor rejects one's development step, an iteration is required.

Marfisi-Schottman [16] presents a detailed complete industrial circuit for creating a serious game model. This methodology is composed of 7 steps: (1) client needs, (2) specification of the learning objectives, (3) design, (4) quality control, (5) development, (6) target audience test, and (7) use and maintenance. This model guides the different actors in the game design and helps them collaborate. This model clearly identifies the function of each one and the tasks they must do. This model leads the different actors to fill and share computer-based standard documents.

ARGILE (Architecture for Representations, Games, Interactions, and Learning among Experts) is a methodology to co-design participatory and knowledge-intensive serious games [17]. ARGILE is a methodology allowing addition, modification and discussion of new objects, knowledge, and rules. In this methodology, there are two communities: game designers and players. However, these communities are not totally divided. Some experimented players, who have ideas of improvements could propose modifications. These submissions are discussed by designers through a forum and then voted to be applied or not.

2.2 Existing Works About Game Design-Based Learning

In our research work, we are interested in game design-based learning. So, we present existing studies about this topic. According to [13], 4 key characteristics exist in design-based learning: the project characteristics (open-ended, hands-on-experiences, real life scenarios, multidisciplinary), the role of the teacher, the assessment methods (formative and summative assessment), and the social context (collaborative learning). So, for each study, we specify these relevant dimensions.

In [6], the game design was to create a game about nutrition. A class of ten children of 5th grade have used *GameMaker* to design a game for them to learn and to teach first graders about nutrition. Children have worked on their game design project for two 45-min sessions a week for 8 weeks. Before children design their own game, teachers taught them how to use *GameMaker* and they presented them some game examples designed with *GameMaker*. In this research work, game design was individual. However, the project promoted collaboration. First, children were encouraged to look at and to test the other children's games to give them feedback and to get ideas from the other games for their own game. Then, children could ask for guidance and help at any time during the sessions. The help which has been asked was about programming tasks and nutrition content. Lastly, children have got feedback from first graders who have tested the games. During the design process, scaffolding occurs by not only teachers but also peers. Even though 10 children have participated to the game design project, the authors chose to focus on 3 children during the game design evaluation. Results showed that designing a game: (1) allowed students to represent their understanding of the concepts that they introduced into the game, and (2) increased students' motivation and engagement. For example, one of the children has reported rarely to play games prior to the project. However, he/she has continued designing games 6 months after the project.

In [7], the game design was to create a game about immunology and neurology. Sixteen high school students and three college student mentors have participated to a program called *Game Design through Mentoring and Collaboration* (GDTMC). In this program, the students learned about Science, Technology, Engineering and Mathematics (STEM) through game design with *GameMaker*, while they simultaneously learn about basic immunology and neurology. Students were assigned into 4 groups of 4 students. First, students, who voluntarily enrolled in a training course, during the school year, have learned 3-D computer modelling and animation, computer programming, and video game design one 2-h session a week, on Saturdays, for 10 weeks. Then, students, who wished to go on, have designed a game, during the summer, 4-h a day, for 4 weeks. During the first week, a science subject matter expert gave a brief overview on basic neurology.

Then, students have worked on their game design project for 3 weeks. The class was directed by an instructor with game programming knowledge and skills. The instructor observed the students and kept students on task. Mentors, who were former GDTMC participants and/or who were in college for technology-related fields, were hired to help the students on technical aspects of the games. Before programming their game, students have created an outline for the game. Results showed that game design-based learning occurred through 3 processes. First, designing a game led student to highlight their lack of knowledge and to seek to fill in the gaps. Then, designing a game contributed to a high sense of ownership and responsibility to make the game attractive, engaging and scientifically accurate. Lastly, students have been able to verbally articulate their understandings of the concepts that they introduced into the game.

In [8], the game design was about creating a Mathematics game. Sixty-four middle school children have used *Scratch* to design a game to learn about mathematical operations such as multiplication and division. Students were assigned into 10 groups of 6–7 students. Before designing their games, students have played a collection of computer Math games at their computer classes. Then, they received three 1-h training sessions on using *Scratch*. Students were encouraged to play to the games available on the developer community website, so they could discover *Scratch* functions and potentials. Students have worked on their game design project for two 1-h sessions a week, for 6 weeks. During the game design activity, five graduate students, who were enrolled in an educational game design course, provided scaffolding to the middle school children. They have answered questions on Mathematics content and on game design; they have given feedback and encouragement. The game making process included the design of a paper prototype. During paper prototyping, students have worked together, brainstormed, shared game design ideas, negotiated and explained Mathematics content. Students could program their game once the paper prototype was finished. After paper prototyping, team members have divided tasks. Coalitions have been created in subgroups where 2 students have usually worked together on their game design actions like internet-based resource searching (such as images and music), game programming, and game testing and refining. During the last game design session, each group has uploaded its game on the developer community website, has presented it to the other students, who gave feedbacks. 52% of students reported to have learned mathematical concepts by designing the game. To assess students' attitudes towards Mathematics, participants have completed the Attitudes Towards Math Inventory (ATMI) before and after the game design activity. Results showed that ATMI post-test mean scores significantly increased in comparison with pre-test mean scores (mean difference $= +2.56$; $p = .01$). p is for p-value or probability value. p is used to quantify the idea of statistical significance of evidence.

In [9], the game design was to create a game about Mathematics. Twenty-eight 8th grade students have used *BlockStudio* to design a game to learn about mathematical operations such as bases and exponents. During the previous school year, the authors proposed a game design course, only for teachers, which has enabled to encourage teachers to participate with their students in the research. The Math teacher and the Portuguese teacher have accepted to involve with their students to the research. Students were assigned into 10 groups of 2–3 students. First, students were given a preparatory session about game design, for three 45-min sessions to introduce the project, to explain how to design a game and to present *BlockStudio*. One month later, students have worked on their game design project for eleven 45-min sessions. Each group had to design their game by filling a Game Design Document (GDD). A GDD is a descriptive document which is filled during the game design activity. It includes the game features as the game world, the story of the game, the characters, the storyboard, the rules, the sounds and the music, the user interface, the game controls, *etc*. In the last day, each team tested the other students' games and gave them feedbacks, so each team could modify and improve its game. On a 4-points Likert scale, students reported to have understood the mathematical concepts (M = 3.66; M represents mean value). Students were motivated by the project. Indeed, they reported to have worked during their free time. Teachers also reported that students were motivated (M = 3.5).

2.3 Discussion

Based on Sect. 2.1, we notice that no one methodology is suitable for our context. Indeed, all these three methodologies of game design require experts in the content domain and in design and development. Otherwise, in the content-centric development process model, experts in the content domain are in the center of the process. In our research work, we need a methodology of game design which would be student-centred.

All the research works reviewed on Sect. 2.2 allow us to identify 11 important steps of game co-design: (1) Specify the pedagogical objectives, (2) Identify the game design software, (3) Identify games with similar field, (4) Play games with similar field for inspiration, (5) Deliver learning content to students, (6) Read, watch, listen, understand the learning content, (7) Teach students and teachers about how to design a game, (8) Teach students and teachers about how to use the game design software, (9) Co-design the game, (10) Co-implement and co-develop the game, (11) Evaluate the game. Table 1 details these 11 steps of methodology of game co-design. This methodology involves different actors: the game designer, the researcher, teachers, and, obviously, the nursing students. Each actor has different actions. First, in step 1, the teachers specify the pedagogical objectives. In step 2, the game designer identifies the game design software. In these 4 above-mentioned research works, 3 different game design software have been used: *GameMaker, Scratch*, and *BlockStudio*. These 3 different game design software are freeware (at least temporarily). One of the next steps of our research work will be to lead a game design software review to describe their features and to identify the more suitable game design software for our nursing students (19–20 years old). The game design software will have to be user-friendly, easy, and rapid to use. In step 3, the game designer identifies games with similar field. In our research work, the learning field is about nursing and more specifically in the clinical reasoning field. Thus, the games will be about this area. In step 4, the students play the games with similar field in order to get ideas for their own game. In step 5, the teachers, who are the subject matter experts, deliver pedagogical resources. In our research work, the nursing teachers will deliver the learning content about clinical reasoning. In step 6, the students read, watch, and listen to the pedagogical resources. They share their understanding of the learning content. In step 7, the game designer teaches students how to design a game, overall. In step 8, the game designer teaches students how to use the game design software which will be chosen by the game designer. For examples, the game designer explains the importance to: (1) find a balance between serious content and playful feature to introduce into the game or (2) give feedback. Indeed, immediate feedback fosters flow state [10]. The game designer teaches students and teachers what kind of gameplay mechanics or reward can be used, how to create a sprite or different levels with a progressive level of difficulty. In our research work, the game designer will teach both students and teachers how to design a game and how to use the game design software. In step 9, the students co-design the game. In our research work, students will fill a Game Design Document (GDD). Students will produce a paper prototype. In step 10, they implement their computer game. Lastly, in step 11, the game designer, the researcher, the students, and the teachers assess the game prototype. The students present their game to the other students. In our research work, students will be asked to especially present the serious content introduced into the game. So, it will help them to verbally articulate their understandings of the concepts that they introduced into the game [7]. Moreover, the students test the games of the other students and give them feedback. So, they can improve their game. Through the students' presentation and game prototypes, the teachers assess the accuracy of the learning content introduced into the games.

Table 1. Methodology of game co-design

Steps	Actions	Actors
1	Specify the pedagogical objectives	T
2	Identify the game design software	GD
3	Identify games with similar field	GD
4	Play games with similar field for inspiration	S
5	Deliver learning content to students	T
6	Read, watch, listen, understand the learning content	S
7	Teach students and teachers about how to design a game	GD
8	Teach students and teachers about how to use the game design software	GD
9	Co-design the game	S
10	Co-implement and co-develop the game	S
11	Evaluate the game	GD-R-S-T

GD: Game Designer/R: Researcher/S: Students/T: Teachers

Our research work aims to design and implement a game co-design-based learning activity and to assess its efficacy on motivation and learning. Thus, in our research work, the researcher will measure students' motivation and learning to assess the relevance and effectiveness of the learning activity. The game designer evaluates the gameplay mechanics introduced into the game. Based on the existing works about game design-based learning presented previously, **collaboration** and **scaffolding** are two essential characteristics that can be found in different steps of the game design (6, 9, 10, and 11). **Collaboration** is "*a process in which entities share information, resources, and* *responsibilities to jointly plan, implement, and evaluate a program of activities to achieve a common goal*" [14]. **Scaffolding** is a "*support given by a teacher to a student when performing a task that the student might otherwise not be able to accomplish*" [18]. Scaffolding refers to support that is adapted to the student's needs. Collaboration occurs exclusively between students, while scaffolding occurs between students and teachers, and between students and the game designer. In step 6, students discuss and share their understanding of the learning content. They can search for additional learning content (**collaboration**). Students can help each other to understand the learning content. Teachers can help them too (**scaffolding**). In step 9 and 10, students brainstorm, share ideas and negotiate during the paper prototyping and the computer game programming (**collaboration**). Students help each other in learning content and programming. In the same way, while teachers help students in learning content, the game designer helps students in game programming. Furthermore, teachers and the game designer can also give encouragement. In [7], the authors emphasize the need to support the students who are discouraged for them not to drop out the game design project (**scaffolding**). In step 11, the students test the other games to get ideas for their own game. The teachers and the game designer give feedbacks to students to help them to improve their game (**scaffolding**).

3 Gameplay-Based Learning

In this section, we present studies in which serious games have been used by nursing students for clinical reasoning learning: (1) to identify the games (step 3 in Table 1) students could play for inspiration (step 4), and (2) investigate how games have been assessed (step 11).

In [11], the author has designed a game simulation, a kind of role-playing game, used for pharmacology learning. 4 nursing teachers have been recruited as actors for the game simulation: the new nurse, being unsure with himself/herself and taking care of the patient with hesitation; a preceptor helping the new nurse in caring for the patient; a family member pushing the Patient Controlled Analgesia (PCA) button; a rapid response team nurse bringing the crash cart and administering the reversal agent. A high-fidelity patient simulator was used as the patient. The game simulation has been played in the hall lecture. The storyline starts when a family member pushes the PCA button, resulting in a morphine overdose and the staff nurse begins taking care of the patient. 79 third-year nursing students have participated to the study. During the game simulation, a bell rings 5 times and the actions stop each time. Students have been asked to determinate the next priority action with 4 possible options. Students were given 2 min to discuss the situation with the other students and share their opinions. Then, they have individually answered each question on the Learning Management System (LMS). Actors restart actions, according to the majority vote. After the game simulation, a debriefing was conducted. To assess the effects of the game on pharmacology learning, students have completed pre and post-tests, including 11 questions focusing on care for a postoperative patient receiving morphine. Results show that post-test mean scores significantly increased in comparison with pre-test mean scores (mean difference $= +4.99$; $p < .01$). On a 5-points Likert scale, students reported a high level of self-confidence in learning ($M = 4.37$).

In [3], authors have designed a game called *CareMe*, used for clinical reasoning learning. The game view represents a 3D character (a patient) in an immersive 3D environment representing a hospital ward. The player takes the role of a nurse. The game consists of 5 scenarios. The game sessions last 30 to 40 min. Each student played at its own pace. Students played 2 to 5 scenarios. Some students played the scenarios once, others played scenarios twice or more. The game is a single-player game. However, students can compete against themselves (to improve his own score) or against other students (to compare players scores). The game also has a fast-paced complication mode in which students compete against time (to make more timely decision). The game provides immediate feedback in terms of points, patient reactions, in-game facilitator's comments, and success or failure effects. 166 nursing students have participated to the study. To assess the effects of the game on clinical reasoning learning, nursing students self-filled a 5-points Likert scale, including 14 variables. Nursing students indicated, between «not at all» to «very much», what they think they learned during the game. For example, one of variables was «I learned to collect information by interviewing patient». Results show that students learned mainly to collect information (M = 3.2) and to take actions (M = 3.3).

In [12], authors have designed a game called *e-Baby*, used for preterm infant's oxygenation evaluation learning. The study presents the learning game development based on an emotional design model. Indeed, authors showed that positive emotions foster learning, curiosity, and positive thinking [12]. The game view represents a simulated incubator with a virtual preterm infant. The player had to evaluate the preterm infant oxygenation: respiratory rate, pulmonary auscultation, respiratory tract permeability, oxygen saturation, skin colour, breath sounds, *etc.* Seven real and validated cases of preterm infants have been developed for the game. The opening screen of the game shows a virtual nurse presenting the baby and his/her case. Each case consists of several phases in which the level of difficulty gradually increases. In phase 1, the virtual preterm infant presents less affected oxygenation. In phase 2, the virtual preterm infant presents a worsening respiratory condition. In the last phase, the virtual preterm infant presents a critically affected oxygenation. During the game, the player's knowledge is tested via questions. If the answer is correct, the baby laughs, and if the answer is wrong, the baby cries. According to the student's answers and actions, a blue points sidebar moves up or down. Unfortunately, in this paper, this game has not been evaluated by the researchers.

These games cannot be used by students for inspiration because they are not available online. However, we can learn how researchers evaluate these games from learning and motivation aspects. Based on studies about gameplay-based learning presented previously, learning has been evaluated twice and via pre and post-tests while motivation, more precisely self-efficacy, has been assessed once only after playing the game.

In addition, we have to look to available games that students could play for free. Even, these games have not been described in any scientific publication, they could be used by students for inspiration.

4   Conclusion and Perspectives

In this paper, we identify a methodology to co-design a serious game in the clinical reasoning field by the students. This methodology is composed of 11 steps and involves

4 different actors (game designer, teachers, researcher, and students). It is based on 2 essential characteristics: collaboration and scaffolding. Existing serious games in the field can be an inspiration in the co-design. That is why we review existing research works about gameplay-based learning. In contrast, a further review should be led to identify and describe learning games in the similar field for inspiration.

This proposed co-design methodology will be applied in IFsanté, a nursing school in France. The first evaluation will concern approximately 135 second-year students. Students will be divided into 3 groups. A first experimental group will co-design a game. A second control group will receive a classical teaching approach. A third group will play the developed game. Our aim is to assess the difference in learning and motivation between (1) students who co-design the game and students with classical learning approach, and (2) students who co-design the game and students who play the game.

References

1. Kohn, L.T., Corrigan, J., Donaldson, M.S.: To Err is Human: Building a Safer Health System. National Academy Press, Washington, D.C. (2000)
2. Levett-Jones, T., et al.: The 'five rights' of clinical reasoning: an educational model to enhance nursing students' ability to identify and manage clinically 'at risk' patients. Nurse Educ. Today 30(6), 515–520 (2009). https://doi.org/10.1016/j.nedt.2009.10.020
3. Koivisto, J.-M., Multisilta, J., Niemi, H., Katajisto, J., Eriksson, E.: Learning by playing: a cross-sectional descriptive study of nursing students' experiences of learning clinical reasoning. Nurse Educ. Today 45, 22–28 (2016). https://doi.org/10.1016/j.nedt.2016.06.009
4. Fenouillet, F.: Les théories de la motivation. Dunod, Paris (2016)
5. Kafai, Y.B.: Playing and making games for learning: instructionist and constructionist: perspectives for games studies. Games Cult. 1(1), 36–40 (2006)
6. Baytak, A., Land, S.M.: A case study of educational game design by kids and for kids. Proc. Soc. Behav. Sci. 2, 5242–5246 (2010)
7. Khalili, N., Sheridan, K., Williams, A., Clark, K., Stegman, M.: Students designing video games about immunology: insights for science learning. Comput. Sch. 28, 228–240 (2011)
8. Ke, F., Im, T.: A case study on collective cognition and operation in team-based computer game design by middle-school children. Int. J. Technol. Des. Educ. 24(2), 187–201 (2013). https://doi.org/10.1007/s10798-013-9248-6
9. Martins, A., Oliveira, L.: Educational video game design by 8th graders: investigating processes and outcomes. In: 12th European Conference on Games Based Learning (2018)
10. Heutte, J.: Les fondements de l'éducation positive: Perspective psychosociale et systémique de l'apprentissage. Dunod, Paris (2019)
11. Lancaster, R.J.: Serious game simulation as a teaching strategy in pharmacology. Clin. Simul. Nurs. 10, e129–e137 (2014)
12. Fonseca, L.M.M., et al.: Development of the e-baby serious game with regard to the evaluation of oxygenation in preterm babies: contributions of the emotional design. Comput. Inform. Nurs. 32(9), 428–436 (2014)
13. Gomez Puente, S.M., van Eijck, M., Jochems, W.: A sampled literature review of design-based learning approaches: a search for key characteristics. Int. J. Technol. Des. Educ. 23, 717–732 (2013)
14. Camarihna-Matos, L.M., Afsarmanesh, H.: Concept of collaboration. In: Encyclopedia of Networked and Virtual Organizations, pp. 311–315 (2008)

15. Moreno-Ger, P., Martinez-Ortiz, I., Sierra, J.L., Fernandez-Manjon, B.: A content-centric development process model. Computer **41**(3), 24–30 (2008)
16. Marfisi-Schottman, I.: Méthodologie, modèles et outils pour la conception de Learning Games (2012)
17. El Mawas, N.: Designing learning scenarios for serious games with ARGILE. Knowl. Manag. E-Learn. **6**(3), 227–249 (2014)
18. Van de Pol, J., Volman, M., Beishuizen, J.: Scaffolding in teacher-student interaction: a decade of research. Educ. Psychol. Rev. **22**(3), 271–296 (2010). https://doi.org/10.1007/s10648-010-9127-6

Class-Card: A Role-Playing Simulation of Instructional Experiences for Pre-service Teachers

Philippe Dessus[1]($^{\boxtimes}$) ⓘ, Julie Chabert[1,2], Jean-Philippe Pernin[3],
and Philippe Wanlin[4] ⓘ

[1] Univ. Grenoble Alpes, LaRAC, 38000 Grenoble, France
philippe.dessus@univ-grenoble-alpes.fr
[2] IFTS, 38130 Échirolles, France
[3] Univ. Grenoble Alpes, LIG, CNRS, 38000 Grenoble, France
[4] University of Geneva, 1211 Genèva 4, Switzerland
Philippe.Wanlin@unige.ch

Abstract. This paper introduces to *Class-Card*, a role-playing simulation allowing pre-service teachers to experience a large part of the instructional process, from planning, to post-active phases. The players first have to perform a cognitive analysis of the learning tasks of a lesson, then they are faced with disruptive events they react on, guided by theoretically-sound frameworks. We examined seven pre-service teacher students using *Class-Card* on five simulations. The results show that participants were engaged in rich decisions and verbal interactions about the events they were faced to. We contend that *Class-Card* is a promising way to attenuate the "reality-shock" novice teachers experience and help them build professional knowledge.

Keywords: Role-play simulation · Teacher training · Teacher professional development · Classroom assessment scoring system

1 Introduction

To teach is complex because it implies to make many decisions urgently. So, teachers typically go daily through three intertwined phases [1]: *pre-active*, when they specify learning objectives and content (design phase); *interactive*, when they introduce to the content, manage classroom, and support students' understanding; *post-active*, when they assess the whole instructional session, students' learning, and make adjustments for further implementations.

Pre-service teachers usually encounter difficulties to understand and manage these phases [2], as planning is an articulated process linking curriculum and taught knowledge on one hand, and contextual features, like students or classroom context, influencing these phases on the other [3]. Also, pre-service teachers hardly handle interactive decision making, classroom management or feedback-related information because they heavily rely on numerous and complex cues [4].

I. Marfisi-Schottman et al. (Eds.): GALA 2020, LNCS 12517, pp. 283–293, 2020.
https://doi.org/10.1007/978-3-030-63464-3_27

Even if internships are essential to experience teaching in authentic contexts, they often are difficult to organize, manage, and mentor [5]. Building training devices that would enable pre-service teachers to simulate simplified yet realistic instructional situations would give them the opportunity to experience useful skills in university settings.

2 Instructional Process and Teacher Training

Teacher education should certainly be strongly anchored in real-life practices. However, training of pedagogical skills should not be entirely left to field experiences or internships as it could lead, for teacher university, to loss of control of rich field-experience material allowing to enhance pre-service teachers' academic learning [6]. Simulations and role-playing have been long used to that end in teacher education [7].

Micro-teaching [8] is an efficient way to simulate instructional events and to train teachers. After a self-record of a short teaching session, the teacher, other peers, and their trainer view the session and make feedback and comments. Also, video-displayed events are used in teacher training in an efficient way [9]. On one side, micro-teaching, as a collective role-play, is highly implicative, but makes students focus on improvised turn-taking rather than deliberate participation. Video-based training, on the other side, requires a large database of events, but may not always be adapted to participants' concerns, since the videos are selected by the trainer. Besides, they also may focus novice teachers on details rather than on more general features [10].

Even if micro-teaching and video-based training put risk-free time constraints on the training, they do not address other professional facets like considering alternate teacher behaviors [11], and ways to collaboratively design them and test their likely effects.

3 Learning Teaching Through Role-Play Simulations

The goal of instructional games, role-plays, or simulations is to expose pre-service teachers to situations and help them develop and exercise their decision-making. Games are focused on competition and entertainment, role-plays on fidelity of the players' interactions, whereas simulations are more open-ended situations where some important variables interact [12]. With a large positive overall effect ($g = .85$), simulations are among the most effective means to facilitate learning of complex skills and scaffolding types including feedback and reflection can enhance this effect [13]. The three main features of simulations are the objects or situations they mimic, the tools they use, and their fidelity [14]. Table 1 lists some instructional process simulations.

According to Gredler [12], simulations have to present: (a) an adequate model of the complex real-world situation the participants have to cope with; (b) a defined role, including responsibilities and constraints, for each participant; (c) a rich environment allowing participants to execute strategies; (d) and, feedback for participants' actions. Incorporated in a teacher training simulation, these characteristics enable pre-service teachers to undertake cognitions and behaviors close to those they would be experiencing in real-world teaching contexts.

Table 1. Some simulations of instructional processes.

Simulation	Simulated objects and situation	Tool description	Fidelity
Family Case Simulation [15]	Group discussion on how to help a dysfunctional family	Teachers' cases	Low
Video Card Game [16]	Solving pedagogical problems collaboratively	Bank of short video excerpts to be annotated	Mid
SimSchool [17]	Learners with specific needs behavior simulation	Web-based system	Mid
Cook School District [18]	Simulation of students' engagement and performance	Web-based system	Mid

We designed a study to assess the usefulness, for teacher training, of *Class-Card*, a role-play simulation of the teaching process phases. We address the following research questions: Firstly, can *Class-Card* encompass the different phases of the instructional process? How did the participants tackle with these phases? Did they understand their roles easily? With which role-play flow? Secondly, what information type (e.g., from the lesson plan, the events) do participants process across the simulation? Do the role's and participants' expertise level affect the type of information they use?

4   Method

4.1   *Class-Card* Role-Play Phases

Class-Card is a paper-based role-playing board which simulates the teaching phases (pre-, inter-, and post-action). It is played by three players of whom two are in frontline: The *Teacher* (role taken by a pre-service teacher) and the *Play master* (a pre-service teacher or a teacher trainer depending on the session form, see Sect. 4.3) interact according to *Class-Card*'s lesson plan, see Sect. 4.2, and additional material. The *Discussant* (background function taken by a teacher trainer) initializes the game and manages the discussion. So, a *Class-Card* session has three phases preceded by an initialization phase.

- **Initialization.** The experimenter presents the simulation material and explains the game's purposes, rules, and phases. The *Teacher* reads the Lesson plan (see Sect. 4.2) which is the focus of the Preparation phase.
- **Preparation.** This phase, during which the *Discussant* has the background role of clarifying the rules and note taking for the *Discussion* phase, is composed of two sub-phases. This phase corresponds to teaching's pre-active phase.

  - **Examination.** The *Teacher* analyzes the lesson plan to draw a best mental image of it. Following this analysis, he selects the most appropriate *pupil action cards* [PAC] and *teacher action counters* [TAC] to define, as accurately as possible, respectively pupils' cognitive activity during the lesson sub-sections and how he would concretely implement them. Short notes can be written on sticky notes to detail the situation and help remembering some important points. The result is a sort of a coded lesson shape the *Teacher* has to implement in the simulation phase.

- **Explanation.** The *Teacher* explains what are the main points of his *Examination* to the *Play master* who can request more details. Then, the *Play master* randomly picks between 3 or 5 *Disruptive events cards* [DEC] to be used in the next phase during which the *Teacher* can only refer to the coded lesson.

- **Simulation.** During this phase, which represents the interactive teaching phase, the *Teacher* simulates a real-time role-play of the lesson, as if he were in front of pupils. The *Play master* observes and can interrupt, at any moment, with playing one of the DEC's front-side to simulate a situation the *Teacher* has to react spontaneously on. Then, both *Teacher* and *Play master* read its backside, to assess the soundness of *Teacher*'s reaction. The backside's content ensures a form of theory-grounded lesson assessment. This phase is iterated until the lesson plan is fulfilled.

- **Discussion.** During this phase corresponding to teaching's post-action, the *Discussant* manages a debate between *Teacher* and *Play master* who express their feelings or opinions, discuss the decisions, formulate alternative actions, etc., of the preceding *Class-Card* phases. The following questions serve as a framework to the discussion: "Which problems appeared? Which decisions did you make to solve them? Which ones were difficult to solve? What would you modify if you had to perform this session again? What did you learn during the simulation session?".

4.2   Material

Material of *Class-Card* simulation game comprises a lesson plan and the role-playing material described hereafter.

Lesson Plan. The participants get a lesson plan including 6 phases of a French language lesson on adjective agreement (3rd Grade). Its goal is to deeper characterize illustrated monsters in a problem-solving session.

1. *Problem* (5 min). Students read a monster's description to guess which monster picture, among plenty, matches the description.
2. *Work Phase* (10 min). Students improve the monster's description.
3. *Collective Discussion* (10 min). Some students' descriptions are read out loud, insisting on adjectives, to the whole class; students guess which monster matches them.
4. *Synthesis* (15 min). A collective synthesis is produced: adding adjectives specifies more accurately the nominal group; adjectives are a useful description means.
5. *Transfer task* (10 min). The students write a chosen monster's picture description.
6. *Assessment.* The students play a game consisting in matching their portraits and descriptions.

Role-Playing Material. Alongside the simulation session, theoretically-sound peda-gogical information is delivered to scaffold the gameplay. Three kinds of material exist. *Pupil action cards* [PAC] (see Fig. 1*a*) are selected by the *Teacher* during the preparation phase to define learners' cognitive activity, relying on Bloom et al.'s cognitive taxon-omy [19]. *Teacher action counters* [TAC] are taken from Merrill's [20] classification of instructional activities (tell, show, ask, help, supervise) and are selected by the *Teacher* during the preparation phase to define his teaching acts. *Disruptive event cards* [DEC] (see Fig. 1*b*), which were randomly picked by the *Play master* during the *Teacher*'s explanation, are used during the simulation phase to represent a plausible disruption in the lessons' progression. Their front-side introduce to a disruption, its dimension according to the *Classroom Assessment Scoring System* (CLASS) manual [21], and a question the *Teachers* has to reflect on. Their back-side present a CLASS-based analytic elaboration, to help ground the soundness of players' assessment decisions and stimulate a reflexive practice, rather than to propose unquestionable tips.

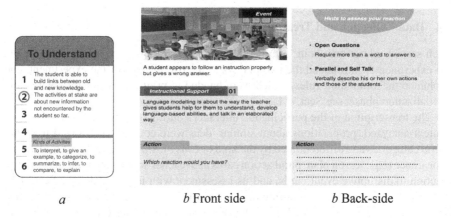

| *a* | *b* Front side | *b* Back-side |

Fig. 1. *a*: Pupil Action Card *b*: Disruptive Event Card

4.3 Participants

We recruited 7 participants and 1 teacher trainer (author 2, experimenter) from the Grenoble Teacher Training Institute. They played a *Class-Card* simulation adopting two different forms depending on the roles' distribution among participants (see Sect. 4.1). All the sessions were audio-recorded upon participants' agreement.

The first form is teacher trainer-led as the experimenter played the role of the *Play master* but also that of *Discussant* during sessions 1, 2 and 3, within which a pre-service teacher took the *Teacher*'s role. The second form is pre-service teacher-led as two pre-service teachers played respectively the *Teacher*'s or the *Play master*'s roles (sessions 4 and 5). Here, the teacher trainer initializes the simulation and discreetly observes the preparation and the simulation phases; for 2 sessions he also took the *Discussant*'s role to undertake a debriefing of the simulation session. This results in five sessions as shown in Table 2 which also details some participants' basic characteristics.

Table 2. Basic information on participants.

Sessions	Roles	Degree	Participants work experience as teachers
Teacher trainer-led sessions			
1	Teacher	Undergraduate	Kindergarten
2	Teacher		Kindergarten, elementary
3	Teacher	2nd-year Master	50 + days kindergarten and elementary
Pre-service teacher-led sessions			
4	Teacher	1st-year Master	40 + days kindergarten and elementary
	Play master	1st-year Master	Kindergarten, elementary, and high schools
5	Teacher	1st-year Master	Kindergarten and elementary
	Play master	1st-year Master	Kindergarten and elementary

4.4 Data Collection and Treatment

Each session (duration, about 90 min) was audio-recorded and transcribed. To begin, the experimenter introduced the two players to the overall goal of the experiment, and explained the simulation rules, which were handed in print format for further reading (Initialization phase; see Sect. 4.1).

The transcription of the participants' utterances during the simulation sessions was content-analyzed: propositions about similar ideas were counted and ranged in meaningful categories and differentiated by the kind of *Class-Card* material that stimulated its appearance (e.g., lesson plan, pupil action cards and teacher action counters, sticky notes, reaction to disruptive event cards, and its assessment with its backside; see Sect. 4.2). Actions or decisions declared during the lesson's pre-active, interactive and post-active phases were coded and counted using the categories named after *Class-Card* material, and the preparation phase's sticky notes. Actions or decisions independent of *Class-Card*'s stimulation were coded as "built ideas". The discussion was neither processed nor analyzed for paper length purposes.

5 Results

5.1 Qualitative Results: Overall Simulation Activity Flow

Table 3 reports the material types' use frequencies during each session. We note a similar use of the material across session forms ($\chi^2_{(3)} = 2, 36; p = 0,50$). However, even if the distribution of the material type adopts a similar shape (more PAC and TAC then sticky notes and reactions to DEC), the teacher trainer-led sessions present about the double of PACs and TACs compared to the pre-service teacher-led ones, which can be an expertise effect. The rest of this section qualitatively analyzes the different phases.

Preparation: Examination Sub-phase. Teachers formulated additional examples and remarks about the content; they elicited expected students' answers and productions (e.g.,

Table 3. *Class-Card* use descriptive data during the whole simulations. Read: During the first session, 15 Pupil Action Cards were used during the examination sub-phase.

Session Form	Teacher trainer-led				Pre-service teacher-led		
Session ID	1	2	3	Total	4	5	Total
Pupil Action Card	15	20	10	45	6	11	17
Teacher Action Counter	14	20	13	47	14	9	23
Sticky Notes	2	7	12	21	6	9	15
Reaction to DEC	3	3	5	11	4	3	7

Session 3: "*Why did you eliminate this monster? How did you do?*"). They described actions they might be engaged in (e.g., Session 3: "*The teacher walks from student to student to gather some students' productions to be displayed on the board*").

Preparation: Explanation Sub-phase. Teachers mentioned likely students' cognitive activities according to Bloom's taxonomy (e.g., Session 3: "*I gonna ask her some questions to check if she's actually reflecting on the task by herself, instead of simply waiting to me.*"). Thus, they accounted for possible events and facts which were not mentioned in the Lesson plan, sometimes further exploring the consequences of a decision (e.g., Session 2: "*If no student answers 'qualificative adjective', I should give one myself, unless I have to explain it because students have usually to elaborate on that idea.*").

Simulation Phase. Two different kinds of elaborations were given. Firstly, before any disruption appearance (DEC), verbalized thoughts were mainly about preparation phase (e.g., Session 3: "*If the monster's description lacks information, I'm expecting that students make several suggestions. If we realize that we're lacking answers, then information about monsters may lack*"). Secondly, after a disruption, *Teachers* often focus on novel elaborations from scratch to bring real-world details that would fit the event better. Expectedly, in both cases, they thought syllogically ("*if… then …*"), and explored alternatives to actions partly based on the CLASS-based information available on the DEC's back-sides.

Discussion Phase. This phase varied across sessions: some *Teachers* used it to perform a deeper analysis of the simulation session while others used it to reflect on their own activity. Three main points were reviewed: – the degree of likeliness or authenticity of the proposed situation or undertaken actions (e.g., Session 4: "*Just keep in mind that during a lesson nothing goes as planned and we've always to adapt to situations… So* events make us see exactly how we adapt."; Session 3: "*I think our reaction to events during the game is close to those in real-life, we can't actually turn things in our head, we decide on-the-fly*"); – the relevance of the simulation acts performed during the session (e.g., Session 3: "*I found it more interesting to plan a lesson and simultaneously think about what pupils would do, because I tend to leave this behind*"); – the efficiency of their own player's role as *Teacher* (e.g., Session 3: "*Just when I was explaining the tasks, I was realizing that they were not so clear*").

5.2   Quantitative Results: Verbalizations Source References

About the information type used and the effect of role definition and players' expertise level, Table 4 shows each *Class-Card* phase and the source material originating the players' discourse to typify the simulated lesson.

Table 4. Verbalizations' sources as percentages of the overall explanation, per phase and play form. Read: In Examination sub-phase, 48.1% of players' talk in the Teacher trainer-led condition referred to the lesson plan.

Source/phase	Teacher trainer-led	Pre-service teacher-led	Statistical test
Prep.–Examination			
Lesson Plan	48.1	41.1	
PAC & TAC	11.9	9.7	
Built Ideas	40.0	49.3	$\chi^2_{(2)} = 1.74$
Reaction to DEC	–	–	$p = 0.42$
Preparation	–	–	
Prep.–Explanation			
Lesson Plan	24.6	60.1	
PAC & TAC	31.4	15.3	$\chi^2_{(2)} = 25.92$
Built Ideas	44.0	24.6	$p < 0.01$
Reaction to DEC	–	–	
Preparation	–	–	$V_c = 0.36$
Simulation			
Lesson Plan	22.2	25.9	
PAC & TAC	0.8	0.4	$\chi^2_{(4)} = 1.87$
Built Ideas	61.7	63.7	$p = 0.76$
Reaction to DEC	2.6	0.9	
Preparation	12.7	9.1	

Typically, after their lesson plan reading, the *Teacher* engaged in the Examination phase equally referring to Lesson plan or expressing new ideas. Then, during Explanation phase, where a more theory-grounded coding of the lesson was supposed to be stimulated, references to the sources adopted a significant and moderate difference according to the session forms: the focus on lesson plan remained for the pre-service teacher-led form, whereas in Teacher trainer-led sessions PACs and TACs quotations and built ideas formulations were more frequent. So, a sort of expertise ensured that Explanation's talks are closer to *Class-Card*'s underlying objectives.

During Simulation phase, even if the reference to DECs was very low, the CLASS-based back-sides of these cards let participants reflect on the pedagogical consequences of events and reactions to them by expressing a growing amount of Built ideas (about 60%), demonstrating a sort of adaptability by giving novel alternatives as well of a "percolation" of the ideas elicited in the previous phases. PACs and TACs information were not mentioned, while references to the Preparation sub-phases were cited (about 10%). These reflections were in line with the Lesson's objectives as the plan still stays a reference (about 25%). There was no statistical difference according to the session form but, as in previous phase *Play master*'s expertise permitted a closer appropriateness to *Class-Card* design objectives, the distance of the Built ideas to theory-based and effective pedagogy should be examined.

6 Discussion

Class-Card is designed to simulate, at small cost, the teaching phases to permit pre-service teachers' engagement and adaptation in a reflective analysis of their upcoming daily activities – planning (pre-active), teaching (interactive), and assessing their instruction (post-active). *Class-Card* creatively enhances the grounding of a two-fold process: the *coding* and *reflective analysis* of instruction based on theoretically-sound material (Bloom's pupil cognitive activities, Merrill's teacher activities, CLASS-based events and teaching classification). This material is pedagogically agnostic and allows the coding of a large diversity of lessons. Results show *Class-Card*'s successful design as it ensures an understanding of a shared vocabulary and an increasing verbalization of alternative teaching acts as many novel ideas were built during its simulation phase.

More specifically, the Preparation phase enabled the *Teacher* to make strong connections between teaching and learning, in precisely defining both his actions by lesson coding, and students' cognitive activities during teaching. This permitted pre-service teachers to surpass possible self-centered concerns. Simulation phase let the *Teacher* act according to his planning and improvise when facing prototypical disruption. The *Teacher*'s reflection was enriched by CLASS dimensions and fostered explanations of pupil behavior and their likely causes, and of *Teacher*'s own reactions' nature and degree of effectiveness. However, this game is most efficient if the *Play Master* has a certain pedagogical expertise to scaffold players' thoughts, notably in the Explanation sub-phase. Unfortunately, it was impossible to examine precisely the effect of this expertise in the discussion phases on talk quality as results present material use frequencies and not the theory or meta-analysis basement of players' talk.

This explorative study has two limitations. The amount of sessions is low and the roles' distribution across sessions is unequal. *Class-Card* simulation's rules are complex and need a time-consuming understanding effort. This leads to the suggestion of next research perspectives: increase the sample's size, equally balance participants among the experimental groups, develop cards and counters relying on meta-analytic results on teacher effectiveness, refine the talks' categorization system (adding a dichotomized category: meta-analysis or theory-based). We also plan to measure the effect of multiple *Class-Card* sessions involving multiple lesson plans, likely built from scratch, about various content and/or disciplines, on pre-service teacher's reflective analysis of his own teaching practice during internships. This would allow to gauge its consequences on the "reality shock" novice teachers often experience [22].

Acknowledgements. This paper has been partially funded by the *Pôle Grenoble Cognition*, Grenoble Alpes university. We wish to thank the participants of this study, Macha Klajnbaum for designing the *Class-Card* material, Hélène Gondrand for her thoughtful help during the experiment, and Ignacio Atal as well as the three anonymous reviewers for their constructive comments on a previous version of this paper.

References

1. Yinger, R.J.: A study of teacher planning. Elem. Sch. J. **80**(3), 107–127 (1980)
2. Hogan, T., Rabinowitz, M., Craven, J.A.: Representation in teaching: inferences from research of expert and novice teachers. Educ. Psychol. **38**(4), 235–247 (2003)
3. Clark, C.M., Dunn, S.: Second-generation research on teachers' planning, intentions, and routines. In: Waxman, H.C., Walberg, H.J. (eds.) Effective Teaching: Current Research, pp. 183–201. McCutchan, Berkeley (1991)
4. Janssen, F., Westbroek, H., Doyle, W., van Driel, J.H.: How to make innovations practical. Teach. Coll. Rec. **115**(7), 1–42 (2013)
5. Dalgarno, B., Gregory, S., Knox, V., Reiners, T.: Practising teaching using virtual classroom role plays. Aust. J. Teach. Educ. **41**(1), 8 (2016)
6. Grossman, P., McDonald, M.: Back to the future: directions for research in teaching and teacher education. Am. Educ. Res. J. **45**(1), 184–205 (2008)
7. Jones, F.H., Eimers, R.C.: Role playing to train elementary teachers to use classroom management "skill package". J. Appl. Behav. Anal. **8**(4), 421–433 (1975)
8. Allen, D., Ryan, K.: Microteaching. Addison-Wesley, Reading (1969)
9. Sherin, M.G., van Es, E.A.: Using video to support teachers' ability to notice classroom interactions. J. Technol. Teach. Educ. **13**(3), 475 (2005)
10. van Es, E.A., Sherin, M.G.: Learning to notice: scaffolding new teachers' interpretations of classroom interactions. J. Technol. Teach. Educ. **10**(4), 571–595 (2002)
11. Hattie, J.: Visible Learning. A Synthesis of Over 800 Meta-Analyses Relating to Achievement. Routledge, New York (2009)
12. Gredler, M.E.: Games and simulations and their relationships to learning. In: Jonassen, D.H. (ed.) Handbook of Research on Educational Communications and Technology, pp. 571–581. Erlbaum, Mahwah (2004)
13. Chernikova, O., Heitzmann, N., Stadler, M., Holzberger, D., Seidel, T., Fischer, F.: Simulation-based learning in higher education: a meta-analysis. Rev. Educ. Res. **90**, 499–541 (2020)
14. Cheong, D., Kim, B.: A simulation for improving teachers' motivational skills. In: Gibson, D., Baek, Y. (eds.) Digital Simulations for Improving Education. Learning Through Artificial Teaching Environments, pp. 227–248. IGI, Hershey (2009)

15. Sottile, J.M., Brozik, D.: The use of simulations in a teacher education program. In: Hawaii International Conference on Education. ERIC Report # ED490383, Honolulu (2004)
16. Routarinne, S., Ylirisku, S.: Video card game as a learning design for teacher education. Proc. Soc. Behav. Sci. **45**, 370–380 (2012)
17. Knezek, G., Fisser, P., Gibson, D.: SimSchool: research outcomes from simulated classrooms. In: SITE 2012, Austin (TX) (2012)
18. Girod, M., Girod, G.: Exploring the efficacy of the cook school district simulation. J. Teach. Educ. **57**(5), 481–497 (2006)
19. Bloom, B.S., Engelhart, M.D., Furst, E.J., Hill, W.H., Krathwohl, D.R.: Taxonomy of Educational Objectives: Handbook I: Cognitive Domain. McKay, New York (1956)
20. Merrill, M.D.: First Principles of Instruction. Pfeiffer, San Francisco (2013)
21. La Paro, K.M., Pianta, R.C., Stuhlman, M.: The classroom assessment scoring system: findings from the prekindergarten year. Elem. Sch. J. **104**(5), 409–426 (2004)
22. Veenman, S.: Perceived problems of beginning teachers. Rev. Educ. Res. **54**(2), 143–178 (1984)

How to Engage Young Adults in Reading H. C. Andersen's Fairy Tale *the Little Mermaid,* Through a Serious Game

Thevakorn K. Lauritsen, Delan Kasim Ali, Niklas Fruerlund Jensen, Irene Ubieto Alamillo, and Thomas Bjørner[✉]

Department of Architecture, Design and Media Technology, Aalborg University, A.C. Meyers Vænge 15, 2450 Copenhagen SV, Denmark
tbj@create.aau.dk

Abstract. For this study, the authors designed a serious game to increase leisure reading engagement in H. C. Andersen's fairy tale, *The Little Mermaid*. The objectives were to increase leisure reading engagement among young Danish adults and to familiarize the group with original version as a supplement to the Disney version. The novelty within this study is the focus on leisure reading engagement and having participants read a story in its original 1837 language. 25 participants were included in a formative evaluation. The evaluation was based on three questionnaires at various stages of the game play, and six participants were selected for in-depth interviews. The findings reveal increased engagement and interest in the story throughout the game. There was a very high level of interest in the story and some good indicators that the users read the entire story. In conclusion, when designing a serious game to promote increased leisure reading engagement, intrinsic motivation is of high importance. Telling the original story of *The Little Mermaid* in a serious game is, to a large extent, about transforming the fairy tale into a digital storytelling with meaningful skills and knowledge for the users.

Keywords: Reading engagement · Digital storytelling · Intrinsic motivation · Formative evaluation

1 Introduction

The Danish author Hans Christian Andersen (1805–1875), usually called H.C. Andersen, is recognized around the world for his fairy tales and stories. From the very first publication, it was H.C. Andersen's intension to target not only children, but also to activate the adult consciousness, and the childlike imagination. His fairy tales are with high complexity of language and contains complicated philosophical, psychological, existential and social issues with life experiences and lost. For the same reason, H.C. Andersen's collection of fairy tales are commonly used as presents for young adults in Denmark, but are rarely read.

The aim of this study was to implement a serious game to achieve leisure reading engagement for H.C. Andersen's fairy tale, *The Little Mermaid*. The story follows the

I. Marfisi-Schottman et al. (Eds.): GALA 2020, LNCS 12517, pp. 294–303, 2020.
https://doi.org/10.1007/978-3-030-63464-3_28

journey of a young mermaid who is willing to give up her life in the sea to gain a human soul. The tale was first published in 1837 and was later adapted to various versions, including musical theatre, ballet, opera, and Disney's well-known animated film [1]. The research question of this study was: How can young Danish adults be engaged in reading H. C. Andersen's fairy tale, *The Little Mermaid*, through a serious game? The background and objectives behind the research question were twofold:

1. To increase reading engagement among young adults aged 18 to 25. Over the past few decades, young adults have changed their habits, reading fewer novels and fairy tales but spending more time reading online than before [2–4]. In Demark, 20% of young adults do not read fiction [13], which is equivalent to other international reporting [4, 14]. On average, across OECD countries, 37% of young adults (students) report that they do not read for enjoyment at all [14]. Reading has always been encouraged through complex and diverse practices. However, there is a huge concern that young adults do not read well enough to cope with the increasing literacy demands of an information society [3–5]. Reading fiction among young adults appears to be positively associated with higher performance on reading assessments [14]. Reading is a skill with many graduations of proficiency, and reading a rather complex tale from 1837 requires a different level of reading ability (compared to, e.g., a newspaper or subtitles on Netflix), which is challenging for many young adults [3–5].

2. To let young adults understand H. C. Andersen's fairy tale, *The Little Mermaid*, as a supplement to the Disney version. The Disney version of *The Little Mermaid* is widely known and has been a bestseller [6], whereas few young adults have read the original fairy tale the Disney version is based on. In both versions, an evil sea witch takes the little mermaid's voice in a trade that allows the mermaid to walk on land. There is also a storm, and the little mermaid must save the prince from drowning. However, there are also major differences. In the original version, there is a narratively influential grandmother, and the little mermaid does not have a name; she is only referred to as the little mermaid. In Disney's version, her name is Ariel. In the Disney version, the sea witch (called Ursula) is killed, and Ariel and Prince Eric live happily after. In the original version, the prince never discovers that the little mermaid actually saved him. In Disney's version, Ariel will belong to the sea witch if she does not complete the task; in the original, she will die if she does not complete the task. The original tale is far more complex than the movie from Disney, as well as far more dystopian, melancholic, and gloomy.

2 Previous Research and Theoretical Framework

Reading engagement is a multidimensional construct including behavioral, affective, and cognitive dimensions [15]. It can be defined as the interest and attitude towards reading and the time used to read a diversity of material for pleasure [7]. Reading engagement for enjoyment is multidimensional and used from various perspectives in various fields; it is also complex, with many variables, including motivation, frequency, emotional engagement, gender preferences, and storytelling.

a) Motivation. Engaging in leisure reading, both in serious games and in other media (analogue included), requires the reader to be motivated [9]. This involves, e.g., important elements within the text's content, comprehending the text, gaining new knowledge, and social interactions with used knowledge and/or lessons learned from the text [8, 9]. Furthermore, to design a motivating reading experience in a serious game, scholars have already emphasized aspects of intrinsic motivation, such as curiosity, a desire for challenge, and involvement [9, 19–23]. However, the success of a serious game for leisure reading purposes depends on players' motivation to start playing the game and spend their time, effort, and energy. Hence, players' intention to interact with the game is crucial [17]. It is assumed that the experiences of flow [18] and enjoyment [19] are crucial in this process. When players have mastered specific challenges, they develop a greater level of skills that can be used and improved with more complex challenges in other levels or games [17, 18]; this can have a positive influence on intrinsic motivation in serious games [20]. Serious games outside a traditional learning context may need to focus more on intrinsic motivation [17, 20–22] in the possible absence of extrinsic motivation from a teacher or learning progression. This means that the learning materials need to invoke curiosity, flow (interplay between challenges and skills), be fun and enjoyable, and eventually allow the player to gain new knowledge.

b) Frequency. The frequency of leisure and educational reading can contribute to one's engagement in reading [7, 10]. Reading engagement and practice allow for more and/or better reading achievements [14] and more motivation towards reading [3, 7, 14]. Better readers tend to be more motivated to read and therefore read more, which leads to improvements in vocabulary and comprehension skills, whereas poor readers experience a decline in skill level [7, 10]. Frequent reading activities also enable readers to discuss an array of topics and comprehend various viewpoints in social groups [11]. In applied approaches, previous research has demonstrated how reading in serious games with self-directed work increases the frequency of reading practice [9, 23].

c) Emotional engagement. Reading engagement in serious games incorporates other forms of engagement in terms of emotional engagement to positively (interest) and negatively (boredom) affect the engagement of the reader. Emotional engagement can be part of cognitive engagement in terms of a reader exerting their mental effort to comprehend the text-based element of a game [7–11]. However, other cognitive activities that distract the reader (media or contextual disturbances) can negatively affect the amount of information the reader can gain or recall [12]. The definition of emotional engagement varies across literature, as it is used within many contexts. However, there is a common understanding that it involves interest, motivation, happiness, fun, anger, empathy, tension, anxiety, and other affective states, any of which could affect gamers' involvement or effort to continue playing [16].

d) Gender preferences. There are no reported gender differences related to reading engagement and reading achievements [10, 13]. However, there are some specific gender differences in terms of motivation for reading. Girls favor narrative and/or continuous texts, whereas boys' reading ability is more affected by their attitude, enjoyment, and interest in the text's content [10].

e) Storytelling. One way to motivate reading engagement is to include a text-based story in a serious game via digital storytelling (DS). This opens an interactive story/world, including both text and game, with the potential to engage a user in the digital storytelling experience and make them focus on the story itself instead of the text or gameplay alone. Digital storytelling is well covered and discussed within serious gaming [24–26]. However, digital storytelling is much more than telling a story in a digital format; in a serious game, it is mainly about making stories engaging and interactive, with meaningful skills and knowledge for the users.

3   Methods

3.1   Participants and Ethical Issues

25 participants were included in a formative evaluation. The participants were young Danish adults aged 18-24 (mean: 21.5) with 20 males and five females. All participants were enrolled in different study programs; 13 were enrolled in IT and design programs, four in humanities, four in engineering, three in medicine, and one from a nursing school. Within the last three months, 18 of the participants had not read any fiction, whereas six participants had read fiction for leisure purposes (reading 1–2 novels each). One participant had read four novels over the last three months. Twenty-two participants had played computer games within the last three months; three participants estimated having played more than 30 h per week. Twelve participants estimated playing 11–20 h per week, five participants played 1–10 h per week, and 3 participants did not play any computer games during the last three months.

All participants gave informed consent and were informed that they could withdraw from the study at any time. We provided all participants with anonymized ID numbers, and all the data were labeled with these IDs. Furthermore, we applied special considerations when recruiting to inform the participants that we respected each individual's reading speed—there was no hurry or judgement based on speed.

3.2   Data Collection, Procedure, and Data Analysis

The 25 participants were recruited by a combination of convenience and snowball sampling via Discord or Facebook. The only criteria for being included in the study was being a young Danish (holding a Danish passport) adult between the ages of 18–30. Due to this study being performed during the outbreak of COVID-19, the data collection and procedure were carried out online.

After giving informed consent and background information, the participants were provided with a link to play the game based on *The Little Mermaid*. The evaluation was divided into three questionnaires provided at various stages of game play. The first (provided after the first level was finalized) and second (provided after finalizing the second level of the game) consisted of three options: a) I would like to continue playing this game; b) I would like to know what is going to happen next in the story; and c) Please write any comments you have regarding what you have experienced until now. We provided only these three options so as not to lose potential user engagement or game flow [18, 19]. After the game was completed, there was a final questionnaire with 9 Likert scale items based on the participants' understanding (knowledge check of the reading) and engagement. The final questionnaire was inspired by the User Engagement Scale, short form (UES-SF) [27], and items from the Narrative Engagement Scale [28]. The rating scale was a 5-point Likert scale (raging from completely disagree to completely agree). Furthermore, six participants were selected for in-depth interviews following a semi-structured interview guide.

The questionnaires were analyzed by cumulative frequency—the total number of answers to specific questions. The interviews were analyzed by traditional coding [29] following four steps: organizing, recognizing, coding, and interpretation. The interviews were transcribed verbatim to be organized and prepared for data analysis. The transcriptions were read several times by two researchers to recognize the concepts and themes, which also included a general sense of the information and an opportunity to reflect on its overall meaning. Researchers then coded and labelled the data in categories/subcategories, followed by interpretation.

4   Design and Implementation

The game was designed in Unity 3D using C# and playable on Mac and PC. The level design is based on four main scenes. The assets used for all the scenes were gathered mainly from the Unity Asset store and Turbosquid. We designed the models and animations of the player and non-player characters (NPCs) using Blender. We used assets to follow a low-polygon aesthetic and implemented a progression system to ensure that the player did not miss any of the story and experienced it chronologically.

The first scene (Fig. 1, left) is under the sea in a water castle and designed mainly to introduce the atmosphere and the premise of the story. Interaction with the little mermaid's sisters.

Fig. 1. Water castle (left) and grandmother's house (right). Top left corner guiding the player of what to do.

The second scene (Fig. 1, right) is under the sea at the witch's house, and it covers the part of the story in which the little mermaid interacts with the witch to get her legs. In the scene, the player needs to speak to the witch, who sets the goal of collecting skulls and passing through rings in order to make the potion.

The third scene (Fig. 2, left) is on the surface near the prince's castle. In this scene, the player needs to interact with the prince and the sisters. In each scene, the player's main goal is to interact with NPCs to get to know (read) the story. Besides those objectives, minor challenges (like gathering oysters or swimming through hoops) were designed to get the players used to the movement of the character, keep them focused, and avoid boredom. The fourth scene (Fig. 2, right) provides some contextual information about the fairy tale.

Fig. 2. The prince's castle (left) and contextual information (right).

To ensure that players are able to experience as much of the story as possible, they can engage with NPCs throughout the game via dialogue-based interactions (implemented as "Press E to start dialogue"). The dialogue bolsters players' perceptions of being part of the game world. This mechanic is introduced early in the game, so the player knows that they can engage in dialogue with various NPCs (Fig. 3). Figure 3 also shows an example of the provided text, which is an old (1837) wording.

5   Findings

5.1   Game Engagement

As seen in Fig. 4, there was a slight increase (mean 3.36 to 3.52) in engagement from "Mid-Game 01" (after the first level) to "Mid-Game 02" (after the second level) based on responses to the statement "I would like to continue playing this game." The engagement was high in general (based on 5-point Likert items, from completely disagree to completely agree). There was also a slight increase (mean 3.96 to 4.08) in interest in the story based on the statement, "I would like to know what is going to happen next in the story." A rather high number of participants reported wanting to read the rest of the story (mean: 3.96). The findings indicate some narrative engagement in this serious game, indicating perceived suspense and relationships between exposure and acceptance of story-related beliefs [28].

Fig. 3. Example of the text (in Danish) from the fairy tale. Grandmother: Now that you are 15 years old, you need to be tested. Go through 7 rings, collect 3 oysters, and then return here.

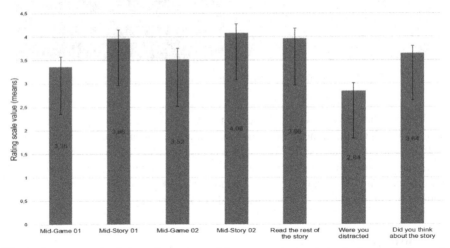

Fig. 4. Engagement levels in various stages of the game; means and standard error. Rating scale 0–5, n = 25.

Even though the number of distracted participants is not very high (mean: 2.84), these data need further investigation. Ten participants answered "neutral" to the statement "I was easily distracted while following the story." Nine participants were not distracted, answering either "completely disagree" or "disagree," while seven participants were distracted. The interviews, based on the question of distractions and boredom, revealed that the game had many positive elements but also some minor issues to be improved upon. Especially, several participants suggested minimizing overly monotonous game elements to maintain flow; they also suggested customizing the text speed, which could be implemented via dynamic difficulty adjustment.

5.2 Story Engagement

The participants read the story throughout the game, as revealed both in time spent on the game (an average of 18 min and 23 s) and the very high percentage of correct answers to the multiple-choice knowledge test (Table 1).

Table 1. Questions, correct and incorrect answers. Based on 5 multiple choice answers, n = 25

Question. The correct answer in the parentheses. Based on 5 multiple-choice answers	Correct answers	Incorrect answers
How old was the little mermaid when she was allowed to swim to the surface? (15)	100%	0
What was the first thing the little mermaid saw after coming to the surface? (a ship)	96%	4%
What did the little mermaid have to sacrifice to get her legs? (her tongue)	96%	4%
How did the witch describe the feeling of wailing with the little mermaid? (as if she were stepping on a knife)	80%	20%
How did the prince see the little mermaid? (as a foundling/little child)	80%	20%
Why did the little mermaid not get the prince? (he was promised to someone else)	92%	8%

The multiple-choice questions were designed to be increasingly difficult to test whether the participants actually read the story or skimmed parts of it. Only one question had 100% correct answers, but all questions had a vast majority of correct answers, meaning that the participants most likely read the story thoroughly enough to answer. It is also very interesting that in the interviews, seven participants mentioned that the story was interesting due the differences from the Disney version.

I've always thought it was a cool story, or a nice story, but I know most about Disney's version of it. But I still want to learn the original story because it tells more. It is just as interesting, if not more interesting. (ID4, female, aged 20 years, nursing school studies).

6 Conclusion

This study was carried out during COVID-19 and the subsequent lockdown, meaning it was difficult to establish a gender-balanced high number of participants and a controlled environment for evaluation—the participants might have experienced various disturbances. In spite of this, our study reveals that it is possible to engage young Danish adults in leisure reading by introducing the text within a serious game. We conclude that the participants read and enjoyed the story via the serious game. There was high intrinsic motivation to read H. C. Andersen's version compared to what most participants were familiar with; namely, the Disney version. It can also be concluded that game progression is very important, and elements to guide the readers to their next action are a prerequisite for success. When developing a serious game focusing on reading engagement, it is very important to focus on narrative engagement [16]. Narrative engagement is related to the story experienced while playing a game and may result in imaginative immersion, narrative involvement, or narrative immersion. The desire to know how the story about the little mermaid unfolds created curiosity, suspense, and excitement, making the players want to continue playing.

As many other scholars have realized when designing serious games, it is a special challenge to find the right balance between skills and challenges, keeping the players in the flow channel [18]. Some of the participants in this study would have liked the game to be a bit more challenging, less monotonous/tedious, and with better links/clues/semiotics to story-specific elements (e.g., making game a bit darker), as well as customizable reading speed to provide dynamic difficulty adjustment.

References

1. The Little Mermaid: Walt Disney Feature Animation and Walt Disney Pictures (1989)
2. Baron, N.S.: Words Onscreen: The Fate of Reading in an Online World. Oxford University Press, Oxford (2015)
3. Ross, R.S., McKechnie, L., Rothbauer, P.M. (eds.) Reading still matters: What the research reveals about reading, libraries, and community. Libraries Unlimited, Santa Barbara (2018)
4. Twenge, J.M., Martin, G.N., Spitzberg, B.H.: Trends in US Adolescents' media use, 1976–2016: the rise of digital media, the decline of TV, and the (near) demise of print. Psychol. Popular Media Culture 8(4), 329–345 (2019)
5. Cai, J., Gut, D.: Literacy and digital problem-solving skills in the 21st century: what PIAAC says about educators in the United States, Canada. Finland and Japan. Teach. Educ. 31(2), 177–208 (2020)
6. Weekly Breakdown Sales For The Little Mermaid DVD. https://www.the-numbers.com/movie/Little-Mermaid-The#tab=video-sales. Accessed 01 July 2020
7. Brozo, W.G., Shiel, G., Topping, K.: Engagement in reading: lessons learned from three PISA countries. J. Adolescent Adult Literacy 51(4), 304–315 (2007)
8. Naumann, J.: A model of online reading engagement: linking engagement, navigation, and performance in digital reading. Comput. Hum. Behav. 53, 263–277 (2015)
9. Guthrie, J.T., Wigfield, A., You, W.: Instructional contexts for engagement and achievement in reading. In: Handbook of Research on Student Engagement, pp. 601–634. Springer, Boston (2012). https://doi.org/10.1007/978-1-4614-2018-7_29
10. Solheim, O., Lundetræ, J., Lundetræ, K.: Can test construction account for varying gender differences in international reading achievement tests of children, adolescents and young adults?–a study based on Nordic results in PIRLS, PISA and PIAAC. Assess. Educ. Principles, Policy Practice 25(1), 107–126 (2018)
11. Cox, K.E., Guthrie, J.T.: Motivational and cognitive contributions to students' amount of reading. Contemporary Educ. Psychol. 26(1), 116–131 (2001)
12. Vanco, B.M., Christensen, J.L.: Ego depletion increases regulatory success in educational digital media environments. Comput. Hum. Behav. 62, 602–612 (2016)
13. Book and literature panel Annual Report: Bogen og litteraturens vilkår 2018 [The book and litteratur 2018]. SLKS, Agency for Culture and Palaces. https://slks.dk/fileadmin/user_upload/0_SLKS/Fotos/Bogpanel/Rapport18/Aarsrapport_2018.pdf. Accessed 01 July 2020

14. OECD 2010/ PISA 2009 Results: Learning to Learn – Student Engagement, Strategies and Practices, vol. III, http://dx.doi.org/10.1787/9789264083943-en. Accessed 01 July 2020

15. Barber, A.T., et al.: Direct and Indirect Effects of Executive Functions, Reading Engagement, and Higher Order Strategic Processes in the Reading Comprehension of Dual Language Learners and English Monolinguals. Contemporary Educational Psychology, p. 101848 (2020)

16. Schønau-Fog, H., Bjørner, T.: "Sure, I Would Like to Continue" a method for mapping the experience of engagement in video games. Bull. Sci. Technol. Soc. **32**(5), 405–412 (2012)

17. De Jans, S., Hudders, L., Herrewijn, L., van Geit, K., Cauberghe, V.: Serious games going beyond the Call of Duty: Impact of an advertising literacy mini-game platform on adolescents' motivational outcomes through user experiences and learning outcomes. Cyberpsychol. J. Psychosoc. Res. Cyberspace **13**(2), article 3 (2019)

18. Csikszentmihalyi, M.: Flow: The Psychology of Optimal Experience. Harper Perennial, New York (1990)

19. Sweetser, P., Wyeth, P.: GameFlow: a model for evaluating player enjoyment in games. Comput. Entertainment (CIE) **3**(3), 14–27 (2005)

20. Wouters, P., Van Nimwegen, C., Van Oostendorp, H., Van Der Spek, E.D.: A meta-analysis of the cognitive and motivational effects of serious games. J. Educ. Psychol. **105**, 249–265 (2013)

21. Prensky, M.: Digital game-based learning. Comput. Entertainment, **1**, 21 (2003)

22. Staiano, A.E., Adams, M. A., Norman, G. J.: Motivation for exergame play inventory: Construct validity and relationship to game play. Cyberpsychol. J. Psychosoc. Res. Cyberspace **13**(3), article 7 (2019)

23. Massler, U., Gantikow, A., Haake, S., Müller, W., Lopes, C., Neofytou, C.: GameLet: Fostering Oral Reading Fluency With a Gamified, Media-Based Approach. In: European Conference on Games Based Learning, pp. 494-XVI. Odense, Denmark. ACIL (2019)

24. Miller, C.H.: Digital Storytelling: A Creator's Guide to Interactive Entertainment, 4th edn. CRC Press, Boca Raton (2019)

25. De Vecchi, N., Kenny, A., Dickson-Swift, V., Kidd, S.: How digital storytelling is used in mental health: a scoping review. Int. J. Mental Health Nursing **25**(3), 183–193 (2016)

26. Vivitsou, M.: Digital storytelling in teaching and research. In: Tatnall, A., Multisilta, J. (eds.) Encyclopedia of Education and Information Technologies. Springer (2018)

27. O'Brien, H.L., Cairns, P., Hall. M.: A practical approach to measuring user engagement with the refined user engagement scale (UES) and new UES short form. Int. J. Hum. Comput. Stud. **112**, 28–39 (2018)

28. Busselle, R., Bilandzic, H.: Measuring Narrative Engagement. Media Psychology **12**(4), 321–347 (2009)

29. Bjørner, T.: Data Analysis and Findings. In. T. Bjørner (ed.). Ualitative Methods for Consumer Research: The Value of the Qualitative Approach in Theory and Practice. Hans Reitzels, Copenhagen (2015)

Serious Game Applications and Studies

Design of a Gameful Application for Individuals with Acquired Brain Injuries to Relearn Social Functioning

Laura-Jane Douch[1], Kristin Gozdzikowska[3], and Simon Hoermann[1,2]([✉])

[1] HIT Lab NZ, University of Canterbury, Christchurch, New Zealand
simon.hoermann@canterbury.ac.nz
[2] School of Product Design, University of Canterbury, Christchurch, New Zealand
[3] Laura Fergusson Trust Inc, Christchurch, New Zealand

Abstract. Acquired brain injuries (ABI) affect over 40 million people each year. Improving social functioning by training the skills needed for success in social interactions is an important, although often underrepresented part, of rehabilitation after ABI. Those who lack social functioning abilities are at risk of becoming socially isolated and typically have high levels of depression and anxiety. Therapy for social functioning after an ABI is limited, with opportunities for practise decreasing as individuals return home from in-patient care facilities. Additionally, training for social functioning is proportionally less focused on than cognitive or physical functioning.

Interactive technology could offer unchartered opportunities for administering parts of this training in an efficient way. Several successful research studies have evaluated rehabilitation of ABI using games and interactive systems. However, these studies are generally focused on the rehabilitation of cognitive and physical functioning rather than the skills needed for social functioning.

This paper presents the research carried out to design and preliminary validate a gameful application known as *SocialMe*. The findings of this research contribute to the area of rehabilitation of social functioning following ABI and the use of gameful intervention technology. The empirically researched design requirements, including interviews and collaboration with domain experts, presented in this paper could be a starting point for interventions for individuals with ABI as well as individuals with a need to learn or improve skills for full social functioning.

Future research will need to be carried out to develop the concept further and evaluate its clinical significance in a randomised controlled trial to see if the use of *SocialMe* can lead to improvements in the social skills needed for social functioning, and to support the social reintegration of individuals with ABI.

Keywords: Social skills · Social functioning · Acquired brain injury · Stroke · Traumatic brain injury · Rehabilitation · Technology · Interactive tool · Gameful application

1 Introduction

Acquired brain injuries (ABI) are debilitating conditions which leave many individuals with ongoing difficulties in undertaking activities of daily living (ADL's). They usually

© Springer Nature Switzerland AG 2020
I. Marfisi-Schottman et al. (Eds.): GALA 2020, LNCS 12517, pp. 307–315, 2020.
https://doi.org/10.1007/978-3-030-63464-3_29

result in physical and cognitive difficulties, and can often cause difficulties with social functioning [1].

Social functioning is defined as the ability of a person to interact successfully with other people in various environments such as at work, during social activities and in relationships with partners, family and friends [2]. Social skills are defined as the skills involved in being able to have successful social interactions, achieve one's goals, collaborate with others and control emotions [3]. Deficits to these skills are a common result of ABI and can have severe negative outcomes for individuals. Deficits to the skills needed for social functioning commonly lead to loss of relationships and friendships, as successful communication is integral in the maintaining of relationships and participation in social activities [4]. The deterioration of interpersonal connections also creates an increased risk of depression in individuals with ABI [5].

Physical and cognitive therapy in the context of ABI rehabilitation are both researched and addressed. There are several examples of literature describing technology-based interventions that aim to improve cognitive abilities after ABI such as memory, attention and orientation [6–8], and physical abilities after ABI such as balance, mobility and motor skills [9–11]. Many of these therapy interventions assist in improving one's social functioning implicitly, however only a few studies explicitly address the issue of impairment to social functioning after an ABI. This gap in the research is the primary focus of this research: designing an interactive tool that aims to improve/rehabilitate social functioning in individuals with ABI.

A range of technologies that could be used for interventions are available. They range from tablet-based interventions, to those that make use of video conferencing, to VR-based and videogame-based interventions. In general, studies presented in the literature report positive outcomes for participants. For example tablet-based interventions, showed significant improvements in linguistic, functional and quality of life measures and generally high usage and retention rates. However, some studies also report low retention rates, dislike of app content and difficulty of use. Tablet-based intervention studies commented on the increase of accessibility tablets provide and the opportunity that they create for independent, home-based therapy practice - and the ability for therapists to monitor this remotely.

Videogame-based interventions and multi-touch device-based interventions can provide highly interactive opportunities for rehabilitating these skills. Reported outcomes of videogame- based interventions included improved communication skills and high acceptance rates. Interventions that made use of multi-touch technologies enabled participants to acquire new communication and language skills and helped them to cope with difficult social situations.

A limitation that was identified is that many of the studies presented in the literature were either pilot or preliminary studies and some did not base the design of the application on an empirical and user centred approach. This could explain the low retention rates reported in some studies as well as suggest that more research to establish design recommendation is required. The research presented in this paper aims to combine user-centred design with a therapeutic intervention, to design a gameful application that is both effective as well as engaging.

2   Methods/Framework

2.1   Design and Research Frameworks

Design methodologies were identified and used to research and develop the design of an interactive tool. These included goal-directed design which includes a process of research, design and evaluation of an intervention [12], user-centred design which has a procedure of identifying and understanding a context of use, specifying user requirements, iterative development of an intervention and evaluation against the user requirements [13] and participatory action research which involves a reflective cycle of exploration of needs, design, implementation in the 'real world', monitoring and analysis, and evaluation [14].

2.2   Semi-structured Interviews

Semi-structured interviews were conducted with domain experts to gather data to inform the design of the interactive tool. Domain experts were health professionals involved in forms of ABI rehabilitation related to social functioning. 8 participants were interviewed in total, including speech and language therapists (n = 5), occupational therapists (n = 1) and neuropsychologists (n = 2). Interview questions were based on three categories: current practices foe ABI rehabilitation specific to social functioning, patient experiences and use of technology-based interventions. Results of the interviews were categorised into nine main themes that emerged: the importance of social functioning rehabilitation, current practises in rehabilitating social functioning, funding of rehabilitation (in New Zealand), social success, common motivations of clients, common obstacles faced by clients, targeted skills for social functioning, usability challenges faced by clients, and health professional training for an intervention.

2.3   Structured Brainstorming

The relevant studies identified in the literature as well as data gathered from background research and the primary data from the semi-structured interviews, were referred to during structured brainstorming sessions. In total, three structured brain storming sessions were conducted with secondary researchers, and several structured brain storming sessions were conducted where the primary researcher brainstormed independently.

The basic procedure followed in structured brain storming sessions involved the following steps:

1. Defining the aim/goal of the brainstorming session.
2. Giving some background information (if a secondary researcher was involved).
3. Re-iterating the problem space (from the aim/goal).
4. Individually creating ideas.
5. After some time individually brainstorming, sharing ideas.
6. Evaluating ideas.
7. Repeat from step 4 until a range of ideas are produced.

Structured brainstorming resulted in the development of personas based on Coopers Personas [12], problem spaces and design requirements including design constraints and essential features. Figure 1 shows Peter, one of our patient personas. Peter was used as the primary persona in brainstorming and concept development.

Peter, 74

Peter had a Stroke four years ago.

He spent four months in in-patient therapy after his Stroke rehabilitating physically. He suffered from aphasia which severely affected his speech.

Challenges

Peters' speech is still slurred, and he has issues with his confidence during social interactions. Peter has anxiety. He avoids using public transport and going to the shops alone, he has trouble initiating conversations with people he's not close with.

Family

Peter lives with his wife. He has two children and one grandchild.

Location

Peter is from Christchurch, New Zealand where he was in in-patient care but now lives on the West Coast. Because this area is rural it is difficult for Peter to access therapy.

Employment

Peter is a retired university lecturer.

Hobbies

Peter plays cricket and enjoys taking his grandson on walks. Before his stroke Peter loved seeing his friends on a Friday night at the pub.

Use of Technology

Peter used a computer regularly when he was working in a university, he likes to use his iPad daily.

Peter hopes the system will **help him** understand his anxiety and reflect on why he doesn't feel as confident as he used to.

Peter hopes the system will **make him feel** more confident initiating conversations with people he doesn't know well.

Peter hopes the system will help him achieve his **long-term goal** of feeling confident using public transport to take his grandson to the park.

Fig. 1. Primary Persona

Specific problem spaces were chosen based on the most common social functioning deficits seen in individuals with ABI – identified in the semi structured interviews with health professionals. An example of a chosen problem space is turn taking, when individuals with ABI are either, overbearing in a conversation and do not let the conversational partner contribute, or they are unassertive in conversation and do not contribute enough.

The design constraints for the interactive tool design were:

- Slow information processing and/or retention.
- Visual deficits.
- Poor precision/dexterity due to motor skill impairments.
- Fatigue.

The essential features to be included in the interactive tool design were:

- A simple, straightforward user interface and short game play. For ease of use if information processing is difficult, and to make sure the interaction is not too long for users who suffer fatigue.
- Help assists throughout the game play and clear instructions that are accessible whenever needed. For ease of use if information processing and/or retention is difficult. Users may need to review current objectives to make progress.
- 'Undo' options throughout the game play. For users who may need to undo decisions or mistakes made due to poor precision.
- Having no time pressure within the game play. For ease of use if information processing and/or retention is difficult.
- Clear text and contrasting background/foreground colours. To ensure readability for those with visual deficits. Auditory playback options for those who are not able to read text.
- Multiple options for text input when needed. For users with poor motor precision who may find it difficult typing.

3 Concept

3.1 SocialMe

The interactive tool design *SocialMe*, is an application designed for mobile devices with touchscreen interaction and camera access such as smartphones or tablets. A design prototype was created using Adobe XD, a user experience design tool for web or mobile apps. The *SocialMe* app was developed to make use of elements from applied gaming including goals, and feedback with the aim of increasing engagement for its users. The app has been gamified and the interaction has been adapted to the needs of its targeted users, individuals with ABI. The user interface (UI) of *SocialMe* was designed considering the design requirements and the targeted user group, individuals with ABI.

SocialMe prompts self-reflection of social skills used for interactions, in the aim of improving self-awareness of deficits that effect these social skills and creating an opportunity to improve them. The app is presented in the context of a self-reflective journal, which includes social simulation through a personalised avatar. To ensure maximum accessibility, the journal aspect of the *SocialMe* interactive tool is designed for users to have either a physical book-based journal or a digital app-based journal. This is to account for some targeted users not having access to devices, or targeted users preferring the use of a physical notebook and pen throughout the day.

Features of the app include: a goal-setting page, where a user can set goals based on their social functioning, and a journal entry process (see Fig. 2), which should be completed several times throughout a day, where users answer simple questions based on social interactions that they have had, their goals and their challenges (Fig. 3). The app also includes a daily 'walkthrough' (see Fig. 4), where at the end of each day the user can view the compiled data from that day via a virtual 'walkthrough' with their avatar. This 'walkthrough' provides follow up questions for further reflection, and is designed to give the user the effect of having a conversation with their avatar.

Conversation/ interaction is had with another person.
Journal page is completed within the book-based journal.
Device camera is used to scan and digitise the answers.
Journal input is completed within the app-based journal.
Answers from all inputs from one day are combined to create a visual 'walkthrough'.
At the end of a day the user goes through the 'walkthrough' and reflects on their results.
Users can view past 'walkthroughs' and visuals of past inputs daily or monthly.

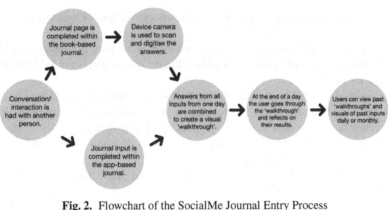

Fig. 2. Flowchart of the SocialMe Journal Entry Process

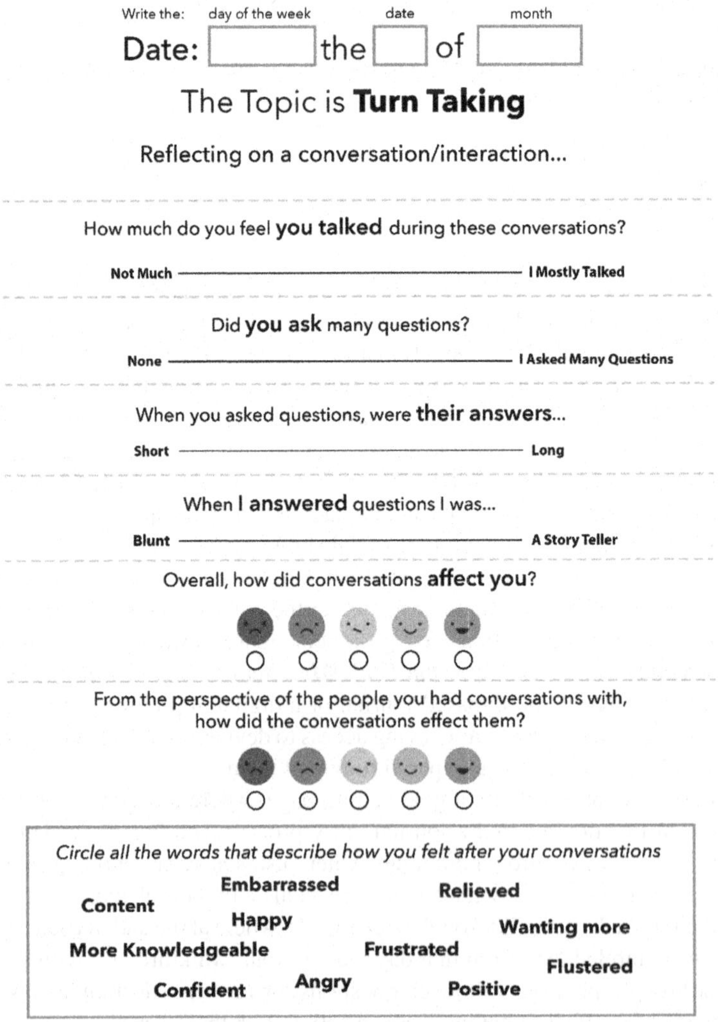

Write the: day of the week date month
Date: the of
The Topic is Turn Taking
Reflecting on a conversation/interaction...
How much do you feel you talked during these conversations?
Not Much
I Mostly Talked
Did you ask many questions?
None
I Asked Many Questions
When you asked questions, were their answers...
Short
Long
When I answered questions I was...
Blunt
A Story Teller
Overall, how did conversations affect you?
From the perspective of the people you had conversations with, how did the conversations effect them?
Circle all the words that describe how you felt after your conversations
Embarrassed
Relieved
Content
Happy
Wanting more
More Knowledgeable
Frustrated
Flustered
Confident
Angry
Positive

Fig. 3. Paper based journal entry

The avatar provides positive interaction and feedback, and may motivate the user to continue with their social practise. Customisation of an avatar is important to give a sense of personalisation within the interactive tool, increasing the motivation of an individual to use it [15]. Ondrejka [15] reports that customisation may make games more 'meaningful' to users and lead them to 'take ownership' over them. Birk, Atkins, Bowey, and Mandryk [16] also show that customisation of an avatar stimulates identification with that avatar and that this identification can lead to higher levels of immersion and more invested effort. The avatar is interacted with throughout the entire app experience providing feedback and encouragement through social simulations.

Users are able to view past data either daily or monthly via a graph (see Fig. 4). These data can also be shared with a health professional and integrated into their rehabilitation process, keeping in mind the importance of this relationship between patient and health professional.

Fig. 4. Daily "Walkthrough" and "Monthly Overview" (rightmost image)

4 Validation of the Concept

4.1 Preliminary Validation

Validation of the design of *SocialMe*, included interviews with health professionals involved in ABI rehabilitation and former patients of ABI. We recruited two former patients of ABI and two health professionals involved in ABI rehabilitation for these preliminary validation interviews. These participants were asked for general feedback on the *SocialMe* intervention, and to complete perceived ease-of-use (PEU) and perceived usefulness (PU) questionnaires [17, 18].

The results of the general feedback, and PEU and PU questionnaires were analysed by the primary researcher and data were extrapolated for the purpose of validating the design concept. The results of the preliminary validation interviews were positive. Health professionals that were interviewed expressed their interest in using *SocialMe* clinically if it were to be developed further and made into a fully working application. The results of the PU and PEU questionnaires revealed highly positive responses to the *SocialMe* design prototype. Both the perceived usefulness (Med = 6.0, IQR = 1.0) and the perceived ease of use (Med = 6.0, IQR = 1.0) had medians that were well above the neutral midpoint of 4.0. This suggests that the participants found that the *SocialMe* intervention has the potential to be both useful and easy to use for individuals with ABI.

5 Conclusion

This research project found that the rehabilitation of social functioning in individuals with ABI is generally identified as a highly important area of rehabilitation, but that research of the use of technology-based interventions, which offer unchartered opportunities, for the rehabilitation of social functioning following ABI is limited. Scientific literature presents a few technology-based interventions that aim to rehabilitate social functioning in individuals with ABI, however more research is needed to form strong conclusions that will aid in the development of future technology-based interventions for this type of rehabilitation.

The research presented in this paper contributes to the area of social functioning rehabilitation following ABI and the use of technology-based interventions. We introduce a concept for an interactive tool *SocialMe,* as well as a design prototype that was created. *SocialMe* is an app designed for use on personal device platforms, the app is presented in the context of a self- reflective journal, which includes social simulation through a personalised avatar. The app aims to prompt self-reflection through a process of setting goals, making journal entries and then reflecting on the data collected over time. To the best of our knowledge no intervention similar to *SocialMe* has previously been designed and researched for use of individuals with stroke or TBI.

SocialMe was developed through a process of background research, primary research, structured brainstorming, prototype creation and validation. The design of SocialMe was based on empirically researched design requirements which are presented in this thesis and could be used as a starting point for other technology-based interventions that may be designed for individuals with ABI in the future. The design concept *SocialMe* may also have the potential to be used by people other than individuals with ABI for the purpose of supporting skills needed for full social functioning.

Through the preliminary validation of this interactive tool concept, we found that *SocialMe* has considerable potential for helping to improve social functioning in individuals with ABI.

References

1. Mayo Clinic: Traumatic Brain Injury (2019). https://www.mayoclinic.org/diseases-condit ions/traumatic-brain-injury/symptoms-causes/syc-20378557
2. Bosc, M.: Assessment of social functioning in depression, Comprehensive Psychiatry, pp. 63–69 (2000)
3. OECD Skills Studies: Learning contexts, skills and social progress: a conceptual framework. In: Skills for Social Progress: The Power of Social and Emotional Skills, OECD Publishing, p. 34 (2015)
4. McDonald, S., Togher, L., Code, C.: The Nature of Traumatic Brain Injury: Basic Features and Neuropsychological Consequences, in *Communication Disorders Following Traumatic Brain Injury*, pp. 19–54. Psychology Press, Hove (1999)
5. Bhogal, S.K., Teasell, R.W., Foley, N.C., Speechley, M.R.: Community reintegation after stroke. Topics in Stroke Rehabilitation, pp. 107–129 (2003)
6. Dores, A., et al.: Virtual city neurocognitive rehabilitation of acquired brain injury. In: 7th Iberian Conference on Information Systems and Technologies (CISTI) (2012)

7. Gamito, P., et al.: Cognitive training on stroke patients via virtual reality-based serious games. Disability and Rehabilitation, pp. 385–388 (2017)
8. Sanchez, L.: et al.: The use of a social assistive robot: NAO for post strokes rehabilitation therapy: a preliminary study. In: Computer Methods in Biomechanics and Biomedical Engineering, pp. 478–480 (2019)
9. Cameirão, M., Badia, S., Oller, E., Verschure, P.: Neurorehabilitation using the virtual reality based rehabilitation gaming system: methodology, design, psychometrics, usability and validation. J. NeuroEng. Rehabilit. **7**, 48 (2010)
10. Kizony, R., et al.: Development and validation of tele-health system for stroke rehabilitation. Int. J. Disability Hum. Dev. **13**, 361–368 (2014)
11. Lloréns, R., Colomer-Font, C., Alcaniz, M., Noé-Sebastián, E.: BioTrak virtual reality system: effectiveness and satisfaction analysis for balance rehabilitation in patients with brain injury. Neurologia, **28**, 268–275 (2013)
12. Cooper, A.: The Inmates Are Running the Asylum: Why High-Tech Products Drive Us Crazy and How to Restore the Sanity, Sams Publishing (1999)
13. Norman, D., Draper, S.: User Centered System Design; New Perspectives on Human-Computer Interaction. L. Erlbaum Associates Inc., New Jersey (1986)
14. Baum, F., MacDougall, C., Smith, D.: Participatory action research. J. Epidemiol. Commun. Health, **60**, 854–857 (2006)
15. Ondrejka, C.: Escaping the Gilded Cage: User Created Content and Building the Metaverse, New York Law School Law Review, Forthcoming (2004)
16. Birk, M., Atkins, C., Bowey, J., Mandryk, R.: Fostering intrinsic motivation through avatar identification in digital games. In: CHI, San Jose, CA (2016)
17. Davis, F.: Perceived usefulness, perceived ease of use, and user acceptance of information technology. MIS Q. pp. 319–340 (1989)
18. Davis, F., Bagozzi, R., Warshaw, P.: User acceptance of computer technology: a comparison of two theoretical models. Manage. Sci. **35**, 982–1003 (1989)

Artifactual Affordances in Playful Robotics

George Kalmpourtzis[(⊠)] and Margarida Romero

Laboratoire d'Innovation et Numérique pour l'Education, Université Côte d'Azur, Nice, France
gkalmpourtzis@playcompass.com, Margarida.Romero@unice.fr

Abstract. Programmable toys present interesting tools for the creation and facilitation of learning experiences through gaming and robotics. In order though for educators and game designers to use these tools to their full potential and provide pedagogical opportunities to support problem-solving activities, we should identify and characterise artifactual affordances in playful robotics. In problem-solving activities, supported by educational robotics artifacts, learners need to identify the artifactual affordances through their interaction with the artifact. This study aims to identify artifactual affordances through the analysis of 15 participants' engagement in the CreaCube task. In this playful problem-solving activity, based on the use of modular robotics, players need to manipulate and assemble robotic cubes in order to create independently moving vehicles. This study aims at providing an initial analysis for the study of artifactual affordances in playful educational robotics.

Keywords: Game based learning · Educational robotics · Affordances · Human computer interaction

1 Introduction

The impact of gaming in educational contexts has been in the spotlight of the industry and academia. Without doubt, research interest focuses on the impact of play and games on learning outcomes and experiences [1] but also on approaches and methodologies around educational game design [2] and the design process [3]. The technological resources for DGBL have been diversified recently with the emergence of IoT connected devices, helping facilitate playful experiences that surpass the static screen of the last century. Within these emergent devices and technologies, a growing corpus or research is developed around Educational Robotics (ER) in playful learning contexts [4]. ER supports GBL through their tangible attributes, their aesthetics and visual appearance [5], their use in simulation contexts [6] and their intrinsically motivating aspect [7].

Educational games have been also examined as problem-solving activities [2]. In order however for players to be able to understand and get acquainted with the contexts around which they are asked to engage in problem-solving, they need to identify what each element and component potentially can help them achieve [8]. Educational games can be considered as artifacts when they have material support and are made intentionally with a certain purpose [9]. The ability of objects (games as artifacts) to convey what they afford to players is called affordance [10]. When considering the *artifactual affordances,*

© Springer Nature Switzerland AG 2020
I. Marfisi-Schottman et al. (Eds.): GALA 2020, LNCS 12517, pp. 316–325, 2020.
https://doi.org/10.1007/978-3-030-63464-3_30

we should consider the material properties which are perceived "as features that provide opportunities for, or constraints on, actions" [12, p.162]. The interactional model of Piaget [12] considers that children construct knowledge through actions taken in the world, influenced not only by socio-cultural factors but also the artifactual features of the subject's environment, including tools, objects and artifacts (made with a certain purpose).

The aim of this study is the identification and analysis of the artifactual affordances in a playful problem-solving task supported by educational robotic artifacts. For this objective, the study examines the participants' interactions while playing CreaCube with Cubelets modular robotics in order to characterize the artifactual affordances supporting the problem-solving activity.

1.1 Problem-Solving in GBL and Playful ER

During the previous years, there has been an increasing attention over the field of Game Based Learning (GBL). Different studies have examined GBL's potential on facilitating active learning [13] and supporting the development of computational thinking skills [14]. This study takes root on the existing corpus on problem-solving in GBL [15] with a specific focus on playful ER engaging the player-learner in problem-solving.

Problem-solving has been identified as an important aspect of GBL, since players are frequently asked to solve problems in gaming contexts [16]. The connection between game playing and problem-solving has also guided research towards the examination of the connection between game making and mathematical problem posing [17]. GBL analysis and creation have also been addressed through a variety of frameworks and models, focusing on various aspects, such as the connection between learning and game mechanics [18], the use of game design strategies [19], didactical situations [20] and exploratory learning [21]. Problem-solving in playful ER tasks engages learners in a creative behaviour which requires them to explore and exploit the ER components through an interactionist approach [22]. When using unfamiliar technologies such ER in playful problem-solving tasks, player-learners are confronted with what Norman [23] designates as the *gulf of execution*, the distance between the user's goals (game objective in the ER task) and the means of achieving them through the ER components available. The gulf of execution should be crossed through the exploration of the robotic components available in order to solve the playful problem-situation (execution bridge) and evaluating the effect of player-learners' actions on the ER components (evaluation bridge). Within the gulf of execution, affordances of the ER components are one of the key aspects that learner-players need to explore and conceptualise to solve the problems they face.

1.2 Affordances: From HCI to GBL

The term *affordance*, even if frequently encountered in Human-Computer Interaction and educational research bibliography, tends to be approached differently by different researchers [24]. A term initially proposed by Gibson [25], affordances initially referred to the characteristics of objects to be perceived both in terms of their form and spatial arrangements but also through one's (animals' or humans') interaction with them. This definition approaches affordances as intrinsic characteristics of objects, whether they are perceived or not by animals or humans. A toy for instance may "afford" play, whether a child understands it or not. The notion of affordances was also impacted by the work of Norman [10], who applied in technology and design contexts. Instead of focusing on the intrinsic attributes of objects, Norman focuses on these object aspects that can be perceived by users. Even if Norman makes a distinction between perceived affordances (meaning affordances of objects that are perceived by users) and real affordances (referring to intrinsic object affordances, which may not necessarily be noticed by users), he pays greater emphasis on the perceivable elements of the field of design [26].

In learning contexts, affordances play an important role in helping both educators and students understand and use the tools they have in their possession [24]. From an educator's standpoint, there are several resources, not originally designed to be used in learning contexts, the application of which could prove interesting for their needs [27]. Studies identifying affordances for educators have been conducted for contexts like wearables [24], handheld devices [28], the Web 2.0 [29], and 3D virtual environments [30]. Regarding affordances for students or players, there have been several studies, some of which come from the "maker" movement on topics that include games, robots and biology education [31, 32]. In addition to this, Kirschner and colleagues [33] point out a potential distinction between technological affordances and social and educational ones. According to them, educational affordances refer to resource attributes that would indicate how they could be used in a learning context. Social affordances on the other hand offer some socio-cultural interaction, relevant to the learning context. In the context of game based learning, Deterding [34] establishes a difference among *situational affordances* and the artifact in its situation-specific meaning and use (*artifactual affordances*). For Deterding *situated motivational affordances* are the opportunities of achieving a goal, which are "provided by the relation between the features of an artifact and the abilities of a subject in a given situation" [p. 3].

In playful ER tasks, the game elements of robots provide *artifactual affordances*, which have a situated meaning in playful activities that players engage in. In ER, *artifactual affordances* include the different perceived characteristics of robots that can be used to achieve ER playful problem-solving tasks. In visuo-spatial constructive play objects, Ness and Farenga [35] observe that the more perceivable the affordances of a constructive play object are, the less they contribute to creative processes. Solving creatively a constructive play activity is then better supported by affordances which requires to be discovered through the task.

In their research on artifactual affordances in maker education contexts, Peppler and colleagues [36] identified the following types of affordances: (a) Tinkerability, describing object attributes that allow learners to play, experiment iteratively and continuously reassess their goals exploring new opportunities, (b) Perceptibility, describing ways that objects can provide learners with feedback on their actions, (c) Expressivity, describing objects' ability to be used and adapted to the individual needs for expression or communication of learners, creating an intrinsically motivating aspect, (d) Usability, describing how easily objects can be used to fulfil the tasks that users want to. Despite the fact that Peppler and colleagues focus on affordances in maker education contexts, the transfer of their model into ER is also relevant to the develop, examination and analysis of artifactual affordances in playful ER tasks. Maker education and ER are both based on tangible technological artifacts, which allows for the consideration of the categorisation of affordances proposed by Peppler and colleagues [36].

2 Methodology

The aim of this study is the identification and analysis of artifactual affordances in the scope of a playful problem-solving task. For this objective, the study a set of playful problem-solving sessions were conducted in which the CreaCube playful robotic task [37] was proposed to the participants. Each session featured one individual participant and one facilitator. The role of the facilitator was to arrange the different tangible elements on the desk when necessary, while the instructions were provided by an audio message to all participants ("build a vehicle made of four pieces moving autonomously from the red point to the black point"). Players were asked to build a self-moving construction that would be able to arrive from a point A (red point on the table) to a point B (black point on the table), using four different modular robotic cubes. Participants were provided with no further clarifications or instructions, apart for the ones delivered through the audio recorded instructions. The *gulf of execution* [23] or problem distance is perceived as important by the participants: from one side, students are asked to create a self-moving vehicle, while on the other side of the gulf, they have four cubes on a table the potential affordances of which they do not know yet. The playful challenge in the CreaCube task requires participant to explore the different cubes and find the relevant affordances to achieve the goal to create a self-moving vehicle.

2.1 Participants

For the scope of this study, the recordings of 15 participants were analysed. Participants were from 25–50 years old. All participants heard the same recorded instructions message and were presented with the same set of four different robotic modular cubes. All participants provided their informed consent for their participation in the task. The sessions were audio and video recorded.

2.2 CreaCube, a Playful Activity with Modular Robotics

The CreaCube activity aims to engage players in a playful problem-solving challenge [38]. The task presents the player-learner with a set of four robotic modular cubes. The materials and their capabilities are unknown to the player-learner. As a result, players need to engage in the exploration of the *artifactual affordances*. These affordances are related to the features of each robotic cube, the identification and understanding of which features on each of the cube is required to solve the playful challenge. The white cube has a set of wheels and presents drive affordance, the black cube offers a distance sensor affordance, the blue cube presents an energy activated by a switch button and the red cube an inverter signal affordance (Fig. 1).

Since affordances are not initially known to player-learners, they are required to engage in the playful activity of exploration (trial and error interactions) as a key behaviour in perceiving the affordances [39]. This exploratory behaviour allows the

Fig. 1. Four robotic cubes proposed to solve the CreaCube task. (Color figure online)

emergence of relevant knowledge on the cube materials (the artifactual affordances), which will potentially lead to using and combining materials in ways that allow task accomplishment (Fig. 2).

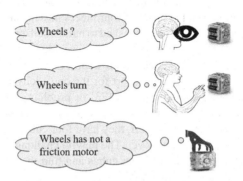

Fig. 2. Exploration of the white cube and its affordances.

Learner-players should interact with all robotic cubes to discover the artifactual affordances they offer, and then assemble the four cubes into a figure which will allow them to succeed in the playful challenge. Figure 3, presents combination leading to task success always (in green), sometimes (orange) and rarely (black).

The CreaCube playful challenge is solved when the player-user succeeds in assembling the four cubes by taking into account the artifactual affordances of each one of them: the activation of the switch button on the blue cube which provides energy to the system, the wheel position on the floor, the red cube placement before the distance sensor in order to invert the signal and provide movement to the vehicle. The game is complete when the *gulf of execution* [23] can be crossed by the reduction of the distance between the user's goals and the means of achieving them through the system. When using technologies that players are unfamiliar with to achieve certain tasks, participants need directly or indirectly bridge the gap between their objectives and their perception of the affordances of the resources in their disposal.

2.3 Data Collection and Analysis

All participants of the study participated in a game-based learning session, where they engaged in the CreaCube task and its feedback. Participants were asked to manipulate and assemble the cubes, in order to create a self-moving vehicle going from an initial point to a final point.

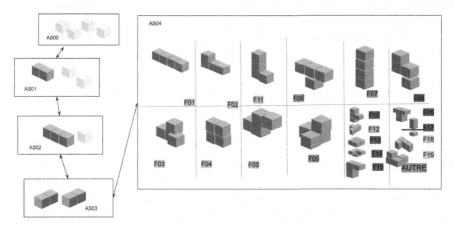

Fig. 3. In green, cubes assembled into a figure allowing to solve the CreaCube task. (Color figure online)

The recordings of the sessions were later analyzed to identify what types of affordances were perceived by participants during the sessions. In this study, the actions, behavior and speech were analyzed in order to identify affordance types during the sessions. A qualitative research methodology was applied, where the analysis took place in an iterative manner in two passes, including an open coding phase, where preliminary thematic categories were proposed and an axial coding phase [40], where the recordings and existing categories were re-examined in terms of categorization and connection. The initial analysis occurred by one coder, while the different produced labels were reviewed by another coder for triangulation purposes at the end of each phase.

Through the continuous revision of data after each recording analysis, every new observation would reinforce or remove existing categories.

3   Results – Affordances in Playful Robotics

The session analysis has led to the proposal of the following types of affordances in the scope of the CreaCube playful robotics sessions: tinkerability, usability (consisting of perceptibility, operability, understandability), aesthetics, playability and feedback.

3.1   Tinkerability

All participants engaged in an exploratory behavior (trial and error) to solve the presented problem with the resources they possessed. During each session, they tried different configurations using the different types of cubes in their disposal, aiming to create a self-driving vehicle. Even if they didn't necessarily understand the logic behind the different combinations they performed, when noticing that specific combinations actually lead to moving structures, they tried to see how they could achieve the intended state of arriving from point A to point B. The affordance of being able to tinker, hence experimenting through a divergent way of problem solving, is defined as tinkering. When dealing with unknown materials, tinkering is a required exploratory divergent thinking behavior permitting the discovery of artifactual affordances.

3.2 Usability

Usability refers to the intuitiveness and ease of use of different objects. In the scope of this study, usability is studied through three sub-categories, which are:

3.2.1 Perceptibility

Perceptibility describes how easily the individual characteristics and elements of cubes are perceived by players. Perceptibility describes for instance users' noticing switches, colors, sensors, wheels and so on. The fact that attributes are perceived however didn't necessarily mean that they are understood by the participants. The analysis of the videos shows that the participants have a better perceptibility of the wheels (white cube), which are the fastest to be detected ($M = 42.52$ s, $SD = 17.17$), followed by the on/off switch blue cube ($M = 56.78$, $SD = 34.15$).

3.2.2 Operability

Operability refers to objects' ability to be operable in the context which they need to be used and by the players that use them. For instance, glossy surfaces and smaller desk sizes did impact cubes' ability to operate under the context of this activity. Operability acquires a special importance in case players have some type of permanent or temporary disability for instance. Additionally, while the sessions took place on a flat desk surface, the possibility of running the same experiment under other situations might potentially impact the operability of CreaCube.

3.2.3 Understandability

Even if the majority of participants noticed the different switches and sensors on the provided cubes, their use was not necessarily understood even if they managed to successfully solve the given problem. This suggests that even if object attributes may be perceived, they may not necessarily be understood. This is the case for the distance sensor and the inverter, which were identified as object attributes but were not correctly understood. The distance sensor was identified later ($M = 65.68$, $SD = 45.49$). However, the participants conceptualized the distance sensor as "two eyes" or "camera", without understanding the existence and functionality of the distance sensor feature when their firstly noticed the "two eyes" or "camera". The red cube has not been correctly conceptualized by any of the participants, which used them to solve the task but without understanding the inverting role it plays on the system.

3.3 Aesthetics

Different objects provide a different perception on how they can be used. CreaCube cubes had different colors and object attributes, each of which gave a hint to players. Even if the object attributes were noticed ("two eyes"), they were not necessarily understood by players (distance sensor).

3.4 Playability

The fact that an item can afford play is not always obvious to players if they engage in the CreaCube task with a performance goal instead of a playful attitude. Even if it was not explicitly asked, the analysis of recordings suggests that some players focused more on the problem-solving aspect of CreaCube during these specific sessions rather than its playful aspect.

3.5 Feedback

The use of the audio recording message as well as the lack of hints on behalf of the facilitator show that feedback, in any way given, plays a key role in playful problem-solving processes involving tangible robotic components. Debriefing after the play activity is of key importance for ensuring the consolidation of the knowledge expected to be developed during the task [41]. A debriefing activity is proposed after the CreaCube playful challenge in order to make sure that players understand the different artifactual affordances, not only within the context of playful tasks, but also in other technological systems. A discussion on exploratory activities (trial and error) and exploitation (developing and testing a hypothesis) is also suggested to support the metacognitive awareness on the different modes of reasoning in creative problem-solving.

4 Discussion

In this study we identified the affordances supporting educational robotics within a playful problem-solving task. In the CreaCube task we observe that players are confronted with a considerable *gulf of execution*, the distance between the user's goals (game objective in the ER task) and the means of achieving them through the ER components available (four robotic cubes). We observed that some object attributes such the wheels and the switch button have a better usability in terms of perceptibility and understandability. On the other hand, distance sensors are not perceived as such at the first task problem-solving stages, which result to players' misconception of the "two eyes" component of the cubes. Despite the misconceptions on the artifactual affordances, the exploration at a component and system level (building the four cubes into a figure) allows players to cross the *gulf of execution* [23] and succeed in the CreaCube playful challenge. Despite that the *gulf of execution* is "crossed" and the playful problem-solving is completed, there is still the need to organize and facilitate a debriefing session to ensure [41] the correct conceptualisation and understanding of the knowledge acquired by players during the task as well as helping them engage the metacognitive awareness of their modes of reasoning during the problem-solving task (exploration vs exploitation) while helping them demystify robotics and develop self-confidence in the use of technologies they are un familiar with. The artifactual affordances in playful tangible artifacts should be considered to help better understand game based learning processes from a cognitive and ergonomic perspective.

References

1. Bellotti, F., et al.: Designing a course for stimulating entrepreneurship in higher education through serious games. Procedia Comput. Sci. **15**, 174–186 (2012)
2. Kalmpourtzis, G.: Connecting game design with problem posing skills in early childhood. Br. J. Educ. Technol. **50**, 846–860 (2019)
3. Romero, M., Ouellet, H., Sawchuk, K.: Expanding the game design play and experience framework for game-based lifelong learning (GD-LLL-PE). In: Romero, M., Sawchuk, K., Blat, J., Sayago, S., Ouellet, H. (eds.) Game-Based Learning Across the Lifespan. AGL, pp. 1–11. Springer, Cham (2017). https://doi.org/10.1007/978-3-319-41797-4_1
4. Zawieska, K., Duffy, B.R.: The social construction of creativity in educational robotics. In: Szewczyk, R., Zieliński, C., Kaliczyńska, M. (eds.) Progress in Automation, Robotics and Measuring Techniques. AISC, vol. 351, pp. 329–338. Springer, Cham (2015). https://doi.org/10.1007/978-3-319-15847-1_32
5. Misirli, A., Komis, V.: Robotics and programming concepts in early childhood education: a conceptual framework for designing educational scenarios. In: Karagiannidis, C., Politis, P., Karasavvidis, I. (eds.) Research on e-Learning and ICT in Education, pp. 99–118. Springer, New York (2014). https://doi.org/10.1007/978-1-4614-6501-0_8
6. Csikszentmihalyi, M.: Flow, The Psychology of Optimal Experience, Steps towards enhancing the quality of life, Harper&Row, Publishers Inc. (1991)
7. Shahid, S., Krahmer, E., Swerts, M.: Child-robot interaction: playing alone or together? In: CHI 2011 Extended Abstracts on Human Factors in Computing Systems, pp. 1399–1404. ACM (2011)
8. Kalmpourtzis, G.: Educational Game Design Fundamentals: A Journey to Creating Intrinsically Motivating Learning Experiences. A K Peters/CRC Press, New York (2018)
9. Hilpinen, R.: On artifacts and works of art1. Theoria. **58**, 58–82 (1992)
10. Norman, D.A.: The Design of Everyday Things. Basic Books Inc, USA (2002)
11. Leonardi, P.M., Barley, S.R.: Materiality and change: Challenges to building better theory about technology and organizing. Inf. Organ. **18**, 159–176 (2008)
12. Piaget, J.: Piaget's theory. In: Mussen, P.H., Kessen, W. (eds.) Handbook of Child Psychology, History, Theory and Methods, vol. 1, pp. 103–126. Wiley, New York (1983)
13. Garris, R., Ahlers, R., Driskell, J.: Games, motivation, and learning: A research and practice model. Simul. Gaming. **33**, 441–467 (2002)
14. Romero, M., Lepage, A., Lille, B.: Computational thinking development through creative programming in higher education. Int. J. Educ. Technol. High. Educ. **14**(1), 1–15 (2017). https://doi.org/10.1186/s41239-017-0080-z
15. Spires, H.A., Rowe, J.P., Mott, B.W., Lester, J.C.: Problem solving and game-based learning: effects of middle grade students' hypothesis testing strategies on learning outcomes. J. Educ. Comput. Res. **44**, 453–472 (2011)
16. Echao, O.F.S., Romero, M.: Creative and collaborative problem solving development through serious games co-creation. In: Presented at the European Conference on Game Based Learning (2017)
17. Kalmpourtzis, G.: Developing kindergarten students' game design skills by teaching game design through organized game design interventions. Multimedia Tools Appl. **78**(14), 20485–20510 (2019). https://doi.org/10.1007/s11042-019-7393-y
18. Arnab, S., et al.: Mapping learning and game mechanics for serious games analysis. Br. J. Educ. Technol. (2015)
19. Kalmpourtzis, G., Romero, M., De Smet, C., Veglis, A.: An Analysis For The Identification Of Use And Development Of Game Design Strategies For Early Childhood Learners. In: Interactive Mobile Communication, Technologies and Learning. Springer (In press)

20. Brousseau, G.: Theory of didactical situations in mathematics: Didactique des mathématiques, 1970–1990. Kluwer Academic Publishing (2002)
21. De Freitas, S., Oliver, M.: How can exploratory learning with games and simulations within the curriculum be most effectively evaluated? Comput. Educ. **46**, 249–264 (2006)
22. Woodman, R.W., Sawyer, J.E., Griffin, R.W.: Toward a theory of organizational creativity. Acad. Manage. Rev. **18**, 293–321 (1993)
23. Norman, D.A.: Cognitive engineering. User Centered Syst. Des. **31**, 61 (1986)
24. Bower, M., Sturman, D.: What are the educational affordances of wearable technologies? Comput. Educ. **88**, 343–353 (2015)
25. Gibson, J.J.: The Theory of Affordances. Hilldale, USA, vol. 1 (1977)
26. Norman, D.A.: Affordance, conventions, and design. Interactions. **6**, 38–43 (1999)
27. Mishra, P., Koehler, M.J.: Technological pedagogical content knowledge: a framework for teacher knowledge. Teach. Coll. Rec. **108**, 1017–1054 (2006)
28. Churchill, D., Churchill, N.: Educational affordances of PDAs: A study of a teacher's exploration of this technology. Comput. Educ. **50**, 1439–1450 (2008)
29. Cochrane, T., Bateman, R.: Smartphones give you wings: pedagogical affordances of mobile Web 2.0. Australas. J. Educ. Technol. **26**, 536–561 (2010)
30. Dalgarno, B., Lee, M.J.W.: What are the learning affordances of 3-D virtual environments?: learning affordances of 3-D virtual environments. Br. J. Educ. Technol. **41**, 10–32 (2010)
31. DiGiacomo, D.K., Gutiérrez, K.D.: Relational equity as a design tool within making and tinkering activities. Mind Cult. Act. **23**, 141–153 (2016)
32. Kafai, Y.B., et al.: Affordances of Digital, Textile and Living Media for Designing and Learning Biology in K-12 Education, p. 8 (2018)
33. Kirschner, P., Strijbos, J.-W., Kreijns, K., Beers, P.J.: Designing electronic collaborative learning environments. Educ. Technol. Res. Dev. **52**, 47–66 (2004)
34. Deterding, S., Sicart, M., Nacke, L., O'Hara, K., Dixon, D.: Gamification using game-design elements in non-gaming contexts. In: Proceedings of the 2011 Annual Conference Extended Abstracts on Human Factors in Computing Systems - CHI EA 2011, p. 2425. ACM Press, Vancouver (2011)
35. Ness, D., Farenga, S.J.: Blocks, bricks, and planks: relationships between affordance and visuo-spatial constructive play objects. Am. J. Play. **8**, 201 (2016)
36. Peppler, K., Halverson, E., Kafai, Y.: Makeology. Routledge, New York (2016)
37. Romero, M., David, D., Lille, B.: CreaCube, a Playful Activity with Modular Robotics. In: Gentile, M., Allegra, M., Söbke, H. (eds.) GALA 2018. LNCS, vol. 11385, pp. 397–405. Springer, Cham (2019). https://doi.org/10.1007/978-3-030-11548-7_37
38. Romero, M., DeBlois, L., Pavel, A.: Créacube, comparaison de la résolution créative de problèmes, chez des enfants et des adultes, par le biais d'une tâche de robotique modulaire. MathémaTICE (2018)
39. Gramsbergen, A.: Motor development. In: Kalverboer, A.F., Genta, M.L., Hopkins, J.B. (eds.) Current Issues in Developmental Psychology. LNCS, pp. 75–106. Springer, Dordrecht (1999). https://doi.org/10.1007/978-94-011-4507-7_4
40. Creswell, J.W.: Educational research: Planning, conducting, and evaluating quantitative and qualitative research. (2012)
41. Sanchez, E., Plumettaz-Sieber, M.: Teaching and learning with escape games from debriefing to institutionalization of knowledge. In: Gentile, M., Allegra, M., Söbke, H. (eds.) GALA 2018. LNCS, vol. 11385, pp. 242–253. Springer, Cham (2019). https://doi.org/10.1007/978-3-030-11548-7_23

A Board Game to Fight Against Misinformation and Fake News

Christophe Maze[1], Arthur Haye[1], Joshua Sarre[1], Michel Galaup[2],
Pierre Lagarrigue[3(✉)], and Catherine Pons Lelardeux[4]

[1] University of Toulouse, INU Champollion, Toulouse, France
[2] Serious Game Research Lab, EFTS, University of
Toulouse, INU Champollion, Toulouse, France
[3] Serious Game Research Lab, ICA, University of
Toulouse, INU Champollion, Toulouse, France
pierre.lagarrigue@univ-jfc.fr
[4] Serious Game Research Lab, IRIT, University of
Toulouse, INU Champollion, Toulouse, France

Abstract. Today, access to daily news is easier than ever. Online misinformation is increasing and is making our societies face great challenges. Our goal aims at providing a support for media education programs, which can help raise young adults' conscientiousness of the dangers related to fake news. Following on from this idea, we designed a board game, called UNISON in partnership with an academic library. The board game has been tested in real conditions. First results show that the majority of participants learnt new knowledge about fake news and media.

Keywords: Serious game · Fake news · Board game · Digital media education · Misinformation

1 Context

Over the last decade, the number of sources of information has exploded and we have information overload. As it has become easier and easier to spread fake news through the internet and social media, it is necessary to decipher real news from fake news. Fake news is, according to the Cambridge English Dictionary, "false stories that appear to be news, spread on the internet or using other media, usually created to influence political views or as a joke" [1]. Over 79% of American adults are on Facebook [1] and 62% got news on social media in 2016, while in 2012, only 49% reported seeing news on social media [2]. 71% of young French adults (15–34 years old) consult the daily news via the social networks. For this generation, social networks are the first media to access to the news (83% use Facebook, 35% Twitter, 32% Youtube). However, social media create the basis for developing fake news and misinformation [3]. Bots on social media are dedicated to spread political fake news especially during political campaigns [4, 5].

Recent events have shown how fake news can impact our daily lives. They can have a serious impact on evidence-based decision making such as consumer purchasing, societal

I. Marfisi-Schottman et al. (Eds.): GALA 2020, LNCS 12517, pp. 326–334, 2020.
https://doi.org/10.1007/978-3-030-63464-3_31

issues, behaviors about climate change or vaccinations [6–8]. Facing this challenge, authorities recommend a board spectrum of solutions. One of them concerns Education and proposes to include digital media literacy in the school curricula [9].

Serious games can be used as a support for media education programs, which can help to raise young people's conscientiousness of the dangers related to fake news. Following on from this idea, we designed a board game to help young adults to defend themselves against these phenomena and inform them of the threat from declining quality news.

This board game called UNISON (United Nations' Intervention Squad on Online Networks) aims at helping people develop more resistance against fake news.

Staff from a French Academic Library helped us to design the content, which focuses on Digital Citizenship and Media Education. In order to distribute the game to a wide audience, all the game components have been designed to be printable from whatever location.

In this paper, we present the board game in Sect. 3. Sections 5 and 6 present the experiment carried out in two academic libraries and the analysis of students' perceptions about knowledge and skills related to misinformation and fake news.

2 Related Work

2.1 Existing Serious Games About Fake News

Some studies focus on misinformation and fake news. This is the case of Roozenbeek et al. [7] who developed an interactive choice-based adventure game. They aims at conferring cognitive resistance against fake news strategies. The game called "Bad News" proposes to take the role of a fake news creator. The mission consists of attracting as many followers as possible while also maximizing your credibility

The more your article is credible the more followers you get. You get an explanation of the consequences of your articles and the different kinds of subjects in the fake news genre. They provide evidence that people's ability to spot and resist misinformation improves after gameplay, irrespective of education, age, political ideology, and cognitive style. In the field of entertainment, Fake News (©Breaking Games) is a board game based on the famous card game "Cards Against Humanity" [8]. In this game, players must complete gaps in a sentence by choosing the correct word or phrase. The goal aims at creating the most appropriate headline. Three categories of headlines allow the player to classify headlines, one of them is "fake news". The goal in this game is really how to create clickbait head titles and to understand why it affects people's choices. Another example concerns a generator of fake news, you can break your own news by choosing your own headline, picture and ticker [9]. A French National Report [10] mentions that Education on media and information has a positive impact on young adults from 15 to 34 years old. Sixty-five percent of young adults who followed the courses on Media and Information check the news.

2.2 A Conflict to Provoke a Debate

Situational awareness is the perception of elements in the environment within a volume of time and space, the comprehension of their meaning, and the projection of their status into the near future. Kaber et Endsley [11] consider the situation awareness as "the sum of operator perception and comprehension of process information and the ability to make projections of system states on this basis". Communication and debate help individuals to build their own representation of the world and make their own decisions. In our case, the first point is to create a context that is likely to launch a debate. It consists of providing the team with a conflictual problem to solve. The implicit rules of a group decision-making is composed of different elements: (1) identifying a topic, (2) identifying who is responsible for the decision, (3) identifying who has the best expertise for the discussion topic, (4) identifying and ranking the different alternatives and their consequences. Some research develops digital applications for learning purposes which support debate [10–12]. This is the case of Tong et al. [10] who developed a digital learning environment which supports the decision-making process. They use both a tactile tabletop and tablets. The tabletop presents the context and the possible alternatives whereas the tablets supports the data browsing. They follow the analytical process of the decision-making activity, which involves four broad categories of decision-making behaviors: exploring, discussing, awareness and regulation. Their system helps students to develop their own ideas and make reasonable decisions providing justifications to support them. In our study, we decide to structure the educational scenario on a set of problems to solve in order to involve students in the group decision-making process. To that end, we follow the model of two famous existing board games to involve a team of players in a collaborative task and use the game to launch a debate.

3 UNISON: A Board Game Against Fake News

UNISON (United Nations' Intervention Squad on Online Networks) is a serious and cooperative board game where a team of players (between 3 and 6 players) is expected to fulfill a mission that aims at solving a mystery in a near future. UNISON has been inspired by two board games: The Dungeon of Naheulbeuk [13] & Times'Up! [14].

3.1 Materials

The board game is composed of (see Fig. 1):

– a set of playing cards, which represent typical characters (Agent) such as 'Granny Germaine" a grandmother, "H4ck3rm4n" an IT enthusiast, a reporter, an authority agent...

Fig. 1. UNISON is a board game composed of playing cards, handbooks and a set of mini board games.

- a set of handbooks, which depict the storytelling (Situation) and summarizes all the right answers
- a set of playing cards attached to mini board games such as a mime game, a quiz, or a game to guess a word connected to the topic of "fake news" (Tests)
- a set of handbooks which depict different media in which players must detect "Fake News" (Investigations)
- tokens that represent the badges earned by the team
- a timer

3.2 Roles

Each teammate chooses an Agent and takes into account their abilities, strengths and weaknesses. At each step, one of the teammates has a particular role: the leader role. The leader exposes the script (detailed on the handbook) to the other players. He is the one who is responsible for the timer. A gaming session must be completed in a limited time.

3.3 Script: Fun and Humour

The design process supports three goals: learning vocabulary related to Fake News, debating and exploring a method to detect "fake news". Actually, all scripts proposed in UNISON are bizarre and fill out with jokes and caricatured references to the real world. The characters are also parodies of celebrities or stereotypes. Their names and abilities recall famous actors, politicians and many cultural references. For example, the team must read an article explaining how a character wants to build a wall all around its great and beloved country.

3.4 Handbook and Leader Role

The handbook depicts the storytelling, which is represented with a tree-like structure (see Fig. 2). Only the leader can access the handbook. The handbook mentions each node of the tree-structure and all the possible alternatives that can be chosen by the team. All good answers to the quiz or mini board games are available in the handbook. It is the main support to lead a gaming session.

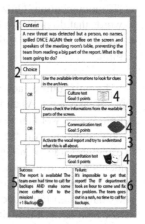

2- Tree-like structure of alternatives: The players must choose between several options (**3**), each option leads to a mini board game (a quiz or an investigation) (**4**). The leader keeps the answer secret until the team finishes the mini game and then he reads the correct answer.

5- End of the script (success): If the team succeeds in the mini game, the leader reads the feedback tagged as a 'Success' and the team obtains a badge.

6- End of the script (failure): If the team fails in the quiz, the leader reads the feedback tagged as a "Failure".

Fig. 2. 1- Script: The leader introduces the storytelling by reading the script to the teammates.

Example of a script: The team is supposed to work in an international company. The daily meeting begins when a threat emerges but someone, nameless, spills once again their coffee on the screen of the meeting room table and on the loudspeakers. It prevents the team from reading a big part of the report. What is your team going to do? Three alternatives are available.

Alternative 1	Use the available pieces of information to look for clues in the archives.
Alternative 2	Cross-check the pieces of information still available on the report
Alternative 3	Activate the vocal report and try to understand what is going on.

Each alternative leads to a new mini board game.

3.5 Mini Board Games

A mini board game is either a quiz on or an investigation into documents or resources to detect fake news or real news.

Quiz: Culture is crucial to understand the world. The more informed you are, the more able you are to detect fake news and the less vulnerable you are to be manipulated. The board game is supposed to transmit knowledge through quizzes of overall culture. The quizzes are composed of a set of close-ended and open-ended questions. There are four different types of quiz, all inspired by the famous board games such as Taboo [16], Cranium [17] and Time's Up [14]:

- "Culture" quiz: the leader reads questions to the team
- "Thinking" quiz: the leader reads three possible definitions of a word while the other players have to find out which is the right one.
- "Communication" Quiz: the leader must make the other teammates guess a word using words that do not belong to the same word root as the word to be discovered [16].
- "Interpretation" Quiz: the leader must make the other players guess a word through mimes [14].

The quiz aims at acknowledging definitions of words and concepts related to the topic of fake news. As an illustration, during a mini game, a teammate must elaborate a definition of a word and express it to the other teammates to make it understandable.

Investigation: An investigation consists of studying an article, a video or comparing two pictures and pointing out the inconsistencies and arguing. The game must help students to discover some tricks and initiate the French official methodology [18] to detect fake news. To that end, UNISON proposes a set of situations in which some fake news have been introduced along with a guideline that mentions a reliable strategy to detect fake news. Each situation is used as a support to launch a debate between the teammates.

When a mini-game is over, the leader presents the right answers. If the team succeeds, the leader delivers a token, which gives additional time to complete the final investigation. The more tokens the team gets, the more time you spend to investigate the final step.

3.6 Design Process

A template has been defined to elaborate a large variety of gaming scenarios. A scenario refers to a mission. A mission is composed of a number of different storytelling scripts (see Fig. 3). Each mission includes a set of scripted situations, which are depicted in the handbooks. The number of scripted situations defines the level of difficulty related to a mission. Players are supposed to have a broad knowledge base related to pop-culture, films and political events to investigate and detect fake news.

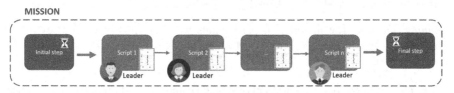

Fig. 3. Structure of a Mission

A new handbook is available at the beginning of each step.

The mini-game scripts were designed using the 3 main categories of Fake News which were depicted by Wardle [15]: misinformation, disinformation, mal-information. The 7 different types of Fake News were included in the design stage: satire or parody, false connection, misleading content, false context, impostor context, manipulated content, and fabricated context.

The successive steps included in a mission aim at making student developing basic verification skills discovering the five pillars of information verification are provenance, source, date, location, motivation. This is a support to introduce a methodology to verify information and elaborate a checklist.

4 Objectives and Method

To determine whether the board game is adapted to the target audience, we conceived two questionnaires. The first one must be completed before the gaming session. It aims to identify the player's profile, their level of experience in board games, their level of knowledge of the subject matter..

The second one (post-test) questionnaire must be completed at the end of a gaming session. It aims at studying the level of acceptability of the board game and the players' experience concerning the skills and knowledge the participants sensed they acquired.

5 Experiment

The experiment was carried out in two Academic libraries located in the immediate campus of a French University. They both involved volunteer students recruited by the Academic library staff. The French academic library organizes board game nights each month. These events are organized in partnership with a gaming organization to entertain students. On these board game nights, the game UNISON has been tested. The participants were divided into 3 gaming groups. Each group played successively and separately. Before starting a gaming session, a student read the rules.

Participants: 15 players participated in this experiment.

Genre: 53% were men and 47% women.

Age: A third were 18 years old, another third were between 19 and 20; and the last third was composed of participants between 21 and 24.

Training Courses: The majority of participants were students in IT courses (60%). The others were in Sciences (13%), Mechanical Field (13%), Literature (7%) and Logistics(7%).

Board Game Experience: 7% never played board games, 13% play rarely, 67% regularly play and 13% often play.

Knowledge of Fake News: Participants were asked to self-assess their prior knowledge of "fake news" on a scale between 1 (low level of knowledge) to 10 (high level of knowledge). 66 percent of the participants rate their own knowledge on "Fake News" at 5 or lower out of 10, showing that they feel that they lack knowledge about fake news.

6   Data and Results

One hundred percent of students completed the pre and post questionnaire. The game was tested by three groups. Each group played one gaming session. One group was composed of three students. The other two groups were composed of six students. None of the students quit the gaming session during the test. Each gaming session lasted on average an hour. The game usually began calmly as the players read the rules. It became much more animated when they had to choose a character to play with and when they created their own Mission. All throughout a gaming session, there was a lot of talking and a great ambiance.

Collaboration to Foster the Debate: The script encourages the teammates to investigate, express their point of view, exchange in order to make a collaborative decision. The experiment shows that the students were extremely involved in the gaming session. They look for clues and argue their opinion to the other teammates.

Satisfaction and Acceptability: The results show a high level of overall satisfaction (see Fig. 4). All ratings fall between 7 and 10 out of 10. The levels of satisfaction per element allowed us to determine which gaming component needed to be improved, corrected or even deleted. For example, we reworked some agents' advantages and disadvantages to balance them out and make them understandable and fun. At one point we also entirely revamped the "thinking" tests as their rules were not clear enough. The average ratings are all high, ranging from 7 to 8.5 out of 10.

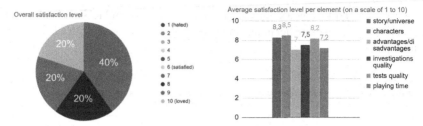

Fig. 4. On the right: users' satisfaction according to gaming elements (1-low level; 10-high level) (right) – On the left: overall satisfaction (0-low level; 6-high level)

The high level of scores concerning the satisfaction on the storytelling, universe, playing time shows a good acceptability.

We've been able to crosscheck those results with some open questions in the post-test questionnaire related to the strong and weak points of the game. We have noticed that the most mentioned weak points are the clarity of the rules (33%) and the shortness of the timers (20%). On the bright side, the players have cited the instructional aspect of the game (33%) and the fun it brings (20%) as the strong points of UNISON.

New Skills and Knowledge about Fake News: The analysis of the questionnaire shows that UNISON fits the theme of "Fake News". Eighty-six per cent of participants sensed they acquired new knowledge relative to "Fake News" that could help them to fight against misinformation. 7% answered that they felt not to be concerned. 7% judged that they did not feel to learn new skills. In conclusion, even if the number of participants was limited, first results show that the majority of participants learnt new knowledge about fake news and media. 86% consider that UNISON brought them new skills and knowledge. These results may anticipate that people were really made aware of fake news. Therefore, they probably are able to spot and fight against misinformation after gameplay. Some other research is in line with this. The French National Report on Young Adults and Information [19] and the study of Roozenbeek et al. [20] showed that people who have been educated about Information and Media, or misinformation and fake news, have improved their ablility to spot and resist misinformation.

7 Conclusion

Our goal aims at providing a support for media education programs, which can help raise young people's conscientiousness of the danger related to fake news. Therefore, we designed a board game in partnership with the academic library staff. This board game has been tested in real conditions with students. Participants who tested UNISON were involved during two board game nights in the academic library at the University. Our study shows that the board game UNISON is user-friendly, fun and amazing to play. The high level of scores concerning the satisfaction on the storytelling, universe, playing time demonstrates a good acceptability. Even though the number of players was limited, first results reveal that the bulk of participants learnt new knowledge about fake news and media. Therefore, as people who have been educated on Information and Media, or misinformation and fake news, improve their ability to spot and resist misinformation, we plan to examine in more detail this improvement in future work with a larger sample of participants.

Acknowledgement. The authors would like to thank Carole Rahoux, Aricia Bassinet, Camille Bertin, Rémy Ginestet, Gaëlle Jan and Florence Lunardi for their contributions.

References

1. Greenwood, S., Perrin, A., Duggan, M.: Social media update 2016. Pew Research Center. **11**, 1–18 (2016)
2. Gottfried, J., Shearer, E.: News use across social media platforms 2016, https://www.journalism.org/2016/05/26/news-use-across-social-media-platforms-2016/. Accessed 22 June 2020
3. Varol, O., Ferrara, E., Davis, C.A., Menczer, F., Flammini, A.: Online human-bot interactions: detection, estimation, and characterization. In: Eleventh International AAAI Conference on Web and Social Media (2017)
4. Ferrara, E.: Disinformation and social bot operations in the run up to the 2017 French presidential election. arXiv preprint arXiv:1707.00086 (2017)
5. Allcott, H., Gentzkow, M.: Social media and fake news in the 2016 election. J. Econ. Perspectives **31**, 211–236 (2017)
6. Poland, G.A., Spier, R.: Fear, misinformation, and innumerates: how the Wakefield paper, the press, and advocacy groups damaged the public health. Vaccine **28**, 2361–2362 (2010). https://doi.org/10.1016/j.vaccine.2010.02.052
7. van der Linden, S.: Beating the hell out of fake news. Ethical Record: Proc. Conway Hall Ethical Soc. **122**, 4–7 (2017)
8. Lazer, D.M.J., et al.: The science of fake news. Science **359**, 1094–1096 (2018). https://doi.org/10.1126/science.aao2998
9. Council of Europe: Freedom of expression. https://www.coe.int/en/web/commissioner/thematic-work/media-freedom. Accessed 09 July 2020
10. Tong, L., Serna, A., George, S., Tabard, A.: Supporting Decision-making Activities in Multi-Surface Learning Environments. https://hal.archives-ouvertes.fr/hal-01493815 (2017)
11. Linn, M.C., Bell, P., Davis, E.A.: Specific design principles: Elaborating the scaffolded knowledge integration framework. Internet environments for science education, pp. 315–340 (2004)
12. Dillenbourg, P., Evans, M.: Interactive tabletops in education. Int. J. Comput. Supported Collaborative Learn. **6**, 491–514 (2011)
13. The Dungeon Of Naheulbeuk : Amulet Of Chaos. https://amuletofchaos.com/. Accessed 03 July 2020
14. Time's Up!
15. Wardle, C.: Fake news. It's complicated. First Draft. 16 (2017)
16. Taboo Game
17. Cranium Game. (1998)
18. French Gouvernement: Fake news : guide des questions à se poser face à une information. https://www.gouvernement.fr/fake-news-guide-des-questions-a-se-poser-face-a-une-information. Accessed 09 July 2020
19. Mediametrie, Ministère de la Culture: Les jeunes et l'information – Synthèse. https://fr.readkong.com/page/les-jeunes-et-l-information-synthese-8696293. Accessed 03 July 2020
20. Roozenbeek, J., van der Linden, S.: The fake news game: actively inoculating against the risk of misinformation. J. Risk Res. **22**, 570–580 (2019). https://doi.org/10.1080/13669877.2018.1443491

A Serious Game for Students to Acquire Productivity Habits

Wouter Raateland, Konstantinos Chronas, Tim Wissel, Tim Bruyn,
Bertan Konuralp, Mijael Bueno, Nestor Z. Salamon,
and Rafael Bidarra[✉]

Delft University of Technology, Delft, The Netherlands
R.Bidarra@tudelft.nl

Abstract. In recent years there has been an increasing shift from traditional work to knowledge work. Students are not always well prepared
for such a work mode and struggle with time and energy management,
leading to stress and long unhealthy study sessions. There are many
applications aimed at developing productivity habits. A few of them are
somewhat gamified, although they are especially focused on real-world
to-do lists, lacking a strong narrative and appeal, especially to students.
We present the serious game *BusyBusy*, specifically designed for college
students. The game revolves around the *capture* and *reflection* steps of
David Allen's *Getting Things Done* methodology. By simulating aspects
of student life, *BusyBusy* facilitates students to practice capturing action-
related thoughts in their real life and reflect upon study activity choices
in an entertaining and engaging environment.

Keywords: Serious games · Getting Things Done · Habit building ·
Personal productivity · Mobile games

1 Introduction

The rapid growth of globalization and the evolution of technology has created
an overwhelming amount of information that people have to adapt to. One part
of society that struggles to adapt are academic students, who face the challenge of balancing their academic goals and other activities in their life. The
current education system falls short in preparing students for knowledge work
[16]. Hence, an increase in anxiety and procrastination among students is being
noticed [7,13]. Traditionally, procrastination is defined as the undesirable behavior of irrationally delaying a course of intended action, with the understanding
that it may result in not ideal outcomes. Nonetheless, researchers found out that
50% of students procrastinate consistently at university [18]. Students who often
procrastinate generally encounter less stress at the beginning of a semester, more
stress later on, and generally suffer more often from anxiety than the ones who
do not [20].

A common reason for stress is the overload of information and possible activities. As the amount of time is finite, this overload means a number of potentially

© Springer Nature Switzerland AG 2020
I. Marfisi-Schottman et al. (Eds.): GALA 2020, LNCS 12517, pp. 335–346, 2020.
https://doi.org/10.1007/978-3-030-63464-3_32

important items can no longer be processed. This creates a lack of control that results in stress [9].

This paper presents *BusyBusy*, a serious game for students to acquire productivity habits that gamifies the *capture* step of the *Getting Things Done* (GTD) methodology. The game is lighthearted simulation of student life in the style of Dumb Ways to Die[1]. Its design focuses on learning how to clear up daily thoughts, when struggling with stress and procrastination. We incorporate a constructivist learning approach [6] to train students to balance different responsibilities while keeping their minds clear. This is achieved by the player performing a series of activities in the form of mini-games, while dealing with thoughts that pop up on the screen, resembling the distracting thoughts occurring to a student.

2 Related Work

We revisit stress-reducing research, applications and games to improve productivity, in the form of task managers or GTD guides. While students use different types of task managers and to-do lists, either gamified or not, these are not focused on integrating the daily student routine.

Stress Reduction and Prevention. Several stress reducing methods focus on reducing stress through physical exercise [12] and yoga or meditation [10]. To prevent stress from occurring, a currently popular methodology that helps students is called Getting Things Done® [2] (GTD) and was proposed by David Allen in 2001 as 'the art of stress-free productivity' [1]. Allen outlined a five-step method for reducing stress while staying on top of an increasingly complex world: "We **(1) capture** things that command our attention; **(2) clarify** what they mean and what to do with them; and **(3) organize** the results, on which we **(4) reflect** as options for what we choose to **(5) engage** with". According to research, GTD can mitigate feelings of stress, anxiety and information overload that are often experienced during knowledge work by restoring a sense of control [9]. It does so by outsourcing thoughts to an external memory [3]. Furthermore, by providing focus and structure, GTD reduces switching of mental context, which costs time and energy [4].

GTD-related Task Managers. Structuring activities according to the GTD methodology can be done with a task manager. In the book Getting Things Done [1], seven different lists, or destinations for *stuff*, are mentioned: Next Actions, Waiting for, Calendar, Someday/Maybe, Trash, Archive and Projects list. In addition, there should be an Inbox, that functions as a bucket to quickly capture whatever needs later clarification. Many task managers give users the option to define their own lists or come with predefined lists for GTD. Examples

---

[1] http://www.dumbwaystodie.com/.

[2] https://gettingthingsdone.com/.

of this are nTask [15] and Nirvana HQ [14]. GTD-related task managers help a user to structure their to-do list while still relying on the intrinsic motivation of the user. Nonetheless, they assume that the user is already familiar with the GTD methodology.

Productivity Related Games. Recently, incorporating gamification in task managers has received significant attention. Games such as Habitica [8], Super-Better [19] and EpicWin [17] are gamified task managers which include elements such as completing quests and role-playing for engagement, and experience points and leveling up as a reward system. However, similar to the GTD-related task managers, these games target users who are already motivated to improve their productivity habits, rather than users who do not consider changing their daily routine of habits.

Theories of Learning. Effective knowledge transfer with stress reduction methods has been the target of frameworks such as the constructivism theory of learning. Constructivism equates learning with creating meaning from experience [6]. Students learn by fitting new information together with previous knowledge and current beliefs and attitudes [2]. By perceiving new experiences, students update their mental model to reflect the new information and use it to construct their interpretation of reality [5]. Hence, it directly proposes an effective way of creating habits.

BusyBusy applies Constructivism learning theory by simulating a scenario that demonstrates the use of GTD. We create an environment where the player experiences a loss of control and can regain control by applying the *capture* and *reflection* steps of GTD. *BusyBusy* advises the players to bring order to the learning process by sorting their thoughts and gaining experience with the mini-games in a virtual experience, without confronting the player with real life tasks.

3   Game Design

The goal of the game is to help students to cope with stress by acquiring the *capturing* habit. To satisfy this goal, the game should: (i) be relatable to the player, (ii) strike a balance between fun and learning, (iii) let the player experience the *capturing* habit, and (iv) be played for consecutive days while *reflecting* about the learned behavior.

To create a game that is relatable to the player, we developed a simulation game wherein the player takes the role of a virtual student. Just like a real student, the virtual student needs to complete courses, keep their room clean, stay healthy, and be entertained. To successfully achieve this, the virtual student needs to balance studying with other activities. The game strikes a balance between fun and learning by visualizing the activities that the student has to do as fast-paced mini-games. During these mini-games the player experiences the *capturing* habit: thoughts related to other must-do activities appear on the screen and the player has to manage them.

The game includes different courses that last multiple game-days. Additionally, to stimulate students to come back daily to the game, we included a streak system rewarding the player for playing consecutive days.

3.1 Game Activities

There are currently 5 activities in the game that the player has to complete: doing homework, working out, cleaning room, socializing and playing games. The activities are grouped into three categories and presented in the form of mini-games. The productivity category encapsulates any productive activity, represented in *BusyBusy* with working out. The organizational category consists of activities that influence the virtual student's room/environment. Finally, the entertainment category includes social and fun activities. Learning efficiency and course progress is affected by a balance of the studying activity and all of these categories.

3.2 Thoughts in the Game

During the mini-games, thought bubbles pop up, related to other activities, representing the thoughts of the virtual student. While floating around the screen, these thought bubbles distract the player from playing the mini-games. However, they also let the player experience how capturing thoughts affects the performance of their daily activities, in a direct and visual way: the player can act on each thought bubble by either capturing it, i.e. dragging it to the collection box, or by trashing it, i.e. dragging it to the trash bin. When more than 5 thoughts are floating around simultaneously, the oldest thoughts get forgotten. If at the end of a game-day, the player has properly dealt with enough thoughts (i.e. there are at most 2 left floating), they will be positively rewarded on each score; otherwise, the player will be penalized on the scores for each forgotten thought. This mechanism encourages the player to perform the capturing habit inside the game. More importantly, the captured thought bubbles control the game cycle: the player's next activity is namely determined by the captured thoughts during the current activity.

3.3 Game Cycle

In *BusyBusy*, virtual student life takes place turn-based, in game-days. Each game-day consists of one to three mini-games. Figure 1 illustrates the complete game flow. Each game-day takes about 1–2 min, specially designed so a student can do a short game-play session without the burden of having yet another time consuming task. On the first day, after a short tutorial, a new course starts and the player is left on the main menu (the student room). From here, the player can start a new game-day with its mini-games. The game-day ends when no thoughts are captured during a mini-game or when 3 mini-games have been played. At the end of the game-day, the player is presented with the score screen. This is repeated till the end of the current course, when the player receives feedback on their grades. Thereafter, a new course can be started with zero scores and progress – hence, the game cycle restarts.

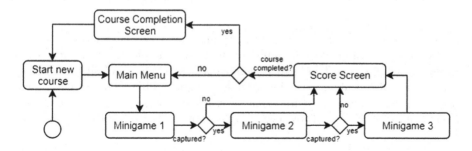

Fig. 1. The game loop of *BusyBusy*.

3.4 Scoring

During the game, we track four scores. The primary score is the virtual student's progress on their current course. Course progress is reset each time a new course is started, and has to be sufficiently high when the course ends. The other three scores relate to activities a student has to perform in their life: productivity, organization and entertainment, and start at 50%.

The effect of each mini-game on their respective scores is presented in Table 1. During the game, the scores are displayed in the main menu and on the scoring screen. At the end of a game-day, the player score is computed based on the played activities. By being shown their scores, players are also encouraged to *reflect* on their progress.

When a player plays at least one game-day on an actual day, their streak is incremented; otherwise, it is reset to zero. For each streak, the player will gain a multiplier on progress they get for one score.

Table 1. The mini-games and its effects on each score on the virtual student life.

Score	Activity	Mini-game	Amount
(P)roductivity	Working out	Jumping rope (timing)	+10%
(O)rganization	Cleaning room	Navigation game	+10%
(E)ntertainment	Social activities	Block-breaker	+10%
	Gaming	Pinball	+10%
Study progress	Studying	Memory	$1 + (P) + (O) + (E)$

3.5   Mini-Game Design

Each activity in *BusyBusy* is relatable to student life domains: study, socialize, clean, workout and have fun. The player engages in these domains by playing the corresponding mini-games, having to balance their activities in the game.

Study. The study mini-game is a memory quiz where the player has to select the correct answer within the time limit. In the game, the player experiences stress from the toughness of trying to remember all the shapes and their respective colors while also dealing with the floating thought bubbles. This memory game was chosen because it is reminiscent of studying, remembering concepts of a course and testing yourself by answering questions. The mini-game is shown in Fig. 2a.

Workout. The workout mini-game focuses on the reflexes of the player. The player has to tap on the screen at the right time to make the virtual student jump a rope within the time limit. Jumping rope is an easy and effective cardio workout and like in the game, depends on the reflexes of a person to time and jump at the downswing of the rope. The mini-game is shown in Fig. 2b.

Socialize. The socialize mini-game is a block-breaker variant where the player controls a paddle and has to hit beer glasses with a ball, also within the time limit. This game is a fun experience, representing the player going out with friends, as one of the multiple social interactions students like to have. The mini-game is shown in Fig. 2c.

Fun. The fun mini-game is a classic pinball game where the player has to touch all targets with the ball. Many students play games to have fun, and pinball represents a relaxing arcade game. The mini-game is shown in Fig. 2d.

Cleaning. In the cleaning mini-game, the player has to clear objects around the room by controlling a hose with a gamepad during the allocated time. This mini-game is a straightforward representation of the domain, vacuuming your room to clean it. Furthermore, the controls and the feel of the game correlate well with the idea of vacuuming a room. The mini-game is shown in Fig. 2e.
All mini-games are integrated in one web-based application[3], meant to be played on mobile devices, with all player data being stored locally.

---

[3] Freely available at https://busy-busy.netlify.com/.

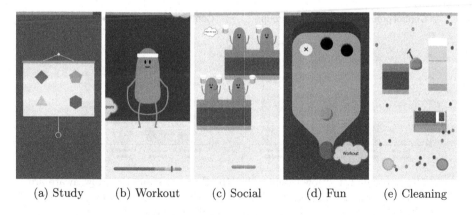

(a) Study   (b) Workout   (c) Social   (d) Fun   (e) Cleaning

Fig. 2. The mini-games in *BusyBusy*.

4   Evaluation

We conducted two studies to evaluate *BusyBusy*: the first considers the effects of playing *BusyBusy* only once, while the second considers the effects of playing it for a longer period.

4.1   Study 1

This study considered the effect of playing *BusyBusy* only once. Our hypothesis was that participants who play *BusyBusy* will be more aware of the value of capturing thoughts than the participants who only answered the survey.

Method. The study was conducted as a double blind trial, with two groups: the experimental group first played *BusyBusy* for five minutes on their phone and then took the survey in Appendix A; the control group only took the survey.

Results. Figure 3 shows the responses of both the control group and the experimental group for two survey questions. Table 2 presents a statistical analysis of the responses. Figure 3a shows that the experimental group considers the value of capturing thoughts very valuable or extremely valuable more often than the control group, with 79% versus 56%. With a P-value of 0.035, this difference is statistically significant. Figure 3b shows that the control group actually found themselves less often unaware of the value of capturing thoughts. However, with a P-value of 0.945, no statistical difference between the groups is found.

Discussion. The statistically significant difference in the respondents answers to Q4 shows that *BusyBusy* indeed makes players aware of the value of capturing thoughts after playing it once. Q5 could have strengthened this evidence, but its answers fail to show any significant difference between the groups.

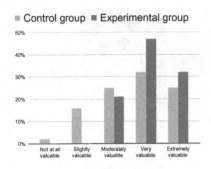

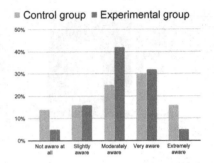

(a) Responses on Q4: "How valuable do you think it is to capture your thoughts outside of your head?"

(b) Responses on Q5: "How aware are you of the value of capturing thoughts outside of your head?"

Fig. 3. Responses on survey questions for study 1.

4.2   Study 2

This study considered the effect of playing *BusyBusy* for a period long enough for creating/changing a personal habit. Our hypothesis was that participants to this study would have developed or strengthened their capturing habit after playing the game.

Method. This study was limited to 5 students (referred to as P1 to P5) who classified themselves as experiencing stress. At the start of the study they filled in the survey in Appendix B, they then played *BusyBusy* for seven days in a row, and afterwards they filled in the survey in Appendix C.

Results. Out of the five people who took part of the experiment, two people already used to capture their thoughts externally before the experiment, two other people used to capture about half of the time, and the remaining person only sporadically. After the experiment, this stayed the same, except that one of the people who said about half the time answered sometimes, and the person who had answered sometimes answered about half the time. This means that their habits did not visibly change in the one-week period in which they played the

Table 2. Significance of responses to Q4 and Q5 in study 1.

Question	Group	n	Mean	Standard deviation	Variance	P-value
Q4	Experimental	19	4.11	0.72	0.87	0.035
	Control	43	3.60	1.10	1.22	
Q5	Experimental	19	3.16	0.93	0.87	0.945
	Control	43	3.18	1.27	1.60	

game; however 4 out of the 5 did confirm that playing the game did help them to practice capturing their thoughts. This can mean that the game helped to remind them of capturing their thoughts, possibly in a more organized manner. These results also reinforce the conclusion of Study 1, because 4 out of 5 people answered that they got more familiar with the thought capturing habit after the experiment ended. The results before and after are shown, respectively, on Tables 3 and 4. Refer to Appendix B and C for the questions.

Table 3. Answers before playing the game in study 2.

Q#	1	2	3	4	5
P1	1	Most of the Time	Always	I only keep them in my head	4
P2	1	About Half the Time	Always	On Paper	5
P3	1	Most of the time	Most of the Time	On Paper	5
P4	1	Sometimes	Sometimes	Digitally	3
P5	5	About Half the Time	About Half the Time	On Paper	3

Table 4. Answers after playing the game in study 2.

Q#	1	2	3	4	5	6
P1	1	Most of the time	About half the time	I only keep them in my head	4	All the time
P2	3	Sometimes	Sometimes	On paper	2	Sometimes
P3	4	Most of the time	Most of the time	On paper	5	Sometimes
P4	4	About half the time	Always	On paper	5	All the time
P5	3	About half the time	About half the time	On paper	5	Never

Discussion. The number of participants was limited and, in hindsight, the study should have been longer for the hypothesis being tested. In addition, it is hard to say how truthful the answers are. Nonetheless, it seems clear that playing everyday for about a week is not enough to increase the habit of a player to capture their thoughts externally. We believe a longer study will be needed to assess with more accuracy the effectiveness of the game for actually forming a habit.

5   Conclusion

Strong productivity habits are crucial for the next generation of knowledge workers, but most students are not sufficiently supported in developing such habits.

Due to their ability to engage players for extended periods, games have the potential to help create such habits. We presented *BusyBusy*, a serious game that helps students learn to capture and clear up their thoughts, following the steps of the proven Getting Things Done (GTD) methodology.

Preliminary evaluation has shown that playing *BusyBusy* raises the player's awareness of the value of capturing. Further research will be required to assess how effective *BusyBusy* is in creating and strengthening the player's capturing habit and what the limits of its applicability are.

We believe that *BusyBusy* provides a solid base to explore the acquisition of other habits in the GTD methodology. A natural development could include, for example, mini-games aimed at creating an in-game daily plan, to build the habits related to the *organizing* step. As always, the key for such habit building mechanisms will have to focus on keeping players engaged and rewarded for longer streaks. This, in turn, will require more content to be developed, most likely using advanced adaptation and procedural generation methods [11].

Acknowledgment. We thank David Allen and Arjan Broere for their support, enthusiasm and inspiring comments throughout this project.

Appendix A   Survey Short Term Study

(Introduction) Thank you for taking the time to participate in this study measuring awareness and valuation of the capturing habit. The capturing habit is introduced by David Allen in his work Getting Things Done®. It refers to the habit of capturing your thoughts related to actions (such as buy milk, call a friend, study a chapter for a course) in a medium outside of your head. The survey contains 5 multiple choice questions and should take 2 min to complete. Your response will be completely anonymous.

(Q1) How familiar are you with the capturing principle?
(Q2) Where do you capture your thoughts?
(Q3) How often do you currently capture your thoughts, related to an action, outside of your head?
(Q4) How valuable is it for you to capture your thoughts outside of your head?
(Q5) How aware are you of the value of capturing thoughts outside of your head?

Appendix B   Survey Before Long Term Study

(Introduction) Thank you for taking the time to participate in this study measuring awareness and valuation of the capturing habit. The capturing habit is introduced by David Allen in his work Getting Things Done. It refers to the habit of capturing your thoughts related to actions (which take more than say 2 min, such as buy milk, call a friend, study a chapter for a course) in a medium outside of your head.

(**Q1**) How familiar are you with the capturing principle?
(**Q2**) How often do you currently capture your thoughts, related to an action, outside of your head?
(**Q3**) How often would you like to capture your thoughts, related to an action, outside of your head?
(**Q4**) Where do you capture your thoughts?
(**Q5**) How valuable is it for you to capture your thoughts outside of your head?

Appendix C   Survey After Long Term Study

(**Introduction**) Thank you for taking the time to participate in this study measuring awareness and valuation of the capturing habit. This is the final step of the experiment, hope you enjoyed it :)

(**Q1**) How familiar are you with the capturing principle?
(**Q2**) How often do you currently capture your thoughts, related to an action, outside of your head?
(**Q3**) How often would you like to capture your thoughts, related to an action, outside of your head?
(**Q4**) Where do you capture your thoughts?
(**Q5**) How valuable is it for you to capture your thoughts outside of your head?
(**Q6**) Has playing the game helped you capture your own thoughts externally?

References

1. Allen, D.: Getting Things Done: The Art of Stress-Free Productivity. Penguin, New York (2001)
2. Bada, S.O., Olusegun, S.: Constructivism learning theory: a paradigm for teaching and learning. J. Res. Method Educ. **5**(6), 66–70 (2015)
3. Clark, A., Chalmers, D.: The extended mind. Analysis **58**, 1 (1998)
4. Czerwinski, M., Horvitz, E., Wilhite, S.: A diary study of task switching and interruptions. In: Conference on Human factors in Computing Systems (SIGCHI) (2004)
5. Driscoll, M.P.: Psychology of Learning. Allyn and Bacon, Boston (2000)
6. Duffy, T.M., Bednar, A.K.: Attempting to come to grips with alternative perspectives. Educ. Technol. **31**(9), 12–15 (1991)
7. Evans, W., Kelly, B.: Pre-registration diploma student nurse stress and coping measures. Nurse Educ. Today **24**(6), 473–482 (2004)
8. HabitRPG Inc: Habitica (2020). nirvanahq.com. Accessed 05 July 2020
9. Heylighen, F., Vidal, C.: Getting things done: the science behind stress-free productivity. Long Range Plan. **41**(6), 585–605 (2008)
10. Jin, P.: Efficacy of tai chi, brisk walking, meditation, and reading in reducing mental and emotional stress. J. Psychosom. Res. **36**(4), 361–370 (1992)

11. Lopes, R., Eisemann, E., Bidarra, R.: Authoring adaptive game world generation. IEEE Trans. Games **10**(1), 42–55 (2018)
12. Stults-Kolehmainen, M., Sinha, R.: The effects of stress on physical activity and exercise. Sports Med. **44**(1), 81–121 (2014). https://doi.org/10.1007/s40279-013-0090-5
13. Murphy, R.J., Gray, S.A., Sterling, G., Reeves, K., DuCette, J.: A comparative study of professional student stress. J. Dent. Educ. **73**(3), 328–337 (2009)
14. Nirvanahq Inc: Nirvana for GTD (2020). nirvanahq.com. Accessed 05 July 2020
15. nTask: nTask (2020). ntaskmanager.com. Accessed 05 July 2020
16. Raelin, J.A.: Work-based (not classroom) learning as the apt preparation for the practice of management. Manag. Teach. Rev. **1**(1), 43–51 (2016)
17. Raelin, J.A.: Work-based (not classroom) learning as the apt preparation for the practice of management. Manag. Teach. Rev. **1**(1), 43–51 (2016)
18. Solomon, L.J., Rothblum, E.D.: Academic procrastination: frequency and cognitive-behavioral correlates. J. Couns. Psychol. **31**(4), 503 (1984)
19. SuperBetter, LLC: SuperBetter (2020). superbetter.com Accessed 05 July 2020
20. Tice, D.M., Baumeister, R.F.: Longitudinal study of procrastination, performance, stress, and health: the costs and benefits of dawdling. Psychol. Sci. **8**(6), 454–458 (1997)

A Serious Game for Changing Mindsets About Loans for Home Retrofitting

Olivier Dikken, Kushal Prakash, Bart Roseboom, Ana Rubio, Sander Østvik, Mijael Bueno, Nestor Z. Salamon, and Rafael Bidarra[✉]

Delft University of Technology, Delft, The Netherlands
R.Bidarra@tudelft.nl

Abstract. Adding energy-saving products to your house can benefit the economy, the environment and your living comfort. However, these products are very costly, and many people cannot afford them using their own savings. There exist several options for funding these projects, but people do not take advantage of such due to lack of information and the common negative view on using external funding. Psychological objections on taking loans include future time perspective, perception of short time rewards and connotation of loans itself. This paper presents a serious game aimed at changing people's mindset on taking loans to retrofit energy into their homes; *Supreme Green Time Machine* is a tycoon game in which you can acquire energy-saving products for your home. A main mechanic in the game is the opportunity to take loans to fund the purchase of these upgrades. Combined with other underlying mechanics, such as the time progress and social feedback, the game targets the different psychological objections to long term loans for home retrofitting. From a preliminary evaluation, we conclude that Supreme Green Time Machine effectively succeeds in making players more positive towards using loans to retrofit their homes.

Keywords: Serious games · Persuasive games · Home retrofitting · Energy finance · Future time perspective · Sustainability

1 Introduction

Due to environmental considerations, there is an increasing pressure to lower our gas emissions and use cleaner energy. Having energy-saving products in a house helps to lower such emissions and brings benefits to the house owner and the people living there. Still, people are hesitant to invest on retrofitting energy to their house due to the high investment cost.

One of the solutions to the high cost of products is for private home owners to take loans to fund their retrofitting project. These loans are often encouraged by the government [10] and have some of the lowest interest rates on the market [14]. However, this is still not a popular solution, as many home owners do not realize the benefits. We approach this problem with the following question: *How could*

© Springer Nature Switzerland AG 2020
I. Marfisi-Schottman et al. (Eds.): GALA 2020, LNCS 12517, pp. 347–361, 2020.
https://doi.org/10.1007/978-3-030-63464-3_33

a game help change people's mindset about using loans to fund energy-saving products for their house?

We target this question by designing and testing a serious game. The game aims at positively changing the player's mindset on taking loans for installing energy-saving products at home. Using games for educative and persuasive purposes has grown in popularity the last years, including environmental awareness [1,3,13,16]. The financial aspect makes the retrofitting a complex problem, and there are several underlying psychological factors that need to be tackled together in order to change someone's mindset. Nonetheless, people's generally negative connotation to loans, the general focus on short term rewards - and the unavailability of *future time perspective* (FTP) visualizations, weight heavily on how home owners feel about taking loans for investments such as retrofitting.

We present *Supreme Green Time Machine*, a serious game to change this mindset and create a positive view on the long-term benefits of loans applied to retrofitting. The FTP problem is tackled by speeding up time to quickly show the player the long term rewards. The game provides a simplified loan system that allows the player to pay back their loans using their savings - providing a more positive connotation towards repaying loans. As for the problem of people's unawareness of the short term benefits of energy-saving products, we use a feedback system providing both visual and statistical instructional information, which emphasises the immediate impact of their actions.

Supreme Green Time Machine was evaluated through surveys, answered during playtest-sessions, with people in the target audience of private home owners.

2   Related Work

Serious games, when integrated into real life, have previously been shown to have positive impact on the attitude and behaviour of household owners when it comes to energy conservation [7]. Quite a few games have been made within the energy domain, including: The Power House [2], Energy Chickens [13], EcoIsland [11] and Powersaver Game [8]. The latter study contains a comparison of previous energy games and points out some shortcomings when it comes to the implementation of gamification and the lack of pre- and post-measurements.

Previous research [9,12] point out that the lack of information about the different aspects of house retrofitting is an important factor as to why there have been so few home retrofits. In a research done on energy labels for dwellings [5], they conclude that the use of energy efficiency labels on homes can help with stimulating people to get a retrofit for their home. This shows that using visual feedback can give people a more positive mindset towards retrofitting their house. Nonetheless, the main reason people have interest in installing insulation is to improve comfort, while the main driver behind the interest in installing solar panels is the perceived cost reductions [4].

Furthermore, people discount the utility of future rewards depending on their future time perspective - the concept on how people perceive results that are happening in the distant future. Most of the people do not appreciate rewards that will happen in more than fifteen to twenty years into the future [15]. This raises a challenge in our domain, as it usually takes several years before home owners reap the rewards from retrofitting their houses. Research suggests that rewards at a time beyond a player's "future window" have no value at all to the player [6]. This is mainly due to lack of interest and not because impulsive instant-reward decisions get priority. Interestingly, different players have different future time perspectives: a player with a deep/long FTP sees their current actions as more valuable because they lead to future goals that are more strongly valued [15]. These findings can be useful to interpret why a player does not partake in a project with guaranteed long term profits. These are mindsets that we try to overcome in the design and evaluation of our game.

Finally, different incentives have different effects on the present performance of an individual. Generally stating that an activity serves the participant's future does not yield positive effects, as it does not allow the participant to fully grasp the specific meaning and importance of the activity [15]. Furthermore, pointing out the future importance of one's present behaviour might only result in beneficial effects if people have an optimistic outlook toward their future. This shows the importance of not only stating long term gains to the player, but also make them aware of the short term benefits. These aspects are targeted within our game and described in the following.

3   Game Design

Supreme Green Time Machine aims at changing the player's mindset on taking a loan to fund the retrofitting of their house. To achieve this, we address psychological aspects such as future time perspective (FTP), perception of short term rewards and the negative connotation of loans.

The game is a tycoon-type game aimed at private home owners. The essence of the game is to upgrade your house with energy-saving products to benefit from living comfort and environmental improvements. It encourages players to consider taking loans to help paying for these upgrades. The game also combines a time speed-up mechanism and a reinforced feedback system, which increases the impact of the simulation by highlighting the positive outcome of investing, through loans, on energy retrofitting. An interactive play-through lasts about ten minutes, running an experience of fifteen years of in-game time. This strongly helps realizing the long term rewards, as well as the short term personal, environmental and social benefits.

3.1   Gameplay

The gameplay revolves around the player's house in a virtual neighborhood. The player will be interacting with and observing the simulation to monitor how their upgrade-choices and outside events play out. During this time, the player will also be buying energy-saving products to improve their home, while facing seasonal challenges (e.g., weather, power failures, etc.) and receiving occasional feedback (e.g., the neighbors' competition for greener and more efficient homes). The player has to balance the environmental and living comfort scores of the house along with their finances.

To help the player on the financial side, the option of taking a loan is available to fully or partially pay for buying a product. An upgrade menu shows players the products they can install into the house along with the funding alternative. Through a clear information overview, the player can keep track of the progression of his/her house, as well as compare the different strategies used by the neighbors – from which useful insights can be drawn. The game mechanic is balanced to help the player get the best of the possible loans: if desired, a joker can be used once to go back in time two years and try applying a different strategy. At the end of the game, players get to see how well they fared against the neighbors, and who managed to achieve the best environmental impact, living comfort and financial outcome. An overview of the gameplay is illustrated in Fig. 1.

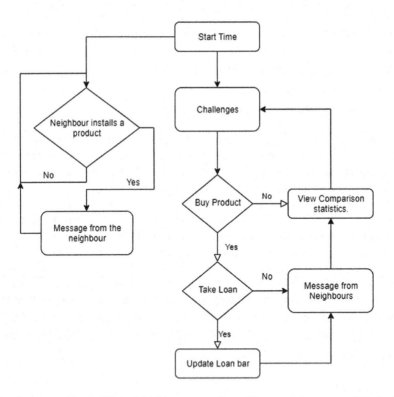

Fig. 1. Supreme Green Time Machine game flow. Players take care of their home by buying and installing energy-saving products, while, in parallel, the neighborhood runs similar retrofitting actions. At the end of a fast-forward simulation, players are presented with the benefits of taking a loan to upgrade their houses.

3.2   Persuasion Mechanisms

The mechanisms included in the game design of Supreme Green Time Machine to facilitate a gentle change in the players' mindset include: (i) providing a future time perspective (FTP) through an accelerated simulation, (ii) a visual feedback system that shows the benefits of greener retrofitting solutions for the house and neighborhood, (iii) a social feedback loop based on common neighborhood emotions, and (iv) a simplified financial model that encourages the players to confidently take a loan with long term returns. In the following, we describe the design and mechanics details.

Accelerated Time Simulation. While home owners could read about the benefits of house retrofitting in, say, a brochure or website, the non-personal character of these texts does not provide a direct FTP, nor the appeal to research how that would apply on their own house and neighborhood. Instead, through actively visualizing and experiencing their options in the game, the long term effects of the players' choices are brought directly to their attention, elucidating what otherwise would just seem abstract to them. This simulation allows players to "quickly" experience events that would spread over fifteen years, and draw practical conclusions of their consequences.

Visual Feedback System. The visual feedback system notifies players of the effects of their different actions. Instead of plainly telling the player 'what causes what', we chose to discretely raise awareness of the short term benefits that come with installing energy-saving products to their homes. After deploying a product, the player scores on financial, environmental and living comfort are updated and visualized in the environment. Seeing these direct benefits of each product, players get encouraged to consider buying specific products that further increase scores on the long term. Moreover, these notifications help conveying the impact on the environment around the player's house. For example, if environmental

Fig. 2. Fog is present while the environmental score is low (left), and will disappear as the player install greener products and influences the neighbors to take similar actions (right).

scores get low, pollution clouds represented by fog start forming, in analogy to the bad air quality in the real world. Implicitly, players are stimulated to take action, installing greener products (see Fig. 2).

Social Feedback Loop. In addition to the visual feedback above, players can also be socially challenged to improve the overall neighborhood environmental conditions, by being confronted with their neighborhood score. Living in the same area, and often with similar financial and social status, neighbors tend to do status comparisons in real life. This recognizable behavior is mimicked in the game, further increasing the player's immersion and influencing their choices.

Receiving feedback from your neighbors – who know what you have installed – is another effective form of short term reward. This is achieved in the game through short messages from the neighbors, which target player's emotions, namely satisfaction and jealousy. At times, a neighbor will compliment after the player installed a product that improves the whole environment. This might induce a positive, satisfactory emotion, creating positive feelings as instantaneous rewards. Conversely, some neighbors might be a step ahead within the game, exhibiting better scores due to a smarter strategy; in that case, they will unmistakably make the player aware of this through appropriate messages. These might induce some jealousy, but hopefully also inspire to reflect and learn, as well as strive for competition.

Financial Model. Supreme Green Time Machine is supported by a simplified financial model to enable taking loans and purchasing energy-saving products. The player starts with a base capital that can be used to buy products. In addition, the player receives a yearly amount representing the household income. Depending on the price of the product of your choice, it can be either integrally paid with saved money or partially financed by taking a loan. Loan amounts are limited each year, and the total needs to be taken into consideration when choosing a purchasing strategy.

Each product in the game will "give back" a certain amount of money every year, i.e. the value of its energy savings. Each year after the product is installed, its savings will be subtracted from the loan that was used for that product; when this loan gets to zero, that amount will go directly into the capital of the player. The incoming capital is also affected by simulation challenges the player is faced with, such as a variety of Winter and Summer events. In case the household is not prepared for such seasonal events, a certain amount is deduced; otherwise, the household withstands it, indicating a well planned investment. With such events and a measurable return on investment, the financial model allows players to quantify the extent to which the the invested capital is returned, as well as to get a clear insight into the timeline of that process. A complete overview of the financial model used is presented in Fig. 3.

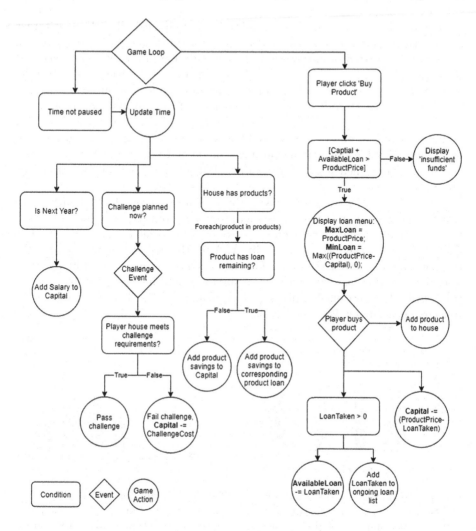

Fig. 3. Complete diagram of the financial model, including loans, seasonal events, annual salary and return on investment.

4   Evaluation

Supreme Green Time Machine's potential on changing people's mindset was validated through a user study based on the following hypothesis: *A game can be significantly more effective than a plain informative text in positively changing the mindset of a house owner, regarding taking loans to retrofit their house.* Assessing this hypothesis allows us to validate if the game adds any value to the solutions already in use to inform people about retrofitting and loans. We evaluated whether the game positively informs players on this matter by conducting multiple playtesting sessions with pre- and post-game questionnaires.

The playtesting sessions had a total of 51 participants, all within our target group: private home owners. The participants were presented with an informative text, which consisted of information on energy-saving products, their price and their impact. The text also stressed the importance and advantages of having more house owners retrofit their homes. Additional information on how to use loans to fund these products was also provided. The reason for an informative text as part of the (pre-)evaluation is to comply with our hypothesis, and also minimize potential bias of uninformed home owners: participants knowing little or nothing about energy-saving products might have answered that the game heavily improved their mindset as a substantial volume of novel information was presented.

Next, the participants were given the pre-game survey. In this survey, we asked about their mindset towards energy-saving products, using loans to fund them as well as some general questions on their current living situation. The questionnaire is available on Appendix A. After the first survey was conducted, the participants played the game for one session (ten minutes). Finally, they were requested to answer the follow up survey, evaluating their new mindset on the previously questioned aspects (see Appendix B). Evaluated answers were collected as a 7 point Likert-scale.

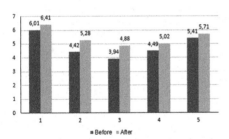

Fig. 4. Outcome of both surveys before and after the game. Questions are presented in Appendices A and B. (Color figure online)

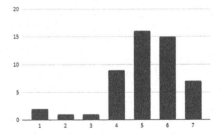

Fig. 5. Distribution of participants' answers to question B #8, on the perceived degree of extra information provided by the game.

Figure 4 shows the survey results for the Likert answers. Blue and the orange bars show the average score given by the participants for the question in the pre- and post-game surveys, respectively. The average score is higher for all of the questions in the survey after the game. The first two questions (Appendix A #7 and #8 (pre), Appendix B #2 and #3 (post)) consist of choices regarding six different products. In order to generate the score per participant, we averaged the scores per product given by the participant. In the third bar (questions #9 and #4, pre- and post), we asked how likely the participant was to use loans to fund the installation of an energy-saving product and observed an increase of almost one point. The participants went from averaging at almost 4 (neutral) to just roughly 5 (somewhat likely) after playing the game. Overall, the questionnaires show that the game did change the participants attitude towards being more likely to acquire energy-saving products and use loans to fund them.

The participants were also asked to which degree they felt that the game provided them with new information. Figure 5 shows that a majority of the participants felt that the game gave them extra information, averaging a score of 5.14 (1 equals "no new information" and 7 "a lot of new information"). With regards to our hypothesis, we can affirm that the game does add value to existing solutions, and manages to improve the mindset of the people playing it in a positive way with regards to using loans to retrofit their houses.

5   Conclusion

Despite all its advantages, retrofitting a house with energy-saving products still struggles with a number of financial, social and psychological objections, including: a lack of future time perspective, deficient perception on short term benefits, and a general negative connotation of taking loans.

We investigated how a game could help change people's mindset on taking loans to fund such projects. For this research, we designed *Supreme Green Time Machine*, a novel tycoon-type game aimed at private home owners. The game design features a careful combination of persuasion mechanisms, providing future time perspective through accelerated simulation, instant visual feedback, a powerful social feedback loop, and an effective financial model.

Our prototype game evaluation has shown that people previously hesitant did adopt a more positive attitude towards taking loans for greener energy after playing the game. We can therefore conclude that Supreme Green Time Machine positively helps change people's mindset about taking loans to fund their home retrofitting projects.

Acknowledgments. The authors thank Gerard van Smeden and De Energiebespaarders for their help and expertise during the development and evaluation of the game.

A   Survey after text

Thank you for participating in this survey! You have read an informative text about energy savings. We would now like to know about some of your views on this topic and your thoughts on installing energy saving products to your home.

*Required

1. **Please enter your name (This will only be used to link your two surveys together)** *

   _____

2. **What is your age?** *
   Mark only one oval.

   ◯ Under 20
   ◯ 20 - 29
   ◯ 30 - 39
   ◯ 40 - 49
   ◯ 50 - 59
   ◯ 60 - 69
   ◯ 70 - 79
   ◯ 80+

3. **In what type of home do you live in?** *
   Mark only one oval.

   ◯ Apartment
   ◯ Cornerhouse
   ◯ Detached house
   ◯ Duplex
   ◯ Row house
   ◯ Other

4. **For how many years have you been living in your current house?** *
   Mark only one oval.

   ◯ Less than 1 year
   ◯ 1 - 2 years
   ◯ 2 - 3 years
   ◯ 3 - 5 years
   ◯ 5 - 7 years
   ◯ 7 - 10 years
   ◯ 10+ years

5. **Do you have any of the following energy saving products in/on your house already?** *
   Tick all that apply.

   ☐ Solar Panels

   ☐ Floor insulation

   ☐ Roof insulation

   ☐ Wall insulation

   ☐ Window insulation

   ☐ Electric heating pump

   ☐ None of the above

6. **If you have one of the above mentioned energy saving products, did you use a loan to fund the installation of that product?** *
   Mark only one oval.

   ◯ Yes, for all of them

   ◯ Yes, for some of them

   ◯ No

   ◯ I did not install them

7. **If these products were free, how likely would you be to install them?** *
   Mark only one oval per row.

	Very unlikely	Unlikely	Somewhat unlikely	Neutral	Somewhat likely	Likely	Very likely
Solar Panels	◯	◯	◯	◯	◯	◯	◯
Floor insulation	◯	◯	◯	◯	◯	◯	◯
Roof insulation	◯	◯	◯	◯	◯	◯	◯
Wall insulation	◯	◯	◯	◯	◯	◯	◯
Window insulation	◯	◯	◯	◯	◯	◯	◯
Electric heating pump	◯	◯	◯	◯	◯	◯	◯

8. **With their normal cost, how likely are you to install any of the energy saving products?** *
   Mark only one oval per row.

	Very unlikely	Unlikely	Somewhat unlikely	Neutral	Somewhat likely	Likely	Very likely
Solar Panels	◯	◯	◯	◯	◯	◯	◯
Floor insulation	◯	◯	◯	◯	◯	◯	◯
Roof insulation	◯	◯	◯	◯	◯	◯	◯
Wall insulation	◯	◯	◯	◯	◯	◯	◯
Window insulation	◯	◯	◯	◯	◯	◯	◯
Electric heating pump	◯	◯	◯	◯	◯	◯	◯

9. **How likely are you to use a loan to fund the installation of a energy saving product?** *
Mark only one oval.

	1	2	3	4	5	6	7	
Very unlikely	◯	◯	◯	◯	◯	◯	◯	Very likely

Survey after text

10. **How important are the following factors to you when it comes to the reason for installing energy saving products to your home?** *
Mark only one oval per row.

	Not important	Neutral	Important
Good for the environment	◯	◯	◯
Increased living comfort	◯	◯	◯
Saving money	◯	◯	◯

11. **How likely are you to further explore your options when it comes to getting loans and/or subsidies for installing energy saving products?** *
Mark only one oval.

	1	2	3	4	5	6	7	
Very unlikely	◯	◯	◯	◯	◯	◯	◯	Very likely

12. **You have read the example of the solar panels paying down their own price in 10 years. How does this fact impact your decision on acquiring energy saving products?** *
Mark only one oval.

	1	2	3	4	5	6	7	
Very negatively	◯	◯	◯	◯	◯	◯	◯	Very positively

B   Survey after game

Thank you for participating in this survey! You have played our game about retrofitting your house with energy saving products. We would now, again, like to know about some of your views on this topic and your thoughts on installing energy saving products to your home.

*Required

1. **Please enter your name (This will only be used to link your two surveys together) ***

2. **If these products were free, how likely would you be to install them? ***
Mark only one oval per row.

	Very unlikely	Unlikely	Somewhat unlikely	Neutral	Somewhat likely	Likely	Very likely
Solar Panels	◯	◯	◯	◯	◯	◯	◯
Floor insulation	◯	◯	◯	◯	◯	◯	◯
Roof insulation	◯	◯	◯	◯	◯	◯	◯
Wall insulation	◯	◯	◯	◯	◯	◯	◯
Window insulation	◯	◯	◯	◯	◯	◯	◯
Electric heating pump	◯	◯	◯	◯	◯	◯	◯

3. **With their normal cost, how likely are you to install any of the energy saving products? ***
Mark only one oval per row.

	Very unlikely	Unlikely	Somewhat unlikely	Neutral	Somewhat likely	Likely	Very likely
Solar Panels	◯	◯	◯	◯	◯	◯	◯
Floor insulation	◯	◯	◯	◯	◯	◯	◯
Roof insulation	◯	◯	◯	◯	◯	◯	◯
Wall insulation	◯	◯	◯	◯	◯	◯	◯
Window insulation	◯	◯	◯	◯	◯	◯	◯
Electric heating pump	◯	◯	◯	◯	◯	◯	◯

4. **How likely are you to use a loan to fund the installation of a energy saving product? ***
Mark only one oval.

	1	2	3	4	5	6	7	
Very unlikely	◯	◯	◯	◯	◯	◯	◯	Very likely

5. **How important are the following factors to you when it comes to the reason for installing energy saving products to your home? ***
Mark only one oval per row.

	Not important	Neutral	Important
Good for the environment	◯	◯	◯
Increased living comfort	◯	◯	◯
Saving money	◯	◯	◯

6. **How likely are you to explore your options when it comes to getting loans and/or subsidies for installing energy saving products? ***
Mark only one oval.

	1	2	3	4	5	6	7	
Very unlikely	◯	◯	◯	◯	◯	◯	◯	Very likely

7. **After playing the game, you have hopefully seen how the product savings pay back the loans. How does this fact impact your decision on acquiring energy saving products? ***
Mark only one oval.

	1	2	3	4	5	6	7	
Very negatively	◯	◯	◯	◯	◯	◯	◯	Very positively

8. **To what degree do you feel that the game gives you extra information beyond the text you read earlier? ***
Mark only one oval.

	1	2	3	4	5	6	7	
No new information	◯	◯	◯	◯	◯	◯	◯	A lot of new information

References

1. Appel, Y., et al.: A serious game to inform young citizens on canal water maintenance. In: Liapis, A., Yannakakis, G.N., Gentile, M., Ninaus, M. (eds.) GALA 2019. LNCS, vol. 11899, pp. 394–403. Springer, Cham (2019). https://doi.org/10.1007/978-3-030-34350-7_38
2. Bang, M., Torstensson, C., Katzeff, C.: The powerhhouse: a persuasive computer game designed to raise awareness of domestic energy consumption. In: IJsselsteijn, W.A., de Kort, Y.A.W., Midden, C., Eggen, B., van den Hoven, E. (eds.) PERSUASIVE 2006. LNCS, vol. 3962, pp. 123–132. Springer, Heidelberg (2006). https://doi.org/10.1007/11755494_18
3. Mac an Bhaird, L., et al.: Learning geothermal energy basics with the serious game hotpipe. In: Liapis, A., Yannakakis, G.N., Gentile, M., Ninaus, M. (eds.) GALA 2019. LNCS, vol. 11899, pp. 312–321. Springer, Cham (2019). https://doi.org/10.1007/978-3-030-34350-7_30
4. Collins, M., Curtis, J.A.: Identification of the information gap in residential energy efficiency: how information asymmetry can be mitigated to induce energy efficiency renovations. Technical report, The Economic and Social Research Institute (ESRI), Dublin (2017)
5. Comerford, D.A., Lange, I., Moro, M.: Proof of concept that requiring energy labels for dwellings can induce retrofitting. Energy Econo. **69**, 204–212 (2018)
6. Fellows, L.K., Farah, M.J.: Dissociable elements of human foresight: a role for the ventromedial frontal lobes in framing the future, but not in discounting future rewards. Neuropsychologia **43**(8), 1214–1221 (2005)
7. Fijnheer, J.D., van Oostendorp, H.: Steps to design a household energy game. In: de De Gloria, A., Veltkamp, R. (eds.) GALA 2015. LNCS, vol. 9599, pp. 12–22. Springer, Cham (2016). https://doi.org/10.1007/978-3-319-40216-1_2
8. Fijnheer, J.D., van Oostendorp, H., Veltkamp, R.: Household energy conservation intervention: a game versus dashboard comparison. Int. J. Serious Games **6**(3), 23–26 (2019)

9. Hrovatin, N., Zorić, J.: Determinants of energy-efficient home retrofits in slovenia: the role of information sources. Energy and Buildings **180**, 42–50 (2018)

10. Kerr, N., Winskel, M.: Private Household Investment in Home Energy Retrofit-Reviewing the Evidence and Designing Effective Public Policy. ClimateXChange, Edinburgh (2018)

11. Kimura, H., Nakajima, T.: Designing persuasive applications to motivate sustainable behavior in collectivist cultures. PsychNology J. **9**, 7–28 (2011)

12. Li, I., Magner, P., Sanders, C.: Increasing homeowner demand for energy efficiency retrofits: recommendations for the north carolina building performance association. Master's thesis, Nicholas School of the Environment, Duke University, North Carolina, USA (2017)

13. Orland, B., Ram, N., Lang, D., Houser, K., Kling, N., Coccia, M.: Saving energy in an office environment: a serious game intervention. Energy and Buildings **74**, 43–52 (2014)

14. Schleich, J., Faure, C., Meissner, T.: Adoption of retrofit measures among homeowners in eu countries: The effects of access to capital and debt aversion. Technical report, Working Paper Sustainability and Innovation (2019)

15. Simons, J., Vansteenkiste, M., Lens, W., Lacante, M.: Placing motivation and future time perspective theory in a temporal perspective. Educ. Psychol. Rev. **16**(2), 121–139 (2004). https://doi.org/10.1023/B:EDPR.0000026609.94841.2f

16. Yiannakoulias, N., Gordon, J.N., Darlington, J.C.: The decision game: a serious game approach to understanding environmental risk management decisions. J. Risk Res. **23**(1), 81–94 (2020)

Intrinsic Motivation in Serious Gaming
A Case Study

Heinrich Söbke[1]($\boxtimes$) (ID), Uwe Arnold[2], and Michael Montag[3] (ID)

[1] Bauhaus-Universität Weimar, Bauhaus-Institute for Infrastructure Solutions (b.is),
Coudraystr. 7, 99423 Weimar, Germany
heinrich.soebke@uni-weimar.de

[2] AHP GmbH & Co. KG, Karl-Heinrich-Ulrichs-Strasse 11, 10787 Berlin, Germany
arnold@ahpkg.de

[3] Hochschule Magdeburg-Stendal, Wendstraße 30, 39576 Stendal, Germany
michael.montag@h2.de

Abstract. Gaming is intrinsically motivated – the motivation for gaming lies within the activity itself. One of the rationales for serious gaming, i.e. using the medium of games for purposes other than entertainment, is the assumption of high motivation fostered by games. Both theoretical discourses and evidence-based meta studies question this assumption. However, together with this assumption, a central justification of high production efforts required for games would also be eliminated, since an equivalent learning effectiveness could presumably also be achieved with media produced more efficiently. Therefore, this study examines whether serious gaming achieves a higher motivation than other learning activities. For three learning activities (serious gaming, lecture and field trip) being part of a Master's program in Environmental Engineering, the motivation is measured using the instruments SIMS (Situational Motivational Scale) and QCM (Questionnaire to Assess Current Motivation in Learning Situations). The results show an increased intrinsic motivation for serious gaming at higher perceived learning outcomes and lower perceived mental load. Thus, it appears that serious gaming can contribute to an increased motivation. Further, by discussing factors that influence the selection and application of games, the article contributes to attainment of high intrinsic motivation in serious gaming.

Keywords: Intrinsic motivation · Extrinsic motivation · Learning activity · SIMS · QCM

1 Introduction

One of the factors used in serious gaming to achieve further goals besides entertainment, such as learning, is the motivating effect of games [1]. Motivation is a complex construct used to explain the direction, persistence and intensity of activities [2]. One categorization of motivation distinguishes between intrinsic motivation, i.e. motivation directed towards the activity itself, and extrinsic motivation, i.e. motivation directed towards external stimuli outside the activity [3]. The effects of games on motivation usually refer

© Springer Nature Switzerland AG 2020
I. Marfisi-Schottman et al. (Eds.): GALA 2020, LNCS 12517, pp. 362–371, 2020.
https://doi.org/10.1007/978-3-030-63464-3_34

to intrinsic motivation. For example, Callois [4] defines games as unproductive, i.e. no external results are expected. There is a discussion whether the unproductive character of games and their use for other purposes outside the game are contradictory, since the intrinsic motivation is compromised by the combination of both, e.g. [5, 6]. Specific measuring instruments for serious games also substantiate the fact that serious games hold a special status regarding motivation. The instrument EGameFlow [7], for example, was developed to measure the extent to which players are in a state of flow that is considered most suitable for learning processes. Furthermore, there is some evidence that the development of serious games is very complex and hence not always fruitful, i.e. partly resulting in reduced motivation. Papert [8] mentions "shavian reversals – offspring that keep the bad features of each parent and lose the good ones – are visible in most software products that claim to come from a mating of education and entertainment". The repeatedly quoted term "choco dipped broccoli" (or "chocolate covered broccoli") goes back to Bruckman [9]: "fun is often treated like a sugar coating to be added to an educational core". Furthermore, Egenfeldt-Nielsen [10] comments "edutainment started as a serious attempt to create computer games that taught children different subjects. Arguably it ended up as a caricature of computer games and a reactionary use of learning theory". Likewise, Dondi and Moretti [11] argue that there is not yet a common regulatory structure for the generation of high-quality games. Additionally, not all learners are receptive to serious games, e.g. a fraction of learners prefers to learn using conventional media [12].

All the phenomena mentioned tend to reduce the motivational effect of games in serious gaming. Accordingly, a meta-study by Wouters et al. [13] is not able to prove any effect of serious games on motivation. However, if no motivational effects of games can be demonstrated, then the question arises as to whether – in view of the high production efforts of games – other media showing a comparable learning effectiveness, that are more efficient to produce, might be preferred. Thus, this study examines the research question of whether higher motivation can be proven for games in educational contexts.

The following terms are used in this article: serious game stands for a game developed specifically for purposes beyond entertainment. Serious gaming is used whenever a game – be it an entertainment game or a serious game – is used for purposes beyond entertainment. This distinction is relevant as in the learning activity investigated the game SimCity, originally developed as an entertainment game, is used for learning purposes. When referring to the specific learning activities of the study, the term gaming is used for short, although it is actually serious gaming due to the definition above. The further article is structured as follows: In the next section the methodology is described, in Sect. 3 the results are presented, which are then discussed in Sect. 4. Finally, the article ends with the conclusions.

2 Methodology

Context. The study is intended to measure the motivation of students involved in a serious gaming learning activity. To facilitate the evaluation of the measured values, same measurements should be taken for further learning activities. A reasonable opportunity for such a series of measurements was offered by the course *Infrastructure Management*" of the Master's program *Environmental Engineering*. The course consists of block events, which are held at two-week intervals. Part of the course is an established block event based on the simulation game SimCity, using an open, competitive game scenario spurring students achieving best possible results in the development of an industrial area [14]. The SimCity serious gaming block event is followed in the next block event by a field trip into the real industrial area that is also the subject of the SimCity serious gaming block event. During this field trip, which lasts about 8 h, six different locations are visited using a bus chartered. At the locations, a tour guided by stakeholders takes place giving opportunities for questioning and discussion. The third learning activity is a lecture in the block event following the excursion block event. All three learning activities are led by the same person, an experienced lecturer involved in teaching this course for almost 20 years.

Study Design and Demographics. In the three block event-based learning activities being part of the course (*gaming, field trip, lecture*) the students were asked to complete a questionnaire consisting of four sections. Participation in both the learning activities and the questionnaire was voluntary. According to the impressions of the lecturer, no student refused to fill out the questionnaire. Therefore, it should be assumed that all participants in the learning activities also completed the questionnaire being identical for all three learning activities. Out of the 29 students of the course, 17 students answered for the learning activity *gaming*, 21 students for the learning activity *field trip*, and 15 students for the learning activity *lecture*. All three learning activities were part of the same course in the same semester. The questionnaires were answered anonymously and were not assigned across the different learning activities to individual students. Age and gender of the students participating have not been surveyed. However, by conducting the course in the second semester of the Master's program, an average age of the students of about 23 years is to be assumed. An equal distribution of gender should also be concluded, since 15 of the 29 students of the course were female and 14 were male. The students' experience with the game SimCity is to be derived from a study in the same course in earlier semesters [14]: 30% of the students involved in the earlier study indicated prior experiences with SimCity.

Standardized Instruments. The questionnaire included two standardized instruments. These two instruments and their relevance for this study are described subsequently.

Situational Motivational Scale. The 16 items of the Situational Motivation Scale (SIMS) [15] were used to measure intrinsic and extrinsic motivation. The SIMS measures four types of motivation on subscales, which are attributed to the work of Ryan and Deci on self-determination theory (SDT) [3]: (1) *Intrinsic motivation* leads to activities, which are carried for the sake of the activity itself (sample item: "Because I think that this activity is interesting"). (2) *Identified regulation* belongs to extrinsic motivation and underlies self-chosen activities, which are performed for a specific external purpose (sample item: "Because I am doing it for my own good"). (3) *External regulation*, also an extrinsic motivation, is given, if a reward is to be achieved or if negative consequences are to be avoided by fixed, non-choosable behavior (sample item: "Because I am supposed to do it"). (4) Finally, *amotivation* occurs when goals do not appear to be achievable through one's own activities (sample item: "I do this activity, but I am not sure it is a good thing to pursue it"). For games, *intrinsic motivation* should be the main motivation type, since games are meant not pursuing external purposes. From the perspective of SDT, which describes the motivation for behavior as dependent on the extent to which the basic human needs of autonomy, social relatedness and competence are satisfied, *identified regulation* is to be considered more motivating than *external regulation* as *identified regulation* allows for a higher grade of autonomy. The four types of motivation are to be understood as continuum where, from the point of view of serious gaming *intrinsic motivation* is most desired and *amotivation* should be avoided.

QCM: Current Motivation in Learning Situations. Since learning is always in the focus of the examined activities, it appears reasonable to examine the motivation also from the perspective of learning. The instrument *Current Motivation in Learning Situations (QCM)* [16] is well-established in this respect. This instrument comprises 18 items and covers the four subscales *interest* (appreciation of the content of the task), *probability of success* (confidence with which the learning situation can be successfully handled), *anxiety* (fear of not being able to learn optimally due to the pressure in the learning situation) and *challenge* (interpretation of the task as a performance situation). The subscale *interest* is partly associated with intrinsic motivation.

3 Results

In the following, the results of the questionnaire are presented and discussed section by section.

3.1 Situational Motivational Scale

Figure 1 illustrates the mean values measured for the four types of motivation. The highest *intrinsic motivation* is just about reached by *gaming* (5.3), compared to the value of 5.2 for *field trip*. The *intrinsic motivation* value for *lecture* is relatively weak at 3.8. The values indicate that *gaming* achieves high *intrinsic motivation* and clearly surpasses *lecture*. This is the theoretically expected but also essential result to illustrate the strengths of serious gaming. The learning activity *field trip* achieves the highest value for *identified regulation* in addition to the very high value regarding *intrinsic motivation*. This high value may be justified by the schedule of the field trip, which on the one hand sets an external framework to be adhered to, thus reducing autonomy, but on the other hand provides a lot of information that is of interest to the students.

The learning activity *lecture* achieves the lowest motivation with the lowest values for *intrinsic motivation* (mean = 3.8) and *identified regulation* (mean = 4.6) and the highest values for *external regulation* (mean = 4.6) and *amotivation* (mean = 3.5). Of interest is the relatively high value for *amotivation* in *gaming*. A possible explanation for high *amotivation* is the non-matching gaming preferences of some of the students. This fraction of the students seems to be not challenged by the game. It is also striking that *external regulation* and *amotivation* spread more (averaged standard deviations = 1.34, min = 1.22, max = 1.46)) than *intrinsic motivation* and *identified regulation* (averaged standard deviations = 0.90, min = 0.79, max = 0.96).

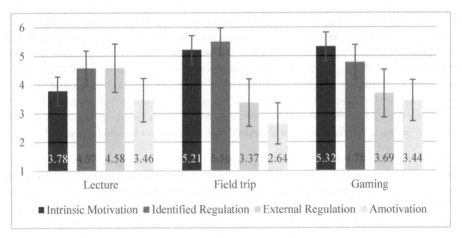

Fig. 1. SIMS subscale values per learning activity (7-point Likert scale)

To examine statistical effects, a MANOVA was conducted for all of the four subscales and revealed significant differences between the three groups ($V = 0.574$, $F(8,94) = 4.727$, $p < .001$). Univariate effects were found for *intrinsic motivation* ($F(2,49) = 13.469$, $p < .001$) and *identified regulation* ($F(2,49) = 5.285$, $p = .008$), but not for *external regulation* ($F(2, 49) = 3.070$, $p = .055$) or *amotivation* ($F(2,49) = 2.536$, $p = .089$).

Pairwise t-tests were conducted to analyze the sources of the significant univariate effects. The intrinsic motivation is significantly lower for *lecture* (mean = 3.783) compared to *field trip* (mean = 5.214; $t(34) = 4.552$, $p < .001$) as well as *gaming* (mean = 5.324; $t(30) = 4.803$, $p < .001$). No significant differences regarding intrinsic motivation were found between *field trip* and *gaming* ($t(36) = 0.368$, $p = .715$). The students also showed higher *identified regulation*, after absolving the *field trip* (mean = 5.500) compared to *lecture* (mean = 4.567; $t(34) = 3.200$, $p = .003$) and *gaming* (mean = 4.794; $t(36) = 2.595$, $p = .014$), but *identified regulation* does not differ significantly between *gaming* and *lecture* ($t(30) = 0.699$, $p = .490$).

Generally, it can be concluded in this case study that *gaming* receives better motivation than *lecture*, while the motivation shown in *gaming* and *field trip* are similar.

3.2 Mental Load and Learning Outcomes

The second section consisted of the self-defined items "How much mental load does the activity put on you?" and "How much do you learn during the activity?", each based on a 7-point Likert scale. The first item was intended to capture the perceived mental load of the student, the second item was meant to assess the personally perceived learning outcome. Interestingly, the values in Table 1 show that *lecture* seems to be by far the most demanding (mean = 4.67) before *field trip* (mean = 3.71) and *gaming* (mean = 3.65), whereas the reverse order is almost exactly the case for learning outcomes. Here *field trip* is most educative (mean = 5.38) before *gaming* (mean = 5.24). Thereafter, *lecture* follows by far (mean = 4.67). The high standard deviation for the values of *field trip* is remarkable. Both the mental load (SD = 1.454) and the learning outcomes (SD = 1.117) have the highest values compared to the other learning activities. Overall, it can be seen that *gaming* has much more advantageous values for perceived mental load and perceived learning outcomes compared to *lecture*. Again, *field trip* reaches similar mean values as *gaming*.

Table 1. Perceived mental load and perceived learning outcomes per learning activity.

		Lecture	Field trip	Gaming
Perceived mental load	Mean	4.67	3.71	3.65
	SD	0.976	1.454	1.169
Perceived learning outcome	Mean	4.53	5.38	5.24
	SD	0.834	1.117	0.970

3.3 QCM: Current Motivation in Learning Situations

Remarkable in the mean values shown in Fig. 2 are again the similar mean values for *field trip* and *gaming*. Compared to *lecture*, *interest* is one point higher, which can be explained by the more practical tasks in *field trip* and *gaming*, while in *lecture* comparatively abstract matters are explained. Similarly, the values for *anxiety* are higher for *field trip* and *gaming* - possibly due to the uncertainty if the abstract facts of the lectures are understandable. Regarding the subscale *probability of success* there are consistently high values for all learning activities, which may be explained by the lack of formal tests in all learning activities – students do not fear needing to prove their understanding immediately. In the subscale *challenge*, *gaming* achieves the highest mean value, possibly spurred on by the competition between groups during the gaming. Interestingly, *lecture* and *field trip* show the same mean value for the subscale *challenge*. Compared to reference values taken from [16], the adopted mean values of this study are within the ranges. The adopted (to the 7-point Likert scale originally suggested) mean values of the subscales *interest* and *probability of success* are to be considered quite high for the learning activities *field trip* and *gaming*.

3.4 Comments

In the last section of the questionnaire, there is an open question to comment on the learning activity and the questionnaire. The frequency of the comments varies according to the activity. For *gaming* only three comments were received (18%), two of which praised the activity highly and one of which pointed out that previous experience with SimCity is helpful. In the five comments regarding *lecture* (33%), there are three comments on how motivation could be improved: by a different form than block events, by presenting larger contexts rather than details, and by more interaction. Most of the comments (nine; 43%) are referring to *field trip*. Here it is pointed out several times

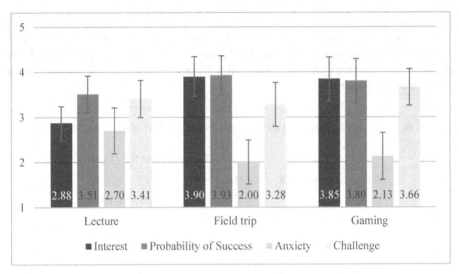

Fig. 2. QCM subscale values per learning activity (5-point Likert scale)

that due to the many locations visited the questionnaire gives only an average measure, but in fact there were large differences in the individual locations affecting motivation. Furthermore, the density of the activities is highlighted, which were perceived as very strenuous. A negative note is made of the high amount of time required for field trips in general.

The respective participation in the learning activities, measured in the questionnaires handed in, can also be seen as a measure of the attractiveness of the respective learning activity. Having 21 participants, *field trip* is the most motivating learning activity ahead of *gaming* (17 participants) and *lecture* (15 participants). In relation to this, however, it should be noted that *field trip* took place on a Friday, while the other two learning activities were offered on Saturdays, a day that is normally free of official learning activities.

4 Discussion and Limitations

The results of the study show high intrinsic motivation values for the learning activity *gaming* compared to conventional *lectures* and thus confirm the use of games for teaching. Simultaneously, it becomes clear that the learning activity *field trip* has similar levels of motivation qualifying field trips as interesting learning activity. However, *field trips* have some disadvantages compared to *gaming*: the effort to conduct *field trips* is much higher in terms of time and costs. External dependencies, such as the availability of field trip guides, are as little prevalent to *gaming* as potential physical threats to the participants on field trip sites. In addition, this case study pointed to the individual locations of the field trip being heterogeneous regarding the interest of the students. In contrast, gaming allows providing a standardized learning environment enhancing intrinsic motivation.

In the following, the limitations of the study are discussed.

Single Gaming Activity. One main limitation of the study is looking at only one serious gaming activity and thus not being universally valid.

Selection Bias. Relatively high mean values for intrinsic motivation may have arisen because participation in the events was voluntary. Due to the lack of obligation to participate, it can be assumed that a selection bias is given, since the students are usually well informed about the expected content of the learning activities by word of mouth.

Game. The game used, SimCity, a classic that has reached an audience of millions and has proven that the game can spark a high player motivation. The didactic setting under investigation has also been used for almost 20 years and can therefore be considered mature. Therefore, the values determined for motivation may not be representative and may be difficult to achieve, for example, through specifically developed serious games, although dedicated serious games may sometimes develop motivation to such an extent that these games are also used as entertainment games (e.g. [17]). Overall, it is assumed that the particular game and the **didactic setting,** in which the game is used have a significant influence on motivation. Therefore, directives to increase the efficiency of serious gaming exist, referring to the game and the didactic setting. Wouters und van Oostendorp [18] name nine instructional techniques, such as content integration, context integration, and feedback, to be considered purposefully designed in serious gaming. Westera [19] highlights challenges and recipes for the design of motivational serious games and addresses the tension between motivational game mechanics and learning effectiveness.

Coordination of the Learning Activities. The coordination regarding time and content of *gaming* and *field trip* may have had an influence on the results, while the content of the *lecture* examined was not related to the content of the two learning activities *gaming* and *field trip*. Furthermore, the order of *gaming* and *field trip* was determined based on previous experience and the assumption that the very illustrative *field trip* could be prepared best by the more abstract learning activity *gaming* (and not the other way around). However, it is necessary to examine what influence the sequence of the learning activities might have on motivation.

Subjective Measurements. Scores for *perceived learning outcomes* and *perceived mental load* were queried from the students. The extent to which these subjective values correspond to the objective learning content must be questioned and clarified individually [20]. A further inaccuracy might be caused by students' subjective interpretations of the terms *mental load* and *learning*. In addition, the motivation only was examined, but not the knowledge imparted, and the learning outcomes achieved. Thus, no statement can be made about learning efficiency.

Measurement Granularity. The measurements were taken only at one point during events lasting several hours each. As described in the student comments on the field trip, the motivation may, however, vary with time, which limits the significance of the measurement results.

Fun and Motivation. Iten and Petko [21] show that the perceived fun of playing a serious game is not sufficient to predict learning success. This result indicates motivation being a complex construct, which may consist of several components. Beyond the fun of playing a game, extrinsic motivation is certainly significantly involved in the setting of Iten and Petko. This again opens the question raised at the beginning of the article, to what extent gaming and intentions beyond gaming are combinable. Design guidelines for serious games and serious gaming depend on the answer to this question.

Despite all limitations, the significance of the results regarding motivational differences between the learning activities *lecture* and *gaming* has been statistically validated in this case study.

5   Conclusions

For serious gaming to work as intended, games have to be able to generate intrinsic motivation in the player and thus achieve a high level of engagement with the learning content. In this study, it has been shown, using the case of an established serious gaming scenario, that the intrinsic motivation of students involved in serious gaming is actually higher than the intrinsic motivation of students in a lecture of the same course. Thus, intrinsic motivation as a theoretically established characteristic of serious gaming is also empirically confirmed in the scenario studied. Future work should – in a first step – consist of making similar measurements for specifically developed serious games that are expected to be less effective in generating intrinsic motivation. A second step is expected to identify the determining factors for achieving intrinsic motivation to transfer these results to other games and to further serious gaming scenarios respectively in a constructive manner, considering and proving the guidelines existing.

References

1. Squire, K.R.: Video Games and Learning: Teaching and Participatory Culture in the Digital Age. Teachers College Press, New York (2011)
2. Zander, S., Heidig, S.: Motivations design bei der Konzeption multimedialer Lernumgebungen. In: Niegemann, H., Weinberger, A. (eds.) Handbuch Bildungstechnologie, pp. 393–415. Springer, Heidelberg (2020). https://doi.org/10.1007/978-3-662-54368-9_37
3. Ryan, R.M., Deci, E.L.: Self-Determination Theory: Basic Psychological Needs in Motivation, Development, and Wellness. Guilford Publications, New York (2017)
4. Caillois, R.: Man, Play and Games. University of Illinois Press, Urbana (2001)
5. Garris, R., Ahlers, R., Driskell, J.E.: Games, motivation, and learning: a research and practice model. Simul. Gaming **33**, 441–467 (2002)
6. Rockwell, G.M., Kee, K.: Game Studies - The Leisure of Serious Games: A Dialogue. Game Stud. - Int. J. Comput. Game Res. **11** (2011)
7. Fu, F.L., Su, R.C., Yu, S.C.: EGameFlow: a scale to measure learners' enjoyment of e-learning games. Comput. Educ. **52**, 101–112 (2009)
8. Papert, S.: Does easy do it? children, games, and learning. Game Developer **5**, p. 88 (1998)
9. Bruckman, A.: Can educational be fun? In: Game Developer's Conference, San Jose, California, pp. 75–79 (1999)

10. Egenfeldt-Nielsen, S.: Educational Potential of Computer Games (Continuum Studies in Education). Continuum, London (2007)
11. Dondi, C., Moretti, M.: A methodological proposal for learning games selection and quality assessment. Br. J. Educ. Technol. **38**, 502–512 (2007)
12. Söbke, H., Weitze, L.: The challenge to nurture challenge. In: Wallner, G., Kriglstein, S., Hlavacs, H., Malaka, R., Lugmayr, A., Yang, H.S. (eds.) ICEC 2016. LNCS, vol. 9926, pp. 15–23. Springer, Cham (2016). https://doi.org/10.1007/978-3-319-46100-7_2
13. Wouters, P., van Nimwegen, C., van Oostendorp, H., van der Spek, E.D.: A meta-analysis of the cognitive and motivational effects of serious games. J. Educ. Psychol. **105**, 249–265 (2013)
14. Arnold, U., Söbke, H., Reichelt, M.: SimCity in infrastructure management education. Educ. Sci. **9**, 209 (2019)
15. Guay, F., Vallerand, R.J., Blanchard, C.: On the assessment of situational intrinsic and extrinsic motivation: the situational motivation scale (SIMS). Motiv. Emot. **24**, 175–213 (2000)
16. Rheinberg, F., Vollmeyer, R., Burns, B.D.: QCM : a questionnaire to assess current motivation in learning situations. Diagnostica **47**, 57–66 (2001)
17. Söbke, H., Harder, R., Planck-Wiedenbeck, U.: Two decades of traffic system education using the simulation game mobility. In: Göbel, S., et al. (eds.) JCSG 2018. LNCS, vol. 11243, pp. 43–53. Springer, Cham (2018). https://doi.org/10.1007/978-3-030-02762-9_6
18. Wouters, P., van Oostendorp, H.: Overview of instructional techniques to facilitate learning and motivation of serious games. In: Wouters, P., van Oostendorp, H. (eds.) Instructional Techniques to Facilitate Learning and Motivation of Serious Games. AGL, pp. 1–16. Springer, Cham (2017). https://doi.org/10.1007/978-3-319-39298-1_1
19. Westera, W.: Why and how serious games can become far more effective. J. Educ. Technol. Soc. **22**, 59–69 (2019)
20. Carpenter, S.K., Witherby, A.E., Tauber, S.K.: On students' (Mis)judgments of learning and teaching effectiveness. J. Appl. Res. Mem. Cogn. **9**, 137–151 (2020)
21. Iten, N., Petko, D.: Learning with serious games: is fun playing the game a predictor of learning success? Br. J. Educ. Technol. **47**, 151–163 (2016)

Two Years After: A Scoping Review of GDPR Effects on Serious Games Research Ethics Reporting

Patrick Jost[1]([⊠]) [iD] and Marisa Lampert[2]

[1] Department of Computer Science, Norwegian University of Science and Technology,
Trondheim, Norway
patrick.jost@ntnu.no
[2] Educational Science Studies, University of Hagen, Hagen, Germany

Abstract. On May 25th, 2018, the EU General Data Protection Regulation (GDPR) came into force. Recognised as a comprehensive regulation for improving privacy and data protection, a substantial impact on data processing disciplines such as Serious Games (SG) research was expected.

By conducting a scoping review, this paper explores the effects of GDPR on reporting of ethics approval, informed consent, ethics guidelines and data protection in SG studies. Five scientific databases were searched for research between 2016 and 2020 addressing Serious Games, Exergames and Applied Games. A total of 2146 full-text studies split into equal collections before and after GDPR were included. Lexicometric and keyword-in-context analysis were conducted and comparatively evaluated regarding ethics reporting and trends.

Results unexpectedly show that GDPR so far hardly left a mark. While a slight increase of 12% in general ethics reporting can be observed, less than 6% of the studies after GDPR coming-into-force report on data protection. Ethics procedures remained consistent with most researchers reporting the approval from their home university committee and stating the Declaration of Helsinki as followed guidelines. Overall, the verifiable impact of GDPR was found negligibly small, with only 0.5% of studies referring to the regulation in the two years after introduction. Conclusively, further research is suggested to focus on integrating ethics and data protection guided on GDPR from an early conceptual stage to the reporting of the findings.

Keywords: Serious games · Scoping review · Data protection guidelines · Research ethics · Ethics approval · GDPR

1 Introduction

1.1 Two Years After – Effects of GDPR on Serious Games Studies

The comprehensive EU General Data Protection Regulation (GDPR) [44] that came into effect in May 2018 aims to provide guidance in privacy and data protection and improve scientific integrity of human-related studies. Since GDPR is believed to have a

© The Author(s) 2020
I. Marfisi-Schottman et al. (Eds.): GALA 2020, LNCS 12517, pp. 372–385, 2020.
https://doi.org/10.1007/978-3-030-63464-3_35

global impact [25], the question arises to what extent the regulations actually changed the scientific conduct and the resulting publications at conferences and in journals.

One area of research concerned with evaluating personal data are applied digital games. Serious Games (SG) have gradually become an instrument for investigation and scientific analysis. Application in research extends from analysis of learning in games [6] over investigating the use of medication [1] and treat phobias [11] to researching decision making and team behaviour [16, 27]. Nearly all SG research is thereby affected by the GDPR as not only experiments with in-game assessment [27] involve data collection but also qualitative interviews that utilise games as a proxy to elicit information [28]. Other, more interactive, research approaches such as participatory SG creation workshops [9] equally require recording participant behaviour.

This paper is thus concerned with investigating the impact of GDPR on scientific reporting of Serious Games (SG) research. With a scoping review [41] of SG studies between 2016 and 2020, split to before and after GDPR came into effect, the reporting of ethics standards and data protection is analysed.

1.2 Research Ethics and Data Protection – Authorities and Guidelines

While for data protection, the legal frame has been laid out more precise with GDPR, guidelines on research ethics are more diverse and loosely defined. Whereas the APA code of conduct, for example, combines guidelines on ethics with data sharing/privacy [5], many European nations regard the two aspects separately. This becomes evident when exemplary, looking at Northern Europe. In Sweden (datainspektionen.se), Norway (datatilsynet.no), Finland (tietosuoja.fi), and Denmark (datatilsynet.dk) data protection is supervised by a single authority. On the other hand, there are generally multiple regional research committees and ethics authorities of different scientific or professional fields. While Sweden just recently moved to a single nationally controlled committee (etikprovningsmyndigheten.se) to administer ethics approvals other Scandinavian countries such as Denmark (nvk.dk) and Finland (tukija.fi) maintain a distributed structure with several regional committees.

Data protection, instead, is supervised much more centrally with single authorities per country that have adopted the GDPR legislative even if not an EU member (e.g. Norway). The far-reaching scope of the regulation may be attributed to the principle of territoriality, which effectively protects every EU citizen with the GDPR even if the data processing party is non-EU related [34]. Thus, researchers from other countries must comply with GDPR if European participants are included in the study. Therefore, it can be assumed that research practices and reporting have adapted widely since coming into force of the regulation.

Much like the diverse structure of ethics boards, numerous ethical guidelines are potentially applicable in the research context. Concerning Serious Games, human-centric research is mostly either medically oriented or related to social science. Ethical considerations regarding vulnerable groups such as children or elderly become specifically relevant when considering Exergames [43]. These SG are developed for improving health or medical conditions and are often researched in clinical trials. Such SG research does not differ from other medical research settings and must follow the same ethical standards. A basic foundation for a medical code of conduct was laid with the Nuremberg Code

[37]. However, more actual and elaborated ethical guidelines that are widely quoted in research are the Declaration of Helsinki (DoH) [48] and Good Clinical Practice (GCP) [21] on a worldwide perspective as well as the Clinical Trials Directive in Europe [22]. While the DoH is widely followed in medical research, there has been controversy regarding conflicts with other codes of conduct. Such conflicting guidelines, for example, exist in the UNESCO Universal Declaration on Bioethics and Human Rights [42] and the guidelines of the Nuffield Council [14]. The USA, for example, do not support the regulations any further but instead recommend the orientation on GCP and their own Common Rule [45].

1.3   Research Objectives

As has been outlined, GDPR is a far-reaching directive which is affecting all SG researchers that collect data from European participants. SG researchers are thus compelled to report on their ethical conduct and data protection when publishing articles to respect publication ethics [32]. This paper is therefore concerned with analysing SG research in the last two years (June 2018 to June 2020) and compare research practice with an equal number of SG studies before GDPR came into effect on May 25th, 2018. A scoping review is conducted as the scientific approach to analyse the broad body of research since 2016 for ethical reporting practice [29]. The specific aim of this review is to give insight into the following questions:

1. What are the reporting practices in SG studies from 2016 to 2020 regarding ethics approval, ethics guidelines and data protection?
2. Which ethical principles/guidelines and data protection policies are most reported in SG studies, and are there notable changes after GDPR introduction?
3. How did the coming-into-effect of GDPR affect SG publication ethics concerning reporting the data protection policy or ethical conduct?

2   Method

The scoping review methodology is suitable for gaining insight into applied research concepts and policies as it is concerned with analysing a large body of literature [4]. The following sections outline the mapping methodology followed in this study, as suggested by Peters et al. [31]. According to the guidelines, no quality appraisal was conducted for the studies. Potential bias influences are further reduced by the lexicometric analysis approach [46]. A preliminary search of existing overviews of ethics reporting in SG studies was conducted in all search engines applied for the SG study search but did not find any hits on the specific topic.

2.1   Information Sources and Search

The keyword search was conducted on different online databases with a time limit from 2016 to 2020 while using the university internet connection to have broad access to full-text publications. The search results were downloaded with Zotero reference management software (zotero.com) that automatically retrieves accessible full texts when importing the records. To get a comprehensive overview of reporting practice, the most popular SG terms were defined as keywords, and no further limitations were made in the search strings. Table 1 lists the search engines and search strings for the search that was conducted on May 6th, 2020.

Table 1. Searched databases and applied search settings

Online databases	URL	Search strings applied to all databases
ACM Digital Library	dl.acm.org	"serious game"; "serious games"; "applied game"; "applied games"; "exergame"; "exergames"
Web of Science	apps.webofknowledge.com	
Science direct	sciencedirect.com	
Scopus	scopus.com	
IEEE Xplore	ieeexplore.ieee.org	

2.2 Screening and Eligibility

The broad search strategy resulted in duplicates which were excluded at the screening stage. Also records not relevant for examining research ethics reporting such as book chapters or reports were defined and excluded (see Sect. 3.1). Moreover, all entries without full-text access were excluded at screening since ethics approval and data protection are generally not reported in title or abstract. Finally, review studies and studies not reported in English were excluded.

2.3 Data Analysis Process

Selected studies are building a literature corpus that is divided into two subcorpora before and after the coming-into-effect of GDPR. The applied process corresponds to the corpus linguistic approach [40] on a closed, large collection with authentic and representative language. The subsequent lexicometric analysis follows suggestions of Dzudzek et al. [19] and Wiedemann [47] by (1) calculating frequencies of terms regarding research ethics and data protection reporting, (2) key phrase-in-context analysis and (3) comparison of the reporting trends before/after GDPR between the two subcorpora. For the context-observing content analysis, the key terms listed in Table 2 were applied on both subcorpora with the software MAXDictio (maxqda.com). The included records were first imported, and meta-data analyses regarding study characteristics were performed. Successively, frequency examination was run with the outlined word set on each subcorpus separately. The analysis thereby focused on the number of papers reporting the terminology. Next, key phrase in-context analysis was conducted for discovered phrases, and related meaning was evaluated. Studies not reporting the respective phrase in the intended context were excluded from the result tables and figures. For example, when data protection measures were not reported concerning the study conduct but rather as a general requirement in the introduction or when a term was only found in a title in the reference list. Finally, the comparative trends before and after GDPR coming-into-force were analysed to answer the research questions.

Table 2. Key phrases applied in lexicometric analysis of SG studies before and after GDPR coming-into-force

Research ethics & Ethics guidelines		Data protection & GDPR
Consent form	Clinical Trials Directive	Anonymised
Ethics approval	Code of Ethics	Data protection
Ethics committee	Common Rule	Data security
Ethical conduct	Ethical Guidelines	Encrypted
Ethics principles	Good Clinical Practice	GDPR
Informed consent	Guidelines for Research Ethics	General Data Protection Regulation
	Helsinki Declaration	Privacy policy
	Nuffield Council on Bioethics	Pseudonymised
	Universal Declaration on Bioethics	

Note. Phrases were lemmatised (e.g. ethics/ethical), British/US spelling, and lower/uppercase were included

3   Results

3.1   Literature Search

The database searches resulted in 20767 citations (Table 3). After exclusion of duplicates, improperly allocated meta-tags were corrected. Proceedings papers listed as book chapters were classified as conference papers during this step. Mostly, the distinction was identifiable from metadata as proceedings or conferences were mentioned in the fields. In rare cases, the full text (if available) was opened for verification.

The subsequent selection process outlined in Fig. 1 left 2186 studies to divide before and after GDPR coming-into-effect. When splitting according to this date, 1073 studies were eligible for inclusion since May 25th, 2018. To allow for comparative lexicometric examination, the same number of studies before May 25th, 2018 were included in the analysis by going backwards in publication dates. Thus, the resulting cut-off date was February 8th, 2016 and the 40 studies before that date were excluded. The selection procedure resulted in two SG subcorpora of journal and conference papers with 1073 before and 1073 after GDPR coming-into-force.

Table 3. Search results total between January 1ˢᵗ, 2016 and May 6ᵗʰ, 2020

Online database	Serious game	Serious games	Applied game	Applied games	Exergame	Exergames
ACM Digital Library	437	850	82	35	195	266
Web of Science	1411	2267	43	50	353	487
Science direct	793	1056	141	35	404	404
Scopus	4125	4125	94	94	521	593
IEEE Xplore	437	1304	7	4	63	91
Sum	7203	9602	367	218	1536	1841

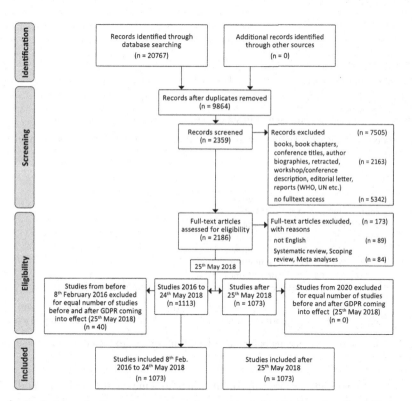

Fig. 1. Study flow selection process; steps of screening and exclusion of studies with reasons

3.2 Ethics Approval and Informed Consent

Lexicometric analysis showed that SG studies report little about their ethical conduct. Only about 29% of the studies before GDPR introduction were reporting one of the investigated ethical aspects. However, overall ethics reporting increased in the more recent study corpus, with about 42% of studies reporting at least one of the elements.

This rising tendency in ethics reporting can be observed in Table 4 as all terms were found more frequently in the more current research. Reporting about ethics committees and approval has increased, although both still are stated by fewer than 10%. Context analysis (Fig. 2) then revealed that the vast majority of researchers were reporting to get approval from a committee at their own university or hospital in both periods before GDPR [10] and after [26].

Table 4. Percentages of papers before/after GDPR reporting on ethics approval and consent

Terminology	Word quantity	Paper quantity (total)	% papers before GDPR	% papers after GDPR
Informed consent	451	312	12.4	16.7
Consent form	272	109	4.4	5.8
Ethics committee	221	169	6.2	9.6
Ethical approval	174	149	5.9	8.0
Ethical principles	21	17	0.5	1.2
Ethical conduct	4	4	0.1	0.3
Total % reporting on research ethics in subcorpus:			29.4	41.6

Note. Phrases include singular and plural forms and lower/uppercase variations; % in relation to subcorpus

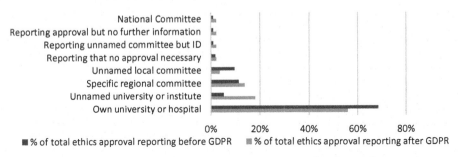

Fig. 2. Ethics approval reporting before/after GDPR in per cent of total reporting per subcorpus

Moreover, two trends became apparent when looking at the approval bodies and comparing before and after subcorpora:

First, researchers are turning more towards not naming the committee but rather stating only that a university has approved [7]. Second, the reporting becomes more diverse with researchers indicating the reference number of the approval document but not the approval body [49] and others reporting just approval without any other information [2] or stating an approval was not necessary [17]. Generally, it can be noticed, that roughly half of the studies (51% before and 44% after GDPR) reporting ethics committee/approval are Exergame studies as compared to only about 20% in each subcorpus total share.

3.3 Ethics Guidelines

By analysing ethics guidelines reporting, even fewer studies can be found that refer to that aspect. About 100 studies of 2146 in total are reporting the application of ethics guidelines which is only 3.6% before and 6.3% of the SG studies after GDPR introduction (Table 5). Again, the proportion of Exergame studies in the rare papers that refer to ethical guidelines is high, with about 60% in the before and 47% in the after subcorpus. SG researchers are only reporting with four of the nine examined phrases. None of the studies has directly stated to follow the Clinical Trials Directive, the Common Rule, any national or international Guidelines for Research Ethics, the Nuffield Council on Bioethics, or the Universal Declaration on Bioethics (UNESCO). Context investigation then disclosed that the Declaration of Helsinki (DoH) was by far the most cited ethical code reported before [8] and after the GDPR effective date [12] (Table 5).

Table 5. Percentages of papers before/after GDPR reporting on ethical guidelines

Terminology	Word quantity	Paper quantity (total)	% papers before GDPR	% papers after GDPR
Declaration of Helsinki	105	84	2.6	5.2
Ethical guidelines	22	13	0.5	0.7
Code of ethics	18	1	0.0	0.1
Good clinical practice	10	6	0.3	0.3
Total % reporting on ethical guidelines in subcorpus:			3.6	6.3

Note. Phrases include singular/plural and lower/uppercase variations; % in relation to subcorpus

3.4 Data Protection

In the concluding analysis of data protection coverage, the authors of SG studies showed an equally reduced reporting behaviour as for the ethical guidelines (Table 6). Although there is a small increase in data protection reporting between the two study collections, both are at low percentages. Only about 3.7% (before) and 5.6% (after) report on the data protection aspects that were examined. The share of Exergame studies in reporting data protection is, however, lower as within reporting of ethics committees/approval and ethics guidelines. In the period before GDPR introduction, eight studies or roughly 27% and in the period after nine studies or about 19% are concerned with Exergames when reporting on data protection.

Examining the context of data protection phrases revealed that authors emphasised most the anonymisation of study artefacts such as transcripts [30], spreadsheets [38], blog-posts [35] or usage/interaction and activity profiles [24]. In both sub-collections, studies only sporadically reported on anonymisation of participants while also sometimes referring to "anonymising" when actually "pseudonymising" was performed [39]. Only two studies reported concrete pseudonymising after the GDPR introduction [13, 20].

Table 6. Percentages of papers before/after GDPR reporting on privacy and data protection

Terminology	Word quantity	Paper quantity (total)	% papers before GDPR	% papers after GDPR
Anonymised	71	56	2.0	3.3
Data protection	46	12	0.5	0.7
Encrypted	43	21	1.0	0.9
GDPR	26	5	0.0	0.5
Data security	15	3	0.3	0.0
Privacy policy	5	1	0.0	0.1
Pseudonymised	2	2	0.0	0.2
Total % reporting on data protection in subcorpus:			3.7	5.6

Note. Phrases include upper/lower case and British/American spelling; GDPR was counted only once when both full phrase and acronym was reported in one paper; % in relation to subcorpus

Equally rare was coverage about encryption with only 1% of authors referring to it in each subcorpus by describing, for instance, secured communication [15] and encrypted storage context [23].

As regards compliance with GDPR and reporting thereof, none of the studies in the subcorpus before the GDPR effective date were found mentioning the regulation. However, remarkably there were also only five studies in the two years after GDPR coming-into-force that reported some form of compliance with the directive. By examining the characteristics of GDPR usage in these studies, it became apparent that the regulation was referred to in terms of compliance [18, 36] but also to clarify privacy requirement [13], identifying the two GDPR data-related roles (controller and processor) in connection with the study [15] and demands concerning data storage [20].

4   Discussion

In the light of the outlined findings, it can be noticed that all three investigated areas, research ethics, ethics guidelines and data protection are in general reported in a minimal range. Analysis of the broad collection of studies between 2016 and 2020 revealed little support for changing trends in reporting practice of research ethics or data protection. Researchers kept referring to Serious Games for their game-oriented studies while Exergaming claims a stable share and the term Applied Game did hardly gain a foot in the community. Concerning the first research question, lexicometric analysis showed a minor rising trend reporting ethics approval and informed consent.

However, the slightly higher quota of journal articles in the after GDPR study collection could have contributed to this under the assumption that authors report more details in journals than in conference papers. The most important ethics approval board for SG researchers before and after GDPR introduction remains their home university ethics committee. There is, however, some indication that designating the approving body generally becomes less regarded. Although SG research is predominantly human-centred, only between 10 and 15% of studies are reporting on their ethics approval or informed consent. There is also no evidence from the comparative before/after analysis that would indicate a fast or considerable change of practice. This could present a considerable hindrance for SG applied in research to be trusted as effective and ethically sound. Especially considering that often children, elderly or disabled people are the ones who should benefit from SG. Thus, instead of keeping a low ethics reporting profile, ethical conduct should become an integral part of a SG from the start. In-game informed consent and modular game structures with secure data communication as well as pseudonymised storage of data should become the basis, not the exception of SG research. A transparent process for participants that also involves briefing and debriefing during a research-game session is an attainable objective.

The second question asked on reporting of ethical guidelines and privacy policies can be answered with clear findings from this review. About 80% of studies reporting guidelines declared to follow the DoH. There is no indication of a change of this from the data analysis. Rather, a consistent picture has been revealed over the last four years of SG research. However, the overall reporting of followed ethical principles remains very low ($< 6\%$) in SG studies.

Regarding the third question and data protection policy, there was no preferred use/reporting of guidelines visible in neither the subcorpus of SG studies before nor after GDRP introduction. Data protection and privacy policy are extremely rarely addressed with only one study out of 2146 reporting on privacy policy [33]. Although the GDPR was broadly discussed long before the date of coming-into-effect [3] authors of the examined SG studies chose not to participate in this discussion. Equally remarkable, two years after the binding regulation has come into force, only five studies out of about a thousand are referring to the directive. Indeed, that is the impact of the GDPR on SG publication revealed from comparatively analysing the two study-sets. The findings do not allow for conclusions on a general rising trend in ethics reporting as practices from other time periods would need consideration in this regard. Yet, a considerable contribution from GDPR to such a potential trend could not be found in the data of this study.

Since the results on reporting of ethics and data protection are concerning, it is suggested to repeat the scoping review protocol of this study in a two-year interval to investigate the course of impact of GDPR. At this point, however, Albrecht's [3] question of how GDPR will change the world can be answered from the perspective of SG research reporting: If at all, then hardly noticeable.

5 Conclusion

The conducted scoping review has provided insight in ethics reporting practices of Serious Games researchers. While researchers showed some increase in reporting on parts of scientific integrity, there was no substantial change found when looking at the writing about ethical guidelines, data protection or the GDPR. Aside from finding only marginal change from GDPR, the scoping review has found that most SG researchers who report on ethics obtain ethics approval from a review board at their own university and follow the Declaration of Helsinki. The outlined problems of conduct and transparency could be addressed in future studies by not only making the situation visible but by supporting SG creation in research with ideation toolsets that include data protection advice and building blocks that comply with GDPR from the very beginning of the development. Ultimately, with GDPR, there are now clear data protection regulations that can be operationalised. Since designing SGs frequently involves matching rules of a domain into a game, data protection rules can be part of the balancing process. Accordingly, this process could then be facilitated with design toolsets oriented on SG research.

Acknowledgements. This research was supported by the Research Council of Norway (Norges Forskningsråd) by funding the IKTPLUSS project ALerT, #270969.

References

1. Abraham, O. et al.: Investigating serious games that incorporate medication use for patients: systematic literature review. JMIR Serious Games **8**(2), e16096 (2020)
2. Adinolf, S. et al.: Towards designing agent based virtual reality applications for cybersecurity training. In: Proceedings of the 31st Australian Conference on Human-Computer-Interaction. pp. 452–456, Fremantle, WA, Australia. Association for Computing Machinery (2019)
3. Albrecht, J.P.: How the GDPR will change the world. Eur. Data Prot. L. Rev. **2**, 287 (2016)
4. Anderson, S., et al.: Asking the right questions: scoping studies in the commissioning of research on the organisation and delivery of health services. Health Res. Policy Syst. **6**, 7 (2008)
5. APA: Ethical principles of psychologists and code of conduct. The American Psychological Association, Washington, D.C. (2017)
6. Bachvarova, Y., et al.: Measuring the effectiveness of learning with serious games in corporate training. Procedia Comput. Sci. **15**, 221–232 (2012)
7. Baker, S. et al.: Interrogating social virtual reality as a communication medium for older adults. Proc. ACM Hum. Comput. Interact. **3**(CSCW), 1–24 (2019)
8. Benzing, V. et al.: Acute cognitively engaging exergame-based physical activity enhances executive functions in adolescents. PLoS One. **11**(12), e0167501 (2016)
9. Bergen, Erlend., et al.: Supporting the co-design of games for privacy awareness. In: Auer, M.E., Tsiatsos, T. (eds.) ICL 2018. AISC, vol. 916, pp. 888–899. Springer, Cham (2020). https://doi.org/10.1007/978-3-030-11932-4_82
10. Birk, M.V. et al.: Age-based preferences and player experience: a crowdsourced cross-sectional study. In: Proceedings of the Annual Symposium on Computer-Human Interaction in Play, pp. 157–170, Amsterdam The Netherlands. ACM (2017)
11. Botella, C., et al.: Treating cockroach phobia using a serious game on a mobile phone and augmented reality exposure: a single case study. Comput. Hum. Behav. **27**(1), 217–227 (2011)
12. de Bruin, E.D., et al.: Playing exergames facilitates central drive to the ankle dorsiflexors during gait in older adults; a quasi-experimental investigation. Front. Aging Neurosci. **11**, 263 (2019)
13. Calvo-Morata, A., et al.: Validation of a cyberbullying serious game using game analytics. IEEE Trans. Learn. Technol. **13**(1), 186–197 (2020)
14. Carlson, R.V., et al.: The revision of the declaration of helsinki: past, present and future. Br. J. Clin. Pharmacol. **57**(6), 695–713 (2004)

15. Chaudy, Y., Connolly, T.: Specification and evaluation of an assessment engine for educational games: integrating learning analytics and providing an assessment authoring tool. Entertainment Comput. **30**, 100294 (2019)

16. Coovert, M.D., et al.: Serious games are a serious tool for team research. IJSG **4**, 1 (2017)

17. Cowley, B., Bateman, C.: Green my place: evaluation of a serious social online game designed to promote energy efficient behaviour change. Int. J. Serious Games **4**(4), 71–90 (2017)

18. Derks, S., et al.: Effectiveness of the serious game "You & I" in changing mentalizing abilities of adults with mild to borderline intellectual disabilities: a parallel superiority randomized controlled trial. Trials **20**(1), 500 (2019)

19. Dzudzek, I., et al.: 11 Verfahren der lexikometrischen Analyse von Textkorpora. In: Glasze, G., Mattissek, A. (eds.) Handbuch Diskurs und Raum: Theorien und Methoden für die Humangeographie sowie die sozial- und kulturwissenschaftliche Raumforschung, p. 334. Transcript, Bielefeld (2009)

20. Ehrari, H., et al.: Effects of playful exercise of older adults on balance and physical activity: a randomized controlled trial. J. Popul. Ageing **13**(2), 207–222 (2020). https://doi.org/10.1007/s12062-020-09273-8

21. EMA/ICH: Good Clinical Practice. European Medicines Agency, London (2017)

22. Commission, European: Directorate General for Research: Ethics for Researchers: Facilitating Research Excellence in FP7. Publications Office, Luxembourg (2013)

23. Francillette, Y., et al.: Development of an exergame on mobile phones to increase physical activity for adults with severe mental illness. In: Proceedings of the 11th Pervasive Technologies Related to Assistive Environments Conference, pp. 241–248, Corfu Greece. ACM (2018)

24. Fraternali, P., et al.: enCOMPASS - an integrative approach to behavioural change for energy saving. In: GIoTS 2017 - Global Internet of Things Summit, Proceedings (2017)

25. Goddard, M.: The EU general data protection regulation (GDPR): European regulation that has a global impact. Int. J. Market Res. **59**(6), 703–705 (2017)

26. Hodge, J., et al.: Relational, flexible, everyday: learning from ethics in dementia research. In: Proceedings of the 2020 CHI Conference on Human Factors in Computing Systems, pp. 1–16, Honolulu, HI, USA. Association for Computing Machinery (2020)

27. Jost, P.: The quest game-frame: balancing serious games for investigating privacy decisions. In: 11th Scandinavian Conference on Information Systems (SCIS), Sundsvall, Sweden August 10 (2020). https://aisel.aisnet.org/scis2020/5/

28. Jost, P., Divitini, M.: Game elicitation: exploring assistance in delayed-effect supply chain decision making. In: NordiCHI 2020, Tallinn, Estonia October 29 (2020). https://doi.org/10.1145/3419249.3420154

29. Lockwood, C., et al.: Practical guidance for knowledge synthesis: scoping review methods. Asian Nurs. Res. **13**(5), 287–294 (2019)

30. Marshall, J., et al.: Designing brutal multiplayer video games. In: Proceedings of the 2016 CHI Conference on Human Factors in Computing Systems, San Jose, California, USA, pp. 2669–2680. Association for Computing Machinery (2016)

31. Peters, M., et al.: Chapter 11: Scoping Reviews (2020 version). In: Aromataris, E., Munn, Z. (eds.) Joanna Briggs Institute Reviewer's Manual. JBI, Adelaide (2020)

32. Poff, D.C., Ginley, D.S.: Publication Ethics. In: Iphofen, R. (ed.) Handbook of Research Ethics and Scientific Integrity, pp. 107–126. Springer, Cham (2020). https://doi.org/10.1007/978-3-030-16759-2_61

33. Rauschenberger, M., et al.: Designing a new puzzle app to target dyslexia screening in pre-readers. In: ACM International Conference Proceeding Series (2019)

34. Ryngaert, C., Taylor, M.: The GDPR as global data protection regulation? AJIL Unbound **114**, 5–9 (2020)

35. Scamell, M., Hanley, T.: Innovation in preregistration midwifery education: web based interactive storytelling learning. Midwifery **50**, 93–98 (2017)
36. Schlögl, R., et al.: Hyper typer: a serious game for measuring mobile text entry performance in the wild. In: Extended Abstracts of the 2019 CHI Conference on Human Factors in Computing Systems, pp. 1–6, Glasgow Scotland UK. ACM (2019)
37. Shuster, E.: Fifty years later: the significance of the nuremberg code. N. Engl. J. Med. **337**(20), 1436–1440 (1997)
38. Sipiyaruk, K., Gallagher, J.E., Hatzipanagos, S., Reynolds, P.A.: Acquiring critical thinking and decision-making skills: an evaluation of a serious game used by undergraduate dental students in dental public health. Technol. Knowl. Learn. **22**(2), 209–218 (2017). https://doi.org/10.1007/s10758-016-9296-6
39. Smale, R., Kloppenburg, S.: Platforms in power: householder perspectives on the social, environmental and economic challenges of energy platforms. Sustainability. **12**(2), 692 (2020)
40. Stefanowitsch, A.: Corpus linguistics: A guide to the methodology. Zenodo, Washington, D.C. (2020)
41. Sucharew, H., Macaluso, M.: Methods for research evidence synthesis: the scoping review approach. J. Hosp. Med. **14**, 7 (2019)
42. UNESCO: Universal Declaration on Bioethics and Human Rights. United Nations Educational, Scientific and Cultural Organization, Paris (2015)
43. Uzor, S., Baillie, L.: Investigating the long-term use of exergames in the home with elderly fallers. In: Proceedings of the SIGCHI Conference on Human Factors in Computing Systems, pp. 2813–2822 (2014)
44. Voigt, P., von dem Bussche, A.: The EU general data protection regulation (GDPR). Springer, Cham (2017). https://doi.org/10.1007/978-3-319-57959-7
45. Weinmeyer, R.: New developments in human subjects protections: proposed updates to the common rule. AMA J. Ethics **17**(12), 1147–1151 (2015)
46. Wiedemann, G.: Computer-assisted text analysis in the social sciences. Text Mining for Qualitative Data Analysis in the Social Sciences. KSD, pp. 17–54. Springer, Wiesbaden (2016). https://doi.org/10.1007/978-3-658-15309-0_2
47. Wiedemann, G.: Opening up to big data: computer-assisted analysis of textual data in social sciences. Historical Social Research/Historische Sozialforschung **38**(4), 332–357 (2013)
48. World Medical Association: Declaration of Helsinki–Ethical Principles for Medical Research Involving Human Subjects. The World Medical Association: Ferney-Voltaire, France (2018)
49. Yoo, S. et al.: Embedding a VR game studio in a sedentary workplace: use, experience and exercise benefits. In: Proceedings of the 2020 CHI Conference on Human Factors in Computing Systems, pp. 1–14, Honolulu, HI, USA. Association for Computing Machinery (2020)

Posters

Office Madness: Design and Pilot Evaluation of a Serious Game for Learning the C++ Programming Language

Savvas Eleftheriadis$^{(\boxtimes)}$ and Stelios Xinogalos ⓘ

University of Macedonia, Egnatia 156, 54636 Thessaloniki, Greece
{mai19015,stelios}@uom.edu.gr

Abstract. In this paper, a new serious game (SG) called Office Madness, is presented. The game is about learning basic and advanced concepts of the programming language C++. Its design was carried out using the EFM design model, while its pilot evaluation was carried out using the MEEGA evaluation model. The main goal of the game is to introduce users to the C++ programming language in a fun and serious way. In contrast with most of the existing programming SGs that are based on puzzles, this game uses an office metaphor and the player undertakes the role of a candidate programmer. The game uses techniques and mechanisms that ultimately aim to stimulate the learner's sense of seriousness and responsibility when learning C++ and not just to entertain him/her during training.

Keywords: Serious game (SG) · Programming · C++ · Serious game design model · Serious game evaluation model

1 Introduction

Video games aim to satisfy the feeling of fun and are now part of everyone's life, with universal acceptance and use. Serious games (SGs) are a special category of video games that aim not only at entertaining, but also at educating [1]. SGs are designed from the ground up for a different purpose than simple entertainment, usually with the help of a special design model, like EFM (Effective learning environment, Flow experience and Motivation) [2]. They are computer-based mental games that are based on specific rules and use the fun factor simply as a driving force to make it easier to convey educational content to users, in several areas such as education, health, business, politics, etc. [1]. However, although the main purpose of SGs is education, they are still video games in which the entertainment factor must be at a high level in order to be attractive and entertaining [3].

This paper is about designing and implementing a SG for learning the programming language C++. There are several games that undertake to train users in a programming language. Most of these games use entertainment as the driving force to keep players from getting tired during their training. But what does "fun" mean? It is a fairly abstract term that cannot be easily measured (let alone designed, implemented and ultimately

© Springer Nature Switzerland AG 2020
I. Marfisi-Schottman et al. (Eds.): GALA 2020, LNCS 12517, pp. 389–394, 2020.
https://doi.org/10.1007/978-3-030-63464-3_36

displayed on the screen) while being greatly altered by many factors, such as content, age, occupation, psychology, motivation. In some cases, the type of "fun" in a game may be repelled by certain groups of users because these groups cannot be identified with the offered type of entertainment. The bottom line is that there are various types of players. The BrainHex model [4] attempted to group players from a sample of 50,000 players into "archetypes". Each archetype has common characteristics on games and therefore prefers certain types of games. The proposed game satisfies mainly the following BrainHex archetypes: the Achiever (goal oriented, long-term achievements); Mastermind (puzzle solver, efficiency based); and the Seeker (memory, patterns). In the game proposed in this paper, a harmonious combination of educational content with several realistic elements is attempted, which is expected to arouse interest and motivate the user to move forward, while at the same time enhancing the seriousness and responsibility for what the player wants to achieve.

The rest of the paper is structured as follows. In Sect. 2, a brief review of serious games for programming is presented. In Sect. 3, the design of the game is analyzed, while in Sect. 4 the pilot evaluation of the game is presented using the MEEGA evaluation model [5]. Finally, in Sect. 5 some conclusions are drawn.

2 Relevant Work

Several SGs that aim to teach programming concepts or even specific programming languages are available nowadays. The existing games are targeted to specific ages, usually beginners or kids. Most of the games refer either to popular programming languages, such as Java and Python, or the well-known interlocking blocks provided by Blockly. Consequently, all the games provide some kind of text editor or an editor for dragging and dropping interlocking blocks that correspond to programming concepts/constructs. The majority of the SGs for programming are puzzle games, but there are also some games that use the mechanics of a typical platform or RPG video game in order to transfer educational content through a motivating scenario.

SQL Island is a *text-based adventure* game aiming at teaching the SQL query language. Robocode [6] is a *multiplayer* programming game, where the goal is to program a robot in order to compete against other robot tanks, programmed by other users in Java and C#. ColoBot is a *puzzle adventure* game and the technological evolution of CeeBot, that uses a pseudo-language that is similar to C++ and Java, called CBOT. Lightbox is an isometric *puzzle* game, developed for Web, iOS & Android. Hakitzu: Code of the Warrior is a *turn-based strategy* game, where users have to create their own robot, which they have to train in order to battle the robots of other users. Codespells is an *action adventure* game, developed for Windows & MacOS X, which trains users in the Java programming language where the players take on the role of a wizard in a country full of gnomes. Human Resource Machine is a cross-platform commercial programming *puzzle game* where the player takes the role of a corporate office worker, assigned to perform tasks in order to get promoted. The tasks include moving objects that correspond to commands in order to assemble complex instructions, like as in Assembly. Code Hunt is a programming *puzzle game* for Java and C#, in which the player solves programming puzzles in a predefined amount of time, with the aid of some clues in the form of predefined results.

In this paper, the SG Office Madness is presented. The game is a hybrid job & programming simulator, which trains users in the C++ programming language. In contrast with most of the programming SGs that are based on a fantastic scenario, Office Madness gives emphasis on realism.

3 Design of the Serious Game Office Madness

Office Madness is a hybrid job & programming simulator. The user plays the role of a candidate programmer who is trying to get hired by a software company. The main inspiration for designing Office Madness came from the successful commercial video games "Papers, Please" and "Not Tonight". The main features of these games are their minimalistic graphics, the realistic scenario and game mechanisms, the sense of responsibility and the daily struggle the player must show while playing, which makes these games addictive. The design of Office Madness was based on the features of the aforementioned games to present a game with a realistic scenario and mechanisms, having as main purpose to stimulate the players' sense of seriousness and responsibility, along with their sense of fun. Moreover, the EFM design model [2] was taken into account. In this design model, a connection between *motivation, flow, efficient learning environment and educational game* is described, aiming in a better process of user learning. Due to space limitations it is not possible to analyze how Office Madness implemented the EFM characteristics, but some of them are referenced in parentheses using italics while describing the game.

Based on the game scenario, the candidate programmer has applied for a job in the company for one of the following positions: *Entry level* or *Junior developer*. This indirectly plays the role of the game's difficulty level, as it presents a different educational content and tasks, based on the selected position by the user (*balance of challenge & skills*). The company tests the candidate employee for a period of one (1) day, evaluating him/her through a number of programming assignments, in a virtual working office. The candidate employee is required to complete the assignments correctly (*specific goals and procedures*) and within an in-game time frame of eight (8) h (working schedule of 07:30 to 15:30), which lasts, roughly, about thirty (30) minutes in real-time (*constant sense of challenge*). This doesn't mean that the trainee cannot finish earlier than the end of working schedule, which happens if he/she completes all the programming assignments. In this case, the game proceeds with the candidate's evaluation. The user can save the current progress for continuing another time, simply by clicking the appropriate application (save) on the virtual monitor. After the final evaluation of the candidate, the user can still load a previously saved game, for reasons of improvement (*motivation*).

The programming assignments take the form of small code snippets written in C++ and (usually) have syntax problems. The user must correct the problematic parts of the code in the built-in code editor (Fig. 1), then compile the code by using the built-in compiler & submit it for evaluation (*autotelic experience*).

After a code submission, the user is informed about the result of the evaluation, which can be either positive or negative (*unambiguous feedback*). In the case of a negative result, the user is presented with a description box, showing the error(s) and some hints for correcting them. In a negative evaluation, the code editor displays the correct

Fig. 1. Virtual built-in code editor

output for the task (if there is an output), as well as a list of corrections e.g. "the x()
function doesn't exist". The educational content (XML file) contains a number of coded
commands for validating code correctness, for each task. When the user's code needs
to be validated, those validating commands are executed on written code, building and
displaying an appropriate text of hints for all the user's errors. The tasks have a specific
order of appearance, which doesn't change in a new game. However, the trainee may
elect to skip some tasks, leaving them for later. The game doesn't take into account the
trainee's performance in order to change the sequence of tasks, for reasons of realism. In
real-world interviews, the candidate is usually asked to solve some predefined problems
in specific time and order, and this is essentially simulated in the game. At the end of the
day, the user is informed about his/her evaluation with a success rate and he/she is either
hired or rejected (*motivation*). The users are trained in new programming concepts by
reading the programming guides that appear gradually, found under a directory on the
virtual monitor's desktop. Each guide is presented as a, properly named, virtual PDF
file. The name describes its educational content.

The game doesn't maintain a score or ranking list among players, as it gives emphasis
on realistic procedures and the seriousness of the situation (virtual interview). However,
in a future multiplayer version of the game, a ranking list could be introduced, such as
the points scored by each candidate for the job.

The game takes place entirely in a 2D environment, simulating the virtual office of
the candidate employee, having all the tools at his/her disposal to complete his/her work
(*sense of direct interaction with the environment*). These tools include the computer
monitor, the C++ code editor, the built-in compiler, the programming guides to read
from, the programming assignments and current time. The game's environment was
deliberately designed to be simple, almost minimalistic, with few and repetitive functions
for the user, however as realistic as possible. The goal in future versions of the game
is to increase the number of these functions, adding to the necessary complexity and
challenge, but still keeping an eye on realism. The game supports English and Greek,
requires Windows with OpenGL 2.0+ support to run and its storage requirements is
about 30 MB. The educational content of the game is stored in an external XML file.

This implementation allows the modification of the XML file to support different content. For example, various XML files could be created, with educational content focused only on specific C++ programming concepts, however with greater coverage. In technical level, the system uses the C++ library PugiXML [7] to manage its XML content. The main reasons of using it was the flexible license (MIT), its extended portability, the widespread usage and finally its full Unicode support, allowing the game to display content in other languages (e.g. Greek). The game evaluates the accuracy of the source code that is written by the user, using the C/C++ compiler from Digital Mars [8]. This compiler runs only in a command line environment and is used to compile and execute the players' code snippets. The executable output that is generated, as well as specific sections of text the user must have written in the code snippet, are evaluated by Office Madness for their accuracy (*intensity of interaction & feedback*). The overall result at the end of day leads to the hiring or rejection of the candidate developer by the company.

4 Pilot Evaluation

For the pilot evaluation of the game, the MEEGA evaluation model [5] was used. This model aims at the evaluation of educational games [5, 9], and it provides useful feedback through a properly structured questionnaire. The MEEGA questionnaire includes questions that have been classified into a set of quality factors & dimensions. The *motivation* quality factor includes the dimensions *attention, relevance, confidence* and *satisfaction*; the *user experience* quality factor includes the dimensions *immersion, social interaction, challenge, fun, competence* and *digital game*; and the *learning* quality factor includes the dimensions *short-term learning* and *long-term learning*. The questions of the *social interaction* dimension have not been used, as the game doesn't support social interaction (single player game). The questions use a five-point Likert scale, where: 1 = strongly disagree, and 5 = strongly agree.

An invitation with a link for downloading the game and a link to the questionnaire (Google Form) was sent to MSc students that had attended a course on "Serious Games Programming". Eleven students (10 male, 1 female) older than 18 years old (4 in the age group 18–28, 4 in the age group 29–39 and 3 in the age group 40–50) played the game and filled in the questionnaire anonymously over a period of ten (10) days.

The pilot evaluation showed that the game did well in most dimensions, achieving a median of 4. The best performance was achieved in the dimensions *Attention, Relevance, Confidence* and *Digital Game*. However, in the dimension of *Immersion*, the game did not perform so well, having the worst performance with a median of 2 on fully concentration on the game, and a median of 3 on losing the sense of time and surroundings. It is clear that accomplishing a high degree of immersion is quite challenging and further work is needed for the specific game. Moreover, the game has to be play-tested and evaluated by more end-users in order to draw safer conclusions regarding the motivation provided, user experience and learning.

5 Conclusions

Several SGs have been developed for introducing novices to programming. Most of the SGs refer to young students and aim to cultivate computational thinking skills through programming [10]. Fewer games for programming are targeted to real world programming languages, such as C [11]. The study presented in this paper aimed at the design and pilot evaluation of a SG for supporting the learning of C++. The game, called Office Madness, aims to stimulate the players' sense of seriousness and professional responsibility. The design of Office Madness was guided by the EFM model, while its pilot evaluation was based on the MEEGA model. The eleven participants of the pilot study evaluated positively the game and made clear that more mechanisms are needed in the game in order to more successfully immerse the player. However, it is clear that in order to draw safer conclusions about the overall quality of the game, an evaluation with more participants is needed.

References

1. Zyda, M.: From visual simulation to virtual reality to games, pp. 25–32, IEEE Computer Society, Information Sciences Institute, California (2005)
2. Song, M., Zhang, S.: EFM: a model for educational game design. In: Pan, Z., Zhang, X., El Rhalibi, A., Woo, W., Li, Y. (eds.) Edutainment 2008. LNCS, vol. 5093, pp. 509–517. Springer, Heidelberg (2008). https://doi.org/10.1007/978-3-540-69736-7_54
3. Abt, C.: Serious Games, University Press of America (1970, reprint 2002)
4. Nacke, E., L., Bateman, C., Mandryk, L., R.: BrainHex: Preliminary Results from a Neurobiological Games Typology Survey. In: 10th International Conference, ICEC 2011, Vancouver, Canada
5. Savi, R. Wangenheim, G. C., Borgatto, F.A.: MEEGA: a model for the evaluation of educational games for teaching software engineering. In: Conference: 25th Brazilian Symposium on Software Engineering (SBES), Sao Paulo, Brazil (2011)
6. Hartness, K.: Robocode: using games to teach artificial intelligence. J. Comput. Small Coll. 19(4), 287–291 (2004)
7. PugiXML - Light-weight, simple and fast XML parser for C++. https://pugixml.org. Accessed 10 Sep 2020
8. DigitalMars C/C++ Compilers. https://www.digitalmars.com. Accessed 18 Jun 2020
9. Petri, G., Wangenheim, G.C., Borgatto, F.A.: MEEGA+: an evolution of a model for the evaluation of educational games, INCoD, Brazilian Institude for Digital Convergence. Federal University of Santa Catarina, Brazil, p. 8, (2016)
10. Giannakoulas, A., Xinogalos, S.: A review of educational games for teaching programming to primary school students. In: Kalogiannakis, M., Papadakis, S., (ed.), Handbook of Research on Tools for Teaching Computational Thinking in P-12 Education, pp. 1–30. IGI Global (2020)
11. Malliarakis, C., Satratzemi, M., Xinogalos, S.: CMX: the effects of an educational MMORPG on learning and teaching computer programming. IEEE Trans. Learn. Technol. 10(2), 219–235 (2017)

What if "Lara Croft" Becomes a Video Game Designer? When Archaeologists "Dig" Serious Games

Samanta Mariotti[(✉)] [iD]

University of Siena, 53100 Siena, Italy
samanta.mariotti@unisi.it

Abstract. Over the last decades, video games have become a pervasive part of society. Today they represent one of the biggest sectors in the entertainment industry and their market share continues to increase. Archaeological content has been often used as a triggering subject but archaeologically inspired interactive entertainment titles are often an outlet for some of the worst kinds of pseudo-archaeological ideas (e.g. *Tomb Raider* series). Given the significant numbers of the video gaming industry, an evident fascination with the past by designers and consumers of games, and a marked risk of archaeology misconception, I suggest archaeologists should engage more with this medium and especially in SGs becoming the domain experts who select the educational contents and provide scientific validity and reliability. The paper focuses on the Italian experience in the last years where archaeological SGs are finally getting more academic recognition and underlines the positive effects of this approach in terms of educational goals for both kids and adults, widespread accurate knowledge for a wider and more diversified public, and eventually touristic outcomes. These are all aspects that the most recent and significant European conventions and documents concerning cultural heritage sustainable development stressed. Archaeological sites and museums can be greatly benefited by the use of SGs as much as archaeologists: as active agents in this process, they can inject a measure of ethical archaeology in the game industry and reach groups of people that, traditionally, have been relatively untouched by previous public education and outreach.

Keywords: Serious games · Archaeology · Heritage enhancement

1 It Could Work!

In the twenty-first century video gaming has become a major component of Western lifestyles. Today they represent one of the biggest sectors in the entertainment industry and their market share continues to increase. According to the most recent report [1], Italian situation respects these trends: in 2019 the industry turnover was EUR 1.787 million with a growth of 1.7% compared to 2018. In this context, a brief perusal of games' content also reveals themes that often incorporate archaeological content, sometimes highly accurate, other times (most frequently) not so much. In the last decades, the number of multimedia products developed within the archaeological community has certainly increased. However, the focus on peer-to-peer communication and university-based courseware has remained quite entrenched. As a result, the increasing public desire for sensational representations of the human past has been largely fulfilled by commercial interactive media producers that rarely have anywhere near the level of expertise necessary to produce titles that conform to the high content standards that archaeologists desire and that archaeology deserves.

Given the above - the significant numbers of the video gaming industry, an evident fascination with the past by designers and consumers of games, and a marked risk of archaeology misconception – we, as archaeologists, would be well advised to engage further with the world of gaming. It is not a coincidence that video games, or better, SGs, are a growing concern in academic research and present a considerable attraction for archaeologists who wish to present their research to audiences that may not be engaged with other forms of academic literature or media regarding archaeology [2–4]. The path, especially in Italy where these topics are still in an experimental stage, hasn't been easy. However, what Watrall stated back in 2002 with respect to the US [5] applies nowadays for Italy too: in fact, the recent development of institutionalized public archaeology programs has had the potential not only to face the interactive entertainment industry's increasing encroachment into archaeology but also to change the sentiments that many archaeologists hold toward interactive entertainment.

The above concerns, as well as the primary thrust of this discussion, is that archaeologically inspired interactive entertainment titles are often an outlet for some of the worst kinds of pseudo-archaeological ideas. One of the most obvious examples of this is the *Tomb Raider* series and its featured "archaeologist" Lara Croft which had a massive impact on the public's perception of archaeology and archaeologists. Given that I totally believe that it remains necessary to work in a multidisciplinary team since a SG requires a complex mix of professional skills, isn't perhaps time for us archaeologists to contribute to creating accurate narratives about the past through SGs?

In this paper, I will try to highlight the advantages that can derive from this approach from an archaeological perspective and underline the benefits of an archaeological SG in terms of educational goals for both kids and adults, widespread accurate knowledge for a wider and more diversified public, and eventually touristic outcomes.

2 Making Learning Fun

In the last years, SGs in the archaeological heritage domain in Italy have received more and more attention, gaining the interest of museum institutions, academics, and local administrations. They appear in a wide variety of forms, spanning from trivia, puzzles and mini-games, to engage in interactive exhibitions/visit, to mobile applications for museums or sites motivated by some reward/engagement mechanism, to adventures set in faithful reconstructions and/or digital counterparts of real sites [6].

The popularity of video games, especially among younger people (digital natives), makes them an ideal medium for educational purposes. All the researchers tell us kids learn things through play: they learn to interact with each other, to follow rules, the executive functions and problem-solving skills. Video games are successful because they seem to address today's approaches to challenges and are consistent with the needs of our time [7]. Moreover, SGs can provide player engagement by creating a fun experience for users while also supporting them to achieve learning objectives [8]. That is why games can also aid in familiarizing young and adult people with specific cultural heritage topics, and significantly increase their interest levels and engagement. The main feature of a SG is, in fact, its objective of supporting the player to achieve learning targets through a fun experience. The fun aspect of a SG can be determined by several factors like storyboard, graphics, usability, collaboration/competition mechanisms, and interaction devices [9]. The learning aspect implements a pedagogical approach, by structuring the educational content and organizing its presentation. An appealing and meaningful environment, a compelling narrative, and a suited and intuitive interaction paradigm are the three main elements to create engagement. Moreover, SGs for cultural heritage seem particularly suited for the affective domain. Empathy with a game character and plot may be very helpful for understanding historical events, different ancient cultures, problems, and behaviors, on the one hand, and the beauty and value of the past, architecture, art, and heritage, on the other one. Adventure games are particularly suited to implement the "learning by doing" approach, which is related to the constructivism theory, where the player learns by constructing knowledge while doing a meaningful activity [8]. In this approach to education, the learner does not passively receive information but rather actively constructs new knowledge by finding information in the game, understanding it, and then applying the new knowledge to fulfill tasks [10]. Moreover, SGs allow a personalized approach to learning: in most cases they can be consumed at home or at school, or both; a game can even be played partially at school, in small groups and with the support of the teacher, and partially at home for example as a tool to review the acquired knowledge.

3   Who Wants to Play?

Archeologists have their area of expertise regarding the historical and archeological content, the narrative, the storytelling. However, while designing a SG, different professionalism and different competence are essential for a good result: the technological aspects should be determined by other professionals whose knowledge about the game industry better fits the requests. Since we, as archeologists, are entering a completely new way of communicating, we have at least to understand the "new rules" of video game form. Knowing the audience we are addressing is fundamental, as it is crucial in every practice of communication, however, one of the main risks is to be too didactic since we are used to telling historical events and explain processes. In a SG, this would be totally wrong. In that case, in fact, you have to create the system to *show* the player, don't tell them.

Public engagement and the communication of the archaeological data have been on the top list of the major concern in Italian archeology debate in the last decade and the natural development of multiple strategies exploiting different mediums was a natural consequence of this new experimental attitude in which technology has been playing a central role. Video games, in particular, are a form of new media, whose novel affordances facilitate active participation and agency through player interaction with both content and digital systems, thus providing the player with the ability to direct or alter the course and outcome of the game as it progresses. The thrill of discovery and exploration combined with the opportunity to relive the past is something that appeals both on an instinctive and emotional level. Video games have played into this desire in several ways because they allow players - young and adults - to immerse themselves in the experience: in case of a SG set in the past, the authenticity of the space (whether stylized or not) and of the narrative is fundamental. In this sense archaeological expertise becomes essential and it can be easily translated both in set dressing and in information conveyed through boxes, dialogues, meaningful objects, etc. [11].

In order to encourage an actively involved player, free to explore and to interact, the creation of a "safe" setting in which errors, mistakes, wrong moves are allowed and have no "real" consequences is necessary. This "safe virtual space" is also supported by the "avatar" or in general by the possibility to play through someone else (a character) and with an interface screen that provides you the "right distance" between what is real and what is not.

4   From Virtual to Real and Return

According to recent studies, as in the case of films or books, video games should be considered as a driver of tourism [12]. A very recent survey of 827 Italian gamers confirmed that the majority of them (79,9%) are willing to visit a place they got to know through a video game and that 47,9% already did [13]. This possibility deserves to be carefully considered and exploited for many good reasons: to enhance the knowledge and the value of cultural heritage in general, to address public engagement and audience development, and to promote archaeological sites, parks, museums. The development of public archaeology as a field of study and the significant European conventions and documents released in the new millennium [14, 15] contributed to placing sustainable development through the promotion of cultural heritage at the center of the archaeological discourse. The commitment to public participation is of pivotal importance for archaeology, given the need to clearly demonstrate the extent of its economic and sociocultural impacts.

Once again, archeological SGs can be a strategical asset for achieving these objects. Games, in fact, are increasingly being played on mobile devices and this occurrence has a great potential to engage museum visitors. Mobile applications typically feature images, QR codes and exploit GPS position. One popular type of feature in this perspective is "location-gaming": the mechanic is that players go to places, do fast, simple tasks and win a reward. The possibility given by this mechanism motivates players on one hand and concretely involves cultural spaces on the other. This also allows museums, cultural institutions, and even local administrations to make themselves known, to develop a network of multiple connections, and to share common benefits deriving from this growth.

The "visiting time expansion" is another very interesting key point and it is probably the litmus test for the effectiveness of the SG project, because it allows us to evaluate what links the virtual scenario offered by SGs and the real space they represent. A SG offers the opportunity to expand visitors' time "in" the site and it can provide further information about it (potentially much more than any guide can do during a generic visit – just think for example of the *Assassin's Creed Discovery Tours* - and more fun than a book for the majority of people). Moreover, it gives players the chance to choose when to access that information: before, after, or during the visit. SGs can be adjusted and conceived to offer a tailored experience and to overcome time and space limitations. However, as we have seen, SGs can also be extremely convenient to engage a larger and more diversified audience and by doing so, to attract the public and bring people physically to specific places.

5   Conclusions

While several archaeological SGs have been developed in the last years, still the literature stresses a lack of significant, extensive user tests. This applies all the more to Italy where SGs are now slowly starting to be recognized as effective tools and applied in the field of cultural heritage enhancement. Further research is necessary to investigate in greater detail the real effectiveness of the various types of SGs, to define a methodology based on metrics and evaluation tools [16], even more so those with archaeological content.

Having said that, SGs are an acknowledged tool for several purposes. Amongst this range of possibilities, they can meet archaeological aims and so, represent an extraordinary medium for archeological heritage enhancement too: they are a potential for public outreach and education, because they can strongly motivate learners and create awareness about a topic; they can also provide immersive environments where a large variety of users can practice knowledge and skills; they can be used as an asset to promote tourism and sustainable cultural heritage development. The design of a SG requires the iterative collaboration of various experts with specific competences and skills. A SG in the archaeological heritage field cannot ignore the domain experts who select the educational contents and provide scientific validity and reliability. This teamwork aims at preventing the project from being just a game with an extra layer of pedagogical and pseudo-archaeological content. There needs to be a new breed of archaeologists who take an active participatory role, as consultants, developers, and writers. This is an ethical responsibility and a very stimulating possibility for archaeologists who are interested in exploring new ways to engage the public, share their research and promote archaeological sites and knowledge: actually, this kind of new interdisciplinary professional profiles can take up the challenge and, through SGs, create a brand new set of opportunities for professionals and archaeological heritage. By doing so, archaeologists can also have the chance to explore how and why creating and communicating through SGs might provide powerful new ways to think about, do, and present the past.

In this way, perhaps, we, real Lara Croft (and Indiana Jones), might become "change agents" in the interactive entertainment industry to ensure the ethical and proper representation of the archaeological discipline as well as human culture, both past and present.

References

1. Italian Interactive Digital Entertainment Association: I videogiochi in Italia nel 2019. Dati sul mercato e sui consumatori. Electronic document, (2020) https://bit.ly/2GiOMW9. Accessed 29 Jun 2020
2. Mol, A.A., Ariese-Vandemeulebroucke, C.E., Boom, K.H.J., Politopoulos, A. (eds.): The Interactive Past: Archaeology, Heritage, and Video Games. Sidestone Press, Leiden (2017)
3. Reinhard, A.: Archaeogaming: An Introduction to Archaeology in and of Video Games, 1st edn. Berghahn Books, New York (2018)
4. Hageneuer, S., (ed.): Communicating the Past in the Digital Age Proceedings of the International Conference on Digital Methods in Teaching and Learning in Archaeology (12–13 October 2018). Ubiquity Press, London (2020)
5. Watral, E.: Digital pharaoh: archaeology, public education, and interactive entertainment. Public Archaeol. 2(3), 163–169 (2002)
6. Mariotti, S.: Serious games and Archaeology: Rough Notes on Crafting Archaeological Data for Heritage Enhancement. In: de Carvalho Antunes, A., Angjeliu, G., Bellanova, M. (eds.): Advances in Interdisciplinary Cultural Heritage Studies, forthcoming
7. Shapiro, J.: The New Childhood: Raising Kids to Thrive in a Connected World, 1st edn. Little, Brown and Company, New York (2018)
8. Mortara, M., Catalano, C.E., Bellotti, F., Fiucci, G., Houry-Panchetti, M., Petridis, P.: Learning cultural heritage by SGs. J. Cult. Heritage 15(3), 318–325 (2014)
9. Mariotti, S., Marotta, N.: Gioco e storydoing: strumenti didattici per l'insegnamento della Storia nella Scuola Primaria. Didattica della Storia - Journal of Research and Didactics of History 2(1S), 608–629 (2020)
10. Froschauer, J.: Serious Heritage Games: Playful Approaches to Address Cultural Heritage. PhD Dissertation, Faculty of Informatics, Wien University of Technology, May 2012 (2012)
11. Anderson, E.F., McLoughlin, L., Liarokapis, F., Peters, C., Petridis, P., de Freitas, S.: Developing SGs for cultural heritage: a state-of-the-art review. Virtual Reality 14, 255–275 (2010). https://doi.org/10.1007/s10055-010-0177-3
12. Dubois, L.E., Gibbs, C.: Video game–induced tourism: a new frontier for destination marketers. Tourism Rev. 73(2), 186–198 (2018)
13. IVIPRO: Videogiochi e luoghi reali: analisi del questionario IVIPRO. Electronic document, (2019). https://bit.ly/32NtR5b. Accessed 07 Jul 2020
14. Council of Europe: Framework Convention on the Value of Cultural Heritage for Society (Faro Convention), Electronic Document, (2005). https://rm.coe.int/1680083746. Accessed 01 Jul 2020
15. Council of the european union: council conclusions on participatory governance of cultural heritage. Official J. Eur. Union C 463, 1–3 (2014)
16. Bellotti, F., Berta, R., De Gloria, A.: Designing effective SGs: opportunities and challenges for research. Int. J. Emerg. Technol. Learn. 5(3), 22–35 (2010)

The Colectyng Model for the Evaluation of Game-Based Learning Activities

Antoine Taly[1,2]([✉]) [ID], Damien Djaouti[3], and Julian Alvarez[4]

[1] CNRS, Universite de Paris, Lab. de Biochimie Théorique, UPR9080 Paris, France
[2] Institut de Biologie Physico -Chimique, Fondation Edmond de Rotchild,
PSL Research University, Paris, France
`taly@ibpc.fr`
[3] LIRDEF, University of Montpellier, Montpellier, France
`damien.djaouti@umontpellier.fr`
[4] EA2445 - DeVisu, University of Valenciennes, ESPE Lille NdF,
Valenciennes, France
`julian.alvarez@espe-lnf.fr`

Abstract. Games and/or play are often used in educational context as mediation. The resulting teaching or training activities are however difficult to assess. To set up a model to allow evaluating these activities, we choose to enrich an existing grid, that was developed in 2006 by Sara de Freitas and Martin Oliver, centered on pedagogical considerations. We propose to add dimensions relating to the game, the humans involved, and their interactions with the game. The resulting grid takes into account COntext, LEarner, Course scenario, Teacher, plaY aNd Game, making the Colectyng framework. The model was confronted to literature to see if we could complete the grid and whether all elements could fit in the model. Altogether our analysis suggest that the colectyng framework acts as a meta-model that could give a general view and could facilitate the articulation between more specialized models.

Keywords: Game-based learning · Evaluation

1 Introduction

Game Based Learning (GBL) is a controversial subject, prompting for a rigorous/agnostic framework to evaluate game-based learning activities and tools. As noted by Tahir and Wang it is not the case yet: "most studies focused only on one or two dimensions of GBL [...] highlighting the need for a comprehensive evaluation framework" [23]. One seminal work is the study by Sara de Freitas and Martin Oliver [7] that considers four criteria: Context, Learner specification, Pedagogic considerations, Mode of representation (Tools for use). The 'CEPAJe' model has then been proposed as an attempt to present a more complete model [2]. First, a new dimension was added for the trainer, because teachers play a key

Supported by the French Agency for Research ANR-11-LABX-0011 (AT).

I. Marfisi-Schottman et al. (Eds.): GALA 2020, LNCS 12517, pp. 401–407, 2020.
https://doi.org/10.1007/978-3-030-63464-3_38

role in the manner in which a play activity is introduced within the lesson and the debriefing is carried out once the activity has ended [7,21]. Furthermore, a second entry was added to take into account the key stages in the activity, namely the brief, activity animation and debriefing. Horizontally, the assessment criteria were put in relation to these key stages. The resulting CEPAJe model is presented in Fig. 1.

Criteria / Dimensions	Game culture	Play skills	Introduction to the activity	Carrying out the activity	Debriefing the activity
Context (1 Context)	–	–	Does the place affect this phase of the activity?	Does the place affect this phase of the activity?	Does the place affect this phase of the activity?
Trainer (New dimension)	History, resources, markets, vocabulary...	Play skills patterns understanding	Ability to engage students in the game activity	Ability to help students during the game activity	Ability to link game with learning outcomes
Learner/Play (2- Learner specifications)	History, resources, markets, vocabulary...	Play skills patterns understanding	Will to enter in the gaming activity	Ability to use and read the game	Ability to take distance from the game
Pedagogy (3- Pedagogic considerations)	–	–	Games integrated in didactic scenario. Learning objectives?	The scenario takes game limitations into account	The scenario anticipates transfer
Game (4- Mode of representation)	–	–	mapping of games elements vs learning objectives	The game proposes help and accessibility tools	The games gives feedback on players accomplishments.

Fig. 1. The CEPAJe model [2]

In fine, the framework should be as exhaustive as possible to allow better design and evaluation of game-based learning activities. Therefore, the CEPAJe model is confronted to the literature to test whether it allows to take into account all the relevant parameters. **The underlying hypothesis is that the model is a form of meta-model.** It is therefore expected that: i) taking into account new data will allow to fill the grid; ii) no element will fall outside of the grid; iii) Models describing details could be encapsulated in the grid but that the depth of specialized models might not be completely represented in the general grid.

2   Filling the Grid

We explore here the possibility to fill the grid, i.e. do empty boxes in Fig. 1 correspond to known situations? We also try to see if the framework is exhaustive, i.e. if there are known situations that do not fit in the framework.

The Context. As noted by De freitas, "it is important to consider all the possible implications of adopting game-based learning in your practice such as context of use, duration of study periods, technical support, community of practitioners." [6]. The experience of the organization with games and game-based learning will therefore impact the activity. De Freitas also noted that game-based learning involves "greater flexibility not least in terms of learning session durations, assessment modes and accreditation" [6]. We therefore propose to add 'Technical context' to the 'Play skill' column to illustrate the influence of the context on the play potential.

The Trainer. Even though the teacher is not required to play the games, she must guide play during the activity and provide support for learners. The experience of teachers with games is far from obvious [22], and therefore needs to be taken into account. In parallel, the teacher must ensure there is a connection with the 'educational scenario'. This implies a specific skill as the successful association is not easy [18]. The (lack of) play skills and game culture has been cited as one of the main reasons to not use games in education [20]. The trainer playskills are therefore important and should be added.

The Learner. A given game can have different signification for different players [13]. The experience of a 'game' used for learning can be dramatically modified by a participant previous play experience [17,19]. The enjoyment of e-learning games, or flow, can be considered as shown by the EGameFlow scale [9] or the EduFlow model [12]. We therefore propose to add flow factors and playskills to the learner dimension.

The Pedagogy. Defining the pedagogical objective is of course a prerequisite before the creation of a serious game [4], and should appear in the antecedent column. There also needs to be a connection between the game mechanics and pedagogy [3], which might require the possibility to alter the game (see below). Interestingly, skills can be developed by gamers regarding their fine dexterity and their aptitude for carrying out several tasks simultaneously [5] or visual abilities linked to attention [11]. As a consequence, skills developed by the game need to be studied.

The Game. In term of context, a question that should be asked is who produced the game, as this might raise ethical issues[15]. The game genre can have an impact on pedagogical considerations. Indeed, a game that has a sandbox mode would allow a teacher to design an exercise. We therefore propose to alter the game culture entry to take into account the game genre. That allows to create an intersection between the game and trainer/learner/pedagogy. The serious goal implies that the game needs to be adapted to everyone, including non-gamers [16] and in case of disability [26,27]. They should provide appropriate challenges so that the player's skill level can be easily matched by varying the level of difficulty [9].

3   Including Other Models from the Literature

This section confront the grid with models found in the literature. Articles were identified in a literature survey looking for "game-based learning" and (framework or model). The following articles were selected after abstract review:

All, et al. 2015. The study by All and collaborators is centered on assessing the effectiveness of digital game-based learning [1]. One crucial aspect of the study is the evaluation of learning outcomes. Learning outcomes, and their evaluation, is not present in CEPAJe but can be added in the pedagogy line.

Kiili, 2005. Kiili focuses on flow [14] which corresponds to the learner/play line. The study identifies three times: Flow antecedents, Flow experience and Flow consequences that correspond to the briefing, Activity animation and debrief stages. The term antecedent is however larger than just the introduction phase and encompass aspect that have been proposed above. We therefore propose to adopt the name 'Antecedent' for the second column. Interestingly Flow antecedent has three poles (Person/Task/Artefact) that correspond to intersection between game and learner/play and points to the need to add connection between boxes (see below).

Gosper, et al. 2012. The MAPLET framework analyses the alignment between learning outcomes, students' expertise and assessment methods [10]. The elements of the framework are: Students expertise, Aims/outcomes, Processes, activities and Assessment. Each element can be placed in the grid. Student expertise finds its place at the Learner/Antecedent intersection. Aim/outcomes are already present but would rather fit under the antecedent category. Processes and activities correspond to the column devoted to the activity, respectively in the Pedagogy and Game lines. The assessment is already present at the intersection of Pedagogy and Debriefing.

Tan, et al. 2007. The "Adaptive digital game-based learning framework" proposes design principles for game-based learning [24]. The framework explores two dimensions, learner and game design, that fit easily the learner and game dimensions. For the learner dimension two essential aspects identified are psychological needs and cognitive development, that match the student expertise added above. In addition, learning behaviors is proposed as a significant factor which fits with the flow factors. The game design dimension corresponds to the intersection of the Game line and the activity column. The task corresponds to the activity added above, whereas, feedback and narration could be added at that level.

Foster, et al. 2012. The study by Foster combines two elements, the TPACK and the PCaRD framework and methodology [8]. The idea of combining two models is congruent with the notion of a meta-model coordinating more specialized models. The TPACK framework takes into account the Technological, pedagogical and content knowledge, which corresponds to the antecedent for the learner. The PCaRD model considers the link of the game with the learning outcomes, the role of the debriefing, including reflection and discussion, and the influence of context, which are all present in the grid.

Van Staalduinen, et al. 2011. The study by van Staalduinen and de Freitas brings together three frameworks to create a new one, again in agreement with the notion of a meta-model [25]. In their proposed framework, the main elements are: i) the pedagogy (background, learning objectives, instructional design, assessment and alignment), ii) users behavior and system feedback, iii) gameplay and player motivation/flow. All of those aspects are already present in the colectyng framework.

4 Conclusion and Perspectives

Starting out with the CEPAJe model, and by taking into account the various suggestions, we obtain the enriched model recorded in Fig. 2. The five dimensions, can be renamed Course scenario, Teacher, plaY aNd Game, making the Colectyng framework. We have then looked for missing parameters, as well as for other models/frameworks, to see if we could complete the grid and whether all elements could fit in the model. We found that it was possible to reach a much more complete framework (compare Figs. 1 and 2). We note however that to reach that goal we had to change names and that our literature review was not exhaustive. Thus, although we might thus have missed exceptions, altogether our analysis suggest that the colectyng framework indeed acts as a meta-model that could give a general view and could facilitate the articulation between more specialized models. Our analysis remains however preliminary. In particular the framework will have to be operationalized: e.g. made more uniform, with items transformed in questions, with direct connections to specialized models. It will then have to be tested in real life...

Criteria / Dimensions	Game culture Game genre ludopedagogic alignment	Antecedent Technical aspects Abilities, Play skills	Introduction to the activity	Carrying out the activity	Debriefing the activity
Context (1 Context)	Organization game culture	Technical context (cost, material, time, etc)	Does the place affect this phase of the activity?	Does the place affect this phase of the activity?	Does the context affect this phase of the activity?
Trainer (New dimension)	History, resources, markets, vocabulary...	Ability to read patterns	Ability to engage students in the game activity	Ability to help students during the game activity	Ability to link game with learning outcomes
Learner/Play (2- Learner specifications)	History, resources, markets, vocabulary... Player type	Ability to read patterns Student expertise	Will to enter in the gaming activity	Ability to use and read the game Flow factors	Ability to take distance from the game Reflection, discussion
Pedagogy (3- Pedagogic considerations)	Does the game allow for content creation?	Learning objectives? Do special need learner need accommodation?	Games integrated in didactic scenario.	Processes (->activities). Game limitations considered	The scenario anticipates transfer Assessment
Game (4- Mode of representation)	Who produced the game? Game genre (-> pedagogy)	Adapted to all players? Accessibility /scaffolding	mapping of games elements vs learning objectives	Activities (-> Processes) The game proposes help and accessibility tools	The games gives feedback on players accomplishments.

Fig. 2. The Colectyng framework

References

1. All, A., Castellar, E.P.N., Van Looy, J.: Towards a conceptual framework for assessing the effectiveness of digital game-based learning. Comput. Educ. **88**, 29–37 (2015)
2. Alvarez, J., Chaumette, P.: Présentation d'un modèle dédié à l'évaluation d'activités ludo-pédagogiques et retours d'expériences. Recherche et pratiques pédagogiques en langues de spécialité **36**(2), (2017)
3. Arnab, S., et al.: Mapping learning and game mechanics for serious games analysis. British J. Educ. Technol. **46**(2), 391–411 (2015)
4. Baaden, M., Delalande, O., Ferey, N., Pasquali, S., Waldispühl, J., Taly, A.: Ten simple rules to create a serious game, illustrated with examples from structural biology (2018)
5. Berry, V.: Les cadres de l'expérience virtuelle: Jouer, vivre, apprendre dans un monde numérique: analyse des pratiques ludiques, sociales et communautaires des joueurs de jeux de rôles en ligne massivement multi-joueurs: Dark Age of Camelot et World of Warcraft. Ph.D. thesis, Paris 13 (2009)

6. De Freitas, S.: Learning in immersive worlds: A review of game-based learning (2006)

7. De Freitas, S., Oliver, M.: How can exploratory learning with games and simulations within the curriculum be most effectively evaluated? Comput. Educ. **46**(3), 249–264 (2006)

8. Foster, A.: Assessing learning games for school content: the TPACK-PCaRD framework and methodology. In: Ifenthaler, D., Eseryel, D., Ge, X. (eds.) Assessment in Game-Based Learning, pp. 201–215. Springer, New York (2012). https://doi.org/10.1007/978-1-4614-3546-4_11

9. Fu, F.L., Su, R.C., Yu, S.C.: Egameflow: a scale to measure learners' enjoyment of e-learning games. Comput. Educ. **52**(1), 101–112 (2009)

10. Gosper, M., McNeill, M.: Implementing game-based learning: the MAPLET framework as a guide to learner-centred design and assessment. In: Ifenthaler, D., Eseryel, D., Ge, X. (eds.) Assessment in Game-Based Learning. Springer, New York (2012). https://doi.org/10.1007/978-1-4614-3546-4_12

11. Green, C.S., Bavelier, D.: Action video game modifies visual selective attention. Nature **423**(6939), 534 (2003)

12. Heutte, J., Fenouillet, F., Kaplan, J., Martin-Krumm, C., Bachelet, R.: The Edu-Flow model: a contribution toward the study of optimal learning environments. In: Harmat, L., Ørsted Andersen, F., Ullén, F., Wright, J., Sadlo, G. (eds.) Flow Experience, pp. 127–143. Springer, Cham (2016). https://doi.org/10.1007/978-3-319-28634-1_9

13. Juul, J.: The game, the player, the world: Looking for a heart of gameness. PLURAIS-Revista Multidisciplinar **1**(2), 248–270 (2018)

14. Kiili, K.: Digital game-based learning: towards an experiential gaming model. Internet High. Educ. **8**(1), 13–24 (2005)

15. Lavigne, M.: Les faiblesses ludiques et pédagogiques des serious games. In: Actes du Colloque international TICEMED. vol. 9 (2014)

16. Law, E., Ahn, L.V.: Human computation. Synth. Lect. Artif. Intell. Mach. Learn. **5**(3), 1–121 (2011)

17. Linderoth, J.: Why gamers don't learn more: an ecological approach to games as learning environments. J. Gaming Virtual Worlds **4**(1), 45–62 (2012)

18. Marfisi-Schottman, I.: Méthodologie, modèles et outils pour la conception de Learning Games. Ph.D. thesis, Lyon, INSA (2012)

19. Martin, L.: Entraves à l'attitude ludique avec un jeu sérieux intégré dans une formation managériale: un exercice plus qu'un jeu? Sciences du jeu (7) (2017)

20. Ruggill, J.E., McAllister, K.S.: Against the use of computer games in the classroom: The wickedness of ludic pedagogies. The Game Culture Reader. Eds. Ouellette, Marc A., Jason, C., Thompson. Newcastle: Cambridge Scholars Publishing (2013)

21. Sanchez, E.: Le paradoxe du marionnettiste. Ph.D. thesis, Université Paris Descartes (2014)

22. Sun-Lin, H.Z., Chiou, G.F.: Instruments for facilitating science teachers' awareness of general and learning games (April 2012)

23. Tahir, R., Wang, A.I.: State of the art in game based learning: dimensions for evaluating educational games. In: European Conference on Games Based Learning. pp. 641–650. Academic Conferences International Limited (2017)

24. Tan, P.H., Ling, S.W., Ting, C.Y.: Adaptive digital game-based learning framework. In: Proceedings of the 2nd international conference on Digital interactive media in entertainment and arts, pp. 142–146. ACM (2007)

25. Van Staalduinen, J.P., de Freitas, S.: A game-based learning framework: linking game design and learning. Learn. Play Exploring Future Educ. Video Games **53**, 29 (2011)

26. Westin, T., Dupire, J.: Design of a curriculum framework for raising awareness of game accessibility. In: Miesenberger, K., Bühler, C., Penaz, P. (eds.) ICCHP 2016. LNCS, vol. 9758, pp. 501–508. Springer, Cham (2016). https://doi.org/10.1007/978-3-319-41264-1_68

27. Westin, T., Dupire, J.: Evaluation and redesign of a curriculum framework for education about game accessibility. In: Wallner, G., Kriglstein, S., Hlavacs, H., Malaka, R., Lugmayr, A., Yang, H.-S. (eds.) ICEC 2016. LNCS, vol. 9926, pp. 217–222. Springer, Cham (2016). https://doi.org/10.1007/978-3-319-46100-7_20

Farming Simulation Game for Sufficient Economy Theory Learning in Thailand

Ronakrit Taweechainaruemitr[(⊠)] and Tanasai Sucontphunt

Graduate School of Applied Statistics, National Institute of Development Administration, Bangkok, Thailand
peach.ronakrit@gmail.com

Abstract. A farming game is a very entertaining and popular simulation game. The main goal of this game genre is to successfully manage resources by expanding farms, growing more resources, and generating more income. In this work, instead, the main goal of our game is to sufficiently use of resources and to be ready for a crisis according to a sufficiency economy theory. This theory is the way of life and it can intuitively be explained by examples using games. Thus, we develop V-Survival, a sufficient farming game to be played and, on some level, subconsciously learnt the theory. Our evaluation illustrates that our game can help players understand some concepts of sufficient economy theory better than those who did not play the game.

Keywords: Farming game · Sufficient economy · Self-immunity · Mixed gardening · Educational game

1 Introduction

Sufficient economy theory [1] is a way of life and a philosophy developed by the late King Bhumibol Adulyadej of Thailand. The theory comprises three main pillars which are moderation, reasonableness, and self-immunity. There are many concepts in the theory and they can be found in Mongsawad's article [6]. In this work, we focus only on a fraction of the self-immunity part which is a mixed gardening concept. It is the overall idea of self-reliance i.e. being independent from the modern trading system and having immunity to a crisis. The mixed gardening concept utilizes the use of land to grow a variety of plants for creating an ecosystem rather than to grow one type of plant that requires extra attentions. Instead of selling a single type of high price farming product and spending the money to buy food, the ecosystem produces food by itself and the left out farming products can then be sold for money. The theory can be demonstrated intuitively by practicing with scenarios and activities in the simulation game.

Typical farming games such as Stardew Valley and Hay Day focuses their gameplay on expanding farming production and construction by growing more resources. Their main simulation is about manipulation the resources to achieve to the next and bigger level. The bigger farm means more success in the game.

© Springer Nature Switzerland AG 2020
I. Marfisi-Schottman et al. (Eds.): GALA 2020, LNCS 12517, pp. 408–414, 2020.
https://doi.org/10.1007/978-3-030-63464-3_39

In our game, the main simulation is also about balancing resources but, instead of growing a bigger farm, the goal is to be able to survive in a crisis when the system is no longer the same such as when a disaster making a shortest of external resources. In our game, V-Survival, players have to survive only by consuming farming products. If they were not able to generate enough products within the time limit, the game is over. To generate the products, they have an option to grow their products all by themselves or buy some of them with money. The money can be obtained from selling products which are vegetables, chickens, eggs, and organic fertilizer. Some products can be sold at high prices. With limited space, players have to choose between products to grow each time. At a typical game time, buying some products is doable and players can survive without problems. However, at a crisis time when the resources are limited, product cost will be a lot higher than typical price and some products are no longer available at all. Thus, players need to balance between selling their products for money and keeping all resources balanced to consume by themselves. In our game, we attempt to give realistic simulation parameters rather than biasing the game to one direction so that players can try to survive with their own choices and see it by themselves about the benefit of each direction especially on having an immunity to a crisis.

2 Related Work

Digital games which are carefully designed for education are an effective method for learning [2]. Several works illustrate that the method can be used in a variety of subjects. Some games focus on sending direct learning messages to students via interactive games. Appel et al. [3] develops a game to raise awareness of canal maintenance for children by let's players recognize what objects are harmful to the canal. Miletic and Lesaja [5] use e-learning software to encourage students to comprehend linear programming. Vanbecelaere et al. [10] develop number sense and reading games for math and reading practices. Holz et al. [4] develops a mobile game for german dyslexic children by designing a stress pattern.

Some others focus on using a simulation game to give students indirect learning messages. Petri et al. [8] evaluate digital and non-digital games in Project Management learning via role-play games. Ouariachi et al. [7] study the effect of playing a strategic climate change game on spanish and american teenagers. Tan and Okamoto [9] investigate an effectiveness of a game-based strategy of sustainable tourism simulation. Our game is also a simulation game attempting to give students indirect learning messages via its gameplay.

3 Game Design

The goal of our V-Survival game (Fig. 1) is to survive on an exotic planet (V-planet). The game is developed using Unity Game Engine for Android mobile phone. The V-planet is an earth-like planet where the seasons and soil are very similar to earth as shown in Fig. 1. This will give players a stronger sense of being

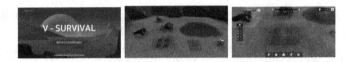

Fig. 1. Left: splash screen of V-Survival: a self-sufficient farming game, middle: the game's environment, right: starter status of the game.

isolated and independent since there is a different social system than earth. The only way to survive is to farm a vegetable and animal. Every some period of time, players are required to refill their health by having a complete set of nutritions. There are five types of nutritions (in Thai nutritions) which are Protein (P), Carbohydrate (C), Mineral (M), Vitamin (V), and Fat (F). Each farming product contains some types of the nutritions. Figure 1 shows an example set of farming products to refill the health. If some of the farming products are not enough, players can buy them with money which is limited. The money can be also obtained from selling the farming products.

4 Game Mechanic

Each player starts the game with given vegetable seeds, water, fertilizer, and money. From Fig. 1 (rightmost), the required nutritions are shown on the middle-left of the screen and the player's job is to fill the nutritions with farming products to be ready to refill the health bar showing on the top-left when the health bar reaches 0 percent.

4.1 Farming Products

There are 10 vegetable and 2 animal products. Figure 2 shows the products, their nutritions, and the health refill portion. The vegetable products are Soy Bean, Cucumber, Rice, Corn, Bean sprouts, Kale, Carrot, Basil, Cabbage, Paprika. The animal products are chicken's Meat and Eggs. The player will start farming vegetable products by selecting which vegetable to grow on the limited garden space using a menu shown in Fig. 3 and the growing process will be shown in Fig. 3. To grow the vegetables, the player needs seeds, water, and fertilizer. If they are not enough, the player can buy them with money. Each vegetable contains its best-yielding season showing as an icon on the top left of the vegetable thumbnail. There are 3 seasons of Summer, Raining, and Winter showing in Fig. 3 (middle). If the vegetables are grown in different seasons than the best-yielding season, the yielding will be a lot less than it should be. Once the garden is harvested, it will generate seeds for the next farming. This will give the player the knowledge about gardening.

To farm the animal products, the player needs to pay with money to buy the animals using a menu showing in Fig. 3 and the progress will be shown in Fig. 3. Each animal will require some rice to raise. If there are not enough rice in the farm, it can also be bought with money.

Nutrition	Product	Refill Portion
Protein	Soy Bean	5.56%
	Cucumber	7.14%
	Meat	6.67%
Carbohydrate	Rice	8.33%
	Corn	5.88%
	Egg	4.00%
Minerals	Bean sprouts	6.25%
	Kale	7.69%
Vitamin	Carrot	6.67%
	Basil	7.69%
Fat	Cabbage	7.14%
	Paprika	5.56%

Fig. 2. Left: the nutritions and their farming products with the refill portion to the health. Right: an example set of farming products to refill the health.

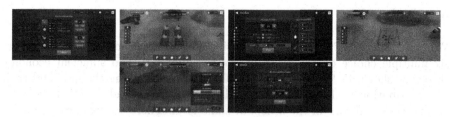

Fig. 3. Top two leftmost: the gardening system for vegetable selection. Top two rightmost: the animal farming system. Bottom: water and fertilizer system.

4.2 Water and Fertilizer

Water and fertilizer are the main resources to grow vegetables. The water can only be obtained from nature especially in the rainy season as shown in Fig. 3. The fertilizer can be obtained from unyield (rotten) vegetables and/or animal waste using a menu in Fig. 3.

4.3 Selling Farming Product by Exporting

To sell the farming products for money, the player can use a menu showing in Fig. 4 by clicking on the spaceship. It will show the farming products in the inventory to be selected for exporting to a space market by the spaceship (Fig. 4). Some farming product prices are a lot higher than an average price e.g. chicken and carrot. Thus, the player is tempted to farm only some specific products to get more money rather than farm a mix of products for self-sufficiency and having immunity to the crisis.

Fig. 4. Two leftmost: the export system. Two rightmost: the crisis scene

4.4   Crisis

After the player refilled the health for a second time, there will be a disaster (a comet storm) as shown in Fig. 4 which destroys the export system as well as makes all the farming product costs a lot higher than usual. After this period of time, the player will now have to survive mainly by the farming products since the money will run out very quickly. The player will now have to survive until the next health refill period when the rescue spaceship arrives (Fig. 4). The trick to survive in the crisis is to be self-sufficient and try not to depend on the trading system which is the core idea of the self-immunity.

5   Evaluation

We evaluate the V-Survival game by using a sufficient economy quiz. There are six multiple choice questions about the self-immunity and sufficient economy theory as shown in Fig. 5. There are 30 participants taking the quiz and their age distribution is shown in Fig. 5. All of them had already studied the sufficient economy theory in the school at some level. There are two groups in this evaluation: Never-Play group and Played group. Fifteen of them did not play the V-Survival game are in Never-Play group while the other fifteen played the game (about 10 min each) are in Played group. Figure 5 shows the number of the correct answers for each question of each group. Figure 6 shows box-plot of the scores of the two groups. From the Figure, P-value is about 0.1014 and we cannot reject the null hypothesis. However, if we focus only on three main questions (1–3) which are the core ideas of the game about the self-immunity and sufficient economy concept, the Fig. 6 shows its box plot in which P-value is about 0.0376 where we can reject the null hypothesis. This suggests that our V-Survival game can help students to recall the core concept of the self-immunity and sufficient economy theory at some level.

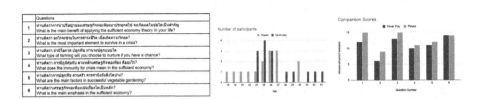

Fig. 5. Left: the sufficient economy questions for the participants. Middle: the age distribution of all 30 participants. Right: the correct answers of each question of all participants.

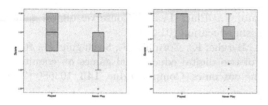

Fig. 6. The box plot of 30 participants. Left: 6 question scores. Right: 3 main question scores.

6   Conclusion and Future Work

In this work, we develop a game called V-Survival, a farming simulation game, to assist students to learn about a mixed gardening concept of the sufficient economy theory. The evaluation shows that our game can help the players to understand and recall the self-immunity concepts while entertaining by its gameplay. In the future, we are planning to develop the other concepts of the sufficient economy theory and to evaluate more on the effectiveness of our method especially in the entertaining part. The V-Survival can be downloaded and played on Android phones at https://sites.google.com/view/v-survival-isproject (only in Thai for now).

References

1. https://www.chaipat.or.th/eng/concepts-theories/sufficiency-economy-new-theory.html
2. All, A., Castellar, E.P.N., Van Looy, J.: Assessing the effectiveness of digital game-based learning. Comput. Educ. **92**, 90–103 (2016)
3. Appel, Y., Dimitrov, Y., Gnodde, S., van Heerden, N., Kools, P., Swaab, D., Salamon, N.Z., Balint, J.T., Bidarra, R.: A serious game to inform young citizens on canal water maintenance. In: Liapis, A., Yannakakis, G.N., Gentile, M., Ninaus, M. (eds.) GALA 2019. LNCS, vol. 11899, pp. 394–403. Springer, Cham (2019). https://doi.org/10.1007/978-3-030-34350-7_38
4. Holz, Heiko., Brandelik, Katharina., Brandelik, Jochen., Beuttler, Benedikt., Kirsch, Alexandra., Heller, Jürgen, Meurers, Detmar: Prosodiya – a mobile game for german dyslexic children. In: Dias, João, Santos, Pedro A., Veltkamp, Remco C. (eds.) GALA 2017. LNCS, vol. 10653, pp. 73–82. Springer, Cham (2017). https://doi.org/10.1007/978-3-319-71940-5_7
5. Miletic, L., Lesaja, G.: Research and evaluation of the effectiveness of e-learning in the case of linear programming. Croatian Oper. Res. Rev. **7**, 109–127 (2016)
6. Mongsawad, P.: The philosophy of the sufficiency economy: a contribution to the theory of development. Asia-Pacific Dev. J. **5**, 123–143 (2017)
7. Ouariachi, T., Olvera-Lobo, M.D., Gutiérrez-Perez, J.: Can serious games help to mitigate climate change? exploring their influence on Spanish and American teenagers. Psyecology **9**, 1–31 (2018)
8. Petri, G., Calderón, A., von Wangenheim, C.G., Borgatto, A.F., Ruiz, M.: Games for teaching software project management: an analysis of the benefits of digital and non-digital games. J. UCS **24**, 1424–1451 (2018)

9. Tan, E., Okamoto, Y.: iPlay, iLearn, iConserve: digital game-based learning for sustainable tourism education (01 2018)
10. Vanbecelaere, S., Berghe, K., Cornillie, F., Sasanguie, D., Reynvoet, B., Depaepe, F.: The effects of two digital educational games on cognitive and non-cognitive math and reading outcomes. Comput. Educ. **143**, 103680 (2019)

Game Mechanics of a Character Progression Multiplayer Role-Playing Game with Science Content

Varvara Garneli[(✉)], Konstantinos Patiniotis, and Konstantinos Chorianopoulos

Ionian University, Corfu, Greece
{c13garn,c15pati,choko}@ionio.gr

Abstract. Current game-based learning designs incorporate the multiplayer component as delegation of tasks, with the meaning that individuals accept the game rules, interact with each other, but they do not necessarily share the same goals. We employed gameplay mechanics of the Multiplayer Role-Playing Games (MRPGs), such as character's progression and a turn-based battle system to encapsulate multiple aspects of science learning and to provide students with a tighter collaborative learning experience. SAIR is a chemistry MRPG that can be played with up to 4 persons. Further research should evaluate with students the influence of collaborative gameplay in science learning.

Keywords: Multiplayer Role-Playing games · Game design · Science education · Chemistry

1 Introduction

Role-Playing Games (RPGs) are a popular game genre that provides affordances for the integration of science and technology courses in playful learning environments [4]. There is a variety of serious games with chemistry content that have been designed to influence student attitudes towards Chemistry [8] or to integrate formal school curriculum [2, 4], employing game elements, such as pop-quiz questions, quests to be performed, and even a turn-based battle system [2, 4]. Minecraft in Education is a popular learning environment that combines the creative mode for building representations and applying the blocks' functionality [9] with the survival mode to give a playful character to the game. Although Minecraft has a first-person perspective, it incorporates the multiplayer component [13]. Ideally, collaboration requires players to share the same goal and to act together to maximize the team's utility [16]. From this viewpoint, collaboration in Minecraft occurs in a freeform (See Table 1. Multiplayer Science Games and this feature does not necessarily generate social game learning [9]. Similarly, Alkhimia is a Multiplayer Role-Playing Game (MRPG) with chemistry content. Players individually perform separation techniques, improving their weapons in a virtual lab and test them against monsters, making comparisons to understand the educational content (See Table 1. Multiplayer Science Games [12]. Massively Multiplayer Online (MMO) games

© Springer Nature Switzerland AG 2020
I. Marfisi-Schottman et al. (Eds.): GALA 2020, LNCS 12517, pp. 415–420, 2020.
https://doi.org/10.1007/978-3-030-63464-3_40

could be also used in science classes to teach fundamental concepts to a big number of players. Shudayfat, et al. (2014) suggested a 3D MMO environment where students solve reaction quests by exploring for elements and solving puzzles to get the necessary materials. The game is cooperative, and therefore, students can communicate and help each other during the game, if they want (See Table 1. Multiplayer Science Games).

Table 1. Multiplayer science games with focus to chemistry

Chemistry game	Educational content	Connecting gaming with learning	Game's use in science classes	Multiplayer element
Mincraft Education	Open ended sandbox/science content	No	free form	cooperative
Alkhimia	A science inquiry/Chemistry	Separation techniques/improving the weapons.	Extra in-class curricula materials	cooperative
3D MMO	Chemical reactions	Reaction quests/searching & puzzle solving	Online use	cooperative

Game mechanics could strictly require players to act together to achieve the group's common goal. However, we did not find games that integrate science learning in such collaborative gameplay mechanics. Our aim is to integrate chemistry content in the game-play mechanics of the MRPGs, We designed and developed MaSters of AIR (SAIR) for students who are 14 years old to learn and practice the school curriculum, connecting the content with real world applications and supporting meaningful collaborative learning. We decided to integrate the chapter of oxygen which includes the oxygen properties, the oxides, and the combustions, as they are described in the schoolbook [17]. We expect that this effort will become a blueprint for integrating chemistry content in the structure of MRPGs, providing an alternative educational tool for students and their teachers.

The rest of the paper is organized into the following sections. Section 2 describes the Game Design and Development while Sect. 3 discusses and concludes the study.

2   Game Design and Development

SAIR is an educational MRPG with chemistry content that can be played by up to 4 players, integrating social mechanics that can motivate student creativity and enhance learning. The game story is about a hidden formula with great powers which covers the earth, but that valuable information has been stolen. The alchemist guides our heroes to reveal those information through a series of challenges, such as exploration, riddles and problems to be solved, combats [1] etc. Through those processes, players increase their strength and progress the game-plot [10]. The storytelling, a core element of all RPGs [15] supported our effort to effectively present the content, using a graphic environment and various Non Playable Characters (NPCs) [11] and connecting the world of atoms and molecules with observations of the macroscopic world. At the same time, the players learn and practice introductory chemistry curriculum, making connections with real-world applications. The integrated educational content regards oxygen, a basic component of the atmospheric air [17]. Learning occurs in the game through the interaction with the NPCs and the game world and additionally through collaboration among the party members.

The game's sequence in a rough timeline is used to identify the concrete components of the serious game activities and their connections, presenting the game's structure [3]. Therefore, SAIR is described from the following timeline (See Table 2).

Table 2. Game sequence

Game periods	Activities	Description
Game Intro.	Gaming	Introduction. Game period selection
Game period 1:	Gaming	Players reveal valuable information. Each one acquires a special skill. Players collaborate, combining those skills against their first enemy.
	Learning	Students learn the oxygen attributes. Students produce/detect oxygen.
	Instructional	NPCs introduce curriculum and guide players to perform tasks. NPCs challenge players & reward them with skills.
Game period 2:	Gaming	Players reveal more valuable information. Each player solves a problem to acquire a special skill. Players look for the volcano cave to find Chimera and combine their skills against it.
	Learning	Students learn to define oxides, to give examples, and to solve the chemical equations
	Instructional	NPCs introduce curriculum and guide players to perform tasks. NPCs challenge players & reward them with skills.
Game period 3:	Gaming	Players reveal more valuable information. Each player solves a problem and acquires a special skill of combustions. They travel with a hydrogen balloon, looking for the dragon. Players combine their skills, fighting the dragon to claim important materials.
	Learning	Students learn to define combustions, to give examples, and to solve chemical equations
	Instructional	NPCs introduce curriculum and guide players to perform tasks. NPCs challenge players & reward them with skills.
Game end	Gaming	Characters celebrate their victories

SAIR is based on a narrative and, therefore, players move in a 2D space, using their avatars and interacting with the game world. Players act as a party, performing together several quests in a free form, such as exploring the game world to find special items or locations, using items to observe their reactions under the guidance of the NPCs etc. Moreover, SAIR uses a skill system that links student experimental observations and chemical equations solving with a turn-based battle system. The correct solution of riddles and problems awards players with skills that are required for the game progression, as enemies cannot be defeated without them. After all players have used their skills, it is possible to defeat an enemy on the turn-based battle system, a system that does not require quick reaction, but the players' acquired skills and strength (See Fig. 1). In particular, the battle system of SAIR is based on the feature of invulnerability, a state in which specified characters of the game are impervious to all damage. The fight with an invulnerable enemy is a fight that can force players to search for a special item or to acquire a special skill. Therefore, in SAIR each player must combine his/her skills with those of the other players against the invulnerability of an enemy (See Fig. 1). This will give the party the opportunity to defeat this enemy. That way, we facilitate collaboration among players in the game.

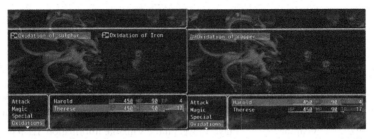

Fig. 1. Harold uses the oxidation of copper skill and therese uses the oxidations of sulfur and iron skills to defeat the chimera's invulnerability).

At the same time, students play the game to learn through active experimentation and reflective observation (See Fig. 2)

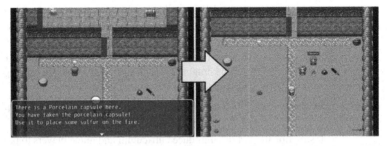

Fig. 2. Sulfur oxidation experiment.

Moreover, the students must not only remember and understand the educational content but additionally, they must be able to identify the content and to respond to related phenomena (See Fig. 3.)

Connections with real world applications are used throughout the game to empower science learning. Several examples have been used, e.g. students need to think where

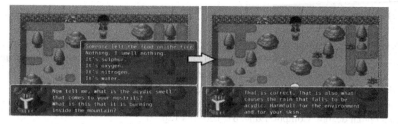

Fig. 3. The riddle of volcano, sulfur dioxide combustion in an active volcano

fish find the oxygen they need, combining the oxygen attributes curriculum with their observations. Another example is that players use hydrogen as a fuel to fly to the dragon's land with a balloon, after learning about the hydrogen combustion or they collect woods to set up a fire for keeping themselves warm in the forest, learning, at the same time about the carbon combustion. In this way, the game activities promote meaningful learning through connections with the real world.

The instructional activities concern the ways that are used from the instructors or the game designers to facilitate learning. The various NPCs guide players to actively participate in the learning setting, providing guidance, feedback, and enhancing retention and transfer.

The game was developed with RPG MAKER MV (RMMV), a roleplaying game development engine published by Degica and developed by Kadokawa Games. [11].

3   Discussion and Future Research

We designed SAIR, a MRPG for 14 years old students to learn and practice science curriculum, connecting the content with real world applications and supporting students towards meaningful collaborative learning. The integration methods of science content with the MRPGs gameplay mechanics was achieved through a series of choices. The learning and the gaming activities were tightly connected through the RPGs storytelling and the characters' evolution features. Players in SAIR need to solve riddles and problems to acquire the necessary for the game's progression educational skills, under the guidance of the NPCs. Each player must combine his/her own educational skills with those of the other players against their enemy's invulnerability, in a turn-based battle system. Therefore, the integrated educational content is tightly connected with the playful character of the MRPGs, supporting collaborative science learning. Students have the opportunity to work together in small groups toward a common goal, becoming responsible for their own learning and gaining critical thinking [6].

Further research will elaborate on the game's design document as it could provide useful guidelines in the design and development of educational MRPGs. Another interesting parameter is the assessment of the collaborative gameplay with students.

Acknowledgements. This research is co-financed by Greece and the European Union (European Social Fund- ESF) through the Operational Programme « Human Resources Development, Education and Lifelong Learning 2014-2020 » in the context of the project "Designing a Multiplayer Role Playing Game with Science Content" (MIS 5047802)."

References

1. Adams, E.: Fundamentals of Role-Playing Game Design. New Riders, Thousand Oaks (2014)
2. Ahmad, W.F.W.; Rahman, N.F.A.: AKAMIA: chemistry mobile game-based tutorial. In: Proceedings of the 3rd International Conference on User Science and Engineering (i-USEr), Shah Alam, Malaysia, pp. 221–226. 2–5 September 2014
3. Carvalho, M.B., et al.: An activity theory-based model for serious games analysis and conceptual design. Comput. Educ. **87**, 166–181 (2015)
4. Garneli, V., Patiniotis, K., Chorianopoulos, K.: Integrating science tasks and puzzles in computer role playing games. Multimodal Technol. Interact. **3**(3), 55 (2019)
5. Gillespie, R.G.: Commentary: reforming the general chemistry textbook. J. Chem. Educ. **74**(5), 484 (1997)
6. Gokhale, A. A. Collaborative learning enhances critical thinking. J. Technol. Educ. 7(1), 1995
7. Vella, K., Koren, C.J., Johnson, D.: The impact of agency and familiarity in cooperative multiplayer games. In: Proceedings of the Annual Symposium on Computer-Human Interaction in Play (CHI PLAY 2017), pp. 423–434. Association for Computing Machinery, New York (2017). https://doi.org/10.1145/3116595.3116622
8. Legerén Lago, B.: Al-Kimia: how to create a video game to help high school students enjoy chemistry. In: Ma, M., Oikonomou, A. (eds.) Serious Games and Edutainment Applications, pp. 259–272. Springer, Cham (2017). https://doi.org/10.1007/978-3-319-51645-5_11
9. Nebel, S., Schneider, S., Rey, G.D.: Mining learning and crafting scientific experiments: a literature review on the use of minecraft in education and research. J. Educ. Technol. Soc. **19**(2), 355–366 (2016)
10. Oxland, K.: Gameplay and Design. Pearson Education, Harlow (2004)
11. Perez, D.: Beginning RPG Maker MV. Apress, Berkeley (2016). https://doi.org/10.1007/978-1-4842-1967-6
12. Chee, Y.S., Tan, K.C.D., Tan, E.M., Jan, M.: Learning chemistry performatively: epistemological and pedagogical bases of design-for-learning with computer and video games. In: Tan, K., Kim, M. (eds.) Issues and Challenges in Science Education Research, pp. 245–262. Springer, Dordrecht (2012). https://doi.org/10.1007/978-94-007-3980-2_16
13. Sanchez, E.: Competition and collaboration for game-based learning: a case study. In: Wouters, P., van Oostendorp, H. (eds.) Instructional Techniques to Facilitate Learning and Motivation of Serious Games. AGL, pp. 161–184. Springer, Cham (2017). https://doi.org/10.1007/978-3-319-39298-1_9
14. Shudayfat, E.A., Moldoveanu, F., Moldoveanu, A., Grâdinaru, A., Dascalu, M.I.: 3D game-like virtual environment for chemistry learning. Sci. Bull. UPB **76**(3), (2014)
15. Tychsen, A.: Role playing games: comparative analysis across two media platforms. In: Proceedings of the 3rd Australasian Conference on Interactive Entertainment, Perth, Australia, pp. 75–82. 4–6 December 2006
16. Zagal, J.P., Rick, J., Hsi, I.: Collaborative games: Lessons learned from board games. Simul. Gaming **37**(1), 24–40 (2006)
17. http://ebooks.edu.gr/modules/ebook/show.php/DSGYM-B202/11/1997,301/

Guess Who? - A Serious Game for Cybersecurity Professionals

Sameer Gupta[1]([✉]), M. P. Gupta[2], Manmohan Chaturvedi[2], M. S. Vilkhu[3], Srishti Kulshrestha[2], Devottam Gaurav[2], and Ansh Mittal[2]

[1] National Institute of Technology, Kurukshetra, India
sameer.lego@gmail.com
[2] Indian Institute of Technology, Delhi, India
mpgupta@iitd.ac.in, mmchat7@gmail.com, srish.kul@gmail.com,
gauravpurusho@gmail.com, anshm18111996@gmail.com
[3] New Delhi, India

Abstract. Cybersecurity education has been a challenge for organizations that rely heavily on digitization and automation. Despite the advent of technological advancements, human intervention still plays a significant role in mitigating increasingly complex cybersecurity threats. We have developed an interactive serious game to aid cybersecurity professionals by addressing two crucial aspects, that are: a) how to identify sophisticated phishing emails and b) threat hunting to detect insider threats using a simulated Security Information and Event Management (SIEM) tool. We have developed this game so that organizations can adapt it to their environment by creating custom scenarios.

Keywords: Serious games · Cybersecurity · Insider threats

1 Introduction

The ordinary user has become the target of cyber attacks with the advancement of technology. Phishing is the most effective attack vector used to target these users. Social engineering techniques have enabled adversaries to bypass spam detection systems. Thus, users should be able to identify subtle giveaways of complex phishing emails. Moreover, insider threats are continuously expanding and automated systems for their detection suffer from problems like false positives and the inability to identify complex scenarios that build over time. Hence, security professionals should be trained to identify hidden adversaries in organizations.

We have developed "Guess Who? - A Serious Game for Cybersecurity Professionals" to address these issues. This game aims to train players to identify complex phishing attacks and insider threats in an organization. Serious games

This work is supported by funding received from Government of India, for the IMPRINT project no. 7804.

I. Marfisi-Schottman et al. (Eds.): GALA 2020, LNCS 12517, pp. 421–427, 2020.
https://doi.org/10.1007/978-3-030-63464-3_41

have proved to be an effective approach for cybersecurity education [6,8]. Zyda [9] defines serious games as "a mental contest, played with a computer in accordance with specific rules that uses entertainment to further government or corporate training, education, health, etc.". Serious games society[1] and International Journal of Serious Games under its aegis have attempted to shape future research in this important and emerging field since 2014.

The current approach towards serious games used for cybersecurity focuses on simulated environments in which cybersecurity elements are *gamified* [5]. These games have addressed phishing [1], insider threats [3], and network security fundamentals [2,4]. They target a variety of audiences, ranging from students to experienced network security professionals [7]. Nagarajan et al. [6] and Pastor et al. [7] discuss the drawbacks of current serious games approaches: Many of these games are static and do not account for differences in the player's knowledge, they do not focus on specific tools and instead give a brief understanding of cybersecurity concepts. Moreover, they do not provide a comprehensive scoring mechanism or tangible feedback to the player.

Our approach aims to improve these drawbacks. We use Unity3D [2] to create a game that targets a) identifying complex phishing emails in an organization and b) using a simulated Security Incident and Event Management (SIEM) tool to unearth an insider threat. We create email examples that capture a wide array of features present in complex phishing emails. We also provide a quiz based interface for the player to identify phishing emails and their distinctive features. For our insider threat hunting examples, we use the MITRE ATT&CK framework[3] as the backbone, enumerating the adversary tactics. Here, the player is tasked with unearthing the trail of an insider threat by investigates different offenses, their parameters, and network based clues. Our game combines constructive feedback and innovative testing examples to ensure that players experience a gentle learning curve. Some features of our game are:

1. A realistic organizational setting with a minimalist user interface (UI), providing an easy-to-navigate environment.
2. An adaptive difficulty setting which factors in a user's playing style, creating a dynamic learning environment.
3. Ample feedback systems combined with repetitive testing procedures to ensure a better learning experience.
4. Ability to customize the Insider Threat and the Phishing levels to adapt to specific organizations.

2 Related Work

Serious games for cybersecurity span a variety of themes. Pastor et al. [7] present a comprehensive survey on the state of the art serious games for cybersecurity, giving design insights as well as guidelines for development.

---

[1] https://seriousgamessociety.org/.

[2] https://unity3d.com/get-unity/download.

One of the most comprehensive serious games created for cybersecurity training is CyberCIEGE [4]. It is a simulation wherein the player acts as the decision-maker of an IT organization and is tasked with protecting systems. This game also includes a Scenario Development Kit to develop custom scenarios. Though this game gives an overview of cybersecurity concepts and practices, it does not cover any specific tool in depth.

There are, however, many games that focus on dedicated concepts of cybersecurity. CyberProtect [2] is an interactive computer network training aid for novice network security professionals. It familiarizes players with security terminologies, concepts, and policies of information systems. The Weakest Link [3] is a decision based insider threat game wherein a user has to answer real life questions that reflect their security awareness. AntiPhishing Phil [1] is an online game that teaches users good habits to help them avoid phishing attacks. They use learning science principles to design the game and also iteratively refine the game.

These games provide a surface level understanding of the elements of cybersecurity and thus can't be used for training purposes. To tackle this, we have developed an in-depth mechanism for comprehensive user learning by combining

3 Game Design

The game's story-line proceeds under well defined rules. It is interspersed with challenges and timely feedback to simulate a real-life scenario, where the player needs to use their skills and domain knowledge to succeed. The player takes the role of a security analyst of an organization, "Cyber Bank" and is tasked with upholding its cybersecurity. We use the ATT&CK (Adversarial Tactics, Techniques & Common Knowledge)[3] framework to structure our game. This framework is a knowledge base of adversary tactics and techniques based on real-world observations.

Figure 1 shows the steps of an insider in one of the levels of our game. The adversary's malicious actions trigger "rules" pre-configured in a SIEM tool. A group of rules trigger an offense that needs to be investigated by a security analyst. We embed the malicious steps in the SIEM tool as offenses that get triggered when these actions occur. The player, as a Security Analyst, has to find this hidden trail. This is discussed at length in Sect. 4.2.

4 Game Description

4.1 Game Elements

We provide a player login and sign-up functionality and use Firebase [4] by Google for authentication and database needs. Moreover, we collect information such as

---

[3] https://attack.mitre.org/.
[4] https://firebase.google.com/.

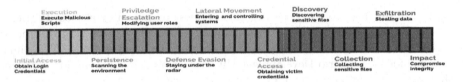

Fig. 1. The MITRE ATT&CK Framework. The different colors, yellow (P3), orange (P2), and red (P1), represent an increasing order of risk and escalation. (Color figure online)

a) name, b) designation, c) age bracket, and d) experience with cybersecurity. These inputs are taken on the player's discretion and consent. Moreover, we have an in-game computer display to act as a navigation system. It has an inbox for the player, which acts as a communication system between the game and the player. There is a network structure which gives a high level diagram of the organization's network infrastructure, it also serves as a reference for the insider threat training. Lastly, A SIEM tool interface is used for insider threat training.

4.2 Game Mechanism

Phishing Quiz. In the quiz, the player has to distinguish the phishing emails and identify their features, such as poor syntax and grammar, malicious sender addresses, links, attachments in the form of word, PDF, or zip files as shown in Fig. 2. A feedback screen is displayed once a player selects all the elements they can, which contains the correct answers and how many the player got right. To challenge the player, we incorporate a timer, and limit the number of clicks for every email example in the quiz.

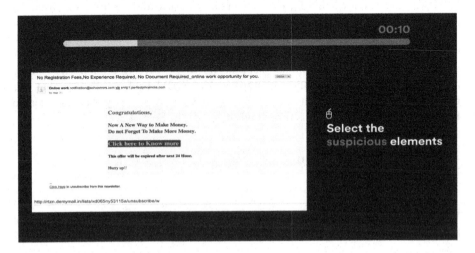

Fig. 2. Phishing quiz interface. The player can hover on different links and view their address as shown.

Insider Threat Hunting on a SIEM Tool. This training exercise is divided into 3 time segments, with the time limit scaled and embedded as the *Security Score* of the organization. A player is presented with a list of 10 offenses in each segment and has to a) investigate every offense and b) chain a given number of offenses after investigating their parameters, as shown in Fig. 3.

Fig. 3. SIEM Tool console. Offenses are displayed along with their different parameters.

Offense Investigation: A successful offense investigation, from the perspective of our game, is when a player can answer the question "What triggered the offense?", that pops up when the user interacts with the "Investigate" button. Based on the correctness of the user, we provide feedback along with a brief explanation for the correct answer.

Chaining Offenses: The players are required to chain together a given number of offences to find an insider's trail after investigating the offenses for a time segment. The number of attempts allowed to find the correct trail of offenses is represented by the *Threat Level* shown in Fig. 3. Flow diagram for threat hunting is shown in Fig. 4. The player can view the complete trajectory of the attack after chaining all offenses of the segments. This gives an overview of the steps taken by the attacker to breach security, and a visual reference to the player.

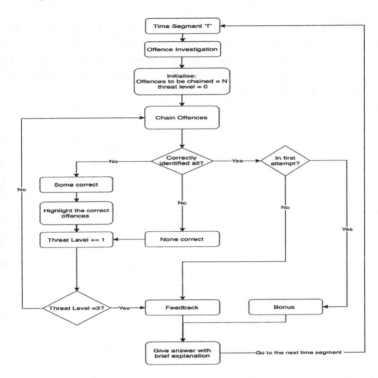

Fig. 4. Flow diagram for Threat Hunting on the SIEM tool console.

5 Conclusion and Future Work

We have described the motivation, approach, and design of "Guess Who?", a serious game for cybersecurity professionals. The main objectives for developing this game are to (a) provide a learning framework to teach the concepts of phishing, and (b) delve into the intricacies of insider threats by investigating offenses. We plan to employ a player feedback questionnaire to evaluate the objectives of our game. From the design perspective, we aim to build progressively complex scenarios for both insider threats and phishing.

References

1. Anti-phishing phil - carnegie mellon university. https://www.cmu.edu/iso/aware/phil/index.html
2. CyberProtect - SGS&C. http://sgschallenge.com/cyber-protect/
3. The weakest link: A user security game. https://www.isdecisions.com/user-security-awareness-game/
4. Irvine, C.E., et al.: Cyberciege: gaming for information assurance. IEEE Secur. Privacy **3**(3), 61–64 (2005)

5. Le Compte, A., et al.: A renewed approach to serious games for cyber security. In: 2015 7th International Conference on Cyber Conflict: Architectures in Cyberspace, pp. 203–216 (2015)
6. Nagarajan, A., et al.: Exploring game design for cybersecurity training. In: 2012 IEEE International Conference on Cyber Technology in Automation, Control, and Intelligent Systems (CYBER), pp. 256–262 (2012)
7. Pastor, V., et al.: State-of-the-art simulation systems for information security education, training and awareness. In: IEEE EDUCON 2010 Conference, pp. 1907–1916 (2010)
8. Raman, R., et al.: Serious games based approach to cyber security concept learning: Indian context. In: 2014 International Conference on Green Computing Communication and Electrical Engineering (ICGCCEE), pp. 1–5 (2014)
9. Zyda, M.: From visual simulation to virtual reality to games. Computer **38**(9), 25–32 (2005)

Challenges in Developing an Adaptive Serious Game and in Creating a Learning Data Model

Sandra Schulz, Antonia Stagge(✉), Cornelia Schade(✉),
Björn Adelberg(✉), and Sam Toorchi Roodsari(✉)

Media Centre, Technische Universität Dresden, 01069 Dresden, Germany
{antonia.stagge,cornelia.schade,bjoern.adelberg,
sam.toorchi_roodsari}@tu-dresden.de

Abstract. The aim of this paper is to present challenges in the development process of an adaptive serious game called "E.F.A." which is directed to employees being responsible for workplace safety. The paper addresses the question of how already existing theories concerning adaptivity serve as a basis for the development of the serious game E.F.A. Therefore at first various theoretical models are explained, then the developmental approach is presented. The result is a set of learning and knowledge entries, tutorial information, and the learner information in a complex model. Finally challenges, limitations, and future research are discussed.

Keywords: Serious game · Adaptivity · Game development · Knowledge

1 Introduction and Aim of the Paper

With the help of adaptive interventions and adjustments in serious games it is possible to control and regulate the learning path according to the learner's capability of fulfilling the learning tasks. This paper focuses on adaptive interventions in order to adjust the learning path of a learner. For the design of these adaptive interventions it is necessary to develop a model which states how knowledge is organised, structured and interdependent (domain model). Besides, there need to be additional models explaining how and which data of the learner is collected (learner model) and how didactic interventions are posed (tutorial model) (see Sect. 2). For the development of an adaptive serious game all these aspects need to be considered [7]. Each serious game is unique though: completely different knowledge domains, competences, or skills can be addressed. Hence, learning objectives and how they are incorporated into learning tasks significantly differ among serious games. Thus, every adaptive serious game development process needs a customized model as basis for shaping adaptive interventions.

The project "E.F.A. – Digital adaptive learning game for vocational education and training"[1] aims at developing an adaptive serious game which enables

---

[1] The project is funded by the European Social Fund and the Free State of Saxony.

© Springer Nature Switzerland AG 2020
I. Marfisi-Schottman et al. (Eds.): GALA 2020, LNCS 12517, pp. 428–434, 2020.
https://doi.org/10.1007/978-3-030-63464-3_42

leaders of social service companies to acquire knowledge on risk assessment. The player takes up the role of a workplace safety expert and has to navigate through a "jungle of obligations". There s*he needs to fulfill different tasks to return to the "real world" by finding a way through four different "temples" representing different subject areas of workplace safety.

This paper shortly presents the current state of research and shows the combination and application of adaptivity models as a basis for the development of the adaptive serious game E.F.A. For this purpose, a prototypical design and the current state of work are presented. The specific research question of the paper is therefore: How can already existing theoretical adaptivity models be transferred into the application context and serve as a basis for the development of an adaptive serious game? Finally, the results are discussed and an outlook on possible follow-up studies is given.

2 State of Research

AI-based, adaptive learning environments are supposed to adapt to users and their learning level in real time. The central components of adaptive learning environments are the domain, the tutorial and the learner model [1,6,7]. The domain model contains information on concepts and content on learning objects (e.g. graphics, examples, or exercises), their relationships to each other or interdependencies. The tutorial model includes information on learning paths, i.e. why a learning object appears at a certain position in the game. Finally, the learner model contains information about the elements of the domain model the learner has already worked on and mastered, how long the learning sessions lasted and how many repetitions and exercises it took to manage a level, etc.

2.1 Flow Theory

The Flow Theory [2] describes the balance between challenges and skills on a given learning path [11]. Reaching the state of "Flow" depends on certain requirements that are included in the activities of a serious game. The most important requirement is the optimal balance of risk of failure and the chance to successfully complete a game [2,11]. To achieve this goal, it is necessary to implement a dynamic system that has the task of, for example, adjusting the degree of difficulty over time (see Sect. 2.3). The goal of an adaptive serious game is that the learner becomes more deeply involved with the game and is motivated to play and learn. The higher the motivation, the more successful the learning will be [9].

2.2 Competence-Based Knowledge Space Theory

One goal of a serious game is to impart knowledge. To achieve this, the game consists of different learning objects (LO). They have the task to convey and test knowledge. A LO is thus related to a "knowledge state" [4]. This refers to a set of knowledge entries that are necessary to fully understand the LO. Since there is a multitude of LO in a serious game, a knowledge structure is created from the individual knowledge entries. Falmagne and Doignon in [4] described the Competence-based Knowledge Space Theory (CbKST). They define a knowledge structure as a pair $(\mathfrak{Q}, \mathfrak{K})$, in which $\mathfrak{Q}$ is the knowledge domain of the knowledge structure and $\mathfrak{K}$ is a family of subsets of $\mathfrak{Q}$, including the domain $\mathfrak{Q}$ itself and the empty set $\emptyset$. "The set $\mathfrak{Q}$ is called the domain of the knowledge structure $(\mathfrak{Q}, \mathfrak{K})$. The elements of $\mathfrak{Q}$ are the items $[w_n]$, and the elements of $\mathfrak{K}$ are the knowledge states, or just the states" [3]. An example of a knowledge structure can be found in Eq. 1.

$$\mathfrak{Q} = \{w_1, w_2, w_3, w_4\}$$
$$\mathfrak{K} = \{\emptyset, \{w_1\}, \{w_2\}, \{w_3\}, \{w_4\}, \{w_1, w_3, w_4\}, \{w_1, w_2, w_3\}, \mathfrak{Q}\} \tag{1}$$

The learner interacts with the LOs in the game. Knowledge states from the knowledge structure are assigned to these objects. The learners have a set of knowledge states that are contained in domain $\mathfrak{Q}$.

2.3 Dynamic Difficulty Adjustment Model

The Dynamic Difficulty Adjustment Model (DDA model) [11] refers to the difficulty of the learning game. Different levels of difficulty are given to the model. Each level requires different skills and parameters from the player, which must be achieved. If the measured performance in the game is below a certain threshold value, the game may be too difficult to play and if the performance is above the threshold value of the current difficulty level, the game is set too simple and the degree of difficulty should be increased. Based on the results provided by the DDA model, the game parameters can be adjusted automatically.

3   The Approach for the Development of E.F.A.

The underlying model for the adaptivity of the serious game E.F.A. needs to be build on a knowledge structure $\mathfrak{K}$ (see Sect. 2.2) displaying which knowledge entries w_n are covered in the game and how this knowledge is linked and interdependent. In a next step means of how to transfer this knowledge to the learner need to be developed and data on the learner needs to be collected in order to make meaningful adaptive interventions to the game (see Sect. 2.3). This ensures that the player remains in a state of flow (see Sect. 2.1).

3.1   Didactic Design of the Domain and Tutorial Model

In the first step of conception the learning objectives were defined, clustered into different content areas and specific knowledge content was assigned to these topics. Finally four subject areas were identified which are represented by four "temples" in the story of the game (see Sect. 1). Then the gameplay of each "temple" was designed in order to transform the underlying learning objectives and knowledge into specific game scenarios. For this purpose all knowledge entries w_n were transferred into LOs and assigned to a specific content of the game (e.g. mini game, dialog, knowledge repository). Each LO aims to convey a specific set of knowledge entries. There are knowledge entries that form the basis for achieving further knowledge states. These prerequisite connections were initially sought, as they form the basis for the adaptivity. Moreover, each LO is supported by information from the tutorial model and allows to collect learner data (see Sect. 2).

In a second step, a learner model was developed that contains all information about the learner's behavior (see Sect. 3.2). The available data about the learner's behavior in relation to a particular LO determines which new content is presented. If content is repeated it can be presented with a newly created didactical representation. This creates an individual, adaptive learning path for each learner.

This specific example will allow a better understanding: at first a content-related link between temple 1 and 2 was found, which means knowledge from the first temple (out of w_x) is needed as a basis for w_y as part of temple 2. To find out whether the player possesses this essential knowledge, it was first looked at what data was collected about the learner for w_x. In total, the player was presented four LOs for w_x: a mini-game, a short and long knowledge repository as well as a quiz question from the temple's exit game. The player's interaction with these LOs provided learner data that allowed the learner to be classified in level one (required knowledge is present), two (required knowledge is partly present), or three (required knowledge is not yet available). Then, corresponding LOs for each category have been developed (a new monolog as a reminder on w_x, repetition of the knowledge repository on w_x, and a newly created audio-visual input on w_x, e.g. an explanation video). Afterwards it was determined when and how these LOs are presented. The new monolog will always be displayed, the presentation of the knowledge repository is only for players that have been classified in level two or three. In addition, players that have been classified as level three will be picked up again with an audio-visual contribution on the topic of w_x in a different way by another media input. This procedure of finding connections between knowledge entries, collecting and evaluating player data, and developing appropriate LOs for different learner classifications will be adapted for all existing connections between knowledge entries.

3.2 Approach to the Learner Model

The adaptivity cycle used in the E.F.A. game is based on the Panarchy principle [5] of Shute et al. [10]. This model can conduct a performance analysis (capture and analyze parameters (first and second phase)) and select the appropriate content with an adaption mechanism (third phase) and finally present it in the game (fourth phase).

If it is known how the learning contents should be presented in phase four (present), according to which principle the appropriate learning paths are selected in phase three (select), how the algorithms have to be designed in phase two (analyze) it finally becomes apparent which data are needed from phase one (capture).

In the first phase, user interaction parameters and the performance of the player are recorded. These data are e.g. the position of the player, his*her number of attempts and the duration of the game. These parameters are measured in different units and are passed on for analysis in the second phase.

The second phase is the analysis of the collected data. One of our approaches to create an automated adaptive model is based on a system called "TwoA" [8] with focus on the DDA model (see Sect. 2.3). One of the ideas of this system is to assess the level of difficulty of an educational game in relation to time. Each task in a serious game is scheduled with several parameters. We refer to this time as t_{ex}. If the player is able to complete the task within t_{ex}, then the learning content is correctly adapted to the user's level of difficulty. If the player is able to complete the task clearly above or below this time, then it can be assumed that the task was too difficult or easy. At this point the system must adjust the level of difficulty according to the DDA model and select the corresponding content in the third phase (Select). Besides time, we try to consider a full scope of player-centric parameters (e.g. number of attempts, correctness) for evaluating the difficulty of tasks for users. Afterwards, with the help of the Time-Complexity and Space-Complexity [12] a suitable function can be selected which has the task to distribute suitable weights to each attempt of the player. Finally, the recalculated parameters can provide information about the player's performance.

In the third phase, depending on the result of the second phase, the parameters of the serious game are automatically changed and the content is adapted for the further course of the game. At this point a data model is necessary which selects the appropriate contents based on the values given by the second phase and makes them available for the fourth phase.

Finally, the game can be redesigned and presented directly with the given contents and parameters. This phase has to take place at runtime and be more like changing properties in the background. The player should only subconsciously realize that the game has adapted according to his*her performance.

3.3 Challenges and Limitations

In the development of the serious game E.F.A., various challenges and limitations become apparent. From a technical perspective, the small knowledge domain Ω and missing connections inside the knowledge structure K are challenges and will make it difficult to identify suitable classes via an AI. The challenge of a small knowledge domain is the initial allocation of the learner model. Start values classifying the player need to be assigned in a meaningful way in order to keep the player's flow.

A conceptual challenge lies in the provision of learning objects. If the system wants to satisfy individual learning needs, one has to provide a large and varied range of learning objects (e.g. prepare learning content for various forms of learning). With regard to the content-related connections between the knowledge entries in the "temples", being consistent with the story-line of the game represent another challenge.

4 Conclusion

On the basis of different theories for the development of adaptive serious games, the E.F.A. project developed its own approach to determine, process, and adaptively use learner data for its special case. The result is a set of learning objects and knowledge entries (domain model), the tutorial model, and the learner model. Due to the challenges described above, the future research in E.F.A. is to extend these three models, to specify and refine them. Another task is the development of a mathematical model to analyze the collected data. In addition, the E.F.A. project researches a classification based on the given game environment (e.g. size of the knowledge domain, number of learning objects) so that solution options can be selected more quickly during game creation. Depending on the condition of the knowledge structure and the three components of adaptive learning environments, different implementations are classified. At the end of this path, a framework would be created that is optimally adapted to different game scenarios. The E.F.A. project is also interested in the problem of the initial pre-allocation of the learner model. Here the project team strives for a classification of the players which allows a reasonable pre-allocation.

References

1. Bagheri, M.M.: Intelligent and adaptive tutoring systems: how to integrate learners. Int. J. Educ. **7**(2), 1–16 (2015). https://doi.org/10.5296/ije.v7i2.7079
2. Csikszentmihalyi, M., Csikzentmihaly, M.: Flow: The Psychology of Optimal Experience, vol. 1990. Harper & Row, New York (1990)
3. Doignon, J.P., Falmagne, J.C.: Knowledge Spaces and Learning Spaces (2015)
4. Falmagne, J.-C., Doignon, J.-P.: Learning Spaces. Springer, Heidelberg (2011). https://doi.org/10.1007/978-3-642-01039-2
5. Holling, C.S., Gunderson, L.H.: Panarchy: Understanding Transformations in Human and Natural Systems. Island Press, Washington, DC (2002)
6. Matthews, C.: Grammar frameworks in intelligent CALL. CALICO J. **11**(1), 5–27 (1993). https://doi.org/10.1558/cj.v11i1.5-27
7. Meier, C.: KI-basierte, adaptive Lernumgebungen. In: Wilbers, K. (ed.) Handbuch E-Learning, pp. 1–21. Deutscher Wirtschaftsdienst/Luchterhand/Wolters Kluwer, Köln (2019). https://www.alexandria.unisg.ch/257285/
8. Nyamsuren, E.: Adaptation and Assessment (TwoA) Asset in TypeScript (v1. 0) (2016)
9. Sailer, M.: Die Wirkung von Gamification auf Motivation und Leistung: Empirische Studien im Kontext manueller Arbeitsprozesse. Springer, Wiesbaden (2016). https://doi.org/10.1007/978-3-658-14309-1
10. Shute, V.J., Zapata-Rivera, D.: Adaptive educational systems. Adapt. Technol. Train. Educ. **7**(27), 1–35 (2012)

11. Streicher, A., Smeddinck, J.D.: Personalized and adaptive serious games. In: Dörner, R., Göbel, S., Kickmeier-Rust, M., Masuch, M., Zweig, K. (eds.) Entertainment Computing and Serious Games. LNCS, vol. 9970, pp. 332–377. Springer, Cham (2016). https://doi.org/10.1007/978-3-319-46152-6_14

12. Wegener, I.: Komplexitätstheorie: Grenzen der Effizienz von Algorithmen. Springer, Heidelberg (2013). https://doi.org/10.1007/978-3-642-55548-0

Developing Stethoscope Replicas for Cardiac Auscultation Training: A Comparison Between Virtual Reality, Mobile, and Makerspace

Tatiana Ortegon-Sarmiento[1], Mario Vargas-Orjuela[1], Alvaro Uribe-Quevedo[2,3](✉) ⓘ, David Rojas[4], Bill Kapralos[2,3] ⓘ, Norman Jaimes[1], and Byron Perez-Gutierrez[1]

[1] Universidad Militar Nueva Granada, Bogota, Colombia
{u1801928,norman.jaimes,byron.perez}@unimilitar.edu.co,
marvaror@gmail.com
[2] Software and Informatics Research Centre, Ontario Tech University, Oshawa, ON, Canada
{alvaro.quevedo,bill.kapralos}@ontariotechu.ca
[3] maxSIMhealth, Ontario Tech University, Oshawa, ON, Canada
[4] University of Toronto, Toronto, ON, Canada
davidrojasgualdron@gmail.com

Abstract. Currently, virtual reality and makerspace consumables are being adopted in education for creating engaging simulation learning experiences. Traditional user input devices can break immersion and may not be suitable for developing psychomotor skills due to the differences with real medical equipment. In this paper, we present the development of a stethoscope replica for cardiac auscultation training and focus on understanding the usability effects on diagnosis practices employing a virtual reality controller, touch gestures, and the proposed makerspace replica, when compared to a simulation manikin. Our preliminary results from four examination scenarios shows that immersive and non-immersive VR are found more usable than a simulation manikin, thus showing an opportunity to further engage learners with interactive learning experiences. Additionally, based on the auscultation examination, it was clear that the participant pool had a diverse range of cardiac auscultation skills, with several failing at diagnosing the murmurs, thus highlighting the importance of our proposed approach.

Keywords: Cardiac auscultation · Virtual reality · Simulation · Immersive technologies

1 Introduction

Developing proficient cardiac auscultation skills requires extensive training to properly interpret heat murmurs and avoid possible misdiagnosis [1]. The significant variation of heart murmurs pitch and the subjectivity associated with the human auditory perceptual system, adds difficulty to the examination [2]. Current auscultation training includes the use of manikin-based simulations that provide safe and re-configurable scenarios for developing cognitive and psychomotor skills, which can lead to improved trainee

© Springer Nature Switzerland AG 2020
I. Marfisi-Schottman et al. (Eds.): GALA 2020, LNCS 12517, pp. 435–440, 2020.
https://doi.org/10.1007/978-3-030-63464-3_43

performance [3]. While current training practices favor manikin-based simulation and the use of diagnostic equipment such as ultrasound, access to such tools often limited to educational facilities, given the associated costs with the acquisition, and maintenance of the manikins, equipment, and facilities [4].

Advances in cardiac auscultation simulation have provided numerous tools, including manikins comprised of simulated organs with murmurs, high-quality recordings of numerous cardiac conditions, and wireless stethoscopes to improve the training realism [5]. In the field of cardiopulmonary examination, the Harvey patient simulator is the most popular manikin platform for medical training, and it has been compared to traditional teaching/training (that included books and heart sound recordings), finding that those who trained using Harvey performed better than those who did not [6].

In this paper, we present the development of a makerspace-based stethoscope replica developed specifically to be incorporated into virtual reality and mobile cardiac auscultation training applications. A between subjects study was conducted to examine the usability perception on the VR and two non-immersive VR scenarios employing touch-based interactions and a 3D printed stethoscope replica towards determining which system is more likely to be used for cardiac auscultation practices.

2   Development Overview

To develop the virtual cardiac auscultation simulation, first, the heart examination procedure itself was analyzed to determine the necessary inputs and outputs of every subsystem. Listening to heart murmurs requires operating the stethoscope, a device comprised of: i) a chest piece including the bell and the diaphragm for listening to low and high pitch sounds respectively, ii) earpieces and iii) a rubber tube connects the components [7]. The bell and the diaphragm of the stethoscope vibrate due to the physiological and/or pathological sounds of the organism and transmit this vibration through the stethoscope tubes to the ear [8], thus the bell captures low frequency murmurs, while the diaphragm captures high frequencies.

Using the cardiac auscultation procedure, we designed our VR experience to replicate that of an examination room. Additionally, we included Graphical User Interface (GUI) components to provide visual information to the user regarding their score through the examination. The users can navigate the examination room and locate the virtual stethoscope before approaching the virtual patient. Once the procedure begins, the receive prompts containing information about the patient so that they can start with the auscultation. The GUI adopts elements from games design as users receive feedback based on their choices, visualizing their global score throughout the examination. To provide visual realism, we added two male and two female virtual patients with different physical characteristics (e.g., height, skin color, hairstyle, and clothing). We decided to include only four murmurs, a normal sound best heard with the diaphragm over the Mitral area, a Mitral Stenosis best heard with the ell over the Mitral area, a Mitral Regurgitation best heard with the diaphragm over the Mitral area, and an Aortic Stenosis best heard with the diaphragm over the Aortic area. The goal is for trainees to identify the heart murmurs in quick exercises where they are awarded 100 points for right murmur identification and zero points for misidentification.

2.1 Immersive VR Stethoscope Replica

The HTC Vive controllers were configured to provide an intuitive form for examining the virtual patient. The Grip buttons were configured to allow for grasping the stethoscope, mimicking the finger movement needed to operate a real stethoscope. During the virtual examination, the audio feedback was provided through noise-cancelling headphones connected to the HMD.

2.2 Non-immersive VR Makerspace Stethoscope Replica

Unlike the VR system, the non-immersive VR approach relies on tablet touch-based interactions and the 3D printed stethoscope replica. The 3D printed replica is comprised of the following: i) a chest piece with capacitive pads on the bell and diaphragm surfaces with push buttons to detect which is being used, ii) a processing unit case, iii) a left and right earpiece with their binaural, and iv) the tubing. The connection between the processing unit and the examination scenario was accomplished employing Ardunity, which is a Unity 3D asset, used to create, compile, and run Arduino alongside the game engine scripting.

3   Experimental Methods

A between subjects study was used to compare the usability perception on a virtual patient employing the VR room-scale scenario, and the non-immersive VR with the touch-based and the 3D printed stethoscope replica. It is worth noting that all systems (e.g., manikin, VR, and non-immersive VR) present the same murmurs and the audio recordings were chosen to be as similar as possible to the those of the auscultation manikin. We conducted a pre-test where all participants performed the diagnosis and rated the usability of a Student Auscultation Manikin (SAM) [9]. The participants were randomly assigned to one of the three examination tools. Once assigned, they were required to examine the virtual patients and identify the type of heart murmur. After completing the auscultation, the participants were asked to complete the System Usability Scale (SUS) questionnaire. The SUS is a usability tool employed to study a variety of aspects related to system usability, including the need for support, training, and complexity. A single score ranging from 0 to 100 that represents the composite measure of the overall usability of the system being studied is calculated, resulting in scores above 68/100 considered usable [10].

Third and fourth-year medical undergraduate students from Universidad Militar Nueva Granada were invited to voluntarily participate in our preliminary study. The participants included nine female and seven males aged between 20 and 21 years old. Participants using the simulation manikin, the immersive and non-immersive VR are presented in Fig. 1 and (Table 1).

 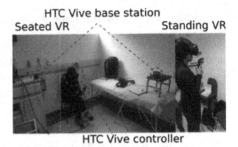

Fig. 1. Stethoscope replicas in use. The picture on the right shows the virtual reality system. The picture on the left shows the makerspace stethoscope replica, the simulation manikin, and the touch-based application.

Table 1. Usability results.

	Group 1		Group 2		Group 3	
Participant	VR	Manikin	Touch	Manikin	Makerspace replica	Manikin
1	85	62.5	92.5	50	100	100
2	55	20	65	65	87.5	95
3	85	92.5	57.5	60	67.5	77.5
4	82.5	27.5	75	57.5	67.5	100
5	82.5	77.5	85	80	80	85
Mean	78	56	75	62.5	80.5	91.5

4   Results

The results from the pre-test show that the manikin simulator was below 68/100, indicating that it is thus considered not usable. We believe this score may be due to the complexity associated with using the system and the corresponding decrease in confidence when performing the examination as a result. In contrast, the SUS corresponding to the group assigned to the stethoscope replica found that the simulation manikin was easy to use, thus obtaining the highest SUS score (see Table 2). Regarding the three interactions for VR, the participants found them usable with particular attention to items related to ease of use and the perceived need of practice to gain confidence. Here, the stethoscope replica was found to be more usable, followed by the room-scale VR and the touch interactions.

Table 3 presents the average scores obtained during the pre- and test following the same assessment. Although the results on auscultation diagnosis show where the participants performed best when exposed to the simulation scenarios, we conducted a univariate analysis of variance to determine any significant differences between at the pre- and test examination levels. At the pre-test level, there was no significant difference ($p = 0.183$), indicating that all groups performed the same; this was expected as all pre-tests were performed on the manikin. In terms of device use, room scale, touch,

Table 2. Examination scores obtained during the study.

Sound	Pre-			Test		
	Manikin			Room-scale VR	Touch	Stethoscope replica
	Group 1	Group 2	Group 3			
Normal	40	100	100	80	80	80
Aortic Stenosis	0	0	0	40	0	80
Mitral Stenosis	20	0	0	80	20	0
Mitral Regurgitation	0	0	0	40	0	0

and the stethoscope replica interactions showed no significant differences (p = 282), on how accurate the participants were at diagnosing the murmurs. Interestingly, a significant difference was found between the accuracy of diagnosing the normal sound, compared to two conditions: "Mitral Regurgitation" and "Mitral Stenosis". Results also showed that participants were significantly better at determining the normal sound condition, compared to determining "Mitral Regurgitation" and "Mitral Stenosis" murmurs, in addition to a significant difference between those diagnosing with the room-scale solution in comparison to the simulation manikin.

5 Conclusion

Here we have studied the usability perception and diagnosis performance on three simulation tools including a simulation manikin, a room-scale immersive VR scenario, a non-immersive VR touch-based and stethoscope replica scenario for cardiac auscultation. Results indicate that VR and non-immersive VR were more usable, where the room-scale solution had a significant difference in performance when compared to the pre-test results. Although no statistical significance was found amongst the interactions between our tools, participants rated the 3D printed stethoscope replica as the most usable of the three. Based on our observation and the SUS scores, operating the replica was more natural given their previous practices with the real stethoscope, while touch and VR controllers added complexity and an unrealistic interaction to conduct the heart examination.

With regards to the examination results, we observed a trend on differences between the room-scale and the touch versions. Although the participants in the room-scale scenario were more accurate at determining/diagnosing murmurs compared to the touch version. However, this difference was not significant (P = .140). Additionally, participants were better at diagnosing normal sounds, which could be attributed to their level of expertise and practice with simulation manikins. However, it is important to highlight the poor performance showing how some students struggled with the examination. Finally, we can conclude that the user input interface plays an important role in the virtual cardiac auscultation and further research is needed to understand how our approach articulates with a serious games design approach towards retention and transferrable skills.

Future work will focus additional experiments will be conducted to develop a greater understanding regarding the difficulties associated with diagnosing heart murmurs other than normal, and how the training tools can help overcoming these difficulties.

Acknowledgements. Authors thank the financial support of Universidad Militar Nueva Granda under project INV-ING-2363/2017.

References

1. Vukanovic-Criley, J.M., Criley, S., Warde, C.M., Boker, J.R., Guevara-Matheus, L., Churchill, W.H., Nelson, W.P., Criley, J.M.: Competency in cardiac examination skills in medical students, trainees, physicians, and faculty: a multicenter study. Arch. Intern. Med. **166**, 610–616 (2006)
2. Alam, U., Asghar, O., Khan, S., Hayat, S., Malik, R.: Cardiac auscultation: an essential clinical skill in decline. Br. J. Cardiol. **17**, 8–10 (2010)
3. Torregrosa, T., Fennigkoh, L., Weston, J.: Fabrication of a nursing manikin overlay for simulation of chest drainage management. In: 2015 IEEE Great Lakes Biomedical Conference (GLBC), pp. 1–4. IEEE (2015)
4. Zendejas, B., Wang, A.T., Brydges, R., Hamstra, S.J., Cook, D.A.: Cost: the missing outcome in simulation-based medical education research: a systematic review. Surgery **153**, 160–176 (2013)
5. Ruthenberg, B., Wasylewski, N., Beard, J.: An experimental device for investigating the force and power requirements of a powered gait orthosis. J. Rehabil. Res. Dev. **4**, 203–213 (1997)
6. Gordon, M.: Cardiology patient simulator: Development of an animated manikin to teach cardiovascular disease. Am. J. Cardiol. **34**, 350–355 (1974)
7. Chizner, M.A.: Cardiac auscultation: rediscovering the lost art. Curr. Probl. Cardiol. **33–7**, 326–408 (2008)
8. McGee, S.M.: Auscultation of the heart: general principles. Evidence-Based Phys. Diagnosis **4**, 327–332 (2017)
9. Quinn, A., Kaminsky, J., Adler, A., Eisner, S., Ovitsh, R.: Cardiac auscultation lab using a heart sounds auscultation simulation Manikin. MedEdPORTAL **15**, 1–6 (2019)
10. Brooke, J.: SUS: a "quick and dirty" usability. Usability evaluation in industry, **189** (1996)

Digital Versus Analogue Simulation Games: Influence on Validity, Play(er) Experience and Learning Outcomes

Maria Freese$^{(\boxtimes)}$ and Geertje Bekebrede

Faculty of Technology, Policy and Management, Delft University of Technology, Jaffalaan 5, 2628 BX Delft, The Netherlands
{M.Freese,G.Bekebrede}@tudelft.nl

Abstract. The aim of this paper is to analyse whether the design decision in terms of the choice between a digital or an analogue simulation game does have an influence on validity, play(er) experience, and learning outcomes. Therefore, we analysed and compared a digital and analogue version of a simulation game for port management regarding their validity, play(er) experience, and learning outcomes. Our results showed that engagement is one of the key factors for learning, but that simulation games need to be realistic enough to also guarantee specific learning outcomes. Further research is needed to statistically evaluate our findings and the applicability of these results in other games.

Keywords: Simulation gaming · Digital games · Analogue games · Complex systems · Socio-technical systems · Learning · Immersion · Validity

1 Introduction

Societies have grown in complexity due to the increasing dynamics and different functional systems that are interconnected [1, 2]. A complex system can very broadly be defined as *"one in which there are multiple interactions between many different elements of the system [...]"* [3]. Due to the characteristics as emergence, self-organization and adaptation [4], complex systems are difficult to analyse and to design. Simulation games open the opportunity to analyse the behaviour of (individual) actors within a social network and in relation with changes in the physical environment [5]. This creates an unique learning environment, while other instruments focus on solely the technical-physical aspects without taking into account personal choices or social network aspects [5, 6].

In general, it is said that simulation games work [7] and that they are suitable tools for learning. But what is the powerful element of such games? Why do they work? Simulation games can be understood as a special method for multilogue communication [8] and of participatory modelling which makes it possible to provide an environment that is structured and safe to (inter-)actively learn about complex problems [9]. Learning occurs on different levels and activates and generates different resources [10]. Simulation

© Springer Nature Switzerland AG 2020
I. Marfisi-Schottman et al. (Eds.): GALA 2020, LNCS 12517, pp. 441–446, 2020.
https://doi.org/10.1007/978-3-030-63464-3_44

games can be build upon these different learning levels and resources, so the process of understanding specific game dynamics and also of playing a game can be defined as (parts of the) learning (process) as well. Gee [11] stated that learning always takes place in well-constructed games, but how can we guarantee a proper design and development of such games. To the best of the authors' knowledge, there are just a few publications about the consequences different design decisions have. Theories and approaches related to the design and development of simulation games, such as Harteveld [12], focus more on the general level of gaming, but what is the difference between digital and analogue games especially for games with the objective to the analysis and design of complex socio-technical systems?

2 Digital and Analogue Games

From the 1980s, the use of computer simulations has increased and also the first computer games were developed. The idea was that by using computers more detailed and valid data could be given about the future. In addition, the idea was that graphics would increase the experience. However, the resources needed to develop these highly realistic digital environments also increases and it is not sure that the outcomes and impact of games are indeed better. Meijer [13] compared low-tech and high-tech games for innovation with each other and showed that *"[…] despite the higher precision, fidelity of high-tech simulators was not necessarily better than that of low-tech cases"*.

Another study was conducted by Kurapati et al. [14]. They explored the similarities and differences of learning outcomes after playing a digital and analogue version of a similar game. Therefore, they organized gaming sessions in different countries, let group of players play either the analogue or the digital game and analysed differences through a post-game survey that measured the learning experiences. Their results showed that the type of a game had just a limited effect on the learning experience, but more research in this domain is needed to derive valid conclusions.

Portelli and Khaled [15] stated that *"analogue games […] are more than capable of eliciting very real emotional responses in their players […]. They are also much simpler to design in a complete way in a shorter span of time; both in terms of concept as well as mechanics"*.

Fang, Chen and Huang [16] did a study in which they wanted to know if analogue games evoke different social interactions and reactions than digital games do. They let their participants play different versions (desktop, tablet, analogue) of Monopoly and Jenga and measured the emotional satisfaction of the players through a questionnaire. They found out that analogue games evoked stronger emotional reactions of the participants. In addition to this, analogue games improved the social interaction as well. This fact has also been given attention by Freese, Schier and Mühlhausen [17] who compared the gameplay of a digital and analogue version of an airport management game.

To conclude, digital as well as analogue games showed their effectiveness for understanding complex problems. However, one of the main question is still what the difference is between digital and analogue games and what this means for characteristics of a game(play), such as validity, play(er) experiences, and learning outcomes. So far and to the best of the authors' knowledge, research articles focused very often just on single concepts but not on the mentioned variables as a whole.

3 Analysis Based on Hands-on Experience

In the following, the focus will be on the description and comparison of a digital and analogue version of a port management simulation game. Although both games have some differences, such as a different number of players, we believe that both versions are comparable with each other because these are validated and evaluated games, they were played with students, so the target groups of the gameplay sessions can be compared with each other, and the same facilitators moderated the gaming sessions.

3.1 SimPort-MV2 Versus PortConstructor

SimPort-MV2 and PortConstructor both simulate the strategic decisions of the port planning of Maasvlakte 2 in the Port of Rotterdam. The first version of SimPort-MV2 has been launched in 2005, while PortConstructor is developed later, based on the success of SimPort-MV2, in 2018. The objective of both games is to develop Maasvlakte 2, the newest extension of the Port of Rotterdam, taking into account the objectives of the Port of Rotterdam.

SimPort-MV2 is a hybrid game, where a team of 3 to 6 players represents the board of the Port Authority, consisting of three roles building director, commercial director and general director. Each role is responsible for certain actions, such as building the port area, negotiate with clients and keep track on finance and performance. Decisions have to be added in a computer program and the effects of the decisions are visible on a beamer, representing the 'current' state of the port area. The game takes about 5 to 8 h to play, including briefing and debriefing [see 18 for a more extensive description of the game].

PortConstructor on the other hand is an online game. The player represents the general director of the port area and the other roles are presented as a non-player characters providing information about potential clients, placing clients to parcels, and informing the forecasts and news. In PortConstructor an infrastructure manager is added who can build infrastructure in the port area, an element which was not part of SimPort-MV2. The general director is often played by two players as team to increase communication about the decisions.

In both games, participants start with a strategy phase, where they have to decide about their objectives and have to define the Masterplan. After the strategy phase, the participants have to execute the strategy, by contracting clients, assigning the clients to the port, and trying to develop Maasvlakte 2 in the best way.

3.2 Methodological Approach

Sessions of both games have been played with professionals (Port of Rotterdam) and students from different educational institutes (TU Delft, Unesco IHE and in port management programs). These sessions have been evaluated with a pre and post survey. The students in this analysis followed a 'Project Management' course at the Faculty of Technology, Policy and Management at Delft University of Technology. The game SimPort-MV2 is played several years in a row and the game Port Constructor is played two times as this game is released in 2019. Therefore, the number of the respondents is higher for SimPort-MV2. The post-game questionnaire consisted of some open questions, and statements with 5-point Likert scales (from 1 totally disagree to 5 totally agree). The statements involved questions about the quality of the game, the manner in which they have played the game, the use of the computers, and the acquired insights. For the descriptive analysis of the quantitative data from the questionnaires we use the analysis program SPSS (version 25).

3.3 Results

Students playing SimPort-MV2 and Port Constructor both had the feeling that it improved their learning ($M_{PortC} = 3.72$, $SD = .70$; $M_{SimP} = 3.86$, $SD = .75$). However, students of PortConstructor did not agree with the statement that the game was educative ($M_{PortC} = 3.26$, $SD = .86$; $M_{SimP} = 3.88$, $SD = .75$). In addition to this, students playing SimPort-MV2 said that this game better promoted communication ($M_{PortC} = 3.67$, $SD = .82$; $M_{SimP} = 3.86$, $SD = .76$) and integration of different disciplines ($M_{PortC} = 3.57$, $SD = .69$; $M_{SimP} = 3.72$, $SD = .80$), and a higher score of students playing PortConstructor highlighted the technical ($M_{PortC} = 3.72$, $SD = .78$; $M_{SimP} = 3.32$, $SD = .98$) and strategic complexity ($M_{PortC} = 3.98$, $SD = .61$; $M_{SimP} = 3.81$, $SD = .86$) and got a better understanding in terms of the effects of the decisions of the port ($M_{PortC} = 3.70$, $SD = .79$; $M_{SimP} = 3.40$, $SD = .91$).

Although the scores regarding elements of gameplay experience and validity for both games are high, the participants of SimPort-MV2 enjoyed more ($M_{PortC} = 4.02$, $SD = .61$; $M_{SimP} = 4.16$, $SD = .70$) and scored higher on the statement that the game was build up in an interesting and stimulating way ($M_{PortC} = 3.70$, $SD = .90$; $M_{SimP} = 3.40$, $SD = .80$). Participants agreed that the aim of the game was clear and that facilitation was good. They also agreed about the clearness of the instructions; however, these were lower for PortConstructor ($M_{PortC} = 3.38$, $SD = .61$; $M_{SimP} = 3.61$, $SD = .90$).

Both groups of participants agreed that the games are sufficient realistic ($M_{PortC} = 3.61$, $SD = .68$; $M_{SimP} = 3.57$, $SD = .84$). We see a difference in the reflection in the game, which is higher for SimPort-MV2 ($M_{PortC} = 3.56$, $SD = .77$; $M_{SimP} = 3.92$, $SD = .84$). The results also show that participants of SimPort-MV2 played more from the perspective of their roles ($M_{PortC} = 3.59$, $SD = .82$; $M_{SimP} = 3.81$, $SD = .74$) and also other players took a role ($M_{PortC} = 3.73$, $SD = .83$; $M_{SimP} = 4.02$, $SD = .62$), more than in PortConstructor.

4   Discussion, Conclusions and Future Research

The aim of the present paper was to analyse whether the design decision in terms of the choice between a digital or an analogue game would have an influence on the validity, play(er) experience, and learning outcomes. To answer to this question, a comparative analysis of a digital and analogue version of a simulation game for the complex system of a port has been done. The discussion and interpretation of the results is structured around the topics of validity, play(er) experience and learning outcomes.

1. Regarding the *validity*, we were not able to find huge differences in terms of the perceived type of complexity of both games, so further research in this area is needed.

An idea here could be to work on a set-up that makes it possible to test the same sample twice, so that biases based on the sample can be reduced. However, complexity can be understood in different ways. Our observations have shown that you can address technical complexity quite easily in and with a digital simulation game, whereas the more social-related complexity (such as communication-related aspects) can easily be addressed by an analogue game.

2. Regarding the *playability*, the results indicated that digital and analogue games generate a different style of playing a game. In analogue games, the focus is quite often on discussions which sometimes can have a negative influence on the gameplay itself, because the players need too much time for making a decision. In digital games, players very often follow the trial and error approach, meaning that they just do a certain action and directly see what the consequences are (but do not think about it). Secondly, *emotional experiences* play an important role. Here, a correlation analysis showed that identification with an in-game-role has a positive effect on learning ($R_s = .42, p < .001$), so the engagement players show is directly and positive correlated with general learning processes. This could be a point of interest for further research, too. As soon as you work with a role change and a good role description including the description of the tasks and areas of responsibility of this role or have an immersive game, it might have a positive influence on the engagement of the players and on the general learning as well. Thirdly, digital and analogue games generate different *social interactions*. We already discussed this briefly, but the analysis of social interactions in the digital and analogue version of the port management simulation games has confirmed this pattern. Often, digital games are less interactive as their focus is more on technical and/of strategical components and the understanding of effects, whereas the focus of analogue games is more on communication and integration. We want to highlight that the comparison of the two games in terms of the degree of the social interaction might be difficult due to the fact that their set-up was different. Interestingly, you can see this clearly back in the way of how people have played the game.

3. Regarding the *learning outcomes*, players learned (slightly) more about technical complexity in the digital game and about communication in the analogue game. In addition to this, the understanding of consequences on the port design was higher in the digital game, whereas the understanding of how you need to integrate things was higher in the analogue game.

To conclude, the results showed that engagement is one of the key factors for learning. If you are having fun, you feel like you have learned something. But a game needs to be realistic enough to also guarantee specific learning outcomes. The focus of this paper was mainly on the comparison of analogue and digital games, but it is also possible to combine aspects of each game type with each other. Generally spoken, analogue and digital games are both suitable methods for analysing and understanding complex systems and for learning as well.

References

1. Davis, M.C., Challenger, R., Jayewardene, D.N., Clegg, C.W.: Advancing socio-technical systems thinking: a call for bravery. Appl. Ergon. **45**(2), 171–180 (2014)
2. Heylighen, F.: Complexity and information overload in society: why increasing efficiency leads to decreasing control. Inf. Soc. **1**, 1–44 (2002)
3. Ridolfi, G., Mooij, E., Corpino, S.: Complex-systems design methodology for systems-engineering collaborative environment. In: Systems Engineering - Practice and Theory, ch. 2, pp. 40–70 (2012). ISBN 9789535103226
4. Holland, J.H.: Hidden Order; How Adaptation Builds Complexity. Addison-Wesley, Reading (1995)
5. Lukosch, H.K., Bekebrede, G., Kurapati, S., Lukosch, S.G.: A scientific foundation of simulation games for the analysis and design of complex systems. Simul. Gaming **49**(3), 279–314 (2018)
6. Mayer, I.S.: The gaming of policy and the politics of gaming: a review. Simul. Gaming **40**(6), 825–862 (2009)
7. Hofstede, G.J., de Caluwé, L., Peters, V.: Why simulation games work-in search of the active substance: a synthesis. Simul. Gaming **41**(6), 824–843 (2010)
8. Duke, R.D.: Gaming, the Future's Language. SAGE, Beverly Hills (1974)
9. Doyle, D., Brown, F.W.: Using a business simulation to teach applied skills-the benefits and the challenges of using student teams from multiple countries. J. Eur. Ind. Train. **24**(6), 330 (2000)
10. Krathwohl, D.R.: A revision of Bloom's taxonomy: an overview. Theory Pract. **41**(4), 212–218 (2002)
11. Gee, J.P.: Learning by design: good video games as learning machines. E-Learn. Digit. Media **2**(1), 5–16 (2005)
12. Harteveld, C.: Triadic Game Design: Balancing Reality, Meaning and Play. Springer, Heidelberg (2011). https://doi.org/10.1007/978-1-84996-157-8
13. Meijer, S.: The power of sponges: comparing high-tech and low-tech gaming for innovation. Simul. Gaming **46**(5), 512–535 (2015)
14. Kurapati, S., Bekebrede, G., Lukosch, H., Kourounioti, I., Freese, M., Verbraeck, A.: Digital versus analogue multiplayer gaming: comparing learning outcomes. In: Hamada, R., et al. (eds.) Neo-Simulation and Gaming Toward Active Learning. TSS, vol. 18, pp. 463–472. Springer, Singapore (2019). https://doi.org/10.1007/978-981-13-8039-6_44
15. Portelli, J.-L., Khaled, R.: Spectrum: exploring the effects of player experience on game design. In: Proceedings of 1st International Joint Conference of DiGRA and FDG, p. 9 (2016)
16. Fang, Y.-M., Chen, K.-M., Huang, Y.-J.: Emotional reactions of different interface formats: comparing digital and traditional board games. Adv. Mech. Eng. **8**(3), 1–8 (2016)
17. Freese, M., Schier, S., Mühlhausen, T.: Computer - oder Brettspiel? Entwicklungen am Beispiel des Planspieles D-CITE [Computer-based or board game? Developments using the example of the serious game D-CITE]. In: Hühn, C., Schwägele, S., Zürn, B., Bartschat, D., Trautwein, F. (eds.) Planspiele – Interaktion gestalten – Über die Vielfalt der Methode, ZMS-Schriftenreihe, 10, Norderstedt: Book on Demand GmbH (2017). ISBN: 978-3-7528-6192-1
18. Bekebrede, G.: Experiencing complexity. A gaming approach for understanding infrastructure systems. NGI (Ph.D. thesis), Delft (2010)

Predicting Real-Time Affective States by Modeling Facial Emotions Captured During Educational Video Game Play

Vipin Verma[1]([✉])(iD), Hansol Rheem[2](iD), Ashish Amresh[2](iD), Scotty D. Craig[1](iD), and Ajay Bansal[1](iD)

[1] Arizona State University, Mesa, AZ, USA
{vverma9,scotty.craig,ajay.bansal}@asu.edu
[2] Arizona State University, Tempe, AZ, USA
{hrheem,amresh}@asu.edu

Abstract. In an attempt to predict the cognitive-affective states of a player during an educational video game session, this study used a self-emote procedure in which participants' facial expressions and emotions were continuously recorded along with self-reported data about their emotional states. Participants' facial expressions and emotions were captured using Affdex SDK from Affectiva. The captured data were used for binomial logistic regression to predict the cognitive-affective states of flow, frustration, and boredom. The binomial logistic regression uncovered that expressions and emotions could be used to predict these cognitive-affective states of a player. We discuss these predictors and their potential to adapt an educational video game session with non-intrusive and affect-sensitive personalization capabilities. The current study provides a pathway for the educational play design and suggests that it should be non-intrusive while being adaptive to a player's capabilities.

Keywords: Affective computing · Sensor-free · Emotion in human-computer interaction · Educational games

1 Introduction

Recently, there has been a surge in research that aims to enable computer applications to measure and adapt to the emotional states of users [11]. Developing online tutors and serious games that can respond to emotional states of learners is a challenging endeavor since it requires a reliable detection mechanism to capture the emotional states accurately [11]. Without an accurate detection mechanism, online tutors or games may fail to provide an intervention that can accommodate the changes in the learning ability of their users induced by the fluctuations in emotional states. Recognizing learner's emotional state is a difficult task for computers, as well as it is for human instructors [5].

© Springer Nature Switzerland AG 2020
I. Marfisi-Schottman et al. (Eds.): GALA 2020, LNCS 12517, pp. 447–452, 2020.
https://doi.org/10.1007/978-3-030-63464-3_45

2   Affect in Educational Games

Previous work in related educational technology, Intelligent Tutoring Systems, has indicated that flow, frustration, and boredom [4,7] are related to learning with the system. Csikszentmihalyi [6] described flow as a state of sustained focus in an activity, accompanied by a state of delight and satisfaction. Boredom is the opposite of flow and has been shown to have a negative correlation to flow and the opposite effect on learning [4]. A game may frustrate a player if the player is not able to cope with the difficulty level imposed by the game [16]. It is imperative to measure the elements such as flow, frustration, and boredom and develop accurate models to determine if a player is kept within the boundaries of the zone of proximal development.

To use these affective states within educational games there must be reliable methods for detection in real time that are expandable. Luckily, research involving the usage of non-intrusive tools and equipment such as facial emotion tracking [13] has been increasing. These non-intrusive methods are economical and can scale to multiple settings. Most of these methods are focused on the Facial Action Coding System (FACS) [10]. This method categorizes emotions using muscle movements (called Action Units or AUs) in the face. Previous work has used the FACS to identify boredom, flow, and frustration based on AUs [5].

Among the new non-intrusive approaches, the focus of this study is facial emotion tracking using Affdex Software Development Kit (SDK) from Affectiva. This approach utilizes a webcam, which is easily accessible hardware, to record the changes in facial features using the facial feature detection SDK [13]. Provided that the tracking environment is set up correctly and the user is front-facing the camera, it is possible to achieve a relatively high detection rate for facial features [13], which then can be used to predict the basic emotional states of users. While research has provided successful results in the detection of the facial features, only a few methods exist that can accurately predict the affective states and provide these as inputs to curate and personalize the user experience [11,15].

3   Method

3.1   Participants

The current study recruited 107 undergraduate students (78 male, 29 female, average age 18.9 years, standard deviation of 2.6) who participated in the study. Sixty-one participants reported having played games with an average play time of six hours per week and a standard deviation of 8.82 h. Their participation lasted up to 1.5 h (mean playtime of 42.1 min, standard deviation of 8.7 min).

3.2   Material and Procedure

All participants who signed the consent form electronically were instructed to turn off their phones. They were requested to remove their caps and glasses, to prevent any interference in the facial expression detection. Participants were asked to put on headphones and play an educational game for about 1.5 h. They were also instructed to refrain from covering their face with their hands while playing the game.

The game titled "Chemo-o-crypt" is a 2D platformer game developed in Unity3D (v2018.1.9f2) using the Content Agnostic Game Engineering (CAGE) architecture [1,2]. In Chemo-o-crypt, the game play mechanics allow left and right player movement, ladder climbing, and jumping. There are three different types of patrolling enemies which reduces a partial portion of the player's health on collision. The game has four levels in which the player is tasked with collecting the required number of molecules of each element and compound that takes part in the chemical reaction, such that the chemical equation gets balanced.

Chemo-o-crypt is embedded with the Affdex Software Development Kit (SDK) from Affectiva [13]. The SDK tracked participants' facial features and provided the probabilities for various emotions and expressions of each participant at a given time point, with a sampling rate of 20 Hz. The size of the template used to capture the faces of participants was set at 640 by 480px (height by width). The SDK detected the seven basic Ekman emotions which included, Anger, Disgust, Fear, Happiness, Sadness, Surprise, and Contempt. It also quantified physical properties of 15 different facial features (facial expressions) which included Attention, BrowFurrow, BrowRaise, ChinRaise, EyeClosure, InnerBrowRaise, LipCornerDepressor, LipPress, LipPucker, LipSuck, MouthOpen, NoseWrinkle, Smile, Smirk, UpperLipRaise. These expressions correspond to the AUs from the Ekman and Friesen's Facial Action Coding System [10]. As the emotion or facial expression occurs and intensifies, the score rises from 0 (no emotion or expression) to 100 (emotion or expression fully present). A description of these expressions is available on iMotions website [12].

3.3   Emotion Detection

A process similar to the emote aloud procedure used by Craig and colleagues [5] was adopted in this study to capture the fluctuations in the cognitive-affective state. During the game, a pop-up message appeared at the bottom of the screen, whenever the detected value for any emotion exceeded the threshold value of 40, out of the maximum possible value of 100. The pop-up message asked the participants to report their affective state by selecting one of the four available options, which were, bored, frustrated, flow, or other. The self-emote pop-up blinked twice every second until the player selected one of the options, and disappeared once a selection was made. However, the pop-up did not appear until the player was at least 30 s into the game. The interval between the two pop-ups was 90 s at the minimum, to minimize the interruption caused by the pop-ups. There were four game levels and the experiment ended when the player cleared all four levels.

4   Analysis

The tracked emotions and expressions were averaged across all time points between two neighboring pop-ups, with an exception that, for the first pop-up message, the averaging was performed across the time points between the start of the game and the time when the first self-emote pop-up appeared. This process was used to create a data matrix that contained the averaged emotion and expression indices for each time when the pop-up message appeared for all participants. As a result, this data consisted of 1030 observations.

The data were then fitted using the step-wise binomial logistic regression. Each pop-up instance could have had one of the four classes (e.g. boredom, flow, frustration, and other). Therefore, boredom, frustration, and others were relabelled as 'nonflow' states to be able to apply the binomial logistic regression resulting in the two classes of flow and nonflow states. The same procedure was also applied to the boredom and frustration classes, but not to the 'other' class, to examine if the tracked emotion and expression data could predict the states of flow, boredom, and frustration. Emotion or facial expression was set as the predictor. The cognitive-affective state of flow (flow, nonflow), boredom (boredom, nonboredom), or frustration (frustration, nonfrustration) was set as the outcome, resulting in a total of six regression models. The 'other' class was beyond the scope of the study mainly because it is an ambiguous notion or state, thus was not reported.

5   Results

The data consisted of a total of 1030 rows of which 321 rows consisted of flow, 205 consisted of boredom, and 395 consisted of frustration. The results obtain from binary logistic regression are summarized in Table 1.

6   Discussion

Binary logistic regression revealed that emotional states and expressions can be used to predict the cognitive-affective states of flow, boredom, and frustration with AUC and prediction accuracies comparable to previous research that used similar [3,8] and different procedures [9,14]. Moreover, both the emotion and expression models showed comparable prediction accuracies.

In detail, the cognitive-affective states were mainly dependent upon the emotions of Happiness, Fear, and Sadness, and expressions that comprise these emotions. In the emotion model of Flow state, Happiness and Fear were identified as significant predictors. In line with this finding, InnerBrowRaise (associated with Fear and Sadness), Smile (Happiness), and MouthOpen (Sadness) were identified as three of the four significant predictors in the expression model of Flow. The Boredom models showed a similar pattern, which indicated that Happiness and Sadness predicted the Boredom state as well as BrowFurrow (Fear and Sadness), BrowRaise (Happiness), MouthOpen (Sadness), and Smile (Happiness)

Table 1. Modeling results obtained from binary logistic regression ($\alpha = .05$)

Affect	Model input	Model equation	p-value	Accuracy	AUC
Flow	Emotions	$ln(Flow/NonFlow) = -0.84 + (0.4 \times Fear) + (0.09 \times Happiness) + (-0.074 \times Sadness)$	.006	72.8%	.57
	Expressions	$ln(Flow/NonFlow) = 1.5 + (-0.02 \times Attention) + (-0.025 \times EyeClosure) + (-0.037 \times InnerBrowRaise) + (0.02 \times LipPucker) + (-0.02 \times LipSuck) + (0.02 \times MouthOpen) + (0.08 \times Smile)$	<.001	72.33%	.63
Boredom	Emotions	$ln(Boredom/NonBoredom) = -1.24 + (-1.13 \times Fear) + (-0.38 \times Happiness) + (0.15 \times Sadness)$	<.001	83%	.6
	Expressions	$ln(Boredom/NonBoredom) = -8.44 + (0.07 \times Attention) + (0.02 \times BrowFurrow) + (0.06 \times BrowRaise) + (0.02 \times InnerBrowRaise) + (-0.028 \times MouthOpen) + (-0.03 \times Smile)$	<.001	83	.64
Frustration	Emotions	Not significant	.08	54.4%	.55
	Expressions	$ln(Frustration/NonFrustration) = 1.85 + (-0.02 \times Attention) + (-0.03 \times BrowFurrow) + (0.02 \times EyeClosure) + (-0.067 \times LipPress) + (-0.03 \times LipPucker) + (0.03 \times LipSuck)$	<.001	61.1%	.57

in the expression domain. Contrarily, none of the predictors in the emotion domain reached significance in the Frustration model. However, the expressions of BrowFurrow (Fear and Sadness), LipPress (Sadness), and LipSuck (Sadness) were identified as significant predictors, which followed the observations in the Flow and Boredom models.

Another finding from the study was that the expression better explained the variances in the affective states compared to emotion. One reason behind this finding may be that the emotion indices are derived from the expression indices [12]. Therefore, the findings indicate that facial expressions, compared to emotions, may be better predictors of the affective states, which also implies that both domains are not necessarily required at the same time. This finding can help future games to embed a less computationally intensive detection module that allows for a fast and online assessment of players' affective states.

7   Conclusion

Affect detection using facial feature tracking provided considerable accuracy. Expression-based modeling provided better performance over the models built using emotional expressions. Therefore, it is recommended to use expressions instead of emotions while modeling cognitive-affective states of a learner. The current study demonstrates that personalizing educational content in games or online learning systems can be achieved by assessing the cognitive-affective states of a learner in real-time and adapting the system to the learners. In return, the personalized systems may be able to adapt better, be inclusive, and tailor the learning for students from all skill levels.

References

1. Baron, T.: An Architecture for designing content agnostic game mechanics for educational burst games. Ph.D. thesis, Arizona State University (2017)
2. Baron, T., Amresh, A.: Word towers: assessing domain knowledge with non-traditional genres. In: European Conference on Games Based Learning, p. 638. Academic Conferences International Limited (2015)
3. Bosch, N., Chen, H., D'Mello, S., Baker, R., Shute, V.: Accuracy vs. availability heuristic in multimodal affect detection in the wild. In: Proceedings of the 2015 ACM on International Conference on Multimodal Interaction, pp. 267–274 (2015)
4. Craig, S., Graesser, A., Sullins, J., Gholson, B.: Affect and learning: an exploratory look into the role of affect in learning with autotutor. J. Educ. Media **29**(3), 241–250 (2004)
5. Craig, S.D., D'Mello, S., Witherspoon, A., Graesser, A.: Emote aloud during learning with autotutor: applying the facial action coding system to cognitive-affective states during learning. Cogn. Emot. **22**(5), 777–788 (2008)
6. Czikszentmihalyi, M.: Flow: The Psychology of Optimal Experience (1990)
7. D'Mello, S., Graesser, A.: Emotions during learning with autotutor. Adapti. Technol. Training Educ. pp. 169–187 (2012)
8. D'Mello, S., Kappas, A., Gratch, J.: The affective computing approach to affect measurement. Emot. Rev. **10**(2), 174–183 (2018)
9. Dmello, S.K., Craig, S.D., Witherspoon, A., Mcdaniel, B., Graesser, A.: Automatic detection of learner's affect from conversational cues. User Model. User-Adapt. Inter. **18**(1–2), 45–80 (2008). https://doi.org/10.1007/s11257-007-9037-6
10. Ekman, P., Friesen, W.: Facial Action Coding System: A Technique for the Measurement of Facial Movement, Psychologists press. Palo Alto (1978)
11. Harley, J.M.: Measuring emotions: a survey of cutting edge methodologies used in computer-based learning environment research. In: Emotions, Technology, Design, and Learning, pp. 89–114. Elsevier (2016)
12. iMotions Inc.: Affectiva channel explained (2018). https://help.imotions.com/hc/en-us/articles/360011728719-Affectiva-channel-explained. Accessed 17 Apr 2020
13. Magdin, M., Prikler, F.: Real time facial expression recognition using webcam and sdk affectiva. IJIMAI **5**(1), 7–15 (2018)
14. Sabourin, J., Mott, B., Lester, J.C.: Modeling learner affect with theoretically grounded dynamic bayesian networks. In: DMello, S., Graesser, A., Schuller, B., Martin, J.-C. (eds.) ACII 2011. LNCS, vol. 6974, pp. 286–295. Springer, Heidelberg (2011). https://doi.org/10.1007/978-3-642-24600-5_32
15. Tadayon, R., Amresh, A., McDaniel, T., Panchanathan, S.: Real-time stealth intervention for motor learning using player flow-state. In: 2018 IEEE 6th International Conference on Serious Games and Applications for Health (SeGAH), pp. 1–8. IEEE (2018)
16. Yun, C., Shastri, D., Pavlidis, I., Deng, Z.: O'game, can you feel my frustration? improving user's gaming experience via stresscam. In: Proceedings of the SIGCHI Conference on Human Factors in Computing Systems, pp. 2195–2204 (2009)

Author Index

Printed in the United States
By Bookmasters